American Government and Politics Today:

THE ESSENTIALS

2013–2014 EDITION

Barbara A. Bardes
University of Cincinnati

Mack C. Shelley II
Iowa State University

Steffen W. Schmidt
Iowa State University

Australia • Brazil • Japan • Korea • Mexico • Singapore • Spain • United Kingdom • United States

American Government and Politics Today:
THE ESSENTIALS
2013–2014 EDITION
Bardes • Shelley • Schmidt

Publisher: Suzanne Jeans
Executive Editor: Carolyn Merrill
Acquisitions Editor: Anita Devine
Developmental Editor: Rebecca Green
Assistant Editor: Patrick Roach
Editorial Assistant: Scott Greenan
Marketing Manager: Lydia LeStar
Marketing Coordinator: Loreen Towle
Media Editor: Laura Hildebrand
Production Manager: Suzanne St. Clair
Senior Content Project Manager: Ann Borman
Manufacturing Planner: Fola Orekoya
Photo Research: Ann Hoffman
Copy Editor: Jeanne Yost
Proofreaders: Judy Kiviat, Kristi Wiswell
Indexer: Terry Casey
Art Director: Linda May
Interior Design: Ke Design
Cover Design: PHodepohl Design
Cover Images: Beathan/Corbis, Tetra Images/Corbis, Mahesh Patil/Shutterstock
Compositor: Parkwood Composition Service

Library of Congress Control Number: 2012952537

Student Edition:
ISBN-13: 978-1-133-60437-2
ISBN-10: 1-133-60437-4

Wadsworth Political Science
20 Channel Center
Boston, MA 02210

Printed in the United States of America
1 2 3 4 5 6 7 16 15 14 13 12

BRIEF CONTENTS

PART I [illegible]

PART II CIVIL RIGHTS AND [illegible]

PART III [illegible]

PART IV [illegible]

PART V [illegible]

CONTENTS

Yang Lei/ZUMA Press/Newscom

Chapter 2: The Constitution 31

CHAPTER 2 FEATURES

AP Photo/Reed Saxon

Chapter 3: Federalism 81

CHAPTER 3 FEATURES

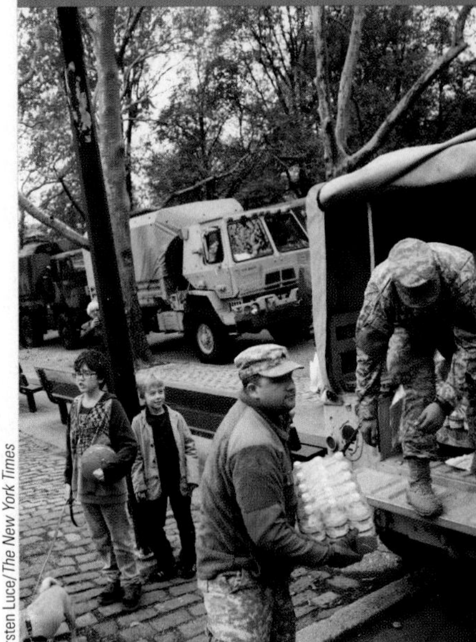

Kirsten Luce/*The New York Times*

PART 2: CIVIL RIGHTS AND LIBERTIES

Chapter 4: Civil Liberties 111

CHAPTER 4 FEATURES

Jim West/REPORT DIGITAL-REA/Redux

Chapter 5: Civil Rights 145

CHAPTER 5 FEATURES

DON EMMERT/AFP/Getty Images

PART 3: PEOPLE AND POLITICS

Chapter 6: Public Opinion and Political Socialization 183

CHAPTER 6 FEATURES

DARREN HAUCK/Reuters/Landov

Chapter 7: Interest Groups 215

CHAPTER 7 FEATURES

DANIEL ACKER/Reuters/Landov

Chapter 8: Political Parties 245

CHAPTER 8 FEATURES

KEVIN LAMARQUE/Reuters/Landov

Chapter 9: Campaigns, Elections, and the Media 279

CHAPTER 9 FEATURES

AP Photo/Steven Senne

PART 4: POLITICAL INSTITUTIONS

Chapter 10: The Congress 321

CHAPTER 10 FEATURES

Gilles Rolla/REA/Redux

Chapter 11: The President 353

CHAPTER 11 FEATURES

GARY C. CASKEY/UPI/Landov

CHAPTER 12 FEATURES

Paul Horsted Stock Connection Worldwide/Newscom

Chapter 12: The Bureaucracy 385

Chapter 13: The Courts 417

CHAPTER 13 FEATURES

AP Photo/Hans Pennink

PART 5: PUBLIC POLICY

Chapter 14: Domestic and Economic Policy 447

CHAPTER 14 FEATURES

EPA/MATTHEW CAVANAUGH/Newscom

Chapter 15: Foreign Policy 479

CHAPTER 15 FEATURES

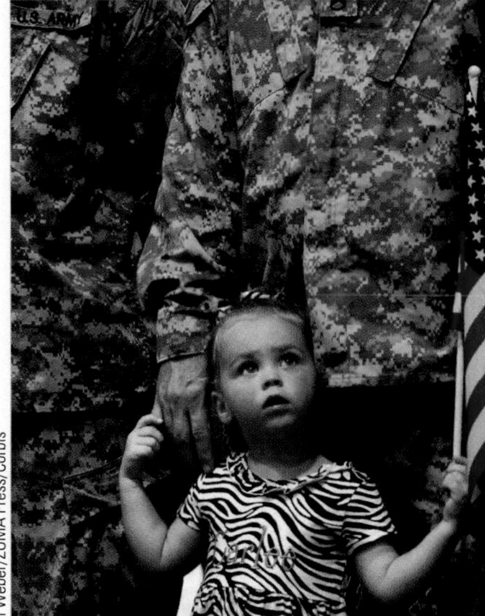

Jim Weber/ZUMA Press/Corbis

PREFACE

The 2012 elections were billed as among the most important ever. If the nation were to reelect Democratic president Barack Obama, then the reforms adopted during his first two years in office would finally come to fruition. These involved wide-ranging changes to the financial industry, but above all, they included the full implementation of the Patient Protection and Affordable Care Act, nicknamed "Obamacare." This act's most important features were not scheduled to go into effect until January 2014.

As an alternative, if Republican presidential candidate Mitt Romney were to win the election and the Republicans were to take control of the U.S. Senate, they promised to set the country on a dramatic new limited-government trajectory. Obamacare would be repealed. Tax rates would fall. The nation's complex program of domestic spending would undergo its most dramatic pruning ever.

For most of 2012, the outcome seemed close. The political campaigns were bitter and hugely expensive. The economy remained troubled, and the unemployment rate was high. In the end, though, Obama prevailed and the Democrats held the Senate. All of these developments and more are covered in the 2013–2014 edition of *American Government and Politics Today: The Essentials.*

2012 Election Results Included and Analyzed

Because we have learned that students respond to up-to-date information about political events, we have included results of the November 2012 elections. We have updated all of the text to reflect these results and have analyzed how the results will affect political processes at all levels of government. In each **2012 elections** feature, we place the election results in the context of the chapter's subject matter.

The Interactive Focus of This Text—Participation

Whether the topic is voter turnout, terrorism, or the problems that face the president, we constantly strive to involve the student in the analysis. We make sure that the student comes to understand that politics is not an abstract process but a very human enterprise. We emphasize how different outcomes can affect students' civil rights and liberties, employment opportunities, and economic welfare.

Emphasis on Critical Thinking

Throughout the text, we encourage the student to think critically. Almost all of the features end with questions designed to engage the student's critical-thinking and analytical skills. A feature titled **Which Side Are You On?** challenges the student to find a connection between controversial issues facing the nation and the student's personal positions on these issues.

End-of-Chapter Questions for Discussion and Analysis

We continue our tradition of engaging students with a section titled **"Questions for Discussion and Analysis,"** which appears at the end of each chapter. This section consists of a series of four questions, each of which asks the student to explore a particular issue relating to a topic covered in the chapter.

Other Interactive Features

We further encourage interaction with the political system by ending each chapter with a feature titled *Why Should You Care about. . . ?*, along with a subsection called **"How You Can Make a Difference."** These show students how to become politically involved and why it is important that they do so.

Special Pedagogy and Features

The 2013–2014 edition of *American Government and Politics Today: The Essentials* contains many pedagogical aids and high-interest features to assist both students and instructors. The *Skill Prep: A Student Study Skills Module, Learning Outcomes, Social Media in Politics,* and the end-of-chapter quizzes are new to this edition. The following list summarizes the special elements that can be found in each chapter:

- *Skill Prep: A Student Study Skills Module*—A new introductory section that opens the book, outlining tips for studying, writing papers and essays, and taking tests.
- *Learning Outcomes*—Listed on the opening page of each chapter, they are designed to help improve students' understanding of the chapter.
- *What If . . .* —A chapter-opening feature that discusses a hypothetical situation concerning a topic to be covered in the chapter.
- *Margin Definitions*—For all important terms.
- *Social Media in Politics*—A margin feature that explains how students can find relevant materials using Facebook, Twitter, and other social media platforms.
- *Did You Know . . . ?*—A margin feature presenting various facts and figures that add interest to the learning process.
- *Which Side Are You On?*—A feature designed to challenge students to take a stand on controversial issues.
- *Politics and . . .* —A feature that examines the influence of politics on a variety of issues. *Politics and Economics* is a common topic, but subjects range from *Politics and Religion* to *Politics and Property Rights.*
- *Beyond Our Borders*—A feature that provides a context for American institutions by looking at the experiences of other countries.
- *Why Should You Care about . . . ?*—A chapter-ending feature that gives the student some specific reasons to care about the topics covered in the chapter and that provides ways in which the student can become actively involved in American politics.
- *Questions for Discussion and Analysis*—A series of questions at the end of each chapter that are designed to promote in-class discussions.
- *Key Terms*—A chapter-ending list, with page numbers, of all terms in the chapter that are **boldfaced** in the text and defined in the margins.
- *Chapter Summary*—A point-by-point summary of the chapter text.
- *Quizzes*—Both fill-in-the-blanks and multiple-choice quizzes, allowing students to test their comprehension of the material.
- *Suggested Readings* and *Media Resources*—An annotated list of suggested scholarly readings as well as popular and timely books, films, and documentaries relevant to chapter topics.
- *E-mocracy*—A feature that discusses politics and the Internet and that offers Web sites and Internet activities related to the chapter's topics.

Appendices

Because we know that this book serves as a reference, we have included important documents for the student of American government to have close at hand. A **fully**

annotated copy of the U.S. Constitution appears at the end of Chapter 2, as an appendix to that chapter. In addition, we have included the following appendices at the end of this text:

- The Declaration of Independence
- How to Read Case Citations and Find Court Decisions
- *Federalist Papers* Nos. 10, 51, and 78
- Justices of the United States Supreme Court since 1900
- Party Control of Congress since 1900
- The Presidents of the United States

Useful material is also located immediately inside the front and back covers of this text. Inside the front cover, you will find a cartogram that distorts the size of the various states to indicate their relative weight in the Electoral College. Inside the back cover, you will find a pictorial diagram of the Capitol of the United States.

Supplements for the Instructor

Aplia for Bardes, Shelley & Schmidt's
American Government and Politics Today: The Essentials, 2013–2014 Edition
Book with Bundle: ISBN-13: 9781285475684
Printed Access Card: ISBN-13: 9781133949121
Instant Access Code: ISBN-13: 9781133949138
Easy to use, affordable, and effective, Aplia helps students learn and saves you time. It's like a virtual teaching assistant! Aplia enables you to have more productive classes by providing assignments that get students thinking critically, reading assigned material, and reinforcing basic concepts—all before coming to class. The interactive questions also help students better understand the relevance of what they're learning and how to apply those concepts to the world around them.

Visually engaging videos, graphs, and political cartoons help capture students' attention and imagination, and an included eBook provides convenient access. Purchase instant access to Aplia via CengageBrain, www.cengagebrain.com, or through the bookstore via the printed access code. Please go to www.aplia.com/politicalscience to view a demo, and contact your local Cengage sales representative for more information.

PowerLecture DVD with ExamView® and JoinIn® for Bardes, Shelley & Schmidt's
American Government and Politics Today: The Essentials, 2013–2014 Edition
ISBN-13: 9781133947240

An all-in-one multimedia resource for class preparation, presentation, and testing, this DVD includes Microsoft® PowerPoint® slides, a test bank in both Microsoft® Word and ExamView® formats, online polling and JoinIn™ clicker questions, an Instructor's Manual, and a Resource Integration Guide.

The **book-specific PowerPoint® slides** of lecture outlines, as well as photos, figures, and tables from the text, make it easy for you to assemble lectures for your course. The **media-enhanced PowerPoint® slides** help bring your lecture to life with audio and video clips, animated learning modules illustrating key concepts, tables, statistical charts, graphs, and photos from the book as well as outside sources.

The **test bank,** offered in Microsoft Word® and ExamView® formats, includes sixty-plus multiple-choice questions with answers and page references, along with ten essay questions for each chapter. ExamView® features a user-friendly testing environment that allows you to publish not only traditional paper and computer-based tests, but also Web-deliverable exams. **JoinIn™** offers "clicker" questions covering key concepts, enabling instructors to incorporate student response systems into their classroom lectures.

The ***Instructor's Manual*** includes Learning Outcomes, chapter outlines, summaries, discussion questions, suggestions for class activities and projects, tips on integrating media into your class, and suggested readings and Web resources. The ***Resource Integration Guide*** provides a chapter-by-chapter outline of all available resources to supplement and optimize learning. Contact your Cengage representative to receive a copy upon adoption.

The Wadsworth News DVD for Bardes, Shelley & Schmidt's
American Government and Politics Today: The Essentials, 2013–2014 Edition
ISBN-13: 9781285053455

This collection of two- to five-minute video clips on relevant political issues serves as a great lecture or discussion launcher.

Political Science CourseMate for Bardes, Shelley & Schmidt's
American Government and Politics Today: The Essentials, 2013–2014 Edition
Printed Access Card: ISBN-13: 9781133949282
Instant Access Code: ISBN-13: 9781133949213

Cengage Learning's Political Science CourseMate brings course concepts to life with interactive learning, study tools, and exam preparation tools that support the printed textbook. Use **Engagement Tracker** to assess student preparation and engagement in the course, and watch student comprehension soar as your class works with the textbook-specific Web site. An **interactive eBook** allows students to take notes, highlight, search, and interact with embedded media. Other resources include video activities, animated learning modules, simulations, case studies, interactive quizzes, and timelines. Students can purchase instant access via www.cengagebrain.com or via a printed access card in your bookstore.

The **American Government NewsWatch** is a real-time news and information resource, updated daily, that includes interactive maps, videos, podcasts, and hundreds of articles from leading journals, magazines, and newspapers from the United States and the world. Also included is the **KnowNow! American Government Blog,** which highlights three current-event stories per week and consists of a succinct analysis of each story, multimedia, and discussion-starter questions. Access your course via www.cengage.com/login.

Instructor Companion Web Site for Bardes, Shelley & Schmidt's
American Government and Politics Today: The Essentials, 2013–2014 Edition
ISBN-13: 9781133938804

This password-protected Web site for instructors features all of the free student assets plus an *Instructor's Manual,* book-specific PowerPoint® presentations, JoinIn™ "clicker" questions, a *Resource Integration Guide,* and a test bank. Access your resources by logging onto your account at www.cengage.com/login.

CourseReader: American Government 0–30 Selections
Printed Access Card: ISBN-13: 9781111479954
Instant Access Code: ISBN-13: 9781111479978

CourseReader: American Government allows you to create your reader, your way, in just minutes. This affordable, fully customizable online reader provides access to thousands of permissions-cleared readings, articles, primary sources, and audio and video selections from the regularly updated Gale research library database. This easy-to-use solution allows you to search for and select the exact material you want for your courses.

Each selection opens with a descriptive introduction to provide context and concludes with critical-thinking and multiple-choice questions to reinforce key points. CourseReader is loaded with convenient tools like highlighting, printing, note taking, and downloadable MP3 audio files for each reading.

CourseReader is the perfect complement to any political science course. It can be bundled with your current textbook, sold alone, or integrated into your learning management system. CourseReader 0-30 allows access to up to thirty selections in the reader. For a demo, please visit www.cengage.com/coursereader, or contact your Cengage sales representative for details.

To access CourseReader materials, go to www.cengage.com/sso, click on "Create a New Faculty Account," and fill out the registration page. Once you are in your new SSO account, search for "CourseReader" from your dashboard, and select "CourseReader: American Government." Then click "CourseReader 0–30: American Government Instant Access Code," and choose "Add to my bookshelf." To access the live CourseReader, click on "CourseReader 0–30: American Government" under "Additional Resources" on the right side of your dashboard.

Election 2012: An American Government Supplement
Printed Access Card: ISBN-13: 9781285090931
Instant Access Code: ISBN-13: 9781285420080

Written by John Clark and Brian Schaffner, this booklet addresses the 2012 congressional and presidential races with real-time analysis and references. Access your course via www.cengage.com/login.

Custom Enrichment Module: Latino-American Politics Supplement
ISBN-13: 9781285184296

This revised and updated thirty-two-page supplement uses real examples to detail political issues related to Latino Americans and can be added to your text via our custom publishing solutions.

Supplements for Students

Free Student Companion Web Site
The text's free companion Web site, accessible at www.cengagebrain.com, contains a wealth of study aids and resources for students. Students will find open access to Learning Outcomes, tutorial quizzes, chapter glossaries, flashcards, and crossword puzzles, all correlated by chapter. At the CengageBrain.com home page, search for the ISBN of your title (from the back cover of your book), using the search box at the top of the page. This will take you to the product page where these resources can be found.

Aplia for Bardes, Shelley & Schmidt's
American Government and Politics Today: The Essentials, 2013–2014 Edition

Easy to use, affordable, and convenient, Aplia helps you learn more and improve your grade in the course. Interactive assignments, including videos, graphs, and political cartoons, enables you to better understand the essential concepts of American government and how they apply to real life.

Aplia helps prepare you to be more involved in class by strengthening your critical-thinking skills, reinforcing what you need to know, and assisting you in understanding why it all matters. For your studying convenience, Aplia includes an eBook, accessible right next to your assignments.

Purchase instant access via CengageBrain or via a printed access card in your bookstore. Visit www.cengagebrain.com for more information. Aplia should be purchased only when assigned by your instructor as part of your course.

Political Science CourseMate for Bardes, Shelley & Schmidt's *American Government and Politics Today: The Essentials, 2013–2014 Edition*
Cengage Learning's Political Science CourseMate brings course concepts to life with interactive learning, study tools, and exam preparation tools that support the printed textbook. The more you study, the better the results. Make the most of your study time by accessing everything you need to succeed in one place. Read your textbook, take notes, watch videos, read case studies, take practice quizzes, and more—online with CourseMate. CourseMate also gives you access to the **American Government NewsWatch** Web site, a real-time news and information resource updated daily, and **KnowNow!,** the go-to blog about current events in American government.

Purchase instant access via CengageBrain or via a printed access card in your bookstore. Visit www.cengagebrain.com for more information. CourseMate should be purchased only when assigned by your instructor as part of your course.

For Users of the Previous Edition

We thank you for your past support of our work. We have made numerous changes to this volume for the 2013–2014 edition, many of which we list below. We have rewritten the text as necessary, added many new features, and updated the book to reflect the events of the past two years.

- **Chapter 1 (The Democratic Republic)**—A new *What If . . .* feature asks what would happen if we had no Bill of Rights. The description of *legitimacy* is updated. The Tea Party and Occupy movements receive new coverage. The section describing American attitudes toward "big government" has been rewritten. The definitions of *conservatism* and *liberalism* are expanded. A final section describes the recent environment of partisanship and gridlock, and connects these attitudes to the 2012 elections.
- **Chapter 2 (The Constitution)**—A new feature discusses the constitutionality of the Affordable Care Act (Obamacare). Other new features explain France's role in defeating the British in the Revolutionary War and the importance of the post-revolutionary economic downturn. *How You Can Make a Difference* has been revised with more-current examples.
- **Chapter 3 (Federalism)**—New sections describe *fiscal federalism* and *competitive federalism*. New features cover the crisis of the European Union, state spending in hard times, and the debate over public employee pensions.
- **Chapter 4 (Civil Liberties)**—The *imminent lawless action test* for advocacy speech is defined. A new section describes the right of assembly. Material on the civil liberties of immigrants has been moved into the chapter. New features deal with gun rights and online piracy.
- **Chapter 5 (Civil Rights)**—The sections on gay and lesbian rights were substantially updated. A major new section details the review standards employed by the United States Supreme Court in assessing potential discrimination—*strict scrutiny, intermediate scrutiny,* and *rational basis review.* A new feature examines the experience of African Americans in the criminal justice system.
- **Chapter 6 (Public Opinion and Political Socialization)**—This chapter received some of the most thorough revisions in the book. The sections on public opinion polls

have been completely redone. New stress is placed on the statistical nature of polling. We also focus on modern polling issues, such as *weighting samples, house effects,* and *robopolls*. A new section discusses the overall political mood of the country. The issue of *framing* is addressed in the text and in a feature. Other new features deal with social media and the growing cultural gap between rich and poor. The many charts and tables have been updated.

- **Chapter 7 (Interest Groups)**—New topics include the political environment faced by the labor movement, global warming and the coal interests, the consumer movement, ideological groups, and identity groups. Features discuss the Keystone XL oil pipeline and the American Legislative Exchange Council.
- **Chapter 8 (Political Parties)**—The section on recent developments is entirely new. It discusses *wave elections* and political overreach by the Democrats and the Republicans. The discussion of proportional representation has been sharpened and includes examples. A new feature addresses the "top-two candidates" primary system in California.
- **Chapter 9 (Campaigns, Elections, and the Media)**—Large-scale revisions include redoing the entire section on campaign finance. *Super PACs* and other independent committees such as *527 and 501(c)4 groups* are now central to the discussion. The concept of the *moneybomb* is introduced. We describe recent changes to the ways in which primaries are managed. A new section discusses photo voter ID laws and the attempts to restrict voter-registration drives. We cover the Republican primary debates and the debates between Obama and Romney. The media section has an enhanced discussion of new media and its appeal to younger citizens.
- **Chapter 10 (The Congress)**—New topics include *reconciliation* and recent attempts to curb earmarks. The section on gerrymandering is enhanced and includes easy-to-understand examples and a feature. Another feature discusses "Taxmageddon," the end-of-2012 financial cliff.
- **Chapter 11 (The President)**—Material on the president's popularity is updated. There is an added discussion of policy "czars" in the White House. A new feature discusses the impact of the state of the economy on the reelection chances of an incumbent president.
- **Chapter 12 (The Bureaucracy)**—A new section provides considerable detail on federal spending, as opposed to federal employment. New features discuss military bureaucracy and Obama's campaign against national security leaks.
- **Chapter 13 (The Courts)**—We clarify how individuals can appeal decisions by bureaucratic agencies. The history of Supreme Court confirmation battles now includes the fight over Robert Bork. The discussion of the Roberts Court contrasts the Court's style of conservatism with the beliefs of the broader conservative movement. A new feature examines *sharia* law.
- **Chapter 14 (Domestic and Economic Policy)**—The sections on health care and immigration are updated. The section on energy and the environment is substantially revised. The impact of energy prices—including the low cost of natural gas—receives fresh treatment, and we discuss such new technologies as *fracking*. The economic policy section now covers conservative criticisms of Keynes and recent proposed changes to the tax system. A new feature addresses the problem of long-term unemployment, and another asks what would happen if we returned to the gold standard.
- **Chapter 15 (Foreign Policy)**—The chapter has new discussions of the "Arab Spring" and the death of Osama bin Laden. We have updated the descriptions of sanctions against Iran and the Israeli-Palestinian conflict. A new section covers the economic crisis in Europe. A new feature asks whether we should attack Iran's nuclear enrichment sites, and another looks at cyberspace attacks against Iran and by China.

Acknowledgments

Since we started this project a number of years ago, a sizable cadre of individuals has helped us in various phases of the undertaking. The following academic reviewers offered numerous constructive criticisms, comments, and suggestions during the preparation of this and all previous editions:

Danny M. Adkison
Oklahoma State University, Stillwater

Ahrar Ahmad
Black Hills State University, South Dakota

Sharon Z. Alter
William Rainey Harper College, Illinois

Pat Andrews
West Valley College, California

Marcos Arandia
North Lake College, Texas

Hugh M. Arnold
Clayton College and State University, Georgia

William Arp III
Louisiana State University

Kevin Bailey
North Harris Community College, Texas

Evelyn Ballard
Houston Community College, Texas

Orlando N. Bama
McLennan Community College, Texas

Dr. Charles T. Barber
University of Southern Indiana, Evansville

Clyde W. Barrow
Texas A&M University

Shari Garber Bax
Central Missouri State University, Warrensburg

Dr. Joshua G. Behr
Old Dominion University, Virginia

David S. Bell
Eastern Washington University, Cheney

David C. Benford, Jr.
Tarrant County Junior College, Texas

Dr. Curtis Berry
Shippensburg University, Pennsylvania

John A. Braithwaite
Coastline College, California

Sherman Brewer, Jr.
Rutgers University–Newark, New Jersey

Lynn R. Brink
North Lake College, Texas

Barbara L. Brown
Southern Illinois University at Carbondale

Richard G. Buckner
Santa Fe Community College, New Mexico

Kenyon D. Bunch
Fort Lewis College, Colorado

Ralph Bunch
Portland State University, Oregon

Carol Cassell
University of Alabama

Dewey Clayton
University of Louisville, Kentucky

Ann Clemmer
University of Arkansas at Little Rock

Frank T. Colon
Lehigh University, Pennsylvania

Frank J. Coppa
Union County College, New Jersey

Irasema Coronado
University of Texas at El Paso

James B. Cottrill
Santa Clara University, California

Robert E. Craig
University of New Hampshire

Beatriz Cuartas
El Paso Community College, Texas

Doris Daniels
Nassau Community College, New York

Carolyn Grafton Davis
North Harris County College, Texas

Paul B. Davis
Truckee Meadows Community College, Nevada

Richard D. Davis
Brigham Young University, Utah

Martyn de Bruyn
Northeastern Illinois University

Ron Deaton
Prince George's Community College, Maryland

Marshall L. DeRosa
Louisiana State University, Baton Rouge

Michael Dinneen
Tulsa Junior College, Oklahoma

Gavan Duffy
University of Texas at Austin

Don Thomas Dugi
Transylvania University, Kentucky

George C. Edwards III
Texas A&M University

Gregory Edwards
Amarillo College, Texas

Mark C. Ellickson
Southwestern Missouri State University, Springfield

Larry Elowitz
Georgia College, Milledgeville

Jodi Empol
Montgomery County Community College, Pennsylvania

John W. Epperson
Simpson College, Indiana

Victoria A. Farrar-Myers
University of Texas at Arlington

Daniel W. Fleitas
University of North Carolina at Charlotte

Elizabeth N. Flores
Del Mar College, Texas

Joel L. Franke
Blinn College, Brenham, Texas

Barry D. Friedman
North Georgia College, Dahlonega

Crystal Garrett
Georgia Perimeter College–Dunwoody

Joseph Georges
El Camino College, California

Robert S. Getz
SUNY–Brockport, New York

Kristina Gilbert
Riverside Community College, California

William A. Giles
Mississippi State University

Jack Goodyear
Dallas Baptist University, Texas

Donald Gregory
Stephen F. Austin State University, Texas

Forest Grieves
University of Montana

Dale Grimnitz
Normandale Community College, Minnesota

Stefan D. Haag
Austin Community College, Texas

Justin Halpern
Northeastern State University, Oklahoma

Willie Hamilton
Mount San Jacinto College, California

Matthew Hansel
McHenry County College, Illinois

Jean Wahl Harris
University of Scranton, Pennsylvania

David N. Hartman
Rancho Santiago College, Santa Ana, California

Robert M. Herman
Moorpark College, California

Richard J. Herzog
Stephen F. Austin State University, Texas

Paul Holder
McClennan Community College, Texas

Michael Hoover
Seminole Community College, Sanford, Florida

Joanne Hopkins-Lucia
Baker College of Clinton Township, Michigan

J. C. Horton
San Antonio College, Texas

Frank Ibe
Wayne County Community College, Michigan

Robert Jackson
Washington State University, Pullman

Willoughby Jarrell
Kennesaw State University, Georgia

Loch K. Johnson
University of Georgia

Donald L. Jordan
United States Air Force Academy, Colorado

Roger Jordan
Baker College of Flint, Michigan

John D. Kay
Santa Barbara City College, California

Charles W. Kegley
University of South Carolina

Jon Kelly
West Valley College, California

Thomas R. Kemp
University of Arkansas at Little Rock

Bruce L. Kessler
Shippensburg University, Pennsylvania

Robert King
Georgia Perimeter College–Dunwoody

Jason F. Kirksey
Oklahoma State University, Stillwater

Kevin Kniess
Lakeland College, Wisconsin

Nancy B. Kral
Tomball College, Texas

Dale Krane
Mississippi State University

Samuel Krislov
University of Minnesota

William W. Lamkin
Glendale Community College, California

Harry D. Lawrence
Southwest Texas Junior College

Ray Leal
Texas State University–San Marcos

Sue Lee
Center for Telecommunications, Dallas County Community College District, Texas

Alan Lehmann
Blinn College, Texas

Carl Lieberman
University of Akron, Ohio

Linda Lien
Westwood College, California

Orma Linford
Kansas State University, Manhattan

James J. Lopach
University of Montana

Eileen Lynch
Brookhaven College, Texas

William W. Maddox
University of Florida

S. J. Makielski, Jr.
Loyola University, Louisiana

Jarol B. Manheim
George Washington University, District of Columbia

J. David Martin
Midwestern State University, Texas

Bruce B. Mason
Arizona State University

Thomas Louis Masterson
Butte College, California

Steve J. Mazurana
University of Northern Colorado, Greeley

James D. McElyea
Tulsa Junior College, Oklahoma

Thomas J. McGaghie
Kellogg Community College, Michigan

William P. McLauchlan
Purdue University, Indiana

Stanley Melnick
Valencia Community College, Florida

James Mitchell
California State University, Northridge

Robert Mittrick
Luzerne County Community College, Pennsylvania

Helen Molanphy
Richland College, Texas

James Morrow
Tulsa Community College, Oklahoma

Keith Nicholls
University of Alabama

Eric Nobles
Atlanta Metropolitan College, Georgia

Sandra O'Brien
Florida Gulf Coast University

Tamra Ortgies Young
Georgia Perimeter College, Decatur

Stephen Osofsky
Nassau Community College, New York

John P. Pelissero
Loyola University of Chicago

Lisa Perez-Nichols
Austin Community College, Texas

Neil A. Pinney
Western Michigan University

George E. Pippin
Jones County Community College, Mississippi

Walter V. Powell
Slippery Rock University, Pennsylvania

Michael A. Preda
Midwestern State University, Texas

Jeffrey L. Prewitt
Brewton-Parker College, Georgia

Mark E. Priewe
University of Texas at San Antonio

About the Authors

BARBARA A. BARDES

Barbara A. Bardes is professor emerita of political science and former dean of Raymond Walters College at the University of Cincinnati. She received her B.A. and M.A. from Kent State University. After completing her Ph.D. at the University of Cincinnati, she held faculty positions at Mississippi State University and Loyola University in Chicago. She returned to Cincinnati, her hometown, as a college administrator. She has also worked as a political consultant and directed polling for a research center.

Bardes has written articles on public opinion and foreign policy, and on women and politics. She has authored *Thinking about Public Policy; Declarations of Independence: Women and Political Power in Nineteenth-Century American Fiction;* and *Public Opinion: Measuring the American Mind* (with Robert W. Oldendick).

Bardes's home is located in a very small hamlet in Kentucky called Rabbit Hash, famous for its 150-year-old general store. Her hobbies include traveling, gardening, needlework, and antique collecting.

MACK C. SHELLEY II

Mack C. Shelley II is professor of political science and statistics at Iowa State University. After receiving his bachelor's degree from American University in Washington, D.C., he completed graduate studies at the University of Wisconsin at Madison, where he received a master's degree in economics and a Ph.D. in political science. He taught for two years at Mississippi State University before arriving at Iowa State in 1979.

Shelley has published numerous articles, books, and monographs on public policy. From 1993 to 2002, he served as elected coeditor of the *Policy Studies Journal.* His published books include *The Permanent Majority: The Conservative Coalition in the United States Congress; Biotechnology and the Research Enterprise* (with William F. Woodman and Brian J. Reichel); *American Public Policy: The Contemporary Agenda* (with Steven G. Koven and Bert E. Swanson); *Redefining Family Policy: Implications for the 21st Century* (with Joyce M. Mercier and Steven Garasky); and *Quality Research in Literacy and Science Education: International Perspectives and Gold Standards* (with Larry Yore and Brian Hand).

His leisure time includes traveling, working with students, and playing with the family dog and cats.

STEFFEN W. SCHMIDT

Steffen W. Schmidt is professor of political science at Iowa State University. He grew up in Colombia, South America, and studied in Colombia, Switzerland, and France. He obtained his Ph.D. in public law and government from Columbia University in New York.

Schmidt has published 12 books and more than 120 journal articles. He is also the recipient of numerous prestigious teaching prizes, including the Amoco Award for Lifetime Career Achievement in Teaching and the Teacher of the Year award. He is a pioneer in the use of Web-based and real-time video courses, as well as a member of the American Political Science Association's section on computers and multimedia. He is on the editorial board of the *Political Science Educator* and is the technology and teaching editor of the *Journal of Political Science Education*.

Schmidt has a political talk show on WOI radio, where he is known as Dr. Politics. The show has been broadcast live from various U.S. and international venues. He is a frequent political commentator for *CNN en Español* and the British Broadcasting Corporation. He is the co-founder of the new Internet magazine InsiderIowa.com.

Schmidt likes to snow ski, ride hunter jumper horses, race sailboats, and scuba dive.

SKILL PREP

A STUDY SKILLS MODULE

WHAT'S INSIDE

After reading through and practicing the material in this study skills module, you will be better prepared to . . .

- **Make good choices** (LifePrep, p. SP–3)
- **Manage your time** (TimePrep, p. SP–5)
- **Be engaged in your studies** (StudyPrep, p. SP–7)
- **Study for quizzes and exams** (TestPrep, p. SP–11)
- **Read your textbook for learning** (ReadPrep, p. SP–13)
- **Write your papers** (WritePrep, p. SP–15)
- **Deliver a speech** (SpeechPrep, p. SP–20)

René Mansi/iStockphoto.com

Welcome!

With this course and this textbook, you've begun what we hope will be a fun, stimulating, and thought-provoking journey into the world of American government and politics. In this course, you will learn all about the foundation of the American system, civil rights and liberties, public opinion, interest groups, political parties, campaigns, elections, the media, our governing institutions, and public policy. Knowledge of these basics will help you think critically about political issues and become an active citizen.

To help you get the most out of this course, and this textbook, we have developed this study skills module. You may be a recent high school graduate, or a working professional continuing your education, or an adult making your way back to the classroom after a few years. Whatever type of student you are, you want RESULTS when you study. You want to be able to understand the issues and ideas presented in the textbook, to be able to talk about them intelligently during class discussions, and to be able to remember them as you prepare for exams and papers.

This kind of knowledge doesn't just come from natural talent. Instead, it comes from the use of good study skills. This module is designed to help you develop the skills and habits you'll need to get the results that you want from this course. With tips on lifestyle decisions, how to manage your time more effectively, how to be more engaged when you study, how to get the most out of your textbook, how to prepare for quizzes and exams, how to write papers, and how to prepare and deliver a speech, this guide will help you become the best learner you can be!

LIFE PREP

Paul Ijsendoorn/iStockphoto.com

It takes several things to succeed in a class—hard work, concentration, and commitment to your studies. In order to work hard, concentrate, and demonstrate commitment, you need energy. When you are full of energy, time seems to pass quickly, and it is easier to get things done. When you don't have energy, time feels as if it is standing still, and even your favorite activities can feel like a burden. To have the energy you need to be a great learner, it is important to make good lifestyle choices. You need to get enough sleep, eat well, take care of yourself, and maintain good relationships. An important part of being a successful student is to pay attention to what goes on in your life so that you have all the ingredients you need to maintain your focus and energy.

Most people who succeed have a plan.

Here are some suggestions that you can use to keep up your energy and develop other aspects of your life so that you can succeed in everything you do.

- Too often, we become so busy with other aspects of our lives that we neglect our health. It is crucial that you eat a balanced diet, exercise regularly, and get enough sleep. If you don't take care of your physical well-being, other areas of your life will inevitably suffer.
- Hearing is not the same thing as listening. Many people are not good listeners. We often hear what we want to hear as we filter information through our own experiences and interests. When talking with friends, instructors, or family members, focus carefully on what they say—it may reveal something unexpected.
- Be very careful about what you post on the Internet. A good rule of thumb is "Don't post anything that you wouldn't want the world to know." Many employers search the Internet for information concerning potential employees, and one embarrassing photo or tweet can have long-term damaging consequences.
- Most people who succeed have a plan—what they want to accomplish and when. Do you have a life plan? If not, you can start by making a list of your lifetime goals, even though they may change later on. You can also create a career plan that includes a list of skills you will need to succeed. Then, choose classes and extracurricular activities that will help you develop these skills.
- When we start doing something new, whether in school or in other areas of life, we usually aren't very good at it. We need feedback from those who are good in that area—such as instructors—to improve and succeed. Therefore, you should welcome feedback, and if it isn't given, you should ask for it.
- Many studies have shown that exercise benefits the mind as well as the body. Students at all levels who participate in organized sports or who regularly engage in their own training programs often do better on standardized math and reading tests than those students who do not. Regular exercise in whatever form should become a part of your daily routine. Not only will you feel great, you'll become a better learner. In other words, exercise should become a habit.

- Do you want to become a better writer? Your college or university probably has a writing center with resources to help you with your writing assignments. If not, you should be able to find a tutor who will help you figure out what you are trying to communicate and how to put it effectively on paper.
- Filing systems are an easy way to keep track of your money. First, label file folders for different categories of income, such as paycheck stubs, bank statements, and miscellaneous. Then, do the same for expenses, such as clothes, food, and entertainment. If you find you need another category, just set up a new folder.
- Do you want to become a better public speaker? Consider using your campus's audiovisual resources to develop this difficult but rewarding skill. Record yourself speaking and then critique your performance. Join a school organization such as a debate or drama club to gain confidence in front of a live audience.
- If you feel that you are overly dependent on family or friends, nurture skills that lead to independence. For example, learn how to cook for yourself. Get a job that does not interfere (too much) with your schoolwork. Save money and pay your own bills. Rent your own living space. Most important, have confidence in yourself.
- More often than not, in school and life, things do not go as planned. When this happens, you need to be flexible. Do not focus on your disappointment. Instead, try to accept the situation as it is, and deal with it by looking at the future rather than dwelling on the past.
- Be thankful for the people who care about you. Your family and good friends are a precious resource. When you have problems, don't try to solve them by yourself. Talk to the people in your life who want you to succeed and be happy, and listen to their advice.
- Critical thinking is a crucial skill, and, as with any other skill, one gets better at it with practice. So, don't jump to conclusions. Whether you are considering a friend's argument, a test question, a major purchase, or a personal problem, carefully weigh the evidence, balance strengths and weaknesses, and make a reasoned decision.
- Rather than constantly seeking approval from others, try to seek approval from the person who matters the most—yourself. If you have good values, then your conscience will tell you when you are doing the right thing. Don't let worries about what others think run, or ruin, your life.

If you don't take care of your physical well-being, other areas of your life will inevitably suffer.

Steven Wynn/iStockphoto.com / Paul Ijsendoorn/iStockphoto.com / Emrah Turudu/iStockphoto.com

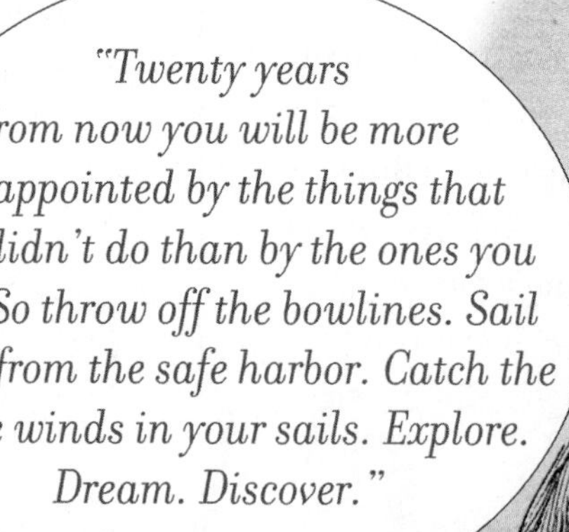

"Twenty years from now you will be more disappointed by the things that you didn't do than by the ones you did. So throw off the bowlines. Sail away from the safe harbor. Catch the trade winds in your sails. Explore. Dream. Discover."

Mark Twain
(American author, 1835–1910)

TIME PREP

Taking a college-level course involves a lot of work. You have to go to class, read the textbook, pay attention to lectures, take notes, complete homework assignments, write papers, and take exams. On top of that, there are other things in the other areas of your life that call for your time and attention. You have to take care of where you live, run daily errands, take care of family, spend time with friends, work a full- or part-time job, and find time to unwind. With all that you're involved in, knowing how to manage your time is critical if you want to succeed as a learner.

Skip Odonnell/iStockphoto.com

The key to managing your time is to know how much time you have and to use it well. At the beginning of every term, you should evaluate how you use your time. How much time is spent working? How much caring for your home and family? On entertainment? How much time do you spend studying? Keep a record of what you do hour by hour for a full week. Once you see where all your time goes, you can decide which activities you might modify in order to have "more" time.

To manage your time well, you need to know where it is going.

Here are some other helpful tips on how to make the most of your time.

- Plan your study schedule in advance. At the beginning of each week, allocate time for each subject that you need to study. If it helps, put your schedule down on paper or use one of the many "calendar" computer programs for efficient daily planning.
- Don't be late for classes, meetings with professors, and other appointments. If you find that you have trouble being on time, adjust your planning to arrive fifteen minutes early to all engagements. That way, even if you are "late," in most cases you will still be on time.
- To reduce the time spent looking for information on the Internet, start with a clear idea of your research task. Use a trusted search engine and focus only on that subject. Do not allow yourself to be sidetracked by other activities such as checking e-mail or social networking.
- Set aside a little time each day to assess whether you are going to meet the deadlines for all of your classes—quizzes, papers, and exams. It is critical to ensure that deadlines don't "sneak up" on you. A great way to do this is to use a calendar program or app, which can help you keep track of target dates and even give you friendly reminders.
- Nothing wastes more time—or is more aggravating—than having to redo schoolwork that was somehow lost on your computer. Back up all of your important files periodically. You can copy them onto an external hard drive, a DVD, or a USB flash drive.

Paul Ijsendoorn/iStockphoto.com

Concentrate *on doing* **one thing** *at a time.*

- Concentrate on doing one thing at a time. Multitasking is often a trap that leads you to do several things quickly but poorly. When you are studying, don't carry on a text conversation with a friend or have one eye on the Internet at the same time.
- Set deadlines for yourself, not only with schoolwork but also with responsibilities in other areas of your life. If you tell yourself, "I will have this task done by Monday at noon and that other task finished before dinner on Wednesday," you will find it much easier to balance the many demands on your time.
- Regularly checking e-mail and text messages not only interrupts the task at hand, but also is an easy excuse for procrastination. Set aside specific times of the day to check and answer e-mail, and, when necessary, make sure that your cell phone is off or out of reach.
- Sometimes, a task is so large that it seems impossible, making it more tempting to put off. When given a large assignment, break it into a

series of small assignments. Then, make a list of the assignments, and as you finish each one, give yourself the satisfaction of crossing it off.

- Many of us have a particular time of day when we are most alert—early morning, afternoon, or night. Plan to do schoolwork during that time, when you will be most efficient, and set aside other times of the day for activities that do not require such serious concentration.
- Because we like to be helpful, we may have a hard time saying "no" when others ask for favors that take up our time. Sometimes, though, unless the person is experiencing a real emergency, you have to put your schoolwork or job first. If you are worried that the person will be offended, explain why and trust that she or he will understand how important your schoolwork or job is.
- Slow down. You may think that you are getting more work done by rushing, but haste inevitably leads to poor decisions, mistakes, and errors of judgment, all of which waste time. Work well, not quickly, and you will wind up saving time.
- If you can, outsource. Give someone else some of your responsibilities. If you can afford to, hire someone to clean your house. Send your dirty clothes to a laundry. If money is tight, split chores with friends or housemates so that you can better manage your work-life responsibilities.
- In marketing, *to bundle* means to combine several products in one. In time management, it means combining two activities to free up some time. For example, if you need to exercise and want to socialize, bundle the two activities by going on a jog with your friends. Take along some schoolwork when you head to the laundromat—you can get a lot done while you're waiting for the spin cycle. Or you can record class lectures (ask the professor for permission) so that you can review class material while you're out running errands.
- Develop a habit of setting time limits for tasks, both in and out of school. You will find that with a time limit in mind, you will waste less time and work more efficiently.
- Even the best time management and organization can be waylaid by forgetfulness. Most e-mail systems have free calendar features that allow you to send e-mail reminders to yourself concerning assignments, tests, and other important dates.
- A Chinese adage goes, "The longest journey starts with a single step." If you are having trouble getting started on a project or assignment, identify the first task that needs to be done. Then do it! This helps avoid time-wasting procrastination.

Paul Ijsendoorn/iStockphoto.com

Bundling, or combining two activities, will help you save time.

Rubberball/iStockphoto.com

STUDY PREP

What does it take to be a successful student? Like many people, you may think that success depends on how naturally smart you are, that some people are just better at school than others. But in reality, successful students aren't born, they're made. What this means is that even if you don't consider yourself naturally "book smart," you can do well in this course by developing study skills that will help you understand, remember, and apply key concepts.

There are five things you can do to develop good study habits:

be engaged
ask questions
take notes
make an outline
mark your text

SV-Art/iStockphoto.com

BE ENGAGED

If you've ever heard elevator music, you know what easy listening is like—it stays in the background. You know it's there, but you're not really paying attention to it, and you probably won't remember it after a few minutes. That is *not* what you should be doing in class. You have to be engaged. Being *engaged* means listening to discover (and remember) something. In other words, listening is more than just hearing. Not only do you have to hear what the professor is saying in class, you have to pay attention to it. And as you listen with attention, you will hear what your instructor believes is important. One way to make sure that you are listening attentively is to take notes. Doing so will help you focus on the professor's words and will help you identify the most important parts of the lecture.

ASK QUESTIONS

If you are really engaged in your American government course, you will ask a question or two whenever you do not understand something. You can also ask a question to get your instructor to share her or his opinion on a subject. However you do it, true engagement requires you to be a participant in your class. The more you participate, the more you will learn (and the more your instructor will know who you are!).

TAKE NOTES

Note-taking has a value in and of itself, just as outlining does. The physical act of writing makes you a more efficient learner. In addition, your notes provide a guide to what your instructor thinks is important. That means you will have a better idea of what to study before the next exam if you have a set of notes that you took during class.

MAKE AN OUTLINE

As you read through each chapter of your textbook, you might want to make an outline—a simple method for organizing information. You can create an outline as part of your reading or at the end of your reading. Or you can make an outline when you reread a section before moving on to the next. The act of physically writing an outline for a chapter will help you retain the material in this text and master it, thereby obtaining a higher grade in class. Even if you make an outline that is no more than the headings in this text, you will be studying more efficiently than you would be otherwise.

To make an effective outline, you have to be selective. Outlines that contain all the information in the text are not very useful. Your objectives in outlining are, first, to identify the main concepts and, then, to add the details that support those main concepts.

Your outline should consist of several levels written in a standard format. The most important concepts are assigned Roman numerals; the second most important, capital letters; the third most important, numbers; and the fourth most important, lowercase letters. Here is a quick example:

I. Why Is Government Necessary?
 A. The Need for Security
  1. Order: a state of peace and security
  2. The example of Afghanistan
 B. Protecting Citizens' Freedoms
  1. To protect the liberties of the people: the greatest freedom of the individual that is equal to the freedom of other individuals in the society
 C. Authority and Legitimacy
  1. Authority: The right and power of a government to enforce its decisions and compel obedience
  2. Legitimacy: Popular acceptance of the right and power of government authority
   a. Iraq as an example of authority without legitimacy

MARK YOUR TEXT

Now that you own your own textbook for this course, you can greatly improve your learning by marking your text. By doing so, you will identify the most important concepts of each chapter, and at the same time, you'll be making a handy study guide for reviewing material at a later time.

WAYS OF MARKING The most common form of marking is to underline important points. The second most commonly used method is to use a felt-tipped highlighter, or marker, in yellow or some other transparent color. Marking also includes circling, numbering, using arrows, jotting brief notes, or any other method that allows you to remember things when you go back to skim the pages in your textbook prior to an exam.

IMPORTANT

winterling/iStockphoto.com

WHY MARKING IS IMPORTANT Marking is important for the same reason that outlining is—it helps you to organize the information in the text. It allows you to become an active participant in the mastery of the material. Researchers have shown that the physical act of marking, just like the physical acts of note-taking during class and outlining, helps you better retain the material. The better the material is organized in your mind, the more you'll remember. There are two types of readers—passive and active. The active reader outlines or marks. Active readers typically do better on exams. Perhaps one of the reasons that active readers retain more than passive readers is that the physical act of outlining and/or marking requires greater concentration. It is through greater concentration that more is remembered.

TWO POINTS TO REMEMBER WHEN MARKING

- Read one section at a time before you do any extensive marking. You can't mark a section until you know what is important, and you can't know what is important until you read the whole section.
- Don't overmark. Just as an outline cannot contain everything that is in a text (and notes can't include everything), marking can't cover the whole book. Don't fool yourself into thinking that you have done a good job just because each page is filled up with arrows, asterisks, circles, and underlines. If you do mark the whole book, when you go back to review the material, your markings will not help you remember what was important.

Take a look at the two paragraphs below:

In our democratic republic, citizens play an important role by voting. Although voting is extremely important, it is only one of the ways that citizens can exercise their political influence. Americans can also join a political organization or interest group, stage a protest, or donate funds to a political campaign or cause. There are countless ways to become involved. Informed participation begins with knowledge, however, and this text aims to provide you with a strong foundation in American government and politics. We hope that this book helps introduce you to a lifetime of political awareness and activity.

Paul Ijsendoorn/iStockphoto.com

In our democratic republic, citizens play an important role by voting. Although voting is extremely important, it is only one of the ways that citizens can exercise their political influence. Americans can also join a political organization or interest group, stage a protest, or donate funds to a political campaign or cause.

There are countless ways to become involved. Informed participation begins with knowledge, however, and this text aims to provide you with a strong foundation in American government and politics. We hope that this book helps introduce you to a lifetime of political awareness and activity.

The second paragraph, with all of the different markings, is hard to read and understand because there is so much going on. There are arrows and circles and underlines all over the place, and it is difficult to identify the most important parts of the paragraph. The first paragraph, by contrast, has highlights only on a few important words, making it much easier to identify quickly the important elements of the paragraph. The key to marking is *selective* activity. Mark each page in a way that allows you to see the most important points at a glance. You can follow up your marking by writing out more in your subject outline.

With these skills in hand, you will be well on your way to becoming a great student. Here are a few more hints that will help you develop effective study skills.

We study best when we are free from distractions.

- Read textbook chapters actively! Underline the most important topics. Put a check mark next to material that you do not understand. After you have completed the entire chapter, take a break. Then, work on better comprehension of the check-marked material.
- As a rule, do schoolwork as soon as possible when you get home after class. The longer you wait, the more likely you will be distracted by television, video games, phone calls from friends, or social networking.

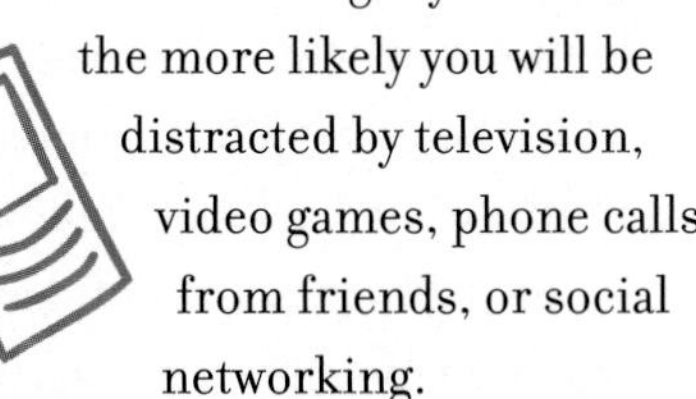

- Many students are tempted to take class notes on a laptop computer. This is a bad idea for two reasons. First, it is hard to copy diagrams or take other "artistic" notes on a computer. Second, it is easy to get distracted by checking e-mail or surfing the Web.
- We study best when we are free from distractions such as the Internet, cell phones, and our friends. That's why your school library is often the best place to work. Set aside several hours a week of "library time" to study in peace and quiet.
- Reward yourself for studying! From time to time, allow yourself a short break for surfing the Internet, going for a jog, taking a nap, or doing something else that you enjoy. These interludes will refresh your mind and enable you to study longer and more efficiently.
- When you are given a writing assignment, make sure you allow yourself enough time to revise and polish your final draft. Good writing takes time—you may need to revise a paper several times before it's ready to be handed in.
- A neat study space is important. Staying neat forces you to stay organized. When your desk is covered with piles of papers, notes, and textbooks, things are being lost even though you may not realize it. The only work items that should be on your desk are those that you are working on that day.

- Often, studying involves pure memorization. To help with this task, create flash (or note) cards. On one side of the card, write the question or term. On the other side, write the answer or definition. Then, use the cards to test yourself on the material.

- Mnemonic (pronounced ne-mon-ik) devices are tricks that increase our ability to memorize. A well-known mnemonic device is the phrase ROY G BIV, which helps people remember the colors of the rainbow—Red, Orange, Yellow, Green, Blue, Indigo, Violet. Of course, you don't have to use mnemonics that other people made. You can create your own for whatever you need to memorize. The more fun you have coming up with mnemonics for yourself, the more useful they will be.
- Take notes twice. First, take notes in class. Then, when you get back home, rewrite your notes. The rewrite will act as a study session by forcing you to think about the material. It will also, invariably, lead to questions that are crucial to the study process.
- Notice that each major section heading in this textbook has been written in the form of a question. By turning headings or subheadings in all of your textbooks into questions—and then answering them—you will increase your understanding of the material.

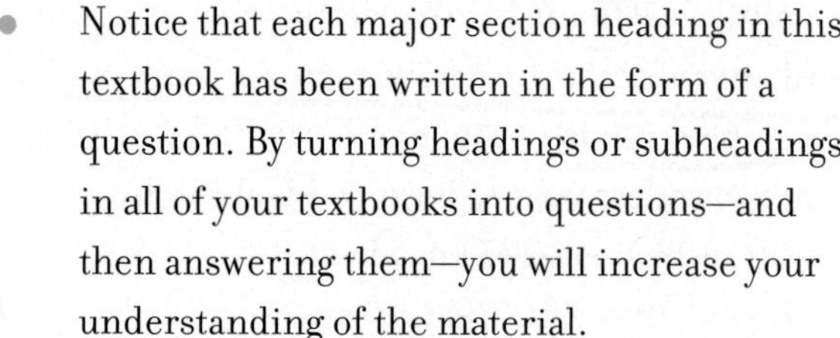

- Multitasking while studying is generally a bad idea. You may think that you can review your notes and watch television at the same time, but your ability to study will almost certainly suffer. It's OK to give yourself TV breaks from schoolwork, but avoid combining the two.

Paul Ijsendoorn/iStockphoto.com

Troels Graugaard/iStockphoto.com

TEST PREP

You have worked hard throughout the term, reading the book, paying close attention in class, and taking good notes. Now it's test time, when all that hard work pays off. To do well on an exam, of course, it is important that you learn the concepts in each chapter as thoroughly as possible, but there are additional strategies for taking exams. You should know which reading materials and lectures will be covered. You should also know in advance what type of exam you are going to take—essay or objective or both. (Objective exams usually include true/false, fill-in-the-blank, matching, and multiple-choice questions.) Finally, you should know how much time will be allowed for the exam. By taking these steps, you will reduce any anxiety you feel as you begin the exam, and you'll be better prepared to work through the entire exam.

Petek ARICI/iStockphoto.com

FOLLOW DIRECTIONS

Students are often in a hurry to start an exam, so they take little time to read the instructions. The instructions can be critical, however. In a multiple-choice exam, for example, if there is no indication that there is a penalty for guessing, then you should never leave a question unanswered. Even if only a few minutes are left at the end of an exam, you should guess on the questions that you remain uncertain about.

Additionally, you need to know the weight given to each section of an exam. In a typical multiple-choice exam, all questions have equal weight. In other types of exams, particularly those with essay questions, different parts of the exam carry different weights. You should use these weights to apportion your time accordingly. If the essay portion of an exam accounts for 20 percent of the total points on the exam, you should not spend 60 percent of your time on the essay.

Finally, you need to make sure you are marking the answers correctly. Some exams require a No. 2 pencil to fill in the dots on a machine-graded answer sheet. Other exams require underlining or circling. In short, you have to read and follow the instructions carefully.

Jesus Jauregui/iStockphoto.com

OBJECTIVE EXAMS

An objective exam consists of multiple-choice, true/false, fill-in-the-blank, or matching questions that have only one correct answer. Students usually commit one of two errors when they read objective/exam questions: (1) they read things into the questions that do not exist, or (2) they skip over words or phrases. Most test questions include key words such as:

- all
- never
- always
- only

If you miss any of these key words, you may answer the question wrong even if you know the information. Consider the following example:

True or False?
The First Amendment to the U.S. Constitution prohibits all restrictions on free speech.

In this instance, you may be tempted to answer "True," but the correct answer is "False," because the First Amendment applies only to governmental restrictions on free speech. In addition, certain types of speech, such as obscenity, are not protected by the First Amendment.

Whenever the answer to an objective question is not obvious, start with the process of elimination. Throw out the answers that are clearly incorrect. Typically, the easiest way to eliminate incorrect answers is to look for those that are meaningless, illogical, or inconsistent. Often, test authors put in choices that make perfect sense and are indeed true, but they are not the answer to the question under study.

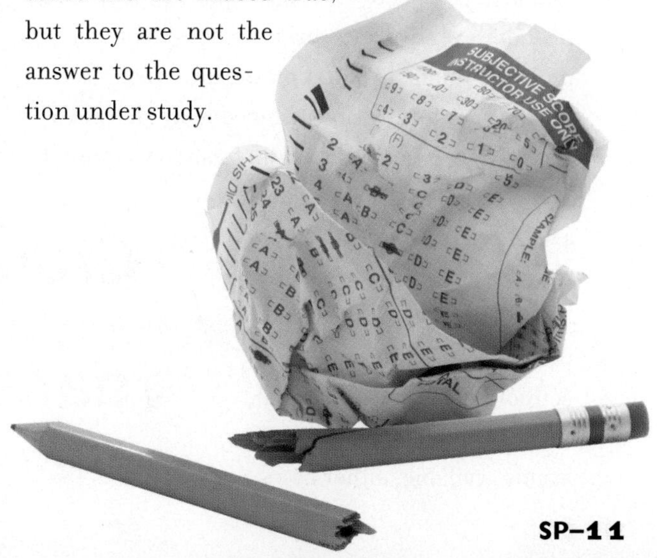

If you follow the above tips, you will be well on your way to becoming an efficient, results-oriented student. Here are a few more that will help you get there.

- Instructors usually lecture on subjects they think are important, so those same subjects are also likely to be on the exam. Therefore, be sure to take extensive notes in class. Then, review your notes thoroughly as part of your exam preparation.
- At times, you will find yourself studying for several exams at once. When this happens, make a list of each study topic and the amount of time needed to prepare for that topic. Then, create a study schedule to reduce stress and give yourself the best chance for success.
- When preparing for an exam, you might want to get together a small group (two or three other students) for a study session. Discussing a topic out loud can improve your understanding of that topic and will help you remember the key points that often come up on exams.
- If the test requires you to read a passage and then answer questions about that passage, read the questions first. This way, you will know what to look for as you read.
- When you first receive your exam, look it over quickly to make sure that you have all the pages. If you are uncertain, ask your professor or exam proctor. This initial scan may uncover other problems as well, such as illegible print or unclear instructions.
- Grades aren't a matter of life and death, and worrying too much about a single exam can have a negative effect on your performance. Keep exams in perspective. If you do poorly on one test, it's not the end of the world. Rather, it should motivate you to do better on the next one.
- Review your lecture notes immediately after each class, when the material is still fresh in your mind. Then, review each subject once a week, giving yourself an hour to go back over what you have learned. Reviews make tests easier because you will feel comfortable with the material.
- Some professors make old exams available, either by posting them online or by putting them on file in the library. Old tests can give you an idea of the kinds of questions the professor likes to ask. You can also use them to take practice exams.
- With essay questions, look for key words such as "compare," "contrast," and "explain." These will guide your answer. If you have time, make a quick outline. Most important, get to the point without wasting your time (or your professor's) with statements such as "There are many possible reasons for . . . ."
- Cramming just before the exam is a dangerous proposition. Cramming tires the brain unnecessarily and adds to stress, which can severely hamper your testing performance. If you've studied wisely, have confidence that the information will be available to you when you need it.
- When you finish a test early, your first instinct may be to hand it in and get out of the classroom as quickly as possible. It is always a good idea, however, to review your answers. You may find a mistake or an area where some extra writing will improve your grade.
- Be prepared. Make a list of everything you will need for the exam, such as a pen or pencil, watch, and calculator. Arrive at the exam early to avoid having to rush, which will only add to your stress. Good preparation helps you focus on the task at hand.
- Be sure to eat before taking a test. Having food in your stomach will give you the energy you need to concentrate. Don't go overboard, however. Too much food or heavy foods will make you sleepy during the exam.

Grades aren't a matter of life and death, and worrying about them can have a negative effect on your performance.

Cramming *just before the exam is a* **dangerous** *proposition.*

READ PREP

This textbook is the foundation for your introduction to American government. It contains key concepts and terms that are important to your understanding of what American government is all about. This knowledge will be important not only for you to succeed in this course, but for your future as you pursue a career in politics and government, or learn to be a good citizen. For this reason, it is essential that you develop good reading skills so that you get the most out of this textbook.

Of course, all students know how to read, but reading for a college-level course goes beyond being able to recognize words on a page. As a student, you must read to learn. You have to be able to read a chapter with the goal of understanding its key points and how it relates to other chapters. In other words, you have to be able to read your textbook and be able to explain what it is all about. To do this, you need to develop good reading habits and reading skills.

READING FOR LEARNING REQUIRES FOCUS

Reading (and learning from) a textbook is not like reading a newspaper or a magazine or even a novel. The point of reading for learning isn't to get through the material as fast as you can or to skip parts to get to the stuff you're interested in. A textbook is a source of information about a subject, and the goal of reading a textbook is to learn as much of that information as you can. This kind of reading requires attention. When you read to learn, you have to make an effort to focus on the book and tune out other distractions so that you can understand and remember the information it presents.

READING FOR LEARNING TAKES TIME

When reading your textbook, you need to go slow. The most important part of reading for learning is not how many pages you get through or how fast you get through them. Instead, the goal is to learn the key concepts of American government that are presented in each chapter. To do that, you need to read slowly, carefully, and with great attention.

READING FOR LEARNING TAKES REPETITION

Even the most well-read scholar will tell you that it's difficult to learn from a textbook just by reading through it once. To read for learning, you have to read your textbook a number of times. This doesn't mean, though, that you just sit and read the same section three or four times. Instead, you should follow a preview-read-review process. Here's a good guide to follow:

THE FIRST TIME The first time you read a section of the book, you should preview it. During the preview, pay attention to how the chapter is formatted. Look over the title of the chapter, the section headings, and highlighted or bolded words. This will give you a good preview of the important ideas in the chapter. You should also pay close attention to any graphs, pictures, illustrations, or figures that are used in the chapter, since these provide a visual illustration of important concepts. You should also pay special attention to the first and last sentence of each paragraph. First sentences usually introduce the main point of the paragraph, while last sentences usually sum up what was presented in each paragraph.

The goal of previewing the section is to answer the question "What is the main idea?" Of course, you may not be able to come up with a detailed answer yet, but that's not the point of previewing. Instead, the point is to develop some general ideas about what the section is about so that when you do read it in full, you can have a guide for what to look for.

THE SECOND TIME After the preview, you'll want to read through the passage in detail. During this phase, it is important to read with a few of questions in mind: What is the main point of this paragraph? What does

Andrzej Tokarski/iStockphoto.com

the author want me to learn from this? How does this relate to what I read before? Keeping these questions in mind will help you to be an attentive reader who is actively focusing on the main ideas of the passage.

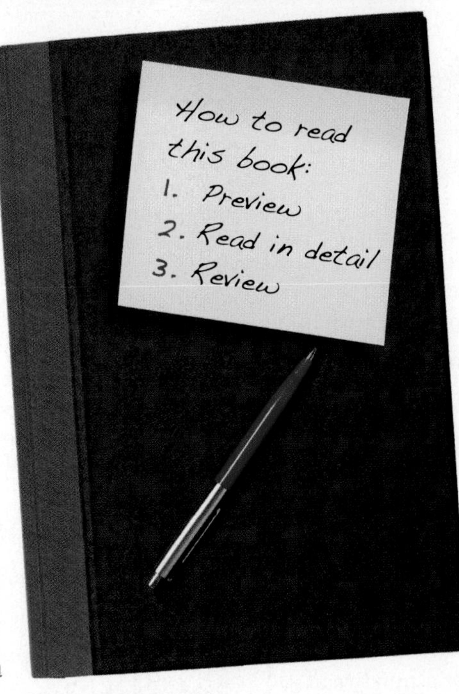

clu/iStockphoto.com

It is helpful to take notes while reading in detail. There are several different methods of doing this—you can write notes in the margin, highlight important words and phrases, or write an outline. Whatever method you prefer, taking notes will help you read actively, identify important concepts, and remember them. Then when it comes time to review for the exam, the notes you've made will make your studying more efficient. Instead of reading through the entire chapter again, you can focus your studying energy on the areas that you've identified as most important.

After you have completed a detailed read of the chapter, take a break so that you can rest your mind (and your eyes). Then you should write up a summary or paraphrase of what you just read. You don't need to produce a detailed, lengthy summary of the whole chapter. Instead, try to produce a brief paraphrase that covers the most important ideas of the chapter. This paraphrase will help you remember the main points of the chapter, check the accuracy of your reading, and provide a good guide for later review.

THE THIRD TIME (AND BEYOND) After you've finished a detailed reading of the chapter, you should take the time to review the chapter (at least once, but maybe even two, three, or more times). During this step, you should review each paragraph and the notes you made, asking this question: "What was this paragraph about?" At this point, you'll want to answer the question in some detail—that is, you should develop a fairly good idea of the important points of what you read before.

A reading group is a great way to review the chapter. After completing the reading individually, group members should meet and take turns sharing what they learned from their reading. Sharing what you learned from reading and explaining it to others will reinforce and clarify what you already know. It also provides an opportunity to learn from others. Getting a different perspective on a passage will increase your knowledge, since different people will find different things important during a reading.

Whether you're reading your textbook for the first time or reviewing it for the final exam, here are some tips that will help you be an attentive and attuned reader.

Set aside time and space.

To read effectively, you need to be focused and attentive, and that won't happen if your phone is ringing every two minutes, if the TV is on in the background, if you're updating Twitter, or if you're surrounded by friends or family. Similarly, you won't be able to focus on your book if you're trying to read in a room that is too hot or too cold, or sitting in an uncomfortable chair. So when you read, find a quiet, comfortable place that is free from distractions where you can focus on one thing—learning from the book.

Take frequent breaks.

Reading your textbook shouldn't be a test of endurance. Rest your eyes and your mind by taking a short break every twenty to thirty minutes. The concentration you need to read attentively requires lots of energy, and you won't have enough energy if you don't take frequent breaks.

Keep reading.

Effective reading is like playing sports or a musical instrument—practice makes perfect. The more time that you spend reading, the better you will be at learning from your textbook. Your vocabulary will grow, and you'll have an easier time learning and remembering information you find in textbooks.

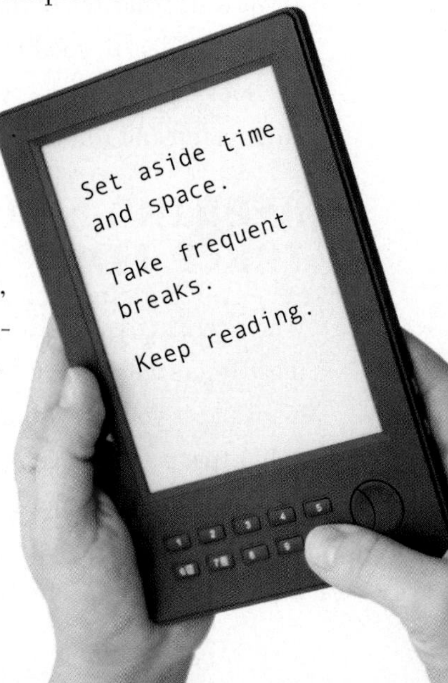

brave-carp/iStockphoto.com

WRITE PREP

kyoshino/iStockphoto.com

A key part of succeeding as a student is learning how to write well. Whether writing papers, presentations, essays, or even e-mails to your instructor, you have to be able to put your thoughts into words and do so with force, clarity, and precision. In this section, we outline a three-phase process that you can use to write almost anything.

1. Getting ready to write
2. Writing a first draft
3. Revising your draft

PHASE 1: GETTING READY TO WRITE

First, make a list. Divide the ultimate goal—a finished paper—into smaller steps that you can tackle right away. Estimate how long it will take to complete each step. Start with the date your paper is due and work backward to the present: For example, if the due date is December 1, and you have about three months to write the paper, give yourself a cushion and schedule November 20 as your targeted completion date. Plan what you want to get done by November 1, and then list what you want to get done by October 1.

PICK a TOPIC To generate ideas for a topic, any of the following approaches work well:

- **Brainstorm with a group.** There is no need to create in isolation. You can harness the energy and the natural creative power of a group to assist you.
- **Speak it.** To get ideas flowing, start talking. Admit your confusion or lack of clear ideas. Then just speak. By putting your thoughts into words, you'll start thinking more clearly.
- **Use free writing.** Free writing, a technique championed by writing teacher Peter Elbow, is also very effective when trying to come up with a topic. There's only one rule in free writing: Write without stopping. Set a time limit—say, ten minutes—and keep your fingers dancing across the keyboard the whole time. Ignore the urge to stop and rewrite. There is no need to worry about spelling, punctuation, or grammar during this process.

ReFIne YOUR IDea After you've come up with some initial ideas, it's time to refine them:

- **Select a topic and working title.** Using your instructor's guidelines for the paper or speech, write down a list of topics that interest you. Write down all of the ideas you think of in two minutes. Then choose one topic. The most common pitfall is selecting a topic that is too broad. "Political Campaigns" is probably not a useful topic for your paper. Instead, consider "The Financing of Political Campaigns."
- **Write a thesis statement.** Clarify what you want to say by summarizing it in one concise sentence. This sentence, called a *thesis statement,* refines your working title. A thesis is the main point of the paper; it is a declaration of some sort. You might write a thesis statement such as "Recent decisions by the Supreme Court have dramatically changed the way that political campaigns are funded."

SeT GOaLS Effective writing flows from a purpose. Think about how you'd like your reader or listener to respond after considering your ideas.

- If you want someone to think differently, make your writing clear and logical. Support your assertions with evidence.
- If your purpose is to move the reader into action, explain exactly what steps to take and offer solid benefits for doing so.

To clarify your purpose, state it in one sentence—for example, "The purpose of this paper is to discuss and analyze the various explanations for the increasing partisanship in Congress."

Begin Research At the initial stage, the objective of your research is not to uncover specific facts about your topic. That comes later. First, you want to gain an overview of the subject. Say that you want to persuade the reader to vote against a voter ID requirement in your state. You must first learn enough about voter ID laws to summarize for your reader the problems such laws may cause for some voters and whether the laws actually deter voting fraud.

Make an Outline An outline is a kind of map. When you follow a map, you avoid getting lost. Likewise, an outline keeps you from wandering off topic. To create your outline, follow these steps:

1. Review your thesis statement and identify the three to five main points you need to address in your paper to support or prove your thesis.
2. Next, look closely at those three to five major points or categories and think about what minor points or subcategories you want to cover in your paper. Your major points are your big ideas. Your minor points are the details you need to fill in under each of those ideas.
3. Ask for feedback. Have your instructor or a classmate review your outline and offer suggestions for improvement. Did you choose the right categories and subcategories? Do you need more detail anywhere? Does the flow from idea to idea make sense?

Do In-Depth Research Three-by-five-inch index cards are an old-fashioned but invaluable tool for in-depth research. Simply write down one idea or piece of information per card. This makes it easy to organize—and reorganize—your ideas and information. Organizing research cards as you create them saves time. Use rubber bands to keep *source cards* (cards that include the bibliographical information for a source) separate from *information cards* (cards that include nuggets of information from a source) and to maintain general categories.

When creating your cards, be sure to:

- Copy all of the information correctly.
- Always include the source and page number on information cards.
- Be neat and organized. Write legibly, using the same format for all of your cards.

In addition to source cards and information cards, generate *idea cards*. If you have a thought while you are researching, write it down on a card. Label these cards clearly as containing your own ideas.

Phase 2: Writing a First Draft

To create your draft, gather your index cards and confirm that they are arranged to follow your outline. Then write about the ideas in your notes. It's that simple. Look at your cards and start writing. Write in paragraphs, with one idea per paragraph. As you complete this task, keep the following suggestions in mind:

- **Remember that the first draft is not for keeps.** You can worry about quality later. Your goal at this point is simply to generate lots of words and lots of ideas.
- **Write freely.** Many writers prefer to get their first draft down quickly and would advise you to keep writing, much as in free writing. Of course, you may pause to glance at your cards and outline. The idea is to avoid stopping to edit your work.
- **Be yourself.** Let go of the urge to sound "official" or "scholarly" and avoid using unnecessary big words or phrases. Instead, write in a natural voice.

stuartbur/iStockphoto.com

Address your thoughts not to the teacher but to an intelligent student or someone you care about. Visualize this person, and choose the three or four most important things you'd say to her about the topic.

- **Make writing a habit.** Don't wait for inspiration to strike. Make a habit of writing at a certain time each day.
- **Get physical.** While working on the first draft, take breaks. Go for a walk. Speak or sing your ideas out loud. From time to time, practice relaxation techniques and breathe deeply.
- **Hide your draft in your drawer for a while.** Schedule time for rewrites before you begin, and schedule at least one day between revisions so that you can let the material sit. The brain needs that much time to disengage itself from the project.

PHASE 3: REVISING YOUR DRAFT

During this phase, keep in mind the saying "Write in haste; revise at leisure." When you are working on your first draft, the goal is to produce ideas and write them down. During the revision phase, however, you need to slow down and take a close look at your work. One guideline is to allow 50 percent of writing time for planning, researching, and writing the first draft. Then use the remaining 50 percent for revising.

There are a number of especially good ways to revise your paper:

1. **Read it out loud.**
   The combination of voice and ears forces us to pay attention to the details. Is the thesis statement clear and supported by enough evidence? Does the introduction tell your reader what's coming? Do you end with a strong conclusion that expands on what's in your introduction rather than just restating it?
2. **Have a friend look over your paper.**
   This is never a substitute for your own review, but a friend can often see mistakes you miss. Remember, when other people criticize or review your work, they are not attacking you. They're just commenting on your paper. With a little practice, you will learn to welcome feedback because it is one of the fastest ways to approach the revision process.

Izabela Habur/iStockphoto.com

3. **Cut.**
   Look for excess baggage. Avoid at all costs and at all times the really, really terrible mistake of using way too many unnecessary words, a mistake that some student writers often make when they sit down to write papers for the various courses in which they participate at the fine institutions of higher learning that they are fortunate enough to attend. (Example: The previous sentence could be edited to "Avoid unnecessary words.") Also, look for places where two (or more sentences) could be rewritten as one. Resist the temptation to think that by cutting text you are losing something. You are actually gaining a clearer, more polished product. For maximum efficiency, make the larger cuts first—sections, chapters, pages. Then go for the smaller cuts—paragraphs, sentences, phrases, words.
4. **Paste.**
   In deleting both larger and smaller passages in your first draft, you've probably removed some of the original transitions and connecting ideas. The next task is to rearrange what's left of your paper or speech so that it flows logically. Look for

consistency within paragraphs and for transitions from paragraph to paragraph and section to section.

5. **Fix.**

Now it's time to look at individual words and phrases. Define any terms that the reader might not know, putting them in plain English whenever you can. In general, focus on nouns and verbs. Using too many adjectives and adverbs weakens your message and adds unnecessary bulk to your writing. Write about the details, and be specific. Also, check your writing to ensure that you are:

- Using the active voice. Write "*The research team began the project*" rather than (passively) "*A project was initiated.*"
- Writing concisely. Instead of "*After making a timely arrival and perspicaciously observing the unfolding events, I emerged totally and gloriously victorious,*" be concise with "*I came, I saw, I conquered.*"
- Communicating clearly. Instead of "*The speaker made effective use of the television medium, asking in no uncertain terms that we change our belief systems,*" you can write specifically, "*The senatorial candidate stared straight into the television camera and said, 'Take a good look at what my opponent is doing! Do you really want six more years of this?'*"

6. **Prepare.**

In a sense, any paper is a sales effort. If you hand in a paper that is wearing wrinkled jeans, its hair tangled and unwashed and its shoes untied, your instructor is less likely to buy it. To avoid this situation, format your paper following accepted standards for margin widths, endnotes, title pages, and other details. Ask your instructor for specific instructions on how to cite the sources used in writing your paper. You can find useful guidelines in the *MLA Handbook for Writers of Research Papers*, a book from the Modern Language Association. If you cut and paste material from a Web page directly into your paper, be sure to place that material in quotation marks and cite the source. Before referencing an e-mail message, verify the sender's identity. Remember that anyone sending e-mail can pretend to be someone else. Use quality paper for the final version of your paper. For an even more professional appearance, bind your paper with a plastic or paper cover.

7. **Proof.**

As you ease down the home stretch, read your revised paper one more time. This time, go for the big picture and look for the following:

Proofreading checklist

- ☐ A clear thesis statement.
- ☐ Sentences that introduce your topic, guide the reader through the major sections of your paper, and summarize your conclusions.
- ☐ Details—such as quotations, examples, and statistics—that support your conclusions.
- ☐ Lean sentences that have been purged of needless words.
- ☐ Plenty of action verbs and concrete, specific nouns.
- ☐ Finally, look over your paper with an eye for spelling and grammar mistakes. Use contractions sparingly if at all. Use your word processor's spell-check by all means, but do not rely on it completely as it will not catch everything.

Feng Yu/iStockphoto.com

When you are through proofreading, take a minute to savor the result. You've just witnessed something of a miracle—the mind attaining clarity and resolution. That's the *aha!* in writing.

ACADEMIC INTEGRITY: AVOIDING PLAGIARISM

Using another person's words, images, or other original creations without giving proper credit is called *plagiarism*. Plagiarism amounts to taking someone else's work and presenting it as your own—the equivalent of cheating on a test. The consequences of plagiarism can range from a failing grade to expulsion from school. Plagiarism can be unintentional. Some students don't understand the research process. Sometimes, they leave writing until the last minute and don't take the time to organize their sources of information. Also, some people are raised in cultures where identity is based on group membership rather than individual achievement. These students may find it hard to understand how creative work can be owned by an individual.

To avoid plagiarism, ask an instructor where you can find your school's written policy on this issue. Don't assume that you can resubmit a paper you wrote for another class for a current class. Many schools will regard this as plagiarism even though you wrote the paper. The basic guidelines for preventing plagiarism are to cite a source for each phrase, sequence of ideas, or visual image created by another person. While ideas cannot be copyrighted, the specific way that an idea is *expressed* can be. You also need to list a source for any idea that is closely identified with a particular person. The goal is to clearly distinguish your own work from the work of others. There are several ways to ensure that you do this consistently:

- **Identify direct quotes.** If you use a direct quote from another writer or speaker, put that person's words in quotation marks. If you do research online, you might find yourself copying sentences or paragraphs from a Web page and pasting them directly into your notes. This is the same as taking direct quotes from your source. To avoid plagiarism, identify such passages in an obvious way.
- **Paraphrase carefully.** Paraphrasing means restating the original passage in your own words, usually making it shorter and simpler. Students who copy a passage word for word and then just rearrange or delete a few phrases are running a serious risk of plagiarism. Remember to cite a source for paraphrases, just as you do for direct quotes. When you use the same sequence of ideas as one of your sources—even if you have not paraphrased or directly quoted—cite that source.
- **Note details about each source.** For books, details about each source include the author, title, publisher, publication date, location of publisher, and page number. For articles from print sources, record the article title and the name of the magazine or journal as well. If you found the article in an academic or technical journal, also record the volume and number of the publication. A librarian can help identify these details. If your source is a Web page, record as many identifying details as you can find—author, title, sponsoring organization, URL, publication date, and revision date. In addition, list the date that you accessed the page. Be careful when using Web resources, as not all Web sites are considered legitimate sources. Wikipedia, for instance, is not regarded as a legitimate source, but the National Institute of Justice's Web site is.
- **Cite your sources as endnotes or footnotes to your paper.** Ask your instructor for examples of the format to use. You do not need to credit wording that is wholly your own. Nor do you need to credit general ideas, such as the suggestion that people use a to-do list to plan their time. When you use your own words to describe such an idea, there's no need to credit a source. But if you borrow someone else's words or images to explain the idea, do give credit.

SPEECH PREP

In addition to reading and writing, your success as a student will depend on how well you can communicate what you have learned. Most often, you'll do so in the form of speeches. Many people are intimidated by the idea of public speaking, but it really is just like any other skill—the more often you do it, the more you practice, the better you will get.

Developing a speech is similar to writing a paper. Begin by writing out your topic, purpose, and thesis statement. Then carefully analyze your audience by using the strategies listed below.

If your topic is new to listeners . . .

- Explain why your topic matters to them.
- Relate the topic to something that they already know and care about.
- Define any terms that they might not know.

If listeners already know about your topic . . .

- Acknowledge this fact at the beginning of your speech.
- Find a narrow aspect of the topic that may be new to listeners.
- Offer a new perspective on the topic, or connect it to an unfamiliar topic.

If listeners disagree with your thesis . . .

- Tactfully admit your differences of opinion.
- Reinforce points on which you and your audience agree.
- Build credibility by explaining your qualifications to speak on your topic.
- Quote experts who agree with your thesis—people whom your audience is likely to admire.
- Explain to your listeners that their current viewpoint has costs for them and that a slight adjustment in their thinking will bring significant benefits.

If listeners might be uninterested in your topic . . .

- Explain how listening to your speech can help them gain something that matters deeply to them.
- Explain ways to apply your ideas in daily life.

Remember that audiences generally have one question in mind: *So what?* They want to know that your presentation relates to their needs and desires. To convince people that you have something worthwhile to say, think of your main topic or point. Then see if you can complete this sentence: I'm telling you this because . . . .

ORGANIZE YOUR PRESENTATIONS

Consider the length of your presentation. Plan on delivering about one hundred words per minute. Aim for a lean presentation—enough words to make your point but not so many as to make your audience restless. Leave your listeners wanting more. When you speak, be brief and then be seated. Speeches are usually organized in three main parts: the introduction, the main body, and the conclusion.

1. **The introduction.**

Rambling speeches with no clear point or organization put audiences to sleep. Solve this problem by making sure your introduction conveys the point of your presentation. The following introduction, for example, reveals the thesis and exactly what's coming. It reveals that the speech will have three distinct parts, each in logical order:

Illegal immigration is a serious problem in many states. I intend to describe the degree of illegal immigration around the country, the challenges it presents, and how various states are addressing the issue.

Some members of an audience will begin to drift during any speech, but most people pay attention for at least the first few seconds.

Highlight your main points in the beginning sentences of your speech. People might tell you to open your introduction with a joke, but humor is tricky. You run the risk of falling flat or offending somebody. Save jokes until you have plenty of experience with public speaking and know your audiences well. Also avoid long, flowery introductions in which you tell people how much you like them and how thrilled you are to address them. If you lay it on too thick, your audience won't believe you. Draft your introduction, and then come back to it after you have written the rest of your speech. In the process of creating the main body and conclusion, your thoughts about the purpose and main points of your speech might change.

2. **The main body.**

The main body of your speech accounts for 70 to 90 percent of your speech. In the main body, you develop your ideas in much the same way that you develop a written paper. Transitions are especially important in speeches. Give your audience a signal when you change points. Do so by using meaningful pauses, verbal emphasis, and transitional phrases: "On the other hand, until the public realizes what is happening to children in these countries . . ." or "The second reason that the national debt is . . ." In long speeches, recap from time to time. Also preview what's to come. Hold your audience's attention by using facts, descriptions, expert opinions, and statistics.

3. **The conclusion.**

At the end of the speech, summarize your points and draw your conclusion. You started with a bang—now finish with drama. The first and last parts of a speech are the most important. Make it clear to your audience when you have reached the end. Avoid endings such as "This is the end of my speech." A simple standby is "So, in conclusion, I want to reiterate three points: First . . . ." When you are finished, stop speaking. Although this sounds quite obvious, a good speech is often ruined by a speaker who doesn't know when, or how, to wrap things up.

Speeches are usually organized in three main parts: the introduction, the main body, and the conclusion.

SUPPORT YOUR SPEECH WITH NOTES AND VISUALS

To create speaking notes, you can type out your speech in full and transfer key words or main points to a few three-by-five-inch index cards. Number the cards so that if you drop them, you can quickly put them in order again. As you finish the information on each card, move it to the back of the pile. Write information clearly and in letters large enough to be seen from a distance. The disadvantage of the index card system is that it involves card shuffling—so some speakers prefer to use standard outlined notes.

You can also create supporting visuals. Presentations often include visuals such as PowerPoint slides or handwritten flip charts. These visuals can reinforce your main points and help your audience understand how your presentation is organized. Use visuals to *complement* rather than *replace* speech. If you use too many visuals or visuals that are too complex, your audience might focus on them and forget about you. To avoid this fate, follow these tips:

- Use fewer visuals rather than more. For a fifteen-minute presentation, a total of five to ten slides is usually enough.
- Limit the amount of text on each visual. Stick to key words presented in short sentences or phrases and in bulleted or numbered lists.
- Use a consistent set of plain fonts. Make them large enough for all audience members to see.
- Stick with a simple, coherent color scheme. Use light-colored text on a dark background or dark text on a light background.

OVERCOME FEAR OF PUBLIC SPEAKING

You may not be able to eliminate fear of public speaking entirely, but you can take steps to reduce and manage it.

PREPARE THOROUGHLY Research your topic thoroughly. Knowing your topic inside and out can create a baseline of confidence. To make a strong start, memorize the first four sentences that you plan to deliver, and practice them many times. Delivering them flawlessly when you're in front of an audience can build your confidence for the rest of your speech.

ACCEPT YOUR PHYSICAL SENSATIONS You have probably experienced the physical sensations that are commonly associated with stage fright: dry mouth, a pounding heart, sweaty hands, muscle jitters, shortness of breath, and a shaky voice. One immediate way to deal with such sensations is to simply notice them. Tell yourself, "Yes, my hands are clammy. Yes, my stomach is upset. Also, my face feels numb." Trying to deny or

gehringj/iStockphoto.com

ignore such facts can increase your fear. In contrast, when you fully accept sensations, they start to lose power.

Focus on content, not delivery If you view public speaking simply as an extension of a one-to-one conversation, the goal is not to perform but to communicate your ideas to an audience in the same ways that you would explain them to a friend. This can reduce your fear of public speaking. Instead of thinking about yourself, focus on your message. Your audience is more interested in what you have to say than in how you say it. Forget about giving a "speech." Just give people valuable ideas and information that they can use.

PRACTICE YOUR PRESENTATION

The key to successful public speaking is practice.

- ☐ **Use your "speaker's voice."** When you practice, do so in a loud voice. Your voice sounds different when you talk loudly, and this fact can be unnerving. Get used to it early on.
- ☐ **Practice in the room in which you will deliver your speech.**
- ☐ **Get familiar with the setting.** If you can't practice your speech in the actual room in which it will be given, at least visit the site ahead of time. Also make sure that the materials you will need for your speech, including any audiovisual equipment, will be available when you want them.
- ☐ **Make a recording.** Many schools have video recording equipment available for student use. Use it while you practice. Then view the finished recording to evaluate your presentation. Pay special attention to your body language—how you stand, your eye contact, how you use your hands.
- ☐ **Listen for repeated words and phrases.** Examples include *you know, kind of,* and *really,* plus any instances of *uh, umm,* and *ah.* To get rid of them, tell yourself that you intend to notice every time they pop up in your daily speech.
- ☐ **Keep practicing.** Avoid speaking word for word, as if you were reading a script. When you know your material well, you can deliver it in a natural way. Practice your presentation until you could deliver it in your sleep. Then run through it a few more times.

DELIVER YOUR PRESENTATION

Before you begin, get the audience's attention. If people are still filing into the room or adjusting their seats, they're not ready to listen. Wait for people to settle into their seats before you begin.

For a great speech, keep these tips in mind:

Dress for the occasion The clothing you choose to wear on the day of your speech delivers a message that's as loud as your words. Consider how your audience will be dressed, and then choose a wardrobe based on the impression you want to make.

Project your voice When you speak, talk loudly enough to be heard. Avoid leaning over your notes or the podium.

Maintain eye contact When you look at people, they become less frightening. Remember, too, that it is easier for people in the audience to listen to someone when that person is looking at them. Find a few friendly faces around the room, and imagine that you are talking to each of these people individually.

Oleg Prikhodko/iStockphoto.com

NOTICE YOUR NONVERBAL COMMUNICATION, YOUR BODY LANGUAGE Be aware of what your body is telling your audience. Contrived or staged gestures will look dishonest. Hands in pockets, twisting your hair, chewing gum, or leaning against a wall will all make you appear less polished than you want to be.

WATCH THE TIME You can increase the impact of your words by keeping track of the time during your speech. It's better to end early than to run late.

PAUSE WHEN APPROPRIATE Beginners sometimes feel that they have to fill every moment with the sound of their voice. Release that expectation. Give your listeners a chance to make notes and absorb what you say.

HAVE FUN Chances are that if you lighten up and enjoy your presentation, so will your listeners.

REFLECT ON YOUR PRESENTATION

Review and reflect on your performance. Did you finish on time? Did you cover all of the points you intended to cover? Was the audience attentive? Did you handle any nervousness effectively? Welcome evaluation from others. Most of us find it difficult to hear criticism about our speaking. Be aware of resisting such criticism, and then let go of your resistance. Listening to feedback will increase your skill.

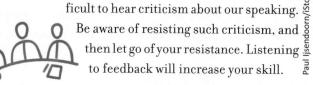

Paul Ijsendoorn/iStockphoto.com

TALKING ABOUT PRACTICE

When practicing your speech, you'll need to do more than just read through it silently. While it's good to use practice sessions to memorize the contents of your speech, they are also important times to work on how you use your voice and body as you speak. To make your practice time efficient and beneficial, follow the two-step process shown below and repeat it two or three (or more times) until you're ready to deliver a masterful speech.

1. Practice

- If possible, practice your speech in the location where you will be actually giving it. If this is not possible, make your practice setting as similar to the actual setting as possible.
- Record your practice so that you can analyze it later.
- Working from your outline or notes, go through the entire speech without stopping. If you make mistakes, try to fix them as you go along.

2. Review

Watch the recording of your first practice and ask yourself:

- Did I leave out important ideas?
- Did I focus too much on one point and not enough on others?
- Did I talk too fast or too slow?
- Did I speak clearly?
- Was my body language distracting or helpful?
- Did I maintain good eye contact?

After watching the recording, write down three or four specific changes that you will make to improve your speech.

OATH PROFANES THE DIVINITY

1 The Democratic Republic

The eight learning outcomes below are designed to help improve your understanding of this chapter. After reading this chapter, you should be able to:

- Learning Outcome 1: **Define the terms *politics* and *government*.**
- Learning Outcome 2: **Explain some of the ways in which Americans interact with their government.**
- Learning Outcome 3: **State what is meant by the words *order, liberty, authority,* and *legitimacy*.**
- Learning Outcome 4: **Distinguish the major features of direct democracy and representative democracy.**
- Learning Outcome 5: **Describe majoritarianism, elite theory, and pluralism as theories of how democratic systems work.**
- Learning Outcome 6: **Summarize the conflicts that can occur between the principles of liberty and order, and also those of liberty and equality.**
- Learning Outcome 7: **Discuss conservatism, liberalism, and other popular American ideological positions.**
- Learning Outcome 8: **Determine how the basic political principles addressed in this chapter were reflected in the 2012 elections.**

U.S. flags wave in front of Los Angeles City Hall during a ceremony to mark the tenth anniversary of the 9/11 terror attacks. (© Yang Lei/ZUMA Press/Newscom)

(AP Photo/Paul Sakuma)

GRAND THEFT AUTO is a violent video game. With no Bill of Rights, would it likely be unavailable to children?

What if...

WE HAD NO BILL OF RIGHTS?

BACKGROUND

You know that you have the right to speak freely about the government without fear of being arrested for what you say. You have probably heard of the right to bear arms. These rights come from the Bill of Rights, the first ten amendments to the U.S. Constitution. Because of these amendments, the government may not pass laws that limit freedom of speech, religion, and many other freedoms. You will learn more about the civil liberties guaranteed by the Bill of Rights in Chapter 4, on pages 113–114.

The Bill of Rights is built into the founding document that guides our government. As a result, it commands a certain reverence. Merely by its existence, it can dissuade citizens and government leaders from impairing the civil liberties of fellow Americans.

WHAT IF WE HAD NO BILL OF RIGHTS?

Because the Bill of Rights protects our fundamental liberties, some people jump to the conclusion that, without it, we would have no rights. Consider, though, that almost all state constitutions enumerate many of the same rights. It is true that if the rights of the people were not written into state and national constitutions, these rights would be entirely dependent on the political process—on elections and on laws passed by the U.S. Congress and state legislatures. Popular rights would still be safe. Unpopular ones would be in danger.

THE RIGHT TO BEAR ARMS

Take as an example the Second Amendment, which guarantees to citizens the right to bear arms. If the Bill of Rights did not exist, would it mean that individuals would be unable to keep firearms in their homes? Probably not. Few localities in the United States have tried to ban handguns completely. Almost all states have gun laws that are far more permissive than they have to be under the Constitution. Indeed, it was not until 2008 and 2010 that the highest court in the land, the Supreme Court, even addressed this issue. The Court ruled that complete bans on possessing handguns are unconstitutional.

THE RIGHTS OF CRIMINAL DEFENDANTS

According to the Sixth Amendment, accused individuals have the right to a speedy and public trial. Also, according to the Fifth Amendment, no accused "shall be compelled in any criminal case to be a witness against himself, nor be deprived of life, liberty, or property, without due process of law." These rules protect people who are accused of crimes. Certainly, without the Bill of Rights, we could imagine many more restrictions on the rights of criminal defendants. Why? Because those accused of crimes are not a popular group of people. Many of the protections now given to criminal defendants would probably not exist if there were no Bill of Rights.

FREE SPEECH

Without the Bill of Rights, we would probably see many more laws restricting political contributions and advertising. We could expect laws against violent video games and pornography on the Internet. In contrast, given current popular attitudes, it is unlikely that "subversive" speech would be greatly restricted. Most Americans and their elected representatives support the right to denounce the government.

FOR CRITICAL ANALYSIS

1. *The Fifth Amendment guarantees that no one can lose her or his liberty or property without due process. Yet, during World War II, we imprisoned tens of thousands of Japanese American citizens, based solely upon their race. Could that happen today to some other group of citizens, such as Muslim Americans? Why or why not?*
2. *Which of the rights mentioned in this feature do you think are the most important? Why?*

Politics, for many people, is the "great game"—better than soccer, better than chess. Scores may be tallied only every two years, at elections, but the play continues at all times. The game, furthermore, is played for high stakes. Politics can affect what you spend. It can determine what you can legally do in your spare time. (The *What If . . .* feature that opened this chapter examined some of the ways in which your freedoms might be restricted if the Bill of Rights did not exist.) In worst-case circumstances, politics can even threaten your life.

Few topics are so entertaining as politics—and so important. How did the great game turn out in the elections held on November 6, 2012? We address that question in the *Elections 2012* feature on the following page.

In our democratic republic, citizens play an important role by voting. Although voting is extremely important, it is only one of the ways that citizens can exercise their political influence. Americans can also join a political organization or interest group, stage a protest, or donate funds to a political campaign or cause. There are countless ways to become involved. Informed participation begins with knowledge, however, and this text aims to provide you with a strong foundation in American government and politics. We hope that this book helps introduce you to a lifetime of political awareness and activity.

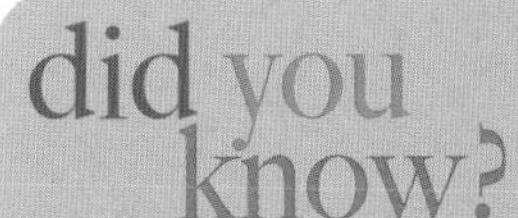

The Greek philosopher Aristotle favored enlightened authoritarianism over democracy, which to him meant mob rule.

Politics and Government

■ Learning Outcome 1: **Define the terms *politics* and *government*.**

What is politics? **Politics** can be understood as the process of resolving conflicts and deciding, as political scientist Harold Lasswell put it in his classic definition, "who gets what, when, and how."[1] More specifically, politics is the struggle over power or influence within organizations or informal groups that can grant benefits or privileges.

Politics
The process of resolving conflicts and deciding "who gets what, when, and how." More specifically, politics is the struggle over power or influence within organizations or informal groups that can grant benefits or privileges.

Institution
An ongoing organization that performs certain functions for society.

Government
The preeminent institution within society in which decisions are made that resolve conflicts and allocate benefits and privileges. It is unique because it has the ultimate authority for making these decisions.

We can identify many such organizations and groups. In families, all members may meet to decide on values, priorities, and actions. In every community that makes decisions through formal or informal rules, politics exists. For example, when a church group decides to construct a new building or hire a new minister, the decision is made politically. Politics can be found in schools, social groups, and any other organized collection of individuals. Of all the organizations that are controlled by political activity, however, the most important is the government.

What is the government? Certainly, it is an **institution**—that is, an ongoing organization that performs certain functions for society and that has a life separate from the lives of the individuals who are part of it at any given moment in time. The **government** can be defined as an institution within which decisions are made that resolve conflicts and allocate benefits and privileges. The government is also the preeminent institution within society because it has the ultimate authority for making these decisions.

Government Is Everywhere

The government is even more important than politics. Many people largely ignore politics, but it is impossible to ignore government. It is everywhere, like the water you drink and the air you breathe. Both air and water, by the way, are subject to government pollution standards. The food you eat comes from an agricultural industry that is heavily regulated and subsidized by the government. Step outside your residence, and almost immediately you will walk down a government-owned street or drive on a government-owned highway.

1. Harold Lasswell, *Politics: Who Gets What, When, and How* (Gloucester, Mass.: Peter Smith Publisher, 1990; originally published in 1936).

■ Learning Outcome 2: **Explain some of the ways in which Americans interact with their government.**

From Your Birth

The county government records your birth. Your toys, crib, and baby food must meet government safety standards. After a few years, you'll start school, and 86 percent of all children attend public—which is to say, government—schools. Some children attend private schools or are home schooled, but their education must also meet government standards. Public school students spend many hours in an environment designed and managed by teachers and other government employees. If you get into trouble, you'll meet government employees you'd rather not see: the police, court employees, or even jail staff.

Throughout Your Life

Most young people look forward eagerly to receiving their government-issued driver's license. Many join the military on graduating from high school, and for those who do, every minute of the next several years will be 100 percent government issue. (That's why we call soldiers "GIs.") A majority of young adults attend college at some point, and if you are reading this textbook, you are probably one of them. Many private colleges and universities exist, but 73 percent of all college students attend public institutions. Even most private universities are heavily dependent on government support.

In nearly all states, you began paying sales taxes from the moment you had your own funds to spend. Some of those funds are made up of currency issued by the government. When you enter the workforce, you'll begin paying payroll and income taxes to the government. If, like most people, you are an employee, government regulations will set many of your working conditions. You might even work for the government itself—17 percent of employees do. If you are unfortunate enough to lose a job or fall into poverty, government programs will lend you a hand.

2012 elections
THE OUTCOME OF THE ELECTION

Throughout 2012, political observers predicted a very close election. To a degree, that prediction was accurate. Democratic president Barack Obama was reelected. The Democrats kept control of the U.S. Senate, adding two seats for a total of fifty-five out of one hundred. Democratic gains in the U.S. House, however, were not even close to the number necessary to take that chamber away from the Republicans. The estimated result was 201 Democrats and 234 Republicans. (These figures, though, include some close races in which the outcome could change.) Elections for state governors and legislatures were somewhat of a wash for both parties.

The election year 2010 had been a "wave" year for the Republicans, who took control of the U.S. House with a large number of seats. By 2012, however, the Republican advantage had largely disappeared. In 2010, many Americans were concerned about the perceived growth in the size of the federal government. Conservative voters turned out in large numbers, while many other voters stayed home. The effects of the Great Recession also hurt the incumbent Democrats.

If the Democrats engaged in overreach in 2009 and 2010, the Republicans also went overboard in 2011 and 2012. They advocated economic and social policies that many moderate voters found unpalatable. Voter turnout among Democratic-oriented groups was also well up in 2012. The result was a nation once again divided right down the middle in its political preferences.

To Your Death

Later in life, you may have health problems. One way or another, the government provides 50 percent of all health-care spending, and that is without President Barack Obama's health-care plan, which was approved in 2010. Much of that spending comes from the federal Medicare program, which funds health care for almost everyone over the age of sixty-five. At that point in your life, you'll probably receive Social Security, the national government's pension plan that covers most employees. Eventually, the county government will record your death, and a government judge will oversee the distribution of your assets to your heirs.

Why Is Government Necessary?

Perhaps the best way to assess the need for government is to examine circumstances in which government, as we normally understand it, does not exist. What happens when multiple groups compete with one another for power within a society? There are places around the world where such circumstances exist. A current example is the African nation of Somalia. Since 1991, Somalia has not had a central government capable of controlling the country. The regions of the country are divided among various warlords and factions, each controlling a block of territory. When Somali warlords compete for control of a particular locality, the result is war, generalized devastation, and famine. Normally, multiple armed forces compete by fighting, and the absence of a unified government is equivalent to ongoing civil war.

■ Learning Outcome 3: **State what is meant by the words *order, liberty, authority,* and *legitimacy.***

The Need for Security

As the example of Somalia shows, one of the original purposes of government is the maintenance of security, or **order.** By keeping the peace, a government dispenses justice and protects its people from violence at the hands of private or foreign armies and criminals. If order is not present, it is not possible for the government to provide any of the other benefits that people expect from it.

Order
A state of peace and security. Maintaining order by protecting members of society from violence and criminal activity is one of the oldest purposes of government.

(AA/ABACA/Newscom)

These protestors in Libya are burning the "green book" of Muammar Qaddafi, their dictator, which instructed them on politics and how to conduct their lives. When Qaddafi was overthrown and killed, what happened to security in that nation?

The Example of Afghanistan. Consider the situation in Afghanistan. The former rulers of that country, the Taliban, were allied with the al Qaeda network, which organized the terrorist attacks of September 11, 2001, from bases in Afghanistan.[2] Soon after the attacks, the United States, Britain, and other nations intervened to overthrow the Taliban regime by providing air support and special operations assistance to the Northern Alliance, an Afghan faction at war with the Taliban. The Northern Alliance soon occupied Kabul, the capital of the nation.

The Loss of Security in Afghanistan. Unfortunately, the new Afghan government never gained full control of its territory. The Taliban regrouped, and its units killed humanitarian workers, blew up newly constructed wells, and burned schools. The government, afflicted by massive corruption, survived only because the United States and its allies moved substantial ground forces into the country.

Today, millions of Afghans do not enjoy the benefits of personal security, pinned as they are between the Taliban and the government's international allies. Afghanistan has the highest infant mortality rate in the world. It has been rated as having the world's second most serious corruption problem (after Somalia). A third of the economy is based on the production of illegal drugs. Clearly, Afghanistan has a considerable distance to go before order is restored. Order is a political value to which we will return later in this chapter.

Limiting Government Power

A complete collapse of order and security, as seen in Somalia and parts of Afghanistan, is actually an uncommon event. Much more common is the reverse—too much government control. In 2012, the human rights organization Freedom House judged that 48 of the world's countries were "not free." These nations contain 35 percent of the world's population. Such countries may be controlled by individual dictators. Libya's Muammar Qaddafi and Hosni Mubarak of Egypt were obvious examples. Alternatively, a political party, such as the Communist Party of China, may monopolize all the levers of power. The military may rule, as in Myanmar (also called Burma).

In all of these examples, the individual or group running the country cannot be removed by legal means. Freedom of speech and the right to a fair trial are typically absent. Dictatorial governments often torture or execute their opponents. Such regimes may also suppress freedom of religion. Revolution, whether violent or nonviolent, is often the only way to change the government.

In short, protection from the violence of domestic criminals or foreign armies is not enough. Citizens also need protection from abuses of power by their own government. To protect the liberties of the people, it is necessary to limit the powers of the government.

Liberty
The greatest freedom of the individual that is consistent with the freedom of other individuals in the society.

Liberty—the greatest freedom of the individual consistent with the freedom of other individuals—is a second major political value, along with order. We discuss this value in more detail later in this chapter.

Authority and Legitimacy

Authority
The right and power of a government or other entity to enforce its decisions.

Every government must have **authority**—that is, the right and power to enforce its decisions. Ultimately, the government's authority rests on its control of the armed forces and the police. Few people in the United States, however, base their day-to-day activities on fear of the government's enforcement powers. Most people, most of the time, obey the law because this is what they have always done. Also, if they did not obey the law, they would face the disapproval of friends and family. Consider an example: Do you avoid

2. *Taliban* means "students" in the Pashto language of Afghanistan. *Al Qaeda* is Arabic for "the base."

injuring your friends or stealing their possessions because you are afraid of the police—or because if you undertook these actions, you no longer would have friends?

Under normal circumstances, the government's authority has broad popular support. People accept the government's right to establish rules and laws. When authority is broadly accepted, we say that it has **legitimacy.** Authority without legitimacy is a recipe for trouble.

Legitimacy
Popular acceptance of the right and power of a government or other entity to exercise authority.

Events in several Arab nations in 2011 serve as an example. The dictators who ruled Egypt, Libya, and Tunisia had been in power for decades. All three dictators had some popular support when they first gained power. None of these nations had a tradition of democracy, and so it was possible for dictatorial rulers to enjoy a degree of legitimacy. After years of oppressive behavior, however, these regimes slowly lost that legitimacy. The rulers survived only because they were willing to employ violence against any opposition. In Egypt and Tunisia, the end came when soldiers refused to use force against large numbers of demonstrators. Having lost all legitimacy, the rulers of these two countries now lost their authority as well. Unfortunately, the downfall and death of Qaddafi in Libya came only after a seven-month civil war.

Democracy and Other Forms of Government

The different types of government can be classified according to which person or group of people controls society through the government.

■ Learning Outcome 4:
Distinguish the major features of direct democracy and representative democracy.

Types of Government

At one extreme is a society governed by a **totalitarian regime.** In such a political system, a small group of leaders or a single individual—a dictator—makes all decisions for the society. Every aspect of political, social, and economic life is controlled by the government. The power of the ruler is total (thus, the term *totalitarianism*).

A second type of system is authoritarian government. **Authoritarianism** differs from totalitarianism in that only the government itself is fully controlled by the ruler. Social and economic institutions, such as churches, businesses, and labor unions, exist that are not under the government's control.

Many of our terms for describing the distribution of political power are derived from the ancient Greeks, who were the first Western people to study politics systematically. One form of rule was known as **aristocracy,** literally meaning "rule by the best." In practice, this meant rule by wealthy members of ancient families. Another term from the Greeks is **theocracy,** which literally means "rule by God" (or the gods). In practice, theocracy means rule by religious leaders, who are typically self-appointed. Iran is a rare example of a country in which supreme power is in the hands of a religious leader, the grand ayatollah Ali Khamenei. One of the most straightforward Greek terms is **oligarchy,** which simply means "rule by a few."

Anarchy is a term derived from a Greek word meaning the absence of government. Advocates of anarchy envision a world in which each individual makes his or her own rules for behavior. In reality, the absence of government typically results in rule by competing armed factions, many of which are indistinguishable from gangsters. This is the state of affairs in Somalia, which we described earlier.

Finally, the Greek term for rule by the people was **democracy.** Within the limits of their culture, some of the Greek city-states operated as democracies. Today, in much of the world, the people will not grant legitimacy to a government unless it is based on democracy.

Totalitarian Regime
A form of government that controls all aspects of the political, social, and economic life of a nation.

Authoritarianism
A type of regime in which only the government itself is fully controlled by the ruler. Social and economic institutions exist that are not under the government's control.

Aristocracy
"Rule by the best"; in reality, rule by members of the upper class.

Theocracy
"Rule by God," or the gods; in practice, rule by religious leaders, typically self-appointed.

Oligarchy
"Rule by a few."

Anarchy
The condition of no government.

Democracy
A system of government in which political authority is vested in the people. The term is derived from the Greek words *demos* ("the people") and *kratos* ("authority").

Direct Democracy
A system of government in which political decisions are made by the people directly, rather than by their elected representatives; probably attained most easily in small political communities.

Legislature
A governmental body primarily responsible for the making of laws.

Initiative
A procedure by which voters can propose a law or a constitutional amendment.

Referendum
An electoral device whereby legislative or constitutional measures are referred by the legislature to the voters for approval or disapproval.

Recall
A procedure allowing the people to vote to dismiss an elected official from state office before his or her term has expired.

Consent of the People
The idea that governments and laws derive their legitimacy from the consent of the governed.

Direct Democracy as a Model

The Athenian system of government in ancient Greece is usually considered the purest model for **direct democracy** because the citizens of that community debated and voted directly on all laws, even those put forward by the ruling council of the city. The most important feature of Athenian democracy was that the **legislature** was composed of all of the citizens. (Women, resident foreigners, and slaves, however, were excluded because they were not citizens.) This form of government required a high level of participation from every citizen. That participation was seen as benefiting the individual and the city-state. The Athenians believed that although a high level of participation might lead to instability in government, citizens, if informed about the issues, could be trusted to make wise decisions.

Direct democracy also has been practiced at the local level in Switzerland and, in the United States, in New England town meetings. At these town meetings, which may include all of the voters who live in the town, important decisions—such as levying taxes, hiring city officials, and deciding local ordinances—are made by majority vote. Some states provide a modern adaptation of direct democracy for their citizens. In these states, representative democracy is supplemented by the **initiative** or the **referendum.** Both processes enable the people to vote directly on laws or constitutional amendments. The **recall** process, which is available in many states, allows the people to vote to remove an official from state office.

The Dangers of Direct Democracy

Although they were aware of the Athenian model, the framers of the U.S. Constitution were opposed to such a system. Democracy was considered to be dangerous and a source of instability. But in the 1700s and 1800s, the idea of government based on the **consent of the people** gained increasing popularity. Such a government was the main aspiration of the American Revolution in 1775, the French Revolution in 1789, and many subsequent revolutions. At the time of the American Revolution, however, the masses were still considered to be too uneducated to govern themselves, too prone to the influence of demagogues (political leaders who manipulate popular prejudices), and too likely to subordinate minority rights to the tyranny of the majority.

James Madison, while defending the new scheme of government set forth in the U.S. Constitution, warned of the problems inherent in a "pure democracy":

> *A common passion or interest will, in almost every case, be felt by a majority of the whole . . . and there is nothing to check the inducements to sacrifice the weaker party or an obnoxious individual. Hence it is that such democracies have ever been spectacles of turbulence and contention, and have ever been found incompatible with personal security or the rights of property; and have in general been as short in their lives as they have been violent in their deaths.*[3]

Like other politicians of his time, Madison feared that pure, or direct, democracy would deteriorate into mob rule. What would keep the majority of the people, if given direct decision-making power, from abusing the rights of those in the minority?

These Woodbury, Vermont, residents cast their ballots after a town meeting. They voted on the school budget and sales taxes. What type of political system does the town meeting best represent?

(AP Photo/Toby Talbot)

3. James Madison, in Alexander Hamilton, James Madison, and John Jay, *The Federalist Papers,* No. 10 (New York: Mentor Books, 1964), p. 81. See Appendix C of this textbook.

A Democratic Republic

The framers of the U.S. Constitution chose to craft a **republic,** meaning a government in which sovereign power rests with the people, rather than with a king or a monarch. A republic is based on **popular sovereignty.** To Americans of the 1700s, the idea of a republic also meant a government based on common beliefs and virtues that would be fostered within small communities. The rulers were to be amateurs—good citizens who would take turns representing their fellow citizens.

The U.S. Constitution created a form of republican government that we now call a **democratic republic.** The people hold the ultimate power over the government through the election process, but all national policy decisions are made by elected officials. For the founders, even this distance between the people and the government was not sufficient. The Constitution made sure that the Senate and the president would not be elected by a direct vote of the people, although later changes to the Constitution allowed the voters to elect members of the Senate directly.

Despite these limits, the new American system was unique in the amount of power it granted to the ordinary citizen. Over the course of the following two centuries, democratic values became more and more popular, at first in Western nations and then throughout the rest of the world. The spread of democratic principles gave rise to another name for our system of government—**representative democracy.** The term *representative democracy* has almost the same meaning as *democratic republic,* with one exception. Recall that in a republic, not only are the people sovereign, but there is no king. What if a nation develops into a democracy but preserves the monarchy as a largely ceremonial institution? That is exactly what happened in Britain. Not surprisingly, the British found the term *democratic republic* to be unacceptable, and they described their system as a representative democracy instead.

Republic
A form of government in which sovereign power rests with the people, rather than with a king or a monarch.

Popular Sovereignty
The concept that ultimate political authority is based on the will of the people.

Democratic Republic
A republic in which representatives elected by the people make and enforce laws and policies.

Representative Democracy
A form of government in which representatives elected by the people make and enforce laws and policies; may retain the monarchy in a ceremonial role.

Universal Suffrage
The right of all adults to vote for their government representatives.

Majority
More than 50 percent.

Majority Rule
A basic principle of democracy asserting that the greatest number of citizens in any political unit should select officials and determine policies.

Principles of Democratic Government.

All representative democracies rest on the rule of the people as expressed through the election of government officials. In the 1790s in the United States, only free white males were able to vote, and in some states they had to be property owners as well. Women in many states did not receive the right to vote in national elections until 1920, and the right to vote was not secured in all states by African Americans until the 1960s. Today, **universal suffrage** is the rule.

Because everyone's vote counts equally, the only way to make fair decisions is by some form of **majority** will. But to ensure that **majority rule** does not become oppressive, modern democracies also provide guarantees of minority rights. If political minorities were not protected, the majority might violate the fundamental rights of

(AP Photo/Chuck Burton)

The U.S. Constitution allows the people to hold the ultimate power over the government through the election process. This process does not work well, however, unless a large percentage of eligible Americans not only register to vote, but vote. This campaign worker at Davidson College in Davidson, North Carolina, explains the voter-registration process to a student. What do we call the form of republican government created by the U.S. Constitution for this country?

■ Learning Outcome 6: **Summarize the conflicts that can occur between the principles of liberty and order, and also those of liberty and equality.**

educational system. (See Chapter 6 for a more detailed discussion of the political socialization process.)

The most fundamental concepts of the American political culture are those of the dominant culture. The term *dominant culture* refers to the values, customs, and language established by the groups that traditionally have controlled politics and government in a society. The dominant culture in the United States has its roots in Western European civilization. From that civilization, American politics inherited a bias toward individualism, private property, and Judeo-Christian ethics.

Liberty versus Order

Civil Liberties
Those personal freedoms, including freedom of religion and freedom of speech, that are protected for all individuals. The civil liberties set forth in the U.S. Constitution, as amended, restrain the government from taking certain actions against individuals.

Bill of Rights
The first ten amendments to the U.S. Constitution.

In the United States, our **civil liberties** include religious freedom—both the right to practice whatever religion we choose and the right to be free from any state-imposed religion. Our civil liberties also include freedom of speech—the right to express our opinions freely on all matters, including government actions. Freedom of speech is perhaps one of our most prized liberties, because a democracy could not endure without it. These and many other basic guarantees of liberty are found in the **Bill of Rights,** the first ten amendments to the Constitution, which we described in the *What If . . .* feature at the beginning of this chapter. Americans are often more protective of their civil liberties than are citizens of other democratic countries, a point that we discuss in this chapter's *Beyond Our Borders* feature below.

Beyond Our Borders

RESTRICTIONS ON CIVIL LIBERTIES IN OTHER DEMOCRATIC COUNTRIES

(© kyoshino / iStockphoto) (© mattjeacock / iStockphoto)

Americans tend to value civil freedoms more than the people of most other democratic countries do. Americans, in particular, prize freedom of speech. Not all democratic countries value it so highly. In Germany, for example, it is illegal to display the swastika, the emblem adopted by the Nazis. Swastikas cannot be affixed to plastic models of World War II–era aircraft. It is even a crime to give a Nazi-style straight-arm salute. Recently, a German sculptor got into serious trouble by crafting a satirical statue of a garden gnome giving such a salute. The German constitution gives the government the power to ban organizations that threaten the democratic order.

Finally, if you are on German soil and you want—even for historical purposes—to purchase a copy of Hitler's autobiography and political statement, *Mein Kampf* (*My Struggle*), you'll have to get it from another country via the Internet. The German state of Bavaria, which owns the rights to the book, has blocked reprints of *Mein Kampf* in Germany.

Most Americans are concerned about crime. Many Americans, however, would be even more concerned about possible injustices if they learned that 99.8 percent of all criminal prosecutions resulted in a conviction. Yet that is exactly what happens in democratic Japan. In that country, suspects can be held for up to twenty-three days before they are charged. The high conviction rate in Japan stems from a high confession rate. Those who are detained have no access to defense lawyers and no idea how long interrogation sessions will last. The Japanese constitution guarantees detainees the right to remain silent, but few Japanese citizens who are arrested are able to take advantage of that right. In several recent cases, innocent people have been browbeaten into making false confessions that are almost impossible to retract.

FOR CRITICAL ANALYSIS

Why would Germany continue to criminalize Nazi symbols more than sixty years after the end of World War II?

Liberty, however, is not the only value widely held by Americans. A substantial portion of the American electorate believes that certain kinds of liberty threaten the traditional social order. The right to privacy is a particularly controversial liberty. The United States Supreme Court has held that the right to privacy can be derived from other rights that are explicitly stated in the Bill of Rights. The Supreme Court has also held that under the right to privacy, the government cannot ban either abortion[7] or private homosexual behavior by consenting adults.[8] Some Americans believe that such rights threaten the sanctity of the family and the general cultural commitment to moral behavior. Of course, others disagree with this point of view.

Security is another issue that follows from the principle of order. When Americans have felt particularly fearful or vulnerable, the government has emphasized national security over civil liberties. Such was the case after the Japanese attack on Pearl Harbor in 1941, which plunged the United States into World War II. Thousands of Japanese Americans were arrested and held in internment camps, based on the assumption that their loyalty to this country was in question. More recently, the terrorist attacks on the World Trade Center and the Pentagon on September 11, 2001, renewed calls for greater security at the expense of some civil liberties.

(Bob Adelman/Corbis)

One of the most fundamental rights Americans have is the right to vote. Here, African Americans in Camden, Alabama, vote for the first time after passage of the 1965 Voting Rights Act. Does voting affect political socialization?

Equality versus Liberty

The Declaration of Independence states, "All men are created equal." The proper meaning of *equality,* however, has been disputed by Americans since the Revolution.[9] Much of American history—and, indeed, world history—is the story of how the value of **equality**—the idea that all people are of equal worth—has been extended and elaborated.

Equality
As a political value, the idea that all people are of equal worth.

First, the right to vote was granted to all adult white males, regardless of whether they owned property. The Civil War (1861–1865) resulted in the end of slavery and established that, in principle at least, all citizens were equal before the law. The civil rights movement of the 1950s and 1960s sought to make that promise of equality a reality for African Americans. Other movements have sought equality for additional racial and ethnic groups, for women, for persons with disabilities, and for gay men and lesbians. We discuss many of these movements in Chapter 5.

Although many people believe that we have a way yet to go in obtaining full equality for all of these groups, we clearly have come a long way already. No American in the nineteenth century could have imagined that the 2008 Democratic presidential primary

did you know?

The phrase "In God We Trust" was made the national motto on July 30, 1956, but had appeared on U.S. coins as early as 1864.

7. *Roe v. Wade,* 410 U.S. 113 (1973).
8. *Lawrence v. Texas,* 539 U.S. 558 (2003).
9. Gary B. Nash, *The Unknown American Revolution: The Unruly Birth of Democracy and the Struggle to Create America* (New York: Viking, 2005); and Alfred F. Young, ed., *Beyond the American Revolution: Explorations in the History of American Radicalism* (DeKalb: Northern Illinois University Press, 1993).

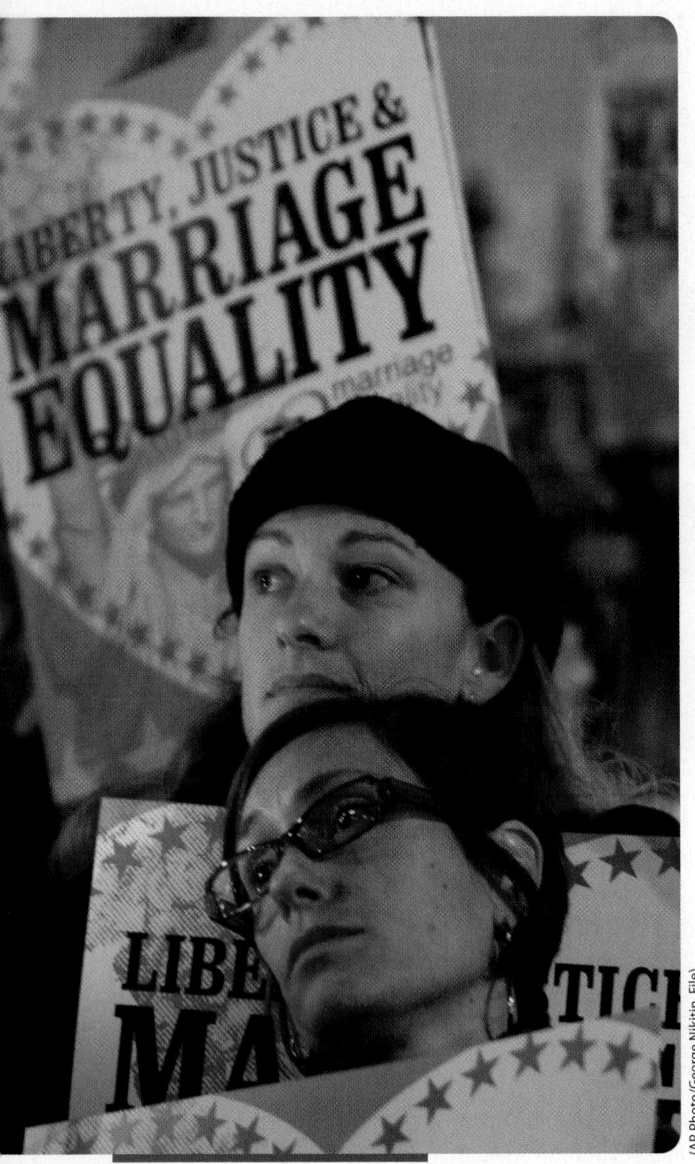

(AP Photo/George Nikitin, File)

The legality of same-sex marriages remains a controversial issue. These two supporters of same-sex marriages demonstrate in San Francisco. What, if anything, does the Bill of Rights have to say about this topic?

elections would be closely fought contests between an African American man (Illinois senator Barack Obama) and a white woman (New York senator Hillary Rodham Clinton). The idea that same-sex marriage could even be open to debate would have been mind-boggling as well.

Promoting equality often requires placing limits on the right to treat people unequally. In this sense, equality and liberty are conflicting values. Today, the right to deny equal treatment to the members of a particular race has very few defenders. Yet as recently as fifty years ago, this right was a cultural norm.

Economic Equality. Equal treatment regardless of race, religion, gender, or other characteristics is a popular value today. Equal opportunity for individuals to develop their talents and skills is also a value with substantial support. Equality of economic status, however, is a controversial value.

For much of history, the idea that the government could do anything about the division of society between rich and poor was not something about which people even thought. Most people assumed that such an effort was either impossible or undesirable. This assumption began to lose its force in the 1800s. As a result of the growing wealth of the Western world and a visible increase in the ability of government to take on large projects, some people began to advocate the value of universal equality, or egalitarianism. Some radicals dreamed of a revolutionary transformation of society that would establish an egalitarian system—that is, a system in which wealth and power were redistributed more equally.

Many others rejected this vision but still came to endorse the values of eliminating poverty and at least reducing the degree of economic inequality in society. Antipoverty advocates believed then and believe now that such a program could prevent much suffering. In addition, they believed that reducing economic inequality would promote fairness and enhance the moral tone of society generally.

Property Rights and Capitalism. The value of reducing economic inequality is in conflict with the right to **property.** This is because reducing economic inequality typically involves the transfer of property (usually in the form of tax dollars) from some people to others. For many people, liberty and property are closely entwined. Our capitalist system is based on private property rights. Under **capitalism,** property consists not only of personal possessions but also of wealth-creating assets such as farms and factories. The investor-owned corporation is in many ways the preeminent capitalist institution. The funds invested by the owners of a corporation are known as *capital*—hence, the very name of the system. Capitalism is also typically characterized by considerable freedom to make binding contracts and by relatively unconstrained markets for goods, services, and investments.

Property—especially wealth-creating property—can be seen as giving its owner political power and the liberty to do whatever he or she wants. At the same time, the ownership of property immediately creates inequality in society. The desire to own property, however, is so widespread among all classes of Americans that radical egalitarian movements have had a difficult time securing a wide following in this country. We discuss

Property
Anything that is or may be subject to ownership. As conceived by the political philosopher John Locke, the right to property is a natural right superior to human law (laws made by government).

Capitalism
An economic system characterized by the private ownership of wealth-creating assets, free markets, and freedom of contract.

Which Side Are You On?

IS INEQUALITY NECESSARILY BAD?

This nation was founded on a belief that everyone is created equal. Clearly, this does not mean that everybody should have the same income or wealth. Income inequality exists today, as it always has. The immigrants who came to our shores from England in the 1600s certainly knew about income inequality. England was a class-based society then. Not only did a limited number of families control most of the nation's wealth, but members of the aristocracy had specified privileges written into the law. To be sure, modern-day America isn't seventeenth-century England. Nonetheless, in recent years, the incomes of the richest few percent have grown much faster than the incomes of everyone else.

THE AMERICAN DREAM IS DEAD

The gap between the rich and the poor has increased dramatically in the last twenty years. In the last ten years, the inflation-adjusted salaries of average workers have not risen at all. Yet the number of millionaires and billionaires has skyrocketed. Today, a small minority live in opulence, while the majority struggle with little hope of getting rich. It is actually harder for a poor person to make it big in today's America than in most other wealthy countries.

Americans do not object to wealth when it is earned by making a real contribution to society. Bill Gates and the late Steve Jobs are very popular. Much of the new wealth, however, has gone to financial wizards who reap billions by gaming the system. Members of Occupy Wall Street and other movements claim that the very rich, not ordinary people, control our government. They have a point. We need to reduce the wealth and the political power of the "1 percent." We could start by raising taxes on the wealthy so that they pay their fair share. Tax rates for the rich were much higher in the 1950s and 1960s than today, and those were boom years for the economy.

INEQUALITY CAN BE FAIR AND BENEFICIAL

There is a huge amount of migration in and out of the top tenth of income earners— in one study, 74 percent of men born to families in the top tenth fall out of that bracket when they become adults. There is similar movement in and out of the bottom tenth. Over time, the rich are not always the same people, and the same goes for the poor.

Investors often reap large rewards from funding innovative products and services. That promotes inequality. Yet studies show that the rest of society benefits five to twenty times more from such innovations than the investor. The more inequality, the larger the incentive to make such investments.

Economists have determined one reason that the rich have become richer over the last twenty years: an increasing number of companies have started to use performance-pay systems. In other words, the harder employees work, the more they are paid. That can't be bad, even if it leads to more income inequality. The growing incidence of performance pay explains about a quarter of the growth in the inequality of male wages in recent years.

It is not fair for the government to take away benefits earned by hard work. Further—do we even want a government that is powerful enough to massively redistribute income? Such a government could threaten everyone's freedoms.

(© kyoshino / iStockphoto) (© Dean Mitchell / iStockphoto)

recent debates over the value of equality in this chapter's *Which Side Are You On?* feature above.

The Proper Size of Government

Opposition to "big government" has been a constant theme in American politics. Indeed, the belief that government is overreaching dates back to the years before the American Revolution. Tensions over the size and scope of government have plagued Americans ever since. Citizens often express contradictory opinions on the size of government and the role that it should play in their lives. Those who complain about the amount of taxes that they pay each year may also worry about the lack of funds for teachers in the local schools. Individuals who believe that the government must act to create jobs may rebel against

(Andrew Stern/Redux)

The Occupy movement started in Wall Street. Against what issue were these protesters expressing their outrage?

government spending programs that are intended to do exactly that. In general, Americans are most likely to call for the benefits of big government when they are reacting to a crisis.

Big Government: The Response to Terrorism. American politics in the twenty-first century can be described largely in terms of ambivalence about big government. In two subsequent administrations, apparent overreach by the national government provoked a popular reaction. In 2000, the Republican and Democratic parties were almost tied in terms of support. The Republicans won the presidency and control of both chambers of Congress in the 2000 elections, but they did so with some of the narrowest victory margins in history.

The terrorist attacks of September 11, 2001, popularly known as 9/11, appeared to require a major response. Many of the subsequent actions taken by President George W. Bush were popular. Others were not. In March 2003, U.S. forces occupied Iraq and overthrew Saddam Hussein, that nation's dictator. Grounds for the attack included the beliefs, later proved incorrect, that Hussein was associated with the 9/11 terrorists and was attempting to develop nuclear weapons. Members of the administration also believed that a democratic Iraq would have a strong positive influence on the entire Middle East. Instead of a quick victory and an early withdrawal, however, U.S. forces in Iraq faced an apparently endless insurrection. The war became a symbol of an over-ambitious government gone astray, and in 2006 the Republicans lost control of the U.S. House and Senate to the Democrats.

The Tea Party movement is not a political party. Rather, its supporters want less government spending and less government regulation. How does it differ from the Occupy movement?

Big Government: The Great Recession. The recession that began in December 2007 proved to be a much more severe crisis than the war in Iraq. In September 2008, a financial meltdown threatened the entire world economy with collapse. Americans demanded government action to save the economy, yet almost every program aimed at accomplishing that goal turned out to be unpopular. The first of these, undertaken in the last days of the Bush administration, was a $700 billion bipartisan bailout of banks and other financial institutions. Even though most of these funds were eventually repaid, the bailout angered Republicans and Democrats alike.

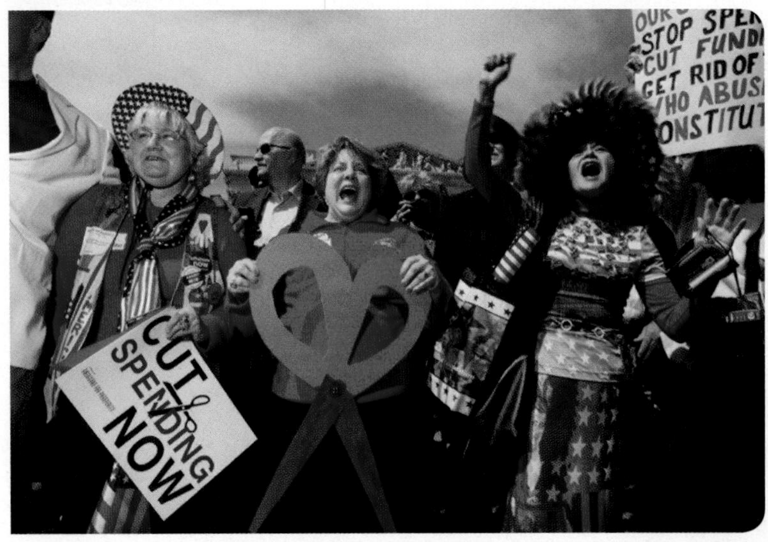

(Mark Peterson/Redux)

As they usually do, a majority of Americans held the incumbent president responsible for the state of the economy. The retiring incumbent was President Bush, a Republican, and in November 2008, the voters handed Democrat Barack Obama a solid victory in the presidential elections. Democrats increased their margins in the House and Senate. The new administration took major actions in an attempt to combat the recession, including an $800 billion stimulus package in February 2009, the rescue of the automobile companies General Motors and

Chrysler, and large increases to the federal budget. Each of these steps proved to be unpopular in the end.

In March 2010, Congress and President Obama approved a major health-care initiative that included the Patient Protection and Affordable Care Act. Also known as Obamacare, the health-care package had no direct connection to fighting the recession, and it completed the picture of big government out of control. In November 2010, voters swung heavily to the Republicans, granting them control of the House. Political scientists had expected voters to turn to the Republicans, given the continued poor state of the economy, but the 2010 swing was substantially greater than what was predictable based on the economy alone.

Political Ideologies

A political **ideology** is a closely linked set of beliefs about politics. The concept of *ideology* is often misunderstood. Many people think that only individuals whose beliefs lie well out on one or the other end of the political spectrum have an ideology—in other words, people with moderate positions are not ideological. Actually, almost everyone who has political opinions can be said to have an ideology. Some people may have difficulty in explaining the principles that underlie their opinions, but the principles are there nonetheless. To give one example: a belief in moderation is itself an ideological principle.

Ideology
A comprehensive set of beliefs about the nature of people and about the role of an institution or government.

Political ideologies offer people well-organized theories that propose goals for society and the means by which those goals can be achieved. At the core of every political ideology is a set of guiding values. The two ideologies most commonly referred to in discussions of American politics are *conservatism* and *liberalism.* In addition to their importance for electoral politics, ideologies such as liberalism and conservatism have helped inspire popular movements. We look at two such movements in this chapter's *Politics and Popular Movements* feature on the following page.

■ Learning Outcome 7:
Discuss conservatism, liberalism, and other popular American ideological positions.

Conservatism

Traditionally, those who favored the ideology of **conservatism** sought to conserve traditional practices and institutions. In that sense, conservatism is as old as politics itself. In America, limited government is a key tradition. For much of our history, limited government included major restrictions on government's ability to interfere with business. In the past, enterprises were largely free to act as they pleased in the marketplace and in managing their employees. Government regulation of business increased greatly in the 1930s, as Democratic president Franklin D. Roosevelt (1933–1945) initiated a series of massive interventions in the economy in an attempt to counter the effects of the Great Depression. Many conservatives look back at the Roosevelt administration as a time when America took a wrong turn.

Conservatism
A set of beliefs that includes a limited role for the national government in helping individuals, support for traditional ideals and life choices, and a cautious response to change.

Conservative Movement
An American movement in the 1950s that provided a comprehensive ideological framework for conservative politics.

Modern Conservatism. It was in the 1950s, however, that American conservatism took its modern shape. The **conservative movement** that arose in that decade provided the age-old conservative impulse with a comprehensive ideological framework. The new movement first demonstrated its strength in 1964, when Senator Barry Goldwater of Arizona was nominated as the Republican presidential candidate. Goldwater lost badly to Democrat Lyndon Johnson, but from that time forward *movement conservatives* occupied a crucial position in the Republican Party.

Social Media IN POLITICS
To find out more about conservative politics in the United States, go to Facebook and search on "national review." You'll see posts by the staff of *National Review,* a conservative magazine.

Conservative Values. American conservatives generally place a high value on the principle of order. This includes support for patriotism and traditional ideals. As a result, conservatives typically oppose such social innovations as same-sex marriage. Conservatives strongly endorse liberty, but they generally define it as freedom from government support of

Politics AND Popular Movements

THE TEA PARTY AND THE OCCUPY TOGETHER MOVEMENTS

The tumultuous politics of the past few years have given us two new popular movements, one conservative and one liberal. On the political right, the Tea Party movement grew explosively after it was first organized in February 2009. On the political left, the Occupy Together movement spread across the nation and the world following the Occupy Wall Street protests in September 2011.

THE TEA PARTY MOVEMENT

The Tea Party movement is named after the Boston Tea Party of 1773, a protest by American colonists in the months leading up to the Revolutionary War. The protesters, who were opposed to a British tax on tea, dumped tea taken from British ships into Boston Harbor. The Tea Party movement is not a political party—the word *party* in its name simply refers to the historical event.

Not all Tea Party advocates share the same political views, but some ideas are widely held. The Obama administration is generally seen as a major threat to American freedom. Tea Partiers believe that government has grown too large, that taxes are too high, and that federal budget deficits are a threat to our future. The belief is widespread that much government spending goes to "freeloaders." These may include bankers, but also illegal immigrants and sometimes even American youth—many Tea Party supporters are middle-aged.

Most Tea Party supporters vote for Republicans. In 2010, many Tea Party–favored candidates triumphed in Republican primary elections. In the November general elections, only about a third of the Tea Party candidates were elected to office. Still, Tea Party supporters in Congress were able to organize a caucus (a club) with 66 members.

THE OCCUPY TOGETHER MOVEMENT

The Occupy Wall Street protest began in September 2011, when members set up a tent encampment to "occupy" Wall Street. (The camp was actually set up in Zuccotti Park, two blocks away from Wall Street.) Within days of the Wall Street event, Occupy protests took place in about six hundred other U.S. cities and college campuses—and in almost one hundred locations around the world. The protests were supported by a number of labor unions and celebrities.

Many of the Occupy Together encampments were involved in confrontations with local police. The movement tended to gain support when the police appeared to be heavy-handed. When the protesters were seen as causing the conflict, however, they lost favor.

A main demand of the Occupy movement is to end the corrupting effect of money on politics. Supporters want bank reform and more jobs, especially for those entering the labor force—most Occupy members are young. Income inequality is a major theme of the movement, as shown by the slogan "We Are the 99%." This slogan refers to the concentration of wealth among the top 1 percent of income earners. While the Occupy movement took little part in the 2012 elections, it did succeed in drawing attention to income inequality in the United States and elsewhere.

FOR CRITICAL ANALYSIS

What might cause you to participate in either the Tea Party or the Occupy Together movements?

(© kyoshino / iStockphoto) (© Evelyn Peyton / iStockphoto)

nontraditional ideals or as freedom from government interference in business. Conservatives believe that the private sector probably can outperform the government in almost any activity. Therefore, they usually oppose initiatives that would increase the role of the government in the economy, such as Obama's health-care reform. Conservatives place a relatively low value on equality. Believing that individuals and families are primarily responsible for their own well-being, conservatives typically oppose high levels of antipoverty spending and government expenditures to stimulate the economy. They usually favor tax-rate cuts instead.

Liberalism
A set of beliefs that includes the advocacy of positive government action to improve the welfare of individuals, support for civil rights, and tolerance for political and social change.

Liberalism

The term **liberalism** stems from the word *liberty* and originally meant "free from prejudice in favor of traditional opinions and established institutions." Liberals have always been skeptical of the influence of religion in politics, but in the nineteenth century they were skeptical of government as well. From the time of Democratic presidents Woodrow Wilson (1913–1921) and Franklin D. Roosevelt, however, American liberals increasingly sought to use the power of government for nontraditional ends. These goals included support for organized labor and for the poor. New programs instituted by the Roosevelt administration included Social Security and unemployment insurance.

Modern Liberalism. American liberalism took its modern form in the 1960s. Liberals rallied to the Civil Rights movement, which sought to obtain equal rights for African Americans. As the feminist movement grew in importance, liberals supported it as well. Liberals won new federal health-care programs such as Medicare and Medicaid, and the promotion of such programs became a key component of liberal politics. Finally, liberals reacted more negatively to U.S. participation in the Vietnam War (1965–1975) than did other Americans, and for years thereafter liberalism was associated with skepticism about the use of U.S. military forces abroad.

Liberal Values. Those who favor liberalism place a high value on social and economic equality. As we have seen, liberals champion the rights of minority group members and favor substantial antipoverty spending. In the recent health-care policy debates, liberals strongly endorsed the principle that all citizens should have access to affordable insurance. In contrast to conservatives, liberals often support government intervention in the economy. They believe that capitalism works best when the government curbs its excesses through regulation. Like conservatives, liberals place a high value on liberty, but they tend to view it as the freedom to live one's life according to one's own values. Liberals, therefore, usually support gay rights, often including the right to marry. Liberals are an influential force within the Democratic Party.

The Traditional Political Spectrum

A traditional method of comparing political ideologies is to arrange them on a continuum from left to right, based primarily on how much power the government should exercise to promote economic equality. Table 1–1 below shows how ideologies can be arrayed in a traditional political spectrum. In addition to liberalism and conservatism, this example includes the ideologies of socialism and libertarianism.

Socialism falls on the left side of the spectrum.[10] Socialists play a minor role in the American political arena, although socialist parties and movements have been important

10. The terms *left* and *right* in the traditional political spectrum originated during the French Revolution, when revolutionary deputies to the Legislative Assembly sat to the left of the assembly president and conservative deputies sat to the right.

Social Media IN POLITICS

To learn more about liberal politics, go to Twitter and locate "thenation." You'll see tweets by the staff of *The Nation*, a liberal publication.

did you know?

About 14 percent of all legal immigrants to the United States plan to live in the Los Angeles/Long Beach, California, area.

Socialism
A political ideology based on strong support for economic and social equality. Socialists traditionally envisioned a society in which major businesses were taken over by the government or by employee cooperatives.

Table 1–1 ▶ The Traditional Political Spectrum

	Socialism	Liberalism	Conservatism	Libertarianism
How much power should the government have over the economy?	Active government control over major economic sectors.	Positive government action in the economy.	Positive government action to support capitalism.	Almost no regulation over the economy.
What should the government promote?	Economic equality, community.	Economic security, equal opportunity, social liberty.	Economic liberty, morality, social order.	Total economic and social liberty.

in other countries around the world. In the past, socialists typically advocated replacing investor ownership of major businesses with either government ownership or ownership by employee cooperatives. Socialists believed that such steps would break the power of the very rich and lead to an egalitarian society. In more recent times, socialists in Western Europe have advocated more limited programs that redistribute income.

Libertarianism
A political ideology based on skepticism or opposition toward most government activities.

On the right side of the spectrum is **libertarianism,** a philosophy of skepticism toward most government activities. Libertarians strongly support property rights and typically oppose regulation of the economy and redistribution of income. Libertarians support *laissez-faire* capitalism. (*Laissez faire* is French for "let it be.") Libertarians also tend to oppose government attempts to regulate personal behavior and promote moral values.

Problems with the Traditional Political Spectrum

Many political scientists believe that the traditional left-to-right spectrum is not sufficiently complete. Take the example of libertarians. In Table 1–1 on the previous page, libertarians are placed to the right of conservatives. If the only question is how much power the government should have over the economy, this is where they belong. Libertarians, however, advocate the most complete freedom possible in social matters. They oppose government action to promote traditional moral values, although such action is often favored by other groups on the political right. Their strong support for cultural freedoms seems to align them more closely with modern liberals than with conservatives.

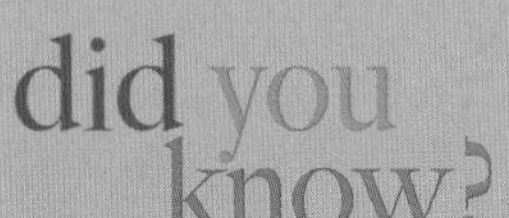

A poll of New York University students revealed that one-fifth of them would give up their vote in the next election for an iPhone and that half of them would renounce their vote permanently for $1 million.

Liberalism is often described as an ideology that supports "big government." If the objective is to promote equality, the description has some validity. In the moral sphere, however, conservatives tend to support more government regulation of social values and moral decisions than do liberals. Thus, conservatives tend to oppose gay rights legislation and propose stronger curbs on pornography. Liberals usually show greater tolerance for alternative life choices and oppose government attempts to regulate personal behavior and morals.

A Four-Cornered Ideological Grid

For a more sophisticated breakdown of recent American popular ideologies, many scholars use a four-cornered grid, as shown in Figure 1–1 on the facing page. The grid includes four possible ideologies. Each quadrant contains a substantial portion of the American electorate. Individual voters may fall anywhere on the grid, depending on the strength of their beliefs about economic and cultural issues.

Economic Liberals, Cultural Conservatives. Note that there is no generally accepted term for persons in the lower-left position, which we have labeled "economic liberals, cultural conservatives." Some scholars have used terms such as *populist* to describe this point of view, but these terms can be misleading. *Populism* more accurately refers to a hostility toward political, economic, or cultural elites, and it can be combined with a variety of political positions.

Individuals who are economic liberals and cultural conservatives tend to support government action both to promote the values of economic equality and fairness and to defend traditional values, such as the family and marriage. These individuals may describe themselves as conservative or moderate. They may vote for a Republican candidate, based on their conservative values. Alternatively, they may be Democrats based on their support for economic liberalism. Many of these Democrats are African Americans or members of other minority groups.

Libertarians. On our four-way grid, the term *libertarians* does not represent the small Libertarian Party, which has only a minor role in the American political arena. Rather, libertarians more typically support the Republican Party. Economically successful individuals are more likely than members of other groups to hold libertarian opinions.

Conservatives and Progressives. Even though all four ideologies are popular, the various labels we have used in the four-cornered grid are not equally favored. Voters are much more likely to describe themselves as conservative than as liberal. There are a variety of reasons for this, but one is that *liberal* has come to imply "radical" to many people, whereas *conservative* often implies "moderate." Because most Americans value moderation, the conservative label has an advantage. One consequence of the unpopularity of the word *liberal* is that few politicians are willing to accept it, even when they clearly support liberal policies. Instead, left-of-center Democrats typically say that they are **progressive.** This term dates back to the years before World War I (1914–1918), when it referred to advocates of reform in both of the major political parties. Public opinion polls reveal that the label *progressive* is relatively popular.

Figure 1-1 ▸ A Four-Cornered Ideological Grid

In this grid, the colored squares represent four different political ideologies. The vertical choices range from cultural order to cultural liberty. The horizontal choices range from economic equality to economic liberty.

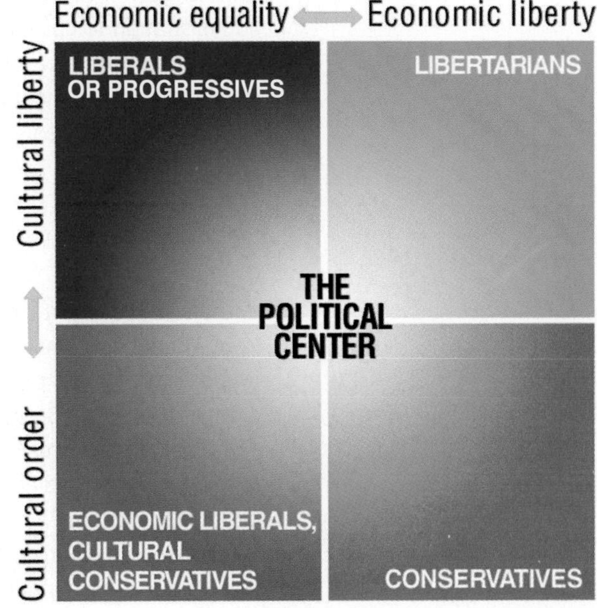

One Nation, Divided

In the past, the ideology of conservatism did not dominate the Republican Party in the way that it does today. Likewise, liberalism was much less tightly linked to the Democrats. Forty years ago, the Republican Party contained a liberal faction that was especially numerous in the northeastern states. Thirty years ago, some of the most ardent conservatives in Congress were Democrats, many of them from the South. Much history lay behind these factions—they represented allegiances dating back to the U.S. Civil War.

Progressive
A popular alternative to the term *liberal.*

In recent decades, however, liberal Republicans have all but vanished. A number of Americans continue to describe themselves as conservative Democrats, but almost none of them serve in Washington, D.C. By 2008, the most conservative Democrats in Congress had voting records that were more liberal than the records of the most moderate Republicans. The major parties no longer exhibited any ideological overlap—progressives and conservatives had sorted themselves completely into opposing political parties.

■ Learning Outcome 8:
Determine how the basic political principles addressed in this chapter were reflected in the 2012 elections.

The result has been political polarization. In Congress, the two major political parties have never been more disciplined. Republicans, and to a lesser extent Democrats, have become used to voting as a monolithic block. Neither progressives nor conservatives trust the intentions of the other camp. In bookstores, among political bloggers on the Web, and on radio and television, political rhetoric is more intense and furious than it has been in a long time. The other side is not just wrong. It is evil.

Political Gridlock

One consequence of political polarization is that most of the major Democratic initiatives in 2009 and 2010 passed with no Republican votes whatsoever. These strict party-line votes were a relatively new development in American politics.

A second consequence followed from the Republican takeover of the U.S. House after the 2010 elections. In 2010, the Democrats enjoyed a 255 to 180 majority in the House. After the elections, the Republican majority was 243 to 192. Many of the new Republican members identified with the Tea Party movement, and these legislators were sworn to reject any compromise with the Democrats. Yet the Democrats still controlled the presidency and the U.S. Senate. Observers questioned whether Congress would be able to accomplish anything at all.

In fact, the 112th Congress passed less legislation than any congress in the sixty-five years since such records were first kept. In two years, Congress did not pass a single budget resolution. To the disgust of farmers, it failed to adopt even a temporary new farm bill. The low point came in the summer of 2011. House Republicans decided to use a periodically scheduled vote to raise the federal government's debt ceiling as a lever to force the administration to cut spending.

A compromise was reached at the last minute, and the federal government was able to meet all of its obligations. The crisis damaged public confidence in the economy, however, and led one credit rating company to strip the federal government of its AAA rating for the first time in history. A team of political scientists has calculated that the 112th Congress was more polarized politically than any congress since the Reconstruction Era that followed the American Civil War.

The Republicans Lose Their Advantage

House Republicans nailed their colors to the mast in 2011 and 2012 by adopting budget proposals in almost complete party-line votes. The plans were authored by Paul Ryan, chair of the House Budget Committee and later the Republican candidate for vice president. In addition to major tax rate cuts, the proposed budgets would greatly restrict future funding for Medicaid and would privatize Medicare for anyone currently under the age of fifty-five.

As we noted earlier, Americans tend to oppose "big government" in principle even as they endorse its benefits. By 2012, for many independents, concern over Democratic affection for the government was counterbalanced by fears that the Republicans might cut valued social programs. These concerns were enough to cost the Republicans their 2010 edge.

These concerns were not strong enough, however, to give the Democrats an advantage. The result in the 2012 elections was a closely—even bitterly—divided electorate. The outcome was also a function of underlying economic conditions, which seemed to predict a very close election.

President Barack Obama and First Lady Michelle Obama celebrate victory on election night, 2012, along with Vice President Joe Biden and his wife, Jill.

(AP Photo/Chris Carlson)

Why Should You Care about... OUR DEMOCRACY?

(© spxChrome/iStockphotos.com)

Americans, for the most part, take our democracy for granted. We assume that our leaders, including the president, will uphold our democratic traditions. Nonetheless, the history of other nations has shown that even elected leaders can become overbearing and move a country away from its democratic underpinnings. In America, however, because most of us take democracy for granted, many of us do not even bother to vote.

In any democracy, citizens must, nonetheless, remain vigilant. A lot is at stake—our way of life in particular. How does an individual stay vigilant? One way is to stay informed about what's going on in government. Staying informed is a lot easier today than it was, say, a hundred years ago. Newspapers and news magazines are everywhere. Perhaps more importantly, the Internet allows you to stay in constant touch with what your government is doing. There are blogs galore of all political stripes created by Democrats, Republicans, independents, libertarians, and socialists.

OUR DEMOCRACY AND YOUR LIFE

Consider local legislative bodies. They can have a direct impact on your life. For example, city councils or county commissions typically oversee the police or the sheriff's department, and the behavior of the police is a matter of interest, even if you live on campus. If you live off campus, local authorities are responsible for an even greater number of issues that affect you directly. Are there items that your local sanitation department refuses to pick up? You might be able to change its policies by lobbying your councilperson.

Even if there are no local issues that concern you, there are still benefits from observing a local legislative session. You may discover that local government works differently from what you expected. You might learn, for example, that the representatives of your political party do not serve your interests as well as you thought—or that the other party is much more sensible than you had presumed.

HOW YOU CAN MAKE A DIFFERENCE

If you want to affect our democracy, you have to learn firsthand how a democratic government works. The easiest way is to attend a session of a local legislative body. To do so, look up the phone number of the city hall or county building on the Internet. Call the clerk of your local council or city commission. Find out when the next city council or county board meeting is. If you live in a state capital such as Baton Rouge, Louisiana, or Santa Fe, New Mexico, you can view a meeting of the state legislature instead. In many communities, city council meetings and county board meetings can be seen on public-access TV channels.

Before attending a business session of the local council or commission, try to find out how the members are elected. Are the members chosen by the "at-large" method of election, so that each member represents the whole community? Or are they chosen by specific geographic districts or wards? What are the responsibilities of this body?

When you visit, keep in mind the theory of representative democracy. The commissioners or council members are elected to represent their constituents. Observe how often the members refer to their constituents or to the special needs of their communities. Listen for sources of conflict. If, for example, there is a debate over a zoning proposal that involves the issue of land use, try to figure out why some members oppose the proposal.

If you want to follow up on your visit, try to get a brief interview with one of the members of the council or board. In general, legislators are very willing to talk to students, particularly students who also are voters. Ask the member how he or she sees the job of representative. How can the wishes of constituents be identified? How does the representative balance the needs of the particular ward or district that she or he represents with the good of the entire community? You can also write to many legislators via e-mail.

Questions for Discussion and Analysis

1. Review the *Which Side Are You On?* feature on page 17. Does inequality of wealth and income necessarily lead to negative consequences? If so, what are they? Are arguments about the benefits of inequality credible? Why or why not?
2. In Australia and Belgium, citizens are legally required to vote in elections. Would such a requirement be a good idea in the United States? What changes might take place if such a rule were in effect?
3. In your own life, what factors have contributed to your political socialization? To what extent were your political values shaped by your family, by school experiences, by friends, and by the media?
4. Following the terrorist attacks of September 11, 2001, the U.S. government imposed various restrictions, notably on airline passengers, in the belief that these measures would enhance our national security. How effective do you think these measures have been? In general, what limits on liberty should we accept as the price of security?

Key Terms

anarchy 9
aristocracy 9
authoritarianism 9
authority 8
Bill of Rights 14
capitalism 16
civil liberties 14
consent of the people 10
conservatism 19
conservative movement 19
democracy 9
democratic republic 11
direct democracy 10
elite theory 12
equality 15
government 5
ideology 19
initiative 10
institution 5
legislature 10
legitimacy 9
liberalism 20
libertarianism 22
liberty 8
limited government 12
majoritarianism 12
majority 11
majority rule 11
oligarchy 9
order 7
pluralism 13
political culture 13
political socialization 13
politics 5
popular sovereignty 11
progressive 23
property 16
recall 10
referendum 10
representative democracy 11
republic 11
socialism 21
theocracy 9
totalitarian regime 9
universal suffrage 11

Chapter Summary

1. Politics is the process by which people decide which members of society receive certain benefits or privileges and which members do not. It is the struggle over power or influence within institutions or organizations that can grant benefits or privileges. Government is an institution within which decisions are made that resolve conflicts and allocate benefits and privileges. It is the predominant institution within society because it has the ultimate decision-making authority.
2. Two fundamental political values are order, which includes security against violence, and liberty, the greatest freedom of the individual consistent with the freedom of other individuals. To be effective, government authority must be backed by legitimacy.
3. Many of our terms for describing forms of government came from the ancient Greeks. In a direct democracy, such as in ancient Athens, the people themselves make the important political decisions. The United States is a democratic republic, also called a representative democracy, in which the people elect representatives to make the decisions.
4. Theories of American democracy include majoritarianism, in which the government does what the majority wants; elite theory, in which the real power lies with one or more elite groups; and pluralism, in which organized interest groups contend for power.
5. Fundamental American values include liberty, order, equality, and property. Not all of these values are fully compatible. The value of order often competes with civil liberties, and economic equality competes with property rights.
6. Popular political ideologies can be arrayed from left (liberal) to right (conservative). We can also analyze economic liberalism and conservatism separately from cultural liberalism and conservatism.

Quiz Multiple Choice

1. Government affects the life of most American citizens in all of the following ways except:
   a. **collecting sales taxes.**
   b. **guaranteeing employment to every citizen.**
   c. **funding health-care services for older persons.**

2. When citizens of a nation do not enjoy liberty, the government frequently will:
   a. **abolish the right to a fair trial.**
   b. **provide government funds to churches.**
   c. **hold regular elections.**

3. A state of affairs in which no government exists is called:
   a. **totalitarianism.**
   b. **oligarchy.**
   c. **anarchy.**

4. A democratic republic is based on all of the following principles except:
   a. **popular sovereignty.**
   b. **majority rule.**
   c. **unlimited government.**

5. The first ten amendments to the United States Constitution, which detail many of our basic liberties, are called:
   a. **the Magna Carta.**
   b. **the Bill of Rights.**
   c. **the Declaration of the Rights of Man.**

6. A major theme of American politics during the twenty-first century has been:
   a. **arguments over whether all citizens should have the right to vote.**
   b. **controversies over the proper size of government.**
   c. **disputes as to whether the government should assume the ownership of major banks.**

7. Popular American ideologies include:
   a. **conservatism, liberalism, and libertarianism.**
   b. **conservatism, liberalism, and socialism.**
   c. **communism, liberalism, and libertarianism.**

8. In recent years, American politics have been characterized by all of the following except:
   a. **a high degree of political polarization.**
   b. **swings in support from one political party to another.**
   c. **bipartisan agreement on economic issues.**

ANSWERS: 1. b, 2. a, 3. c, 4. c, 5. b, 6. b, 7. a, and 8. c.

Quiz Fill-Ins

9. Government is the preeminent __________ in which decisions are made that resolve conflicts or allocate benefits.

10. When government protects the people from the violence of foreign armies and domestic criminals, it is enforcing the principle of _____.

11. When authority is broadly accepted, we say that it has __________.

12. When the citizens themselves meet to establish the laws, the governmental system is known as ________________.

13. An alternative term for *democratic republic* is ____________________.

14. _________ theory describes our democratic system in terms of competition among groups.

15. Various kinds of equality are possible. The most controversial of these is _________________.

16. Under __________, property consists not only of personal possessions but of wealth-creating assets.

17. ______________ is an ideology based on skepticism toward most government activities.

18. A common term that has come to replace liberalism in current American politics is ____________.

ANSWERS: 9. institution, 10. order, 11. legitimacy, 12. direct democracy, 13. representative democracy, 14. Pluralist, 15. economic equality, 16. capitalism, 17. Libertarianism, and 18. progressivism.

Selected Print & Media Resources

SUGGESTED READINGS

Bogus, Carl T. *Buckley: William F. Buckley, Jr., and the Rise of American Conservatism.* New York: Bloomsbury Press, 2011. Bogus, a law professor at Roger Williams University, depicts the conservative movement through the life of William F. Buckley, one of the movement's most important thinkers.

Fukuyama, Francis. *The Origins of Political Order: From Prehuman Times to the French Revolution.* New York: Farrar, Straus and Giroux, 2011. Fukuyama, a well-known political theorist, analyzes key characteristics of the modern state. These include freedom from family and tribal allegiances, adherence to the rule of law, and political accountability.

Remnick, David. *The Bridge: The Life and Rise of Barack Obama.* New York: Knopf, 2010. Remnick, editor of the *New Yorker,* describes the influences that shaped our most recent progressive president.

Skocpol, Theda, and Vanessa Williamson. *The Tea Party and the Remaking of Republican Conservatism.* New York: Oxford University Press, 2012. Skocpol is a political science professor at Harvard, and Williamson is her research assistant. Their account of the Tea Party movement is based on a large number of personal interviews with movement activists.

Stewart, Jon, and the writers of *The Daily Show*. *America (the Book): A Citizen's Guide to Democracy Inaction.* New York: Grand Central Publishing, 2006. This book, a triumph of liberal snark, actually contains a considerable amount of useful information.

Zakaria, Fareed. *The Future of Freedom: Liberal Democracy at Home and Abroad* (revised edition). New York: W. W. Norton & Co., 2007. Zakaria, a prominent journalist and commentator, argues that elections are not enough to guarantee a democratic system. To function properly, democracy also requires acceptance of the rule of law and the defense of basic freedoms.

MEDIA RESOURCES

American Feud: A History of Conservatives and Liberals—Directed by Richard Hall, this 2008 documentary explores popular American ideologies through interviews with leading political commentators.

The Best of The Colbert Report—This 2005 compilation of episodes from Stephen Colbert's political parody includes such classics as the definition of *truthiness,* the "truth" that feels right without reference to logic or facts.

E-mocracy

CONNECTING TO AMERICAN GOVERNMENT AND POLITICS

The Web has become a virtual library, a telephone directory, a contact source, and a vehicle to improve your understanding of American government and politics today.

Increasingly, governments at all levels are using the Web to do business and communicate with citizens. In some states, individuals filing for unemployment compensation do so entirely online. Other states are using the Web to post public notices that in the past were published in newspapers. To help you become familiar with Web resources, we conclude each chapter in this book with an *e-mocracy* feature.

A word of caution about Internet use: Many students surf the Web for political resources. When doing so, you need to remember to approach these sources with care. For one thing, you should be very careful when giving out information about yourself. You also need to use good judgment, because the reliability or intent of any given Web site is often unknown. Some sites are more concerned with accuracy than others, and some sites are updated to include current information while others are not.

LOGGING ON

You may want to visit the home page of Dr. Politics—offered by Steffen Schmidt, one of the authors of this book—for some interesting ideas and activities relating to American government and politics. To do so, use a search engine such as Google or Yahoo to locate the following phrase: "dr politics iowa."

1. Searching on "us government" will bring up a page containing sites with information about the federal government and its programs. One is USA.gov, which provides access to all federal government offices and agencies.
2. Another site is Immigrationdirect.com, a project of U.S. Citizenship and Immigration Services, a federal agency. The site provides information about the rules and requirements for immigration and citizenship.
3. A third site brought up by searching on "us government" is the article on the federal government in Wikipedia, the giant online encyclopedia written by volunteers. You might also consult the Wiki article entitled "Political Ideologies in the United States." Note that while the quality of Wiki articles is usually high, the site is occasionally subject to attacks by vandals who insert dangerously false material into articles. Such false information is usually detected and deleted quickly, however.
4. The Web is a good place to learn about political science as a profession. To do so, search on "political science association." This search will yield the sites of the American Political Science Association, state and regional associations, and the International Political Science Association.

Corporations
We the People
of the United States,
in order to form a more perfec
establish justice, insure do
provide for the common defen
general welfare, and secu
Liberty to ourselves a
and estab
for the U
KOCH
amazon.com
Mobil
NDAA
OCCUPIED
OCCUPY
OREGON

2 The Constitution

The nine learning outcomes below are designed to help improve your understanding of this chapter. After reading this chapter, you should be able to:

- **Learning Outcome 1: Explain how the colonial experience prepared Americans for independence.**
- **Learning Outcome 2: Discuss the restrictions that Britain placed on the colonies and the American response.**
- **Learning Outcome 3: Describe how the Declaration of Independence came to be written and the importance of its second paragraph.**
- **Learning Outcome 4: Detail the Articles of Confederation and some of their weaknesses.**
- **Learning Outcome 5: Discuss the most important compromises reached at the Constitutional Convention and the basic structure of the resulting government.**
- **Learning Outcome 6: Summarize the arguments in favor of adopting the Constitution and the arguments against it.**
- **Learning Outcome 7: Explain how and why the Bill of Rights came to be adopted.**
- **Learning Outcome 8: Describe the process for amending the Constitution.**
- **Learning Outcome 9: Consider the informal ways in which the meaning of the Constitution has adjusted to modern circumstances.**

Occupy the Rose Parade protesters carry an oversize copy of the preamble to the U.S. Constitution, followed by a "corporate" version of the document, as they march in a prearranged demonstration at the end of the 123rd Rose Parade in Pasadena, California, in 2012. (AP Photo/Reed Saxon)

Abraham Lincoln was elected president in 1860 even though he received less than 40 percent of the popular vote. (His name was not even on the ballot papers in most of the South.) Lincoln did win 59 percent of the *electoral vote*, which is described below. What problems can result when a president is elected with few popular votes?

(Library of Congress Prints and Photographs Division Washington, D.C.)

What if... WE ELECTED THE PRESIDENT BY POPULAR VOTE?

BACKGROUND

When you vote for president, the names of the candidates appear before you on the ballot. You don't, however, choose one of these candidates directly. As established by the U.S. Constitution, you vote for a slate of *electors* who are pledged to support a particular candidate. There are 538 electors, one for each member of Congress plus three for the District of Columbia. Although the electors never gather together in one place, they are known collectively as the *electoral college*. This body was created by the founders in the hope that the people would delegate the choice of president to a group of notables. The plan did not survive contact with reality. Electors publicly pledged themselves to candidates almost from the start, and so voters knew whom they were choosing for president.

While the electoral college system has not prevented the people from choosing a president, it does have a side effect. A president can be elected without winning a majority of the popular vote. Of the 33 presidents elected since 1824, a full 16—about half—failed at least once to win 50 percent of the popular vote. A candidate can even win a majority of the popular votes but lose the election. This has happened. In 2000, Democrat Al Gore received 540,000 more votes than George W. Bush, the Republican. Still, Bush won enough electoral college votes to become president. Some citizens believe that the existing electoral college system should be abolished.

WHAT IF WE ELECTED THE PRESIDENT BY POPULAR VOTE?

Under the current system, in all but two small states, the winner of the state's popular vote takes all of the state's electoral votes. This winner-take-all provision is called the *unit rule*. As a result, presidential candidates have little reason to campaign in states where they are certain either to win or to lose by a large margin. During the last presidential elections, major campaigns took place in only a few key states, such as Florida, Ohio, and Virginia. The "spectator" states included some of the nation's most populous—California, Illinois, New York, and Texas. If presidential candidates had to win a majority of the popular vote, they would be forced to campaign in every state.

Some believe, however, that without the electoral college and the unit rule, small states would be ignored. Also, the current system typically encourages certainty in elections by exaggerating the winner's margin of victory. Finally, under the existing system if the election is close and votes must be recounted, the recounts will take place in only a few jurisdictions. If the popular vote determined the winner, votes might have to be recounted in every corner of the country.

HOW A POPULAR VOTE SYSTEM COULD BE ESTABLISHED

Abolishing the electoral college would mean amending the Constitution, and that is very difficult. The unit rule could be abolished more easily, but political scientists have calculated that such a change might make it even less likely that the popular vote winner would carry the election. As an alternative, some people have proposed an interstate compact that would allow presidents to be elected by popular vote. Under the proposal, participating states would award their electoral votes to the candidate who wins the national popular vote. The plan would go into effect when enough states joined to control the electoral college. So far, the compact has been joined by eight states and the District of Columbia. These jurisdictions cast a combined total of 140 electoral votes—270 are needed to activate the plan.

FOR CRITICAL ANALYSIS

1. *Defenders of the existing system argue that it reduces voter fraud. How might that reduction happen?*
2. *Critics of the system argue that it prevents us from ever electing a third-party presidential candidate. Do you agree? Why or why not? And is this really a problem?*

> *We the People of the United States, in Order to form a more perfect Union, establish Justice, insure domestic Tranquility, provide for the common defence, promote the general Welfare, and secure the Blessings of Liberty to ourselves and our Posterity, do ordain and establish this Constitution for the United States of America.*

Every schoolchild in America has at one time or another been exposed to these famous words from the Preamble to the U.S. Constitution. The document itself is remarkable. The U.S. Constitution, compared with others in the fifty states and in the world, is relatively short. Because amending it is difficult, it also has relatively few amendments. The Constitution has remained largely intact for more than two hundred years. To a great extent, this is because the principles set forth in the Constitution are sufficiently broad that they can be adapted to meet the needs of a changing society. (Sometimes questions arise over whether and how the Constitution should be adapted, as you read in this chapter's opening *What If . . .* feature.)

did you know?

The first English claim to territory in North America was made by John Cabot, on behalf of King Henry VII, on June 24, 1497.

How and why the U.S. Constitution was created is a story that has been told and retold. It is worth repeating, because knowing the historical and political context in which this country's governmental machinery was formed is essential to understanding American government and politics today. The Constitution did not result just from creative thinking. Many of its provisions were grounded in the political philosophy of the time. The delegates to the Constitutional Convention in 1787 brought with them two important sets of influences: their political culture and their political experience.

In the years between the first settlements in the New World and the writing of the Constitution, Americans had developed a political philosophy about how people should be governed and had tried out several forms of government. These experiences gave the founders the tools with which they constructed the Constitution.

The Colonial Background

■ Learning Outcome 1: **Explain how the colonial experience prepared Americans for independence.**

In 1607, a company chartered by the English government sent a group of settlers to establish a trading post, Jamestown, in what is now Virginia. Jamestown was the first permanent English colony in the Americas. The king of England gave the backers of this colony a charter granting them "full power and authority" to make laws "for the good and welfare" of the settlement. The colonists at Jamestown instituted a **representative assembly,** a legislature composed of individuals who represented the population, thus setting a precedent in government that was to be observed in later colonial adventures.

Representative Assembly
A legislature composed of individuals who represent the population.

Separatists, the *Mayflower*, and the Compact

The first New England colony was established in 1620. A group made up in large part of extreme Separatists, who wished to break with the Church of England, came over on the ship *Mayflower* to the New World, landing at Plymouth (Massachusetts). Before going onshore, the adult males—women were not considered to have any political status—drew up the Mayflower Compact, which was signed by forty-one of the forty-four men aboard the ship on November 21, 1620. The reason for the compact was obvious. This group was outside the jurisdiction of the Virginia Company of London, which had chartered its settlement.

The Separatist leaders feared that some of the *Mayflower* passengers might conclude that they were no longer under any obligations of civil obedience. Therefore, some form of public authority was imperative. As William Bradford (one of the Separatist leaders) recalled in his accounts, there were "discontented and mutinous speeches that some of the strangers [non-Separatists] amongst them had let fall from them in the ship; That when they came ashore they would use their owne libertie; for none had power to command them."[1]

The Significance of the Compact. The compact was not a constitution. It was a political statement in which the signers agreed to create and submit to the authority of a government, pending the receipt of a royal charter. The Mayflower Compact's historical and political significance is twofold: it depended on the consent of the affected individuals, and it served as a prototype for similar compacts in American history. By the time of the American Revolution, the compact was well on its way toward achieving mythic status. In 1802, John Quincy Adams, son of the second American president, spoke these words at a founders' day celebration in Plymouth: "This is perhaps the only instance in human history of that positive, original social compact, which speculative philosophers have imagined as the only legitimate source of government."[2]

(The Granger Collection)

The signing of the compact aboard the *Mayflower.* In 1620, the Mayflower Compact was signed by almost all of the men aboard the *Mayflower* just before they disembarked at Plymouth, Massachusetts. It stated, "We . . . covenant and combine ourselves togeather into a civil body politick . . . ; and by vertue hearof to enacte, constitute, and frame such just and equal laws . . . as shall be thought [necessary] for the generall good of the Colonie."

Pilgrim Beliefs. Although the Plymouth settlers—later called the Pilgrims—committed themselves to self-government, in other ways their political ideas were not those that are prevalent today. The new community was a religious colony. Separation of church and state and most of our modern civil liberties were alien to the settlers' thinking. By the time the U.S. Constitution was written, the nation's leaders had a very different vision of the relationship between religion and government. We look at some of the founders' beliefs in this chapter's *Politics and Religion* feature on the facing page.

More Colonies, More Government

Another outpost in New England was set up by the Massachusetts Bay Colony in 1630. Then followed Rhode Island, Connecticut, New Hampshire, and others. By 1732, the last of the thirteen colonies, Georgia, was established. During the colonial period, Americans developed a concept of limited government, which followed from the establishment of the first colonies under Crown charters. Theoretically, London governed the colonies. In practice, owing partly to the colonies' distance from London, the colonists exercised a large measure of self-government.

The colonists were able to make their own laws—for example, the Fundamental Orders of Connecticut in 1639. The Massachusetts Body of Liberties in 1641 supported the protection of individual rights. In 1682, the Pennsylvania Frame of Government was passed. Along with the Pennsylvania Charter of Privileges of 1701, it foreshadowed our modern Constitution and Bill of Rights. All of this legislation enabled the colonists to acquire crucial political experience. After independence was declared in 1776, the states quickly set up their own new constitutions.

1. John Camp, *Out of the Wilderness: The Emergence of an American Identity in Colonial New England* (Middleton, Conn.: Wesleyan University Press, 1990).
2. Nathaniel Philbrick, *Mayflower: A Story of Courage, Community, and War* (New York: Penguin, 2007), p. 352. Today, the *Mayflower* Separatists are frequently referred to as the Pilgrims, but that name did not come into common use until two centuries after the colony was founded.

Politics AND Religion

JUST HOW CHRISTIAN WERE THE FOUNDERS?

Christianity utterly permeated the world of the first English settlers in America. The oldest colonial documents are filled with endorsements of Christianity. Regular church attendance was often mandatory. Nine of the colonies had churches that were established by law.

The Declaration of Independence, however, makes no reference to Christ. The word *God* does not appear in the Constitution. By 1790, officially established churches were found only in Connecticut and Massachusetts, and the Congregational Church in Massachusetts had drifted so far from its Puritan origins that many of its members no longer accepted the divinity of Jesus. That is, they belonged to *Unitarian* congregations. One result of this development was that in the national elections of 1796 and 1800, neither major party fielded a presidential candidate who was, by modern definition, a Christian. John Adams, Unitarian, squared off against Thomas Jefferson, freethinker.

These facts raise the question: Just how Christian were the founders? More to the point, did the founders intend the United States to be a "Christian nation"? Scholars and school boards often differ on these issues.

BY AND LARGE, THE FOUNDERS WERE DEVOUT CHRISTIANS . . .

Christian conservatives point out that many American leaders throughout history have characterized the country as a Christian nation, beginning with John Jay, the first chief justice of the United States Supreme Court. The revolutionaries of 1776 often viewed the struggle in religious terms. Quite a few believed that God had a special plan for America to serve as an example to the world. The overwhelming majority of the colonists considered themselves Christians. Today, 78 percent of Americans identify themselves as such. If the term *Christian nation* merely identifies the beliefs of the majority, it is undeniably an accurate label.

To Christian conservatives who would like to change what is taught in the schools, however, the term means much more. They contend that American law is based on the laws of Moses as set down in the Bible. They also believe that America's divine mission is not just an opinion held by many people—it should be taught as literal truth. Finally, according to this group, the separation of church and state is a liberal myth. The language of the First Amendment means only that the national government should not prefer one Protestant denomination over the others.

. . . WHO OPPOSED MIXING CHURCH AND STATE

Mainstream scholars disagree with the above arguments, often vehemently. For example, Steven K. Green, a professor at Willamette University in Oregon, has searched for American court cases that reference the laws of Moses. He has found none.

Ultimately, opponents say, to argue that the founders were not serious about the separation of church and state is to ignore the plain language of the Constitution. True, most of the founders were Christians, but they were also steeped in Enlightenment rationalism that rejected "enthusiasm" in religion. *Enthusiasm* meant the spirit that allowed Protestant and Catholic Europeans to kill one another in the name of God over a period of two centuries. For the founders, mixing church and government was a recipe for trouble.

(© kyoshino / iStockphoto) (© Evelyn Peyton / iStockphoto)

FOR CRITICAL ANALYSIS

Today, candidates for president clearly benefit when they use religious language and when they are comfortable discussing their faith. Is this at all troubling? Why or why not?

British Restrictions and Colonial Reactions

■ Learning Outcome 2: **Discuss the restrictions that Britain placed on the colonies and the American response.**

The conflict between Britain and the American colonies, which ultimately led to the Revolutionary War, began in the 1760s when the British government decided to raise revenues by imposing taxes on the American colonies. Policy advisers to Britain's King George III, who ascended the throne in 1760, decided that it was only logical to require the American colonists to help pay the costs of Britain's defending them during the French

(Painting by William Robinson/The Crown Estate/The Bridgeman Art Library International)

King George III (1738–1820) was king of Great Britain and Ireland from 1760 until his death in 1820. Under George III, the British Parliament attempted to tax the American colonies. Ultimately, the colonies, exasperated at repeated attempts at taxation, proclaimed their independence on July 4, 1776. Why would Britain attempt to tax the colonists?

and Indian War (1756–1763). The colonists, who had grown accustomed to a large degree of self-government and independence from the British Crown, viewed the matter differently.

In 1764, the British Parliament passed the Sugar Act. Many colonists were unwilling to pay the tax imposed by the act. Further regulatory legislation was to come. In 1765, Parliament passed the Stamp Act, providing for internal taxation of legal documents and even newspapers—or, as the colonists' Stamp Act Congress, assembled in 1765, called it, "taxation without representation." The colonists boycotted the purchase of English commodities in return.

The success of the boycott (the Stamp Act was repealed a year later) generated a feeling of unity within the colonies. The British, however, continued to try to raise revenues in the colonies. When Parliament passed duties on glass, lead, paint, and other items in 1767, the colonists again boycotted British goods. The colonists' fury over taxation climaxed in the Boston Tea Party: colonists dressed as Mohawk Indians dumped almost 350 chests of British tea into Boston Harbor as a gesture of tax protest. In retaliation, Parliament passed the Coercive Acts (the "Intolerable Acts") in 1774, which closed Boston Harbor and placed the government of Massachusetts under direct British control. The colonists were outraged—and they responded.

The First Continental Congress

New York, Pennsylvania, and Rhode Island proposed the convening of a colonial gathering, or congress. The Massachusetts House of Representatives requested that all colonies hold conventions to select delegates to be sent to Philadelphia for such a congress.

The First Continental Congress was held at Carpenter's Hall in Philadelphia on September 5, 1774. It was a gathering of delegates from twelve of the thirteen colonies (delegates from Georgia did not attend until 1775). At that meeting, there was little talk of independence. The congress passed a resolution requesting that the colonies send a petition to King George III expressing their grievances. Resolutions were also passed requiring that the colonies raise their own troops and boycott British trade. The British government condemned the congress's actions, treating them as open acts of rebellion.

did you know?

The celebration of King George III's birthday on June 4 gave rise to the custom of summer fireworks, and after 1776, the celebration was rebranded and moved to the 4th of July.

The Second Continental Congress

By the time the Second Continental Congress met in May 1775 (all of the colonies were represented this time), fighting already had broken out between the British and the colonists. One of the main actions of the Second Continental Congress was to establish an army. It did this by declaring the militia that had gathered around Boston an army and naming George Washington as commander in chief. The participants in that congress still attempted to reach a peaceful settlement with the British Parliament. One declaration of the congress stated explicitly that "we have not raised armies with ambitious designs of separating from Great Britain, and establishing independent states." But by the beginning of 1776, military encounters had become increasingly frequent.

Public debate was acrimonious. Then Thomas Paine's *Common Sense* appeared in Philadelphia bookstores. The pamphlet was a colonial best seller. (To do relatively as well today, a book would have to sell between 9 million and 11 million copies in its first year of publication.) Many agreed that Paine did make common sense when he argued that

> *a government of our own is our natural right: and when a man seriously reflects on the precariousness [instability, unpredictability] of human affairs, he will become convinced, that it is infinitely wiser and safer, to form a constitution of our own in a cool and deliberate manner, while we have it in our power, than to trust such an interesting event to time and chance.*[3]

Paine further argued that "nothing can settle our affairs so expeditiously as an open and determined declaration for Independence."[4]

Students of Paine's pamphlet point out that his arguments were not new—they were common in tavern debates throughout the land. Rather, it was the near poetry of his words—which were at the same time as plain as the alphabet—that struck his readers.

Declaring Independence

On April 6, 1776, the Second Continental Congress voted for free trade at all American ports with all countries except Britain. This act could be interpreted as an implicit declaration of independence. The next month, the congress suggested that each of the colonies establish state governments unconnected to Britain. Finally, in July, the colonists declared their independence from Britain.

The Resolution of Independence

On July 2, the Resolution of Independence was adopted by the Second Continental Congress:

> *RESOLVED, That these United Colonies are, and of right ought to be, free and independent States, that they are absolved from allegiance to the British Crown, and that all political connection between them and the state of Great Britain is, and ought to be, totally dissolved.*

In June 1776, Thomas Jefferson already was writing drafts of the Declaration of Independence. When the Resolution of Independence was adopted on July 2, Jefferson argued that a declaration clearly putting forth the causes that compelled the colonies to separate from Britain was necessary. The Second Congress assigned the task to him.

July 4, 1776—The Declaration of Independence

Jefferson's version of the declaration was amended to gain unanimous acceptance (for example, his condemnation of the slave trade was eliminated to satisfy Georgia and North Carolina), but the bulk of it was passed intact on July 4, 1776. On July 19, the modified draft became "the unanimous declaration of the thirteen United States of America." On August 2, it was signed by the members of the Second Continental Congress.

Universal Truths. The Declaration of Independence has become one of the world's most famous and significant documents. The words opening the second paragraph of the Declaration indicate why this is so:

> *We hold these Truths to be self-evident, that all Men are created equal, that they are endowed by their Creator with certain unalienable Rights, that among these are Life, Liberty, and the Pursuit of Happiness—That to secure these Rights, Governments are*

3. *The Political Writings of Thomas Paine,* Vol. 1 (Boston: J. P. Mendum Investigator Office, 1870), p. 46.
4. *Ibid.,* p. 54.

Milestones in Early U.S. Political History

1607	Jamestown established; Virginia Company lands settlers.
1620	Mayflower Compact signed.
1630	Massachusetts Bay Colony set up.
1639	Fundamental Orders of Connecticut adopted.
1641	Massachusetts Body of Liberties adopted.
1682	Pennsylvania Frame of Government passed.
1701	Pennsylvania Charter of Privileges written.
1732	Last of the thirteen colonies (Georgia) established.
1756	French and Indian War begins.
1765	Stamp Act; Stamp Act Congress meets.
1774	First Continental Congress.
1775	Second Continental Congress; Revolutionary War begins.
1776	Declaration of Independence signed.
1777	Articles of Confederation drafted.
1781	Last state (Maryland) signs Articles of Confederation.
1783	"Critical period" in U.S. history begins; weak national government until 1789.
1786	Shays' Rebellion.
1787	Constitutional Convention.
1788	Ratification of Constitution.
1791	Ratification of Bill of Rights.

■ Learning Outcome 3: **Describe how the Declaration of Independence came to be written and the importance of its second paragraph.**

instituted among Men, deriving their just Powers from the Consent of the Governed, that whenever any Form of Government becomes destructive of these Ends, it is the Right of the People to alter or abolish it, and to institute new Government.

Natural Rights and Social Contracts. The statement that "all Men are created equal" and have **natural rights** ("unalienable Rights"), including the rights to "Life, Liberty, and the Pursuit of Happiness," was revolutionary at that time. Its use by Jefferson reveals the influence of the English philosopher John Locke (1632–1704), whose writings were familiar to educated American colonists, including Jefferson. In his *Two Treatises on Government,* published in 1690, Locke had argued that all people possess certain natural rights, including the rights to life, liberty, and property. This claim was not inconsistent with English legal traditions.

Natural Rights
Rights held to be inherent in natural law, not dependent on governments. John Locke stated that natural law, being superior to human law, specifies certain rights of "life, liberty, and property." These rights, altered to become "life, liberty, and the pursuit of happiness," are asserted in the Declaration of Independence.

Social Contract
A voluntary agreement among individuals to secure their rights and welfare by creating a government and abiding by its rules.

Locke went on to argue, however, that the primary purpose of government was to protect these rights. Furthermore, government was established by the people through a **social contract**—an agreement among the people to form a government and abide by its rules. As you read earlier, such contracts, or compacts, were not new to Americans. The Mayflower Compact was the first of several documents that established governments or governing rules based on the consent of the governed.

After setting forth these basic principles of government, the Declaration of Independence goes on to justify the colonists' revolt against Britain. Much of the remainder of the document is a list of what "He" (King George III) had done to deprive the colonists of their rights. (See Appendix A at the end of this book for the complete text of the Declaration of Independence.)

The Significance of the Declaration. The concepts of equality, natural rights, and government established through a social contract were to have a lasting impact on American life. The Declaration of Independence set forth ideals that have since become a fundamental part of our national identity. The Declaration also became a model for use by other nations around the world.

Certainly, most Americans are familiar with the beginning words of the Declaration. Yet, as Harvard historian David Armitage noted in his study of the Declaration of Independence in the international context,[5] few Americans ponder the obvious question: What did these assertions in the Declaration have to do with independence? Clearly, independence could have been declared without these words. Even as late as 1857, Abraham Lincoln admitted, "The assertion that 'all men are created equal' was of no practical use in effecting our separation from Great Britain; and it was placed in the Declaration, not for that, but for future use."[6]

Benjamin Franklin (left) sits with John Adams while Thomas Jefferson looks on during a meeting outside the Second Continental Congress. What important document came out of that congress?

(Jean Léon Gerome Ferris/The Granger Collection)

Essentially, the immediate significance of the Declaration of Independence, in 1776, was that it established the legitimacy of the new nation in the eyes of foreign governments, as well as in the eyes of the colonists themselves. What the new nation needed most were supplies for its armies and a commitment of foreign military aid. Unless it appeared to the world as a political entity separate and independent from Britain, no foreign government would enter into an agreement with its leaders.

5. David Armitage, *The Declaration of Independence: A Global History* (Cambridge, Mass.: Harvard University Press, 2007).
6. As cited in Armitage, *The Declaration of Independence,* p. 26.

In fact, foreign support was crucial to the success of the revolution, as you will discover in the *Beyond Our Borders* feature below.

The Rise of Republicanism

Although the colonists had formally declared independence from Britain, the fight to gain actual independence continued for five more years, until the British general Cornwallis surrendered at Yorktown in 1781. In 1783, after Britain formally recognized the independent status of the United States in the Treaty of Paris, Washington disbanded the army. During these years of military struggles, the states faced the additional challenge of creating a system of self-government for an independent United States.

Some colonists had demanded that independence be preceded by the formation of a strong central government. But others, who called themselves Republicans (not to be confused with today's Republican Party), were against a strong central government. They opposed monarchy, executive authority, and almost any form of restraint on the power of local groups.

From 1776 to 1780, all of the states adopted written constitutions. Eleven of the constitutions were completely new. Two of them—those of Connecticut and Rhode Island—were old royal charters with minor modifications. Republican sentiment led to increased power for the legislatures. In Georgia and Pennsylvania, **unicameral** (one-body) **legislatures** were unchecked by executive or judicial authority. In almost all states, the legislature was predominant.

Unicameral Legislature
A legislature with only one legislative chamber, as opposed to a bicameral (two-chamber) legislature, such as the U.S. Congress. Today, Nebraska is the only state in the Union with a unicameral legislature.

Beyond Our Borders

FRANCE'S ROLE IN DEFEATING THE BRITISH

By the summer of 1781, after six years of war, the American army was struggling. The British occupied New York City. In the South, a British army led by General Cornwallis had captured Charleston in South Carolina and Richmond in Virginia. Cornwallis was now headed toward Chesapeake Bay.

Washington, who was camped outside of New York City, had lost battle after battle. Still, he was never forced to surrender—after each loss, he retreated. In July 1781, a French expeditionary force linked up with Washington's army in New York, doubling the strength of the revolutionary forces. In August, the combined armies marched south to attack Cornwallis.

THE BATTLE OF YORKTOWN

In September, the French navy defeated the British navy in Chesapeake Bay, and the French were temporarily in control of the seas. In October, American and French forces defeated the British army at Yorktown, Virginia. Unable to retreat by sea, Cornwallis was forced to surrender. When the news reached London, the British prime minister resigned in disgrace.

A TRUE WORLD WAR

The war began as an American fight for independence. By the 1780s, however, it had turned into a global conflict. France, the Netherlands, and Spain were also at war with Britain. Battles took place in Gibraltar, India, Ireland, and the West Indies. Fighting in so many places, the British concluded that it would be impossible to replace Cornwallis's army and continue the war with the Americans. In September 1783, the British signed the Treaty of Paris granting independence to the United States.

FOR CRITICAL ANALYSIS

What might have happened if the British had ever been able to force Washington to surrender?

■ Learning Outcome 4: **Detail the Articles of Confederation and some of its weaknesses.**

The Articles of Confederation: Our First Form of Government

The fear of a powerful central government led to the passage of the Articles of Confederation, which created a weak central government. The term **confederation** is important. It means a voluntary association of independent **states,** in which the member states agree to only limited restraints on their freedom of action. As a result, confederations seldom have an effective executive authority.

Confederation
A political system in which states or regional governments retain ultimate authority except for those powers they expressly delegate to a central government; a voluntary association of independent states, in which the member states agree to limited restraints on their freedom of action.

State
A group of people occupying a specific area and organized under one government. It may be either a nation or a subunit of a nation.

In June 1776, the Second Continental Congress began the process of composing what would become the Articles of Confederation. The final draft of the Articles was completed by November 15, 1777. It was not until March 1, 1781, however, that the last state, Maryland, agreed to ratify the Articles. Well before the final ratification of the Articles, however, many of them were implemented: the Continental Congress and the thirteen states conducted American military, economic, and political affairs according to the standards and the form specified by the Articles.[7]

The Articles Establish a Government

Under the Articles, the thirteen original colonies, now states, established on March 1, 1781, a government of the states—the Congress of the Confederation. The Congress was a unicameral assembly of so-called ambassadors from each state, with each state possessing a single vote. Each year, the Congress would choose one of its members as the president of the Congress (that is, the presiding officer), but the Articles did not provide for a president of the United States.

The Congress was authorized in Article X to appoint an executive committee of the states "to execute in the recess of Congress, such of the powers of Congress as the United States, in Congress assembled, by the consent of nine [of the thirteen] states, shall from time to time think expedient to vest with them." The Congress was also allowed to appoint other committees and civil officers necessary for managing the general affairs of the United States. In addition, the Congress could regulate foreign affairs and establish coinage and weights and measures. But it lacked an independent, direct source of revenue and the necessary executive machinery to enforce its decisions throughout the land. Article II of the Articles of Confederation guaranteed that each state would retain its sovereignty. Figure 2–1 alongside illustrates the structure of the government under the Articles of Confederation. Table 2–1 on the facing page summarizes the powers—and the lack of powers—of Congress under the Articles of Confederation.

Figure 2–1 ▸ The Confederal Government Structure under the Articles of Confederation

Congress
Congress had one house. Each state had two to seven members, but only one vote. The exercise of most powers required approval of at least nine states. Amendments to the Articles required the consent of *all* the states.

↓

Committee of the States
A committee of representatives from all the states was empowered to act in the name of Congress between sessions.

↓

Officers
Congress appointed officers to do some of the executive work.

↓

The States

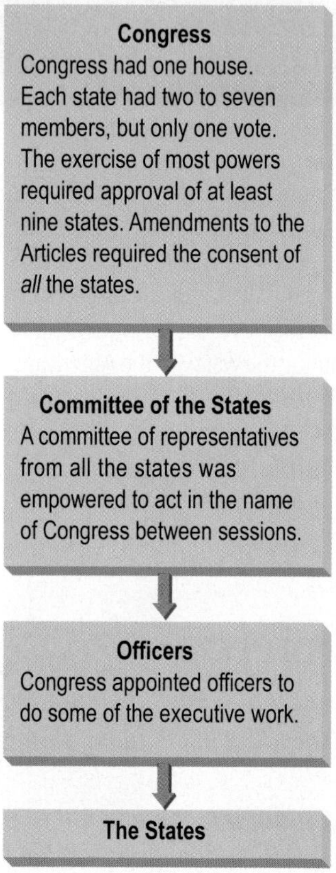

Accomplishments under the Articles

The new government had some accomplishments during its eight years of existence under the Articles of Confederation. Certain states' claims to western lands were settled. Maryland had objected to the claims of the Carolinas, Connecticut, Georgia, Massachusetts, New York, and Virginia. It was only after these states consented to give up their land claims to the United States as a whole that Maryland signed the Articles of Confederation. Another accomplishment under the Articles was the passage of the Northwest Ordinance of 1787, which established a basic pattern of government for new territories north of the Ohio River. All in all, the Articles represented the first real pooling of resources by the American states.

Weaknesses of the Articles

In spite of these accomplishments, the Articles of Confederation had many defects. Although Congress had the legal right to declare war and to conduct foreign policy, it did not have the right to demand revenues from the states. It could only ask for them.

7. Keith L. Dougherty, *Collective Action under the Articles of Confederation* (New York: Cambridge University Press, 2006).

Additionally, the actions of Congress required the consent of nine states. Any amendments to the Articles required the unanimous consent of the Congress and confirmation by every state legislature. Furthermore, the Articles did not create a national system of courts.

Basically, the functioning of the government under the Articles depended on the goodwill of the states. Article III simply established a "league of friendship" among the states—no national government was intended.

Probably the most fundamental weakness of the Articles, and the most basic cause of their eventual replacement by the Constitution, was the lack of power to raise funds for the militia. The Articles contained no language giving Congress coercive power to raise revenue (by levying taxes) to provide adequate support for the military forces controlled by Congress. Due to a lack of resources, the Continental Congress was forced to disband the army after the Revolutionary War, even in the face of serious Spanish and British military threats.

Why did Daniel Shays take possession of the courthouse in western Massachusetts?

Shays' Rebellion and the Need to Revise the Articles

Because of the weaknesses of the Articles of Confederation, the central government could do little to maintain peace and order in the new nation. The states bickered among themselves and increasingly taxed each other's goods. By 1784, the country faced a serious economic depression. Banks were calling in old loans and refusing to make new ones. People who could not pay their debts were often thrown into prison.

In August 1786, mobs of musket-bearing farmers led by former revolutionary captain Daniel Shays seized county courthouses and disrupted the trials

Table 2–1 ▸ Powers of the Congress of the Confederation

Congress Had Power to	Congress Lacked Power to
• Declare war and make peace. • Enter into treaties and alliances. • Establish and control armed forces. • Requisition men and revenues from states. • Regulate coinage. • Borrow funds and issue bills of credit. • Fix uniform standards of weight and measurement. • Create admiralty courts. • Create a postal system. • Regulate Indian affairs. • Guarantee citizens of each state the rights and privileges of citizens in the several states when in another state. • Adjudicate disputes between states on state petition.	• Provide for effective treaty-making power and control foreign relations—it could not compel states to respect treaties. • Compel states to meet military quotas—it could not draft soldiers. • Regulate interstate and foreign commerce—it left each state free to tax imports from other states. • Collect taxes directly from the people—it had to rely on states to collect and forward taxes. • Compel states to pay their share of government costs. • Provide and maintain a sound monetary system or issue paper money—this was left up to the states, and the paper currencies in circulation differed tremendously in value.

did you know?

The Articles of Confederation specified that Canada could be admitted to the Confederation if it ever wished to join.

of debtors in Springfield, Massachusetts. Shays and his men then launched an attack on the federal arsenal at Springfield, but they were repulsed. Shays' Rebellion demonstrated that the central government could not protect the citizenry from armed rebellion or provide adequately for the public welfare. The rebellion spurred the nation's political leaders to action.

The Constitutional Convention

■ Learning Outcome 5: **Discuss the most important compromises reached at the Constitutional Convention and the basic structure of the resulting government.**

The Virginia legislature called for a meeting of all the states to be held at Annapolis, Maryland, on September 11, 1786—ostensibly to discuss commercial problems only. It was evident to those in attendance (including Alexander Hamilton and James Madison) that the national government had serious weaknesses that had to be addressed if it was to survive. Among the important problems to be solved were the relationship between the states and the central government, the powers of the national legislature, the need for executive leadership, and the establishment of policies for economic stability.

The result of this meeting was a petition to the Continental Congress for a general convention to meet in Philadelphia in May 1787 "to consider the exigencies of the union." Congress approved the convention in February 1787. When those who favored a weak central government realized that the Philadelphia meeting would in fact take place, they endorsed the convention. They made sure, however, that the convention would be summoned "for the sole and express purpose of revising the Articles of Confederation." Those in favor of a stronger national government had different ideas.

The designated date for the opening of the convention at Philadelphia, now known as the Constitutional Convention, was May 14, 1787. Few of the delegates had actually arrived in Philadelphia by that time, so the Convention was delayed. It was formally opened in the East Room of the Pennsylvania State House on May 25.[8] Fifty-five of the seventy-four delegates chosen for the convention actually attended. (Of those fifty-five, only about forty played active roles at the convention.) Rhode Island was the only state that refused to send delegates.

Who Were the Delegates?

Who were the fifty-five delegates to the Constitutional Convention? They certainly did not represent a cross section of American society in the 1700s. Indeed, most were members of the upper class. Consider the following facts:

1. Thirty-three were members of the legal profession.
2. Three were physicians.
3. Almost 50 percent were college graduates.
4. Seven were former chief executives of their respective states.
5. Six were owners of large plantations.
6. Eight were important businesspersons.

They were also relatively young by today's standards: James Madison was thirty-six, Alexander Hamilton was only thirty-two, and Jonathan Dayton of New Jersey was twenty-six. The venerable Benjamin Franklin, however, was eighty-one and had to be carried in on a portable chair borne by four prisoners from a local jail. Not counting Franklin, the average age was just over forty-two.

did you know?

James Madison was the only delegate to attend every meeting of the Constitutional Convention.

The Working Environment

The conditions under which the delegates worked for 115 days were far from ideal and were made even worse by the necessity of maintaining total secrecy. The framers of the Constitution believed that if public debate took place on particular positions, delegates

8. The State House was later named Independence Hall. This was the same room in which the Declaration of Independence had been signed eleven years earlier.

would have a more difficult time compromising or backing down to reach agreement. Consequently, the windows were usually shut in the East Room of the State House. Summer quickly arrived, and the air became humid and hot by noon of each day. The delegates did, however, have a nearby tavern and inn to which they retired each evening—the Indian Queen. It became the informal headquarters of the delegates.

(Collection of the New-York Historical Society, USA/The Bridgeman Art Library International)

Alexander Hamilton (shown in an 1804 portrait) was among those who wanted a monarchy.

Factions among the Delegates

We know much about the proceedings at the convention because James Madison kept a daily, detailed personal journal. A majority of the delegates were strong nationalists—they wanted a central government with real power, unlike the central government under the Articles of Confederation. George Washington and Benjamin Franklin were among those who sought a stronger government.

Among the nationalists, some—including Alexander Hamilton—went so far as to support monarchy. Another important group of nationalists were of a more republican stripe. Led by James Madison of Virginia and James Wilson of Pennsylvania, these republican nationalists wanted a central government founded on popular support.

Many of the other delegates from Connecticut, Delaware, Maryland, New Hampshire, and New Jersey were concerned about only one thing—claims to western lands. As long as those lands became the common property of all of the states, these delegates were willing to support a central government.

Finally, there was a group of delegates who were totally against a national authority. Two of the three delegates from New York quit the convention when they saw the nationalist direction of its proceedings.

Politicking and Compromises

The debates at the convention started on the first day. James Madison had spent months reviewing European political theory. When his Virginia delegation arrived ahead of most of the others, it got to work immediately. By the time George Washington opened the convention, Governor Edmund Randolph of Virginia was prepared to present fifteen resolutions proposing fundamental changes to the nation's government. In retrospect, this was a masterful stroke on the part of the Virginia delegation. It set the agenda for the remainder of the convention—even though, in principle, the delegates had been sent to Philadelphia for the sole purpose of amending the Articles of Confederation.

did you know?

The word *democracy* does not appear once in the U.S. Constitution.

The Virginia Plan. Randolph's fifteen resolutions proposed an entirely new national government under a constitution. Basically, it called for the following:

1. A **bicameral** (two-chamber) **legislature,** with the lower chamber chosen by the people and the smaller upper chamber chosen by the lower chamber from nominees selected by state legislatures. The number of representatives would be proportional to a state's population, thus favoring the large states. The legislature could void any state laws.
2. The creation of an unspecified national executive, elected by the legislature.
3. The creation of a national judiciary, appointed by the legislature.

Bicameral Legislature
A legislature made up of two parts, called chambers. The U.S. Congress, composed of the House of Representatives and the Senate, is a bicameral legislature.

It did not take long for the smaller states to realize they would fare poorly under the Virginia Plan, which would enable Massachusetts, Pennsylvania, and Virginia to form a majority in the national legislature. The debate on the plan dragged on for a number of weeks. It was time for the small states to come up with their own plan.

The New Jersey Plan. On June 15, William Paterson of New Jersey offered an alternative plan. After all, argued Paterson, under the Articles of Confederation all states had equality. Therefore, the convention had no power to change this arrangement. He proposed the following:

1. The fundamental principle of the Articles of Confederation—one state, one vote—would be retained.
2. Congress would be able to regulate trade and impose taxes.
3. All acts of Congress would be the supreme law of the land.
4. Several people would be elected by Congress to form an executive office.
5. The executive office would appoint a Supreme Court.

Supremacy Doctrine
A doctrine that asserts the priority of national law over state laws. This principle is stated in Article VI of the Constitution, which provides that the Constitution, the laws passed by the national government under its constitutional powers, and all treaties constitute the supreme law of the land.

Great Compromise
The compromise between the New Jersey and Virginia Plans that created one chamber of the Congress based on population and one chamber representing each state equally; also called the Connecticut Compromise.

Basically, the New Jersey Plan was simply an amendment of the Articles of Confederation. Its only notable feature was its reference to the **supremacy doctrine,** which was later included in the Constitution.

The "Great Compromise." The delegates were at an impasse. Most wanted a strong national government and were unwilling even to consider the New Jersey Plan. But when the Virginia Plan was brought up again, the small states threatened to leave. It was not until July 16 that a compromise was achieved. Roger Sherman of Connecticut proposed the following:

1. A bicameral legislature in which the lower chamber, the House of Representatives, would be apportioned according to the number of free inhabitants in each state, plus three-fifths of the slaves.
2. An upper chamber, the Senate, which would have two members from each state elected by the state legislatures.

This plan, known as the **Great Compromise** (it is also called the Connecticut Compromise because of the role of the Connecticut delegates in the proposal), broke the deadlock. It did exact a political price, however, because it permitted each state to have equal representation in the Senate. Having two senators represent each state diluted the voting power of citizens living in more heavily populated states and gave the smaller states disproportionate political power. But the Connecticut Compromise resolved the controversy between small and large states. In addition, the Senate would act as a check on the House, which many feared would be dominated by the masses and excessively responsive to them.

George Washington presided over the Constitutional Convention of 1787.

(Stearns/© Bettmann/Corbis)

The Three-Fifths Compromise. The Great Compromise also settled another major issue—how to deal with slaves in the representational scheme. Slavery was still legal in several northern states, but it was concentrated in the

South. Many delegates were opposed to slavery and wanted it banned entirely in the United States. Charles Pinckney of South Carolina led strong southern opposition to a ban on slavery. Furthermore, the South wanted slaves to be counted along with free persons in determining representation in Congress. Delegates from the northern states objected. Sherman's three-fifths proposal was a compromise between northerners who did not want the slaves counted at all and southerners who wanted them counted in the same way as free whites. Actually, Sherman's Connecticut Plan spoke of three-fifths of "all other persons" (and that is the language of the Constitution itself). It is not hard to figure out, though, who those other persons were.

The three-fifths rule meant that the House of Representatives and the electoral college would be apportioned in part on the basis of *property*—specifically, property in slaves. Modern commentators have referred to the three-fifths rule as valuing African Americans only three-fifths as much as whites. Actually, the additional southern representatives elected because of the three-fifths rule did not represent the slaves at all. Rather, these extra representatives were a gift to the slave owners—the additional representatives enhanced the power of the South in Congress.

The Slave Trade and the Future of Slavery. The three-fifths compromise did not completely settle the slavery issue. There was also the question of the slave trade. Eventually, the delegates agreed that Congress could not ban the importation of slaves until after 1808.

The compromise meant that the matter of slavery itself was never addressed directly. The South won twenty years of unrestricted slave trade and a requirement that escaped slaves in free states be returned to their owners in slave states.

Clearly, many delegates, including slave owners such as George Washington and James Madison, had serious objections to slavery. Why, then, did they allow slavery to continue? Historians have long maintained that the framers had no choice—that without a slavery compromise, the delegates from the South would have abandoned the convention. Indeed, this was the fear of a number of antislavery delegates to the convention. Madison, for example, said, "Great as the evil is, a dismemberment of the Union would be even worse."[9] Other scholars, however, contend that not only would it have been possible for the founders to ban slavery, but by doing so they would have achieved greater unity for the new nation.

A number of historians have made an additional point. Many American leaders believed that slavery would die out naturally. These leaders assumed that in the long run, slave labor could not compete with the labor of free citizens. This assumption turned out to be incorrect.

did you know?

During the four centuries of slave trading, an estimated 10 million to 11 million Africans were transported to North and South America—and only 6 percent of those slaves were imported into the United States.

Other Issues. The South also worried that the northern majority in Congress would pass legislation unfavorable to its economic interests. Because the South depended on agricultural exports, it feared the imposition of export taxes. In return for acceding to the northern demand that Congress be able to regulate commerce among the states and with other nations, the South obtained a promise that export taxes would not be imposed. As a result, the United States is among the few countries that do not tax their exports.

There were other disagreements. The delegates could not decide whether to establish only a Supreme Court or to create lower courts as well. They deferred the issue by mandating a Supreme Court and allowing Congress to establish lower courts. They also disagreed over whether the president or the Senate would choose the Supreme Court justices. A compromise was reached with the agreement that the president would nominate the justices and the Senate would confirm the nominations.

9. Speech before the Virginia ratifying convention on June 17, 1788, as cited in Bruno Leone, ed., *The Creation of the Constitution* (San Diego: Greenhaven Press, 1995), p. 159.

These compromises, as well as others, resulted from the recognition that if one group of states refused to ratify the Constitution, it was doomed.

Working toward Final Agreement

The Connecticut Compromise was reached by mid-July. The makeup of the executive branch and the judiciary, however, was left unsettled. The remaining work of the convention was turned over to a five-man Committee of Detail, which presented a rough draft of the Constitution on August 6. It made the executive and judicial branches subordinate to the legislative branch.

Separation of Powers The principle of dividing governmental powers among different branches of government.

Madisonian Model A structure of government proposed by James Madison in which the powers of the government are separated into three branches: executive, legislative, and judicial.

Checks and Balances A major principle of the American system of government whereby each branch of the government can check the actions of the others.

The Madisonian Model—Separation of Powers.

The major issue of **separation of powers** had not yet been resolved. The delegates were concerned with structuring the government to prevent the imposition of tyranny, either by the majority or by a minority. It was Madison who proposed a governmental scheme—sometimes called the **Madisonian model**—to achieve this: the executive, legislative, and judicial powers of government were to be separated so that no one branch had enough power to dominate the others. The separation of powers was by function, as well as by personnel, with Congress passing laws, the president enforcing and administering laws, and the courts interpreting laws in individual circumstances.

Each of the three branches of government would be independent of the others, but they would have to cooperate to govern. According to Madison, in *Federalist Paper* No. 51 (see Appendix C), "the great security against a gradual concentration of the several powers in the same department consists in giving to those who administer each department the necessary constitutional means and personal motives to resist encroachments of the others."

The Madisonian Model—Checks and Balances.

The "constitutional means" Madison referred to is a system of **checks and balances** through which each branch of the government can check the actions of the others. For example, Congress can enact laws, but the president has veto power over congressional acts. The Supreme Court has the power to declare acts of Congress and of the executive branch unconstitutional, but the president appoints the justices of the Supreme Court, with the advice and consent of the Senate. (The Supreme Court's power to declare acts unconstitutional was not mentioned in the Constitution, although arguably the framers assumed that the Court would have this power—see the discussion of *judicial review* later in this chapter.) Figure 2–2 on the facing page outlines these checks and balances.

James Madison (1751–1836) earned the title "master builder of the Constitution" because of his persuasive logic during the Constitutional Convention. His contributions to the *Federalist Papers* showed him to be a brilliant political thinker and writer.

(Musee Franco-Americaine, Blerancourt, Chauny, France/Giraudon/The Bridgeman Art Library)

Madison's ideas of separation of powers and checks and balances were not new. Indeed, the influential French political thinker Baron de Montesquieu (1689–1755) had explored these concepts in his book *The Spirit of the Laws,* published in 1748. Montesquieu not only discussed the "three sorts of powers" (executive, legislative, and judicial) that were necessarily exercised by any government but also gave examples of how, in some nations, certain checks on these powers had arisen and had been effective in preventing tyranny.

The Development of the Madisonian Model.

In the years since the Constitution was ratified, the checks and balances built into it have evolved into a sometimes complex give-and-take among the branches of government. Generally, for nearly every check that one branch has over another, the branch that has been checked has found a way of getting around it. For example, suppose that the president checks Congress by vetoing a bill.

Figure 2-2 ▸ Checks and Balances

The major checks and balances among the three branches are illustrated here. The U.S. Constitution does not mention some of these checks, such as judicial review—the power of the courts to declare federal or state acts unconstitutional—and the president's ability to refuse to enforce judicial decisions or congressional legislation. Checks and balances can be thought of as a confrontation of powers or responsibilities. Each branch checks the actions of another. Two branches in conflict have powers that can result in balances or stalemates, requiring one branch to give in or both to reach a compromise.

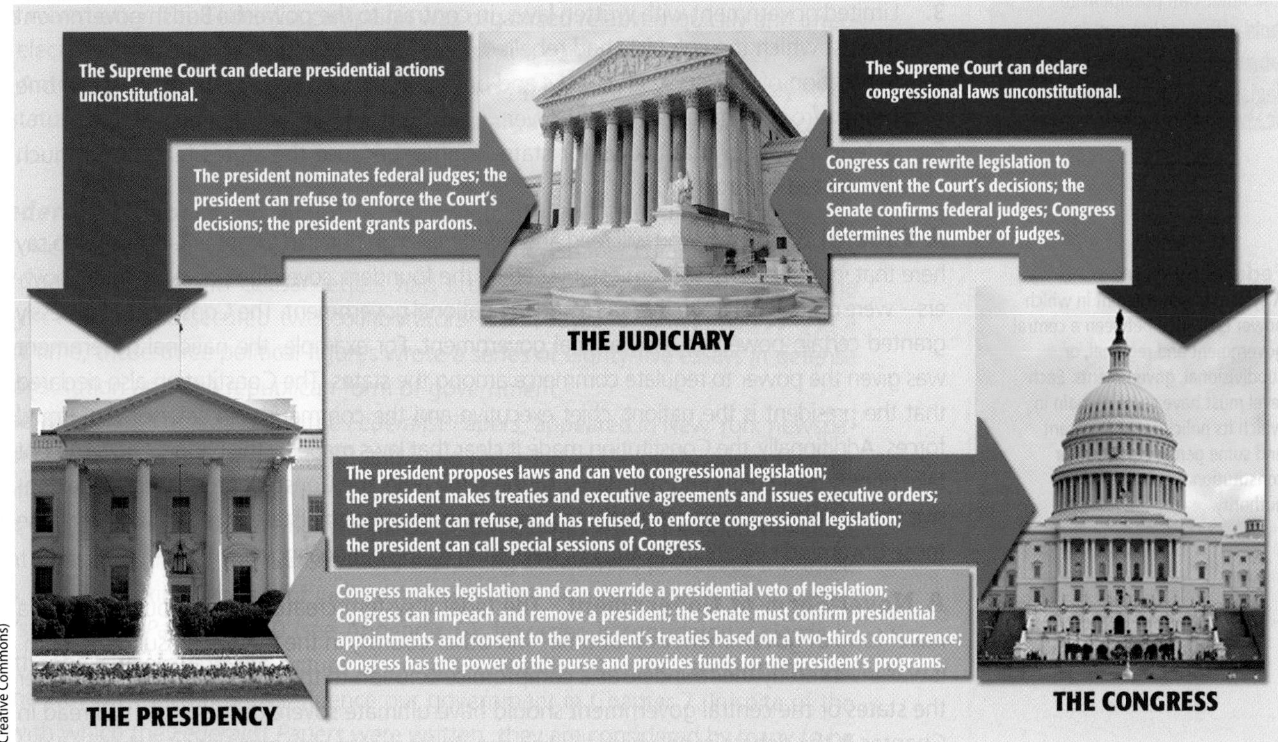

(Creative Commons)

Congress can override the presidential veto by a two-thirds vote. Additionally, Congress holds the "power of the purse." If it disagrees with a program endorsed by the executive branch, it can simply refuse to appropriate the funds necessary to operate that program. Similarly, the president can impose a countercheck on Congress if the Senate refuses to confirm a presidential appointment, such as a judicial appointment. The president can simply wait until Congress is in recess and then make what is called a "recess appointment," which does not require the Senate's approval.

The Executive. Some delegates favored a plural executive made up of representatives from the various regions. This idea was abandoned in favor of a single chief executive. Some argued that Congress should choose the executive. To make the presidency completely independent of the proposed Congress, however, an **electoral college** was adopted. To be sure, the electoral college created a cumbersome presidential election process (see Chapter 9). The process even made it possible for a candidate who comes in second in the popular vote to become president by being the top vote getter in the electoral college, as we explained in this chapter's opening *What If . . .* feature. The electoral college insulated the president, however, from direct popular control.

Electoral College
A group of persons called electors selected by the voters in each state and the District of Columbia (D.C.). This group officially elects the president and vice president of the United States. The number of electors in each state is equal to the number of each state's representatives in both chambers of Congress. The Twenty-third Amendment to the Constitution grants D.C. as many electors as the state with the smallest population.

The Final Document

On September 17, 1787, the Constitution was approved by thirty-nine delegates. Of the fifty-five who had attended originally, only forty-two remained. Three delegates refused to sign the Constitution. Others disapproved of at least parts of it but signed anyway to begin the ratification debate.

include a list of guaranteed liberties, or a bill of rights. Finally, the Anti-Federalists decried the weakened power of the states.[12]

did you know?

The U.S. Constitution, at 4,400 words without its amendments, is the shortest written constitution of any major nation.

The Anti-Federalists cannot be dismissed as unpatriotic extremists. They included such patriots as Patrick Henry and Samuel Adams. They were arguing what had been the most prevalent view in that era. This view derived from the French political philosopher Montesquieu, who, as mentioned earlier, was an influential political theorist. Montesquieu believed that a republic was possible only in a relatively small society governed by direct democracy or by a large legislature with small districts. The Madisonian view favoring a large republic, particularly as expressed in *Federalist Papers* No. 10 and No. 51 (see Appendix C), was actually an exceptional view in those years. Indeed, some researchers believe it was mainly the bitter experiences with the Articles of Confederation, rather than Madison's arguments, that persuaded the state conventions to ratify the Constitution.

The March to the Finish

The struggle for ratification continued. Strong majorities were procured in Connecticut, Delaware, Georgia, New Jersey, and Pennsylvania. After a bitter struggle in Massachusetts, that state ratified the Constitution by a narrow margin on February 6, 1788. By the spring, Maryland and South Carolina had ratified by sizable majorities. Then on June 21 of that year, New Hampshire became the ninth state to ratify the Constitution. Although the Constitution was formally in effect, this meant little without Virginia and New York. Virginia ratified it a few days later, but New York did not join in for another month (see Table 2–2 below).

12. Herbert J. Storing edited seven volumes of Anti-Federalist writings and released them in 1981 as *The Anti-Federalist.* Political science professor Murray Dry has prepared a more manageable, one-volume version of this collection: Herbert J. Storing, ed., *The Anti-Federalist: An Abridgment of the Complete Anti-Federalist* (Chicago: University of Chicago Press, 2006).

Table 2–2 ▸ Ratification of the Constitution

State	Date	Vote For–Against
Delaware	Dec. 7, 1787	30–0
Pennsylvania	Dec. 12, 1787	43–23
New Jersey	Dec. 18, 1787	38–0
Georgia	Jan. 2, 1788	26–0
Connecticut	Jan. 9, 1788	128–40
Massachusetts	Feb. 6, 1788	187–168
Maryland	Apr. 28, 1788	63–11
South Carolina	May 23, 1788	149–73
New Hampshire	June 21, 1788	57–46
Virginia	June 25, 1788	89–79
New York	July 26, 1788	30–27
North Carolina	Nov. 21, 1789*	194–77
Rhode Island	May 29, 1790	34–32

*Ratification was initially defeated on August 4, 1788, by a vote of 84–184.

Did the Majority of Americans Support the Constitution?

In 1913, historian Charles Beard published *An Economic Interpretation of the Constitution of the United States.*[13] This book launched a debate that has continued ever since—the debate over whether the Constitution was supported by a majority of Americans.

(© Peter Steiner/The New Yorker Collection/www.cartoonbank.com)

"Remember, gentlemen, we aren't here just to draft a constitution. We're here to draft the best damned constitution in the world."

Beard's Thesis. Beard argued that the Constitution had been produced primarily by wealthy property owners who desired a stronger government able to protect their property rights. Beard also claimed that the Constitution had been imposed by undemocratic methods. He pointed out that there was never any popular vote on whether to hold a constitutional convention in the first place. Furthermore, even if such a vote had been taken, state laws generally restricted voting rights to property-owning white males.

State Ratifying Conventions. The delegates to the various state ratifying conventions had been selected by only 150,000 of the nation's approximately 4 million total inhabitants. That does not seem very democratic—at least not by today's standards. Some historians have suggested that if a Gallup poll could have been taken at that time, the Anti-Federalists would probably have outnumbered the Federalists.[14] Much has also been made of the various machinations used by the Federalists to ensure the Constitution's ratification, including the purchase of at least one printing press to prevent the publication of Anti-Federalist sentiments.

did you know?

Sixty-four percent of Americans believe that the Constitution declared English to be the national language of the United States.

Support Was Probably Widespread. Many small farmers feared that the Constitution would result in oppressive domination by a wealthy elite. Still, the perception that a strong central government was necessary to keep order and protect the public welfare appears to have been widespread among all classes, rich and poor alike. No doubt an effective national government would benefit the wealthy, as Beard argued. Yet it could help workers and small farmers as well. After all, the economic and political crisis that the nation faced in the 1780s fell even harder on the poor than on the rich. For details on the economic troubles of that decade, see the *Politics and Economics* feature on the following page.

Further, although the need for strong government was a major argument in favor of adopting the Constitution, even the Federalists sought to craft a limited government. Compared with constitutions adopted by other nations in later years, the U.S. Constitution, through its checks and balances, favors limited government over "energetic" government to a marked degree.

The Bill of Rights

■ Learning Outcome 7: **Explain how and why the Bill of Rights came to be adopted.**

The U.S. Constitution would not have been ratified in several important states if the Federalists had not assured the states that amendments to the Constitution would be passed to protect individual liberties against incursions by the national government. Many of the recommendations of the state ratifying conventions included specific rights that were considered later by James Madison as he labored to draft what became the Bill of Rights. (We introduced the Bill of Rights in the *What If . . .* feature that opened Chapter 1.)

13. Charles A. Beard, *An Economic Interpretation of the Constitution of the United States* (New York: Macmillan, 1913; New York: Free Press, 1986).
14. Jim Powell, "James Madison—Checks and Balances to Limit Government Power," *The Freeman,* March 1996, p. 178.

Politics AND Economics

THE POST-REVOLUTIONARY DEPRESSION

Americans today are very aware that the condition of the economy has a great effect on politics. When the economy is creating a large number of jobs in the months before presidential elections, an incumbent president gains an advantage. If the reverse is true, the incumbent is in trouble. Although many people don't realize it, the state of the economy was also politically important in the years following the American Revolution.

After Britain recognized the independence of the United States, our trade with that country was no more than half what it had been before the revolution. Total exports to all countries from the Upper South fell by almost 40 percent. Exports from the Lower South dropped 50 percent.

The collapsing economy damaged America's cities. In 1774, Charleston, Boston, New York City, and Philadelphia together had 5.1 percent of the nation's population. By 1790, that figure was down to 2.7 percent. Earnings of urban workers collapsed, and many of them fled from the cities to become farm workers. In short, the years between the revolution and the adoption of the Constitution were scarred by a tremendous depression. The nation did not recover fully until after 1800.[a]

a. Peter H. Lindert and Jeffrey G. Williamson, "America's Revolution: Economic Disaster, Development, and Equality," *VoxEU* (online journal of the Centre for Economic Policy Research, London), July 15, 2011.

FOR CRITICAL ANALYSIS

The economy began to pick up again in the 1790s, after the Constitution was adopted. What impact would this development have had on how Americans viewed their new government?

(© kyoshino / iStockphoto) (© Evelyn Peyton / iStockphoto)

The American Civil Liberties Union (ACLU) is the nation's leading civil liberties advocacy group. If you friend "ACLU" on Facebook, you'll get a regular stream of updates on efforts to protect the rights guaranteed by the Constitution.

A "Bill of Limits"

Although called the Bill of Rights, the first ten amendments to the Constitution essentially were a "bill of limits," because the amendments limited the powers of the national government over the rights and liberties of individuals.

Ironically, a year earlier Madison had told Jefferson, "I have never thought the omission [of the Bill of Rights] a material defect" of the Constitution. Jefferson's enthusiasm for a bill of rights apparently influenced Madison, however.

Was a Bill of Rights Necessary? Many framers thought that it was dangerous to enumerate specific civil liberties in a bill of rights. Future governments might assume that rights that were not listed did not exist. (This concern was addressed in the Bill of Rights itself by the Ninth Amendment.)

Also, the Constitution already listed certain rights. The original document prohibits *bills of attainder*—laws that impose punishment on named individuals without trial. The original Constitution also bars *ex post facto* laws, which make an act illegal after it has already happened. A trial by jury is required in federal criminal cases. Finally, individuals may not be jailed without due process of law. A judge can demand to know why a particular person is in custody (the demand is called a *writ of habeas corpus*). If no proper explanation is given, the judge can order the individual's release.

Madison Drafts the Bill. Madison had to cull through more than two hundred state recommendations. It was no small task, and in retrospect he chose remarkably well. One of the rights appropriate for constitutional protection that he left out was equal protection under the laws—but that was not commonly regarded as a basic right at that time. Not until 1868 was the Constitution amended to guarantee that no state shall deny equal protection to any person.

The final number of amendments that Madison and a specially appointed committee came up with was seventeen. Congress tightened the language somewhat and eliminated five of the amendments. Of the remaining twelve, two—dealing with the apportionment of representatives and the compensation of the members of Congress—were not ratified immediately by the states. Eventually, Supreme Court decisions led to reform of the apportionment process. The amendment on the compensation of members of Congress was ratified 203 years later—in 1992![15]

Adoption of the Bill of Rights

On December 15, 1791, the national Bill of Rights was adopted when Virginia agreed to ratify the ten amendments. On ratification, the Bill of Rights became part of the U.S. Constitution. The basic structure of American government had already been established. Now the fundamental rights and liberties of individuals were protected, at least in theory, at the national level. The proposed amendment that Madison characterized as "the most valuable amendment in the whole lot"—which would have prohibited the states from infringing on the freedoms of conscience, press, and jury trial—had been eliminated by the Senate. Thus, the Bill of Rights as adopted did not limit state power, and individual citizens had to rely on the guarantees contained in a particular state constitution or state bill of rights. The country had to wait until the violence of the Civil War before significant limitations on state power in the form of the Fourteenth Amendment became part of the national Constitution.

Altering the Constitution: The Formal Amendment Process

As amended, the U.S. Constitution consists of about 7,000 words. It is shorter than any state constitution except that of Vermont, which has 6,880 words. The federal Constitution is short because the founders intended it to be only a framework for the new government, to be interpreted by succeeding generations. One of the reasons it has remained short is that the formal amending procedure does not allow for changes to be made easily. Article V of the Constitution outlines the ways in which amendments may be proposed and ratified (see Figure 2–3 on the following page).

■ Learning Outcome 8: **Describe the process for amending the Constitution.**

Two formal methods of proposing an amendment to the Constitution are available: (1) a two-thirds vote in each chamber of Congress or (2) a national convention that is called by Congress at the request of two-thirds of the state legislatures. This second method has never been used.

Ratification can occur by one of two methods: (1) by a positive vote in three-fourths of the legislatures of the various states or (2) by special conventions called in the states and a positive vote in three-fourths of them. The second method has been used only once, to repeal Prohibition (the ban on the production and sale of alcoholic beverages). That situation was exceptional—it involved an amendment (the Twenty-first) to repeal another amendment (the Eighteenth, which had created Prohibition). State conventions were necessary for repeal of the Eighteenth Amendment because prohibitionist forces were in control of the legislatures in many states where a majority of the population actually supported repeal. (Note that Congress determines the method of ratification to be used by all states for each proposed constitutional amendment.)

did you know?

The Constitution explicitly says that no amendment can alter the equal representation of the states in the Senate. This is the only such "entrenched" provision in the document.

15. For perspectives on these events, see Richard E. Labunski, *James Madison and the Struggle for the Bill of Rights* (New York: Oxford University Press, 2008); and Steven Waldman, *Founding Faith: How Our Founding Fathers Forged a Radical New Approach to Religious Liberty* (New York: Random House Trade Paperbacks, 2009).

Figure 2-3 ▸ The Formal Constitutional Amending Procedure

There are two ways of proposing amendments to the U.S. Constitution and two ways of ratifying proposed amendments. Among the four possibilities, the usual route has been proposal by Congress and ratification by state legislatures.

PROPOSING AMENDMENTS
EITHER . . . By a two-thirds vote in both chambers of Congress . . .
OR . . . By a national convention called by Congress at the request of two-thirds of the states.
RATIFYING AMENDMENTS
EITHER . . . By the legislatures of three-fourths of the states . . .
OR . . . By conventions in three-fourths of the states.
Typical (used for all except one amendment)
Used only once (Twenty-first Amendment)
Never used

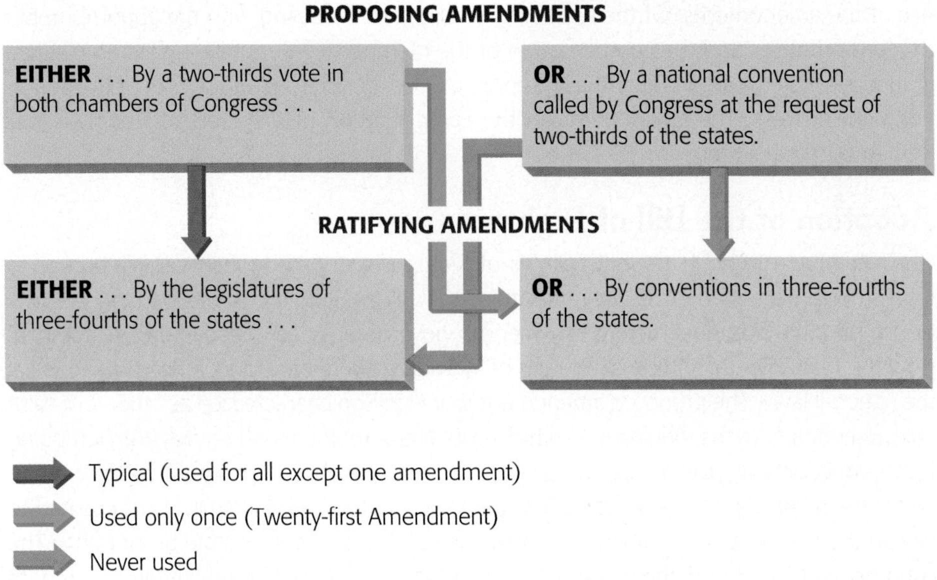

Many Amendments Proposed, Few Accepted

Congress has considered more than eleven thousand amendments to the Constitution. Only thirty-three amendments have been submitted to the states after having been approved by the required two-thirds vote in each chamber of Congress, and only twenty-seven have been ratified—see Table 2–3 on the facing page. (The full, annotated text of the U.S. Constitution, including its amendments, is presented in a special appendix at the end of this chapter.) It should be clear that the amendment process is much more difficult than a graphic depiction such as Figure 2–3 above can indicate. Because of competing social and economic interests, the requirement that two-thirds of both the House and the Senate approve the amendments is hard to achieve.

After an amendment has been approved by Congress, the process becomes even more arduous. Three-fourths of the state legislatures must approve the amendment. Only those amendments that have wide popular support across parties and in all regions of the country are likely to be approved.

Why was the amendment process made so difficult? The framers feared that a simple amendment process could lead to a tyranny of the majority, which could pass amendments to oppress disfavored individuals and groups. The cumbersome amendment process does not seem to stem the number of amendments that are proposed in Congress, however, particularly in recent years. Proposing an amendment that will never pass is an effective way for a legislator to engage in grandstanding.

Limits on Ratification

A reading of Article V of the U.S. Constitution reveals that the framers of the Constitution specified no time limit on the ratification process. The Supreme Court has held that Congress can specify a time for ratification as long as it is "reasonable." Since 1919, most proposed amendments have included a requirement that ratification be obtained within seven years. This was the case with the proposed Equal Rights Amendment, which sought to guarantee equal rights for women. When three-fourths of the states had not ratified it

Table 2-3 ▸ Amendments to the Constitution

Amendment	Subject	Year Adopted	Time Required for Ratification
1st–10th	The Bill of Rights	1791	2 years, 2 months, 20 days
11th	Immunity of states from certain suits	1795	11 months, 3 days
12th	Changes in electoral college procedure	1804	6 months, 3 days
13th	Prohibition of slavery	1865	10 months, 3 days
14th	Citizenship, due process, and equal protection	1868	2 years, 26 days
15th	No denial of vote because of race, color, or previous condition of servitude	1870	11 months, 8 days
16th	Power of Congress to tax income	1913	3 years, 6 months, 22 days
17th	Direct election of U.S. senators	1913	10 months, 26 days
18th	National (liquor) prohibition	1919	1 year, 29 days
19th	Women's right to vote	1920	1 year, 2 months, 14 days
20th	Change of dates for congressional and presidential terms	1933	10 months, 21 days
21st	Repeal of the Eighteenth Amendment	1933	9 months, 15 days
22d	Limit on presidential tenure	1951	3 years, 11 months, 3 days
23d	District of Columbia electoral vote	1961	9 months, 13 days
24th	Prohibition of tax payment as a qualification to vote in federal elections	1964	1 year, 4 months, 9 days
25th	Procedures for determining presidential disability and presidential succession and for filling a vice-presidential vacancy	1967	1 year, 7 months, 4 days
26th	Prohibition of setting the minimum voting age above eighteen in any election	1971	3 months, 7 days
27th	Prohibition of Congress's voting itself a raise that takes effect before the next election	1992	203 years

in the allotted seven years, however, Congress extended the limit by an additional three years and three months. That extension expired on June 30, 1982, and the amendment still had not been ratified. Another proposed amendment, which would have guaranteed congressional representation for the District of Columbia, fell far short of the thirty-eight state ratifications needed before its August 22, 1985, deadline.

On May 7, 1992, Michigan became the thirty-eighth state to ratify the Twenty-seventh Amendment (on congressional compensation)—one of the two "lost" amendments of the twelve that originally were sent to the states in 1789. Because most of the amendments proposed in recent years have been given a time limit of only seven years by Congress, it was questionable for a time whether the amendment would take effect even if the necessary number of states ratified it. Is 203 years too long a lapse of time between the proposal and the final ratification of an amendment? It apparently was not, because the amendment was certified as legitimate by the National Archives on May 18, 1992.

(AP Photo/Ann Heisenfelt)

These protesters in Washington, D.C., argue that the Constitution should be changed so that corporations are not considered persons. Would such a change interfere with freedom of speech?

The National Convention Provision

The Constitution provides that a national convention requested by the legislatures of two-thirds of the states can propose a constitutional amendment. Congress has received approximately 400 convention applications since the Constitution was ratified—every state has applied at least once. Fewer than 20 applications were submitted during the Constitution's first hundred years, but more than 150 have been filed in the past two decades. No national convention has been held since 1787, and many national political and judicial leaders are uneasy about the prospect of convening a body that conceivably could do what the Constitutional Convention did—create a new form of government.

The state legislative bodies that originate national convention applications, however, do not appear to be uncomfortable with such a constitutional modification process at the state level—more than 230 state constitutional conventions have been held.

Informal Methods of Constitutional Change

■ Learning Outcome 9: **Consider the informal ways in which the meaning of the Constitution has adjusted to modern circumstances.**

Formal amendments are one way of changing our Constitution, and, as is obvious from their small number, they have been resorted to infrequently. If we discount the first ten amendments (the Bill of Rights), which were adopted soon after the ratification of the Constitution, there have been only seventeen formal alterations of the Constitution in the more than two hundred years of its existence.

But looking at the sparse number of formal constitutional amendments gives us an incomplete view of constitutional change. The brevity and ambiguity of the original document have permitted great alterations in the Constitution by way of varying interpretations over time. As the United States grew, both in population and in territory, new social and political realities emerged. Congress, presidents, and the courts found it necessary to interpret the Constitution's provisions in light of these new realities. The Constitution has proved to be a remarkably flexible document, adapting itself time and again to new events and concerns.

Congressional Legislation

The Constitution gives Congress broad powers to carry out its duties as the nation's legislative body. For example, Article I, Section 8, of the Constitution gives Congress the power to regulate foreign and interstate commerce. Although there is no clear definition of foreign commerce or interstate commerce in the Constitution, Congress has cited the *commerce clause* as the basis for passing thousands of laws.

Similarly, Article III, Section 1, states that the national judiciary shall consist of one supreme court and "such inferior courts, as Congress may from time to time ordain and establish." Through a series of acts, Congress has used this broad provision to establish the federal court system of today.

In addition, Congress has frequently delegated to federal agencies the legislative power to write regulations. These regulations become law unless challenged in the court system. Nowhere does the Constitution outline this delegation of legislative authority.

did you know?

The states have still not ratified an amendment (introduced by Congress in 1810) barring U.S. citizens from accepting titles of nobility from foreign governments.

Presidential Actions

Even though the Constitution does not expressly authorize the president to propose bills or even budgets to Congress,[16] presidents since the time of Woodrow Wilson (1913–1921) have proposed hundreds of bills to Congress each year that are introduced by the president's supporters in Congress. Presidents have also relied on their Article II authority as commander in chief of the nation's armed forces to send American troops abroad into combat, although the Constitution provides that Congress has the power to declare war.

Presidents have also conducted foreign affairs by the use of **executive agreements,** which are legally binding understandings reached between the president and a foreign head of state. The Constitution does not mention such agreements.

Executive Agreement
An international agreement between chiefs of state that does not require legislative approval.

Judicial Review

Another way that the Constitution adapts to new developments is through judicial review. **Judicial review** refers to the power of U.S. courts to examine the constitutionality of actions undertaken by the legislative and executive branches of government. A state court, for example, may rule that a statute enacted by the state legislature violates the state constitution. Federal courts (and ultimately, the United States Supreme Court) may rule unconstitutional not only acts of Congress and decisions of the national executive branch, but also state statutes, state executive actions, and even provisions of state constitutions.

Judicial Review
The power of the Supreme Court and other courts to declare unconstitutional federal or state laws and other acts of government.

Not a Novel Concept. The Constitution does not specifically mention the power of judicial review. Those in attendance at the Constitutional Convention, however,

16. Note, though, that the Constitution, in Article II, Section 3, does state that the president "shall from time to time . . . recommend to [Congress's] Consideration such Measures as he shall judge necessary and expedient." Some scholars interpret this phrase to mean that the president has the constitutional authority to propose bills and budgets to Congress for consideration.

U.S. Supreme Court justices are (first row, left to right) Justice Clarence Thomas, Justice Antonin Scalia, Chief Justice John Roberts, Justice Anthony M. Kennedy, Justice Ruth Bader Ginsburg, (second row, left to right) Justice Sonia Sotomayor, Justice Stephen G. Breyer, Justice Samuel Alito, Justice Elena Kagan.

(Steve Petteway, The Collection of the Supreme Court of the United States/Wikimedia Commons)

probably expected that the courts would have some authority to review the legality of acts by the executive and legislative branches, because, under the common law tradition inherited from England, courts exercised this authority. Indeed, Alexander Hamilton, in *Federalist Paper* No. 78 (see Appendix C), explicitly outlined the concept of judicial review. In 1803, the Supreme Court claimed this power for itself in *Marbury v. Madison,*[17] in which the Court ruled that a particular provision of an act of Congress was unconstitutional.

Allows Court to Adapt the Constitution. Through the process of judicial review, the Supreme Court adapts the Constitution to modern situations. Electronic technology, for example, did not exist when the Constitution was ratified. Nonetheless, the Court has used the Fourth Amendment guarantees against unreasonable searches and seizures to place limits on the use of wiretapping and other electronic eavesdropping methods. In 2012, the Court issued one of the most important rulings in many years—on the constitutionality of the Patient Protection and Affordable Care Act of 2010. We discuss the relevant issues in this chapter's feature *Which Side Are You On? Is the Supreme Court Right about Health-Care Reform?* on the facing page.

Additionally, the Court has changed its interpretation of the Constitution in accordance with changing values. It ruled in 1896 that "separate-but-equal" public facilities for African Americans were constitutional. By 1954, however, the times had changed, and the Court reversed that decision.[18] Woodrow Wilson summarized the Court's work when he described it as "a constitutional convention in continuous session." Basically, the law is what the Supreme Court says it is at any point in time.

Interpretation, Custom, and Usage

The Constitution has also been changed through interpretation by both Congress and the president. Originally, the president had a staff consisting of personal secretaries and a few others. Four small departments reported to President Washington. Today, because Congress delegates specific tasks to the president and to the executive branch, this branch of government has grown to include hundreds of departments, agencies, and organizations that employ about 2.7 million civilians.

Executive Order
A rule or regulation issued by the president that has the effect of law. Executive orders can implement and give administrative effect to provisions in the U.S. Constitution, treaties, or statutes.

One of the ways in which presidents have expanded their powers is through **executive orders.** (Executive orders will be discussed in Chapter 11, in the context of the presidency.) Executive orders have the force of legislation and allow presidents to significantly affect the political landscape. Consider, for example, that affirmative action programs have their origin in executive orders.

Changes in ways of doing political business have also led to the reinterpretation of the Constitution. The Constitution does not mention political parties, yet these informal, "extraconstitutional" organizations make the nominations for offices, run the campaigns, organize the members of Congress, and in fact change the election system from time to time. In many ways, the Constitution has been adapted from a document serving the needs of a small, rural republic to one that provides a framework of government for an industrial giant with vast geographic, natural, and human resources.

17. 5 U.S. 137 (1803). See Chapter 13 for a further discussion of the *Marbury v. Madison* case.
18. *Brown v. Board of Education of Topeka,* 347 U.S. 483 (1954).

Which Side Are You On?

IS THE SUPREME COURT RIGHT ABOUT HEALTH-CARE REFORM?

The 2010 Patient Protection and Affordable Care Act and associated legislation, called *Obamacare* by its opponents and many journalists, will massively transform the health-care system. The changes will be phased in over many years. The nation will not approach universal health-care insurance coverage until 2014. At that time, an *individual mandate* will go into effect that requires almost everyone either to have health insurance or to pay a penalty on his or her income tax return. Many state governors and attorneys general have challenged the constitutionality of the health-care reform legislation. In 2012, the issue reached the United States Supreme Court.

In June 2012, the Court ruled five to four that the greater part of the Affordable Care Act was constitutional.[a] Chief Justice John Roberts supplied the crucial vote in this verdict, and Roberts wrote the Court's opinion. Justice Anthony Kennedy, usually the swing vote on the Court, sided with the three most conservative justices in opposing the act.

(© kyoshino / iStockphoto) (© Dean Mitchell / iStockphoto)

THE LEGISLATION SHOULD HAVE BEEN STRUCK DOWN

Opponents of Obamacare believe that the Court's verdict was wrong. The principal argument against the constitutionality of the health-care legislation was that individuals cannot be required to purchase health insurance. Opponents of the legislation argued that the federal government cannot regulate inactivity. If the tax that enforces the individual mandate is deemed constitutional by the Supreme Court, there would be no limits on government actions. After all, opponents claimed, the government could go on to tax those who are overweight, those who don't exercise, those who smoke, or those who buy foreign cars. If the individual mandate were permitted to stand, Congress would have the power to regulate Americans "merely because they exist."

In his ruling, Chief Justice Roberts agreed that the individual mandate could not be defended under the Constitution's commerce clause. Roberts argued that the government could only regulate commerce, not require individuals to engage in it. Roberts also found, however, that because the enforcement mechanism was an income tax penalty, the mandate could be defended as part of the government's taxation powers. Opponents of Obamacare argued that Roberts missed the point. If the individual mandate were unconstitutional, than any means of accomplishing it should be unconstitutional as well.

THE HEALTH-CARE REFORMS SHOULD STAND

Supporters of the health-care legislation applauded the Court's decision. Constitutional experts who support Obamacare contended that the arguments of opponents are illusory. It is not the health-care legislation that grants Congress the right to regulate Americans "because they exist." Congress, these experts say, has had that power since 1789. Right now, the government effectively imposes higher rates of income tax on those who do not marry or do not have children. It should certainly be able to impose higher taxes on those who do not buy insurance.

The Democratic members of Congress who drafted the health-care reform bills were aware that there might be constitutional challenges. They argued, however, that failing to buy insurance "substantially affects interstate commerce." This is the Supreme Court's standard for federal authority under the Constitution's commerce clause.

Obamacare supporters were relieved that Roberts had rescued the legislation, even if they believed he should have done so through the commerce clause. They opposed one other part of Roberts's ruling, however. The Affordable Care Act threatened to cut all of a state's Medicaid funding if it did not agree to an expansion of the Medicaid program. The Court found this penalty too severe. This is one piece of the Court's ruling that liberals would like to overturn.

a. *National Federation of Independent Business v. Sebelius*, ___ U.S. ___, 132 S.Ct. 2566, 183 L.Ed.2d 450 (2012).

Why Should You Care about... THE CONSTITUTION?

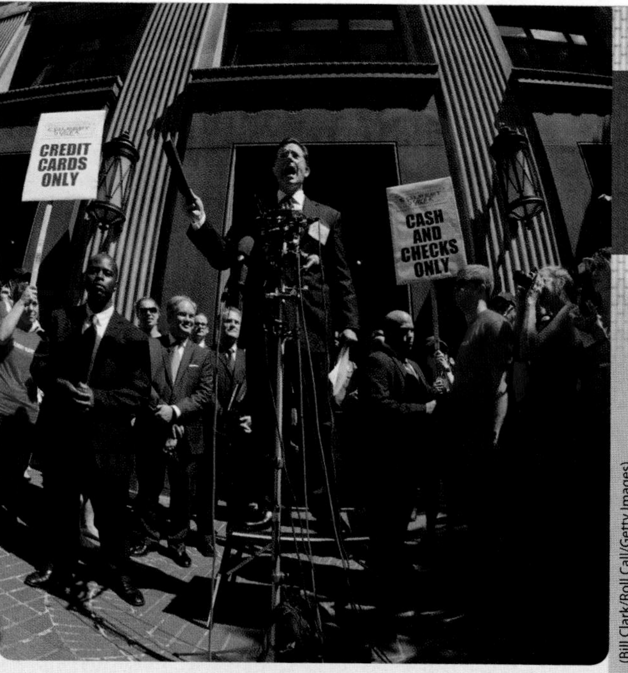

(Bill Clark/Roll Call/Getty Images)

Comedian and political satirist Stephan Colbert makes a speech outside of the Federal Election Commission. He founded a super PAC called "Making a Better Tomorrow, Tomorrow."

The U.S. Constitution is an enduring document that has survived more than two hundred years of turbulent history. It is also a changing document, however. Twenty-seven amendments have been added to the original Constitution. Why should you, as an individual, care about the Constitution?

THE CONSTITUTION AND YOUR LIFE

The laws of the nation have a direct impact on your life, and none more so than the Constitution—the supreme law of the land. The most important issues in society are often settled by the Constitution. For example, for the first seventy-five years of the republic, the Constitution implicitly protected the institution of slavery. If the Constitution had never been changed by an amendment, the process of abolishing slavery would have been much different and might have involved revolutionary measures.

Since the passage of the Fourteenth Amendment in 1868, the Constitution has defined who is a citizen and who is entitled to the protections the Constitution provides. Constitutional provisions define our liberties. The First Amendment protects our freedom of speech more thoroughly than do the laws of many other nations. Few other countries have constitutional provisions governing the right to own firearms (the Second Amendment). Disputes involving these rights are among the most fundamental issues we face.

HOW YOU CAN MAKE A DIFFERENCE

At the time of this writing, national coalitions of interest groups support or oppose a number of constitutional amendments. One hotly debated proposal would create a constitutional requirement to balance the federal budget. In late 2011, a constitutional amendment to do just that failed in both the U.S. House and the Senate. The measure would have required a three-fifths majority in both chambers of Congress to approve any future deficit spending. If such an amendment sounds like a good idea to you, there are a variety of organizations you might investigate using a search engine on your computer. These include Americans for a Balanced Budget, Americans for a Balanced Budget Amendment, Americans for Prosperity, and the Tea Party Patriots.

Other Americans have different concerns. In 2010, the Supreme Court struck down a wide range of campaign finance laws in *Citizens United v. Federal Election Commission*. One result of this ruling was the "super PACs" that flooded television networks with attack advertisements during the 2012 elections. Often funded by very wealthy individuals, super PACs can spend as much as they want, provided that they do not openly coordinate their activities with a candidate's campaign. A proposed constitutional amendment would overturn the *Citizens United* ruling. If getting the money out of politics is of interest to you, you can examine the activist groups that support this amendment. They include Common Cause, Democracy Is for People, MoveOn.org, and OccupyWallStreet.

Questions for Discussion and Analysis

1. Review the *Which Side Are You On?* feature on page 59. Consider that hospitals are required by law to accept critically ill or injured patients even if those persons cannot pay for services. Given that fact, should individuals have the constitutional right to go without health-care insurance? Why or why not?
2. Naturalized citizens—immigrants—have almost all of the rights of natural-born citizens, but under the Constitution they cannot be elected president. If the Constitution were changed to allow an immigrant to become president, do you think that today's voters would be reluctant to vote for such an individual? Why might a naturalized leader be more nationalistic than a natural-born one?
3. Consider what might have happened if Georgia and the Carolinas had stayed out of the Union because of a desire to protect slavery. What would subsequent American history have been like? Would the eventual freedom of the slaves have been delayed—or advanced?
4. A result of the Great Compromise is that representation in the Senate dramatically departs from the one-person, one-vote rule. The 38 million people who live in California elect two senators, as do the half-million people living in Wyoming. What political results might occur when the citizens of small states are much better represented than the citizens of large ones? Do you see any signs that your predictions have actually come true?

Key Terms

Anti-Federalist 48
bicameral legislature 43
checks and balances 46
confederation 40
electoral college 47
executive agreement 57
executive order 58
federal system 48
Federalist 48
Great Compromise 44
judicial review 57
Madisonian model 46
natural rights 38
ratification 48
representative assembly 33
separation of powers 46
social contract 38
state 40
supremacy doctrine 44
unicameral legislature 39

Chapter Summary

1. The first permanent English colonies were established at Jamestown in 1607 and Plymouth in 1620. The Mayflower Compact created the first formal government in New England.
2. In the 1760s, the British began to impose a series of taxes and legislative acts on their increasingly independent-minded colonies. The colonists responded with protests and boycotts of British products. Representatives of the colonies formed the First Continental Congress in 1774. The Second Continental Congress established an army in 1775 to defend the colonists against attacks by British soldiers.
3. On July 4, 1776, the Second Continental Congress approved the Declaration of Independence. Perhaps the most revolutionary aspects of the Declaration were its statements that people have natural rights to life, liberty, and the pursuit of happiness; that governments derive their power from the consent of the governed; and that people have a right to overthrow oppressive governments. During the Revolutionary War, the states signed the Articles of Confederation, creating a weak central government with few powers. The Articles proved to be unworkable because the national government had no way to ensure compliance by the states with such measures as securing tax revenues.
4. Dissatisfaction with the Articles of Confederation prompted the call for a convention at Philadelphia in 1787. Delegates focused on creating a constitution for a new form of government. The Virginia Plan, which favored the larger states, and the New Jersey Plan, which favored smaller ones, did not garner sufficient support. A compromise offered by Connecticut provided for a bicameral legislature and thus resolved the large-state/small-state controversy. The final version of the Constitution provided for the separation of powers, checks and balances, and a federal form of government.
5. Fears of a strong central government prompted the addition of the Bill of Rights to the Constitution. The Bill of Rights, which includes the freedoms of religion, speech, and assembly, was initially applied only to the federal government, but amendments to the Constitution following the Civil War were interpreted to ensure that the Bill of Rights would apply to the states as well.
6. An amendment to the Constitution may be proposed either by a two-thirds vote in each chamber of Congress or by a national convention called by Congress at the request of two-thirds of the state legislatures. Ratification can occur either by the approval of three-fourths of the legislatures of the states or by special conventions called in the states for the purpose of ratifying the amendment and approval by three-fourths of these conventions. Informal methods of constitutional change include reinterpretation through congressional legislation, presidential actions, and judicial review.

Quiz Multiple Choice

1. When the First Continental Congress convened in 1774, the British government:

a. welcomed the advice offered by the colonists.
b. agreed to allow the colonies to form a separate government.
c. treated the meeting as an act of rebellion.

2. A major defect in the Articles of Confederation was:

a. the lack of power to raise funds for military forces.
b. the lack of treaty-making power.
c. the inability to easily communicate with citizens.

3. In our system of checks and balances, the Supreme Court can "check" congressional and presidential actions:

a. by declaring that the executive and legislative branches cannot be funded.
b. by refusing to enforce congressional laws.
c. by declaring laws passed by Congress and accepted by the president to be unconstitutional.

4. Those who wrote the *Federalist Papers* were, in general, in favor of:

a. a system of government similar to the one under the Articles of Confederation.
b. a strong central government based on the new Constitution.
c. a decade-long period of debate over the new Constitution.

5. Which of the following fundamental principles was not established by the Constitution of 1787:

a. popular sovereignty, or control by the people.
b. limited government with written laws.
c. a system in which the central government had complete power over the states.

6. The major drafter of the Bill of Rights was:

a. Washington.
b. Jefferson.
c. Madison.

7. The reason the U.S. Constitution has so few amendments is that:

a. the formal amendment process is exceedingly difficult.
b. the Constitution was written so well that it hasn't needed to be amended.
c. Congress doesn't have time to consider new amendments.

8. When the Supreme Court examines the validity of a law, it is engaging in:

a. research on better ways to implement the law.
b. an examination of how other countries will react to the law.
c. judicial review to determine the constitutionality of the law.

ANSWERS: 1. c, 2. a, 3. c, 4. b, 5. c, 6. c, 7. a, and 8. c.

Quiz Fill-Ins

9. In 1620, the members of New England's first colony signed the _________ _________ at Plymouth (Massachusetts).

10. The Second Continental Congress established an _________ and named _________ _________ as commander in chief.

11. The Declaration of Independence established as unalienable rights those of life, _________, and the pursuit of happiness.

12. Under the Articles of Confederation, it became clear that the central government could not protect the citizenry from armed rebellion when _________ _________ occurred in August 1786.

13. When no branch of government—executive, legislative, or judicial—is able to dominate the others, we call this the _________ of powers.

14. Because under the Constitution the states have many rights that the central government does not have, our system is called a _________ system.

15. Those who opposed the ratification of the Constitution were called _________-_________.

16. When an amendment to the Constitution is proposed by a two-thirds vote in both the Senate and the House, then the legislatures of _________-_________ of the states must approve it if it is to be adopted.

17. Informal methods of constitutional change involve congressional and presidential actions as well as power of the federal courts to exercise _________ _________.

18. One of the ways in which presidents expand their powers is through _________ orders.

ANSWERS: 9. Mayflower Compact, 10. army, George Washington, 11. liberty, 12. Shays' Rebellion, 13. separation, 14. federal, 15. Anti-Federalists, 16. three-fourths, 17. judicial review, 18. executive.

(© Aleksandar Jovicic/iStockphoto)

Selected Print & Media Resources

SUGGESTED READINGS

Bodenhamer, David J. *The Revolutionary Constitution.* New York: Oxford University Press, 2012. Bodenhamer, a professor of history, emphasizes the novelty of the Constitution and describes how interpretations of the document have changed as our nation developed.

Maier, Pauline. *Ratification: The People Debate the Constitution, 1787–1788.* New York: Simon & Schuster, 2011. Maier, a professor at M.I.T., charts the Constitution's uncertain course toward ratification.

Okrent, Daniel. *Last Call: The Rise and Fall of Prohibition.* New York: Scribner, 2010. Okrent, an editor at the *New York Times,* tells the story of America's greatest constitutional folly—the 1919 amendment to ban alcoholic beverages. The result was a huge crime wave that did not abate until Prohibition was repealed by another amendment in 1933.

Wood, Gordon S. *The Idea of America: Reflections on the Birth of the United States.* New York: Penguin Press, 2011. Wood, a professor at Brown University, may be the most prominent living scholar of the revolutionary era. This collection of essays summarizes his life's work. Wood emphasizes the radicalism of the American Revolution, which truly did result in an entirely new conception of politics.

MEDIA RESOURCES

John Adams—A widely admired 2008 HBO miniseries on founder John Adams and his wife, Abigail Adams, and other prominent Americans of the revolutionary period. The series is largely based on David McCullough's book *John Adams.*

Thomas Jefferson—A 1996 documentary by acclaimed director Ken Burns. The film covers Jefferson's entire life, including his writing of the Declaration of Independence, his presidency, and his later years in Virginia. Historians and writers interviewed include Daniel Boorstin, Garry Wills, Gore Vidal, and John Hope Franklin.

(© PashaIgnatov/iStockphoto)

E-mocracy THE INTERNET AND OUR CONSTITUTION

Today, you can find many important documents from the founding period online, including descriptions of events leading up to the American Revolution, the Articles of Confederation, notes on the Constitutional Convention, the Federalists' writings, and the Anti-Federalists' responses.

You are able to access the Internet and explore a variety of opinions on every topic imaginable because you enjoy the freedoms—including freedom of speech—guaranteed by our Constitution. Even today, more than two hundred years after the U.S. Bill of Rights was ratified, citizens in some countries do not enjoy the right to free speech. Nor can they surf the Web freely, as U.S. citizens do.

For example, the Chinese government employs a number of methods to control Internet use. One method is to use filtering software to block electronic pathways to objectionable sites, including the sites of Western news organizations. Another technique is to prohibit Internet users from sending or discussing information that has not been publicly released by the government. Still another practice is to monitor the online activities of Internet users. None of these methods is foolproof, however. Indeed, some observers claim that the Internet, by exposing citizens in politically oppressive nations to a variety of views on politics and culture, will eventually transform those nations.

We should note that such restrictions also can exist in the United States. For example, there have been persistent efforts by Congress and many courts to limit access to Web sites deemed pornographic. Free speech advocates have attacked these restrictions as unconstitutional, as you will read in Chapter 4.

LOGGING ON

1. You can, of course, find a considerable amount of information about the U.S. Constitution simply by searching on "us constitution," using your favorite Internet search engine. You can enhance your search, however, if you add to the search term the name of one of the several universities that offer commentary and collections of relevant documents. For example, you might try entering "us constitution emory" or "us constitution cornell" into your search engine.
2. Searching on "constitution center" will yield the site of the National Constitution Center, which provides a variety of information on the document in an entertaining format.
3. Entering "state constitutions" will bring up several collections of state constitutions.

shall have been elected, and he shall not receive within that Period any other Emolument from the United States, or any of them.

The president maintains the same salary during each four-year term. Moreover, she or he may not receive additional cash payments from the government. Originally set at $25,000 per year, the salary is currently $400,000 a year plus $169,000 in various expense accounts.

Clause 8: The Oath of Office. Before he enter on the Execution of his Office, he shall take the following Oath or Affirmation: "I do solemnly swear (or affirm) that I will faithfully execute the Office of President of the United States, and will to the best of my Ability, preserve, protect and defend the Constitution of the United States."

The president is "sworn in" prior to beginning the duties of the office. The taking of the oath of office occurs on January 20, following the November election. The ceremony is called the inauguration. *The oath of office is administered by the chief justice of the United States Supreme Court.*

Section 2. Powers of the President

Clause 1: Commander in Chief. The President shall be Commander in Chief of the Army and Navy of the United States, and of the Militia of the several States, when called into the actual Service of the United States; he may require the Opinion, in writing, of the principal Officer in each of the executive Departments, upon any Subject relating to the Duties of their respective Offices, and he shall have Power to grant Reprieves and Pardons for Offences against the United States, except in Cases of Impeachment.

The armed forces are placed under civilian control because the president is a civilian but still commander in chief of the military. The president may ask for the help of the head of each of the executive departments (thereby creating the cabinet). The cabinet members are chosen by the president with the consent of the Senate, but they can be removed without Senate approval.

The president's clemency powers extend only to federal cases. In those cases, he or she may grant a full or conditional pardon, or reduce a prison term or fine.

Clause 2: Treaties and Appointment. He shall have Power, by and with the Advice and Consent of the Senate, to make Treaties, provided two thirds of the Senators present concur; and he shall nominate, and by and with the Advice and Consent of the Senate, shall appoint Ambassadors, other public Ministers and Consuls, Judges of the supreme Court, and all other Officers of the United States, whose Appointments are not herein otherwise provided for, and which shall be established by Law; but the Congress may by Law vest the Appointment of such inferior Officers, as they think proper, in the President alone, in the Courts of Law, or in the Heads of Departments.

Many of the major powers of the president are identified in this clause, including the power to make treaties with foreign governments (with the approval of the Senate by a two-thirds vote) and the power to appoint ambassadors, Supreme Court justices, and other government officials. Most such appointments require Senate approval.

Clause 3: Vacancies. The President shall have Power to fill up all Vacancies that may happen during the Recess of the Senate, by granting Commissions which shall expire at the end of their next Session.

The president has the power to appoint temporary officials to fill vacant federal offices without Senate approval if the Congress is not in session. Such appointments expire automatically at the end of Congress's next term.

Section 3. Duties of the President

He shall from time to time give to the Congress Information of the State of the Union, and recommend to their Consideration such Measures as he shall judge necessary and expedient; he may, on extraordinary Occasions, convene both Houses, or either of them, and in Case of Disagreement between them, with Respect to the Time of Adjournment, he may adjourn them to such Time as he shall think proper; he shall receive Ambassadors and other public Ministers; he shall take Care that the Laws be faithfully executed, and shall Commission all the Officers of the United States.

Annually, the president reports on the state of the union to Congress, recommends legislative measures, and proposes a federal budget. The State of the Union speech is a statement not only to Congress but also to the American people. After it is given, the president proposes a federal budget and presents an economic report. At any time, the president may send special messages to Congress while it is in session. The president has the power to call special sessions, to adjourn Congress when its two chambers do not agree on when to adjourn, to receive diplomatic representatives of other governments, and to ensure the proper execution of all federal laws. The president further has the ability to empower federal officers to hold their positions and to perform their duties.

Section 4. Impeachment

The President, Vice President and all civil Officers of the United States, shall be removed from Office on Impeachment for, and Conviction of, Treason, Bribery, or other high Crimes and Misdemeanors.

Treason *denotes giving aid to the nation's enemies. The phrase* high crimes and misdemeanors *is usually considered to mean serious abuses of political power. In either case, the president or vice president may be accused by the House (called an* impeachment*) and then removed from office if convicted by the Senate. (Note that impeachment does not mean removal but rather refers to an accusation of treason or high crimes and misdemeanors.)*

ARTICLE III. (Judicial Branch)

Section 1. Judicial Powers, Courts, and Judges

The judicial Power of the United States, shall be vested in one supreme Court, and in such inferior Courts as the Congress may from time to time ordain and establish. The Judges, both of the supreme and inferior Courts, shall hold their Offices during good Behaviour, and shall, at stated Times, receive for their Services a Compensation, which shall not be diminished during their Continuance in Office.

The Supreme Court is vested with judicial power, as are the lower federal courts that Congress creates. Federal judges serve in their offices for life unless they are impeached and convicted by Congress. The payment of federal judges may not be reduced during their time in office.

Section 2. Jurisdiction

Clause 1: Cases under Federal Jurisdiction. The judicial Power shall extend to all Cases, in Law and Equity, arising under this Constitution, the Laws of the United States, and Treaties made, or which shall be made, under their Authority;—to all Cases affecting Ambassadors, other public Ministers and Consuls;—to all Cases of admiralty and maritime Jurisdiction;—to Controversies to which the United States shall be a Party;—to Controversies between two or more States; [—between a State and Citizens of another State;—][9] between Citizens of different States;—between Citizens of the same State claiming Lands under Grants of different States, [and between a State, or the Citizens thereof, and foreign States, Citizens or Subjects.][10]

The federal courts take on cases that concern the meaning of the U.S. Constitution, all federal laws, and treaties. They also can take on cases involving citizens of different states and citizens of foreign nations.

Clause 2: Cases for the Supreme Court. In all Cases affecting Ambassadors, other public Ministers and Consuls, and those in which a State shall be a Party, the supreme Court shall have original Jurisdiction. In all the other Cases before mentioned, the supreme Court shall have appellate Jurisdiction, both as to Law and Fact, with such Exceptions, and under such Regulations as the Congress shall make.

In a limited number of situations, the Supreme Court acts as a trial court and has original jurisdiction. These cases involve a representative from another country or involve a state. In all other situations, the cases must first be tried in the lower courts and then can be appealed to the Supreme Court. Congress may, however, make exceptions. Today, the Supreme Court acts as a trial court of first instance on rare occasions.

Clause 3: The Conduct of Trials. The Trial of all Crimes, except in Cases of Impeachment, shall be by Jury; and such Trial shall be held in the State where the said Crimes shall have been committed; but when not committed within any State, the Trial shall be at such Place or Places as the Congress may by Law have directed.

Any person accused of a federal crime is granted the right to a trial by jury in a federal court in that state in which the crime was committed. Trials of impeachment are an exception.

Section 3. Treason

Clause 1: The Definition of Treason. Treason against the United States, shall consist only in levying War against them, or, in adhering to their Enemies, giving them Aid and Comfort. No Person shall be convicted of Treason unless on the Testimony of two Witnesses to the same overt Act, or on Confession in open Court.

Treason *is the making of war against the United States or giving aid to its enemies.*

Clause 2: Punishment. The Congress shall have Power to declare the Punishment of Treason, but no Attainder of Treason shall work Corruption of Blood, or Forfeiture except during the Life of the Person attainted.

Congress has provided that the punishment for treason ranges from a minimum of five years in prison and/or a $10,000 fine to a maximum of death. "No Attainder of Treason shall work Corruption of Blood" prohibits punishment of the traitor's heirs.

ARTICLE IV. (Relations among the States)

Section 1. Full Faith and Credit

Full Faith and Credit shall be given in each State to the public Acts, Records, and judicial Proceedings of every other State. And the Congress may by general Laws prescribe the Manner in which such Acts, Records and Proceedings shall be proved, and the Effect thereof.

All states are required to respect one another's laws, records, and lawful decisions. There are exceptions, however. A state does not have to enforce another state's criminal code. Nor does it have to recognize another state's grant of a divorce if the person obtaining the divorce did not establish legal residence in the state in which it was given.

Section 2. Treatment of Citizens

Clause 1: Privileges and Immunities. The Citizens of each State shall be entitled to all Privileges and Immunities of Citizens in the several States.

A citizen of a state has the same rights and privileges as the citizens of another state in which he or she happens to be.

Clause 2: Extradition. A Person charged in any State with Treason, Felony, or other Crime, who shall flee from Justice, and be found in another State, shall on Demand of the executive Authority of the State from which he fled, be delivered up, to be removed to the State having Jurisdiction of the Crime.

Any person accused of a crime who flees to another state must be returned to the state in which the crime occurred.

Clause 3: Fugitive Slaves. [No Person held to Service or Labour in one State, under the Laws thereof, escaping into another, shall, in

9. Modified by the Eleventh Amendment.
10. Modified by the Eleventh Amendment.

Consequence of any Law or Regulation therein, be discharged from such Service or Labour, but shall be delivered up on Claim of the Party to whom such Service or Labour may be due.][11]

This clause was struck down by the Thirteenth Amendment, which abolished slavery in 1865.

Section 3. Admission of States

Clause 1: The Process. New States may be admitted by the Congress into this Union; but no new State shall be formed or erected within the Jurisdiction of any other State; nor any State be formed by the Junction of two or more States, or Parts of States, without the Consent of the Legislatures of the States concerned as well as of the Congress.

Only Congress has the power to admit new states to the Union. No state may be created by taking territory from an existing state unless the state's legislature so consents.

Clause 2: Public Land. The Congress shall have Power to dispose of and make all needful Rules and Regulations respecting the Territory or other Property belonging to the United States; and nothing in this Constitution shall be so construed as to Prejudice any Claims of the United States, or of any particular State.

The federal government has the exclusive right to administer federal government public lands.

Section 4. Republican Form of Government

The United States shall guarantee to every State in this Union a Republican Form of Government, and shall protect each of them against Invasion; and on Application of the Legislature, or of the Executive (when the Legislature cannot be convened) against domestic Violence.

Each state is promised a republican form of government—that is, one in which the people elect their representatives. The federal government is bound to protect states against any attack by foreigners or during times of trouble within a state.

ARTICLE V. (Methods of Amendment)

The Congress, whenever two thirds of both Houses shall deem it necessary, shall propose Amendments to this Constitution, or on the Application of the Legislatures of two thirds of the several States, shall call a Convention for proposing Amendments, which, in either Case, shall be valid to all Intents and Purposes, as Part of this Constitution, when ratified by the Legislatures of three fourths of the several States, or by Conventions in three fourths thereof, as the one or the other Mode of Ratification may be proposed by the Congress; Provided that no Amendment which may be made prior to the Year One thousand eight hundred and eight shall in any Manner affect the first and fourth Clauses in the Ninth Section of the First Article; and that no State, without its Consent, shall be deprived of its equal Suffrage in the Senate.

Amendments may be proposed in either of two ways: by a two-thirds vote of each chamber (Congress) or at the request of two-thirds of the states. Ratification of amendments may be carried out in two ways: by the legislatures of three-fourths of the states or by the voters in three-fourths of the states. No state may be denied equal representation in the Senate.

ARTICLE VI. (National Supremacy)

Clause 1: Existing Obligations. All Debts contracted and Engagements entered into, before the Adoption of this Constitution shall be as valid against the United States under this Constitution, as under the Confederation.

During the Revolutionary War and the years of the Confederation, Congress borrowed large sums. This clause pledged that the new federal government would assume those financial obligations.

Clause 2: Supreme Law of the Land. This Constitution, and the Laws of the United States which shall be made in Pursuance thereof; and all Treaties made, or which shall be made, under the Authority of the United States, shall be the supreme Law of the Land; and the Judges in every State shall be bound thereby, any Thing in the Constitution or Laws of any State to the Contrary notwithstanding.

This is typically called the supremacy clause; *it declares that federal law takes precedence over all forms of state law. No government at the local or state level may make or enforce any law that conflicts with any provision of the Constitution, acts of Congress, treaties, or other rules and regulations issued by the president and his or her subordinates in the executive branch of the federal government.*

Clause 3: Oath of Office. The Senators and Representatives before mentioned, and the Members of the several State Legislatures, and all executive and judicial Officers, both of the United States and of the several States, shall be bound by Oath or Affirmation, to support this Constitution; but no religious Test shall ever be required as a Qualification to any Office or public Trust under the United States.

Every federal and state official must take an oath of office promising to support the U.S. Constitution. Religion may not be used as a qualification to serve in any federal office.

ARTICLE VII. (Ratification)

The Ratification of the Conventions of nine States shall be sufficient for the Establishment of this Constitution between the States so ratifying the Same.

Nine states were required to ratify the Constitution. Delaware was the first and New Hampshire the ninth.

11. Repealed by the Thirteenth Amendment.

Done in Convention by the Unanimous Consent of the States present the Seventeenth Day of September in the Year of our Lord one thousand seven hundred and Eighty seven and of the Independence of the United States of America the Twelfth. In witness whereof we have hereunto subscribed our Names,

Go. WASHINGTON
Presid't.
and deputy from Virginia

Attest William Jackson Secretary

DELAWARE: Geo. Read, Gunning Bedford jun, John Dickinson, Richard Bassett, Jaco. Broom

MARYLAND: James McHenry, Dan of St. Thos. Jenifer, Danl. Carroll

VIRGINIA: John Blair, James Madison Jr.

NORTH CAROLINA: Wm. Blount, Richd. Dobbs Spaight, Hu. Williamson

SOUTH CAROLINA: J. Rutledge, Charles Cotesworth Pinckney, Charles Pinckney, Pierce Butler

GEORGIA: William Few, Abr. Baldwin

NEW HAMPSHIRE: John Langdon, Nicholas Gilman

MASSACHUSETTS: Nathaniel Gorham, Rufus King

CONNECTICUT: Wm. Saml. Johnson, Roger Sherman

NEW YORK: Alexander Hamilton

NEW JERSEY: Wh. Livingston, David Brearley, Wm. Paterson, Jona. Dayton

PENNSYLVANIA: B. Franklin, Thomas Mifflin, Robt. Morris, Geo. Clymer, Thos. FitzSimons, Jared Ingersoll, James Wilson, Gouv. Morris

AMENDMENTS TO THE CONSTITUTION OF THE UNITED STATES[12]

Articles in addition to, and amendment of, the Constitution of the United States of America, proposed by Congress and ratified by the Legislatures of the several states, pursuant to the Fifth Article of the original Constitution.

AMENDMENT I.

(Religion, Speech, Assembly, and Petition)

Congress shall make no law respecting an establishment of religion, or prohibiting the free exercise thereof; or abridging the freedom of speech, or of the press; or the right of the people peaceably to assemble, and to petition the Government for a redress of grievances.

Congress may not create an official church or enact laws limiting the freedom of religion, speech, the press, assembly, and petition. These guarantees, like the others in the Bill of Rights (the first ten amendments), are not absolute—each may be exercised only with regard to the rights of other persons.

AMENDMENT II.

(Militia and the Right to Bear Arms)

A well regulated Militia, being necessary to the security of a free State, the right of the people to keep and bear Arms, shall not be infringed.

To protect itself, each state has the right to maintain a volunteer armed force. States and the federal government may regulate but not completely ban the possession and use of firearms by individuals.

AMENDMENT III.

(The Quartering of Soldiers)

No Soldier shall, in time of peace be quartered in any house, without the consent of the Owner, nor in time of war, but in a manner to be prescribed by law.

Before the Revolutionary War, it had been common British practice to quarter soldiers in colonists' homes. Military troops do not have the power to take over private houses during peacetime.

AMENDMENT IV.

(Searches and Seizures)

The right of the people to be secure in their persons, houses, papers, and effects, against unreasonable searches and seizures, shall not be violated, and no Warrants shall issue, but upon probable cause, supported by Oath or affirmation, and particularly describing the place to be searched, and the persons or things to be seized.

Here the word warrant *means "justification" and refers to a document issued by a magistrate or judge indicating the name, address, and possible offense committed. Anyone asking for the warrant, such as a police officer, must be able to convince the magistrate or judge that an offense probably has been committed.*

AMENDMENT V.

(Grand Juries, Self-Incrimination, Double Jeopardy, Due Process, and Eminent Domain)

No person shall be held to answer for a capital, or otherwise infamous crime, unless on a presentment or indictment of a Grand Jury, except in cases arising in the land or naval forces, or in the Militia, when in actual service in time of War or public danger; nor shall any person be subject for the same offence to be twice put in jeopardy of life or limb; nor shall be compelled in any criminal case to be a witness against himself, nor be deprived of life, liberty, or property, without due process of law; nor shall private property be taken for public use, without just compensation.

There are two types of juries. A grand jury *considers physical evidence and the testimony of witnesses and decides whether there is sufficient reason to bring a case to trial. A* petit jury *hears the case at trial and decides it. "For the same offence to be twice put in jeopardy of life or limb" means to be tried twice for the same crime. A person may not be tried for the same crime twice or forced to give evidence against herself or himself. No person's right to life, liberty, or property may be taken away except by lawful means, called the* due process of law. *Private property taken for public use must be paid for by the government.*

AMENDMENT VI.

(Criminal Court Procedures)

In all criminal prosecutions, the accused shall enjoy the right to a speedy and public trial, by an impartial jury of the State and district wherein the crime shall have been committed, which district shall have been previously ascertained by law, and to be informed of the nature and cause of the accusation; to be confronted with the witnesses against him; to have compulsory process for obtaining witnesses in his favor, and to have the Assistance of Counsel for his defence.

Any person accused of a crime has the right to a fair and public trial by a jury in the state in which the crime took place. The charges against that person must be indicated. Any accused person has the right to a lawyer to defend him or her and to question those who testify against him or her, as well as the right to call people to speak in his or her favor at trial.

AMENDMENT VII.

(Trial by Jury in Civil Cases)

In Suits at common law, where the value in controversy shall exceed twenty dollars, the right of trial by jury shall be preserved, and no fact tried by jury, shall be otherwise re-examined in any Court of the United States, than according to the rules of the common law.

A jury trial may be requested by either party in a dispute in any case involving more than $20. If both parties agree to a trial by a judge without a jury, the right to a jury trial may be put aside.

---

12. On September 25, 1789, Congress transmitted to the state legislatures twelve proposed amendments, two of which, having to do with congressional representation and congressional pay, were not adopted. The remaining ten amendments became the Bill of Rights. In 1992, the amendment concerning congressional pay was adopted as the Twenty-seventh Amendment.

AMENDMENT VIII.
(Bail, Cruel and Unusual Punishment)

Excessive bail shall not be required, nor excessive fines imposed, nor cruel and unusual punishments inflicted.

Bail *is an amount of money that a person accused of a crime may be required to deposit with the court as a guaranty that she or he will appear in court when requested. The amount of bail required or the fine imposed as punishment for a crime must be reasonable compared with the seriousness of the crime involved. Any punishment judged to be too harsh or too severe for a crime is prohibited.*

AMENDMENT IX.
(The Rights Retained by the People)

The enumeration in the Constitution, of certain rights, shall not be construed to deny or disparage others retained by the people.

Many civil rights that are not explicitly enumerated in the Constitution are still held by the people.

AMENDMENT X.
(Reserved Powers of the States)

The powers not delegated to the United States by the Constitution, nor prohibited by it to the States, are reserved to the States respectively, or to the people.

Those powers not delegated by the Constitution to the federal government or expressly denied to the states belong to the states and to the people. This amendment in essence allows the states to pass laws under their "police powers."

AMENDMENT XI.
(Ratified on February 7, 1795—
Suits against States)

The Judicial power of the United States shall not be construed to extend to any suit in law or equity, commenced or prosecuted against one of the United States by Citizens of another State, or by Citizens or Subjects of any Foreign State.

This amendment has been interpreted to mean that a state cannot be sued in federal court by one of its own citizens, by a citizen of another state, or by a foreign country.

AMENDMENT XII.
(Ratified on June 15, 1804—
Election of the President)

The Electors shall meet in their respective states, and vote by ballot for President and Vice-President, one of whom, at least, shall not be an inhabitant of the same State with themselves; they shall name in their ballots the person voted for as President, and in distinct ballots the person voted for as Vice-President, and they shall make distinct lists of all persons voted for as President, and of all persons voted for as Vice-President, and of the number of votes for each, which lists they shall sign and certify, and transmit sealed to the seat of the government of the United States, directed to the President of the Senate;—The President of the Senate shall, in the presence of the Senate and House of Representatives, open all the certificates and the votes shall then be counted;—The person having the greatest number of votes for President, shall be the President, if such number be a majority of the whole number of Electors appointed; and if no person have such majority, then from the persons having the highest numbers not exceeding three on the list of those voted for as President, the House of Representatives shall choose immediately, by ballot, the President. But in choosing the President, the votes shall be taken by States, the representation from each State having one vote; a quorum for this purpose shall consist of a member or members from two-thirds of the States, and a majority of all States shall be necessary to a choice. [And if the House of Representatives shall not choose a President whenever the right of choice shall devolve upon them, before the fourth day of March next following, then the Vice-President shall act as President, as in the case of the death or other constitutional disability of the President.][13]—The person having the greatest number of votes as Vice-President, shall be the Vice-President, if such number be a majority of the whole number of Electors appointed, and if no person have a majority, then from the two highest numbers on the list, the Senate shall choose the Vice-President; a quorum for the purpose shall consist of two-thirds of the whole number of Senators, and a majority of the whole number shall be necessary to a choice. But no person constitutionally ineligible to the office of President shall be eligible to that of Vice-President of the United States.

The original procedure set out for the election of president and vice president in Article II, Section 1, resulted in a tie in 1800 between Thomas Jefferson and Aaron Burr. It was not until the next year that the House of Representatives chose Jefferson to be president. This amendment changed the procedure by providing for separate ballots for president and vice president.

AMENDMENT XIII.
(Ratified on December 6, 1865—
Prohibition of Slavery)

Section 1.

Neither slavery nor involuntary servitude, except as a punishment for crime whereof the party shall have been duly convicted, shall exist within the United States, or any place subject to their jurisdiction.

Some slaves had been freed during the Civil War. This amendment freed the others and abolished slavery.

Section 2.

Congress shall have power to enforce this article by appropriate legislation.

13. Changed by the Twentieth Amendment.

AMENDMENT XIV.
(Ratified on July 9, 1868— Citizenship, Due Process, and Equal Protection of the Laws)

Section 1.

All persons born or naturalized in the United States, and subject to the jurisdiction thereof, are citizens of the United States and of the State wherein they reside. No State shall make or enforce any law which shall abridge the privileges or immunities of citizens of the United States; nor shall any State deprive any person of life, liberty, or property, without due process of law; nor deny to any person within its jurisdiction the equal protection of the laws.

Under this provision, states cannot make or enforce laws that take away rights given to all citizens by the federal government. States cannot act unfairly or arbitrarily toward, or discriminate against, any person.

Section 2.

Representatives shall be apportioned among the several States according to their respective numbers, counting the whole number of persons in each State, excluding Indians not taxed. But when the right to vote at any election for the choice of electors for President and Vice President of the United States, Representatives in Congress, the Executive and Judicial officers of a State, or the members of the Legislature thereof, is denied to any of the male inhabitants of such State, being [twenty-one][14] years of age, and citizens of the United States, or in any way abridged, except for participation in rebellion, or other crime, the basis of representation therein shall be reduced in the proportion which the number of such male citizens shall bear to the whole number of male citizens twenty-one years of age in such State.

Section 3.

No person shall be a Senator or Representative in Congress, or elector of President and Vice President, or hold any office, civil or military, under the United States, or under any State, who having previously taken an oath, as a member of Congress, or as an officer of the United States, or as a member of any State legislature, or as an executive or judicial officer of any State, to support the Constitution of the United States, shall have engaged in insurrection or rebellion against the same, or given aid or comfort to the enemies thereof. But Congress may by a vote of two-thirds of each House, remove such disability.

This provision forbade former state or federal government officials who had acted in support of the Confederacy during the Civil War to hold office again. It limited the president's power to pardon those persons. Congress removed this "disability" in 1898.

Section 4.

The validity of the public debt of the United States, authorized by law, including debts incurred for payment of pensions and bounties for services in suppressing insurrection or rebellion, shall not be questioned. But neither the United States nor any State shall assume or pay any debt or obligation incurred in aid of insurrection or rebellion against the United States, or any claim for the loss or emancipation of any slave, but all such debts, obligations and claims shall be held illegal and void.

Section 5.

The Congress shall have power to enforce, by appropriate legislation, the provisions of this article.

AMENDMENT XV.
(Ratified on February 3, 1870— The Right to Vote)

Section 1.

The right of citizens of the United States to vote shall not be denied or abridged by the United States or by any State on account of race, color, or previous condition of servitude.

No citizen can be refused the right to vote simply because of race or color or because that person was once a slave.

Section 2.

The Congress shall have power to enforce this article by appropriate legislation.

AMENDMENT XVI.
(Ratified on February 3, 1913—Income Taxes)

The Congress shall have power to lay and collect taxes on incomes, from whatever source derived, without apportionment among the several States, and without regard to any census or enumeration.

This amendment allows Congress to tax income without sharing the revenue so obtained with the states according to their population.

AMENDMENT XVII.
(Ratified on April 8, 1913— The Popular Election of Senators)

Section 1.

The Senate of the United States shall be composed of two Senators from each State, elected by the people thereof, for six years; and each Senator shall have one vote. The electors in each State shall have the qualifications requisite for electors of the most numerous branch of the State legislatures.

Section 2.

When vacancies happen in the representation of any State in the Senate, the executive authority of such State shall issue writs of election to fill such vacancies: *Provided,* That the legislature of any State may empower the executive thereof to make temporary appointments until the people fill the vacancies by election as the legislature may direct.

Section 3.

This amendment shall not be so construed as to affect the election or term of any Senator chosen before it becomes valid as part of the Constitution.

14. Changed by the Twenty-sixth Amendment.

This amendment modified portions of Article I, Section 3, that related to election of senators. Senators are now elected by the voters in each state directly. When a vacancy occurs, either the state may fill the vacancy by a special election, or the governor of the state involved may appoint someone to fill the seat until the next election.

AMENDMENT XVIII.
(Ratified on January 16, 1919—Prohibition)

Section 1.
After one year from the ratification of this article the manufacture, sale, or transportation of intoxicating liquors within, the importation thereof into, or the exportation thereof from the United States and all territory subject to the jurisdiction thereof for beverage purposes is hereby prohibited.

Section 2.
The Congress and the several States shall have concurrent power to enforce this article by appropriate legislation.

Section 3.
This article shall be inoperative unless it shall have been ratified as an amendment to the Constitution by the legislatures of the several States, as provided in the Constitution, within seven years from the date of the submission hereof to the States by the Congress.[15]

This amendment made it illegal to manufacture, sell, and transport alcoholic beverages in the United States. It was repealed by the Twenty-first Amendment.

AMENDMENT XIX.
(Ratified on August 18, 1920—Women's Right to Vote)

Section 1.
The right of citizens of the United States to vote shall not be denied or abridged by the United States or by any State on account of sex.

Section 2.
Congress shall have power to enforce this article by appropriate legislation.

Women were given the right to vote by this amendment, and Congress was given the power to enforce this right.

AMENDMENT XX.
(Ratified on January 23, 1933— The Lame Duck Amendment)

Section 1.
The terms of the President and Vice President shall end at noon on the 20th day of January, and the terms of Senators and Representatives at noon on the 3d day of January, of the years in which such terms would have ended if this article had not been ratified; and the terms of their successors shall then begin.

This amendment modified Article I, Section 4, Clause 2, and other provisions relating to the president in the Twelfth Amendment. The taking of the oath of office was moved from March 4 to January 20.

Section 2.
The Congress shall assemble at least once in every year, and such meeting shall begin at noon on the 3d day of January, unless they shall by law appoint a different day.

Congress changed the beginning of its term to January 3. The reason the Twentieth Amendment is called the Lame Duck Amendment is that it shortens the time between when a member of Congress is defeated for reelection and when he or she leaves office.

Section 3.
If, at the time fixed for the beginning of the term of the President, the President elect shall have died, the Vice President elect shall become President. If a President shall not have been chosen before the time fixed for the beginning of his term, or if the President elect shall have failed to qualify, then the Vice President elect shall act as President until a President shall have qualified; and the Congress may by law provide for the case wherein neither a President elect nor a Vice President elect shall have qualified, declaring who shall then act as President, or the manner in which one who is to act shall be selected, and such person shall act accordingly until a President or Vice President shall have qualified.

This part of the amendment deals with problem areas left ambiguous by Article II and the Twelfth Amendment. If the president dies before January 20 or fails to qualify for office, the presidency is to be filled as described in this section.

Section 4.
The Congress may by law provide for the case of the death of any of the persons from whom the House of Representatives may choose a President whenever the right of choice shall have devolved upon them, and for the case of the death of any of the persons from whom the Senate may choose a Vice President whenever the right of choice shall have devolved upon them.

Congress has never created legislation pursuant to this section.

Section 5.
Sections 1 and 2 shall take effect on the 15th day of October following the ratification of this article.

Section 6.
This article shall be inoperative unless it shall have been ratified as an amendment to the Constitution by the legislatures of three-fourths of the several States within seven years from the date of its submission.

AMENDMENT XXI.
(Ratified on December 5, 1933— The Repeal of Prohibition)

Section 1.
The eighteenth article of amendment to the Constitution of the United States is hereby repealed.

Section 2.
The transportation or importation into any State, Territory, or possession of the United States for delivery or use therein of

15. The Eighteenth Amendment was repealed by the Twenty-first Amendment.

intoxicating liquors, in violation of the laws thereof, is hereby prohibited.

Section 3.
This article shall be inoperative unless it shall have been ratified as an amendment to the Constitution by conventions in the several States, as provided in the Constitution, within seven years from the date of the submission hereof to the States by the Congress.

The amendment repealed the Eighteenth Amendment but did not make alcoholic beverages legal everywhere. Rather, they remained illegal in any state that so designated them. Many such "dry" states existed for a number of years after 1933. Today, there are still "dry" counties within the United States, in which the sale of alcoholic beverages is illegal.

AMENDMENT XXII.
(Ratified on February 27, 1951— Limitation of Presidential Terms)

Section 1.
No person shall be elected to the office of the President more than twice, and no person who has held the office of President, or acted as President, for more than two years of a term to which some other person was elected President shall be elected to the office of President more than once. But this Article shall not apply to any person holding the office of President when this Article was proposed by the Congress, and shall not prevent any person who may be holding the office of President, or acting as President, during the term within which this Article becomes operative from holding the office of President or acting as President during the remainder of such term.

Section 2.
This article shall be inoperative unless it shall have been ratified as an amendment to the Constitution by the legislatures of three-fourths of the several States within seven years from the date of its submission to the States by the Congress.

No president may serve more than two elected terms. If, however, a president has succeeded to the office after the halfway point of a term in which another president was originally elected, then that president may serve for more than eight years, but not to exceed ten years.

AMENDMENT XXIII.
(Ratified on March 29, 1961— Presidential Electors for the District of Columbia)

Section 1.
The District constituting the seat of Government of the United States shall appoint in such manner as the Congress may direct:

A number of electors of President and Vice President equal to the whole number of Senators and Representatives in Congress to which the District would be entitled if it were a State, but in no event more than the least populous State; they shall be in addition to those appointed by the States, but they shall be considered, for the purposes of the election of President and Vice President, to be electors appointed by a State; and they shall meet in the District and perform such duties as provided by the twelfth article of amendment.

Section 2.
The Congress shall have power to enforce this article by appropriate legislation.

Citizens living in the District of Columbia have the right to vote in elections for president and vice president. The District of Columbia has three presidential electors, whereas before this amendment it had none.

AMENDMENT XXIV.
(Ratified on January 23, 1964— The Anti–Poll Tax Amendment)

Section 1.
The right of citizens of the United States to vote in any primary or other election for President or Vice President, for electors for President or Vice President, or for Senator or Representative in Congress, shall not be denied or abridged by the United States, or any State by reason of failure to pay any poll tax or other tax.

Section 2.
The Congress shall have power to enforce this article by appropriate legislation.

No government shall require a person to pay a poll tax to vote in any federal election.

AMENDMENT XXV.
(Ratified on February 10, 1967—Presidential Disability and Vice-Presidential Vacancies)

Section 1.
In case of the removal of the President from office or of his death or resignation, the Vice President shall become President.

Whenever a president dies or resigns from office, the vice president becomes president.

Section 2.
Whenever there is a vacancy in the office of the Vice President, the President shall nominate a Vice President who shall take office upon confirmation by a majority vote of both Houses of Congress.

Whenever the office of the vice presidency becomes vacant, the president may appoint someone to fill this office, provided Congress consents.

Section 3.
Whenever the President transmits to the President pro tempore of the Senate and the Speaker of the House of Representatives his written declaration that he is unable to discharge the powers and duties of his office, and until he transmits to them a written declaration to the contrary, such powers and duties shall be discharged by the Vice President as Acting President.

Whenever the president believes she or he is unable to carry out the duties of the office, she or he shall so indicate to Congress in writing. The vice president then acts as president until the president declares that she or he is again able to carry out the duties of the office.

Section 4.

Whenever the Vice President and a majority of either the principal officers of the executive departments or of such other body as Congress may by law provide, transmit to the President pro tempore of the Senate and the Speaker of the House of Representatives their written declaration that the President is unable to discharge the powers and duties of his office, the Vice President shall immediately assume the powers and duties of the office as Acting President.

Thereafter, when the President transmits to the President pro tempore of the Senate and the Speaker of the House of Representatives his written declaration that no inability exists, he shall resume the powers and duties of his office unless the Vice President and a majority of either the principal officers of the executive department or of such other body as Congress may by law provide, transmit within four days to the President pro tempore of the Senate and the Speaker of the House of Representatives their written declaration that the President is unable to discharge the powers and duties of his office. Thereupon Congress shall decide the issue, assembling within forty-eight hours for that purpose if not in session. If the Congress, within twenty-one days after receipt of the latter written declaration, or, if Congress is not in session, within twenty-one days after Congress is required to assemble, determines by two-thirds vote of both Houses that the President is unable to discharge the powers and duties of his office, the Vice President shall continue to discharge the same as Acting President; otherwise, the President shall resume the powers and duties of his office.

Whenever the vice president and a majority of the members of the cabinet believe that the president cannot carry out her or his duties, they shall so indicate in writing to Congress. The vice president shall then act as president. When the president believes that she or he is able to carry out her or his duties again, she or he shall so indicate to the Congress. However, if the vice president and a majority of the cabinet do not agree, Congress must decide by a two-thirds vote within three weeks who shall act as president.

AMENDMENT XXVI.
(Ratified on July 1, 1971— The Eighteen-Year-Old Vote)

Section 1.

The right of citizens of the United States, who are eighteen years of age or older, to vote shall not be denied or abridged by the United States or by any State on account of age.

No one over eighteen years of age can be denied the right to vote in federal or state elections by virtue of age.

Section 2.

The Congress shall have power to enforce this article by appropriate legislation.

AMENDMENT XXVII.
(Ratified on May 7, 1992—Congressional Pay)

No law, varying the compensation for the services of the Senators and Representatives, shall take effect, until an election of representatives shall have intervened.

This amendment allows the voters to have some control over increases in salaries for congressional members. Originally submitted to the states for ratification in 1789, it was not ratified until 203 years later, in 1992.

3 Federalism

In the aftermath of Superstorm Sandy during the fall of 2012, the National Guard was called in to work with city and state agencies. Here, the Guard delivers supplies to the Red Hook Houses in Brooklyn, New York. (Kirsten Luce/The New York Times)

The eight learning outcomes below are designed to help improve your understanding of this chapter. After reading this chapter, you should be able to:

- Learning Outcome 1: **Define the terms *unitary system*, *confederal system*, and *federal system*.**
- Learning Outcome 2: **Explain some of the benefits of the federal system for the United States.**
- Learning Outcome 3: **Describe how the various provisions of the U.S. Constitution provide a framework for federalism.**
- Learning Outcome 4: **Discuss how, in the early years of the republic, the United States Supreme Court confirmed the authority of the national government.**
- Learning Outcome 5: **Summarize the impact of the U.S. Civil War and President Franklin D. Roosevelt's New Deal on the historical development of federalism.**
- Learning Outcome 6: **Define *cooperative federalism*, and discuss its impact on the states.**
- Learning Outcome 7: **Explain the accomplishments of national authority and the arguments for reemphasizing states' rights.**
- Learning Outcome 8: **Detail recent Supreme Court rulings that affect the distribution of power between the national government and the states.**

(DENG JIAN/xinhua/Landov)

What if...

SHOULD ALL STATES have to recognize same-sex marriages? Why or why not?

ONE STATE'S SAME-SEX MARRIAGES HAD TO BE RECOGNIZED NATIONWIDE?

BACKGROUND

In November 2003, the Massachusetts Supreme Judicial Court ruled that same-sex couples have a right to civil marriage under the state constitution.[a] The California Supreme Court legalized same-sex marriages in May 2008, but California voters overturned the ruling in November of that year by amending the state constitution.[b] By 2012, however, Connecticut, the District of Columbia, Iowa, Maine, Maryland, New Hampshire, New York, Vermont, and Washington had all accepted same-sex marriages.

The U.S. Constitution requires that each state give full faith and credit to every other state's public acts. If a man and a woman are married under the laws of Nevada, the other forty-nine states must recognize that marriage. But what if one state recognizes same-sex marriages? Does that mean that all other states must recognize such marriages and give each partner the benefits accorded to partners in opposite-sex marriages?

In 1996, Congress attempted to prevent such a result through the Defense of Marriage Act, which allows state governments to ignore same-sex marriages performed in other states. It is conceivable that the United States Supreme Court could rule the Defense of Marriage Act is unconstitutional. If this happens, then all state laws that refuse to recognize same-sex marriages performed in another state would be unconstitutional as well.

WHAT IF ONE STATE'S SAME-SEX MARRIAGES HAD TO BE RECOGNIZED NATIONWIDE?

If same-sex marriages were recognized nationwide, then same-sex relationships would be much more conspicuous. Marriage is an issue in many contexts—from registering at a hotel to applying for a line of credit. Hotel clerks or bankers who would prefer not to deal with same-sex couples would be forced to confront the reality of these relationships.

The national government has traditionally left marriage laws to the states. In the past, the Internal Revenue Service and other federal agencies recognized marriages when, and only when, the states recognized them. Under the Defense of Marriage Act, however, federal agencies do not recognize same-sex marriages, no matter what the states do. In July 2010, however, a federal district court judge in Massachusetts ruled that it was unconstitutional for the federal government to deny benefits to same-sex couples married under state laws. The judge did not require states to recognize other states' same-sex marriages, however. This ruling is certain to be appealed all the way to the Supreme Court.

ENFORCING THE LAW

Popular attitudes toward same-sex marriages have become much more positive in recent years. By 2011, public opinion polls had begun to suggest that Americans who accept such marriages now outnumber those who do not. Still, either by statute or by constitutional amendment, forty states ban same-sex marriages. If same-sex marriages were legal nationwide, officials in conservative states might refuse to recognize such marriages, regardless of the law. It could take a long campaign of lawsuits to enforce widespread compliance.

FOR CRITICAL ANALYSIS

1. ***Conservatives have proposed an amendment to the U.S. Constitution to ban same-sex marriage. What difficulties do the advocates of this amendment face in getting it adopted?***
2. ***What impact might widespread same-sex marriage have on American culture generally?***

a. *Goodridge v. Department of Public Health,* 798 N.E.2d 941 (Mass. 2003).

b. *In re Marriage Cases,* 183 P.3d 384 (Cal. 2008). California continues to recognize same-sex marriages performed between May and November 2008. Maryland and New York recognize same-sex marriages performed in other states. The question as to whether California voters had the right to overturn the ruling appears to be headed to the United States Supreme Court.

In the United States, rights and powers are reserved to the states by the Tenth Amendment. Since the financial crisis of September 15, 2008, however, it may appear that the federal government, sometimes called the national or central government, predominates. That might be a temporarily exaggerated perception, for there are 89,529 separate governmental units in this nation, as you can see in Table 3–1 alongside.

Visitors from countries such as France and Spain are often awestruck by the complexity of our system of government. Consider that a criminal action can be defined by state law, by national law, or by both. Thus, a criminal suspect can be prosecuted in the state court system or in the federal court system (or both). Often, economic regulation covering exactly the same issues exists at the local level, the state level, and the national level—generating multiple forms to be completed, multiple procedures to be followed, and multiple laws to be obeyed. Many programs are funded by the national government but administered by state and local governments.

Relations between central governments and local units can be structured in various ways. *Federalism* is one of these ways. Understanding federalism and how it differs from other forms of government is important in understanding the American political system. Indeed, many political issues today would not arise if we did not have a federal form of government in which governmental authority is divided between the central government and various subunits. States, for example, might not have the right to set their own marriage laws, as we discussed in this chapter's opening *What If* . . . feature.

Table 3–1 ▶ Governmental Units in the United States

With more than 89,000 separate governmental units in the United States today, it is no wonder that intergovernmental relations in the United States are so complicated. Actually, the number of school districts has decreased over time, but the number of special districts created for single purposes, such as flood control, has increased from about 8,000 during World War II to more than 37,000 today.

Federal government	**1**
State governments and District of Columbia	**51**
Local governments	
Counties	**3,034**
Municipalities (mainly cities or towns)	**19,492**
Townships (less extensive powers)	**16,519**
Special districts (water, sewer, and the like)	**37,381**
School districts	**13,051**
TOTAL	**89,529**

Source: U.S. Census Bureau.

Three Systems of Government

There are almost two hundred independent nations in the world today. Each of these nations has its own system of government. Generally, though, we can describe how nations structure relations between central governments and local units in terms of three models: (1) the unitary system, (2) the confederal system, and (3) the federal system. The most popular, both historically and today, is the unitary system.

■ Learning Outcome 1: **Define the terms *unitary system, confederal system,* and *federal system.***

A Unitary System

A **unitary system** of government is the easiest to define. Unitary systems place ultimate governmental authority in the hands of the national, or central, government. Consider a typical unitary system—France. There are regions, departments, municipalities, and communes in France. The regions, departments, cities, and communes have elected and appointed officials. So far, the French system appears to be very similar to the U.S. system, but the similarity is only superficial. Under the unitary French system, the decisions of the lower levels of government can be overruled by the national government. The national government also can cut off the funding for local government activities. Moreover, in a unitary system such as that in France, all questions of education, police, the use of land, and welfare are handled by the national government.

Britain, Egypt, Ghana, Israel, Japan, the Philippines, and Sweden—in fact, a majority of all nations—have unitary systems of government.[1]

Unitary System A centralized governmental system in which ultimate governmental authority rests in the hands of the national, or central, government.

A Confederal System

You were introduced to the elements of a **confederal system** of government in Chapter 2, when we examined the Articles of Confederation. A *confederation* is the opposite of a unitary governing system. It is a league of independent states, in which a central government or administration handles only those matters of common concern expressly

Confederal System A system consisting of a league of independent states, in which the central government created by the league has only limited powers over the states.

1. Recent legislation has altered somewhat the unitary character of the French political system. In Britain, the unitary nature of the government has been modified by the creation of the Scottish Parliament.

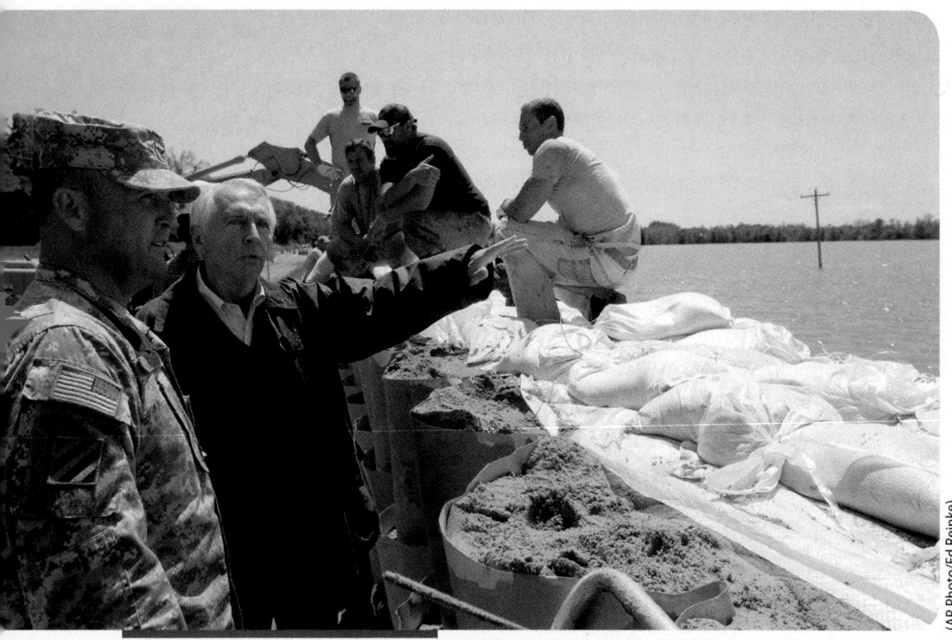
(AP Photo/Ed Reinke)

Governor Steve Beshear of Ohio works with members of the U.S. military to prepare defenses against a threatened major flood. Is this an example of federalism?

delegated to it by the member states. The central government has no ability to make laws directly applicable to member states unless the members explicitly support such laws. The United States under the Articles of Confederation was a confederal system.

Few, if any, confederations of this kind exist. One possible exception is the European Union (EU), a league of countries that has developed a large body of Europe-wide laws that all members must observe. Many members even share a common currency, the euro. Recent problems in the "Eurozone," which we describe in this chapter's *Beyond Our Borders* feature on the facing page, demonstrate the limits of a confederal system.

A Federal System

The federal system lies between the unitary and confederal forms of government. As mentioned in Chapter 2, in a *federal system,* authority is divided, usually by a written constitution, between a central government and regional, or subdivisional, governments (often called *constituent governments*). The central government and the constituent governments both act directly on the people through laws and through the actions of elected and appointed governmental officials. Within each government's sphere of authority, each is supreme, in theory. Thus, a federal system differs sharply from a unitary one, in which the central government is supreme and the constituent governments derive their authority from it. In addition to the United States, Australia, Brazil, Canada, Germany, India, and Mexico are examples of nations with federal systems. See Figure 3–1 on page 86 for a comparison of the three systems.

■ Learning Outcome 2: **Explain some of the benefits of the federal system for the United States.**

Why Federalism?

Why did the United States develop in a federal direction? We look here at that question, as well as at some of the arguments for and against a federal form of government.

A Practical Solution

As you saw in Chapter 2, the historical basis of our federal system was laid down in Philadelphia at the Constitutional Convention, where advocates of a strong national government opposed states' rights advocates. This conflict continued through to the ratifying conventions in the several states. The resulting federal system was a compromise. The supporters of the new Constitution were political pragmatists—they realized that without a federal arrangement, the new Constitution would not be ratified. The appeal of federalism was that it retained state traditions and local power while establishing a strong national government capable of handling common problems.

did you know?

Under Article I, Section 10, of the Constitution, no state is allowed to enter into any treaty, alliance, or confederation.

Even if the founders had agreed on the desirability of a unitary system, size and regional isolation would have made such a system difficult operationally. At the time of the Constitutional Convention, the thirteen states taken together were much larger geographically than England or France. Slow travel and communication, combined with geographic spread, contributed to the isolation of many regions within the states. It could take several weeks for all of the states to be informed about a particular political decision.

Other Arguments for Federalism

For big countries, such as Canada, India, and the United States, federalism allows many functions to be "farmed out" by the central government to the states or provinces. The lower levels of government that accept these responsibilities thereby can become the focus of political dissatisfaction rather than the national authorities. Also, even with modern transportation and communications systems, the large area or population of some nations makes it impractical to locate all political authority in one place.

Finally, federalism brings government closer to the people. It allows more direct access to, and influence on, government agencies and policies, rather than leaving the population restive and dissatisfied with a remote, faceless, all-powerful central authority.

Benefits for the United States. In the United States, federalism historically has yielded many benefits. State governments long have been a training ground for future national leaders. Many presidents made their political mark as state governors. The states themselves have been testing grounds for new government initiatives. As United States Supreme Court justice Louis Brandeis once observed:

(© kyoshino / iStockphoto) (© mattjeacock / iStockphoto)

Beyond Our Borders

THE EUROPEAN UNION GAZES INTO THE ABYSS

The European Union (EU) is a confederation of twenty-seven countries. Seventeen of the countries share a common currency called the euro. When the euro was created in 1999, Germany—the largest Eurozone economy—demanded and received certain guarantees. Nations adopting the euro would have to keep their budget deficits below 3 percent. The European Central Bank (ECB) was barred from aiding any national government that got into trouble. Some economists warned that the Eurozone, as designed, was inherently unstable. For many years, however, everything seemed fine. Most nations, including Germany, ignored the 3 percent rule.

CRISIS IN GREECE

After 1999, investors in wealthy euro nations such as Germany and France invested larger and larger sums in the poorer euro nations. These included Greece, Ireland, Portugal, and Spain. In 2010, however, a newly elected Greek government discovered that previous administrations had "cooked the books." In fact, Greece had rolled up so much debt it would never be able to pay it all back. Much against their will, other euro nations put together a package to bail out the Greek government. But the rot did not stop with Greece. In Ireland, banks had made huge loans on home mortgages, loans that now could not be repaid. The Irish government, which had been running a substantial budget *surplus*, assumed the obligations of its banks—and discovered that it was now stuck as well. A bailout of Ireland was soon followed by a bailout of Portugal.

CRISIS IN THE EUROZONE

If nations such as Greece and Portugal had their own currencies, they could devalue them. Their debts would fall, and their exports would be more competitive. With the euro, that is impossible. Investors began to flee from the bonds issued by the poorer euro nations. Even countries with finances that ought to have been stable—such as Italy and Spain—were in danger of defaulting on their debts, simply because they could no longer borrow. The only alternative to default would be to leave the euro. Either alternative would be a disaster.

Normally, a nation in such a situation would borrow from its own central bank. But the ECB, remember, was prohibited from making such loans. By the end of 2011, however, the ECB began loaning huge sums to European banks. The banks then used the funds to buy the bonds of nations in trouble. In September 2012, the ECB announced that it would buy, from investors, as many bonds issued by troubled nations as would be necessary to save the euro.

FOR CRITICAL ANALYSIS

No one worries that fiscal misbehavior by an American state could threaten the dollar. Why?

Figure 3-1 ▸ The Flow of Power in Three Systems of Government

In a unitary system, power flows from the central government to the local and state governments. In a confederal system, power flows in the opposite direction—from the state governments to the central government. In a federal system, the flow of power, in principle, goes both ways.

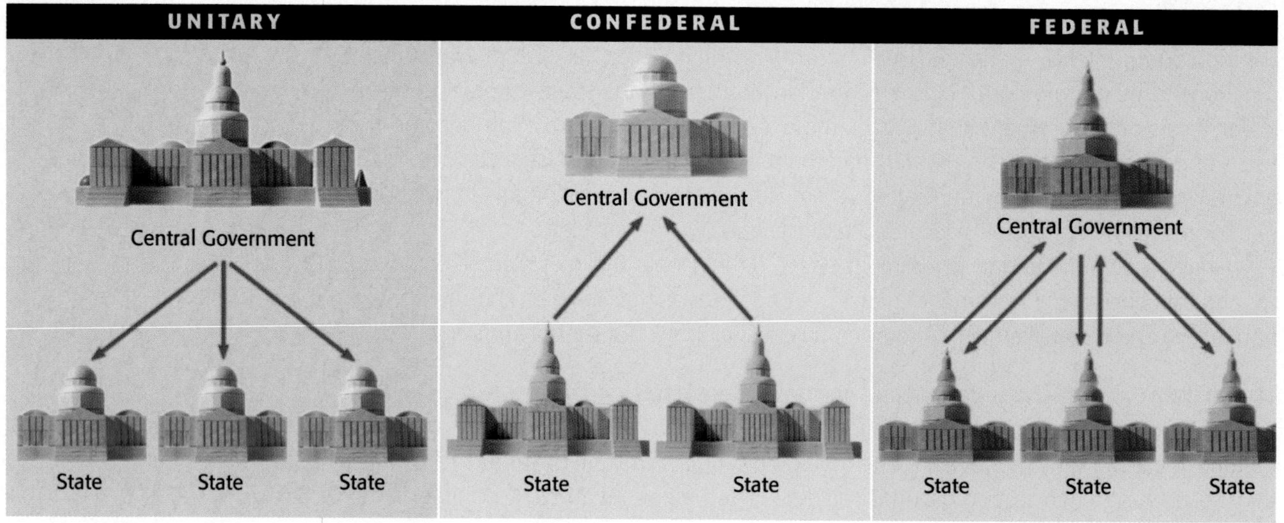

It is one of the happy incidents of the federal system that a single courageous state may, if its citizens choose, serve as a laboratory and try novel social and economic experiments without risk to the rest of the country.[2]

Examples of programs pioneered at the state level include unemployment compensation, which began in Wisconsin, and air-pollution control, which was initiated in California. Today, states are experimenting with policies ranging from education reform to homeland security strategies. Since the passage of the 1996 welfare reform legislation—which gave more control over welfare programs to state governments—states also have been experimenting with different methods of delivering welfare assistance.

Allowance for Many Political Subcultures. The American way of life always has been characterized by a number of political subcultures, which divide along the lines of race and ethnic origin, region, wealth, education, and, more recently, degree of religious commitment and sexual preference. The existence of diverse political subcultures would appear to be incompatible with a political authority concentrated solely in a central government. Had the United States developed into a unitary system, various political subcultures certainly would have been less able to influence government behavior than they have been, and continue to be, in our federal system.

Some federal funds are used to help local elementary schools hire more assistants.

(Matt Smith/Express-Times/Landov)

Arguments against Federalism

Not everyone thinks federalism is such a good idea. Some see it as a way for powerful state and local interests to

2. *New State Ice Co. v. Liebmann*, 285 U.S. 262 (1932). See the *E-mocracy* feature at the end of this chapter for information on how to look up court cases online.

block progress and impede national plans. Smaller political units are more likely to be dominated by a single political group. (This was essentially the argument that James Madison put forth in *Federalist Paper* No. 10, which you can read in Appendix C of this text.) In fact, the dominant groups in some cities and states have resisted implementing equal rights for minority groups. Some argue, however, that the dominant factions in other states have been more progressive than the national government in many areas, such as environmental protection.

Critics of federalism also argue that too many Americans suffer as a result of the inequalities across the states. Individual states differ markedly in educational spending and achievement, crime and crime prevention, and even the safety of their buildings. Not surprisingly, these critics argue for increased federal legislation and oversight. This might involve creating national standards for education and building codes, national expenditure minimums for crime control, and similar measures.

Others see dangers in the expansion of national powers at the expense of the states. President Ronald Reagan (1981–1989) said, "The Founding Fathers saw the federalist system as constructed something like a masonry wall. The States are the bricks, the national government is the mortar. . . . Unfortunately, over the years, many people have increasingly come to believe that Washington is the whole wall."[3]

did you know?

State governments in the United States are unitary governments. As a result, most local governments are mere creatures of the states.

The Constitutional Basis for American Federalism

■ **Learning Outcome 3:** **Describe how the various provisions of the U.S. Constitution provide a framework for federalism.**

The term *federal system* cannot be found in the U.S. Constitution. Nor is it possible to find a systematic division of governmental authority between the national and state governments in that document. Rather, the Constitution sets out different types of powers. These powers can be classified as (1) the powers of the national government, (2) the powers of the states, and (3) prohibited powers. The Constitution also makes it clear that if a state or local law conflicts with a national law, the national law will prevail.

Powers of the National Government

The powers delegated to the national government include both expressed and implied powers, as well as the special category of inherent powers. Most of the powers expressly delegated to the national government are found in the first seventeen clauses of Article I, Section 8, of the Constitution. These **enumerated powers,** also called *expressed powers,* include coining money, setting standards for weights and measures, making uniform naturalization laws, admitting new states, establishing post offices and post roads, and declaring war. Another important enumerated power is the power to regulate commerce among the states—a topic we deal with later in this chapter.

Enumerated Powers
Powers specifically granted to the national government by the Constitution. The first seventeen clauses of Article I, Section 8, specify most of the enumerated powers of the national government.

The Necessary and Proper Clause. The implied powers of the national government are also based on Article I, Section 8, which states that the Congress shall have the power

> *to make all Laws which shall be necessary and proper for carrying into Execution the foregoing Powers, and all other Powers vested by this Constitution in the Government of the United States, or in any Department or Officer thereof.*

This clause is sometimes called the **elastic clause,** or the **necessary and proper clause,** because it provides flexibility to our constitutional system. It gives Congress the power to

Elastic Clause, or Necessary and Proper Clause
The clause in Article I, Section 8, that grants Congress the power to do whatever is necessary to execute its specifically delegated powers.

3. Text of the address by the president to the National Conference of State Legislatures, Atlanta, Georgia (Washington, D.C.: The White House, Office of the Press Secretary, July 30, 1981).

do whatever is necessary to execute its specifically delegated powers. The clause was first used in the Supreme Court decision of *McCulloch v. Maryland*[4] (discussed later in this chapter) to develop the concept of implied powers. Through this concept, the national government has succeeded in strengthening the scope of its authority to meet the many problems that the framers of the Constitution did not, and could not, anticipate.

Inherent Powers. A special category of national powers that is not implied by the necessary and proper clause consists of what have been labeled the *inherent powers* of the national government. These powers derive from the fact that the United States is a sovereign power among nations, and so its national government must be the only government that deals with other nations. Under international law, it is assumed that all nation-states, regardless of their size or power, have an inherent right to ensure their own survival. To do this, each nation must have the ability to act in its own interest among and with the community of nations—by, for instance, making treaties, waging war, seeking trade, and acquiring territory.

Note that no specific clause in the Constitution says anything about the acquisition of additional land. Nonetheless, the federal government's inherent powers allowed it to make the Louisiana Purchase in 1803 and then go on to acquire Florida, Texas, Oregon, Alaska, Hawaii, and other lands. The United States grew from a mere thirteen states to fifty states, plus several territories.

The national government has these inherent powers whether or not they have been enumerated in the Constitution. Some constitutional scholars categorize inherent powers as a third type of power, completely distinct from the delegated powers (both expressed and implied) of the national government.

Powers of the State Governments

The Tenth Amendment states that the powers not delegated to the United States by the Constitution, nor prohibited by it to the states, are reserved to the states, or to the people. These are the *reserved powers* that the national government cannot deny to the states. Because these powers are not expressly listed, there is sometimes a question as to whether a certain power is delegated to the national government or reserved to the states.

Police Power
The authority to legislate for the protection of the health, morals, safety, and welfare of the people. In the United States, most police power is reserved to the states.

State powers have been held to include each state's right to regulate commerce within its borders and to provide for a state militia. States also have the reserved power to make laws on all matters not prohibited to the states by the U.S. Constitution or state constitutions and not expressly, or by implication, delegated to the national government. Furthermore, the states have **police power**—the authority to legislate for the protection of the health, morals, safety, and welfare of the people. Their police power enables states to pass laws governing such activities as crime, marriage, contracts, education, intrastate transportation, and land use.

The ambiguity of the Tenth Amendment has allowed the reserved powers of the states to be defined differently at different times in our history. When there is widespread support for increased regulation by the national government, the Tenth Amendment tends to recede into the background. When the tide turns the other way (in favor of states' rights), the Tenth Amendment is resurrected to justify arguments supporting the states.

(© Mischa Richter/The New Yorker Collection/www.cartoonbank.com)

"They have very strict anti-pollution laws in this state."

4. 17 U.S. 316 (1819).

Prohibited Powers

The Constitution prohibits, or denies, a number of powers to the national government. For example, the national government has expressly been denied the power to impose taxes on goods sold to other countries (exports). Moreover, any power not granted expressly or implicitly to the federal government by the Constitution is prohibited to it. For example, many legal experts believe that the national government could not create a national divorce law system without a constitutional amendment. The states are also denied certain powers. For example, no state is allowed to enter into a treaty on its own with another country.

Concurrent Powers

In certain areas, the states share **concurrent powers** with the national government. Most concurrent powers are not specifically listed in the Constitution—they are only implied. An example of a concurrent power is the power to tax. The types of taxation are divided between the levels of government. For example, states may not levy a tariff (a set of taxes on imported goods). Only the national government may do this. Neither government may tax the facilities of the other. If the state governments did not have the power to tax, they would not be able to function other than on a ceremonial basis.

Concurrent Powers
Powers held jointly by the national and state governments.

Additional concurrent powers include the power to borrow funds, to establish courts, and to charter banks and corporations. To a limited extent, the national government exercises police power, and to the extent that it does, police power is also a concurrent power. Concurrent powers exercised by the states are normally limited to the geographic area of each state and to those functions not granted by the Constitution exclusively to the national government.

The Supremacy Clause

The supremacy of the national constitution over subnational laws and actions is established in the **supremacy clause** of the Constitution. The supremacy clause (Article VI, Clause 2) states the following:

Supremacy Clause
The constitutional provision that makes the Constitution and federal laws superior to all conflicting state and local laws.

> *This Constitution, and the Laws of the United States which shall be made in Pursuance thereof; and all Treaties made . . . under the Authority of the United States, shall be the supreme Law of the Land; and the Judges in every State shall be bound thereby, any Thing in the Constitution or Laws of any State to the Contrary notwithstanding.*

In other words, states cannot use their reserved or concurrent powers to thwart national policies. All national and state officers, including judges, must be bound by oath to support the Constitution. Hence, any legitimate exercise of national governmental power supersedes any conflicting state action. Of course, deciding whether a conflict actually exists is a judicial matter, as you will soon learn when we discuss the case of *McCulloch v. Maryland.*

The National Guard can serve as an example of how federal power supersedes that of the states. Normally, the National Guard functions as a state militia under the command of the governor. It is frequently called out to assist with recovery efforts after natural disasters such as hurricanes, floods, and earthquakes. The president, however, can assume command of any National Guard unit at any time. Presidents Bush and Obama repeatedly "federalized" such units for deployment in Afghanistan and Iraq. In the conflicts in these countries, National Guard members and reservists made up a larger percentage of the forces on combat duty than during any previous war in U.S. history.

National government legislation in a concurrent area is said to *preempt* (take precedence over) conflicting state or local laws or regulations in that area. One of the ways in which the national government has extended its powers, particularly during the twentieth century, is through the preemption of state and local laws by national legislation. In the first decade of the twentieth century, fewer than twenty national laws preempted laws and regulations issued by state and local governments. By the beginning of the twenty-first century, the number had grown into the hundreds.

Vertical Checks and Balances

Recall from Chapter 2 that one of the concerns of the founders was to prevent the national government from becoming too powerful. For that reason, they divided the government into three branches—legislative, executive, and judicial. They also created a system of checks and balances that allowed each branch to check the actions of the others. The federal form of government created by the founders also involves checks and balances. These are sometimes called *vertical checks and balances* because they involve relationships between the states and the national government. They can be contrasted with *horizontal checks and balances,* in which the branches of government that are on the same level—either state or national—can check one another.

For example, the reserved powers of the states act as a check on the national government. The founders also made it impossible for the central government to change the Constitution without the states' consent, as you read in Chapter 2. Finally, many national programs and policies are administered by the states, which gives the states considerable control over the ultimate shape of those programs and policies.

The national government, in turn, can check state policies by exercising its constitutional powers under the clauses just discussed, as well as under the commerce clause (to be examined later). Furthermore, the national government can influence state policies indirectly through federal grants, as you will learn later in this chapter.

Interstate Relations

So far, we have examined only the relationship between central and state governmental units. The states, however, have constant commercial, social, and other dealings among themselves. The national Constitution imposes certain "rules of the road" on interstate relations. These rules have had the effect of preventing any one state from setting itself apart from the other states. The three most important clauses governing interstate relations in the Constitution, all taken from the Articles of Confederation, require each state to do the following:

1. Give full faith and credit to every other state's public acts, records, and judicial proceedings (Article IV, Section 1).
2. Extend to every other state's citizens the privileges and immunities of its own citizens (Article IV, Section 2).
3. Agree to return persons who are fleeing from justice in another state back to their home state when requested to do so (Article IV, Section 2).

Following these constitutional mandates is not always easy for the states. For example, one question that has arisen in recent years is whether states will be constitutionally obligated to recognize same-sex marriages performed in other states. We considered that question in the *What If . . .* feature at the beginning of this chapter.

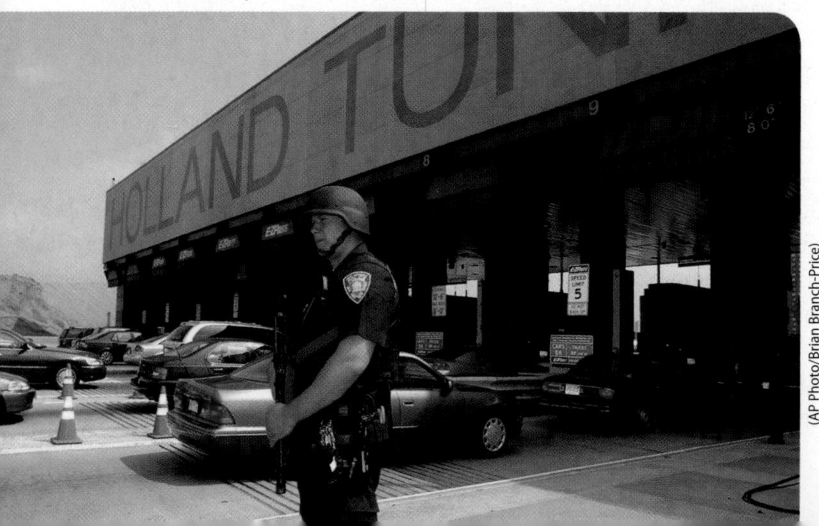

A police officer for the New York-New Jersey Port Authority stands guard at the Holland Tunnel in Jersey City. Was an interstate compact responsible for the Port Authority?

(AP Photo/Brian Branch-Price)

Additionally, states may enter into agreements with one another called **interstate compacts**—if consented to by Congress. In reality, congressional consent is necessary only if such a compact increases the power of the contracting states relative to other states (or to the national government). An example of an interstate compact is the Port Authority of New York and New Jersey, established by an agreement between those two states in 1921.

Interstate Compact
An agreement between two or more states. Agreements on minor matters are made without congressional consent, but any compact that tends to increase the power of the contracting states relative to other states or relative to the national government generally requires the consent of Congress.

The Supreme Court Defines the Powers of the National Government

■ Learning Outcome 4: **Discuss how, in the early years of the republic, the United States Supreme Court confirmed the authority of the national government.**

Although political bodies at all levels of government play important roles in the process of settling disputes over the nature of our federal system, ultimately it is the United States Supreme Court that casts the final vote. As might be expected, the character of the referee will have an impact on the ultimate outcome of any dispute. From 1801 to 1835, the Supreme Court was headed by Chief Justice John Marshall, a Federalist who advocated a strong central government. We look here at two cases decided by the Marshall Court: *McCulloch v. Maryland*[5] and *Gibbons v. Ogden*.[6] Both cases are considered milestones in the movement toward national government supremacy.

McCulloch v. Maryland (1819)

The U.S. Constitution says nothing about establishing a national bank. Nonetheless, at different times Congress chartered two banks—the First and Second Banks of the United States—and provided part of their initial capital. Thus, they were national banks. The government of Maryland imposed a tax on the Second Bank's Baltimore branch in an attempt to put that branch out of business. The branch's cashier, James William McCulloch, refused to pay the Maryland tax. When Maryland took McCulloch to its state court, the state of Maryland won. The national government appealed the case to the Supreme Court.

Commerce Clause
The section of the Constitution in which Congress is given the power to regulate trade among the states and with foreign countries.

One of the issues before the Court was whether the national government had the implied power, under the necessary and proper clause, to charter a bank and contribute capital to it. The other important question before the Court was the following: If the bank was constitutional, could a state tax it? In other words, was a state action that conflicted with a national government action invalid under the supremacy clause?

Chief Justice Marshall held that if establishing a national bank aided the national government in the exercise of its designated powers, then the authority to set up such a bank could be implied. Having established this doctrine of implied powers, Marshall then answered the other question before the Court and established the doctrine of national supremacy. Marshall ruled that no state could use its taxing power to tax a part of the national government. If it could, "the declaration that the Constitution . . . shall be the supreme law of the land, is [an] empty and unmeaning [statement]."

Marshall's decision enabled the national government to grow and to meet problems that the Constitution's framers were unable to foresee. Today, practically every expressed power of the national government has been expanded in one way or another by use of the necessary and proper clause.

When John Marshall (1755–1835) was chief justice of the United States Supreme Court, he championed the power of the federal government. What are the most famous cases that the Marshall Court decided?

(© Corbis)

Gibbons v. Ogden (1824)

One of the most important parts of the Constitution included in Article I, Section 8, is the **commerce clause,** in which Congress is given the power "to regulate Commerce with foreign Nations, and among the several States, and with the Indian Tribes." The meaning of this clause was at issue in *Gibbons v. Ogden*.

5. 17 U.S. 316 (1819).
6. 22 U.S. 1 (1824).

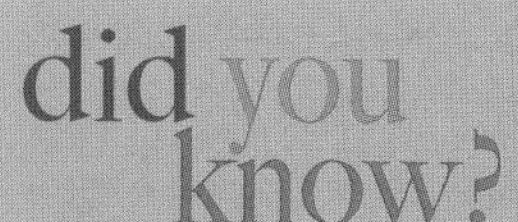

The Liberty Bell cracked when it was rung at the funeral of John Marshall in 1835.

The Background of the Case. Robert Fulton and Robert Livingston secured a monopoly on steam navigation on the waters in New York State from the New York legislature in 1803. They licensed Aaron Ogden to operate steam-powered ferryboats between New York and New Jersey. Thomas Gibbons, who had obtained a license from the U.S. government to operate boats in interstate waters, decided to compete with Ogden, but he did so without New York's permission. Ogden sued Gibbons. New York's state courts prohibited Gibbons from operating in New York waters. Gibbons appealed to the Supreme Court.

There were actually several issues before the Court in this case. The first issue was how the term *commerce* should be defined. New York's highest court had defined the term narrowly to mean only the shipment of goods or the interchange of commodities, *not* navigation or the transport of people. The second issue was whether the national government's power to regulate interstate commerce extended to commerce within a state (*intrastate* commerce) or was limited strictly to commerce among the states (*interstate* commerce). The third issue was whether the power to regulate interstate commerce was a concurrent power (as the New York court had concluded) or an exclusive national power.

■ Learning Outcome 5: **Summarize the impact of the U.S. Civil War and President Franklin D. Roosevelt's New Deal on the historical development of federalism.**

Marshall's Ruling. Marshall defined *commerce* as all commercial interactions—all business dealings—including navigation and the transport of people. Marshall also held that the commerce power of the national government could be exercised in state jurisdictions, even though it could not reach *solely* intrastate commerce. Finally, Marshall emphasized that the power to regulate interstate commerce was an *exclusive* national power. Marshall held that because Gibbons was duly authorized by the national government to navigate in interstate waters, he could not be prohibited from doing so by a state court.

Marshall's expansive interpretation of the commerce clause in *Gibbons v. Ogden* allowed the national government to exercise increasing authority over economic affairs throughout the land. Congress did not immediately exploit this broad grant of power. In the 1930s and subsequent decades, however, the commerce clause became the primary constitutional basis for national government regulation—as you will read later in this chapter.

From the Civil War to the New Deal

The controversy over slavery that led to the Civil War took the form of a dispute over national government supremacy versus the rights of the separate states. Essentially, the Civil War brought to an ultimate and violent climax the ideological debate that had been outlined by the Federalist and Anti-Federalist parties even before the Constitution was ratified.

The Shift Back to States' Rights

As we have seen, while John Marshall was chief justice of the Supreme Court, he did much to increase the power of the national government and to reduce that of the states. During the administration of President Andrew Jackson (1829–1837), however, a shift back to states' rights began. The question of the regulation of commerce became one of the major issues in federal–state relations. When Congress passed a tariff in 1828, the state of South Carolina unsuccessfully attempted to nullify the tariff (render it void), claiming that in cases of conflict between a state and the national government, the state should have the ultimate authority over its citizens.

During the next three decades, the North and South became even more sharply divided, especially over the slavery issue. On December 20, 1860, South Carolina formally repealed its ratification of the Constitution and withdrew from the Union. On February 4, 1861, representatives from six southern states met at Montgomery, Alabama, to form a new government called the Confederate States of America.

War and the Growth of the National Government

The ultimate defeat of the South in 1865 permanently ended the idea that a state could successfully claim the right to secede, or withdraw, from the Union. Ironically, the Civil War—brought about in large part because of the South's desire for increased states' rights—resulted in the opposite: an increase in the political power of the national government.

The War Effort. Thousands of new employees were hired to run the Union war effort and to deal with the social and economic problems that had to be handled in the aftermath of the war. A billion-dollar ($1.3 billion, which is about $18 billion in today's dollars) national government budget was passed for the first time in 1865 to cover the increased government expenditures. The first (temporary) income tax was imposed on citizens to help pay for the war.

The Civil War Amendments. The expansion of the national government's authority during the Civil War was also reflected in the passage of the Civil War amendments to the Constitution. Before the war, it was a bedrock constitutional principle that the national government should not interfere with slavery in the states. The Thirteenth Amendment, ratified in 1865, did more than interfere with slavery—it abolished the institution altogether.

The Fourteenth Amendment, ratified in 1868, defined who was a citizen of each state. It sought to guarantee equal rights under state law, stating that

> *[no] State [shall] deprive any person of life, liberty, or property, without due process of law; nor deny to any person within its jurisdiction the equal protection of the laws.*

In time, the courts interpreted these words to mean that the national Bill of Rights applied to state governments, a development that we will examine in Chapter 4. Finally, the Fifteenth Amendment (1870) gave African Americans the right to vote in all elections, including state elections—although a century would pass before that right was enforced in all states.

Although the outcome of the Civil War firmly established the supremacy of the national government and put to rest the idea that a state could secede from the Union, the war by no means ended the debate over the division of powers between the national government and the states.

Dual Federalism and the Retreat of National Authority

During the decades following the Civil War, the prevailing model of federalism was what political scientists have called **dual federalism**—a doctrine that emphasizes a distinction between national and state

Social Media IN POLITICS

The *New York Times* sponsors a series on the United States Civil War that uses contemporary accounts, diaries, and images. To follow it on Twitter, enter "nytcivilwar."

did you know?

Only after the Civil War did people commonly refer to the United States as "it" instead of "they."

Dual Federalism
A model of federalism in which the states and the national government each remain supreme within their own spheres. The doctrine looks on nation and state as co-equal sovereign powers. Neither the state government nor the national government should interfere in the other's sphere.

President Lincoln meets with some of his generals and other troops on October 3, 1862. While the Civil War was fought over the issue of slavery, it was also a battle over the supremacy of the national government. Once the North won the war, what happened to the size and power of our national government?

(Library of Congress)

(AP Photo)

Child labor was still common in the early 1900s. Why didn't the federal government simply ban it then?

spheres of government authority. This doctrine looks on nation and state as co-equal sovereign powers. Neither the state government nor the national government should interfere in the other's sphere.

Various images have been used to describe different configurations of federalism over time. Dual federalism is commonly depicted as a layer cake, because the state governments and the national government are viewed as separate entities, like separate layers of a cake. The two layers are physically separate; they do not mix. For the most part, advocates of dual federalism believed that the state and national governments should not exercise authority in the same areas.

The doctrine of dual federalism represented a revival of states' rights following the expansion of national authority during the Civil War. Dual federalism, after all, was a fairly accurate model of the prewar consensus on federal–state relations. For many people, it therefore represented a return to normal.

The Civil War crisis drastically reduced the influence of the United States Supreme Court. In the prewar *Dred Scott* decision,[7] the Court had attempted to abolish the power of the national government to restrict slavery in the territories. In so doing, the Court placed itself on the losing side of the impending conflict. After the war, Congress took the unprecedented step of exempting the entire process of southern reconstruction from judicial review. The Court had little choice but to acquiesce.

In time, the Supreme Court reestablished itself as the legitimate constitutional umpire. Its decisions tended to support dual federalism, defend states' rights, and limit the powers of the national government. The Court generally limited the exercise of police power to the states. For example, in 1918, the Court ruled that a 1916 national law banning child labor was unconstitutional because it attempted to regulate a local problem.[8] In effect, the Court placed severe limits on the ability of Congress to legislate under the commerce clause of the Constitution.

The New Deal and the End of Dual Federalism

The doctrine of dual federalism receded into the background in the 1930s as the nation attempted to deal with the Great Depression. Franklin D. Roosevelt was inaugurated as president on March 4, 1933. In the previous year, nearly 1,500 banks had failed (and 4,000 more would fail in 1933). Thirty-two thousand businesses had closed down, and almost one-fourth of the labor force was unemployed. The public expected the national government to do something about the disastrous state of the economy.

The "New Deal." President Herbert Hoover (1929–1933), however, clung to the doctrine of dual federalism and insisted that unemployment and poverty were local issues. The states, not the national government, had the sole responsibility for combating the effects of unemployment and providing relief to the poor. Roosevelt did not feel bound by this doctrine, and his new Democratic administration energetically intervened in the economy. Roosevelt's "New Deal" included large-scale emergency antipoverty programs. In addition, the New Deal introduced major new laws regulating economic activity, such as the National Industrial Recovery Act of 1933, which established the National Recovery Administration (NRA).

The End of Dual Federalism. Roosevelt's expansion of national authority was challenged by the Supreme Court, which continued to adhere to the doctrine of dual federalism. In 1935, the Court ruled that the NRA program was unconstitutional.[9] The NRA had

7. *Dred Scott v. Sandford,* 60 U.S. 393 (1856).
8. *Hammer v. Dagenhart,* 247 U.S. 251 (1918). This decision was overruled in *United States v. Darby,* 312 U.S. 100 (1940).
9. *Schechter Poultry Corp. v. United States,* 295 U.S. 495 (1935).

turned out to be largely unworkable and was unpopular. The Court, however, rejected the program on the ground that it regulated intrastate, not interstate, commerce. This position appeared to rule out any alternative recovery plans that might be better designed.

In 1937, Roosevelt proposed legislation that would allow him to add up to six new justices to the Supreme Court. Presumably, the new justices would be more friendly to the exercise of national power than the existing members were. Congressional Democrats refused to support the measure, and it failed. Still, changes to the membership of the Court from 1937 on proved as effective as the failed "court-packing scheme." After 1937 the Court ceased its attempts to limit the national government's powers under the commerce clause.

(© Bettmann/Corbis)

President Franklin Delano Roosevelt (1933–1945). Roosevelt's national approach to addressing the effects of the Great Depression was overwhelmingly popular, although many of his specific initiatives were controversial. How did the Great Depression change the political beliefs of many ordinary Americans?

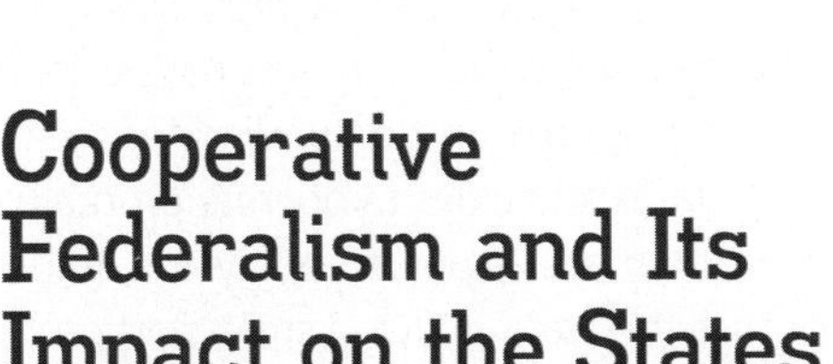

Cooperative Federalism and Its Impact on the States

Some political scientists have described the era since 1937 as characterized by **cooperative federalism,** in which the states and the national government cooperate in solving complex common problems. Roosevelt's New Deal programs, for example, often involved joint action between the national government and the states. The pattern of federal–state relationships during these years gave rise to a new metaphor for federalism—that of a marble cake. Unlike a layer cake, in a marble cake the two types of cake are intermingled, and any bite contains cake of both flavors.

Cooperative Federalism
A model of federalism in which the states and the national government cooperate in solving problems.

As an example of how national and state governments work together under the cooperative federalism model, consider Aid to Families with Dependent Children (AFDC), a welfare program that was established during the New Deal. (In 1996, AFDC was replaced by Temporary Assistance to Needy Families—TANF.) Under the AFDC program, the national government provided most of the funding, but state governments established benefit levels and eligibility requirements for recipients. Local welfare offices were staffed by state, not national, employees. In return for national funding, the states had to conform to a series of regulations on how the program was to be carried out. These regulations tended to become more elaborate over time.

■ Learning Outcome 6:
Define *cooperative federalism*, and discuss its impact on the states.

Federal Grants to the States

Even before the Constitution was adopted, the national government gave grants to the states in the form of land to finance education. The national government also provided land grants for canals, railroads, and roads. In the twentieth century, federal grants increased significantly, especially during Roosevelt's administration throughout the Great Depression and again in the 1960s, when the dollar amount of grants quadrupled. These funds were used for improvements in education, pollution control, recreation, and highways. With this increase in grants, however, came a bewildering number of restrictions and regulations.

Categorical Grant
A federal grant to a state or local government for a specific program or project.

Categorical Grants. In the 1980s, **categorical grants** were spread out across four hundred separate programs, but the five largest accounted for more than 50 percent of the revenues spent. These five programs were Medicaid (health care for the poor), highway construction, unemployment benefits, housing assistance, and welfare programs to assist mothers with dependent children and people with disabilities. For fiscal year 2013, the national government gave about $580 billion to the states. The shift toward a greater role for the central government in the United States can be seen in Figure 3–2 below, which shows the increase in central government spending as a percentage of total government spending.

Before the 1960s, most categorical grants by the national government were *formula grants.* These grants take their name from the method used to allocate funds. They fund state programs using a formula based on such variables as the state's needs, population, or willingness to come up with matching funds. Beginning in the 1960s, the national government began increasingly to offer *program grants.* This funding requires states to apply for grants for specific programs. The applications are evaluated by the national government, and the applications may compete with one another. Program grants give the national government a much greater degree of control over state activities than do formula grants.

Over the decades, federal grants to the states have increased significantly, as shown in Figure 3–3 on the facing page. One reason for this increase is that Congress has decided to offload some programs to the states and provide a major part of the funding for them. Also, Congress continues to use grants to persuade states and cities to operate programs devised by the federal government. Finally, states often are happy to apply for grants because they are relatively "free," requiring only that the state match a small portion of each grant. States can still face criticism for accepting the grants, because their matching funds may be diverted from other state projects.

Figure 3–2 ▸ The Shift toward Central Government Spending

In the years before the Great Depression, local governments accounted for close to three-fifths of all government spending, and the federal government accounted for only about 30 percent. After Franklin D. Roosevelt's New Deal, federal spending began to rival state and local spending combined. The federal share is still about 46 percent today, not counting transfers to state and local governments. The size of the pies reflects total spending.

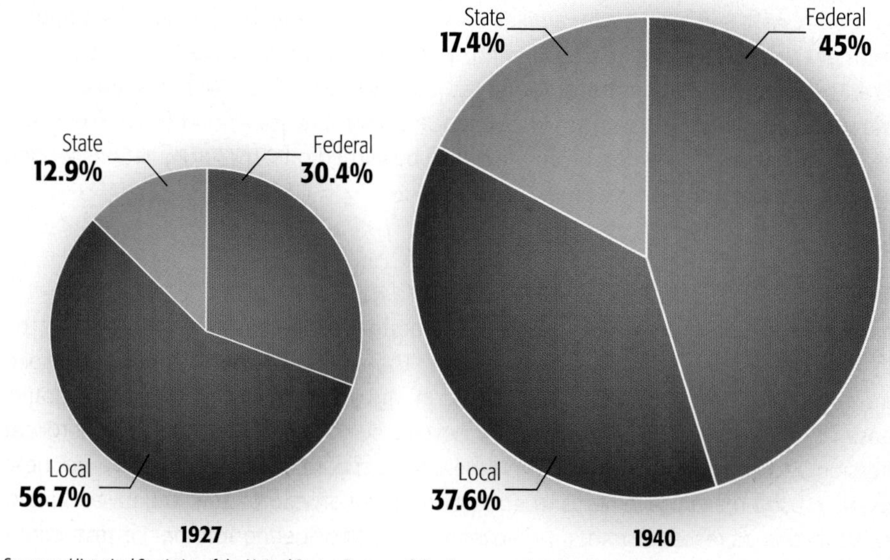

Sources: *Historical Statistics of the United States,* Bureau of the Census, and authors' calculations.

Figure 3–3 ▸ The Rise in Federal Transfers to State and Local Governments

The chart shows the percentage of the nation's state and local revenues supplied by the federal government. The federal government has gained leverage over state and local governments by supplying an increasing share of their revenues. The drop in federal transfers from 1980 to 1990 took place during the presidency of Ronald Reagan, as we explain in "The 'New Federalism'" on pages 100 and 101.

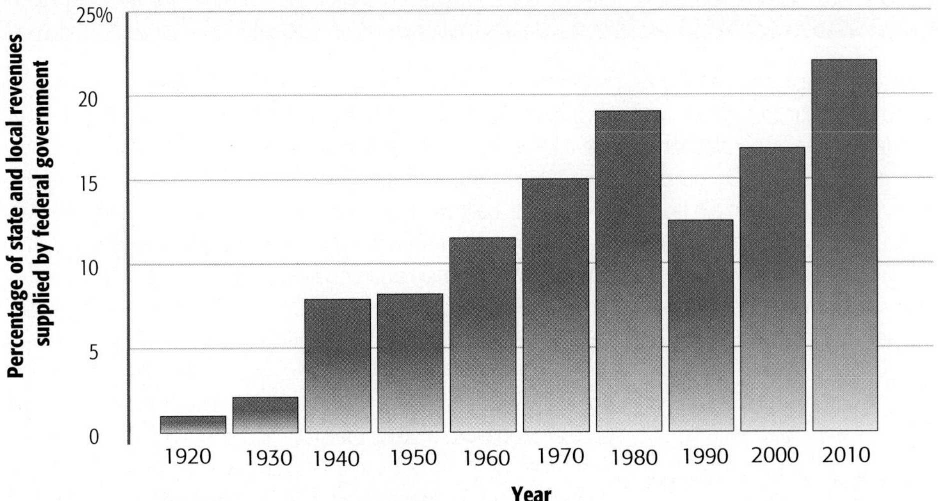

Sources: *Historical Statistics of the United States; Statistical Abstract of the United States, 2008;* and *Budget of the United States Government, FY 2011* and *FY 2012.*

Block Grants. **Block grants** lessen the restrictions on federal grants given to state and local governments by grouping a number of categorical grants under one broad heading. Governors and mayors generally prefer block grants because such grants give the states more flexibility in how the funds are spent.

One major set of block grants provides aid to state welfare programs. The Personal Responsibility and Work Opportunity Reconciliation Act of 1996 ended the AFDC program. The TANF program that replaced AFDC provided a welfare block grant to each state. Each grant has an annual cap. According to some, this is one of the most successful block grant programs. Although state governments prefer block grants, Congress generally favors categorical grants because the expenditures can be targeted according to congressional priorities.

Block Grant
A federal grant that provides funds to a state or local government for a general functional area, such as criminal justice or mental-health programs.

did you know?

Part of the $4.2 million in federal block grants received by four Native American tribes since 1997 has gone toward the building of "smoke shops"—stores that sell discounted cigarettes and pipe tobacco.

Fiscal Federalism and State Budgets

In discussions of government policy, you may have heard the word *fiscal*. This word simply means "having to do with government revenues and expenditures." **Fiscal** policy, therefore, is policy concerning taxing or borrowing—and then spending the revenues. When the federal government makes grants to state and local governments, funds raised through taxation or borrowing by one level of government (the national government) are spent by another level (state and local governments). We can speak of this process as **fiscal federalism.** With more than 20 percent of state and local revenues supplied by the federal government, fiscal federalism clearly has a major impact on the finances of the states.

The Great Recession in the first decade of the 2000s had a devastating impact on state budgets, and in response the federal government substantially increased the amount of funding available to the states in 2009 and 2010. Much of this support came through President Barack Obama's stimulus plan, passed by Congress in February 2009. The new federal funds, however, did not fully compensate the states for the lost revenue and increased expenses resulting from the recession. We look at state spending in this chapter's *Politics and Economics* feature on the following page.

Fiscal
Having to do with government revenues and expenditures.

Fiscal Federalism
A process by which funds raised through taxation or borrowing by one level of government (usually the national government) are spent by another level (typically state or local governments).

Politics AND Economics

SPENDING BY THE STATES IN HARD TIMES

During the boom years in the middle of the first decade of the 2000s, many state governments enjoyed large increases in revenue from taxes and other sources. Quite a few states responded with increased spending. After the Great Recession began in December 2007, however, high-spending states found themselves in big trouble. By 2011, Illinois had a deficit equal to more than half of its entire budget. So great was the impact of the financial calamity, however, that even the most responsible state governments experienced serious difficulties. The states, taken together, faced $125 billion in budget deficits for fiscal year 2012.

THE STATES REACT

Unlike the federal government, most states have a balanced budget requirement written into their constitutions. As a result, there are limits to how much they can borrow, and for how long. Despite these limits, however, state governments were under great pressure to borrow as much as they could in the hope that they could pay back the sums when the economy improved. Many states proved to be remarkably ingenious in finding ways around their constitutional limits.

State and local governments reacted to the budget deficits with dramatic steps. Funds for schools, colleges, and health care were slashed. Some communities even closed schools or libraries. For fiscal year 2012, state governments spent 9.4 percent less than they did in 2008, adjusted for inflation. From January 2009 through the end of 2011, state and local government employment shrunk by 625,000 jobs, and additional losses followed in 2012. Some economists believed that cuts to state spending and employment were an important reason why the economy was so sluggish in 2011, although others disagreed.

Some states also raised tax rates—total revenue from state sales taxes increased by several percent after 2010. In contrast, several Republican governors newly elected in 2010 actually cut tax rates, hoping to boost economic growth but potentially creating additional budget problems. In 2012, the states faced an additional complication. From 2009 to 2011, the federal government supported the states through President Obama's 2009 stimulus package. By 2012, these funds were no longer available.

FOR CRITICAL ANALYSIS

Is the federal government under any obligation to aid state governments that find themselves in financial difficulty? Why or why not?

(© kyoshino / iStockphoto) (© Evelyn Peyton / iStockphoto)

Feeling the Pressure—The Strings Attached to Federal Grants. No dollars sent to the states are completely free of "strings." All funds come with requirements that must be met by the states. Often, through the use of grants, the national government has been able to exercise substantial control over matters that traditionally have been under the purview of state governments. When the federal government gives federal funds for highway improvements, for example, it may condition the funds on the state's cooperation with a federal policy. This is exactly what the federal government did in the 1980s and 1990s to force the states to raise their minimum alcoholic beverage drinking age to twenty-one.

Such carrot-and-stick tactics have been used as a form of coercion in recent years as well. In 2002, for example, President George W. Bush signed the No Child Left Behind (NCLB) Act into law. Under the NCLB, Bush promised billions of dollars to the states to bolster their education budgets. The funds would only be delivered, however, if states agreed to hold schools accountable on standardized tests. Education traditionally had been under state control, and the conditions for receiving NCLB funds effectively stripped the states of some autonomy in creating standards for public schools.

Federal Mandate
A requirement in federal legislation that forces states and municipalities to comply with certain rules.

Federal Mandates. For years, the federal government has passed legislation requiring that states improve environmental conditions or the civil rights of various groups. Since the 1970s, the national government has enacted hundreds of **federal mandates** requiring the states to take some action in areas ranging from voter registration, to ocean-dumping restrictions, to the education of people with disabilities. The Unfunded Mandates Reform Act of 1995 requires the Congressional Budget Office to identify mandates that cost state and local governments more than $50 million to implement. Nonetheless, the federal government routinely continues to pass mandates for state and local governments that cost more than that to put into place. For example, the National Conference of State Legislatures has identified federal mandates to the states in transportation, health care, education, environment, homeland security, election laws, and other areas with a total cost of $29 billion per year. Water-quality mandates appear to be particularly expensive.

One way in which the national government has moderated the burden of federal mandates is by granting *waivers,* which allow individual states to try out innovative approaches to carrying out the mandates. For example, Oregon received a waiver to experiment with a new method of rationing health-care services under the federally mandated Medicaid program.

Competitive Federalism. When state governments have authority in a particular field, there may be great variations from state to state in how they exercise that authority. Such differentials can lead to a competition among the states, which has been called *competitive federalism.* For example, it is widely believed that major corporations are more likely to establish new operations in states with a "favorable business climate." Such a climate could result from state spending on roads and other infrastructure, a well-educated workforce, and other amenities. More often, a favorable business climate means low taxes on businesses and on the executives who run those businesses.

Always and everywhere, citizens tend to favor ample government services, even as they resist the taxes necessary to fund those services. Fiscal problems can be more severe than usual in bad economic times, as just explained in this chapter's *Politics and Economics* feature. State governments can experience fiscal difficulties even in times of economic growth, however, and competitive federalism adds to the pressures. To bridge the gap between demanded services and available revenues, some states have failed to put aside enough revenue to fund state employee pensions adequately. We discuss the pensions issue in this chapter's *Which Side Are You On?* feature on the following page.

The Politics of Federalism

■ Learning Outcome 7: **Explain the accomplishments of national authority and the arguments for reemphasizing states' rights.**

As we have observed, the allocation of powers between the national and state governments continues to be a major issue. We look here at some further aspects of the ongoing conflict between national authority and states' rights in our federal system.

What Has National Authority Accomplished?

Why is it that conservatives have favored the states and liberals have favored the national government? One answer is that throughout American history, the expansion of national authority typically has been an engine of social change. Far more than the states, the national government has been willing to alter the status quo. The expansion of national authority during the Civil War freed the slaves—a major social revolution. During the New Deal, the expansion of national authority meant unprecedented levels of government intervention in the economy. In both the Civil War and the New Deal eras, support for states' rights was a method of opposing these changes and supporting the status quo.

Another example of the use of national power to change society occurred during the presidency of Lyndon B. Johnson (1963–1969). Johnson oversaw the greatest expansion of national authority since the New Deal. Under Johnson, a series of civil rights acts forced the states to grant African Americans equal treatment under the law. Crucially, these acts included the abolition of all measures designed to prevent African Americans from voting. Johnson's

Which Side Are You On?

ARE STATE AND LOCAL GOVERNMENT PENSIONS TOO GENEROUS?

(© kyoshino / iStockphoto) (© Dean Mitchell / iStockphoto)

It's well known that government employees—whether they work for federal, state, or local governments—receive better benefits than most people employed by private businesses. That includes pension benefits. Recently, articles in *USA Today* and other publications claimed that state governments had incurred at least a trillion dollars in unfunded pension liabilities. After the 2010 elections, a number of Republican governors and state legislatures went on the warpath against state employees and state employee pensions in particular. This raises the question: Do state and local government workers, in fact, receive pensions that are too generous?

PUBLIC SECTOR WORKERS ARE THE NEW ELITE

Those who believe that state and local government employees are getting too good of a deal say that these workers have better pay, benefits, vacations, and job security than workers employed in the private sector. Many state and local government employees retire earlier than their counterparts in the private sector. Above all, their pension benefits are considerably more generous than in the private sector. Government employees typically have "defined benefit" plans under which their pension income is guaranteed. Private-sector workers more often have "defined contribution" plans, under which their benefits can rise and fall with the stock market.

Often, state employees receive a promotion during their last year of work to ensure that their annual pension payments are greater. Unless you are a chief executive officer, that won't happen in the private sector. Take California as one example. In recent years, spending on retirement benefits has grown at three times the rate of state revenues. The cost now exceeds $6 billion annually. The result: fewer taxpayer dollars for public schools, higher education, and highways. It is unfair that government workers get a better deal than the rest of us.

PENSIONS AREN'T BANKRUPTING THE STATES

Those who support government workers agree that many state and local governments provide generous compensation to their employees. But those employees on average perform tasks that require more education than the average employee in the private sector. Professors, teachers, health-care workers, and even police officers need to be well educated or trained. Nationwide, current state and local pension payments are about 3 percent of total spending. Unless a government is very badly managed (admittedly, some are), pensions shouldn't "break the bank."

Many pension plans were underfunded recently for a good reason. When the stock market tanked in 2008, so did the value of the funds set aside for pensions. Still, overall, state and local pensions are almost 80 percent funded. Workers do not all retire at the same time, and pension funds are not all drawn down at once. On average, state and local governments can pay out benefits for the next fifteen years *without making additional contributions to pension funds.* Of course, state and local governments will be adding to the pension funds year by year. Most states also require that employees contribute to their own plans.

We shouldn't be worrying that government employee pensions are too generous. Rather, we should be trying to improve pensions of ordinary workers in the private sector.

Great Society and War on Poverty programs resulted in major increases in spending by the national government. As before, states' rights were invoked to support the status quo—states' rights meant no action on civil rights and no increase in antipoverty spending.

The "New Federalism"

Devolution
The transfer of powers from a national or central government to a state or local government.

In the years after 1968, the **devolution** of power from the national government to the states became a major ideological theme for the Republican Party. Republican president Richard Nixon (1969–1974) advocated what he called a "New Federalism" that would devolve authority from the national government to the states. In part, the New Federalism involved the conversion of categorical grants into block grants, thereby giving state governments greater flexibility in spending. A second part of Nixon's New Federalism was *revenue sharing.* Under the revenue-sharing plan, the national government provided direct, unconditional financial support to state and local governments.

Nixon was able to obtain only a limited number of block grants from Congress. The block grants he did obtain, plus revenue sharing, substantially increased financial support to state governments. Republican president Ronald Reagan (1981–1989) was also a strong advocate of federalism, but some of his policies withdrew certain financial support from the states. Reagan was more successful than Nixon in obtaining block grants, but Reagan's block grants, unlike Nixon's, were less generous to the states than the categorical grants they replaced. Under Reagan, revenue sharing was eliminated. You can see the results of these actions in Figure 3–3 on page 97.

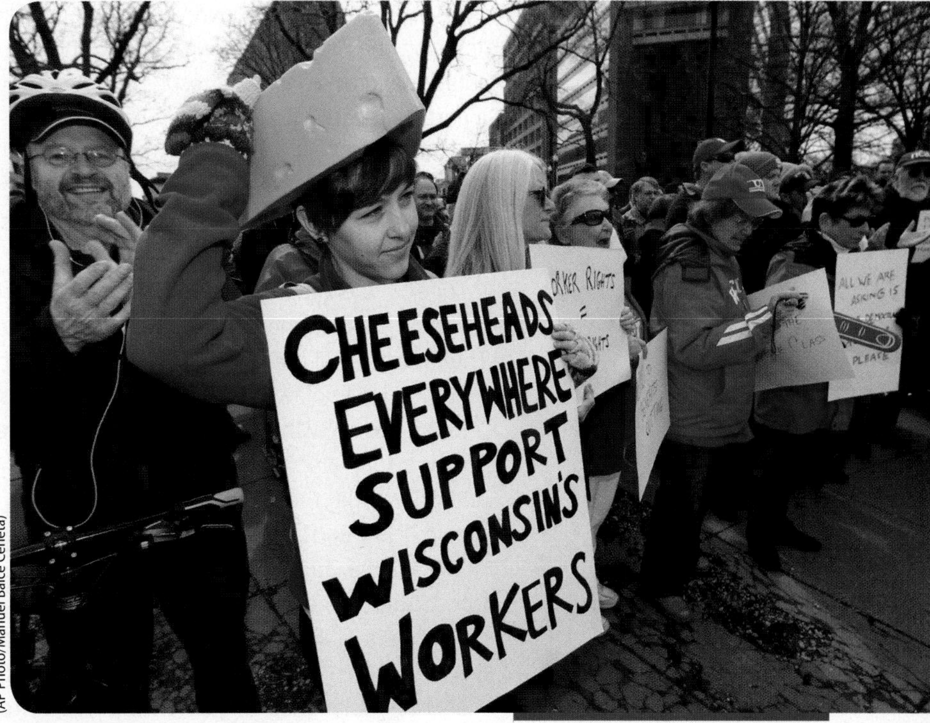

During the continuing economic downturn in the early 2010s, some states attempted to reduce spending. Those affected showed their displeasure (here in Wisconsin). Why wouldn't the federal government just make up any state budget shortfalls, which it had done a few years earlier?

Federalism Today

In recent years, it has not been clear whether competing theories of federalism divide the Republicans from the Democrats at all, at least in practice. Consider that the passage of welfare reform legislation in 1996, which involved transferring significant control over welfare programs to the states, took place under Democratic president Bill Clinton (1993–2001). In contrast, under Republican president George W. Bush, Congress enacted the No Child Left Behind Act of 2001, which was signed into law in 2002. This act increased federal control over education and educational funding, which had traditionally been under the purview of state governments.

Beginning in 2009, however, conservative activists began to rediscover states' rights. One reason may be that in that year the Democrats added the presidency to their control of the U.S. House and Senate. Republicans were shut out at the national level. The ambitious program of the Obama administration also alarmed conservatives. Obama's initiatives generally involved greater federal control of the private sector, not of state and local governments. Still, many conservatives hoped that the states could be a counterweight to the newly active national government.

Federalism and Today's Supreme Court

■ Learning Outcome 8: **Detail recent Supreme Court rulings that affect the distribution of power between the national government and the states.**

The United States Supreme Court, which normally has the final say on constitutional issues, plays a major role in determining where the line is drawn between federal and state powers. Consider the decisions rendered by Chief Justice John Marshall in the cases discussed earlier in this chapter. Since the 1930s, Marshall's broad interpretation of the commerce clause has made it possible for the national government to justify its regulation of almost any activity, even when the activity appears to be completely local in character. In the 1990s and 2000s, however, the Court has evidenced a willingness to impose some limits on the national government's authority under the commerce clause and other constitutional provisions. As a result, it is difficult to predict how today's Court might rule on a particular case involving federalism.

The Trend toward States' Rights

Since the mid-1990s, the Supreme Court has tended to give greater weight to states' rights than it did during previous decades. In a widely publicized 1995 case, *United States v. Lopez,*[10] the Supreme Court held that Congress had exceeded its constitutional authority under the commerce clause when it passed the Gun-Free School Zones Act in 1990. The Court stated that the act, which banned the possession of guns within one thousand feet of any school, was unconstitutional because it attempted to regulate an area that had "nothing to do with commerce, or any sort of economic enterprise." This marked the first time in sixty years that the Supreme Court had placed a limit on the national government's authority under the commerce clause.

In 1999 and in the first decade of the 2000s, the Court also issued decisions that bolstered the authority of state governments under the Eleventh Amendment to the Constitution. The cases involved employees and others who sought redress for state-government violations of federal laws regulating employment. The Court held that the Eleventh Amendment, in most circumstances, precludes lawsuits against state governments for violations of rights established by federal laws unless the states consent to be sued.[11] Additionally, the Court supported states' rights under the Tenth Amendment in 1977 when it invalidated provisions of a federal law that required state employees to check the backgrounds of prospective handgun purchasers.[12]

The Court Sends Mixed Messages

Although the Court has tended to favor states' rights in some decisions, in other decisions it has backed the federal government's position. For example, in two cases decided in 2003 and 2004, the Court, in contrast to its earlier rulings involving the Eleventh Amendment, ruled that the amendment could not shield states from suits by individuals complaining of discrimination based on gender and disability, respectively.[13] In 2005, the Court held that the federal government's power to declare various substances to be illegal drugs superseded California's law legalizing the use of marijuana for medical treatment.[14] Yet less than a year later, the Court favored states' rights when it upheld Oregon's controversial "death with dignity" law, which allows patients with terminal illnesses to choose to end their lives early and thus alleviate suffering.[15]

Arizona Governor Jan Brewer supported a strict immigration law for her state. In 2012, the federal government challenged that law in a Supreme Court case. Were states' rights an issue?

(AP Photo/Matt York)

10. 514 U.S. 549 (1995).
11. See, for example, *Alden v. Maine,* 527 U.S. 706 (1999); and *Kimel v. Florida Board of Regents,* 528 U.S. 62 (2000).
12. *Printz v. United States,* 521 U.S. 898 (1997).
13. *Nevada v. Hibbs,* 538 U.S. 721 (2003); and *Tennessee v. Lane,* 541 U.S. 509 (2004).
14. *Gonzales v. Raich,* 545 U.S. 1 (2005).
15. *Gonzales v. Oregon,* 546 U.S. 243 (2006).

Recent Rulings on States' Rights

As noted, since President Obama took office conservatives have taken a greater interest in states' rights. A growing number of such cases have been brought before the Supreme Court. In its rulings, the Court has shown a degree of sympathy for states' rights. Yet, it has rejected arguments that would transform the relationship between the states and the federal government.

In one important opinion, the Court found that Arizona had gone too far in its attempt to subject unauthorized immigration to state authority. Under the ruling, Arizona cannot make it a crime when illegal immigrants fail to carry identification papers or attempt to find work. Arizona police cannot arrest individuals solely on suspicion of illegal status.[16]

It was the Court's opinion on the Affordable Care Act, though, that was expected to be the most important states' rights ruling in decades. In the end, the Court's verdict was somewhat anti-climactic—it did not find that Obamacare violated the police powers of the states. Chief Justice Roberts's ruling on Medicaid expansion did hearten states' rights advocates, however. By making Medicaid expansion optional for the states, the Court for the first time put limits on the ability of the federal government to coerce states by withholding grants.[17]

16. *Arizona v. United States,* ___ U.S. ___, 132 S.Ct. 2492, 183 L.Ed.2d 351 (2012).
17. *National Federation of Independent Business v. Sebelius,* ___ U.S. ___, 132 S.Ct. 2566, 183 L.Ed.2d 450 (2012).

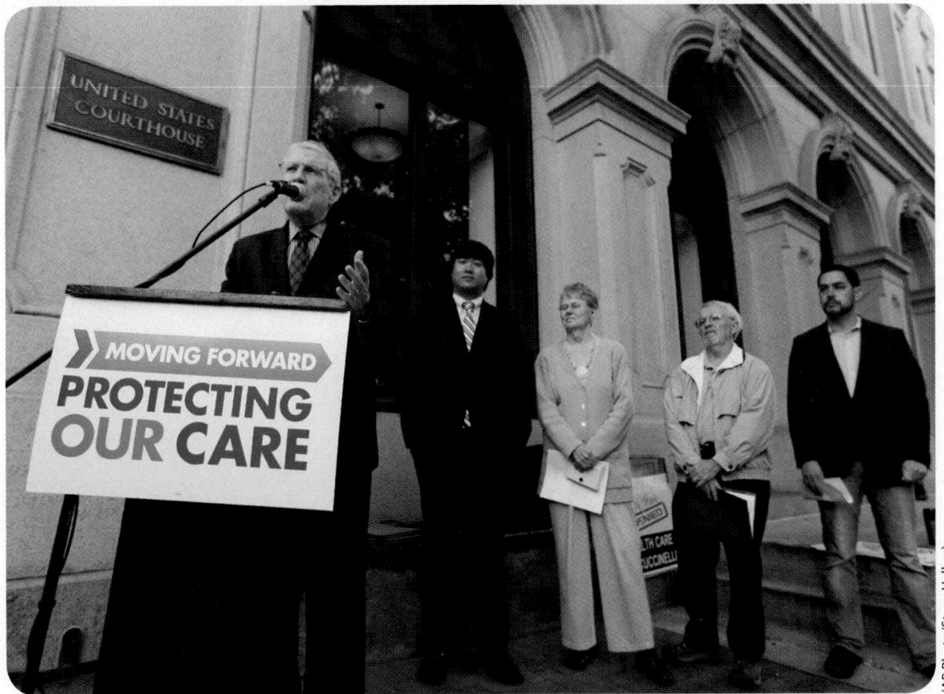

(AP Photo/Steve Helber)

Supporters of President Obama's health-care policies hold a rally in front of federal court in Richmond, Virginia. Overall, was Obamacare popular or unpopular?

Why Should You Care about... THE FEDERAL SYSTEM?

(© Liv Friis-Larsen, 2008. Used under license from Shutterstock.com)

Why should you, personally, care about the federal system? The system encourages debate over whether a particular issue should be a national, state, or local question. Many questions are, in fact, state or local ones, and it is easier for you to make a significant contribution to the discussion on these issues. Even in the largest states, there are many fewer people to persuade than in the nation as a whole. Attempts to influence your fellow citizens can therefore be more effective.

THE FEDERAL SYSTEM AND YOUR LIFE

In this chapter, we have mentioned a variety of issues arising from our federal system that may concern you directly. Although the national government provides aid to educational programs, education is still primarily a state and local responsibility. The total amount of money spent on education is determined by state and local governments. Therefore, you can address this issue at the state or local level. Gambling laws are another state responsibility. Do you enjoy gambling—or do you believe that the effects of gambling make it a social disaster? State law—or state negotiations with American Indian tribes—determines the availability of gambling.

HOW YOU CAN MAKE A DIFFERENCE

In our modern era, the number of ways in which you can communicate your opinion is vast. You can post a response on any of thousands of blogs. You could develop your own mini-video and post it on YouTube. Politicians use Facebook and Twitter to organize their supporters and often have thousands of online "friends." This can provide you with the opportunity to present your views to someone who might be able to act on them.

If you want to effect policy change at the state or local level, however, the local newspaper, in both its paper and its online formats, continues to be essential. Blogs, YouTube, and other online venues tend to be nationally and even internationally oriented. Most newspapers, however, are resolutely local and are the natural hub for discussions of local issues. Most papers allow responses and comments on their Web sites, and you can make a point by contributing in that fashion. Nothing, however, will win you a wider audience than an old-fashioned letter to the editor. Use the following rules to compose an effective communication:

1. Use a computer, and double-space the lines. Use a spelling checker and grammar checker.
2. Include a lead topic sentence that is short, to the point, and powerful.
3. Keep your thoughts on target—choose only one topic to discuss. Make sure it is newsworthy and timely.
4. Make sure your communication is concise; never let it exceed a page and a half in length (double-spaced).
5. If you know that facts were misstated or left out in current news stories about your topic, supply the facts. The public wants to know.
6. Don't be afraid to express moral judgments. You can go a long way by appealing to the reader's sense of justice.
7. Personalize the communication by bringing in your own experiences, if possible.
8. If you are writing a letter, sign it and give your address (including your e-mail address) and your telephone number. Comments posted to blogs and other communications may have their own rules for identifying yourself; follow them.
9. If writing a letter, send or e-mail it to the editorial office of the newspaper of your choice. Almost all publications now have e-mail addresses. Their Web sites usually give information on where you can send mail.

Questions for Discussion and Analysis

1. Review the *Which Side Are You On?* feature on page 100. Do you believe that state government employees are indeed an overpaid labor aristocracy—or do attacks on state employees' compensation divert us from focusing on the true aristocracy, the wealthiest 1 percent? In either case, why?

2. Some members of the Tea Party movement have advocated repealing the Seventeenth Amendment, which provides for electing U.S. senators by popular vote. If the amendment were repealed, state legislatures would choose each state's senators. Advocates of repeal argue that it would strengthen the power of the states within the federal system. Are they right—and would such a change have good or bad consequences? Explain.

3. Traditionally, conservatives have favored states' rights and liberals have favored national authority. Can you think of modern-day issues in which these long-standing preferences might be reversed, with conservatives favoring national authority and liberals favoring states' rights? Explain.

4. Sometimes, state and local governments take action in areas that are normally considered to be the responsibility of the national government. Immigration is one example. A few localities, such as San Francisco and New Haven, Connecticut, have taken measures to protect unauthorized immigrants (also known as illegal immigrants or undocumented workers). A greater number have taken a more negative approach. Arizona and Alabama, for example, have passed laws that severely penalize undocumented workers. Critics of such laws argue that they generate discrimination against Hispanics who are citizens or legal residents. How might this happen?

Key Terms

Chapter Summary

1. There are three basic models for ordering relations between central governments and local units: (a) a unitary system (in which ultimate power is held by the national government), (b) a confederal system (in which ultimate power is retained by the states), and (c) a federal system (in which governmental powers are divided between the national government and the states).

2. The Constitution expressly grants certain powers to the national government in Article I, Section 8. In addition to these enumerated powers, the national government has implied and inherent powers. Implied powers are those that are reasonably necessary to carry out the powers expressly delegated to the national government. Inherent powers are those held by the national government by virtue of its being a sovereign state with the right to preserve itself.

3. The Tenth Amendment to the Constitution states that powers not delegated to the United States by the Constitution, nor prohibited by it to the states, are reserved to the states, or to the people. In certain areas, the Constitution provides for concurrent powers (such as the power to tax), which are powers that are held jointly by the national and state governments. The Constitution also denies certain powers to both the national government and the states.

4. The supremacy clause of the Constitution states that the Constitution, congressional laws, and national treaties are the supreme law of the land. States cannot use their reserved or concurrent powers to override national policies.

5. Chief Justice John Marshall's expansive interpretation of the necessary and proper clause of the Constitution in *McCulloch v. Maryland* (1819), along with his affirmation of the supremacy clause, enhanced the power of the national government. Marshall's broad interpretation of the commerce clause in *Gibbons v. Ogden* (1824) further extended the powers of the national government.

6. The controversy over slavery that led to the Civil War took the form of a fight over national government supremacy versus the rights of the separate states. Since the Civil War,

federalism has evolved through at least two general phases: dual federalism and cooperative federalism. In dual federalism, each of the states and the federal government remain supreme within their own spheres. The era since the Great Depression has sometimes been labeled one of cooperative federalism, in which states and the national government cooperate in solving complex common problems.

7. Categorical grants from the federal government to state governments help finance many projects. By attaching special conditions to federal grants, the national government can effect policy changes in areas typically governed by the states. Block grants usually have fewer strings attached, thus giving state and local governments more flexibility in using the funds. Federal mandates—laws requiring states to implement certain policies—have generated controversy.

8. Traditionally, conservatives have favored states' rights, and liberals have favored national authority. In part, this is because the national government has historically been an engine of change.

Quiz Multiple Choice

1. The United States has the following system of government:
   a. **a unitary system.**
   b. **a confederal system.**
   c. **a federal system.**

2. One reason the founders chose a federal system is that:
   a. **there were no supporters of states' rights.**
   b. **at the time of the Constitutional Convention the United States was already large geographically and it would have been difficult to govern just from the national capital.**
   c. **the thirteen states were smaller geographically than France, so a federal system was appropriate.**

3. The enumerated powers of the national government do not include:
   a. **setting standards for weights and measures.**
   b. **the regulation of commerce among the states.**
   c. **the creation of a national school system.**

4. When both the national government and the state governments share certain powers, we call them:
   a. **prevailing powers.**
   b. **concurrent powers.**
   c. **constitutional powers.**

5. In the Supreme Court case of *McCulloch v. Maryland* (1819), the Court clearly established:
   a. **that the Constitution is the supreme law of the land.**
   b. **that state governments can tax the national government.**
   c. **that the national government can tax the state governments.**

6. The powers of the national government greatly increased during:
   a. **the time of Andrew Jackson's presidency.**
   b. **the period following the Civil War.**
   c. **the period of the Great Depression and Roosevelt's New Deal.**

7. When the federal (national) government sends dollars to state governments, those funds:
   a. **are given without any restrictions.**
   b. **are to be returned to the federal government at a later date.**
   c. **come with many "strings" attached.**

8. Competitive federalism occurs when:
   a. **the federal government sets different standards for different states.**
   b. **state governments decide differently how to exercise their authority.**
   c. **state governments compete to see how quickly they can meet federal mandates.**

ANSWERS: 1. c, 2. b, 3. c, 4. b, 5. a, 6. c, 7. c, 8. b.

Quiz Fill-Ins

9. In a federal system, individuals can express their likes and dislikes for state government policies by "voting __________ __________ __________."

10. The necessary and proper clause is sometimes called __________ __________.

11. The reserved powers that the national government cannot deny to the states are referenced in the __________ Amendment.

12. The Constitution denies a number of powers to the national government. These are called the __________ __________.

13. Each state must give full __________ and __________ to other states' public acts, records, and judicial proceedings.

14. The U.S. Supreme Court case of *Gibbons v. Ogden* (1824) involved regulation of __________ commerce.

15. Dual federalism ended with the __________ __________.

16. When Congress passes a law requiring that the states do certain things, this is called a __________ __________.

17. When monies are raised through taxation or borrowing by the national government but then spent by the state governments, this is an example of __________ __________.

18. __________ __________ are not enumerated in the Constitution, but are derived from the fact that the United States is a sovereign power among nations.

ANSWERS: 9. with their feet, 10. elastic clause, 11. Tenth, 12. prohibited powers, 13. faith, credit, 14. interstate, 15. New Deal, 16. federal mandate, 17. fiscal federalism, 18. inherent powers.

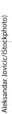

Selected Print & Media Resources

SUGGESTED READINGS

Gerston, Larry N. *American Federalism: A Concise Introduction.* Armonk, N.Y.: M. E. Sharpe, 2007. Gerston, a Cengage author, is a political science professor at San José State University. His survey of federalism focuses on the struggle for power among various levels of government.

Ryan, Erin. *Federalism and the Tug of War Within.* New York: Oxford University Press, 2012. Ryan, a law professor at the College of William & Mary, explores how inconsistent Supreme Court decisions have created problems for the federal system. Her examples include Court decisions involving Hurricane Katrina, environmental law, and health-care reform.

Simon, Scott. *Windy City: A Novel of Politics.* New York: Random House Trade Paperbacks, 2009. The mayor of Chicago is dead, face down in a pizza, and Alderman Sundaran "Sunny" Roopini, the interim mayor, has more than one problem on his hands. Simon's comic novel portrays the gritty urban politics of Illinois.

Van Overtveldt, Johan. *The End of the Euro: The Uneasy Future of the European Union.* Evanston, Ill.: Agate Publishing, 2011. Van Overtveldt describes how the European monetary union was flawed from the start. In addition to depicting the crisis in borrowing countries such as Greece and Spain, he explains the reactions of Germany, the continent's largest lender. Van Overtveldt is the editor of *Trends,* a European business weekly.

MEDIA RESOURCES

The Civil War—The PBS documentary series that made director Ken Burns famous. *The Civil War,* first shown in 1990, marked a revolution in documentary technique. Photographs, letters, eyewitness memoirs, and music are used to bring the war to life. The DVD version was released in 2002.

Street Fight—A 2005 documentary by Marshall Curry, this film chronicles the unsuccessful attempt by young City Council member Cory Booker to unseat longtime Newark mayor Sharpe James in 2002. Curry captures on film James's abuse of police and code enforcement officers to sabotage Booker's campaign. In 2006, the voters elected Booker mayor of Newark. In 2008, James was sentenced to twenty-seven months in prison on corruption charges.

(© PashaIgnatov/iStockphoto)

E-mocracy HOW TO FIND COURT CASES ONLINE

As you have learned in this chapter, the federal courts have a major impact on how federalism has been interpreted and implemented in the United States. Beginning with this chapter and continuing through the rest of the text, you will find many references to court cases, typically ones decided by the United States Supreme Court. An excellent way to find out more about the role of the courts in the American system is to learn about key cases.

You'll notice in the footnotes that refer to cases that there is a standard format for citing them. Consider *New State Ice Co. v. Liebmann,* which is cited on page 86. In addition to the name of the case, the citation includes the rather mysterious term "285 U.S. 262 (1932)." This case was decided by the United States Supreme Court in 1932, and "U.S." is an abbreviation for *United States Reports,* the official edition of the decisions of the Supreme Court; "285" is the volume number, and "262" is the page number on which the decision begins.

There's no need for you to track down these large, dusty volumes when you want to investigate cases, however. Important cases are easy to find on the Web. The cases referred to in this text are almost always famous, and you can find dozens of reports on them simply by typing the name of the case into a search engine such as Google.

Two kinds of results are likely to appear when you employ a search engine. One is the text of the Court's decision. Dozens of sites carry the text of an important case. If you want to read the text, you might find that Findlaw.com does a good job of formatting cases so that they are easy to read. In addition, the search engine will locate articles describing the case and its importance. Wikipedia, for example, has articles on most important cases. You might find it useful to read one or more of these articles first—and then if you want to delve deeper, you can read the Court's decision.

Sometimes, the name of the case is not enough to locate it. What if the name is *United States v. Johnson?* Twelve cases by that name are important enough to merit articles in Wikipedia. If you are searching for such a case, you'll want to enter the full citation into the search engine—for example, "*United States v. Johnson* 457 U.S. 537 (1982)."

LOGGING ON

The Web offers a variety of sites that allow you to learn more about our federal form of government and about current issues relating to federalism.

1. You can access the *Federalist Papers* online to learn the founders' views on federalism. If you enter "federalist papers" into your favorite search engine, you'll find at least a half-dozen collections of the papers on the first results page alone.
2. For the constitutions of other nations, search on "national constitutions." You'll be offered several portals that link to world constitutions. Wikipedia is one option, but you might prefer the constitution finder sponsored by the University of Richmond instead.
3. Two organizations that provide information on state governments and federal–state relations are the Council of State Governments (CSG) and the National Governors Association (NGA). You can find the Web site of each body by searching on its acronym, "csg" or "nga." (You'll also see sites of other organizations with the same acronyms, but the two state government coalitions should be among the top results.)
4. To find opinion pieces on federalism, you can consult two organizations that have very different political views—the Brookings Institution and the Cato Institute. Simply search on "brookings" or "cato." When you reach the home page of either organization, type "federalism" into the search box to bring up a list of articles.

It's About
Freedom!
CORRECTIONS
OCSEA
OHIO

4 Civil Liberties

The eight learning outcomes below are designed to help improve your understanding of this chapter. After reading this chapter, you should be able to:

- Learning Outcome 1: **Describe the Bill of Rights and how it came to be applied to state governments as well as the national government.**
- Learning Outcome 2: **Explain how the First Amendment's establishment clause and free exercise clause guarantee our freedom of religion.**
- Learning Outcome 3: **Specify the limited circumstances, including obscenity and slander, in which governments may override the principle of free speech.**
- Learning Outcome 4: **Define *libel*, and depict how freedom of the press has been extended to new media.**
- Learning Outcome 5: **Provide the constitutional basis of the right to privacy, and explain how the principle has been applied to the abortion and right-to-die controversies.**
- Learning Outcome 6: **Cite examples of how recent security concerns have affected the civil liberties of immigrants and Americans generally.**
- Learning Outcome 7: **Identify the constitutional rights of those who are accused of a crime, and describe the *Miranda* and exclusionary rules.**
- Learning Outcome 8: **Discuss whether or not the death penalty is a cruel and unusual punishment and the extent to which the penalty is in use today.**

These union members and supporters express their views in Columbus, Ohio. Freedom of speech and the right to peaceful assembly are key liberties that all Americans enjoy. (Jim West/Report Digital-REA/Redux)

(Shawn Thew/Epa/Landov)

A PRO-CHOICE PROTESTER debates with a pro-life protester at the Supreme Court during the annual March for Life in Washington, D.C.

What if... *ROE V. WADE* WERE OVERTURNED?

BACKGROUND

The Bill of Rights and other provisions of the U.S. Constitution are the ultimate protections of our civil rights and liberties. But how do these rights work in practice? How do we determine what our rights are in any given situation? One way is through *judicial review,* the power of the United States Supreme Court or other courts to declare laws and other acts of government unconstitutional.

Supreme Court cases are often hotly contested, and the decision in the 1973 case *Roe v. Wade* is one of the most contentious ever handed down. In the *Roe v. Wade* case, the Court declared that a woman's constitutionally protected right to privacy includes the right to have an abortion. The Court concluded that the states cannot restrict a woman's right to an abortion during the first three months of pregnancy. Forty years later, however, the debate over the legality of abortion still rages in the United States.

WHAT IF *ROE V. WADE* WERE OVERTURNED?

If the Supreme Court overturned *Roe v. Wade,* the authority to regulate abortion would fall again to the states. Before the *Roe v. Wade* case, each state decided whether abortion would be legal within its borders. State legislatures made the laws that covered abortion.

Simply overturning *Roe v. Wade* would not make abortion in the United States illegal overnight. In many states, abortion rights are very popular, and the legislatures in those states would not consider measures to ban abortion or to further restrict access to abortion. Some states have laws that would protect abortion rights even if *Roe v. Wade* were overturned. Access to abortions would likely continue in the West Coast states and in much of the Northeast. In most of the South and parts of the Midwest, however, abortion could be seriously restricted or even banned.

Already, twenty-six states require a waiting period between when a woman receives counseling and when the procedure is performed. Nineteen states require counseling that includes information generally considered to be incorrect by the medical profession, such as the proposition that abortions can cause breast cancer. Some states have "trigger laws" that would immediately outlaw abortion if *Roe v. Wade* were overturned.

Women living in conservative states such as the Dakotas, Kentucky, and Mississippi already face serious difficulties in obtaining an abortion. In each of these states, 98 percent of the counties do not have an abortion clinic. Many women desiring the procedure already have to travel long distances at considerable personal expense. Still, if abortion were banned, these women could cross state lines to obtain an abortion. If twenty-one of the most conservative states banned abortion, only 170 providers would be affected—less than 10 percent of the national total. It is also probable that if states could outlaw abortion, most existing state laws restricting the procedure would become irrelevant. The states that have passed such laws are generally the same states that would make abortion illegal.

FOR CRITICAL ANALYSIS

1. *Why do you think that abortion has remained a contentious topic for the forty years since the* Roe v. Wade *decision? Should that decision be revisited? Why or why not?*
2. *How significant a role should the courts play in deciding constitutional questions about abortion? Do you feel that individual states should have a say in the legality of abortion within their own borders? Why or why not?*

"The land of the free." When asked what makes the United States distinctive, Americans will commonly say that it is a free country. Americans have long believed that limits on the power of government are an essential part of what makes this country free. Recall from Chapter 1 that restraints on the actions of government against individuals are generally referred to as *civil liberties.* The first ten amendments to the U.S. Constitution—the Bill of Rights—place such restraints on the national government. Of these amendments, none is more famous than the First Amendment, which guarantees freedom of religion, speech, and the press, as well as other rights.

Most other democratic nations have laws to protect these and other civil liberties, but none of the laws is quite like the First Amendment. Take the issue of "hate speech." What if someone makes statements that stir up hatred toward a particular race or other group of people? In Germany, where memories of Nazi anti-Semitism remain alive, such speech is unquestionably illegal. In the United States, the issue is not so clear. The courts have often extended constitutional protection to this kind of speech.

In this chapter, we describe the civil liberties provided by the Bill of Rights and some of the controversies that surround them. We initially look at the First Amendment. We also discuss the right to privacy, which is at the heart of the abortion issue introduced in the *What If . . .* feature that opened this chapter. We also examine the rights of defendants in criminal cases.

The Bill of Rights

■ Learning Outcome 1: **Describe the Bill of Rights and how it came to be applied to state governments as well as the national government.**

As you read through this chapter, bear in mind that the Bill of Rights, like the rest of the Constitution, is relatively brief. The framers set forth broad guidelines, leaving it up to the courts to interpret these constitutional mandates and apply them to specific situations. Thus, judicial interpretations shape the true nature of the civil liberties and rights that we possess. Because judicial interpretations change over time, so do our liberties and rights. As you will read in the following pages, there have been many conflicts over the meaning of such simple phrases as *freedom of religion* and *freedom of the press.*

To understand what freedoms we actually have, we need to examine how the courts—and particularly the United States Supreme Court—have resolved some of those conflicts. One important conflict was over the issue of whether the Bill of Rights in the federal Constitution limited the powers of state governments as well as those of the national government.

Extending the Bill of Rights to State Governments

Many citizens do not realize that, as originally intended, the Bill of Rights limited only the powers of the national government. At the time the Bill of Rights was ratified, there was little concern over the potential of state governments to curb civil liberties. For one thing, state governments were closer to home and easier to control. For another, most state constitutions already had bills of rights. Rather, the fear was of the potential tyranny of the national government. The Bill of Rights begins with the words, "Congress shall make no law . . . ." It says nothing about states making laws that might abridge citizens' civil liberties. In 1833, in *Barron v. Baltimore,*[1] the United States Supreme Court held that the Bill of Rights did not apply to state laws.

We mentioned that most states had bills of rights. These bills of rights were similar to the national one, but there were some differences. Furthermore, each state's judicial system interpreted the rights differently. Citizens in different states, therefore, effectively had different sets of civil liberties. It was not until after the Fourteenth Amendment was

1. 32 U.S. 243 (1833).

ratified in 1868 that civil liberties guaranteed by the national Constitution began to be applied to the states. Section 1 of that amendment provides, in part, as follows:

> *No State shall . . . deprive any person of life, liberty, or property, without due process of law . . .*

Incorporation of the Fourteenth Amendment

There was no question that the Fourteenth Amendment applied to state governments. For decades, however, the courts were reluctant to define the liberties spelled out in the national Bill of Rights as constituting "due process of law," which was protected under the Fourteenth Amendment. Not until 1925, in *Gitlow v. New York*,[2] did the United States Supreme Court hold that the Fourteenth Amendment protected the freedom of speech guaranteed by the First Amendment to the Constitution from state infringement.

Only gradually did the Supreme Court accept the **incorporation theory**—the view that most of the protections of the Bill of Rights are incorporated into the Fourteenth Amendment's protection against state government actions. Table 4–1 below shows the rights that the Court has incorporated into the Fourteenth Amendment and the case in

2. 268 U.S. 652 (1925).

Social Media IN POLITICS

Two organizations of interest when studying civil liberties issues are the Civil Liberties Defense Center (CLDC), which you can find by searching on "civil liberties" in Facebook, and the National Rifle Association (NRA), which you can locate by entering "nra."

Incorporation Theory
The view that most of the protections of the Bill of Rights apply to state governments through the Fourteenth Amendment's due process clause.

Table 4–1 ▸ Incorporating the Bill of Rights into the Fourteenth Amendment

Year	Issue	Amendment Involved	Court Case
1925	Freedom of speech	I	*Gitlow v. New York*, 268 U.S. 652.
1931	Freedom of the press	I	*Near v. Minnesota*, 283 U.S. 697.
1932	Right to a lawyer in capital punishment cases	VI	*Powell v. Alabama*, 287 U.S. 45.
1937	Freedom of assembly and right to petition	I	*De Jonge v. Oregon*, 299 U.S. 353.
1940	Freedom of religion	I	*Cantwell v. Connecticut*, 310 U.S. 296.
1947	Separation of church and state	I	*Everson v. Board of Education*, 330 U.S. 1.
1948	Right to a public trial	VI	*In re Oliver*, 333 U.S. 257.
1949	No unreasonable searches and seizures	IV	*Wolf v. Colorado*, 338 U.S. 25.
1961	Exclusionary rule	IV	*Mapp v. Ohio*, 367 U.S. 643.
1962	No cruel and unusual punishment	VIII	*Robinson v. California*, 370 U.S. 660.
1963	Right to a lawyer in all criminal felony cases	VI	*Gideon v. Wainwright*, 372 U.S. 335.
1964	No compulsory self-incrimination	V	*Malloy v. Hogan*, 378 U.S. 1.
1965	Right to privacy	I, III, IV, V, IX	*Griswold v. Connecticut*, 381 U.S. 479.
1966	Right to an impartial jury	VI	*Parker v. Gladden*, 385 U.S. 363.
1967	Right to a speedy trial	VI	*Klopfer v. North Carolina*, 386 U.S. 213.
1969	No double jeopardy	V	*Benton v. Maryland*, 395 U.S. 784.
2010	Right to bear arms	II	*McDonald v. Chicago*, 561 U.S. 3025.

which it first applied each protection. As you can see in the table, in the fifteen years following the *Gitlow* decision, the Supreme Court incorporated into the Fourteenth Amendment the other basic freedoms (of the press, assembly, the right to petition, and religion) guaranteed by the First Amendment. These and the later Supreme Court decisions listed in Table 4–1 on the facing page have bound the fifty states to accept for their citizens most of the rights and freedoms that are set forth in the U.S. Bill of Rights.

The most recent ruling that states must abide by protections listed in the Bill of Rights came in 2010. In that year, the Court stated that the freedom to bear arms specified by the Second Amendment was binding on the states. We look at some current gun rights issues in this chapter's *Which Side Are You On?* feature below.

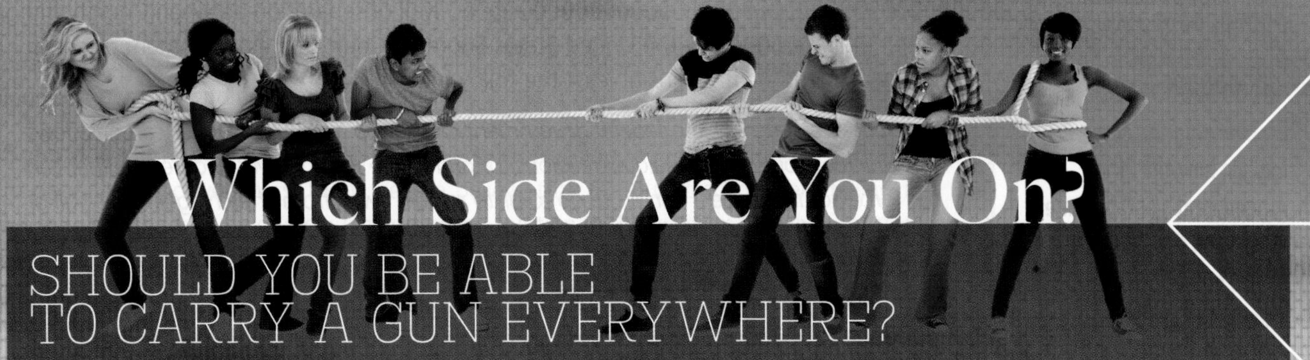

Which Side Are You On?

SHOULD YOU BE ABLE TO CARRY A GUN EVERYWHERE?

The Second Amendment to the United States Constitution provides the right to keep and bear arms. In 2008, the United States Supreme Court recognized that this was a right enjoyed by individuals, not just state militias, and that the national government may not impose complete bans on handgun possession.[a] In 2010, the Court confirmed that state and local governments also cannot impose such complete bans.[b] Gun control advocates were not happy about these decisions, but they did recognize that the Court had affirmed the legitimacy of firearms regulations, as opposed to complete bans.

The gun rights lobby, in contrast, has used these decisions as a springboard to eliminate state laws that regulate firearms. In addition, gun rights advocates have proposed federal legislation that would require every state to recognize "concealed carry" permits issued by any other state. A permit issued in Arizona would be valid in San Francisco. Should anyone who wants to carry a concealed weapon be able to do so everywhere?

IN OUR FEDERAL SYSTEM, THE STATES SHOULD DECIDE

Those who oppose nationwide recognition of state-issued concealed carry permits point out that there are reasons why different states have different laws. We expect that rural states with low population densities, such as Montana and Wyoming, will have different laws regulating firearms than will crowded urban states, such as Massachusetts and New Jersey. Rural people are more familiar with guns. Out in the country, you can hunt ducks or deer. You may need to control predators that attack chickens or other livestock. In a big city, the only thing you can shoot is another human being. Urban areas therefore need to control who can carry a concealed handgun. Not everyone should be eligible. Indeed, some states that contain both large cities and extensive rural areas, such as California and New York, allow their counties to set very different policies on concealed carry permits. If a federal law allowed anyone who obtained a concealed weapon license in Idaho to freely carry in New York City, even these laws would be swept away.

PROTECT GUN OWNERS BY PASSING UNIFORM NATIONAL LAWS

Today, Supreme Court decisions make it clear that all citizens have a fundamental right to protect themselves. Gun rights advocates contend that all individuals should be able to own and carry weapons, both openly and concealed. The different state laws that regulate concealed weapons form a very complicated patchwork. Say we had a concealed carry law at the national level. Someone who had the right to carry a concealed weapon in Kentucky would not have to worry about being arrested simply for crossing the Ohio state line. Those campaigning for a national law point out that states will still have the right to ban concealed carry altogether. (The only state that currently does so is Illinois.)

It is very desirable for a substantial number of citizens to carry concealed weapons. Criminals will then have to worry that anyone they might attack will be able to fight back. States that widely allow concealed carry have murder rates that are 30 percent lower than those of states that are more restrictive.

a. *District of Columbia v. Heller,* 554 U.S. 570 (2008).
b. *MacDonald v. Chicago,* 561 U.S. 3025 (2010).

(AP Photo/The Gleaner/Mike Lawrence)

Can middle school students say morning prayers in front of their public school?

On appeal, however, the Supreme Court ruled that the regents' action was unconstitutional because "the constitutional prohibition against laws respecting an establishment of a religion must mean at least that in this country it is no part of the business of government to compose official prayers for any group of the American people to recite as part of a religious program carried on by any government."

The Debate over School Prayer Continues. Although the Supreme Court has ruled repeatedly against officially sponsored prayer and Bible-reading sessions in public schools, other means for bringing some form of religious expression into public education have been attempted. In *Wallace v. Jaffree,*[7] the Supreme Court struck down as unconstitutional an Alabama law authorizing one minute of silence for prayer or meditation in all public schools. The Court concluded that the law violated the establishment clause because it was "an endorsement of religion lacking any clearly secular purpose."

Since then, the lower courts have interpreted the Supreme Court's decision to mean that states can require a moment of silence in the schools as long as they make it clear that the purpose of the law is secular, not religious.

Forbidding the Teaching of Evolution. For many decades, certain religious groups have opposed the teaching of evolution in the schools. To these groups, evolutionary theory directly counters their religious belief that human beings did not evolve but were created fully formed, as described in the biblical story of the creation. State and local attempts to forbid the teaching of evolution, however, have not passed constitutional muster in the eyes of the United States Supreme Court. For example, in 1968 the Supreme Court held, in *Epperson v. Arkansas,*[8] that an Arkansas law prohibiting the teaching of evolution violated the establishment clause because it imposed religious beliefs on students.

Nonetheless, state and local groups around the country continue their efforts against the teaching of evolution. Some school districts have considered teaching the creationist theory of "intelligent design" as an alternative explanation of the origin of life. Proponents of intelligent design contend that evolutionary theory has "gaps" that can be explained only by the existence of an intelligent creative force (God).

The federal courts took up the issue of intelligent design in 2005. The previous year, the Dover Area Board of Education in Pennsylvania had voted to require the presentation of intelligent design as an explanation of the origin of life. In December 2005, a U.S. district court ruled that the Dover mandate was unconstitutional. Judge John E. Jones III, appointed in 2002 by President George W. Bush, criticized the intelligent design theory in depth.[9] All of the school board members who endorsed intelligent design were voted out of office, and the new school board declined to appeal the decision.

This scientist, who studies human evolution, is surrounded by different human skulls, some dating back many thousands of years. Why is the theory of evolution often attacked?

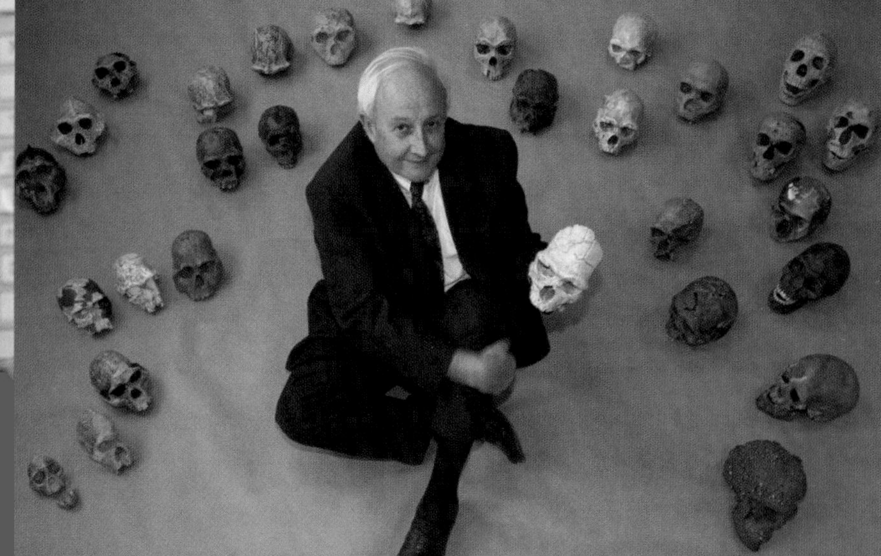
(© Marc Charuel/Sygma/Corbis)

Religious Displays on Public Property. On a regular basis, the courts are asked to determine whether religious symbols placed on public property violate the establishment clause. A frequent source of controversy is the placement of a crèche, or nativity scene, on public property during the Christmas season. The Supreme Court has allowed some displays but prohibited others. In general, a nativity

7. 472 U.S. 38 (1985).
8. 393 U.S. 97 (1968).
9. *Kitzmiller v. Dover Area School District,* 400 F.Supp.2d 707 (M.D.Pa. 2005).

scene is acceptable if it is part of a broader display that contains secular objects such as lights, Christmas trees, Santa Claus figures, and reindeer. A stand-alone crèche is not acceptable.[10] A related issue is whether the Ten Commandments may be displayed on public property. As with nativity displays, acceptability turns on whether the Ten Commandments is part of a larger secular display or whether the context is overtly religious.

In a new twist on the Ten Commandments controversy, the Supreme Court ruled in 2009 that the city of Pleasant Grove, Utah, was not required to accept a monument from Summum, a small religious group, and place it in a city park. The proposed monument would have listed Summum's principles. A variety of donated monuments were already installed in the park, including one that displayed the Ten Commandments. Summum based its argument on freedom of speech grounds, not the establishment clause. In response, the Court ruled that by accepting or not accepting monuments, the city was exercising its own freedom of speech, rather than regulating the speech of others. When New York accepted the Statue of Liberty from France, it was under no obligation also to accept a "statue of autocracy" from somewhere else.[11]

(AP Photo/Craig Ruttle)

This holiday display on public property has a Christmas tree, a Jewish menorah, and an Islamic crescent and star. Would a judge approve it?

The Free Exercise Clause

The First Amendment constrains Congress from prohibiting the free exercise of religion. Does this *free exercise clause* mean that no type of religious practice can be prohibited or restricted by government? Certainly, a person can hold any religious belief that he or she wants, or a person can have no religious belief. When, however, religious *practices* work against public policy and the public welfare, the government can act. For example, regardless of a child's or parent's religious beliefs, the government can require vaccinations.

Churches and other religious organizations are tax-exempt bodies, and as a result they are not allowed to endorse candidates for office or make contributions to candidates' campaigns. Churches are allowed to take positions on ballot proposals, however, and may contribute to referendum campaigns. For example, both the Latter-Day Saints (the Mormons) and the Roman Catholic Church were able to fund the campaign for California's 2008 Proposition 8, a measure to ban same-sex marriage.

The Internal Revenue Service (IRS) rarely bothers to threaten the tax-exempt status of a church based on simple candidate endorsements, however. For example, in September 2008, thirty-three ministers collectively endorsed Republican presidential candidate John McCain in a deliberate challenge to the 1954 law that prohibits such endorsements. The IRS did not respond. In 1995, however, the IRS did revoke the tax-exempt status of Branch Ministries, Inc., and in 2000 a federal district court supported the revocation.[12] Branch Ministries went far beyond simply endorsing a candidate from the pulpit. The church had used tax-exempt income to buy newspaper advertisements denouncing Democratic presidential candidate Bill Clinton.

did you know?

On the eve of the American Revolution, fewer than 20 percent of American adults adhered to a church in any significant way, compared with the 55 percent that do so today.

10. *Lynch v. Donnelly*, 465 U.S. 668 (1984).
11. *Pleasant Grove City v. Summum*, 129 S.Ct. 1125 (2009).
12. *Branch Ministries v. Rossetti*, 211 F.3d 137 (D.C.Cir. 2000).

■ **Learning Outcome 3: Specify the limited circumstances, including obscenity and slander, in which governments may override the principle of free speech.**

Freedom of Expression

Perhaps the most frequently invoked freedom that Americans have is the right to free speech and a free press. Each of us has the right to have our say, and all of us have the right to hear what others say. For the most part, Americans can criticize public officials and their actions without fear of reprisal by any branch of our government.

No Prior Restraint

Restraining an activity before that activity has actually occurred is called **prior restraint.** When expression is involved, prior restraint means censorship, as opposed to subsequent punishment. Prior restraint of expression would require, for example, that a permit be obtained before a speech could be made, a newspaper published, or a movie or TV show exhibited. Most, if not all, Supreme Court justices have been very critical of any governmental action that imposes prior restraint on expression.

Prior Restraint
Restraining an activity before it has actually occurred. When expression is involved, this means censorship.

Symbolic Speech
Expression made through articles of clothing, gestures, movements, and other forms of nonverbal conduct. Symbolic speech is given substantial protection by the courts.

One of the most famous cases concerning prior restraint was *New York Times v. United States,*[13] the so-called Pentagon Papers case. In 1971, the *Times* and the *Washington Post* were about to publish the Pentagon Papers, an elaborate secret history of the U.S. government's involvement in the Vietnam War (1965–1975). The secret documents had been obtained illegally by a disillusioned former Pentagon official. The government wanted a court order to bar publication of the documents, arguing that national security was threatened and that the documents had been stolen. The newspapers argued that the public had a right to know the information contained in the papers and that the press had the right to inform the public. The Supreme Court ruled six to three in favor of the newspapers' right to publish the information. This case affirmed the no-prior-restraint doctrine.

The Protection of Symbolic Speech

Not all expression is in words or in writing. Articles of clothing, gestures, movements, and other forms of nonverbal expressive conduct are considered **symbolic speech.** Such speech is given substantial protection today by our courts. For example, in a landmark decision issued in 1969, *Tinker v. Des Moines School District,*[14] the United States Supreme Court held that the wearing of black armbands by students in protest against the Vietnam War was a form of speech protected by the First Amendment.

William F. Hornsby, Jr., of Euclid, Ohio, was suspended in 1965 for six school days from Euclid High School. Hornsby wore a black armband to classes in mourning for the American and Vietnamese dead in the Vietnam War. Do high school students have the same free speech rights as adults?

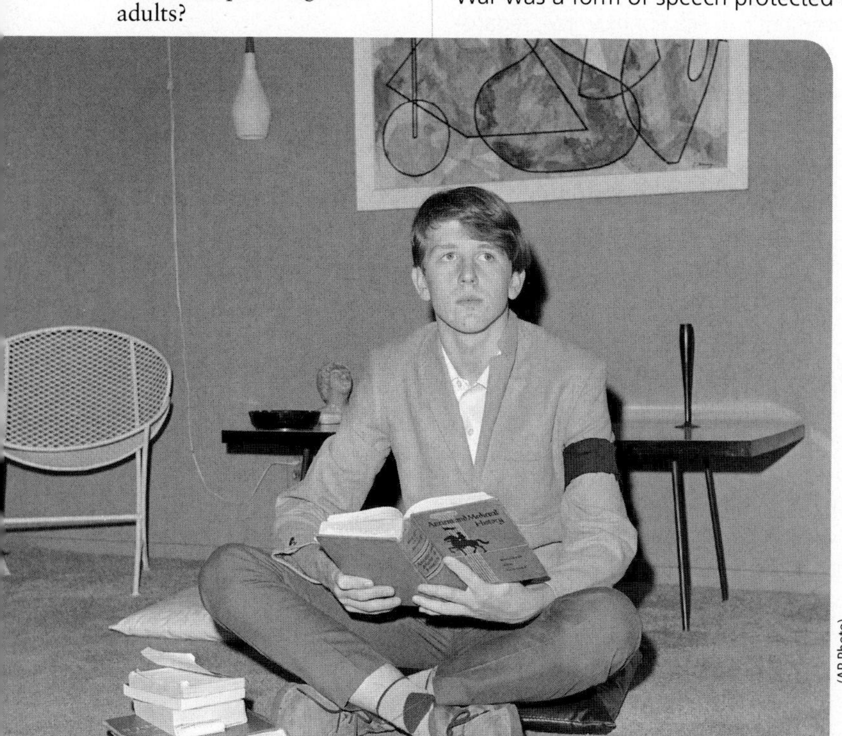

(AP Photo)

Flag Burning. In 1989, in *Texas v. Johnson,*[15] the Supreme Court ruled that state laws that prohibited the burning of the American flag as part of a peaceful protest also violated the freedom of expression protected by the First Amendment. Congress responded by passing the Flag Protection Act of 1989, which was ruled unconstitutional by the Supreme Court in 1990.[16] Congress and President George H. W. Bush immediately pledged to work for a constitutional amendment to "protect our flag"—an effort that has yet to be successful.

Cross Burning. In 2003, the Supreme Court concluded in a Virginia case that a state,

13. 403 U.S. 713 (1971).
14. 393 U.S. 503 (1969).
15. 488 U.S. 884 (1989).
16. *United States v. Eichman,* 496 U.S. 310 (1990).

Everyday
Reach
for a
LUCKY
instead of a
sweet
LUCKY STRIKE
"IT'S TOASTED"
CIGARETTES
ROSALIE ADELE NELSON.
Original "Lucky" Girl
"To keep slender. I reach for a Lucky instead of a sweet"
"It's toasted"- No Throat Irritation - No Cough

(© Bettmann/Corbis)

This cigarette ad is from the 1920s. Would it be protected commercial speech today?

consistent with the First Amendment, may ban cross burnings carried out with the intent to intimidate. The Court reasoned that historically, cross burning was a sign of impending violence, and a state has the right to ban threats of violence. The Court also ruled, however, that the state must prove intimidation and cannot infer it from the cross burnings themselves. In an impassioned dissent, Justice Clarence Thomas, who is African American and usually one of the Court's most conservative members, argued that cross burnings should be automatic evidence of intent to intimidate.[17]

The Protection of Commercial Speech

Commercial Speech
Advertising statements, which increasingly have been given First Amendment protection.

Commercial speech usually is defined as advertising statements. Can advertisers use their First Amendment rights to prevent restrictions on the content of commercial advertising? Until the 1970s, the Supreme Court held that such speech was not protected at all by the First Amendment. By the mid-1970s, however, more and more commercial speech had been brought under First Amendment protection. According to Justice Harry A. Blackmun, "Advertising, however tasteless and excessive it sometimes may seem, is nonetheless dissemination of information as to who is producing and selling what product for what reason and at what price."[18] Nevertheless, the Supreme Court will consider a restriction on commercial speech valid as long as it (1) seeks to implement a substantial government interest, (2) directly advances that interest, and (3) goes no further than necessary to accomplish its objective. In particular, a business engaging in commercial speech can be subject to liability for factual inaccuracies in ways that do not apply to noncommercial speech.

An important recent issue involving the relationship between commerce and free speech has been the question of online piracy—that is, the unauthorized reproduction of copyrighted material using the Internet. To what extent can online piracy be restricted without violating the free speech and other rights of Americans? We examine that question in the *Politics and Property Rights* feature on the following page.

Attempts to Ban Subversive or Advocacy Speech

Over the past hundred years, the United States Supreme Court has established, in succession, a number of doctrines regarding language allegedly subversive to the public order. Descriptions of these doctrines follow.

17. *Virginia v. Black*, 538 U.S. 343 (2003).
18. *Virginia State Board of Pharmacy v. Virginia Citizens Consumer Council, Inc.*, 425 U.S. 748 (1976).

Politics AND Property Rights

ONLINE PIRACY

According to representatives of the music industry, four out of five downloads of music from the Internet are illegal, "pirated" copies. Peer-to-peer sites, many of which foster piracy, receive more than 1 billion views per month. That number is growing at over 25 percent annually. Revenues from album sales have fallen by half since 1999, their peak year.

The sales of Blu-ray discs and DVDs are dropping also. Illegally downloaded movies are becoming a problem for the motion picture industry. E-book sales are growing at the expense of books printed on old-fashioned paper. Online piracy is not yet a major problem for publishers, but it is growing. At least 5 million people read pirated copies of books every day.

THE CONTENT PROVIDERS REACT TO PIRACY

The response by major music labels, big movie studios, and book publishers is a call for more legislation. Trade organizations representing content providers advocate greater punishment for illegal copying. In particular, these organizations want to force major online sites, such as Google, YouTube, Facebook, and Wikipedia, to devote significant new resources to enforcing copyright protection.

A site that did not cooperate adequately with the enforcement effort could face heavy fines or even be put out of business. Such policies were embedded in the Stop Online Piracy Act of 2012. A campaign by major Internet sites and by users, however, forced Congress to abandon this legislation.

HOW MUCH OF A PROBLEM IS ONLINE PIRACY?

Few will deny that creative productions—intellectual property—deserve legal protection. If no one paid for creative works, few people would be able to produce them. Still, there have long been ways to enjoy films, literature, and music without paying for them. You can see advertiser-supported movies on television and listen to advertiser-supported music on the radio. You can borrow books from a library or a friend. Also, you can buy used books, CDs, and DVDs—and rent DVDs from NetFlix. Content providers never see the dollars spent on used materials. In the end, the question becomes, at what point does copying become unacceptable?

According to blogger Matthew Yglesias, "Online piracy is like fouling in basketball. You want to penalize it to prevent it from getting out of control, but any effort to actually eliminate it would be a cure much worse than the disease." Those who agree with this viewpoint support shutting down criminal enterprises that do nothing but provide stolen copies of creative works. They would oppose, however, attempts to ban every instance in which ordinary people freely pass materials to each other.

Many believe that the music and movie industries' estimates of lost revenues from online piracy are seriously exaggerated. The industries assume that every pirated album, movie, or book represents a lost sale. Clearly, though, many who pay nothing for pirated intellectual property would simply do without if they were forced to pay.

Online piracy may be huge and growing, but American consumers have never had so much entertainment available to them. Some would argue that, so far at least, piracy is not severe enough to discourage creative people from creating.

FOR CRITICAL ANALYSIS

Should there be such a thing as freedom to obtain information? If so, how can it be squared adequately with intellectual property rights?

Clear and Present Danger Test
The test proposed by Justice Oliver Wendell Holmes for determining when government may restrict free speech. Restrictions are permissible, he argued, only when speech creates a *clear and present danger* to the public order.

Clear and Present Danger. In 1919, the Supreme Court ruled that when a person's remarks create a clear and present danger to the peace or public order, they can be curtailed constitutionally. Justice Oliver Wendell Holmes used this reasoning when examining the case of a socialist who had been convicted of violating the Espionage Act by distributing a leaflet that opposed the military draft.[19] According to the **clear and present danger test,** expression may be restricted if evidence exists that such expression would cause a dangerous condition, actual or imminent, that Congress has the power to prevent.

19. *Schenck v. United States,* 249 U.S. 47 (1919).

The Bad Tendency Rule. Over the course of the twentieth century, the Supreme Court modified the clear and present danger rule, limiting the constitutional protection of free speech in 1925 and 1951, and then broadening it substantially in 1969. In *Gitlow v. New York,*[20] the Court reintroduced the earlier *bad tendency rule,* which placed greater restrictions on speech than Justice Holmes's formulation. According to this rule, speech may be curtailed if there is a possibility that such expression might lead to some "evil."

In the *Gitlow* case, a member of a left-wing group was convicted of violating New York State's criminal anarchy statute when he published and distributed a pamphlet urging the violent overthrow of the U.S. government. In its majority opinion, the Supreme Court held that the First Amendment afforded protection against state incursions on freedom of expression—the first time that the First Amendment was ever invoked against a state government (see the discussion of incorporation theory on page 114). Nevertheless, Gitlow could be punished legally because his expression would tend to bring about evils that the state had a right to prevent.

The Imminent Lawless Action Test. Some claim that the United States did not achieve true freedom of political speech until 1969. In that year, in *Brandenburg v. Ohio,*[21] the Supreme Court overturned the conviction of a Ku Klux Klan leader for violating a state statute. The statute prohibited anyone from advocating "the duty, necessity, or propriety of sabotage, violence, or unlawful methods of terrorism as a means of accomplishing industrial or political reform." The Court held that the guarantee of free speech does not permit a state "to forbid or proscribe [disallow] advocacy of the use of force or of law violation except where such advocacy is directed to inciting or producing imminent [immediate] lawless actions and is likely to incite or produce such action." The **imminent lawless action test** enunciated by the Court is a difficult one for prosecutors to meet. As a result, the Court's decision significantly broadened the protection given to advocacy speech.

Imminent Lawless Action Test
The current standard established by the Supreme Court for evaluating the legality of advocacy speech. Such speech can be forbidden only when it is "directed to inciting . . . imminent lawless action."

Unprotected Speech: Obscenity

A large number of state and federal statutes make it a crime to disseminate obscene materials. Generally, the courts have not been willing to extend constitutional protections of free speech to what they consider obscene materials. But what is obscenity? Justice Potter Stewart once stated that even though he could not define *obscenity,* "I know it when I see it."

Definitional Problems. The Supreme Court has grappled from time to time with the difficulty of specifying an operationally effective definition of **obscenity.** In 1973, in *Miller v. California,*[22] Chief Justice Warren Burger created a formal list of requirements that must be met for material to be legally obscene. Material is obscene if (1) the average person finds that it violates contemporary community standards, (2) the work taken as a whole appeals to a prurient interest in sex, (3) the work shows patently offensive sexual conduct, and (4) the work lacks serious redeeming literary, artistic, political, or scientific merit. The problem, of course, is that one person's prurient interest is another person's medical interest or artistic pleasure. The Court went on to state that the definition of *prurient interest* would be determined by the community's standards. The Court avoided presenting a definition of *obscenity,* leaving this determination to local and state authorities. Consequently, the *Miller* case has been applied in a widely inconsistent manner.

Obscenity
Sexually offensive material. Obscenity can be illegal if it is found to violate a four-part test established by the United States Supreme Court.

Protecting Children. The Supreme Court has upheld state laws making it illegal to sell materials showing sexual performances by minors. In 1990, in *Osborne v. Ohio,*[23] the

20. 268 U.S. 652 (1925).
21. 395 U.S. 444 (1969).
22. 413 U.S. 5 (1973).
23. 495 U.S. 103 (1990).

■ Learning Outcome 5: **Provide the constitutional basis of the right to privacy, and explain how the principle has been applied to the abortion and right-to-die controversies.**

The Right to Privacy

No explicit reference is made anywhere in the Constitution to a person's right to privacy. Until the second half of the 1900s, the courts did not take a very positive approach toward the right to privacy. For example, during Prohibition, suspected bootleggers' telephones were tapped routinely, and the information obtained was used as a legal basis for prosecution. In *Olmstead v. United States*[37] in 1928, the Supreme Court upheld such an invasion of privacy. Justice Louis Brandeis, a champion of personal freedoms, strongly dissented from the majority decision in this case, though. He argued that the framers of the Constitution gave every citizen the right to be left alone. He called such a right "the most comprehensive of rights and the right most valued by civilized men."

In the 1960s, the highest court began to modify the majority view. In 1965, in *Griswold v. Connecticut*,[38] the Supreme Court overturned a Connecticut law that effectively prohibited the use of contraceptives, holding that the law violated the right to privacy. Justice William O. Douglas formulated a unique way of reading this right into the Bill of Rights. He claimed that the First, Third, Fourth, Fifth, and Ninth Amendments created "penumbras, formed by emanations [shadows, formed by the light] from those guarantees that help give them life and substance," and he went on to describe zones of privacy

37. 277 U.S. 438 (1928). This decision was overruled later in *Katz v. United States,* 389 U.S. 347 (1967).
38. 381 U.S. 479 (1965).

Beyond Our Borders

THE TROUBLE WITH BRITISH LIBEL LAW

Because Americans value free speech highly, it is not easy to sue someone for libel successfully. Britain, in contrast, has a much lower standard for proving libel.

THE DIFFERENCE BETWEEN U.S. AND BRITISH LAWS

To succeed in a libel suit in the United States, the *plaintiff,* the person who is suing, has to prove that the offending speech was false and published with reckless disregard for the truth. In contrast, British law assumes that any offending speech is false. It is the writer or author who must prove that it is in fact true in order to prevail against a libel charge.

Britain also has been willing to hear cases in which the alleged libel took place in another country. As a result, during the past decade, Britain has become the international destination of choice for those who wish to file libel suits. For example, a Tunisian businessperson sued Al Arabiya, a satellite television network based in Dubai and broadcasting in Arabic, in London. The Tunisian disputed allegations that he had ties to terrorist groups. Why London? The Al Arabiya program was available by satellite in Britain. A court awarded the plaintiff $325,000.

A further problem is that defending oneself against a libel suit in Britain is very expensive. A wealthy plaintiff can wind up bankrupting a defendant even if the plaintiff's case is weak.

SOME STATES AND CITIES IN THE UNITED STATES FIGHT BACK

In reaction to easy libel lawsuits in Britain, some states and cities in the United States adopted laws to protect their citizens. An example is New York State's Libel Terrorism Protection Act. It protects New York–based publishers and writers from the enforcement of most foreign libel judgments. In 2010, Congress passed the Securing the Protection of our Enduring and Established Constitutional Heritage (SPEECH) Act. This law makes foreign libel judgments unenforceable in U.S. courts unless the judgments are in accord with the First Amendment. Both the House and the Senate approved the act unanimously, and President Barack Obama immediately signed it into law.

FOR CRITICAL ANALYSIS

British lawmakers are considering reforming their nation's libel laws. Why might they do this?

that are guaranteed by these rights. When we read the Ninth Amendment, we can see the foundation for his reasoning: "The enumeration in the Constitution, of certain rights, shall not be construed to deny or disparage [belittle] others retained by the people." In other words, just because the Constitution, including its amendments, does not specifically talk about the right to privacy does not mean that this right is denied to the people.

Privacy Rights and Abortion

Historically, abortion was not a criminal offense before the "quickening" of the fetus (the first movement of the fetus in the uterus, usually between the sixteenth and eighteenth weeks of pregnancy). During the latter half of the nineteenth century, however, state laws became more severe. By 1973, performing an abortion at any time during pregnancy was a criminal offense in a majority of the states.

Roe v. Wade. In 1973, in *Roe v. Wade,*[39] the United States Supreme Court accepted the argument that the laws against abortion violated "Jane Roe's" right to privacy under the Constitution. The Court held that during the first trimester (three months) of pregnancy, abortion was an issue solely between a woman and her physician. The state could not limit abortions except to require that they be performed by licensed physicians. During the second trimester, to protect the health of the mother, the state was allowed to specify the conditions under which an abortion could be performed. During the final trimester, the state could regulate or even outlaw abortions except when they were necessary to preserve the life or health of the mother.

After the *Roe* case, the Supreme Court issued decisions in a number of cases defining and redefining the boundaries of state regulation of abortion. During the 1980s, the Court twice struck down laws that required a woman who wished to have an abortion to undergo counseling designed to discourage abortions. In the late 1980s and early 1990s, however, the Court took a more conservative approach. For example, in *Webster v. Reproductive Health Services*[40] in 1989, the Court upheld a Missouri statute that, among other things, banned the use of public hospitals or other taxpayer-supported facilities for performing abortions. And, in *Planned Parenthood v. Casey*[41] in 1992, the Court upheld a Pennsylvania law that required preabortion counseling, a waiting period of twenty-four hours, and, for girls under the age of eighteen, parental or judicial permission. As a result, abortions are now more difficult to obtain in some states than others, as noted in the chapter-opening *What If . . .* feature.

Protests at Abortion Clinics. Because of several episodes of violence attending protests at abortion clinics, in 1994 Congress passed the Freedom of Access to Clinic Entrances Act. The act prohibits protesters from blocking entrances to such clinics. In 1997, the Supreme Court upheld the constitutionality of prohibiting protesters from entering a fifteen-foot "buffer zone" around abortion clinics and from giving unwanted counseling to those entering the clinics.[42] In a 2000 decision, the Court upheld a Colorado law requiring demonstrators to stay at least eight feet away from people entering and leaving clinics unless people consented to be approached. The Court concluded that

This protester stands in front of the Planned Parenthood center in Aurora, Illinois. What limits are placed on anti-abortion protesters?

(AP Photo/Stacie Freudenberg)

39. 410 U.S. 113 (1973). Jane Roe was not the real name of the woman in this case. It is a common legal pseudonym used to protect a person's privacy.
40. 492 U.S. 490 (1989).
41. 505 U.S. 833 (1992).
42. *Schenck v. ProChoice Network,* 519 U.S. 357 (1997).

the law's restrictions on speech-related conduct did not violate the free speech rights of abortion protesters.[43]

Partial-Birth Abortion. Another issue in the abortion controversy concerns "partial-birth" abortion. A partial-birth abortion, which physicians call intact dilation and extraction, is a procedure that can be used during the second trimester of pregnancy. Abortion rights advocates claim that in limited circumstances the procedure is the safest way to perform an abortion and that the government should never outlaw specific medical procedures. Opponents argue that the procedure has no medical merit and that it ends the life of a fetus that might be able to live outside the womb.

In 2000, the Supreme Court addressed this issue when it reviewed a Nebraska law banning partial-birth abortions. The Court invalidated the Nebraska law on the ground that, as written, the law could be used to ban other abortion procedures and contained no provisions for protecting the health of the pregnant woman.[44]

In 2003, legislation similar to the Nebraska statute was passed by the U.S. Congress and signed into law by President George W. Bush. In 2007, the Supreme Court, with several changes in membership since the 2000 ruling, upheld the federal law in a five-to-four vote, effectively reversing its position on partial-birth abortion.[45] Furthermore, said the Court, "government has a legitimate and substantial interest in preserving and promoting fetal life." The Court also noted that there was an alternative (though less safe, according to the act's opponents) abortion procedure that could be used in the second trimester. The Court emphasized that the law allowed partial-birth abortion to be performed when a woman's life was in jeopardy. In her dissent to the majority opinion, Justice Ruth Bader Ginsburg said that the ruling "cannot be understood as anything other than an effort to chip away at a right declared again and again by this Court"—that right being a woman's right to choose.

The Controversy Continues. Abortion continues to be a divisive issue. During the early years of the twenty-first century, abortion opponents concentrated on state ballot proposals that could lay the groundwork for an eventual challenge to *Roe*. They were not very successful, however. In one 2011 example, in Mississippi, a conservative state, voters rejected a measure that would have outlawed all abortions and some forms of birth control. Abortion opponents have been more successful in winning new restrictions passed by state legislatures. New state laws became especially common after the 2010 elections, when Republicans took over many state legislative chambers.

Privacy Rights and the "Right to Die"

A 1976 case involving Karen Ann Quinlan was one of the first publicized "right-to-die" cases.[46] The parents of Quinlan, a young woman who had been in a coma for nearly a year and who had been kept alive during that time by a respirator, wanted her respirator removed. In 1976, the New Jersey Supreme Court ruled that the right to privacy includes the right of a patient to refuse treatment and that patients unable to speak can exercise that right through a family member or guardian. In 1990, the Supreme Court took up the issue. In *Cruzan v. Director, Missouri Department of Health,*[47] the Court stated that a patient's life-sustaining treatment can be withdrawn at the request of a family member only if there is "clear and convincing evidence" that the patient did not want such treatment.

43. *Hill v. Colorado,* 530 U.S. 703 (2000).
44. *Stenberg v. Carhart,* 530 U.S. 914 (2000).
45. *Gonzales v. Carhart,* 550 U.S. 124 (2007).
46. *In re Quinlan,* 70 N.J. 10 (1976).
47. 497 U.S. 261 (1990).

What If There Is No Living Will? Since the 1976 *Quinlan* decision, most states have enacted laws permitting people to designate their wishes concerning life-sustaining procedures in "living wills" or durable health-care powers of attorney. These laws and the Supreme Court's *Cruzan* decision have resolved the right-to-die controversy for situations in which the patient has drafted a living will. Disputes are still possible if there is no living will.

An example is the case of Terri Schiavo. The husband of the Florida woman who had been in a persistent vegetative state for more than a decade sought to have her feeding tube removed on the basis of oral statements that she would not want her life prolonged in such circumstances. Schiavo's parents fought this move in court but lost on the ground that a spouse, not a parent, is the appropriate legal guardian for a married person. Although the Florida legislature passed a law allowing Governor Jeb Bush to overrule the courts, the state supreme court held that the law violated the state constitution.[48]

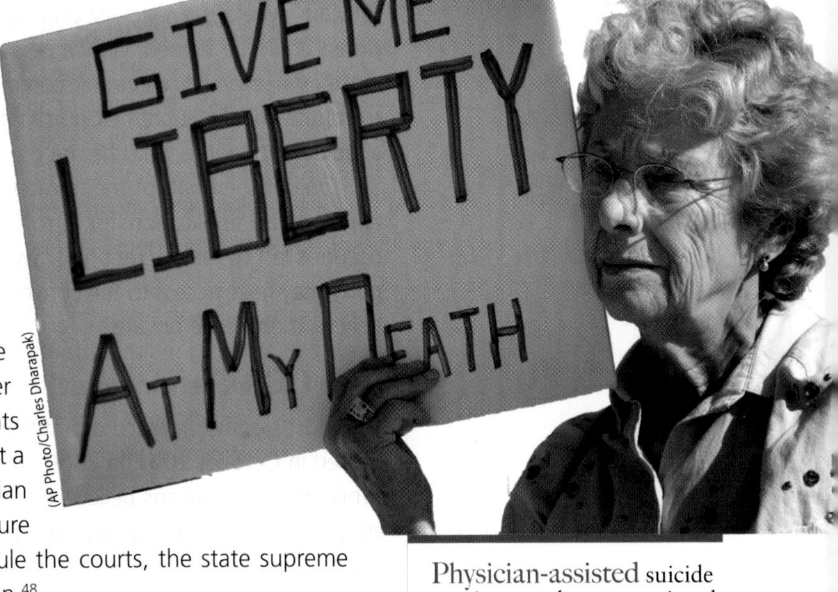

(AP Photo/Charles Dharapak)

Physician-assisted suicide continues to be an emotional issue for many Americans. Only three states allow such action by physicians. Does the Constitution give any guidelines about the "right-to-die" controversy?

In March 2005, the U.S. Congress intervened and passed a law allowing Schiavo's case to be heard in the federal court system. The federal courts, however, essentially agreed with the Florida state courts and refused to order the reconnection of the feeding tube, which had been disconnected a few days earlier. After twice appealing to the United States Supreme Court without success, the parents gave up hope, and Schiavo died shortly thereafter.

Physician-Assisted Suicide. In the 1990s, another issue surfaced: Do privacy rights include the right of terminally ill people to end their lives through physician-assisted suicide? Until 1996, the courts consistently upheld state laws that prohibited this practice. In 1996, after two federal appellate courts ruled that state laws banning assisted suicide were unconstitutional, the issue reached the United States Supreme Court.

In *Washington v. Glucksberg,*[49] the Court stated that the liberty interest protected by the Constitution does not include a right to commit suicide, with or without assistance. In effect, the Supreme Court left the decision as to whether to permit the practice to the states. Since then, assisted suicide has been allowed in only three states—Montana, Oregon, and Washington. In 2006, the Supreme Court upheld Oregon's physician-assisted suicide law against a challenge from the George W. Bush administration.[50]

Civil Liberties versus Security Issues

■ Learning Outcome 6: **Cite examples of how recent security concerns have affected the civil liberties of immigrants and Americans generally.**

As former Supreme Court justice Thurgood Marshall once said, "Grave threats to liberty often come in times of urgency, when constitutional rights seem too extravagant to endure." Not surprisingly, antiterrorist legislation since the attacks on September 11, 2001, has eroded certain basic rights, in particular the Fourth Amendment protections against unreasonable searches and seizures.

48. *Bush v. Schiavo,* 885 So.2d 321 (Fla. 2004).
49. 521 U.S. 702 (1997).
50. *Gonzales v. Oregon,* 546 U.S. 243 (2006).

did you know?

In eighteenth-century England, pocket picking and similar crimes were punishable by the death penalty.

Time Limits for Death Row Appeals

In 1996, Congress passed the Anti-Terrorism and Effective Death Penalty Act. The law limits access to the federal courts for defendants convicted in state courts. It also imposes a severe time limit on death row appeals. Many are concerned that the shortened appeals process increases the possibility that innocent persons may be put to death. Recently, DNA testing has shown that some innocent people may have been convicted unjustly of murder. Since 1973, more than one hundred prisoners have been freed from death row after new evidence suggested that they were convicted wrongfully. On average, it takes about seven years to exonerate someone on death row. Currently, however, the time between conviction and execution has been shortened from an average of ten to twelve years to an average of six to eight years.

Methods of Execution

The most recent controversy concerning the death penalty is whether execution by injecting the condemned prisoner with lethal drugs is a cruel and unusual punishment. Lethal injection is currently used in almost all executions. Evidence exists that when performed incompetently, death by lethal injection can be extremely painful. Some death penalty opponents have claimed that the procedure is painful in so many instances that it constitutes cruel and unusual punishment. The United States Supreme Court took up this matter in a Kentucky case in 2007. In 2008, it ruled by a seven-to-two margin that Kentucky's method of execution by lethal injection was constitutional.[63]

63. *Baze v. Rees*, 553 U.S. 35 (2008).

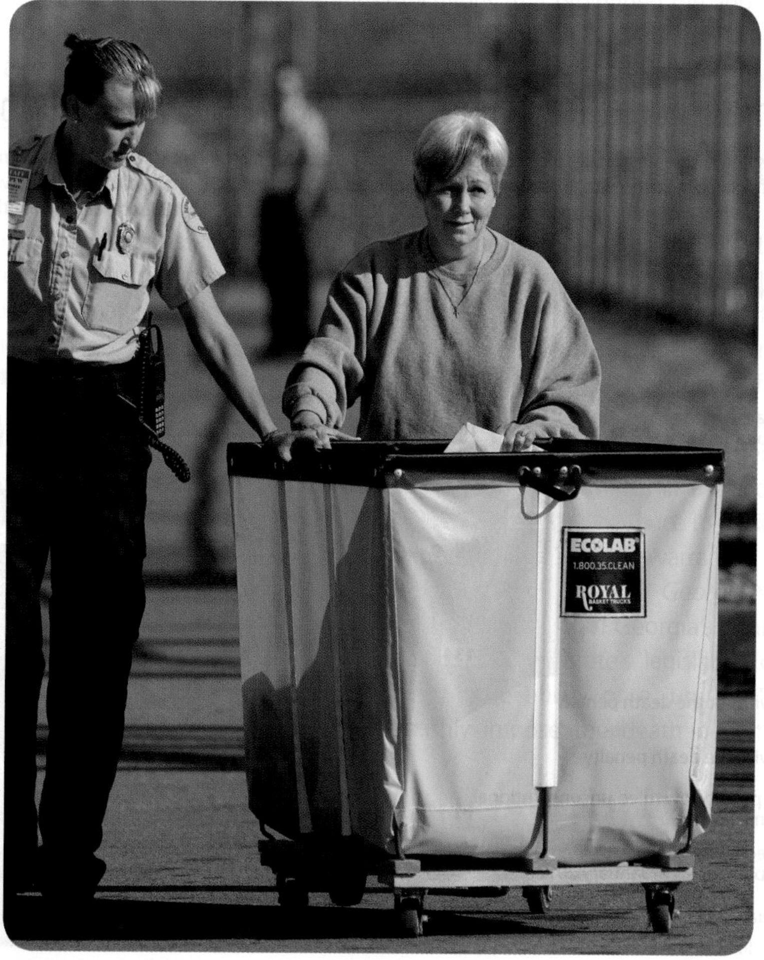

(AP Photo/Mark Humphrey)

Gaile Owens spent 26 years on death row for hiring a stranger to kill her husband. Then her sentence was commuted to life in prison. In 2011, she won parole and was released from prison.

Why Should You Care about... CIVIL LIBERTIES?

(AP Photo/J. Scott Applewhite)

The Bill of Rights includes numerous provisions that protect persons who are suspected of criminal activity. Among these are limits on how the police can conduct searches and seizures.

CIVIL LIBERTIES AND YOUR LIFE

You may be the most law-abiding person in the world, but that will not guarantee that you will never be stopped, arrested, or searched by the police. Sooner or later, the great majority of all citizens will have some kind of interaction with the police. People who do not understand their rights or how to behave toward law enforcement officers can find themselves in serious trouble. The words of advice in this feature actually provide you with key survival skills for life in the modern world.

HOW YOU CAN MAKE A DIFFERENCE

How should you behave if you are stopped by police officers? Your civil liberties protect you from having to provide information other than your name and address. Normally, even if you have not been placed under arrest, the officers have the right to frisk you for weapons, and you must let them proceed. The officers cannot, however, check your person or your clothing further if, in their judgment, no weaponlike object is produced.

The officers may search you only if they have a search warrant or probable cause to believe that a search will likely produce incriminating evidence. What if the officers do not have probable cause or a warrant? Physically resisting their attempt to search you can lead to disastrous results. It is best simply to refuse orally to give permission for the search, if possible in the presence of a witness. Being polite is better than acting out of anger and making the officers irritable. It is usually advisable to limit what you say to the officers. If you are arrested, it is best to keep quiet until you can speak with a lawyer.

If you are in your car and are stopped by the police, the same fundamental rules apply. Always be ready to show your driver's license and car registration. You may be asked to get out of the car. The officers may use a flashlight to peer inside if it is too dark to see otherwise. None of this constitutes a search. A true search requires either a warrant or probable cause. No officer has the legal right to search your car simply to find out if you may have committed a crime. Police officers can conduct searches that are incident to lawful arrests, however.

If you are in your home and a police officer with a search warrant appears, you can ask to examine the warrant before granting entry. A warrant that is correctly made out will state the place or persons to be searched, the object sought, and the date of the warrant (which should be no more than ten days old). It will also bear the signature of a judge or magistrate. If the warrant is in order, you need not make any statement. If you believe the warrant to be invalid, or if no warrant is produced, you should make it clear orally that you have not consented to the search, if possible in the presence of a witness. If the search later is proved to be unlawful, normally any evidence obtained cannot be used in court.

Officers who attempt to enter your home without a search warrant can do so only if they are pursuing a suspected felon into the house. Rarely is it advisable to give permission for a warrantless search. You, as the resident, must be the one to give permission if any evidence obtained is to be considered legal. A landlord, manager, or head of a college dormitory cannot give legal permission. A roommate, however, can give permission for a search of his or her room, which may allow the police to search areas where you have belongings.

If you are a guest in a place that is being legally searched, you may be legally searched as well. But unless you have been placed under arrest, you cannot be compelled to go to the police station or get into a squad car.

If you would like to find out more about your rights and obligations under the laws of searches and seizures, you might want to contact the American Civil Liberties Union. You can find its Web site by entering the initials "aclu" into your favorite search engine.

Questions for Discussion and Analysis

1. Review the *Which Side Are You On?* feature on page 115. Advocates of carrying concealed handguns observe that murder rates in states that readily allow "concealed carry" are lower than in states that are more restrictive. The implication is that concealed carry leads to lower murder rates. It is possible, however, that causation might run in the opposite direction. In other words, some states might prefer restrictive gun laws because they have high murder rates. Which of these cause-and-effect relationships do you think is likely to be more important? Why?
2. The courts have never held that the provision of military chaplains by the armed forces is unconstitutional, despite the fact that chaplains are religious leaders who are employed by and under the authority of the U.S. government. What arguments might the courts use to defend the military chaplain system?
3. The courts have banned the teaching of the theory of creation by intelligent design in public school biology classes, arguing that the theory is based on religion, not science. Indeed, it is not hard to detect a religious basis in the classroom materials recently disseminated by the intelligent design movement. Is it possible to make an argument in favor of intelligent design that would not promote a religious belief?
4. In a surprisingly large number of cases, arrested individuals do not choose to exercise their right to remain silent. Why might a person not exercise his or her *Miranda* rights?

Key Terms

actual malice 127
arraignment 134
clear and present danger test 122
commercial speech 121
defamation of character 124
establishment clause 116
exclusionary rule 135
free exercise clause 116
gag order 127
imminent lawless action test 123
incorporation theory 114
libel 126
obscenity 123
prior restraint 120
public figure 127
slander 124
symbolic speech 120
writ of *habeas corpus* 134

Chapter Summary

1. Originally, the Bill of Rights limited only the power of the national government, not that of the states. Gradually and selectively, however, the Supreme Court accepted the incorporation theory, under which no state can violate most provisions of the Bill of Rights.
2. The First Amendment protects against government interference with freedom of religion by requiring a separation of church and state (under the establishment clause) and by guaranteeing the free exercise of religion. Controversial issues that arise under the establishment clause include aid to church-related schools, school prayer, the teaching of evolution versus creationism, school vouchers, the placement of religious displays on public property, and discrimination against religious speech. The government can interfere with the free exercise of religion only when religious practices work against public policy or the public welfare.
3. The First Amendment protects against government interference with freedom of speech, which includes symbolic speech (expressive conduct). The Supreme Court has been especially critical of government actions that impose prior restraint on expression. Commercial speech (advertising) by businesses has received limited First Amendment protection. Restrictions on expression are permitted when the expression may incite imminent lawless action. Other speech that has not received First Amendment protection includes expression judged to be obscene or slanderous.
4. The First Amendment protects against government interference with the freedom of the press, which can be regarded as a special instance of freedom of speech. Speech by the press that does not receive protection includes libelous statements. Publication of news about a criminal trial may be restricted by a gag order in some circumstances.
5. Under the Ninth Amendment, rights not specifically mentioned in the Constitution are not necessarily denied to the people. Among these unspecified rights protected by the courts is a right to privacy, which has been inferred from the First, Third, Fourth, Fifth, and Ninth Amendments. Whether an individual's privacy rights include a right to an abortion or a "right to die" continues to provoke controversy. Another major challenge concerns the extent to which Americans must forfeit civil liberties to control terrorism.

6. The Constitution includes protections for the rights of persons accused of crimes. Under the Fourth Amendment, no one may be subject to an unreasonable search or seizure or be arrested except on probable cause. Under the Fifth Amendment, an accused person has the right to remain silent. Under the Sixth Amendment, an accused person must be informed of the reason for his or her arrest. The accused also has the right to adequate counsel, even if he or she cannot afford an attorney, and the right to a prompt arraignment and a speedy and public trial before an impartial jury selected from a cross section of the community.

7. In *Miranda v. Arizona* (1966), the Supreme Court held that criminal suspects, before interrogation by law enforcement personnel, must be informed of the right to remain silent and the right to be represented by counsel.

8. The exclusionary rule forbids the admission in court of illegally obtained evidence. There is a "good faith exception" to the exclusionary rule: evidence need not be thrown out owing to, for example, a clerical error in a database. Under the Eighth Amendment, cruel and unusual punishment is prohibited. Whether the death penalty is cruel and unusual punishment continues to be debated.

Quiz Multiple Choice

1. As originally intended, the Bill of Rights limited the powers of:
   - **a. only the state governments.**
   - **b. both the national government and state governments.**
   - **c. only the national government.**

2. The freedom to bear arms is specified by:
   - **a. the First Amendment.**
   - **b. the Second Amendment.**
   - **c. the Fourteenth Amendment.**

3. The freedom of religion consists of two main principles:
   - **a. the establishment clause from the Second Amendment and the due process clause from the Fourteenth Amendment.**
   - **b. the free exercise clause from the Second Amendment and the establishment clause from the Fourteenth Amendment.**
   - **c. the establishment clause and the free exercise clause, both from the First Amendment.**

4. The Supreme Court has held that any law prohibiting the teaching of evolution:
   - **a. violates the establishment clause because it imposes religious beliefs on students.**
   - **b. violates the free exercise clause of the First Amendment because it bars the beliefs of atheists.**
   - **c. violates both the establishment clause and the free exercise clause.**

5. When government restrains an activity before that activity has occurred, it is called a government exercise of:
   - **a. criminal prevention.**
   - **b. prior restraint.**
   - **c. external prohibition.**

6. If you utter a false statement that harms the good reputation of another, it is called slander and such expression is:
   - **a. always protected under the First Amendment.**
   - **b. unprotected speech and a potential basis for a lawsuit.**
   - **c. prosecuted as a felony in most states.**

7. The First Amendment guarantees the right to assemble and to:
   - **a. prevent unwanted people from attending your public meetings.**
   - **b. require attendance at certain meetings, depending on the subject.**
   - **c. petition the government.**

8. The right to privacy:
   - **a. is explicitly guaranteed by the original text of the Constitution.**
   - **b. is explicitly guaranteed by the Fifth Amendment to the Constitution.**
   - **c. has been inferred from other rights by the Supreme Court.**

ANSWERS: 1. c, 2. b, 3. c, 4. a, 5. b, 6. b, 7. c, 8. c.

Quiz Fill-Ins

9. The Supreme Court has ruled that the decision as to whether to permit the practice of assisted suicide must be left to the __________.

10. The most significant antiterrorism legislation is the __________ __________ __________.

11. Limits on the ability of police officers to conduct searches and make arrests are mainly provided by the __________ __________.

12. "You have the right to remain silent. Anything you say can and will be used against you in a court of law." These words come from the Supreme Court case _______ *v.* _______.

13. Illegally seized evidence is not admissible at trial because of the __________ __________.

14. Cruel and unusual punishment is prohibited by the __________ __________.

15. Since 1925, the Supreme Court has gradually accepted the __________ __________ and has therefore extended the Bill of Rights to cover state governments through the Fourteenth Amendment's due process clause.

16. When governments attempt to ban certain types of clothing, gestures, and other forms of expressive conduct, they are attempting to ban __________ __________.

ANSWERS: 9. states, 10. USA Patriot Act, 11. Fourth Amendment, 12. *Miranda v. Arizona*, 13. exclusionary rule, 14. Eighth Amendment, 15. incorporation theory, 16. symbolic speech.

(© Aleksandar Jovicic/iStockphoto)

Selected Print & Media Resources

SUGGESTED READINGS

Kitcher, Philip. *Living with Darwin: Evolution, Design, and the Future of Faith.* New York: Oxford University Press, 2007. This brief book looks at the history of the controversy over evolution as part of a larger conflict between religious faith and the discoveries of modern science.

MacKinnon, Rebecca. *Consent of the Networked: The Worldwide Struggle for Internet Freedom.* New York: Basic Books, 2012. MacKinnon, a journalist and activist, observes that the Internet is a double-edged sword. It has been used to empower people in events such as the Arab Spring, but it has also been employed by oppressive governments and by businesses that would erode our privacy. The ultimate impact of the Internet on our freedoms is up to us.

Mayer, Jane. *The Dark Side: The Inside Story of How the War on Terror Turned into a War on American Ideals.* New York: Doubleday, 2008. Mayer, a staff writer for the *New Yorker,* provides a dramatic account in which she alleges that torture became an unofficial policy of the George W. Bush administration. Mayer contends that up to half of the mistreated individuals were in fact imprisoned by mistake.

Waldron, Jeremy. *The Harm in Hate Speech (Oliver Wendell Holmes Lectures).* New York: Harvard University Press, 2012. Constitutionalists often contend that regulation of hate speech violates the First Amendment. Waldron, a law professor at New York University, makes the opposing case that such regulation is essential to protect human dignity.

MEDIA RESOURCES

***The Abortion War: Thirty Years after* Roe v. Wade**—An ABC News program released in 2003 that examines the abortion issue.

Of Civil Wrongs and Rights: The Fred Korematsu Story—When the U.S. government sent West Coast Americans of Japanese ancestry to internment camps during World War II, Fred Korematsu resisted. His case went all the way to the Supreme Court, which ruled against him. It took thirty-nine years for Korematsu to win vindication. This 2007 PBS documentary was directed by Eric Paul Fournier and stars Fred Korematsu, Rosa Parks, and Bill Clinton.

Gideon's Trumpet—An excellent 1980 movie about the *Gideon v. Wainwright* case. Henry Fonda plays the role of the convicted petty thief Clarence Earl Gideon.

Taxi to the Dark Side—Winner of the 2008 Academy Award for best documentary. Director Alex Gibney focuses on an Afghan taxi driver named Dilawar who was apparently beaten to death by U.S. soldiers at Bagram Air Base. The film goes on to examine America's policy on torture and interrogation in general.

(© PashaIgnatov/iStockphoto)

E-mocracy UNDERSTANDING YOUR CIVIL LIBERTIES

Today, the online world offers opportunities for Americans to easily access information concerning the nature of their civil liberties, how they originated, and how they may be threatened by various government actions.

LOGGING ON

1. A key asset in learning about our civil liberties is the Web site of the American Civil Liberties Union. As noted in *How You Can Make a Difference* on page 139, you can find the Web site by entering the initials "aclu" into your favorite search engine.
2. For a different take on civil liberties, check out the Web site of the Liberty Counsel by searching on "liberty counsel." This conservative group describes itself as "a nonprofit religious civil liberties education and legal defense organization established to preserve religious freedom."
3. Summaries and the full text of Supreme Court decisions concerning constitutional law, plus a virtual tour of the Supreme Court, are available at the Web site of the Oyez Project. The project is housed at the Chicago-Kent College of Law in Illinois. You can locate it by searching on "oyez."
4. Cornell University has a collection of historic Supreme Court decisions. You can find the collection by searching on "cornell supct."
5. The Center for Democracy and Technology (CDT) focuses on how developments in communications technology are affecting the constitutional liberties of Americans. You can access the CDT's site by typing "center democracy technology" into a search engine.
6. The American Library Association's Web site provides information on free speech issues, especially issues of free speech on the Internet. Find it by searching on "ala."
7. You can find current information on Internet privacy issues at the Electronic Privacy Information Center's Web site. Enter the term "electronic privacy."

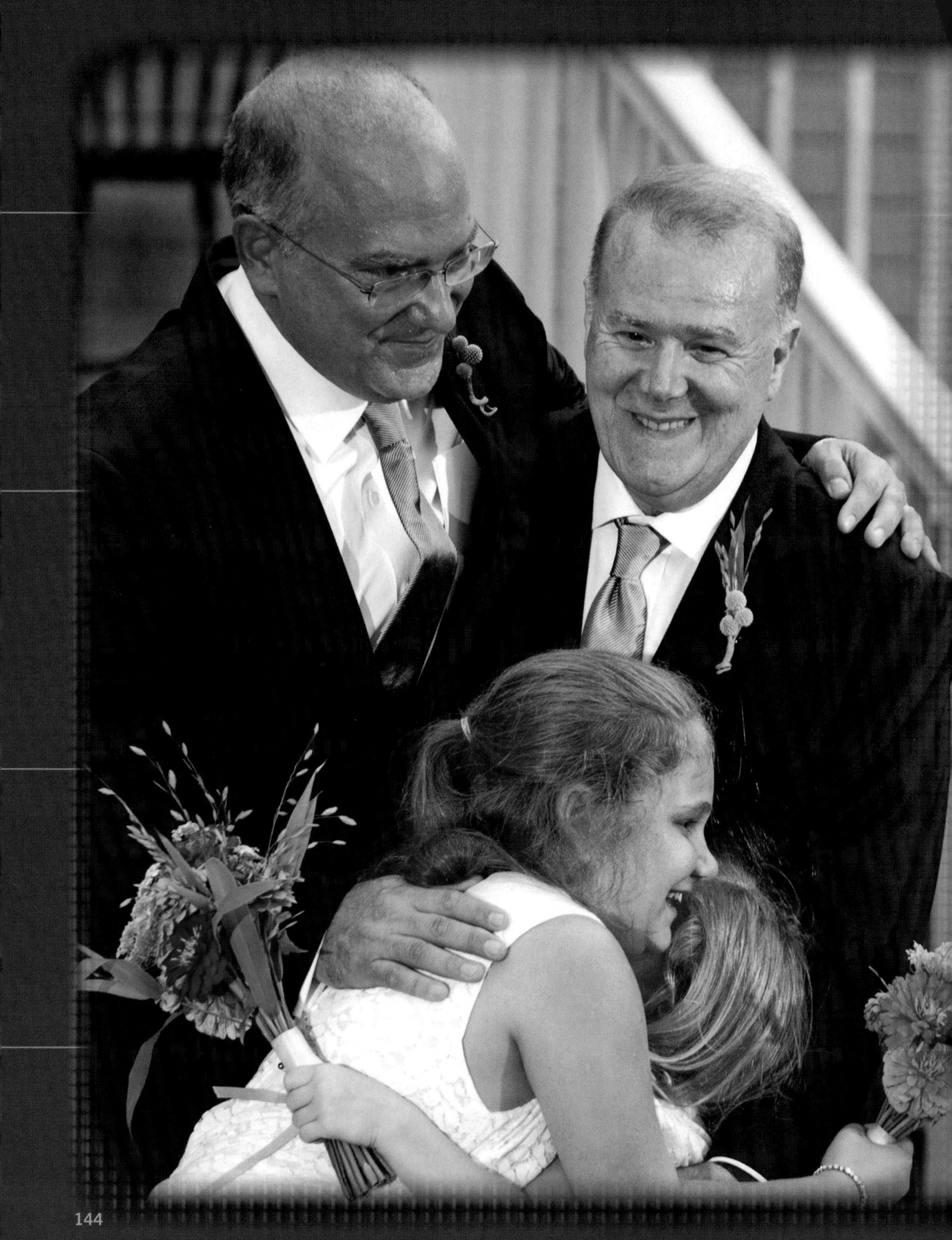

5 Civil Rights

The New York state legislature approved same-sex marriages in 2011, which allowed New York City Mayor Michael Bloomberg to attend this gay marriage ceremony. (Don Emmert/AFP/Getty Images)

The nine learning outcomes below are designed to help improve your understanding of this chapter. After reading this chapter, you should be able to:

- Learning Outcome 1: **Summarize the experience of African Americans under the separate-but-equal doctrine, and state how that doctrine was abolished.**
- Learning Outcome 2: **Describe the philosophies of the civil rights movement and the major civil rights legislation of the 1960s.**
- Learning Outcome 3: **Analyze the three standards used to determine if a law is discriminatory: strict scrutiny, intermediate scrutiny, and rational basis review.**
- Learning Outcome 4: **Contrast the goals of the women's suffrage movement with the goals of modern feminism.**
- Learning Outcome 5: **Explain how immigration is changing the face of America.**
- Learning Outcome 6: **Define *affirmative action*, and provide some of the arguments used against it.**
- Learning Outcome 7: **Detail the rights provided by the Americans with Disabilities Act.**
- Learning Outcome 8: **Summarize the recent revolution in the rights enjoyed by gay men and lesbians.**
- Learning Outcome 9: **Evaluate the rights and status of juvenile citizens.**

(Greenhouse/*The Boston Globe* via Getty Images)

THIS NATIVE Brazilian left his wife and two children behind when he was deported as an illegal immigrant.

What if...

WE DEPORTED MOST UNAUTHORIZED IMMIGRANTS?

BACKGROUND

Today, about 11 million unauthorized immigrants live in the United States. Whether they are called illegal immigrants, illegal aliens, or undocumented workers, for many Americans they represent a problem. Most unauthorized immigrants come from Latin America, with more than 50 percent of them from Mexico alone. For years, Congress has made various attempts at resolving the illegal immigrant issue. Yet nothing has happened. Many proposals have involved programs to move illegal immigrants onto a path that ends in legal status or even citizenship. In contrast, states such as Alabama and Arizona have passed their own very strict immigration laws.

During the 2011–2012 contest for the Republican presidential nomination, former Massachusetts governor Mitt Romney and former Pennsylvania senator Rick Santorum advocated "self-deportation"—that is, making life so hard for unauthorized immigrants that they would leave on their own.

WHAT IF WE DEPORTED MOST UNAUTHORIZED IMMIGRANTS?

Suppose that the federal government initiated a policy of actively searching for unauthorized immigrants and immediately deporting all those it found. Some say that this would be simply following current immigration laws to the letter. Others contend, however, that the United States would suffer from the repercussions of such a policy for years.

To implement such a policy, the government would have to hire hundreds of thousands of additional immigration officers. New prisons would be needed to hold those arrested while they awaited deportation. Expenditures would increase by many billions of dollars per year. Other government programs might have to be cut to fund the expanded deportation program.

SURPRISE—SUCH A PROGRAM MIGHT KILL JOBS

Deportation proponents argue that with fewer illegal immigrants, American citizens would have access to more jobs. Most economists disagree. The number of jobs in the economy is not fixed. There is no static "lump of labor" to be shared out. When the economy grows, the number of jobs rises. Legal and illegal immigrants alike add to net employment because they not only work, they also spend. They buy lodging, food, and entertainment. This spending adds to the demand for goods and services, which leads to more employment, not less. These workers also pay taxes. If they were deported, of course, they would no longer pay these taxes.

Major industries such as agriculture are completely dependent on undocumented workers. A team at the University of Alabama recently estimated that Alabama's stiff immigration law may cost the state almost $2.5 billion per year. A study at the University of California at Davis, Los Angeles, predicted that mass deportation would reduce California tax revenues by 8.5 percent and would shrink the state economy by tens of billions of dollars per year. If the projections for states such as Alabama and California were extended to the entire nation, the reduced economic activity resulting from mass deportation could trigger a major economic recession.

THE EFFECT ON CIVIL RIGHTS

A successful mass deportation effort would require that police at all levels have the ability to "stop and ask." Everyone would have to produce proof of legal status. Questioning could not be limited to unauthorized immigrants. Latinos who are U.S. citizens would be singled out. Many non-Hispanic citizens might be caught in the net as well.

FOR CRITICAL ANALYSIS

1. *If mass deportations were initiated, what might happen to the cost of farm produce?*
2. *Why has the immigration issue remained a political "hot potato" for decades?*

In spite of the words set forth in the Declaration of Independence that "all Men are created equal," the concept of equal treatment under the law was a distant dream in our nation's early years. In fact, the majority of the population had few rights at that time. As you learned in Chapter 2, the framers of the Constitution permitted slavery to continue. Slaves thus were excluded from the political process. Women also were excluded for the most part, as were Native Americans, African Americans who were not slaves, and even white men who did not own property.

Today, in contrast, we have numerous civil rights. Equality is at the heart of the concept of civil rights. Generally, the term **civil rights** refers to the rights of all Americans to equal protection under the law, as provided for by the Fourteenth Amendment to the Constitution. Although the terms *civil rights* and *civil liberties* are sometimes used interchangeably, scholars make a distinction between the two. As discussed in Chapter 4, civil liberties are basically limitations on government. They specify what the government *cannot* do. Civil rights, in contrast, specify what the government *must* do to ensure equal protection and freedom from discrimination.

The history of civil rights in America is the story of the struggle of various groups to be free from discriminatory treatment. In this chapter, we first look at two movements that had significant consequences for civil rights in America: the civil rights movement of the 1950s and 1960s and the women's movement, which began in the mid-1800s and continues today. Each of these movements resulted in legislation that secured important basic rights for all Americans—the right to vote and the right to equal protection under the laws.

As you read in the chapter-opening *What If . . .* feature, most of the 11 million (or more) unauthorized immigrants in the United States come from Latin America. In this chapter, we look at some of the issues related to Hispanic Americans and immigration. Note that most minorities in this nation have suffered—and some continue to suffer—from discrimination. Native Americans, Asian Americans, and Arab Americans all have had to struggle for equal treatment, as have people from other countries and older Americans. The fact that these groups are not singled out for special attention in the following pages should not be construed to mean that their struggle for equality is any less significant than the struggles of those groups that we do discuss. We do, however, take a special look at the catastrophic historical experience of Native Americans in the *Politics and History* feature on the following page.

did you know?

At the time of the American Revolution, African Americans made up 21 percent of the American population of about 2.5 million.

Civil Rights
Generally, all rights rooted in the Fourteenth Amendment's guarantee of equal protection under the law.

■ Learning Outcome 1: **Summarize the experience of African Americans under the separate-but-equal doctrine, and state how that doctrine was abolished.**

African Americans and the Consequences of Slavery in the United States

Before 1863, the Constitution protected slavery and made equality impossible in the sense in which we use the word today. The inferior status of African Americans was confirmed just a few years before the outbreak of the Civil War in the infamous *Dred Scott v. Sandford*[1] case of 1857. The Supreme Court held that slaves and their descendants—even if free—were not citizens of the United States, nor were they entitled to the rights and privileges of citizenship. The *Dred Scott* decision had grave consequences. Many historians contend that the ruling contributed to making the Civil War inevitable.

First Lady Michelle Obama attends the unveiling of a bust of African American leader Sojourner Truth in the U.S. Capitol Building.

(AP Photo/Manuel Balce Ceneta)

1. 60 U.S. 393 (1857).

Politics AND History

THE AGONY OF THE AMERICAN INDIAN

During the years after Columbus discovered America, Native American population numbers—both in the future United States and in the Americas generally—may have experienced the most catastrophic collapse of such numbers in human history. The Europeans brought with them Old World diseases to which American Indians had no immunity. The indigenous population was hit with many diseases at once—including smallpox, cholera, malaria, mumps, yellow fever, influenza, and measles. A person who was able to resist one disease might die from another. By one modern estimate, 90 percent of the inhabitants of the New World died.

To be sure, the European invaders could be brutal, and many Native Americans were killed in wars. Most of those who perished, however, died of disease without ever seeing a white man. For their part, the Europeans had no conception of what caused diseases and did not even understand what was happening. When the Pilgrims landed at Plymouth in 1620, the coast of New England was lined with empty village sites, abandoned due to the epidemics.

WHAT WERE THE ACTUAL NUMBERS?

It is not really possible to determine how many died, because we do not have a good grasp on how many people were living in the Americas in 1500. Fifty to one hundred years ago, the proposed figures were small. One common estimate held that 800,000 people lived in the continental United States. Modern-day estimates are much larger. In 1966, anthropologist Henry Dobyns argued that the true figure was between 10 million and 12 million.[a] A recent consensus estimate puts the sum at a more moderate 3.5 million.

In the United States, the American Indian population continued to decrease straight through the nineteenth century—a time when the European American and African American populations were experiencing explosive growth. The decrease was largely due to the concentration of Native Americans into ever-smaller territories. The U.S. Indian population bottomed out at 250,000 at the end of the nineteenth century. Since that time, however, Native American numbers have recovered substantially. The figure is about 3.2 million today.

a. Charles C. Mann, *1491: New Revelations of the Americas before Columbus* (New York: Vintage Books, 2006).

FOR CRITICAL ANALYSIS

Is there any way that European Americans would have allowed the indigenous tribes to keep more of their lands? Why or why not?

(© kyoshino / iStockphoto) (© Evelyn Peyton / iStockphoto)

Ending Servitude

With the emancipation of the slaves by President Abraham Lincoln's Emancipation Proclamation in 1863 and the passage of the Thirteenth, Fourteenth, and Fifteenth Amendments during the Reconstruction period (1865–1877) following the Civil War, constitutional inequality was ended.

The Thirteenth Amendment (1865) states that neither slavery nor involuntary servitude shall exist within the United States. The Fourteenth Amendment (1868) tells us that *all* persons born or naturalized in the United States are citizens of the United States. It states, furthermore, that "[n]o State shall make or enforce any law which shall abridge the privileges or immunities of citizens of the United States; nor shall any State deprive any person of life, liberty, or property, without due process of law; nor deny to any person within its jurisdiction the equal protection of the laws." Note the use of the terms *citizen* and *person* in this amendment. *Citizens* have political rights, such as the right to vote and run for political office. Citizens also have certain privileges or immunities (see Chapter 3). All *persons,* however, including noncitizen immigrants, have a right to due process of law and equal protection under the law. We discuss the Fourteenth Amendment in greater detail later in this chapter.

Social Media IN POLITICS

Twitter contains a large number of hashtags devoted to civil rights. You could check out #civilrights, #womensrights, or #gayrights.

Finally, the Fifteenth Amendment (1870) reads as follows: "The right of citizens of the United States to vote shall not be denied or abridged by the United States or by any State on account of race, color, or previous condition of servitude."

The Civil Rights Acts of 1865 to 1875

From 1865 to 1875, Congress passed a series of civil rights acts to enforce the Thirteenth, Fourteenth, and Fifteenth Amendments. The Civil Rights Act of 1866 implemented the extension of citizenship to anyone born in the United States and gave African Americans full equality before the law. The act further authorized the president to enforce the law with the national armed forces. The Enforcement Act of 1870 set out specific criminal penalties for interfering with the right to vote as protected by the Fifteenth Amendment and by the Civil Rights Act of 1866.

Equally important was the Civil Rights Act of 1872, known as the Anti–Ku Klux Klan Act. This act made it a federal crime for anyone to use law or custom to deprive an individual of rights, privileges, and immunities secured by the Constitution or by any federal law. The Second Civil Rights Act, passed in 1875, declared that everyone is entitled to full and equal enjoyment of public accommodations, theaters, and other places of public amusement, and it imposed penalties on violators.

The Ineffectiveness of the Early Civil Rights Laws

The Reconstruction statutes, or civil rights acts, ultimately did little to secure equality for African Americans. Both the *Civil Rights Cases* and the case of *Plessy v. Ferguson* (discussed next) effectively nullified these acts. Additionally, various barriers were erected that prevented African Americans from exercising their right to vote.

(AP Photo/Rick Browne)

This member of the Ute tribe attends a ceremony for Ute and Comanche leaders. About how many Native Americans are there today?

The *Civil Rights Cases*. The United States Supreme Court invalidated the 1875 Second Civil Rights Act when it held, in the *Civil Rights Cases*[2] of 1883, that the enforcement clause of the Fourteenth Amendment (which states that "[n]o State shall make or enforce any law which shall abridge the privileges or immunities of citizens") was limited to correcting official actions by states. Thus, the discriminatory acts of *private* citizens were not illegal. ("Individual invasion of individual rights is not the subject matter of the Amendment.") The 1883 Supreme Court decision met with widespread approval throughout most of the United States.

Twenty years after the Civil War, the white majority was all too willing to forget about the Civil War amendments to the U.S. Constitution and the civil rights legislation of the 1860s and 1870s. The other civil rights laws that the Court did not specifically invalidate became dead letters in the statute books, although they were never officially repealed by Congress. At the same time, many former Confederate leaders had regained political power in the southern states.

***Plessy v. Ferguson*: Separate but Equal.** A key decision during this period concerned Homer Plessy, a Louisiana resident who was one-eighth African American. In 1892, he boarded a train in New Orleans. The conductor made him leave the car, which was restricted to whites, and directed him to a car for nonwhites. At that time, Louisiana had a statute providing for separate railway cars for whites and African Americans.

did you know?

Justice John Marshall Harlan, who wrote the only dissent to *Plessy v. Ferguson*, stated in that very dissent, just a few paragraphs after his now-famous words that our Constitution is "color-blind," that Chinese people are members of "a race so different from our own" that it is permissible to deny them citizenship rights.

2. 109 U.S. 3 (1883).

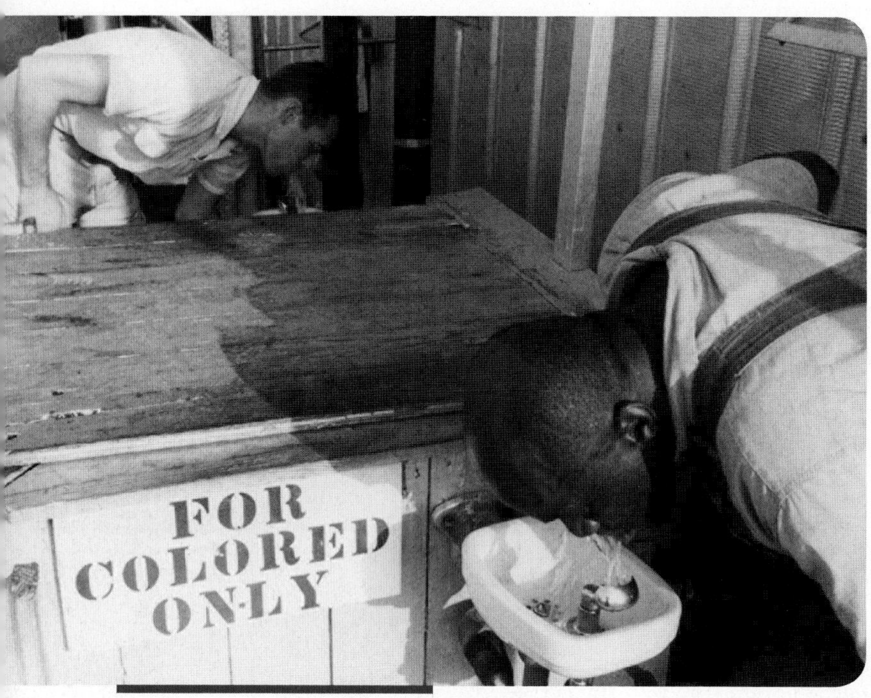

(© Bettmann/Corbis)

Segregated drinking fountains were common in southern states in the late 1800s and during the first half of the twentieth century. What landmark Supreme Court case made such segregated facilities legal?

Plessy went to court, claiming that such a statute was contrary to the Fourteenth Amendment's equal protection clause. In 1896, the United States Supreme Court rejected Plessy's contention. The Court concluded that the Fourteenth Amendment "could not have been intended to abolish distinctions based upon color, or to enforce social . . . equality." The Court stated that segregation alone did not violate the Constitution: "Laws permitting, and even requiring, their separation in places where they are liable to be brought into contact do not necessarily imply the inferiority of either race to the other."[3] So was born the **separate-but-equal doctrine.**

Plessy v. Ferguson became the judicial cornerstone of racial discrimination throughout the United States. Even though *Plessy* upheld segregated facilities in railway cars only, it was assumed that the Supreme Court was upholding segregation everywhere. The result was a system of racial segregation, particularly in the South—supported by state and local "Jim Crow" laws. (Jim Crow was an insulting term for African Americans derived from a song-and-dance show.) These laws required separate drinking fountains; separate seats in theaters, restaurants, and hotels; separate public toilets; and separate waiting rooms for the two races. "Separate" was indeed the rule, but "equal" was never enforced, nor was it a reality.

Separate-but-Equal Doctrine The doctrine holding that separate-but-equal facilities do not violate the equal protection clause of the Fourteenth Amendment to the U.S. Constitution.

White Primary A state primary election that restricted voting to whites only; outlawed by the Supreme Court in 1944.

Grandfather Clause A device used by southern states to disenfranchise African Americans. It restricted voting to those whose grandfathers had voted before 1867.

Poll Tax A special tax that had to be paid as a qualification for voting. In 1964, the Twenty-fourth Amendment to the Constitution outlawed the poll tax in national elections, and in 1966 the Supreme Court declared it unconstitutional in state elections as well.

Literacy Test A test administered as a precondition for voting, often used to prevent African Americans from exercising their right to vote.

Voting Barriers. The brief voting enfranchisement of African Americans ended after 1877, when the federal troops that occupied the South during the Reconstruction era were withdrawn. White supremacist politicians regained control of state governments and, using everything except race as a formal criterion, passed laws that effectively deprived African Americans of the right to vote. By using the ruse that political parties were private entities, the Democratic Party managed to keep black voters from its primaries. The **white primary** was upheld by the Supreme Court until 1944 when, in *Smith v. Allwright,*[4] the Court ruled it a violation of the Fifteenth Amendment.

Another barrier to African American voting was the **grandfather clause,** which restricted voting to those who could prove that their grandfathers had voted before 1867. **Poll taxes** required the payment of a fee to vote. Thus, poor African Americans—as well as poor whites—who could not afford to pay the tax were excluded from voting. Not until the Twenty-fourth Amendment to the Constitution was ratified in 1964 was the poll tax eliminated as a precondition to voting. **Literacy tests** were also used to deny the vote to African Americans. Such tests asked potential voters to read, recite, or interpret complicated texts, such as a section of the state constitution, to the satisfaction of local registrars—who were, of course, rarely satisfied with the responses of African Americans.

Extralegal Methods of Enforcing White Supremacy. The second-class status of African Americans was also a matter of social custom, especially in the South. In their interactions with southern whites, African Americans were expected to observe an informal but detailed code of behavior that confirmed their inferiority. The most serious violation of the informal code was "familiarity" toward a white woman by an African American

3. *Plessy v. Ferguson,* 163 U.S. 537 (1896).
4. 321 U.S. 649 (1944).

man. The code was backed up by the common practice of *lynching*—mob action to murder an accused individual, usually by hanging and sometimes accompanied by torture. Of course, lynching was illegal, but southern authorities rarely prosecuted these cases, and white juries would not convict.[5]

The End of the Separate-but-Equal Doctrine

As early as the 1930s, several court rulings began to chip away at the separate-but-equal doctrine. The United States Supreme Court did not explicitly overturn *Plessy v. Ferguson* until 1954, however, when it issued one of the most famous judicial decisions in U.S. history.

In 1951, Oliver Brown decided that his eight-year-old daughter, Linda Carol Brown, should not have to go to an all-nonwhite elementary school twenty-one blocks from her home, when there was a white school only seven blocks away. The National Association for the Advancement of Colored People (NAACP), formed in 1909, decided to support Oliver Brown. The outcome would have a monumental impact on American society.

Brown v. Board of Education of Topeka. The 1954 unanimous decision of the United States Supreme Court in *Brown v. Board of Education of Topeka*[6] established that the segregation of races in the public schools violates the equal protection clause of the Fourteenth Amendment. Chief Justice Earl Warren said that separation implied inferiority, whereas the majority opinion in *Plessy v. Ferguson* had said the opposite.

"With All Deliberate Speed." The following year, in *Brown v. Board of Education*[7] (sometimes called the second *Brown* decision), the Court declared that the lower courts needed to ensure that African Americans would be admitted to schools on a nondiscriminatory basis "with all deliberate speed." The district courts were to consider devices in their desegregation orders that might include "the school transportation system, personnel, [and] revision of school districts and attendance areas into compact units to achieve a system of determining admission to the public schools on a nonracial basis."

(AP Photo)

Linda Carol Brown was only eight years old when her father started a lawsuit to allow her to attend a nearby white grammar school. The result was the landmark decision *Brown v. Board of Education of Topeka,* rendered in 1954. What was the impact of this Supreme Court decision?

Reactions to School Integration

The white South did not let the Supreme Court ruling go unchallenged. Governor Orval Faubus of Arkansas used the state's National Guard to block the integration of Central High School in Little Rock in September 1957. A federal court demanded that the troops be withdrawn. Finally, President Dwight Eisenhower had to federalize the Arkansas National Guard and send in the Army's 101st Airborne Division to quell the violence. Central High became integrated.

Universities in the South remained segregated. When James Meredith, an African American student, attempted to enroll at the University of Mississippi in Oxford in 1962, violence flared there, as it had in Little Rock. The white riot at Oxford was so intense that President John F. Kennedy was forced to send in 30,000 U.S. combat troops, a larger force than the one then stationed in Korea. There were 375 military and civilian injuries, many from gunfire, and two bystanders were killed. Ultimately, peace was restored, and Meredith began attending classes.

did you know?

The original Constitution failed to describe the status of *citizen* or how this status could be acquired.

De Jure and *De Facto* Segregation

The kind of segregation faced by Linda Carol Brown and James Meredith is called ***de jure* segregation,** because it is the result of discriminatory laws or government actions. (*De jure* is Latin for "by law.") A second kind of public school segregation was common in

***De Jure* Segregation**
Racial segregation that occurs because of laws or administrative decisions by public agencies.

5. One of the most notorious organizations enforcing white supremacy was the Ku Klux Klan, which made its first appearance in 1866.
6. 347 U.S. 483 (1954).
7. 349 U.S. 294 (1955).

***De Facto* Segregation**
Racial segregation that occurs because of past social and economic conditions and residential racial patterns.

many northern communities—***de facto* segregation.** This term refers to segregation that is not due to an explicit law but results from other causes, such as residential patterns. Neighborhoods inhabited almost entirely by African Americans naturally led to *de facto* segregation of the public schools.

Discrimination was still involved, however. In many communities, landlords would only rent to African Americans in specific districts, and realtors would not allow them to view houses outside of these zones. In other words, nongovernmental discrimination confined African Americans to all-black districts, which became known as *ghettos.*[8]

One method used by federal courts in the 1970s and 1980s to address both *de jure* and *de facto* segregation in the public schools was to bus students from black neighborhoods into white ones, and vice versa. Busing proved to be enormously unpopular. In the mid-1970s, about three-fourth of all whites opposed the policy, as did almost half of all African Americans. By the 1990s, federal courts were backing away from the practice. The desegregation of U.S. public schools peaked in 1988, and since then the schools have grown more segregated. Indeed, today, school admissions policies that favor minority applicants in an attempt to reduce *de facto* segregation may end up being challenged on equal protection grounds. (For a further discussion of this issue, see the section on affirmative action later in this chapter.)

■ Learning Outcome 2:
Describe the philosophies of the civil rights movement and the major civil rights legislation of the 1960s.

The Civil Rights Movement

The *Brown* decisions applied only to public schools. Not much else in the structure of existing segregation was affected. In December 1955, an African American woman, Rosa Parks, boarded a public bus in Montgomery, Alabama. When the bus became crowded, Parks was asked to move to the rear of the bus, the "colored" section. She refused, was arrested, and was fined $10. But that was not the end of the matter. For an entire year, African Americans boycotted the Montgomery bus line. The protest was headed by a twenty-seven-year-old Baptist minister, Dr. Martin Luther King, Jr. In the face of overwhelming odds, the protesters won. In 1956, a federal district court issued an injunction prohibiting the segregation of buses in Montgomery. The era of civil rights protests had begun.

Civil Disobedience
A nonviolent, public refusal to obey allegedly unjust laws.

In 1955, Rosa Parks was arrested for refusing to give up her seat on a Montgomery, Alabama, bus and move to the colored section. What happened after her arrest?

(AP Photo/Montgomery County Sheriff's Office)

King's Philosophy of Nonviolence

In the following year, 1957, King formed the Southern Christian Leadership Conference (SCLC). King advocated nonviolent **civil disobedience** as a means to achieve racial justice. The SCLC used tactics such as demonstrations and marches, as well as nonviolent, public disobedience of unjust laws. King's followers successfully used these methods to gain wider public acceptance of their cause.

Nonviolent Demonstrations. For the next decade, African Americans and sympathetic whites engaged in sit-ins, freedom rides, and freedom marches. In the beginning, such demonstrations were often met with violence, and the contrasting image of nonviolent African Americans and violent, hostile whites created strong public support for the civil rights movement. When African Americans in Greensboro, North Carolina, were refused service

8. *Ghetto* was originally the name of a district in Venice, Italy, in which Venetian Jews were required to live.

at a Woolworth's lunch counter, they organized a sit-in that was aided day after day by other African Americans and by sympathetic whites. Within six months of the first sit-in at the Greensboro Woolworth's, hundreds of lunch counters throughout the South were serving African Americans. The sit-in technique also was successfully used to integrate interstate buses and their terminals, as well as railroads engaged in interstate transportation.

The March on Washington. In August 1963, African American leaders A. Philip Randolph and Bayard Rustin organized the massive March on Washington for Jobs and Freedom. Before nearly a quarter-million white and African American spectators and millions watching on television, Dr. Martin Luther King, Jr., told the world: "I have a dream that my four little children will one day live in a nation where they will not be judged by the color of their skin but by the content of their character."

Another Approach—Black Power. Not all African Americans agreed with King's philosophy of nonviolence. Black Muslims and other African American separatists advocated a more militant stance and argued that desegregation should not result in cultural assimilation. During the 1950s and 1960s, when King was spearheading nonviolent protests and demonstrations to achieve civil rights for African Americans, black power leaders such as Malcolm X insisted that African Americans should "fight back" instead of turning the other cheek. Indeed, some would argue that without the fear generated by black militants, a "moderate" such as King would not have garnered such widespread support from white America.

did you know?

By September 1961, more than 3,600 students had been arrested for participating in civil rights demonstrations and 141 students and 58 faculty members had been expelled by colleges and universities for their part in civil rights protests.

Civil Rights Legislation

Attacks on demonstrators using police dogs, cattle prods, high-pressure water hoses, beatings, and bombings—plus the March on Washington—all led to an environment in which Congress felt compelled to act on behalf of African Americans. The second era of civil rights acts, sometimes referred to as the second Reconstruction period, was under way.

The Civil Rights Act of 1964. The Civil Rights Act of 1964, the most far-reaching bill on civil rights in modern times, banned discrimination on the basis of race, color, religion, gender, or national origin. The major provisions of the act were as follows:

1. It outlawed arbitrary discrimination in voter registration.
2. It barred discrimination in public accommodations, such as hotels and restaurants, which have operations that affect interstate commerce.
3. It authorized the federal government to sue to desegregate public schools and facilities.
4. It expanded the power of the Civil Rights Commission, which had been created in 1957, and extended its life.
5. It provided for the withholding of federal funds from programs administered in a discriminatory manner.
6. It established the right to equality of opportunity in employment.

Title VII of the Civil Rights Act of 1964 is the cornerstone of employment-discrimination law. It prohibits discrimination in employment based on race, color, religion, gender, or national origin. Under Title VII, executive orders were issued that banned employment discrimination by firms that received any federal funding. The 1964 Civil Rights Act created a five-member commission, the Equal Employment Opportunity Commission (EEOC), to administer Title VII.

In August 1963, a quarter-million whites and blacks descended on Washington, D.C., for a massive March for Jobs and Freedom. Who was the most important speaker at that event?

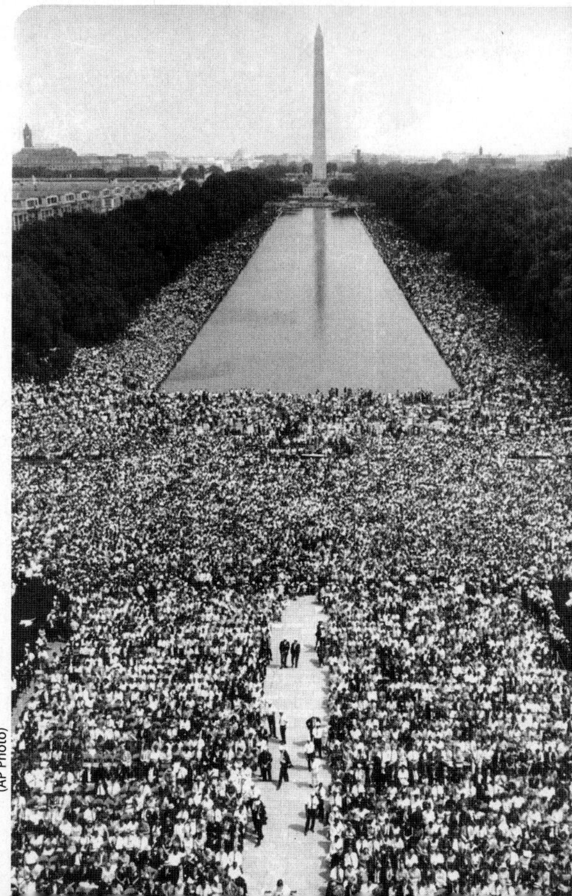
(AP Photo)

(© Bob Adelman/Corbis)

Martin Luther King in a quiet moment as he prepared to speak in Montgomery, Alabama. What type of resistance against segregation did King advocate?

It was not until 1972, however, that Congress gave the EEOC the right to sue employers, unions, and employment agencies. Therefore, litigation became an important activity for the agency.

The Voting Rights Act of 1965. As late as 1960, only 29 percent of African Americans of voting age were registered in the southern states, in stark contrast to 61 percent of whites. The Voting Rights Act of 1965 addressed this issue. The act had two major provisions. The first outlawed discriminatory voter-registration tests. The second authorized federal registration of voters and federally administered voting procedures in any political subdivision or state that discriminated electorally against a particular group. The act also provided that certain political subdivisions could not change their voting procedures and election laws without federal approval.

The act targeted counties, mostly in the South, in which fewer than 50 percent of the eligible population were registered to vote. Federal voter registrars were sent to those areas to register African Americans who had been kept from voting by local registrars. Within one week after the act was passed, forty-five federal examiners were sent to the South. A massive voter-registration drive covered the country.

Urban Riots. Even as the civil rights movement was experiencing its greatest victories, a series of riots swept through African American inner-city neighborhoods. The riots were primarily civil insurrections, although these disorders were accompanied by large-scale looting of stores. Inhabitants of the affected neighborhoods attributed the riots to racial discrimination. The riots dissipated much of the goodwill toward the civil rights movement that had been built up earlier in the decade among northern whites. Together with widespread student demonstrations against the Vietnam War (1965–1975), the riots pushed many Americans toward conservatism.

The Civil Rights Act of 1968 and Other Housing Reform Legislation. Martin Luther King, Jr., was assassinated on April 4, 1968. Despite King's message of peace, his death was followed by the most widespread rioting to date. Nine days after King's death, President Lyndon Johnson signed the Civil Rights Act of 1968, which forbade discrimination in most housing and provided penalties for those attempting to interfere with individual civil rights (giving protection to civil rights workers, among others). Subsequent legislation added enforcement provisions to the federal government's rules against discriminatory mortgage-lending practices.

Consequences of Civil Rights Legislation

As a result of the Voting Rights Act of 1965 and its amendments, and the large-scale voter-registration drives in the South, the number of African Americans registered to vote climbed dramatically. By 1980, 56 percent of African Americans of voting age in the South were registered. In recent national elections, turnout by African American voters has come very close to the white turnout. In 2008, with an African American on the presidential ballot, African American turnout exceeded that of whites for the first time in history.[9]

Political Participation by African Americans. Today, there are more than ten thousand African American elected officials in the United States. The movement of African

9. One widely reported study claimed that African American turnout did not quite match that of whites, but this conclusion was based on an overestimate of the number of African Americans eligible to vote.

American citizens into high elected office has been sure, if exceedingly slow. Notably, recent polling data show that most Americans do not consider race a significant factor in choosing a president. In 1958, when a Gallup poll first asked whether respondents would be willing to vote for an African American as president, only 38 percent of the public said yes. By 2008, this number had reached 94 percent. This high figure may have been attained, at least in part, because of the emergence of African Americans of presidential caliber. Of course, Barack Obama, elected president in 2008 on the Democratic ticket, is African American. Earlier, two Republican African Americans were also mentioned as presidential possibilities: Colin Powell, formerly chair of the Joint Chiefs of Staff and later secretary of state under President George W. Bush; and Condoleezza Rice, who succeeded Powell at the State Department.

Hispanic
Someone who can claim a heritage from a Spanish-speaking country. The term is used only in the United States or other countries that receive immigrants—Spanish-speaking persons living in Spanish-speaking countries normally do not apply the term to themselves.

Latino
An alternative to the term Hispanic that is preferred by many. Latina is the feminine.

Political Participation by Other Minorities. The civil rights movement focused primarily on the rights of African Americans. Yet the legislation resulting from the movement ultimately benefited nearly all minority groups. The Civil Rights Act of 1964, for example, prohibits discrimination against any person because of race, color, or national origin. Subsequent amendments to the Voting Rights Act of 1965 extended its protections to other minorities, including **Hispanic** Americans (or **Latinos**), Asian Americans, Native Americans, and Native Alaskans.

The political participation of non–African American minority groups has increased in recent years. Hispanics, for example, have gained political power in several states. Hispanics do not vote at the same rate as African Americans, in large part because many Hispanics are immigrants who are not yet citizens. Still, there are now about five thousand Hispanic elected officials in the United States. The impact of immigration will be discussed in greater detail later in this chapter.

Lingering Social and Economic Disparities. According to recent census data, social and economic disparities between whites and blacks (and other minorities) persist. Data released by the U.S. Census Bureau following the 2010 census showed that mean incomes in black households were only 59 percent of the incomes in non-Hispanic white households, and incomes of Hispanic households were just 69 percent of those of non-Hispanic whites. White adults were also more likely than black and Hispanic adults to have college degrees and to own their own homes. Whites are also less likely to live in poverty. Consider that the poverty rate for non-Hispanic white persons was 9.9 percent, compared

Half a century ago, not even 40 percent of Americans said they would vote for an African American for president. Since then, many African Americans have emerged as high government officials, including Colin Powell, secretary of state, and Condoleezza Rice, who succeeded him in that office during the Bush administration. What does Barack Obama's victory in the 2008 presidential elections tell you about changing racial attitudes in this country?

(From left to right, Charles Haynes/Creative Commons, AP Photo/J. J. Guillen, and AP Photo/Jae C. Hong)

Social Media IN POLITICS

Some social networks appeal to specific audiences. An examples is BlackPlanet, a site for socializing and debate that is actually older than either Facebook or Twitter. It can be accessed through those networks, however.

with a poverty rate of 27.4 percent for blacks and 26.6 percent for Hispanics. The recent collapse of the housing market also hit minority households much harder than white ones. While median non-Hispanic white households lost 16 percent of their net assets from 2005 to 2009, the figure for African Americans was 53 percent and for Hispanics, 66 percent.

Finally, even today, race consciousness continues to divide African Americans and white Americans. Whether we are talking about media stereotyping, racial profiling, or academic achievement, the black experience is different from the white one. As a result, African Americans often view the nation and many specific issues differently than their white counterparts do. In survey after survey, when blacks are asked whether they have achieved racial equality, few believe that they have. In contrast, whites are much more likely than blacks to believe that racial equality has been achieved.

One of the most troubling contrasts between the races is their differing experiences with the criminal justice system. African Americans, especially men, are far more likely to be arrested and imprisoned than whites. There is widespread disagreement about the reasons for this phenomenon, as you will see in this chapter's *Which Side Are You On?* feature on the facing page.

■ Learning Outcome 3: **Analyze the three standards used to determine if a law is discriminatory: strict scrutiny, intermediate scrutiny, and rational basis review.**

Civil Rights and the United States Supreme Court

As you have just learned, our modern understanding of civil rights developed over a period of many years, and decisions by the United States Supreme Court were crucial in establishing that understanding. Over time, the Supreme Court developed a series of standards to use when deciding cases of alleged discrimination: strict scrutiny, intermediate scrutiny, and rational basis review.

2012 elections
MINORITY-GROUP MEMBERS

2012 was not a banner year for gains in minority representation. The total number of minority-group members elected to the U.S. House and Senate was up by one for each chamber, for a total of five senators and seventy-eight representatives. The Senate now includes two Asian Americans and three Latino Americans, while the House contains forty-two African Americans, twenty-seven Latino Americans, and nine Asian Americans.

Minority-group members were key to the 2012 elections, however, but as voters, not candidates. The white non-Hispanic share of the electorate fell to 72 percent in 2012, down from 75 percent in 2008. The black, "other," and Latino vote shares were all up. Further, Barack Obama did better among Hispanics than he did in 2008—according to a Latino poll, 75 percent instead of 67 percent. Obama's get-out-the-vote drive, possibly the most effective in American history, had something to do with the high turnout.

Another factor was anger among minority-group members at alleged voter suppression tactics. These tactics included stiff voter-ID laws, beefed-up, poll-watching teams in minority precincts, and "robo-calls" instructing blacks and Latinos to vote on Wednesday, not Tuesday. Such measures proved to be counterproductive, as they drove up minority turnout instead.

(© kyoshino / iStockphoto) (© manley099 / iStockphoto)

Which Side Are You On?

IS THE CRIMINAL JUSTICE SYSTEM DISCRIMINATORY?

Since 1980, the rate of drug arrests of African Americans in forty large American cities has increased 250 percent, compared to 75 percent among whites. African Americans make up about 13 percent of the U.S. population. Nonetheless, they represent more than 50 percent of sentenced drug offenders. Nationwide, 43 percent of all inmates in state and federal prisons are black. In New York City, the most recent data show that police make about 575,000 pedestrian stops in a year, of which 55 percent target African Americans. Yet black citizens are only 23 percent of that city's population. Not surprisingly, many believe that the criminal justice system is unfair to African Americans.

THE SYSTEM IS UNFAIR

Those who believe that the system is discriminatory point to a number of statistics. About the same percentage of black and white poll respondents admit to using illegal drugs—between 8.5 and 9 percent. Yet African Americans are three times more likely than whites to be arrested on drug charges. Three-quarters of those sentenced for drug crimes are African American. More than four out of five drug arrests are for simple possession of a banned substance—so the racial disparity in arrests cannot be due to a large class of African American drug dealers. Under New York City mayor Michael Bloomberg, the police department has dramatically increased the number of minor drug arrests. Such targeting tactics result in blacks being arrested for drug possession at seven times the rate of whites. How can that be fair?

BUT RACISM IS NOT THE EXPLANATION

Some observers, however, argue that the disparities just described are legitimate. Certainly, the black-versus-white statistics are clear. But to blame racism is misguided. Police personnel go where the easy "collars" are. As a Chicago police chief admitted, "There is as much cocaine in the stock exchange as there is in the black community. But those guys are harder to catch. Those deals are done in office buildings [and] in someone's home. But the guy standing on the corner, he has almost got a sign on his back. These guys are just arrestable." District attorneys also know they can get higher conviction rates because residents of low-income communities usually cannot hire expensive legal help. Further, some experts contend that trading drugs openly on the streets leads to other crimes, including crimes of violence. This is not true of drug sales that take place in homes and offices. Low-income neighborhoods benefit when open drug markets are shut down. Indeed, homicide rates are now falling in such areas.

(© kyoshino / iStockphoto) (© Dean Mitchell / iStockphoto)

The Fourteenth Amendment

The Fourteenth Amendment to the U.S. Constitution, adopted in 1869 following the Civil War, is the main constitutional basis for civil rights legislation and court decisions. On page 114 in Chapter 4, we discussed the due process clause of the Fourteenth Amendment:

> *No State shall . . . deprive any person of life, liberty, or property, without due process of law . . . .*

This language mirrors that of the Fifth Amendment, which binds the federal government:

> *No person shall . . . be deprived of life, liberty, or property, without due process of law . . . .*

The due process clause was crucial to extending the civil liberties contained in the Bill of Rights to cover the actions of the individual states. The courts have made use of this clause

receiving Federal financial assistance." Title IX's best-known and most controversial impact has been on high school and collegiate athletics, although the original statute made no reference to athletics.

A question that the Supreme Court has not ruled on is whether women should be allowed to participate in military combat. Given that national security is such a compelling government interest, the Court has left this decision up to Congress and the Department of Defense. Recently, women have been allowed to serve as combat pilots and on naval warships. To date, however, they have not been allowed to join infantry direct-combat units, although they are now permitted to serve in combat-support units.

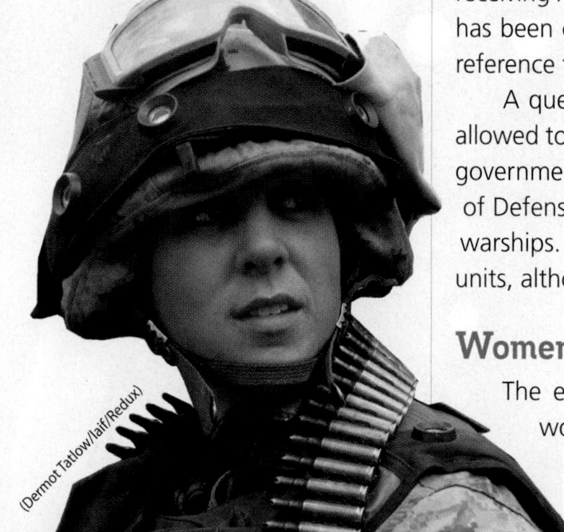

(Dermot Tatlow/laif/Redux)

More women are joining the U.S. Marines today. Are women in the military allowed to participate in on-the-ground combat?

Women in Politics Today

The efforts of women's rights advocates have helped to increase the number of women holding political offices at all levels of government.

Women in Congress. Although a men's club atmosphere still prevails in Congress, the number of women holding congressional seats has increased significantly in recent years. Elections during the 1990s brought more women to Congress than either the Senate or the House had seen before. In 2001, for the first time, a woman was elected to a leadership post in Congress—Nancy Pelosi of California became the Democrats' minority whip in the U.S. House of Representatives. In 2002, she was elected minority leader. In 2006, she was chosen to be the first woman Speaker of the House in the history of the United States—although she was forced to drop back to minority leader again in 2010 when the Republicans regained control of the House.

Women in the Executive and Judicial Branches. In 1984, for the first time, a woman, Geraldine Ferraro, became the Democratic nominee for vice president. In 2008, Hillary Clinton mounted a major campaign for the Democratic presidential nomination, and Sarah Palin became the Republican nominee for vice president. Recent Gallup polls show that close to 90 percent of Americans said they would vote for a qualified woman for president if she was nominated by their party.

Increasing numbers of women are also being appointed to cabinet posts. President George W. Bush appointed several women to cabinet positions, including Condoleezza Rice as his secretary of state in 2005. President Barack Obama named his former rival Hillary Clinton to be secretary of state and added six other women to his cabinet.

Increasing numbers of women are sitting on federal judicial benches as well. President Ronald Reagan (1981–1989) was credited with a historic first when he appointed Sandra Day O'Connor to the United States Supreme Court in 1981. (O'Connor retired in 2006.) President Bill Clinton also appointed a woman, Ruth Bader Ginsburg, to the Court. In 2009, President Obama named Sonia Sotomayor to the Court. She became the third woman and first Hispanic to serve. In 2010, Obama appointed Elena Kagan to the Court, bringing the number of women currently serving on the Court to three.

Around the world, more and more women have succeeded in winning top leadership positions in their national governments. We examine this development in the *Beyond Our Borders* feature on the facing page.

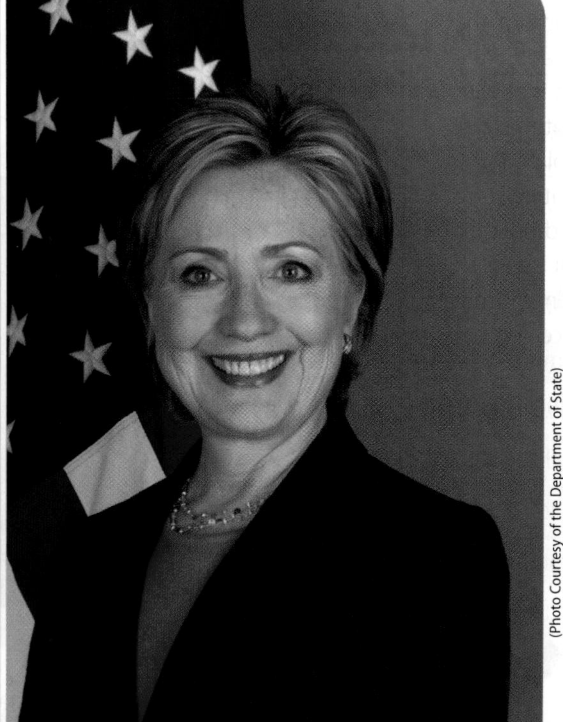

(Photo Courtesy of the Department of State)

Hillary Clinton almost became the first major party female presidential candidate in 2008. She became secretary of state in 2009.

Beyond Our Borders

WOMEN AS WORLD LEADERS

(© kyoshino / iStockphoto) (© mattjeacock / iStockphoto)

Since ancient times, women have occasionally risen to lead their people. When monarchy was in fashion, situations could arise in which a princess had a better claim to the throne than any man. Rulers such as England's Queen Elizabeth I (1558–1603) and Russia's Empress Catherine the Great (1762–1796) proved to be enormously successful. With the onset of elected leaders, however, female heads of government were out of the question for many years. For much of that time, after all, women could not even vote.

The hereditary principle is not limited to elevating queens and empresses. Many women have won elections on that basis. In 1960, Sirimavo Bandaranaike, prime minister of Sri Lanka, became the world's first democratically elected female head of government. Her husband was prime minister until 1959, when he was assassinated. The practice of wives, daughters, and sisters succeeding male leaders continues to this day. President Cristina Kirchner of Argentina is the widow of President Néstor Kirchner. Prime Minister Yingluck Shinawatra of Thailand is the younger sister of exiled former prime minister Thaksin Shinawatra. If Hillary Clinton, wife of President Bill Clinton, had won the presidency, she, too, would have illustrated the hereditary principle.

In recent years, however, more and more women have won elections without succeeding male relatives. The first of these was Prime Minister Golda Meir of Israel (1969–1974). Prime Minister Margaret Thatcher of Britain (1979–1990) famously pushed her nation toward free market capitalism. Today, Australia's Julia Gillard, Brazil's Dilma Rousseff, and Germany's Angela Merkoff lead their nations as the culmination of independent political careers.

FOR CRITICAL ANALYSIS

Prime Minister Jóhanna Sigurðardóttir of Iceland is the world's first lesbian elected chief executive. Could a gay man or lesbian ever be elected in the United States? Why or why not?

Gender-Based Discrimination in the Workplace

Traditional cultural beliefs concerning the proper role of women in society continue to be evident not only in the political arena but also in the workplace. Since the 1960s, however, women have gained substantial protection against discrimination through laws that require equal employment opportunities and equal pay.

Title VII of the Civil Rights Act of 1964. Title VII of the Civil Rights Act of 1964 prohibits gender discrimination in employment and has been used to strike down employment policies that discriminate against employees on the basis of gender. In 1978, Congress amended Title VII to expand the definition of gender discrimination to include discrimination based on pregnancy.

Sexual Harassment. The United States Supreme Court has also held that Title VII's prohibition of gender-based discrimination extends to **sexual harassment** in the workplace. One form of sexual harassment occurs when job opportunities, promotions, salary increases, and the like are given in return for sexual favors. Another form of sexual harassment, called hostile-environment harassment, occurs when an employee is subjected to sexual conduct or comments that interfere with the employee's job performance or are so pervasive or severe as to create an intimidating, hostile, or offensive environment.

Sexual Harassment
Unwanted physical or verbal conduct or abuse of a sexual nature that interferes with a recipient's job performance, creates a hostile work environment, or carries with it an implicit or explicit threat of adverse employment consequences.

Wage Discrimination. Although Title VII and other legislation since the 1960s have mandated equal employment opportunities for men and women, women continue to earn less, on average, than men do.

2012 elections

THE ROLE OF WOMEN

(© kyoshino / iStockphoto) (© manley099 / iStockphoto)

Women continued to gain representation in Congress in the 2012 elections. Every female senator running for reelection was returned. The number of women in the Senate is now twenty, up three. The total in the House is seventy-eight, up six. Several of these victories were notable. Democrat Tammy Baldwin of Wisconsin will be the first openly gay or lesbian senator in American history. Tulsi Gabbard, a Hawaii Democrat, will be the first Hindu American ever to serve in Congress. New Hampshire now has two women as senators, an all-female House delegation, and a female governor.

The hard-fought senate win by Elizabeth Warren in Massachusetts was widely applauded by feminists and liberals—she will be among the Senate's most liberal members. The greatest upset of the 2012 elections, however, starred a moderate Democratic woman, Heidi Heitkamp, who confounded the public opinion polls with a narrow senate victory in North Dakota. White men are now a minority in the House Democratic Caucus.

Women voters were also essential to Democratic victories. They supported Barack Obama 55 percent to 44 percent, while men supported Mitt Romney by 52 percent to 45 percent. The gender gap was especially notable among unmarried women, who backed Obama over Romney 67 percent to 31 percent.

In addition, women voters helped seal the fate of Tea Party–backed Republican senate candidates in Indiana and Missouri. Both men had made highly unfortunate statements in attempts to justify banning abortion in cases of rape. In Missouri, Representative Todd Akin contended that if women experience "legitimate rape," their bodies have a way to avert unwanted pregnancies. In Indiana, Republican Richard Mourdock stated that a pregnancy resulting from a rape was God's will. These remarks cost the Republicans two seats that they otherwise almost certainly would have carried. Further, the controversy may have helped taint the Republican "brand" among women in other states as well.

Exit polls after the elections revealed another fascinating gender-related fact—the impact of the gay and lesbian vote. Respondents who reported that they were gay, lesbian, or bisexual broke for Obama over Romney 76 percent to 22 percent. That was not surprising. What was startling was that voters who were *not* gay, lesbian, or bisexual split their votes 49 percent to 49 percent. One could make the argument, therefore, that the gay and lesbian vote was responsible for Obama's reelection.

The Equal Pay Act was enacted in 1963 as an amendment to the Fair Labor Standards Act of 1938. Basically, the Equal Pay Act requires employers to provide equal pay for substantially equal work. In other words, males cannot legally be paid more than females who perform essentially the same job. The Equal Pay Act did not address the fact that certain types of jobs traditionally held by women pay lower wages than the jobs usually held by men. For example, more women than men are salesclerks and nurses, whereas more men than women are construction workers and truck drivers. Even if all clerks performing substantially similar jobs for a company earned the same salaries, they typically would still be earning less than the company's truck drivers.

More women today are in scientific and high-tech jobs than ever before. Why?

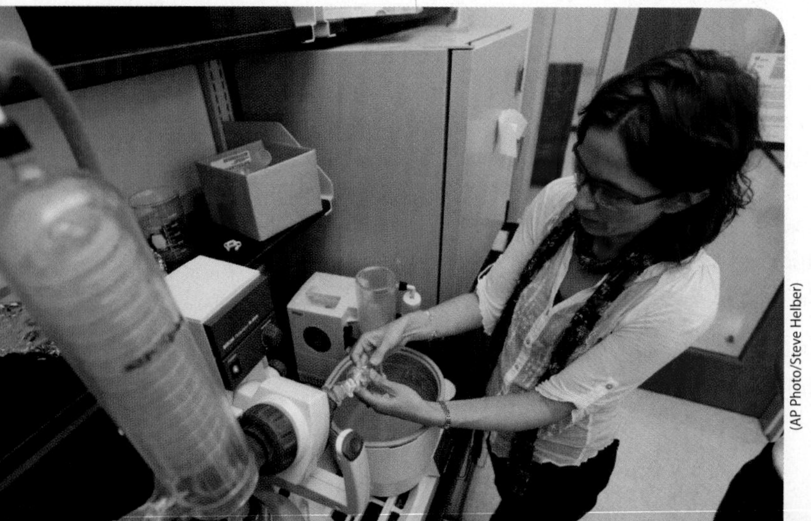

(AP Photo/Steve Helber)

When Congress passed the Equal Pay Act in 1963, a woman, on average, made 59 cents for every dollar earned by a man. By the mid-1990s, this amount had risen to 75 cents. Figures recently released by the U.S. Department of Labor indicate, though, that since then there has been little change. By 2010, women were still earning, on average, 78 cents for every dollar earned by men.

Immigration, Latinos, and Civil Rights

■ Learning Outcome 5: **Explain how immigration is changing the face of America.**

Immigration, and in particular unauthorized immigration, has become one of the hottest political topics under debate. Issues include how we should address the question of unauthorized immigrants, as discussed in the *What If* . . . feature at the beginning of this chapter. A second major topic is how to limit unauthorized immigration in the first place. Closely allied to these issues are those affecting legal immigrants. Are we admitting too many legal immigrants—or not enough? Are laws restricting the rights of immigrants appropriate—or too tough? We examine immigration further in Chapter 14.

A century ago, most immigrants to the United States came from Europe. Today, however, most come from Latin America and Asia. Tables 5–2, 5–3, and 5–4 below and on the following page show the top countries of origin for immigrants, both legal and unauthorized, entering the United States. Note the large number of immigrants from Spanish-speaking, or "Hispanic," countries, which are shown in red in the tables.

The large number of new immigrants from Spanish-speaking countries increases the Hispanic proportion of the U.S. population. The number of persons who identify themselves as *multiracial* is also growing due to interracial marriages.

Hispanic versus *Latino*

To the U.S. Census Bureau, Hispanics can be of any race. They can be new immigrants or members of families that have lived in the United States for centuries. Hispanics may come from any of about twenty primarily Spanish-speaking countries,[17] and as a result, they are a highly diverse population. The four largest Hispanic groups include Mexican Americans, at 65.5 percent of all Hispanics. Puerto Ricans, all of whom are U.S. citizens, constitute 9.1 percent of the total. Salvadorans make up 3.6 percent, and Cuban Americans, 3.5 percent.

The term *Hispanic* itself, although used by the government, is not particularly popular among Hispanic Americans. Many prefer the term *Latino* or *Latina*. When possible, Latinos prefer a name that identifies their heritage more specifically—for example, many Mexican Americans would rather be called that than *Latino* or *Hispanic*. Some Mexican Americans prefer the term *Chicano*.

The Changing Face of America

As a result of immigration, the ethnic makeup of the United States is changing. Yet immigration is not the only factor contributing to changes in the American ethnic mosaic. Another factor is ethnic differences in the *fertility rate*. The **fertility rate** measures the average number of children that women in a given group are expected to have over the course of a lifetime. A fertility rate of 2.1 is the "long-term replacement rate." In other words, if a nation or group maintains a rate of 2.1, its population will eventually stabilize. This can take many years, however. Because of past growth, the median age of the population may be younger than it would otherwise be. This means that there are more potential mothers and fathers. Only after its residents age will the population of a group or country stabilize.

Today, the United States actually has a fertility rate of 2.1 children per woman. Hispanic Americans, however, have a current fertility rate of 2.9. African Americans have a fertility rate of 2.1. Non-Hispanic white Americans

Fertility Rate
A statistic that measures the average number of children that women in a given group are expected to have over the course of a lifetime.

Table 5–2 ▸ Top Eleven Countries of Origin for the Foreign-Born Population

Hispanic countries are shown in red.

Mexico	11,700,000
China	2,200,000
India	1,800,000
Philippines	1,800,000
El Salvador	1,200,000
Vietnam	1,200,000
Cuba	1,100,000
Korea	1,100,000
Dominican Republic	900,000
Canada	800,000
Guatemala	800,000
ALL COUNTRIES	40,000,000

Source: U.S. Bureau of the Census. Figures are for 2010.

17. According to the census definition, *Hispanic* includes the relatively small number of Americans whose ancestors came directly from Spain itself. Few of these people are likely to check the "Hispanic" box on a census form, however.

Table 5–3 ▸ Top Ten Countries of Birth for Unauthorized Immigrants

Also referred to as "illegal" or "undocumented" immigrants. Of necessity, these figures are rough estimates. Hispanic countries are shown in red.

Mexico	6,640,000
El Salvador	620,000
Guatemala	520,000
Honduras	330,000
Philippines	280,000
India	200,000
Brazil*	180,000
Ecuador	180,000
Korea	170,000
China	130,000
ALL COUNTRIES	10,790,000

*Although Brazil is located in South America, its language is Portuguese, and the Bureau of the Census does not consider it a Hispanic country.

Source: U.S. Department of Homeland Security. Figures are for 2010.

Table 5–4 ▸ Top Eight Countries of Origin for Legal Immigrants

The following figures are for a single year only. Legal immigrants are persons obtaining official permanent resident status in that year. Hispanic countries are shown in red.

Mexico	139,120
China	70,863
India	69,162
Philippines	58,173
Dominican Republic	53,870
Cuba	33,573
Vietnam	30,632
Haiti	22,582
ALL COUNTRIES	1,042,625

Source: U.S. Department of Homeland Security. Figures are for 2010.

have a fertility rate of 1.84. Figure 5–1 on the facing page shows the projected changes in U.S. ethnic distribution in future years. These estimates could change if immigration rates fall, as is typical during a recession.

■ Learning Outcome 6: **Define *affirmative action*, and provide some of the arguments used against it.**

Affirmative Action

Affirmative Action
A policy in educational admissions and job hiring that gives special attention or compensatory treatment to traditionally disadvantaged groups in an effort to overcome present effects of past discrimination.

As noted earlier in this chapter, the Civil Rights Act of 1964 prohibited discrimination against any person on the basis of race, color, national origin, religion, or gender. The act also established the right to equal opportunity in employment. A basic problem remained, however: minority groups and women, because of past discrimination, often lacked the education and skills to compete effectively in the marketplace. In 1965, the federal government attempted to remedy this problem by implementing the concept of affirmative action. **Affirmative action** policies attempt to "level the playing field" by giving special preferences in educational admissions and employment decisions to groups that have been discriminated against in the past.

In 1965, President Lyndon Johnson issued Executive Order 11246, which mandated affirmative action policies to remedy the effects of past discrimination. All government agencies, including those of state and local governments, were required to implement such policies. Additionally, affirmative action requirements were imposed on companies that sell goods or services to the federal government and on institutions that receive federal funds, such as universities. Affirmative action policies were also required whenever an employer had been ordered to develop such a plan by a court or by the Equal Employment Opportunity Commission because of evidence of past discrimination. Finally, labor unions

Figure 5-1 ▸ Projected Changes in U.S. Ethnic Distribution

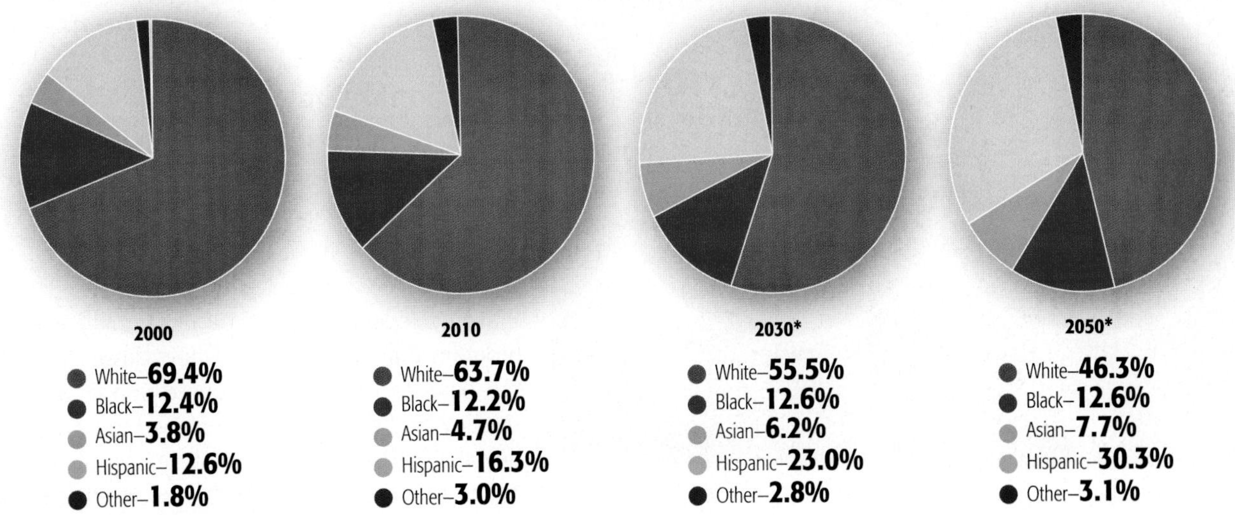

*Data for 2030 and 2050 are projections.
Hispanics may be of any race. The chart categories *White, Black, Asian,* and *Other* are limited to non-Hispanics.
Other consists of the following non-Hispanic groups: *American Indian, Native Alaskan, Native Hawaiian, Other Pacific Islander,* and *Two or more races.*
Sources: U.S. Bureau of the Census and authors' calculations.

that had been found to discriminate against women or minorities in the past were required to establish and follow affirmative action plans.

Affirmative action programs have been controversial because they allegedly result in discrimination against "majority" groups, such as white males (or discrimination against other minority groups that may not be given preferential treatment under a particular affirmative action program). At issue in the current debate over affirmative action programs is whether such programs, because of their discriminatory nature, violate the equal protection clause of the Fourteenth Amendment to the Constitution.

The *Bakke* Case

The first United States Supreme Court case addressing the constitutionality of affirmative action examined a program implemented by the University of California at Davis. Allan Bakke, a white student who had been turned down for medical school at the Davis campus, discovered that his academic record was better than those of some of the minority applicants who had been admitted to the program. He sued the University of California regents, alleging **reverse discrimination.** The UC Davis Medical School had held sixteen places out of one hundred for educationally "disadvantaged students" each year, and the administrators at that campus admitted to using race as a criterion for admission for those particular slots.

Reverse Discrimination
The situation in which an affirmative action program discriminates against those who do not have minority status.

In 1978, the Supreme Court handed down its decision in *Regents of the University of California v. Bakke.*[18] The Court did not rule against affirmative action programs. Rather, it held that Bakke must be admitted to the medical school because its admissions policy had used race as the sole criterion for the sixteen "minority" positions. Justice Lewis Powell, speaking for the Court, indicated that while race can be

(© Roy Delgado/www.CartoonStock.com)

"Sorry, but hiring only men allows me to avoid gender politics."

18. 438 U.S. 265 (1978).

(AP Photo/Paul Sakuma)

Demonstrators protest outside a hearing where a ban on considering race in public college admissions was challenged. Why would nonminority students want to keep laws that favor the admission of more minority students?

considered "as a factor" among others in admissions (and presumably hiring) decisions, race cannot be the sole factor. So affirmative action programs, but not quota systems, were upheld as constitutional.

Additional Limits on Affirmative Action

A number of cases decided during the 1980s and 1990s placed further limits on affirmative action programs. In a landmark decision in 1995, *Adarand Constructors, Inc. v. Peña,*[19] the Supreme Court held that any federal, state, or local affirmative action program that uses racial or ethnic classifications as the basis for making decisions is subject to strict scrutiny by the courts. (We described the strict scrutiny standard earlier in this chapter, on page 158.) The Court's opinion in the *Adarand* case means that an affirmative action program cannot make use of quotas or preferences for unqualified persons. In addition, once the program has succeeded in achieving the purpose it was tailored to meet, the program must be changed or dropped.

In 2003, in two cases involving the University of Michigan, the Supreme Court indicated that limited affirmative action programs continued to be acceptable and that diversity was a legitimate goal. The Court struck down the affirmative action plan used for undergraduate admissions at the university, which automatically awarded a substantial number of points to applicants based on minority status.[20] At the same time, it approved the admissions plan used by the law school, which took race into consideration as part of a complete examination of each applicant's background.[21]

The End of Affirmative Action?

Although in 2003 the United States Supreme Court upheld the admissions plan used by the University of Michigan Law School, a Michigan ballot initiative passed in 2006 prohibited affirmative action programs in all public universities and for state government positions. In addition to Michigan, other states, including California, Florida, Nebraska, and Washington, have banned all state-sponsored affirmative action programs. Colorado voters rejected such a ban in 2008, but Oklahoma banned affirmative action in 2012.

In 2007, the United States Supreme Court heard a case involving voluntary integration plans in school districts in Seattle, Washington, and in Louisville, Kentucky. The schools' racial-integration guidelines permitted race to be a deciding factor if, say, two students sought to be admitted to the school and there was space for only one. The schools' policies were challenged by parents of students, most of them white, who were denied admission because of their race. In a close (five-to-four) decision, the Court ruled that the schools' policies violated the Constitution's equal protection clause. (The Court did not, however, go so far as to invalidate the use of race as a factor in admissions policies.)[22]

Today, the future of affirmative action programs is in doubt. State attempts to ban such programs are not the greatest threat. Rather, affirmative action faces a possible change of heart by the Supreme Court. It is conceivable that in coming years the Court

19. 515 U.S. 200 (1995).
20. *Gratz v. Bollinger,* 539 U.S. 244 (2003).
21. *Grutter v. Bollinger,* 539 U.S. 306 (2003).
22. *Parents Involved in Community Schools v. Seattle School District No. 1,* 551 U.S. 701 (2007).

may find that affirmative action programs can no longer survive the strict scrutiny standard when they are applied to a suspect classification such as race.

Securing Rights for Persons with Disabilities

Persons with disabilities did not fall under the protective umbrella of the Civil Rights Act of 1964. In 1973, however, Congress passed the Rehabilitation Act, which prohibited discrimination against persons with disabilities in programs receiving federal aid. A 1978 amendment to the act established the Architectural and Transportation Barriers Compliance Board. Regulations for ramps, elevators, and the like in all federal buildings were implemented. Congress passed the Education for All Handicapped Children Act in 1975. It guarantees that all children with disabilities will receive an "appropriate" education. The most significant federal legislation to protect the rights of persons with disabilities, however, is the Americans with Disabilities Act (ADA), which Congress passed in 1990.

■ Learning Outcome 7:
Detail the rights provided by the Americans with Disabilities Act.

The Americans with Disabilities Act of 1990

The ADA requires that all public buildings and public services be accessible to persons with disabilities. The act also mandates that employers must reasonably accommodate the needs of workers or potential workers with disabilities. Car rental companies must provide cars with hand controls for disabled drivers. Telephone companies are required to have operators to pass on messages from speech-impaired persons who use telephones with keyboards.

The ADA requires employers to "reasonably accommodate" the needs of persons with disabilities unless to do so would cause the employer to suffer an "undue hardship." The ADA defines persons with disabilities as persons who have physical or mental impairments that "substantially limit" their everyday activities. Health conditions that have been considered disabilities under federal law include blindness, a history of alcoholism, heart disease, cancer, muscular dystrophy, cerebral palsy, paraplegia, diabetes, acquired immune deficiency syndrome (AIDS), and infection with the human immunodeficiency virus (HIV) that causes AIDS.

The ADA does not require that *unqualified* applicants with disabilities be hired or retained. If a job applicant or an employee with a disability, with reasonable accommodation, can perform essential job functions, however, then the employer must make the accommodation. Required accommodations may include installing ramps for a wheelchair, establishing more flexible working hours, creating or modifying job assignments, and creating or improving training materials and procedures.

Limiting the Scope and Applicability of the ADA

Beginning in 1999, the United States Supreme Court issued a series of decisions that effectively limited the scope of the ADA. In 1999, for example, the Court held in *Sutton v. United Airlines, Inc.*,[23] that a condition (in this case, severe nearsightedness) that can be corrected with medication or a corrective device (in this case, eyeglasses) is not considered a disability

23. 527 U.S. 471 (1999).

The Orange County Transportation Authority center uses Americans with Disabilities Act standards to create accessible transportation services. Why didn't buses have these services available fifty years ago?

(Jebb Harris/Zuma Press/Newscom)

under the ADA. In other words, the determination of whether a person is substantially limited in a major life activity is based on how the person functions when taking medication or using corrective devices, not on how the person functions without these measures. Thereafter, the courts held that plaintiffs with bipolar disorder, epilepsy, diabetes, and other conditions do not fall under the ADA's protections if the conditions can be corrected with medication or corrective devices—even if the plaintiffs were discriminated against because of their conditions.

In September 2008, President George W. Bush signed into law the ADA Amendments Act. This legislation overturned limits that the Supreme Court had placed on the ADA. With the exception of eyeglasses, the courts are no longer allowed to consider how a person functions when using "mitigating measures," but must assess whether a person is disabled without such assistance. The new law also struck down a Supreme Court decision that seriously restricted the meaning of "major life activities." In that case, the Court refused to consider carpal tunnel syndrome as a disability because the manual tasks that sufferers were unable to perform did not qualify as a major life activity.[24]

The Supreme Court has also limited the applicability of the ADA by holding that lawsuits under the ADA cannot be brought against state government employers.[25] In a 2001 case, the Court concluded that states, as sovereigns, are immune from lawsuits brought against them by private parties under the federal ADA.

■ Learning Outcome 8: **Summarize the recent revolution in the rights enjoyed by gay men and lesbians.**

The Rights and Status of Gay Males and Lesbians

In the summer of 1969, gay men and lesbians who frequented a New York City bar called the Stonewall Inn had had enough. They were tired of unrelenting police harassment. For two nights, they fought with police. Out of these riots came a "gay power" movement.

On June 27, 1969, patrons of the Stonewall Inn, a New York City bar popular with gay men and lesbians, responded to a police raid by throwing beer cans and bottles because they were angry at what they felt was unrelenting police harassment. In the ensuing riot, which lasted two nights, hundreds of gay men and lesbians fought with police. Before Stonewall, the stigma attached to homosexuality and the resulting fear of exposure had tended to prevent most gay men and lesbians from engaging in activism. In the months immediately after Stonewall, however, "gay power" graffiti began to appear in New York City. The Gay Liberation Front and the Gay Activist Alliance were formed, and similar groups sprang up in other parts of the country.

("DoctorWho," Creative Commons)

Growth in the Gay Male and Lesbian Rights Movement

The Stonewall incident marked the beginning of the movement for gay and lesbian rights. Since then, gay men and lesbians have formed thousands of organizations to exert pressure on legislatures, the media, schools, churches, and other organizations to recognize their right to equal treatment.

To a great extent, lesbian and gay groups have succeeded in changing

24. *Toyota Manufacturing, Kentucky, Inc. v. Williams*, 534 U.S. 184 (2002).
25. *Board of Trustees of the University of Alabama v. Garrett*, 531 U.S. 356 (2001).

public opinion—and state and local laws—that pertain to their status and rights. Nevertheless, they continue to struggle against age-old biases against homosexuality, often rooted in deeply held religious beliefs, and the rights of gay men and lesbians remain an extremely divisive issue in American society.

State and Local Laws Targeting Gay Men and Lesbians

Before the Stonewall incident, forty-nine states had sodomy laws that made various kinds of sexual acts, including homosexual acts, illegal (Illinois, which had repealed its sodomy law in 1962, was the only exception). During the 1970s and 1980s, more than half of these laws were either repealed or struck down by the courts.

The states—mostly in the South—that resisted the movement to abolish sodomy laws received a boost in 1986 with the Supreme Court's decision in *Bowers v. Hardwick*.[26] In that case, the Court upheld, by a five-to-four vote, a Georgia law that made homosexual conduct between two adults a crime. In 2003, however, the Court reversed its earlier position on sodomy with its decision in *Lawrence v. Texas*.[27] In this case, the Court held that laws against sodomy violate the due process clause of the Fourteenth Amendment. The Court stated: "The liberty protected by the Constitution allows homosexual persons the right to choose to enter upon relationships in the confines of their homes and their own private lives and still retain their dignity as free persons." As a result, *Lawrence v. Texas* invalidated the sodomy laws that remained on the books in fourteen states.

Today, twenty-five states, the District of Columbia, and more than 180 cities and counties have enacted laws protecting lesbians and gay men from discrimination in employment in at least some workplaces. Many of these laws also ban discrimination in housing, in public accommodation, and in other contexts. In contrast, Colorado adopted a constitutional amendment in 1992 to invalidate all state and local laws protecting homosexuals from discrimination. Ultimately, however, the Supreme Court, in *Romer v. Evans*,[28] ruled against the amendment, because it violated the equal protection clause of the U.S. Constitution by denying to homosexuals in Colorado—but to no other Colorado residents—"the right to seek specific protection of the law."

did you know?

Albert Einstein was among six thousand persons in Germany in 1903 who signed a petition to repeal a portion of the German penal code that made homosexuality illegal.

The Gay Community and Politics

Politicians at the national level have not overlooked the potential significance of homosexual issues in American politics. While conservative politicians generally have been critical of efforts to secure gay and lesbian rights, liberals, by and large, have been speaking out for gay rights in the past thirty years. In 1980, the Democratic platform included a gay plank for the first time.

As of the 2012 elections, six openly gay men, lesbians, or bisexuals were seated in the House of Representatives. Democrat Tammy Baldwin of Wisconsin was the first gay or lesbian member of the Senate. Gay rights groups continue to work for increased political representation in Congress.

Army National Guard Lieutenant Dan Choi was dismissed as a result of the Army's "don't ask, don't tell" policy described on the following page.

(AP Photo/Damian Dovarganes)

26. 478 U.S. 186 (1986).
27. 539 U.S. 558 (2003).
28. 517 U.S. 620 (1996).

(AP Photo/Mike Derer)

Arrested youths under the age of 18 do not necessarily have the same rights as adults. In some cases, however, they can be tried as adults.

Children's rights and their ability to articulate their rights for themselves in custody matters were strengthened, however, by several well-publicized rulings involving older children. In one case, for example, an eleven-year-old Florida boy filed suit in his own name, assisted by his own privately retained legal counsel, to terminate his relationship with his biological parents and to have the court affirm his right to be adopted by foster parents. The court granted his request, although it did not agree procedurally with the method by which the boy initiated the suit.[39]

Criminal Rights of Juveniles. One of the main requirements for an act to be criminal is intent. The law has given children certain defenses against criminal prosecution because of their presumed inability to have criminal intent. Under the **common law,** children up to seven years of age were considered incapable of committing a crime because they did not have the moral sense to understand that they were doing wrong. Children between the ages of seven and fourteen were also presumed to be incapable of committing a crime, but this presumption could be challenged by showing that the child understood the wrongful nature of the act. Today, states vary in their approaches. Most states retain the common law approach, although age limits vary from state to state. Other states have simply set a minimum age for criminal responsibility.

Common Law
Judge-made law that originated in England from decisions shaped according to prevailing customs. Decisions were applied to similar situations and thus gradually became common to the nation.

All states have juvenile court systems that handle children below the age of criminal responsibility who commit delinquent acts. The aim of juvenile courts is allegedly to reform rather than to punish. In states that retain the common law approach, children who are above the minimum age but are still juveniles can be turned over to the criminal courts if the juvenile court determines that they should be treated as adults. Children sent to juvenile court do not have the right to trial by jury or to post bail. Also, in most states parents can commit their minor children to state mental institutions without allowing the child a hearing.

Although minors usually do not have the full rights of adults in criminal proceedings, they have certain advantages. In felony, manslaughter, murder, armed robbery, and assault cases, traditionally juveniles were not tried as adults. They were often sentenced to probation or "reform" school for a relatively short term regardless of the seriousness of their crimes. Today, however, most states allow juveniles to be tried as adults (often at the discretion of the judge) for certain crimes, such as murder. When they are tried as adults, they are given due process of law and tried for the crime, rather than being given the paternalistic treatment reserved for a juvenile delinquent. Juveniles who are tried as adults may also face adult penalties. These used to include the death penalty. In 2005, however, the United States Supreme Court ruled that executing persons who were under the age of eighteen when they committed their crimes would constitute cruel and unusual punishment. The Court contended that sixteen- and seventeen-year-olds do not have a fully developed sense of right and wrong, nor do they necessarily understand the full gravity of their misdeeds.[40] In May 2010, the Court also ruled that juveniles who commit crimes in which no one is killed may not be sentenced to life in prison without the possibility of parole.[41]

39. *Kingsley v. Kingsley,* 623 So.2d 780 (Fla.App. 1993).
40. *Roper v. Simmons,* 543 U.S. 551 (2005).
41. *Graham v. Florida,* 560 U.S. ___ (2010).

Why Should You Care about... CIVIL RIGHTS?

(AP Photo/Javier Galeano)

Why should you, as an individual, care about civil rights? Some people may think that discrimination is a problem only for members of racial or ethnic minorities. Actually, almost everyone can be affected. Consider that in some instances, white men have actually experienced "reverse discrimination"—and have obtained redress for it. Also, discrimination against women is common, and women constitute half the population. Even if you are male, you probably have female friends or relatives whose well-being is of interest to you. Therefore, the knowledge of how to proceed when you suspect discrimination is another useful tool to have when living in the modern world.

HOW YOU CAN MAKE A DIFFERENCE

Anyone applying for a job may be subjected to a variety of possibly discriminatory practices based on race, color, gender, religion, age, sexual preference, or disability. There may be tests, some of which could have a discriminatory effect. At both the state and the federal levels, the government continues to examine the fairness and validity of criteria used in screening job applicants. As a result, there are ways of addressing the problem of discrimination.

If you believe that you have been discriminated against by a potential employer, consider the following steps:

1. Evaluate your own capabilities, and determine if you are truly qualified for the position.
2. Analyze the reasons why you were turned down. Would others agree with you that you have been the object of discrimination, or would they uphold the employer's claim?
3. If you still believe that you have been treated unfairly, you have recourse to several agencies and services.

You should first speak to the personnel director of the company and explain politely that you believe you have not been evaluated adequately. If asked, explain your concerns clearly. If necessary, go into explicit detail, and indicate that you may have been discriminated against.

If a second evaluation is not forthcoming, contact your local state employment agency. If you still do not obtain adequate help, contact one or more of the following state agencies, usually listed in your telephone directory under "State Government":

1. If a government entity is involved, a state ombudsperson or citizen aide may be available to mediate.
2. You can contact the state civil rights commission, which at least should give you advice, even if it does not wish to take up your case.
3. The state attorney general's office normally has a division dealing with discrimination and civil rights.
4. There may be a special commission or department specifically set up to help you, such as a women's status commission or a commission on Hispanics or Asian Americans. If you are a woman or a member of such a minority group, contact these commissions.

Finally, at the national level, you can contact:

Equal Employment Opportunity Commission
131 M St. NE
Washington, DC 20507
202-663-4900

Search on "eeoc" to locate the agency's Web site.

Questions for Discussion and Analysis

1. Review the *Which Side Are You On?* feature on page 157. What effect would legalizing or decriminalizing drugs have on the relationship between minority group members and the criminal justice system?
2. Not all African Americans agreed with the philosophy of nonviolence espoused by Dr. Martin Luther King, Jr. Advocates of black power called for a more militant approach. Can militancy make a movement more effective (possibly by making a more moderate approach seem like a reasonable compromise), or is it typically counterproductive? Either way, why?
3. Women in the military are currently barred from assignments that are likely to place them in active combat. (Of course, the nature of war is such that support units sometimes find themselves in combat, regardless of assignment.) Such barriers can keep female officers from advancing to the highest levels within the armed services. Are these barriers appropriate? Why or why not?
4. The prevention of terrorist acts committed by adherents of radical Islamism is a major policy objective today. Can we defend ourselves against such acts without abridging the civil rights and liberties of American Muslims and immigrants from predominantly Muslim countries? What measures that might be undertaken by the authorities are legitimate? Which are not?

Key Terms

Chapter Summary

1. Before the Civil War, most African Americans were slaves, and slavery was protected by the Constitution. Constitutional amendments after the Civil War ended slavery, and African Americans gained citizenship, the right to vote, and other rights. This protection was largely a dead letter by the 1880s, however, and African American inequality continued.
2. Segregation was declared unconstitutional by the Supreme Court in *Brown v. Board of Education of Topeka* (1954), in which the Court stated that separation implied inferiority. In 1955, the modern civil rights movement began with a boycott of segregated public transportation in Montgomery, Alabama. The Civil Rights Act of 1964 banned discrimination on the basis of race, color, religion, gender, or national origin in employment and public accommodations.
3. The Voting Rights Act of 1965 outlawed discriminatory voter-registration tests and authorized federal voter registration. The Voting Rights Act and other protective legislation apply not only to African Americans but to other ethnic groups. Minorities have been increasingly represented in national and state politics.
4. Civil rights are protected by the Fourteenth Amendment to the U.S. Constitution and, in particular, by the due process and equal protection clauses. The courts have developed a series of tests to use when considering cases of possible discrimination. Strict scrutiny, the most rigorous of these, applies to such suspect classifications as race, religion, and national origin. Intermediate, or exacting, scrutiny is employed in cases involving women's rights. Rational basis review, used when strict or exacting scrutiny does not apply, is the easiest test to meet.
5. In the early history of the United States, women had no political rights. After the first women's rights convention in 1848, the women's movement gained momentum. Not until 1920, however, when the Nineteenth Amendment was ratified, did women obtain the right to vote nationwide. The modern women's movement began in the 1960s in the wake of the civil rights and anti–Vietnam War movements. Efforts to secure the ratification of the Equal Rights Amendment failed, but the women's movement has been successful in obtaining new laws, changes in

social customs, and increased political representation for women.

6. The number of women in Congress and in other government bodies increased significantly in the 1990s and 2000s. Federal government efforts to eliminate gender discrimination in the workplace include Title VII of the Civil Rights Act of 1964, which prohibits gender-based discrimination, including sexual harassment on the job. Wage discrimination continues to be a problem for women.

7. Today, most immigrants come from Asia and Latin America, especially Mexico. Many are unauthorized immigrants (also called illegal aliens or undocumented workers). The percentage of Latinos, or Hispanic Americans, in the population is growing rapidly. By 2050, non-Hispanic whites will make up less than half of the nation's residents.

8. Affirmative action programs have been controversial because they may lead to reverse discrimination against majority groups or even other minority groups. United States Supreme Court decisions have limited affirmative action programs, and several states now ban state-sponsored affirmative action.

9. The Americans with Disabilities Act of 1990 prohibits job discrimination against persons with physical and mental disabilities. The act requires expanded access to public facilities, including transportation, and to services offered by such private concerns as car rental and telephone companies. The courts have limited the impact of this law, however.

10. Gay and lesbian rights groups became commonplace after 1969. During the 1970s and 1980s, sodomy laws that criminalized specific sexual practices were repealed or struck down by the courts in nearly half of the states. In 2003, a United States Supreme Court decision invalidated all remaining sodomy laws nationwide. Many states and cities have laws prohibiting at least some types of discrimination based on sexual orientation. The military's "don't ask, don't tell" policy, now repealed, fueled extensive controversy, as have same-sex marriages.

11. Children have few rights and protections, in part because it is presumed that their parents protect them. The Twenty-sixth Amendment grants the right to vote to those ages eighteen or older. Minors have some defense against criminal prosecution because of their presumed inability to have criminal intent below certain ages. For those under the age of criminal responsibility, there are state juvenile courts. When minors are tried as adults, they are entitled to the procedural protections afforded to adults and are usually subject to adult penalties.

Quiz Multiple Choice

1. Before the outbreak of the Civil War, the Supreme Court decided in the case *Dred Scott v. Sandford* that:
   - **a. the slaves should be freed.**
   - **b. slaves were U.S. citizens.**
   - **c. slaves and their descendants—even if freed—were not citizens of the United States.**

2. The Thirteenth Amendment to the Constitution provides:
   - **a. that all inhabitants of the United States are citizens.**
   - **b. that slavery and involuntary servitude are illegal within the United States.**
   - **c. protection for the due process of law.**

3. The separate-but-equal doctrine was announced by the Supreme Court:
   - **a. in *Plessy v. Ferguson.***
   - **b. in *Roe v. Wade.***
   - **c. nowhere, because the Supreme Court never addressed the issue.**

4. The difference between *de jure* and *de facto* segregation is that:
   - **a. *de facto* segregation requires governmental approval.**
   - **b. *de jure* segregation does not result from government actions.**
   - **c. *de jure* segregation occurs because of discriminatory laws or government actions.**

5. Arguably the most important civil rights legislation in modern times was the:
   - **a. Civil Rights Act of 1964.**
   - **b. Civil Rights Act of 2012.**
   - **c. Civil Rights Acts of 1856 to 1875.**

6. In 1920, women obtained the right to vote because:
   - **a. of an act of Congress.**
   - **b. in that year, all of the states finally allowed it.**
   - **c. of the passage of the Nineteenth Amendment to the U.S. Constitution.**

7. The Equal Rights Amendment today requires:
   - **a. that women be treated equally to men.**
   - **b. that women be treated equally in the labor market.**
   - **c. nothing at all, because the Equal Rights Amendment never passed.**

8. Currently, most immigrants come from:
   - **a. Europe.**
   - **b. Africa.**
   - **c. Latin America (especially Mexico) and Asia.**

ANSWERS: 1. c, 2. b, 3. a, 4. c, 5. a, 6. c, 7. c, 8. c.

Quiz Fill-Ins

9. Affirmative action policies attempt to "level the playing field" by providing special __________ in educational admissions and employment decisions to groups that have been discriminated against in the past.

10. Individuals with disabilities are protected under the __________ _____ __________ Act of 1990.

11. Since 2011, _____ _____ and __________ can openly serve in the U.S. military.

12. In 1971, because of the __________ __________, citizens eighteen and older were given the right to vote.

13. Past barriers to African American voting included grandfather clauses, poll taxes, and __________ __________.

14. The Supreme Court decision in *Brown v. Board of Education* effectively ended the __________-__________-__________ doctrine.

15. The Fourteenth Amendment requires that no state shall deprive any person of life, liberty, or property, without __________ __________ of __________.

16. In discrimination lawsuits, suspect classifications include race, religion, and __________ __________.

ANSWERS: 9. preferences, 10. Americans with Disabilities, 11. gay men, lesbians, 12. Twenty-sixth Amendment, 13. literacy tests, 14. separate-but-equal, 15. due process of law, 16. national origin.

(© Aleksandar Jovicic/iStockphoto)

Selected Print & Media Resources

SUGGESTED READINGS

Friedan, Betty. *The Feminine Mystique.* New York: W. W. Norton, 2001. Originally published in 1963, Betty Friedan's work is the feminist classic that helped launch the modern women's movement in the United States. This edition contains an up-to-date introduction by columnist Anna Quindlen.

Marquardt, Marie Friedman, Timothy J. Steigenga, Philip J. Williams, and Manuel A. Vasquez. *Living "Illegal": The Human Face of Unauthorized Immigration.* New York: The New Press, 2011. Four professors depict the lives of people who are caught up in one of America's most troubling issues.

Wilkerson, Isabel. *The Warmth of Other Suns: The Epic Story of America's Great Migration.* New York: Vintage Books, 2011. Wilkerson's book describes one of the least-told but most important stories in American history—the great migration of African Americans from the South to the North. Wilkerson, a reporter, won the Pulitzer Prize for earlier work. This volume has won more than half a dozen prizes and was named one of the best books of the year by at least thirty leading newspapers.

MEDIA RESOURCES

The Help—This 2011 film is an ensemble piece focusing on the lives of black maids in the Deep South during the civil rights revolution. A massive box-office success, *The Help* received four Academy Award nominations, including one for best picture. It also won the Screen Actors Guild award for outstanding performance by a cast.

Iron Jawed Angels—This 2004 HBO movie, starring Hilary Swank, Margo Martindale, and Anjelica Huston, depicts the struggles of the women's suffrage movement. It is a stirring film and excellent history, even if the sound track is a bit too modern.

Malcolm X—This 1992 film, directed by Spike Lee and starring Denzel Washington, depicts the life of Malcolm X, the controversial "black power" leader. Malcolm X, who was assassinated on February 21, 1965, clearly had a different vision from that of Martin Luther King, Jr., regarding how to achieve civil rights, respect, and equality for black Americans.

Martin Luther King, Jr.: The Essential Box Set: The Landmark Speeches and Sermons of Dr. Martin Luther King, Jr.—Released in 2009, this CD contains twenty of King's most important speeches and sermons. Hearing King's oratory live is definitely more compelling than just reading it. The advantage of audio over film is that many important talks were recorded, but never filmed.

(© PashaIgnatov/iStockphoto)

E-mocracy CIVIL RIGHTS INFORMATION ONLINE

Today, thanks to the Internet, information on civil rights issues is literally at your fingertips. A host of Web sites offer data on the extent to which groups discussed in this chapter are protected under state and federal laws. You can also find many advocacy sites that describe what you can do to help promote the rights of a certain group.

LOGGING ON

1. The National Organization for Women (NOW) offers online information and updates on the status of women's rights, including affirmative action cases involving women. You can locate its Web site simply by entering "now" into your favorite search engine. Searching on such a common word will yield other results, of course, but NOW should be near or at the top of your results page.
2. An excellent source of information on issues facing African Americans is the Web site of the National Association for the Advancement of Colored People (NAACP). Find it by searching on "naacp."
3. You can find a wealth of information on the Americans with Disabilities Act (ADA) at the U.S. Department of Justice's ADA home page. Just search on "ada." As with NOW, you'll see other results, but the Department of Justice site should be near or at the top of the page.
4. You can access the Web site of the Human Rights Campaign Fund, the nation's largest gay and lesbian political organization, by entering "hrc" into your search engine.
5. If you are interested in children's rights and welfare, try searching on "child welfare." You'll see a variety of relevant sites, including one sponsored by the U.S. Department of Health and Human Services. Another site has a directory of resources provided by the Child Welfare Research Institute.

Recall
Walker!
Wisconsin AFL-CIO · StandWisconsin.org

6 Public Opinion and Political Socialization

The six learning outcomes below are designed to help improve your understanding of this chapter. After reading this chapter, you should be able to:

■ Learning Outcome 1: **Define *public opinion, consensus,* and *divided opinion.***

■ Learning Outcome 2: **Discuss major sources of political socialization, including the family, schools, the media, and political events.**

■ Learning Outcome 3: **Identify the effects of various influences on voting behavior, including party identification, education, income, religion, race, and geography.**

■ Learning Outcome 4: **Describe the characteristics of a scientific opinion poll, and list some of the problems pollsters face in obtaining accurate results.**

■ Learning Outcome 5: **Evaluate the impact of new technologies on opinion polling.**

■ Learning Outcome 6: **Consider the effect that public opinion may have on the political process.**

When the opinions of some citizens become strong enough, in some states a politician can be recalled in a special election. In Madison, Wisconsin, those who wish to oust the governor make their feelings known.

(Darren Hauck/Reuters/Landov)

(Zhang Yongxing/ZUMA Press/Newscom)

THESE INTERVIEWERS are conducting telephone polling. What challenges do they face?

What if...

SCIENTIFIC OPINION POLLING HAD NEVER BEEN INVENTED?

BACKGROUND

Not a day goes by, especially during an election year, without the results of yet another opinion poll being proudly announced in the media. One presidential candidate is pulling away from the other. Or perhaps the candidates are now neck and neck. Or the Republicans might gain a majority of the seats in the U.S. Senate. As you will learn in this chapter, reputable opinion polls use random, representative sampling in an effort to make accurate predictions. Scientific opinion polling was invented in the 1930s and refined in the 1940s and 1950s.

WHAT IF SCIENTIFIC OPINION POLLING HAD NEVER BEEN INVENTED?

Before the development of scientific polling, newspapers frequently carried predictions about who would be elected president. Those predictions were often based on the latest betting odds. In the 1916 presidential elections, for example, more than $200 million (measured in 2013 dollars) was wagered on the election outcome. That sum constituted twice the amount spent on the election campaigns themselves. At that time, a variety of firms were in the business of receiving and placing bets on election outcomes.

Newspapers routinely showed the odds on the two presidential candidates, Woodrow Wilson and Charles Evans Hughes. The betting favored Wilson by a slight margin, and indeed he won. When various state and federal gambling laws were instituted later in the twentieth century, however, betting on political events became illegal. In the United States today, online gambling is illegal under many circumstances.

ENTER THE IOWA ELECTRONIC MARKETS

In 1993, a group of researchers at the University of Iowa obtained permission from the federal government to establish an experimental academic program that allows betting on elections and other predictable events, such as Academy Award winners. Exchanges of this type are called *prediction markets*. The bets are limited to a maximum of $500. The program, called Iowa Electronic Markets, claims that since 1993, its results have been more accurate than the opinion polls 75 percent of the time.

Intrade, a prediction market based in Dublin, Ireland, is widely used by polling experts as a way to check their conclusions. A controversy exists as to whether it is legal for Americans to make bids through Intrade.

THE DIFFERENCE BETWEEN OPINION POLLS AND BETTING

Well-crafted opinion polling requires, as stated above, not only a representative sample but truthful responses by those interviewed. Election prediction markets, in contrast, require neither. When a person can win or lose a $500 bet by predicting who will be the next president and what the margin will be, a lot more care goes into that prediction than might go into the answer to a polling question. The old saying "Put your money where your mouth is" turns out to result in good political predictions.

FOR CRITICAL ANALYSIS

1. ***Is there any difference between "placing a bet" on the future value of a stock by buying it through the stock market and placing a bet on who will become president? Explain.***
2. ***Economist Robin Hanson has suggested that after voters decide on national goals, betting markets could be used to determine optimum policies to reach those goals: "Betting markets are our best known institution for aggregating information." Does his suggestion make any sense? Why or why not?***

In a democracy, the ability of the people to freely express their opinions is fundamental. Americans can express their opinions in many ways. They can write letters to newspapers. They can share their ideas in online forums on Facebook, blogs, and tweets. They can organize politically. They can vote. They can respond to opinion polls. Public opinion clearly plays an important role in our political system, just as it does in any democracy.

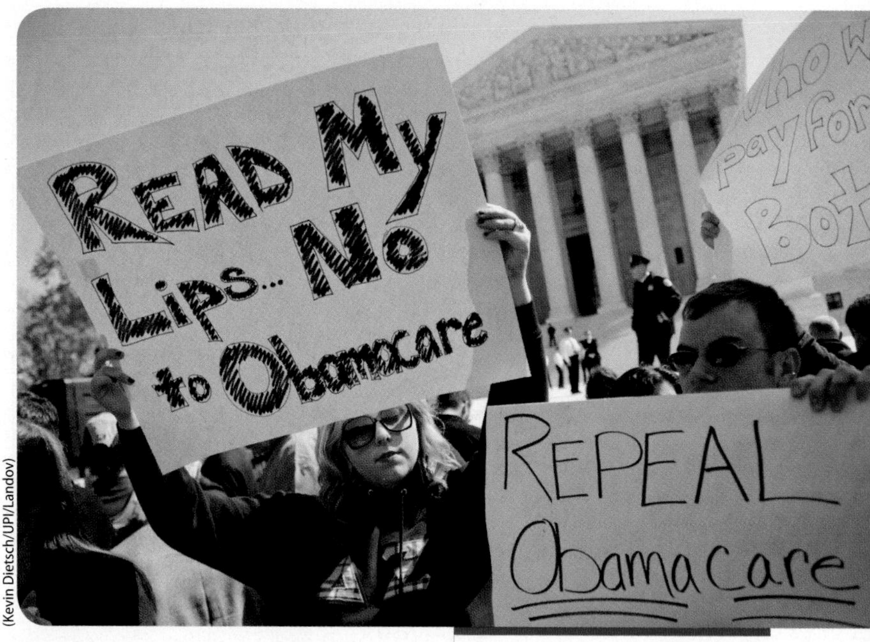

Public opinion can be strongly divided. Why is that so with health care reform legislation?

President Barack Obama and the Republicans in the U.S. House of Representatives found out how important public opinion was in July 2011 during the "debt-ceiling crisis." Congress must specifically authorize any increase in the federal debt, even if the larger debt is required by measures that Congress has already adopted. The debt ceiling has been raised dozens of times over the years without incident. In 2011, however, Republicans in the House seized upon the debt-ceiling vote as a way to force Democrats to agree to major federal budget cuts. They threatened to vote down the debt-ceiling increase if they did not get the cuts. If the debt ceiling had not been raised, someone would not have been paid—perhaps defense contractors, maybe Medicare providers, possibly even those who hold the federal debt itself in the form of Treasury obligations.

On July 31, at the very last moment, a deal was reached that provided for some budget cuts. The dispute had serious consequences. Many economists believed that uncertainty surrounding the vote slowed the recovery from the recession. Both the president and the Congress—especially congressional Republicans—suffered severe blows to their popularity. Obama's job approval rate dropped below 40 percent, his worst showing ever. Congressional job approval fell to 13 percent.

There is no doubt that public opinion can be powerful. The extent to which public opinion affects policymaking is not always so clear, however. For example, suppose that public opinion strongly supports a certain policy. If political leaders adopt that position, is it because they are responding to public opinion or because they share the public's beliefs? Also, political leaders themselves can shape public opinion to a degree.

Defining Public Opinion

■ Learning Outcome 1: **Define *public opinion*, *consensus*, and *divided opinion*.**

There is no single public opinion, because there are many different "publics." In a nation of more than 315 million people, there may be innumerable gradations of opinion on an issue. What we do is describe the distribution of opinions about a particular question. Thus, we define **public opinion** as the aggregate of individual attitudes or beliefs shared by some portion of the adult population.

Typically, public opinion is distributed among several different positions, and the distribution of opinion can tell us how divided the public is on an issue and whether compromise is possible. When polls show that a large proportion of the American public appears to express the same view on an issue, we say that a **consensus** exists, at least at the moment the poll was taken. Figure 6–1 on the following page shows a pattern of opinion that might be called consensual. Issues on which the public holds widely differing attitudes result in **divided opinion** (see Figure 6–2 on the following page). Sometimes, a poll shows a distribution of opinion indicating that most Americans either have no information about the issue

Public Opinion
The aggregate of individual attitudes or beliefs shared by some portion of the adult population.

Consensus
General agreement among the citizenry on an issue.

Divided Opinion
Public opinion that is polarized between two quite different positions.

Figure 6-1 ▶ Consensus Opinion

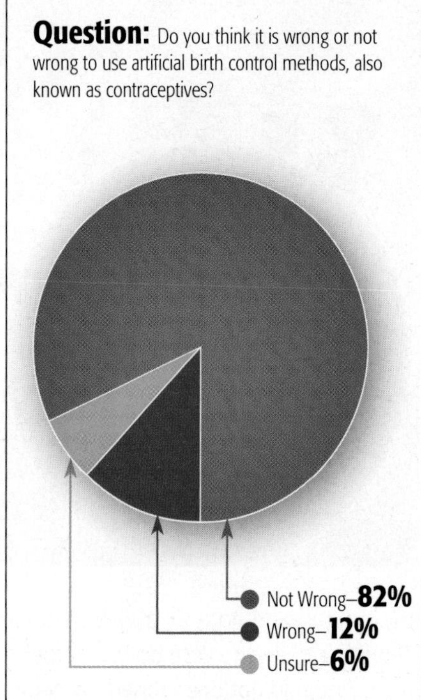
Question: Do you think it is wrong or not wrong to use artificial birth control methods, also known as contraceptives?
Not Wrong–82%
Wrong–12%
Unsure–6%

Source: Quinnipiac University Poll, February 14–20, 2012.

Figure 6-2 ▶ Divided Opinion

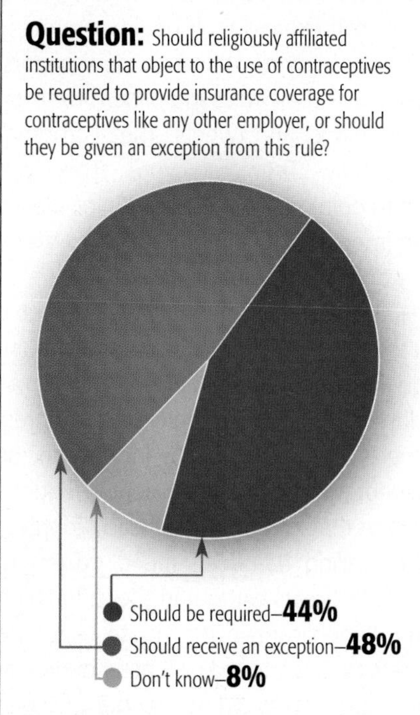
Question: Should religiously affiliated institutions that object to the use of contraceptives be required to provide insurance coverage for contraceptives like any other employer, or should they be given an exception from this rule?
Should be required–44%
Should receive an exception–48%
Don't know–8%

Source: Pew Research Center, February 8–12, 2012. Question asked only of those who had heard about the issue.

or are not interested enough in the issue to formulate a position. Politicians may believe that lack of public knowledge of an issue gives them more room to maneuver, or they may be wary of taking any action for fear that opinion will crystallize after a crisis.

An interesting question arises as to when private opinion becomes public opinion. Everyone probably has a private opinion about the competence of the president, as well as private opinions about more personal concerns, such as the state of a neighbor's lawn. We say that private opinion becomes public opinion when the opinion is publicly expressed and concerns public issues. When someone's private opinion becomes so strong that the individual is willing to take action, then the opinion becomes public opinion. Many kinds of action are possible. An individual may go to the polls to vote for or against a candidate or an issue, participate in a demonstration, discuss the issue at work, speak out online, or participate in the political process in any one of a dozen other ways.

How Public Opinion Is Formed: Political Socialization

Political Socialization The process by which people acquire political beliefs and values.

■ Learning Outcome 2: **Discuss major sources of political socialization, including the family, schools, the media, and political events.**

Most Americans are willing to express opinions on political issues when asked. How do people acquire these opinions and attitudes? Typically, views that are expressed as political opinions are acquired through the process of **political socialization.** By this, we mean that people acquire their political beliefs and values, often including their party identification, through relationships with their families, friends, and co-workers.

Models of Political Socialization

The most important early sources of political socialization are the family and the schools. Individuals' basic political orientations are formed in the family if other family members hold strong views. When the adults in a family view politics as relatively unimportant and

Questions for Discussion and Analysis

1. Review the *Which Side Are You On?* feature on page 209. Conservatives have argued that public school spending is poorly related to educational outcomes. Some liberals claim, however, that to equalize outcomes, we would have to spend *more* on schools that contain large numbers of poor and troubled students than on other schools, and that this rarely happens. Does this argument make any sense? Why or why not?
2. Years ago, people with postgraduate degrees were more likely to vote for Republican than Democratic candidates, but in recent years, highly educated voters have been trending Democratic. Why might physicians and lawyers be more likely to vote Democratic than in the past? For what reasons might college professors tilt to the Democrats?
3. Some political scientists claim that individual polls are relatively meaningless but that a number of polls averaged together can be fairly accurate. Why would a number of polls averaged together have more predictive power?
4. Why do you think the American people express a relatively high degree of confidence in the military as an institution? Why do people express less confidence in Congress than in other major institutions? Could people be holding various institutions to different standards, and if so, what might these standards be?

Key Terms

agenda setting 189
consensus 185
divided opinion 185
Fairness Doctrine 189
framing 209
gender gap 196
generational effect 190
house effect 200
media 189
opinion leader 189
opinion poll 197
peer group 188
political socialization 186
political trust 205
public opinion 185
sampling error 199
socioeconomic status 191
Watergate break-in 190

Chapter Summary

1. Public opinion is the aggregate of individual attitudes or beliefs shared by some portion of the adult population. A consensus exists when a large proportion of the public appears to express the same view on an issue. Divided opinion exists when the public holds widely different attitudes on an issue. Sometimes, a poll shows a distribution of opinion indicating that most people either have no information about an issue or are not interested enough in the issue to form a position on it.
2. People's opinions are formed through the political socialization process. Important factors in this process are the family, educational experiences, peer groups, opinion leaders, the media, and political events. The influence of the media as a socialization factor may be growing relative to the influence of the family. Party identification is one of the most important indicators of voting behavior. Voting behavior is also influenced by demographic factors, such as education, economic status, religion, race and ethnicity, gender, and geographic region. Finally, voting behavior is influenced by election-specific factors, such as perception of the candidates and issue preferences.
3. Most descriptions of public opinion are based on the results of opinion polls. The accuracy of polls depends on sampling techniques. An accurate poll includes a representative sample of the population being polled and ensures randomness in the selection of respondents.
4. Problems with polls include sampling error, the difficulty in obtaining a truly representative sample, the issue of whether responses are influenced by the phrasing and order of questions asked, the use of a yes/no format for answers to the questions, and the interviewer's techniques. Many people are concerned about the use of push polls (in which the questions "push" the respondent toward a particular candidate). "Polls" that rely on self-selected respondents are inherently inaccurate and should be discounted.
5. Advances in technology have changed polling techniques over the years. During the 1970s, telephone polling became widely used. Today, largely because of extensive telemarketing, people often refuse to answer calls, and nonresponse rates in telephone polling have skyrocketed. Many poll takers also fail to include cell phone users. Due to the difficulty of obtaining a random sample in the online environment, Internet polls are often "nonpolls." Whether Internet polling can overcome this problem remains to be seen.
6. Public opinion affects the political process in many ways. The political culture provides a general environment of support for the political system, allowing the nation to weather periods of crisis. The political culture also helps Americans to evaluate their government's performance. At times, the level of trust in government has been relatively high. At other times, the level of trust has declined steeply. Similarly, Americans' confidence in government institutions

varies over time, depending on a number of circumstances. Generally, though, Americans turn to government to solve what they perceive to be the major problems facing the country. In 2012, Americans ranked the economy and unemployment as the two most significant problems facing the nation.

7. Public opinion also plays an important role in policymaking. Although polling data show that a majority of Americans would like policy leaders to be influenced to a great extent by public opinion, politicians cannot always be guided by opinion polls. This is because the respondents often do not understand the costs and consequences of policy decisions or the trade-offs involved in making such decisions. How issues are framed has an important influence on popular attitudes.

Quiz Multiple Choice

1. We can best define *public opinion* as:
   a. **beliefs held by moderate voters.**
   b. **beliefs shared by both Democrats and Republicans.**
   c. **the aggregate of individual beliefs shared by some portion of adults.**
2. Some of the major sources of political socialization include:
   a. **schools and the family.**
   b. **schools and sporting events.**
   c. **schools and literature.**
3. The gender gap refers to:
   a. **the difference in college attendance rates for males and females.**
   b. **the tendency for women to be more likely to vote for a particular candidate than men.**
   c. **the tendency for men to dominate the political process.**
4. For a public opinion poll to be accurate:
   a. **those polled must be picked at random.**
   b. **there must be an equal number of high school dropouts and high school graduates.**
   c. **there can be no businesspersons in the group.**
5. One of the problems with Internet polling is that:
   a. **not enough people have access to the Internet.**
   b. **there is a lack of statistical randomness in the sample of those who respond.**
   c. **people don't reason well when they respond to questions on the Internet.**
6. One way to compensate for underrepresented groups in a polling sample is to:
   a. **eliminate all answers from those who are part of the underrepresented group.**
   b. **reduce the weight given to the underrepresented group so that it does not count excessively.**
   c. **add extra weight to correct for the underrepresented group.**
7. One of the problems with telephone polling today is that:
   a. **not everyone has a telephone.**
   b. **too many people have telephones.**
   c. **many people only have cell phones and therefore cannot easily be polled.**
8. The trend in political satisfaction in this country has:
   a. **always been very high.**
   b. **fallen since around 2001.**
   c. **risen since around 2001.**

ANSWERS: 1. c, 2. a, 3. b, 4. a, 5. b, 6. c, 7. c, 8. b.

Quiz Fill-Ins

9. When most people have similar opinions about a particular policy, we say that a ______________ exists.
10. Political socialization occurs in families because parents ______________ their feelings and preferences to their children.
11. If you are influenced in your political attitudes by your friends and co-workers, that means that a ______________ ______________ affects your attitudes.
12. Traditional media, such as newspapers, radio, and television, are less important for the younger generation because of the ______________ and ______________ ______________.
13. Opinion polls can often be accurate even when fewer than two thousand voters are interviewed because of ______________ ______________.

14. When the results of an opinion poll are given with a margin of plus or minus 3 percent, that 3 percent represents ______________ ______________.

15. When one polling organization's results consistently differ from those of other poll takers, we call this the ______________ effect.

16. Voice-over-Internet phone services, such as Skype, ______________ the accuracy of telephone polls.

17. Since about 2008, the most important problem that Americans say they face is the state of the ______________.

18. The same polling question can result in different responses depending on how that question is ______________.

ANSWERS: 9. consensus, 10. communicate, 11. peer group, 12. Internet; social media, 13. representative sampling, 14. sampling error, 15. house, 16. reduce, 17. economy, 18. phrased.

(© Aleksandar Jovicic/iStockphoto)

Selected Print & Media Resources

SUGGESTED READINGS

Bishop, Bill. *The Big Sort: Why the Clustering of Like-Minded America Is Tearing Us Apart.* New York: Houghton Mifflin, 2008. Jam-packed with polling data, Bishop's book argues that we have clustered into like-minded communities as never before. Results include political polarization and an inability to understand Americans of different backgrounds or beliefs.

Fiorina, Morris P., with Samuel J. Adams and Jeremy C. Pope. *Culture War? The Myth of a Polarized America,* 3d ed. New York: Longman, 2010. Fiorina and his colleagues use polling data to argue that most Americans are politically moderate, even though our political leaders are highly polarized. Topics include abortion, same-sex marriage, school prayer, and gun control. A new chapter in this edition analyzes the 2008 elections.

Lakoff, George. *The Political Mind: A Cognitive Scientist's Guide to Your Brain and Its Politics.* New York: Penguin, 2009. Lakoff is one of the nation's leading experts on framing and other political thought processes. Lakoff's liberal politics may annoy conservative readers, but his theories are not dependent on his ideology.

Sniderman, Paul M., and Edward H. Stiglitz. *The Reputational Premium: A Theory of Party Identification and Policy Reasoning.* Princeton, N.J.: Princeton University Press, 2012. Two political scientists argue that the policy positions of the major political parties are more important in making up voters' minds than are the policies of individual candidates.

MEDIA RESOURCES

Purple State of Mind—A 2009 film, in which two old friends, college roommates, take different political roads—one left, the other right. They meet again and explore their differences.

Wag the Dog—A 1997 film that provides a very cynical look at the importance of public opinion. The film, which features Dustin Hoffman and Robert De Niro, follows the efforts of a presidential political consultant who stages a foreign policy crisis to divert public opinion from a sex scandal in the White House.

(© PashaIgnatov/iStockphoto)

E-mocracy ONLINE POLLING AND POLL DATA

The Internet is an excellent source for finding polling reports and data. All of the major polling organizations have Web sites that include news releases about polls they have conducted. Many sites make the polling data available for free to users. A few require that a user pay a subscription fee before accessing the polling archives on the site.

LOGGING ON

1. The Polling Report Web site offers polls and their results organized by topic. It is up to date and easy to use. To find it, enter "pollingreport" into your favorite search engine.
2. The Gallup organization's Web site offers not only polling data but also information on how polls are constructed, conducted, and interpreted. Search for it using the term "gallup."
3. The Pew Research Center, a major public opinion research group, sponsors projects on journalism, the Internet, religion, Hispanics, global attitudes, and other topics. If you enter "pew" into your favorite search engine, you'll see a full page of Pew sites (along with a handful of sites dealing with church furniture).
4. Real Clear Politics is known for its "poll of polls," which aggregates results from leading pollsters in the run-up to elections. The site also aggregates polls on the president's job approval rating and other indicators. Although the site is run by conservatives, it offers opinion pieces from multiple media sources on its home page. Search for it by entering "rcp" into a search engine.
5. In recent years, Nate Silver has won a reputation as one of the Web's sharpest students of polling data. Follow his analyses and those of his colleagues by searching on "538"—the name of his blog.

NRA
DON'T TREAD
ON MY GUN RIGHTS

7 Interest Groups

The seven learning outcomes below are designed to help improve your understanding of this chapter. After reading this chapter, you should be able to:

- Learning Outcome 1: **Describe the basic characteristics of interest groups and how they are sometimes related to social movements.**
- Learning Outcome 2: **Provide three major reasons why Americans join interest groups.**
- Learning Outcome 3: **List the major types of interest groups, especially those with economic motivations.**
- Learning Outcome 4: **Evaluate the factors that make some interest groups especially powerful.**
- Learning Outcome 5: **Discuss interest group strategies, differentiating between direct and indirect techniques.**
- Learning Outcome 6: **Describe the main ways in which lobbyists are regulated.**
- Learning Outcome 7: **Consider interest groups in terms of elite theory and pluralism.**

The National Rifle Association (NRA) is one of many interest groups that lobby in favor of its members' values. What might those be? (Daniel Acker/Reuters/Landov)

(© Stephen Crowley/*The New York Times*/Redux)

These three lobbyists are shown outside the White House. What would happen if lobbying were eliminated?

What if...

LOBBYING WERE ABOLISHED?

BACKGROUND

Lobbyists—persons hired in an attempt to influence members of Congress (and state legislatures, too)—have been around for a long time. In America, lobbying goes back to colonial times. The Reverend Increase Mather lobbied in London for a new charter for Massachusetts. Benjamin Franklin served as a lobbyist for Pennsylvania and other colonies.

Today, lobbyists are deeply unpopular. Lobbying is often seen as an essentially corrupt activity. All presidential candidates in recent years have promised to stand up against "special interests" and the lobbyists they employ. Congress—the main target of lobbying—has devised many rules and regulations in an attempt to regulate lobbyists. None have had much effect.

Lobbying is protected by the First Amendment to the Constitution, which states that Congress shall make no law abridging the right of the people "to petition the Government for a redress of grievances." Let us assume, however, that the Constitution has been amended in such a way that lobbying could be abolished.

WHAT IF LOBBYING WERE ABOLISHED?

If lobbying were abolished, about 35,000 lobbyists who swarm Capitol Hill in Washington, D.C., would be out of work. Currently, corporate America spends $6 million a day or more on lobbying. The abolition of lobbying would free up these funds. Yet just because these dollars would no longer go to lobbyists does not mean they would go to stockholders, customers, or employees. Doubtless, if lobbying were abolished, big business would spend more on media campaigns to "educate" voters about what kinds of politicians would be best for America. Other interest groups would also spend more to sway the public to vote for favored candidates who would then in turn vote the "right" way on pending legislation.

NO LOBBYING COULD LEAD TO LESS DEMOCRACY, NOT MORE

As you learned in the previous chapter, the "will of the people" in a complex nation such as ours is hard to define. Students of public opinion believe that there are many different "publics" in a country of more than 315 million people. Lobbying improves the public debate by providing an outlet for more constituencies. In this way, lobbying is an expression of democracy. Without lobbyists, Congress might ignore many of the various interests with which Americans identify. In fact, lobbyist Nick Allard has argued in favor of more lobbyists, not fewer. He believes that we need lobbyists for the poor, the young, and all of the people who are not adequately represented today.

LOBBYISTS AND CONGRESSIONAL STAFF

Lobbying provides lawmakers with information—lobbyists try to woo lawmakers with facts, not just campaign donations. Without lobbyists, Congress would have to hire more staff members to research the multitude of issues facing government. Congress would have more staff specializing in energy, health care, education, and other topics. Ultimately, taxpayers would foot the bill for additional staff members, who might be responsive to the political parties instead of interest groups.

FOR CRITICAL ANALYSIS

1. *Why has* lobbying *become a dirty word?*
2. *The American Cancer Society spends $5 million a year on lobbyists and AARP (representing seniors) spends $15 million. Are such lobbying activities open for criticism? Explain.*

The structure of American government invites the participation of **interest groups** at various stages of the policymaking process. Americans can form groups in their neighborhoods or cities and lobby the city council or their state government. They can join statewide groups or national groups and try to influence government policy through Congress or through one of the executive agencies or cabinet departments. Representatives of large corporations may seek to influence the president personally at social events or fund-raisers. When attempts to influence government through the executive and legislative branches fail, interest groups can turn to the courts, filing suits in state or federal courts to achieve their political objectives.

Interest Group
An organized group of individuals sharing common objectives who actively attempt to influence policymakers.

The large number of "pressure points" for interest group activity in American government helps to explain why there are so many—more than one hundred thousand—interest groups at work in our society. Another reason for the multitude of interest groups is that the right to join a group is protected by the First Amendment to the U.S. Constitution (see Chapter 4). Not only are all people guaranteed the right "peaceably to assemble," but they are also guaranteed the right "to petition the Government for a redress of grievances." This constitutional provision encourages Americans to form groups and to express their opinions to the government or to their elected representatives as members of a group. The constitutional protection of groups is one reason that it would be very difficult to satisfy the occasional demand that **lobbyists**—persons hired to represent interest groups to the government—be eliminated. As noted in the chapter-opening *What If . . .* feature, such a change would require a constitutional amendment.

Lobbyist
An organization or individual who attempts to influence legislation and the administrative decisions of government.

■ **Learning Outcome 1: Describe the basic characteristics of interest groups and how they are sometimes related to social movements.**

Interest Group Fundamentals

Interest groups play a significant role in American government at all levels. As you will read later in this chapter and in Chapter 9, one of the ways in which interest groups attempt to influence government policies is through campaign contributions to members of Congress who intend to run for reelection. It is the interplay between campaign financial assistance and legislation favorable to specific interests that has caused some observers to claim that Congress has been sold to the highest bidder. Certainly, devising a system in which campaigns can be financed *without* jeopardizing objectivity on the part of members of Congress is a major challenge for our nation today. Recall from Chapter 1, however, that in our pluralist society, the competition by interest groups for access to lawmakers automatically checks the extent to which any one particular group can influence Congress.

This state representative confers with a lobbyist who was paid to represent one of the cities in her district. Is this legal?

(AP Photo/John Hanna)

Interest Groups: A Natural Phenomenon

Alexis de Tocqueville observed in the early 1830s that "in no country of the world has the principle of association been more successfully used or applied to a greater multitude of objectives than in America."[1] The French traveler was amazed at the degree to which Americans formed groups to solve civic problems, establish social relationships, and speak for their economic or political interests. Perhaps James Madison, when he wrote *Federalist Paper* No. 10 (see Appendix C), had already judged the character of his

1. Alexis de Tocqueville, *Democracy in America,* Vol. 1 [1835], ed. Phillips Bradley (New York: Knopf, 1980), p. 191.

country's citizens similarly. He supported the creation of a large republic with many states to encourage the formation of multiple interests. The multitude of interests, in Madison's view, would work to discourage the formation of an oppressive majority interest.

did you know?

At least half of all lobbyists in Washington, D.C., are women.

Poll data show that more than two-thirds of all Americans belong to at least one group or association. Although the majority of these affiliations could not be classified as "interest groups" in the political sense, Americans certainly understand the principles of working in groups.

Today, interest groups range from the elementary school parent-teacher association and the local "Stop the Sewer Plant Association" to the statewide association of insurance agents. They include small groups such as local environmental organizations and national groups such as the American Civil Liberties Union, the National Education Association, and the American League of Lobbyists.

(© Hulton-Deutsch Collection/Corbis)

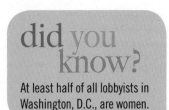

These women wanted the right to vote in 1900. Did they have many supporters then?

Interest Groups and Social Movements

Interest groups are often spawned by mass **social movements.** Such movements represent demands by a large segment of the population for change in the political, economic, or social system. A social movement is often the first expression of latent discontent with the existing system. It may be the authentic voice of weaker or oppressed groups in society that do not have the means or standing to organize as interest groups. For example, the women's movement of the early 1800s suffered disapproval from most mainstream political and social leaders. Because women were unable to vote or take an active part in the political system, it was difficult for women who desired greater freedoms to organize formal groups. After the Civil War, when more women became active in professional life, organizations seeking to win women the right to vote came into being.

African Americans found themselves in an even more disadvantaged situation after the end of the Reconstruction period (1865–1877). They were unable to exercise political rights in many southern states, and their participation in any form of organization could lead to economic ruin, physical harassment, or even death. The civil rights movement of the 1950s and 1960s was clearly a social movement. To be sure, several formal organizations worked to support the movement—including the Southern Christian Leadership Conference, the National Association for the Advancement of Colored People, and the Urban League—but only a social movement could generate the kinds of civil disobedience that took place in hundreds of towns and cities across the country.

Social Movement
A movement that represents the demands of a large segment of the public for political, economic, or social change.

Social movements may generate interest groups with specific goals that successfully recruit members by offering certain incentives. In the example of the women's movement of the 1960s, the National Organization for Women was formed in part out of a demand to end gender-segregated job advertising in newspapers.

■ Learning Outcome 2: **Provide three major reasons why Americans join interest groups.**

Why Do Americans Join Interest Groups?

One puzzle that has fascinated political scientists is why some people join interest groups, while many others do not. Everyone has some interest that could benefit from government action. For many individuals, however, those concerns remain unorganized interests, or **latent interests.**

Latent Interests
Public-policy interests that are not recognized or addressed by a group at a particular time.

According to political theorist Mancur Olson,[2] it simply may not be rational for individuals to join most groups. In his classic work on this topic, Olson introduced the idea of

2. Mancur Olson, *The Logic of Collective Action* (Cambridge, Mass.: Harvard University Press, 1965).

the "collective good." This concept refers to any public benefit that, if available to any member of the community, cannot be denied to any other member, whether or not he or she participated in the effort to gain the good.

Although collective benefits are usually thought of as coming from such public goods as clean air and national defense, benefits are also bestowed by the government on subsets of the public. Price subsidies to dairy farmers and loans to college students are examples. Olson used economic theory to propose that it is not rational for interested individuals to join groups that work for *group* benefits. In fact, it is often more rational for the individual to wait for others to procure the benefits and then share them. How many community college students, for example, join the American Association of Community Colleges, an organization that lobbies the government for increased financial aid to students? The difficulty interest groups face in recruiting members when the benefits can be obtained without joining the groups is referred to as the **free rider problem.**

If so little incentive exists for individuals to join together, why are there thousands of interest groups lobbying in Washington? According to the logic of collective action, if the contribution of an individual *will* make a difference to the effort, then it is worth it to the individual to join. Thus, smaller groups, which seek benefits for only a small proportion of the population, are more likely to enroll members who will give time and funds to the cause. Larger groups, which represent general public interests (the women's movement or the American Civil Liberties Union, for example), will find it relatively more difficult to get individuals to join. People need an incentive—material or otherwise—to participate.

Social Media IN POLITICS

Interest groups are hugely into social media. Entering the name or initials of most large groups into a Facebook search box is likely to bring up a page with scores of recent posts by the group's supporters. For labor, try "afl-cio." The U.S. Chamber of Commerce page at "uschamber" is very active. So is the Consumers Union—enter "consumers union." For more conservative views, try "tea party patriots."

Free Rider Problem
The difficulty interest groups face in recruiting members when the benefits they achieve can be gained without joining the group.

Solidary Incentive
A reason or motive that follows from the desire to associate with others and to share with others a particular interest or hobby.

Material Incentive
A reason or motive based on the desire to enjoy certain economic benefits or opportunities.

Solidary Incentives

Interest groups offer **solidary incentives** for their members. Solidary benefits include companionship, a sense of belonging, and the pleasure of associating with others. Although the National Audubon Society was originally founded to save the snowy egret from extinction, today most members join to learn more about birds and to meet and share their pleasure with other individuals who enjoy bird-watching as a hobby. Even though the incentive might be solidary for many members, this organization nonetheless also pursues an active political agenda, working to preserve the environment and to protect endangered species. Still, most members may not play any part in working toward larger, more national goals unless the organization can convince them to take political action or unless some local environmental issue arises.

Material Incentives

For other individuals, interest groups offer direct **material incentives.** A case in point is AARP (formerly the American Association of Retired Persons), which provides discounts, insurance plans, and organized travel opportunities for its members. Because of its exceptionally low dues ($16 annually) and the benefits gained through membership, AARP has become the largest—and a very powerful—interest group in the United States. AARP can claim to represent the interests of millions of senior citizens and can show that they actually have joined the group. For most seniors, the material incentives outweigh the membership costs.

It's Easy

Anyone 50 or over can get all the great benefits of membership in AARP for only $16 a year. And membership includes your spouse or partner, free! Joining online is fast and secure. You become a member right away and receive your membership number online.

Time to renew? Renew Now!

(Courtesy of http://www.aarp.org)

Another example of such an interest group is the American Automobile Association (AAA).

Purposive Incentive
A reason for supporting or participating in the activities of a group that is based on agreement with the goals of the group. For example, someone with a strong interest in human rights might have a purposive incentive to join Amnesty International.

Most people who join this organization do so for its emergency roadside assistance and trip planning. Many members may not realize that the AAA is also a significant interest group seeking to shape laws that affect drivers.

Many other interest groups offer indirect material incentives for their members. Such groups as the American Dairy Association and the National Association of Automobile Dealers do not give discounts or "freebies" to their members, but they do offer indirect benefits and rewards by, for example, protecting the material interests of their members from government policymaking that is injurious to their industry or business.

did you know?

The activities of interest groups at the state level have been growing faster than those in the nation's capital, with more than 47,000 registered state lobbyists in 2012.

Purposive Incentives

Interest groups also offer the opportunity for individuals to pursue political, economic, or social goals through joint action. **Purposive incentives** offer individuals the satisfaction of taking action when the goals of a group correspond to their beliefs or principles. The individuals who belong to a group focusing on the abortion issue or gun control, for example, do so because they feel strongly enough about the issues to support the group's work with money and time.

Some scholars have argued that many people join interest groups simply for the discounts, magazine subscriptions, and other tangible benefits and are not really interested in the political positions taken by the groups. According to William P. Browne, however, research shows that people really do care about the policy stance of an interest group. Representatives of a group seek people who share the group's views and then ask them to join. As one group leader put it, "Getting members is about scaring the hell out of people."[3] People join the group and then feel that they are doing something about a cause that is important to them.

■ Learning Outcome 3: **List the major types of interest groups, especially those with economic motivations.**

Types of Interest Groups

Thousands of groups exist to influence government. Among the major types of interest groups are those that represent the main sectors of the economy. In addition, a number of "public-interest" organizations have been formed to represent the needs of the general citizenry. Other types of groups include many "single-issue" groups, ideological groups, and groups based on race, sex, or sexual orientation. The interests of foreign governments and foreign businesses are represented in the American political arena as well. The names of some major interest groups are shown in Table 7–1 on the facing page.

This is a greenhouse for growing tobacco plants. Why do tobacco growers hire lobbyists?

(Takaaki Iwabu/MCT/Landov)

Economic Interest Groups

More interest groups are formed to represent economic interests than any other set of interests. The variety of economic interest groups mirrors the complexity of the American economy. Major sectors that seek influence in Washington, D.C., include business, agriculture, labor unions, government workers, and professionals.

3. William P. Browne, *Groups, Interests, and U.S. Public Policy* (Washington, D.C.: Georgetown University Press, 1998), p. 23.

Table 7-1 ▸ A List of Effective Interest Groups

Business
- American Bankers Association
- American Farm Bureau Federation
- American Hospital Association
- America's Health Insurance Plans
- Business Roundtable
- Chamber of Commerce of the United States
- National Association of Home Builders
- National Association of Manufacturers (NAM)
- Pharmaceutical Research and Manufacturers of America

Labor
- American Federation of Labor–Congress of Industrial Organizations (AFL-CIO)
- American Federation of State, County, and Municipal Employees (AFSCME)
- Change to Win (a federation of labor unions)
- International Brotherhood of Teamsters
- National Education Association (NEA)
- Service Employees International Union

Professional
- American Association for Justice
- American Medical Association (AMA, representing physicians)
- National Association of Realtors

Identity
- AARP (formerly the American Association of Retired Persons)
- League of United Latin American Citizens (LULAC)
- National Association for the Advancement of Colored People (the NAACP, representing African Americans)
- National Organization for Women (NOW)

Environmental
- National Audubon Society
- National Wildlife Federation
- Nature Conservancy
- Sierra Club

Other
- American Civil Liberties Union (ACLU)
- American Israel Public Affairs Committee (AIPAC)
- American Legion (veterans)
- American Society for the Prevention of Cruelty to Animals (ASPCA)
- Amnesty International USA (human rights)
- Consumers Union
- Handgun Control, Inc. (favors gun control)
- Mothers Against Drunk Driving (MADD)
- NARAL Pro-Choice America
- National Rifle Association (NRA)
- National Right to Life Committee

Business Interest Groups. Thousands of business groups and trade associations work to influence government policies that affect their respective industries. "Umbrella groups" represent collections of businesses or other entities. The U.S. Chamber of Commerce, for example, is an umbrella group that represents a wide variety of businesses, while the National Association of Manufacturers is an umbrella group that represents only manufacturing concerns.

Some business groups are decidedly more powerful than others. The U.S. Chamber of Commerce, which represents about 3 million member companies, can bring constituent influence to bear on every member of Congress. The National Association of Manufacturers is another powerful group. With a staff of about 150 people in Washington, D.C., the organization can mobilize dozens of well-educated, articulate lobbyists to work the corridors of Congress on issues of concern to its members.

Interest groups are just as active on Twitter as they are on Facebook. Search on Twitter for any of the groups mentioned on page 219 and you will see a long list of recent posts.

Agricultural Interest Groups. American farmers and their employees represent less than 1 percent of the U.S. population. In spite of this, farmers' influence on legislation

did you know?

The names of many interest groups suggest goals opposite from the organization's true objectives—for example, the Palm Oil Truth Foundation does not seek to expose the dangers of palm oil use, but to expand the use of palm oil in food and oppose action against global warming.

beneficial to their interests has been significant. Farmers have succeeded in their aims because they have very strong interest groups. They are geographically dispersed and therefore have many representatives and senators to speak for them.

The American Farm Bureau Federation, or Farm Bureau, established in 1919, represents more than 5.5 million families (a majority of whom are not actually farm families) and is usually seen as conservative. It was instrumental in getting government guarantees of "fair" prices during the Great Depression in the 1930s. Another important agricultural interest organization is the National Farmers' Union (NFU), which is considered more liberal. Single-issue farm groups have emerged. The American Dairy Association, the Peanut Growers Group, and the National Soybean Association, for example, work to support their respective farmers and associated businesses.

Agricultural interest groups have probably been more successful than any other groups in obtaining subsidies from American taxpayers. U.S. farm subsidies cost taxpayers about $16 billion a year. Republicans and Democrats alike have supported agricultural subsidy legislation, showing the success of agricultural lobbying groups. The latest legislation, passed in 2008, created the most expensive agricultural subsidy program ever. Congress began work on a new farm bill in 2012.

As expensive as U.S. agricultural supports may be, many other nations provide their farmers with even greater subsidies. We provide some figures in the *Beyond Our Borders* feature on the facing page.

Labor Movement
The economic and political expression of working-class interests.

Service Sector
The sector of the economy that provides services—such as health care, banking, and education—in contrast to the sector that produces goods.

Labor Interest Groups. Interest groups representing the **labor movement** date back to at least 1886, when the American Federation of Labor (AFL) was formed. In 1955, the AFL joined forces with the Congress of Industrial Organizations (CIO). Today, the combined AFL-CIO is a large federation with a membership of about 10 million workers and an active political arm called the Committee on Political Education. In a sense, the AFL-CIO is a union of unions.

The AFL-CIO remained the predominant labor union organization for fifty years. The AFL-CIO experienced discord within its ranks during 2005, however, as four key unions left the federation and formed the Change to Win Coalition. Today, Change to Win has a membership of about 6 million workers. Many labor advocates fear that the split will reduce organized labor's influence, and in 2009 leaders of the two federations met to discuss the possibility of reunification.

This Goodyear Tire & Rubber Company union employee supports a strike against his employer. Are labor unions still a major lobbying force in the United States?

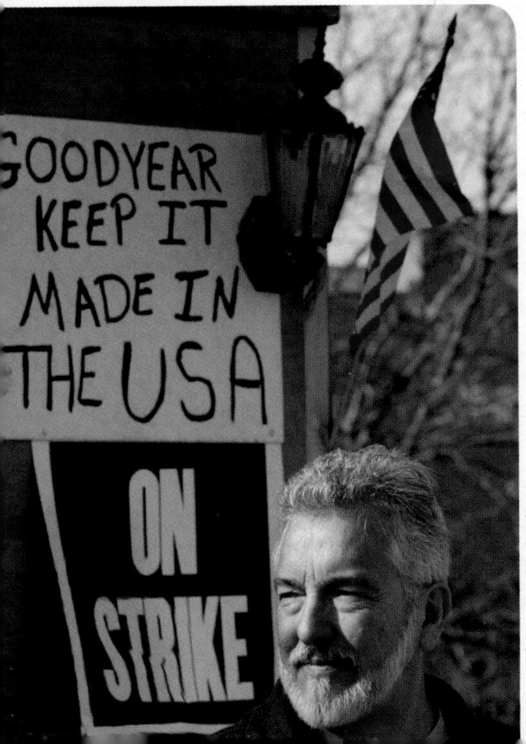

(AP Photo/Tony Dejak)

Even before the split, the role of unions in American society had been waning, as witnessed by the decline in union membership (see Figure 7–2 on page 224). In the age of automation and with the rise of the **service sector,** blue-collar workers in basic industries (autos, steel, and the like) represent a smaller and smaller percentage of the total working population.

Because of this decline in the industrial sector of the economy, national unions are looking to nontraditional areas for their membership, including migrant farmworkers, service workers, and especially public employees—such as police officers, firefighting personnel, teachers, college professors, and even graduate assistants. Indeed, public-sector unions make up an ever-greater share of the labor movement.

Although the proportion of the workforce that belongs to a union has declined over the years, American labor unions have not given up their efforts to support sympathetic candidates for Congress or for state office. Currently, the AFL-CIO, under the leadership of coal miner Richard Trumka, has a large political budget, which it uses to help Democratic candidates nationwide. Labor offers a candidate (such as Democratic presidential candidate Barack Obama in 2008) a corps of volunteers in addition to campaign contributions.

Beyond Our Borders

HOW FOREIGN COUNTRIES SUBSIDIZE AGRICULTURE

(© kyoshino / iStockphoto) (© matjeacock / iStockphoto)

Figure 7–1 ▸ Agricultural Subsidies as a Percent of Production Value

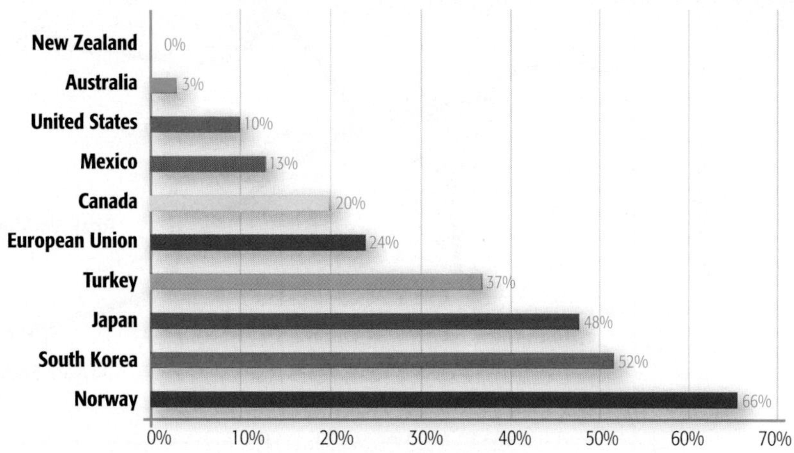

Source: Organization for Economic Cooperation and Development, 2009.

U.S. agricultural subsidies have often been controversial. In the 1930s, when subsidies began, many farmers were seriously impoverished. With today's large farms and high commodity prices, this is no longer true. It is worth noting, however, that the United States is far from the greatest sinner in the farm subsidy game. Most wealthy nations and some middle-income nations provide larger subsidies. Figure 7–1 above shows the size of farm subsidies as a percentage of total agricultural production. We give a single figure for the European Union, a confederation of twenty-seven countries with a Common Agricultural Policy (CAP). While the CAP is generous, it was more so in the past. In the 1980s, it paid out subsidies worth 40 percent of production.

FOR CRITICAL ANALYSIS

Some African countries tax farmers to support people who live in cities. If those countries were on this chart, their figures would actually be negative. Why might such nations have policies so different from those of wealthier countries?

Public Employee Unions. The degree of unionization in the private sector has declined over the past fifty years, but this has been partially offset by growth in the unionization of public employees. Figure 7–2 on the next page displays the growth in public-sector unionization. With a total membership of almost 8 million, public-sector unions are likely to continue expanding.

Both the American Federation of State, County, and Municipal Employees and the American Federation of Teachers are members of the AFL-CIO's Public Employee Department. Over the years, public employee unions have sometimes been involved in strikes. Most of these strikes are illegal, because almost no public employees have the right to strike.

Figure 7–2 ▶ Decline in Union Membership, 1948 to Present

The percentage of the total workforce that consists of labor union members has declined precipitously over the past forty years. The percentage of government workers who are union members, however, increased significantly in the 1960s and 1970s and has remained stable since. (Note that the percentage of the workforce that consists of union members, as shown on this chart, is several points lower than the percentage of workers represented by a union, because most unions represent some nonmembers.)

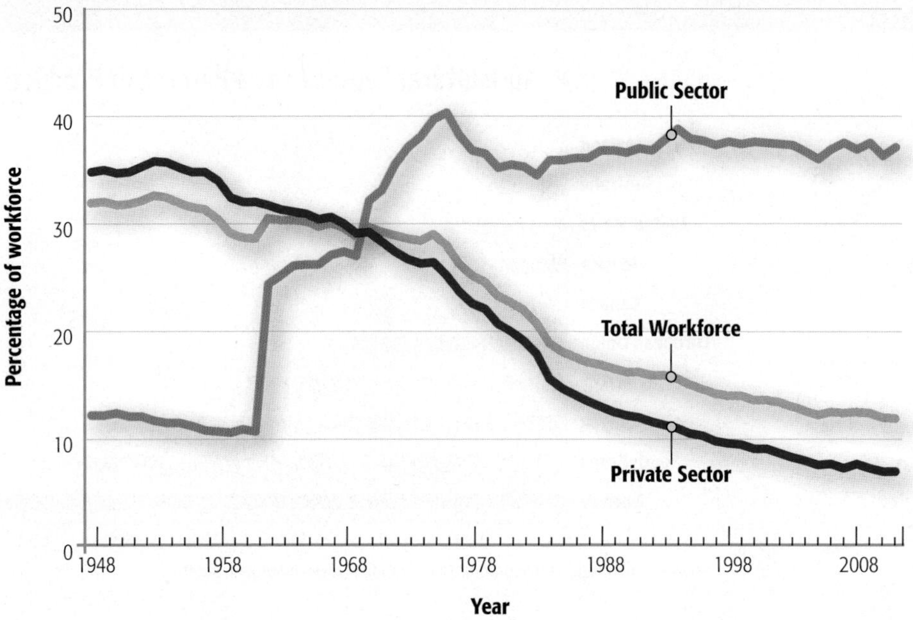

Source: Bureau of Labor Statistics.

A powerful interest group lobbying on behalf of its public employees is the National Education Association (NEA), a nationwide organization of about 3.2 million teachers and others connected with education. Most NEA locals function as labor unions. The NEA lobbies intensively for increased public funding of education.

The Political Environment Faced by Labor. The success or failure of attempts to form unions depends greatly on popular attitudes. Many business-oriented conservatives have never accepted unions as legitimate institutions. In states where this position is widely held, local laws and practices can make it hard for labor to organize. For example, Georgia and North Carolina are major manufacturing states, but the percentages of union members in these two conservative states are 4.6 percent and 5 percent, respectively. States where the voting public is more sympathetic to labor, such as California and New York, have unionization rates of 19.5 percent and 26.6 percent, respectively. These rates are more typical of the world's wealthy nations than are the rates in conservative southern states.

In recent years, conservatives have taken a strong stand against public employee unions, in particular teachers' unions such as the National Education Association and the American Federation of Teachers. In some states, mostly in the South, bargaining with public-sector unions is prohibited. In 2011, Republican governors in several midwestern states—notably including Ohio and Wisconsin—attempted to restrict or abolish the bargaining rights of public employees.

Interest Groups of Professionals. Many professional organizations exist, including the American Bar Association, the Association of General Contractors of America, the Institute of Electrical and Electronics Engineers, and others. Some professional groups, such as those representing lawyers and physicians, are more influential than others because of their ability to restrict entry into their professions. Lawyers have a unique advantage—a large number of members of Congress share their profession. In terms of funds spent on lobbying, however, one professional organization stands head and shoulders above the rest—the American Medical Association. Founded in 1847, it is affiliated with more than 1,000 local and state medical societies and has a total membership of about 216,000.

The Unorganized Poor. Some have argued that the system of interest group politics leaves out poor Americans and U.S. residents who are not citizens and cannot vote. Americans who are disadvantaged economically typically do not join interest groups. If they are members of the working poor, they may hold two or more jobs just to survive, leaving them no time to participate in interest groups. Other groups in the population—including non-English-speaking groups, resident aliens, single parents, Americans with disabilities, and younger voters—may not have the time or expertise even to find out what groups might represent them. Consequently, some scholars suggest that interest groups and lobbyists are the privilege of upper-middle-class Americans and those who belong to unions or other special groups.

R. Allen Hays examines the plight of poor Americans in his book *Who Speaks for the Poor?*[4] Hays studied groups and individuals who have lobbied for public housing and other issues related to the poor and concluded that the poor depend largely on indirect representation. Most efforts on behalf of the poor come from a policy network of groups—including public housing officials, welfare workers and officials, religious groups, public-interest groups, and some liberal general-interest groups—that speak loudly and persistently for the poor. Poor Americans themselves remain outside the interest group network and have little direct voice of their own.

(© Charley Gallay/Getty Images)

These writers are members of the Writers Guild of America in Hollywood, California. If you were to classify this interest group, what kind would it be?

Environmental Groups

Environmental interest groups are not new. We have already mentioned the National Audubon Society, which was founded in 1905 to protect the snowy egret from the commercial demand for hat decorations. The patron of the Sierra Club, John Muir, worked for the creation of national parks more than a century ago. But the blossoming of national environmental groups with mass memberships did not occur until the 1970s.

Today's Environmental Groups. Since the first Earth Day, organized in 1972, many interest groups have sprung up to protect the environment in general or unique ecological niches. The groups range from the National Wildlife Federation, with a membership of more than 4 million and an emphasis on education, to the more elite Environmental Defense Fund, with a membership of 500,000 and a focus on influencing federal policy. The Nature Conservancy uses members' contributions to buy up threatened natural areas and then either gives them to state or local governments or manages them itself. Other groups include the more radical Greenpeace Society and Earth First.

Global Warming. The topic of global warming has become a major focus for environmental groups in recent years. This issue has pitted environmentalists against other interest groups to a much greater degree than in the past. Environmentalists often find themselves in opposition to economic interests representing industries that release

4. R. Allen Hays, *Who Speaks for the Poor? National Interest Groups and Social Policy* (New York: Routledge, 2009).

"greenhouse" gases into the atmosphere. Indeed, the reaction against environmentalism has been strong enough in such coal-oriented states as West Virginia to transform them politically. Once a Democratic bastion, West Virginia now usually supports Republicans in presidential contests.

An example of a recent controversy that lined up oil companies and construction workers against environmentalists and farmers was the dispute over the Keystone XL oil pipeline. We discuss that controversy in this chapter's *Which Side Are You On?* feature below.

Public-Interest Groups

Public Interest
The best interests of the overall community; the national good, rather than the narrow interests of a particular group.

Public interest is a difficult term to define because, as we noted in Chapter 6, there are many publics in our nation of more than 10 million. It is almost impossible for one particular public policy to benefit everybody, which in turn makes it practically impossible to

Which Side Are You On?

DO WE NEED MORE OIL PIPELINES?

With gas prices at more than $4 a gallon in 2012, debate over building more pipelines to bring more oil to American refineries sometimes reached a fever pitch. As far back as 2008, the State Department had given its blessing to the Keystone XL pipeline, which would link oil sands in Alberta, Canada, to U.S. refineries on the Gulf Coast. The project was strongly opposed by environmental groups, however, and President Obama attempted to postpone a decision on it until after the 2012 elections. When Congress forced the administration to make a decision immediately, Obama denied the necessary permit altogether, at least for the time being. This decision did not end the argument over the pipeline—if anything, it raised the temperature of debate.

KEYSTONE XL IS BAD FOR THE ENVIRONMENT

Opponents of the Keystone XL pipeline contend that it is environmentally unsound. They argue that Canadian oil companies, in extracting usable oil from heavy tar sands, scar the environment. To extract the petroleum, the companies must use natural gas to boil vast quantities of water and then inject steam into the ground. According to some, this process creates "the dirtiest oil on earth." Carbon must be emitted into the atmosphere merely to mine the product, never mind the emissions when the oil is finally burned. It should come as no surprise that Alberta's native peoples are uniformly hostile to the development of the oil sands.

The American states through which the pipeline would flow will certainly be at risk from spills. And spills of this type of heavy, corrosive oil are harder to clean up. Nebraskans are particularly worried about such spills contaminating their drinking water. Spills in remote areas might not be detected until they have done toxic damage.

IT'S ALL ABOUT REPLACING "CONFLICT" OIL

Supporters of the pipeline have characterized our existing imported oil as "conflict" oil. The reason for the label is that much of the oil traded in international markets comes from countries in the Middle East and elsewhere that are governed by dictators. The United States imports large quantities of oil from Venezuela, which is run by an anti-American, authoritarian regime.

Canada, in contrast, provides "ethical" oil because it is a Western, liberal democracy. The estimated amount of crude oil that would come through the Keystone XL pipeline is about 800,000 barrels a day—the same amount that we currently get from Venezuela. Also, Venezuelan oil is notoriously "heavy." Producing it creates almost as much pollution as the petroleum from Canadian oil sands.

Allowing more oil to flow from Canada would increase the number of jobs in the United States and eventually lead to lower gasoline prices. In the end, it is better to be dependent on a friend for imported oil than on countries with leaders who regularly proclaim their hostility to America.

define the public interest. Nonetheless, over the past few decades, a variety of lobbying organizations have been formed "in the public interest."

The Consumer Movement. As an organized movement, consumerism began in 1936 with the founding of the Consumers Union, which continues to publish the popular magazine *Consumer Reports.* The movement had antecedents dating back to the earliest years of the twentieth century, when investigative journalists known as "muckrakers" exposed exploitative working conditions and unsafe products in a variety of industries. Upton Sinclair's 1906 novel *The Jungle,* which revealed abuses of the workforce and unsanitary conditions in the meatpacking industry, was a classic of this genre.

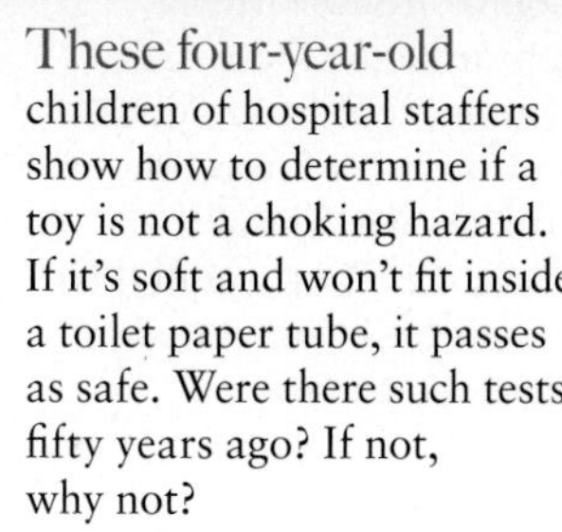

(AP Photo/Reed Saxon)

These four-year-old children of hospital staffers show how to determine if a toy is not a choking hazard. If it's soft and won't fit inside a toilet paper tube, it passes as safe. Were there such tests fifty years ago? If not, why not?

Consumerism took off during the 1960s, a time of social ferment marked by the civil rights, antiwar, and feminist movements. Ralph Nader, who gained notice by exposing unsafe automobiles, was a key figure in the consumer movement. Nader was a major sponsor of a series of new organizations. These included the Public Interest Research Groups (PIRGs)—campus organizations that emerged in the early 1970s and continue to provide students with platforms for civic engagement. Other new groups included the Consumer Federation of America (1968) and Public Citizen (1971).

Partly in response to the PIRG organizations and other groups, several conservative public-interest legal foundations have sprung up that are often pitted against liberal groups in court. Some of these are the Pacific Legal Foundation, the National Right to Work Legal Defense Foundation, the Institute for Justice, and the Mid-Atlantic Legal Foundation.

Other Public-Interest Groups. One of the largest public-interest groups is Common Cause, founded in 1968. Its goal is to reorder national priorities toward "the public" and to make governmental institutions more responsive to the needs of the public. Anyone willing to pay dues of $40 a year ($15 for students) can become a member. Members are polled regularly to obtain information about local and national issues. Another public-interest group is the League of Women Voters, founded in 1920. Although officially nonpartisan, it has lobbied for the Equal Rights Amendment and for government reform.

Other Interest Groups

A number of interest groups focus on just one issue. Single-interest groups, being narrowly focused, may be able to call attention to their causes because they have simple, straightforward goals and because their members tend to care intensely about the issues. Thus, such groups can easily motivate their members to contact legislators or to organize demonstrations in support of their policy goals.

The abortion debate has created groups opposed to abortion (such as the National Right to Life Committee) and groups in favor of abortion rights (such as NARAL

(Scott J. Ferrell/Congressional Quarterly/Getty Images)

Representatives from Facebook, the Association for Competitive Technology, Apple Inc., Google Inc., and Common Sense Media appear before the Senate Commerce Subcommittee on Consumer Protection, Product Safety, and Insurance. Why would this committee be interested in these companies?

Pro-Choice America). Further examples of single-issue groups are the National Rifle Association of America, the National Right to Work Committee (an antiunion group), and the American Israel Public Affairs Committee (a pro-Israel group).

Ideological Groups. Among the most important interest groups are those that unite citizens around a common ideological viewpoint. The Americans for Democratic Action, for example, was founded in 1947 as a home for liberals who were explicitly anti-Communist. On the political right, Americans for Tax Reform, organized by Grover Norquist, has been phenomenally successful in persuading almost all leading Republicans to sign a pledge promising never to vote to raise taxes. The various organizations making up the Tea Party movement are widely seen as ideological interest groups. (Some observers, however, believe that the movement is better considered as a faction of the Republican Party rather than a series of interest groups.)

Identity Groups. Still other groups represent Americans who share a common identity, such as membership in a particular race or ethnic group. The NAACP, founded in 1909 as the National Association for the Advancement of Colored People, represents African Americans. The National Organization for Women (NOW) has championed women's rights since 1966.

Elderly Americans can be considered to have a common identity. AARP, as mentioned earlier, is one of the most powerful interest groups in Washington, D.C., and, according to some, the strongest lobbying group in the United States. It is certainly the nation's largest interest group, with a membership of about 40 million. AARP has accomplished much for its members over the years. It played a significant role in the creation of Medicare and Medicaid, as well as in obtaining annual cost-of-living increases in Social Security payments. (Medicare pays for medical expenses incurred by those who are at least sixty-five years of age; Medicaid provides health-care support for the poor.) In 2009 and 2010, AARP strongly supported the Democratic health-care reform bills and argued against those who feared that the new legislation might harm the Medicare program.

Foreign Interest Groups

Homegrown interest groups are not the only players in the game. Washington, D.C., is also the center for lobbying by foreign governments as well as private foreign interests. The governments of the largest U.S. trading partners, such as Canada, the European Union (EU) countries, Japan, and South Korea, maintain substantial research and lobbying staffs. Even smaller nations, such as those in the Caribbean, engage lobbyists when vital legislation affecting their trade interests is considered. Frequently, these foreign interests hire former members of Congress to promote their positions on Capitol Hill.

What Makes an Interest Group Powerful?

■ Learning Outcome 4:
Evaluate the factors that make some interest groups especially powerful.

At any time, thousands of interest groups are attempting to influence state legislatures, governors, Congress, and members of the executive branch of the U.S. government. What characteristics make some of those groups more powerful than others and more likely to have influence over government policy? Generally, interest groups attain a reputation for being powerful through their membership size, financial resources, leadership, and cohesiveness.

Size and Resources

No legislator can deny the power of an interest group that includes thousands of his or her own constituents among its members. Labor unions and organizations such as AARP and the American Automobile Association are able to claim voters in every congressional district. Having a large membership—about 10 million in the case of the AFL-CIO—carries a great deal of weight with government officials. AARP now has about 40 million members and a budget of more than a billion dollars for its operations. In addition, AARP claims to represent all older Americans, who constitute close to 20 percent of the population, whether they join the organization or not.

Having a large number of members, even if the individual membership dues are relatively small, provides an organization with a strong financial base. Those funds pay for lobbyists, television advertisements, e-mailings to members, a Web site, pages on Facebook, Twitter feeds, and many other resources that help an interest group make its point to politicians. The business organization with the largest membership is probably the U.S. Chamber of Commerce, which represents more than 3 million businesses. The Chamber uses its members' dues to pay for staff and lobbyists, as well as a sophisticated communications network so that it can contact members in a timely way. All of the members can check the Chamber's Web site to get updates on the latest legislative proposals.

Other organizations may have fewer members but nonetheless can muster significant financial resources. The pharmaceutical lobby, which represents many of the major drug manufacturers, is one of the most powerful interest groups in Washington due to its financial resources. This interest group has more than 1,250 registered lobbyists and spent close to $30 million in the 2012 cycle for lobbying and campaign expenditures.

Leadership

Money is not the only resource that interest groups need. Strong leaders who can develop effective strategies are also important. For example, the American Israel Public Affairs Committee (AIPAC) has long benefited from strong leadership. AIPAC lobbies Congress

While running for president, former Massachusetts governor Mitt Romney often spoke before different interest groups, such as the American Israel Public Affairs Committee (AIPAC). Why did both presidential candidates agree to do so during the campaign?

(Kevin Dietsch/UPI/Landov)

and the executive branch on issues related to U.S.-Israeli relations, as well as general foreign policy in the Middle East. AIPAC has been successful in promoting the close relationship that the two nations have enjoyed, which includes foreign aid that the United States annually bestows on Israel, now down to about $3.1 billion a year, but more than $4 billion as recently as 2000. Despite its modest membership size, AIPAC has won bipartisan support for its agenda and is consistently ranked among the most influential interest groups in America.

Other interest groups, including some with few financial resources, succeed in part because they are led by individuals with charisma and access to power. Sometimes, choosing a leader with a particular image can be an effective strategy for an organization. The National Rifle Association (NRA) had more than organizational skills in mind when it elected the late actor Charlton Heston as its president. The strategy of using an actor identified with powerful roles as the spokesperson for the organization worked to improve its image.

Cohesiveness

Regardless of an interest group's size or the amount of funds in its coffers, the motivation of an interest group's members is a key factor in determining how powerful it is. If the members of a group hold their beliefs strongly enough to send letters to their representatives, join a march on Washington, or work together to defeat a candidate, that group is considered powerful. As described earlier, the American labor movement's success in electing Democratic candidates made the labor movement a more powerful lobby.

Although groups that oppose abortion rights have had modest success in influencing policy, they are considered powerful because their members are vocal and highly motivated. Of course, the existence of countervailing pro-choice groups limits their influence. Other measures of cohesion include the ability of a group to get its members to contact Washington quickly or to give extra funds when needed. The U.S. Chamber of Commerce excels at both of these strategies. In comparison, AARP cannot claim that it can get many of its 40 million members to contact their congressional representatives, but it does seem to have some influence on the opinions of older Americans and their views of political candidates.

Interest Group Strategies

■ Learning Outcome 5: **Discuss interest group strategies, differentiating between direct and indirect techniques.**

Interest groups employ a wide range of techniques and strategies to promote their policy goals. Although few groups are successful at persuading Congress and the president to endorse their programs completely, many are able to block—or at least weaken—legislation injurious to their members. The key to success for interest groups is access to government officials. To gain such access, interest groups and their representatives try to cultivate long-term relationships with legislators and government officials. The best of these relationships are based on mutual respect and cooperation. The interest group provides the official with sources of information and assistance, and the official in turn gives the group opportunities to express its views.

The techniques used by interest groups can be divided into direct and indirect techniques. With **direct techniques,** the interest group and its lobbyists approach officials personally to present their case. With **indirect techniques,** in contrast, the interest group uses the general public or individual constituents to influence the government on behalf of the interest group.

Direct Technique
An interest group activity that involves personal interaction with government officials to further the group's goals.

Indirect Technique
A strategy employed by interest groups that uses third parties to influence government officials.

Direct Techniques

Lobbying, publicizing ratings of legislative behavior, building alliances, and providing campaign assistance are four direct techniques used by interest groups.

Lobbying Techniques. As you might have guessed, the term *lobbying* comes from the activities of private citizens regularly congregating in the lobbies of legislative chambers to petition legislators. In the latter part of the 1800s, railroad and industrial groups openly bribed state legislators to pass legislation beneficial to their interests, giving lobbying a well-deserved bad name. Most lobbyists today are professionals. They are either consultants to a company or interest group or members of one of the Washington, D.C., law firms that specialize in providing lobbying services. Such firms employ hundreds of former members of Congress and former government officials who are valued for their network of contacts in Washington. As Ed Rollins, a former White House aide, put it, "I've got many friends who are all through the agencies and equally important, I don't have many enemies. . . . I tell my clients I can get your case moved to the top of the pile."[5] Lobbyists of all types are becoming more numerous. The number of lobbyists in Washington, D.C., has more than doubled since 2000.

did you know?

Federal lobbying expenditures in the United States exceed the gross domestic product (GDP) of fifty-nine countries.

Lobbyists engage in an array of activities to influence legislation and government policy. These activities include the following:

- Meeting privately with public officials to make known the interests of the lobbyists' clients. Although they are acting on behalf of their clients, lobbyists often furnish needed information to senators and representatives (and government agency appointees) that these officials could not easily obtain on their own. It is to the lobbyists' advantage to provide useful information so that the policymakers will rely on them in the future.
- Testifying before congressional committees for or against proposed legislation.
- Testifying before executive rulemaking agencies—such as the Federal Trade Commission or the Consumer Product Safety Commission—for or against proposed rules.
- Assisting legislators or bureaucrats in drafting legislation or prospective regulations. Often, lobbyists furnish advice on the specific details of legislation. Especially at the state level, lobbying firms have been known to write up the complete text of a bill, which is then passed by the legislature. We examine that practice in the *Politics and the States* feature on the following page.
- Inviting legislators to social occasions, such as cocktail parties, boating expeditions, and other events, including conferences at exotic locations. Most lobbyists believe that meeting legislators in a social setting is effective.
- Providing political information to legislators and other government officials. Sometimes, the lobbyists have better information than the party leadership about how other legislators are going to vote. When this is so, the political information they furnish may be a key to legislative success.
- Suggesting nominations for federal appointments to the executive branch.

The Ratings Game. Many interest groups attempt to influence the overall behavior of legislators through their rating systems. Each year, these interest groups identify the legislation that they consider most important to their goals and then monitor how legislators vote on it. Legislators receive scores based on their votes. The usual scheme ranges from 0 to 100 percent. In the ratings scheme of the liberal Americans for Democratic Action, for example, a rating of 100 means that a

Georgia governor Nathan Deal (on the left) meets with a lobbyist during a session of that state's legislature. Why would he willingly be photographed with lobbyists?

(AP Photo/*Atlanta Journal-Constitution*/Jason Getz)

5. As quoted in H. R. Mahood, *Interest Groups in American National Politics: An Overview* (New York: Prentice Hall, 2000), p. 51.

Politics AND the States

PSST—WANT TO BUY A NEW LAW?

If you were a state lobbyist or a member of the state legislature, it would be nice if someone else did the work of writing the bills that you favor or wish to sponsor. New laws are almost always filled with tedious detail. The job of crafting legislation is time consuming if you start from scratch. If you are a conservative, however, you are in luck. The American Legislative Exchange Council (ALEC) has a collection of about eight hundred "model bills" that are ready to go—just fill in the name of your state. ALEC, a nonprofit organization, is based in Washington, D.C. In a recent year, more than one thousand ALEC bills were introduced by state legislators. About two hundred of these became law.

WHO PAYS FOR THESE MODEL BILLS?

ALEC does not release details of its membership and operations. Analysis by a watchdog group, however, suggests that ALEC's members include about two thousand state lawmakers who pay $50 a year in dues. Corporations and trade groups can be members, too. They pay up to $25,000 a year. Some major corporations, such as AT&T and Reynolds American, a tobacco firm, pay $100,000 to become "president level" sponsors. Other major corporate sponsors have included ExxonMobil and the drug companies Allergan and Pfizer.

THE COMMON THREAD OF ALEC'S MODEL LEGISLATION

The model laws provided by ALEC are usually conservative. A common thread is to reduce or prevent the growth of state and local regulation of business. For example, one bill enacts a state ban on requiring restaurants to reveal information about food ingredients or nutritional values. A second goal is to prevent initiatives by publicly financed entities that could potentially compete with private corporations. For example, ALEC has enjoyed great success with state legislation that bans local governments from providing broadband Internet service.

Other ALEC legislation tightens voter identification requirements, which may make it more difficult for students and poor people to vote. Another popular bill requires that a state withdraw from regional agreements to reduce CO_2 emissions. Some of the model legislation, however, encourages more government investment in infrastructure, an objective that can be shared by legislators with a variety of ideologies.

IMPROVING THE EFFICIENCY OF BUSINESS LOBBYING

Traditionally, when a corporation wanted to influence legislation in a particular state, it would hire a lobbyist or a lobbying firm. These lobbyists then would attempt to influence legislators in that state so that either (1) any new laws favor the company's interests, or (2) new legislation at least does the company no harm. ALEC's model legislation acts as a "force multiplier" for its corporate members. When corporations influence ALEC's model legislation, they gain the support of sympathetic legislators all over the country.

FOR CRITICAL ANALYSIS

Most legislators who use ALEC's model bills are Republicans. Is there any reason why there could not be a Democratic equivalent of ALEC? Could there be a problem in funding such an organization?

member of Congress voted with the group on every issue and is, by that measure, very liberal.

Ratings are a shorthand way of describing members' voting records for interested citizens. They can also be used to embarrass members. For example, an environmental group identifies the twelve representatives who the group believes have the worst voting records on environmental issues and labels them "the Dirty Dozen," and a watchdog group describes those representatives who took home the most "pork" for their districts or states as the biggest "pigs."

Building Alliances. Another direct technique used by interest groups is to form a coalition with other groups concerned about the same legislation. Often, these groups will set up a paper organization with an innocuous name to represent their joint concerns. In the early 1990s, for example, environmental, labor, and consumer groups formed an alliance called the Citizens Trade Campaign to oppose the passage of the North American Free Trade Agreement.

Members of such a coalition share expenses and multiply the influence of their individual groups by combining their efforts. Other advantages of forming a coalition are that it blurs the specific interests of the individual groups involved and makes it appear that larger public interests are at stake. These alliances also are efficient devices for keeping like-minded groups from duplicating one another's lobbying efforts.

"Please understand, I don't sell access to the government, I merely sell access to the guys who do sell access to the government."

(© Ed Fisher/The New Yorker Collection/www.cartoonbank.com)

Campaign Assistance. Interest groups have additional strategies to use in their attempts to influence government policies. Groups recognize that the greatest concern of legislators is to be reelected, so they focus on the legislators' campaign needs. Associations with large memberships, such as labor unions, are able to provide workers for political campaigns, including precinct workers to get out the vote, volunteers to put up posters and pass out literature, and people to staff telephone banks at campaign headquarters.

Candidates vie for the groups' endorsements in a campaign. Gaining those endorsements may be automatic, or it may require that the candidates participate in debates or interviews with the interest groups. An interest group usually publicizes its choices in its membership publication, and the candidate can use the endorsement in her or his campaign literature. Traditionally, labor unions have endorsed Democratic Party candidates. Republican candidates, however, often try to persuade union locals at least to refrain from any endorsement. Making no endorsement can then be perceived as disapproval of the Democratic Party candidate.

Citizens United v. FEC. In 2010, the United States Supreme Court shook up the campaign-finance system when it issued its opinion in *Citizens United v. FEC.*[6] The Court

6. 130 S.Ct. 876 (2010).

2012 elections
THE IMPACT OF INTEREST GROUPS

While much spending by interest groups in the 2012 elections came from ideological groups with links to the political parties, industries with narrower interests were also players. Two of these industries were coal and natural gas. During 2012, both flooded the airwaves with ads that did not explicitly name candidates or political parties.

For the natural gas industry, the real issue is how ordinary Americans view the industry. Vast new volumes of natural gas are now in production due to an innovative extraction technique known as hydraulic fracturing, or fracking. This process, however, has its opponents who fear that fracking might contaminate drinking water or even lead to earthquakes. The natural gas industry seeks to head off such concerns and to sell fracking to the public as a safe and effective way to obtain vitally needed energy. The industry is also interested in subsidies for motor vehicles that use natural gas.

The coal industry wants emission standards for mercury and other pollutants released by burning coal to be relaxed. (New standards were recently introduced by the Environmental Protection Agency.) Coal, however, has a more serious problem. New supplies of natural gas are driving down the cost of that fuel to the point where coal cannot compete on price. Utilities across the country are closing coal-based electric power plants and opening new ones that use natural gas. While the coal industry is desperate to win public support, such support will not protect it from more competitive energy sources.

(© kyoshino / iStockphoto) (© manley099 / iStockphoto)

use in the policymaking process. While some groups are composed of members who have high social status and significant economic resources, such as the National Association of Manufacturers, other groups derive influence from their large memberships. AARP, for example, has more members than any other interest group. Its large membership allows it to wield significant power over legislators. Still other groups, such as environmentalists, have causes that can claim strong public support even from people who have no direct stake in the issue. Groups such as the National Rifle Association are well organized and have highly motivated members. This enables them to channel a stream of letters, e-mails, and tweets toward Congress with a few days' effort.

did you know?

On average, there are now sixty lobbyists for each member of Congress.

Even the most powerful interest groups do not always succeed in their demands. Whereas the U.S. Chamber of Commerce may be accepted as having a justified interest in the question of business taxes, many legislators might feel that the group should not engage in the debate over the future of Social Security. In other words, groups are seen as having a legitimate concern in the issues closest to their interests but not necessarily in broader issues. This may explain why some of the most successful groups are those that focus on very specific issues—such as tobacco farming, funding of abortions, and handgun control—and do not get involved in larger conflicts.

Complicating the question of interest group influence is the fact that many groups' lobbyists are former colleagues, friends, or family members of current members of Congress.

(AP Photo/Kenneth Lambert)

James Brady was shot and disabled during an attempt to assassinate President Ronald Reagan in 1981. He and his wife, Sarah, are activists against gun violence. What interest group might oppose the Bradys' attempts to win gun control legislation?

Why Should You Care about... INTEREST GROUPS?

Why should you, as an individual, care about interest groups? True, some interest groups focus on issues that concern only a limited number of people. Others, however, are involved in causes in which almost everyone has a stake. Gun control is one of the issues that concerns a large number of people. The question of whether the possession of handguns should be regulated is at the heart of a long-running heated battle among organized interest groups. The fight is fueled by the 1 million gun incidents occurring in the United States each year—murders, suicides, assaults, accidents, and robberies in which guns are involved.

INTEREST GROUPS AND YOUR LIFE

The passionate feelings that are brought to bear on both sides of the gun control issue are evidence of its importance. The problem of crime is central to the gun control issue. Public opinion poll respondents cited crime as one of the nation's most important problems throughout the 1990s, and it continues to be a major concern today.

Does the easy availability of handguns promote crime? Are guns part of the problem of crime—or part of the solution? Either way, the question is important to you personally. Even if you are fortunate enough not to be victimized by crime, you will probably find yourself limiting your activities from time to time out of a fear of crime.

HOW YOU CAN MAKE A DIFFERENCE

Almost every year, Congress and the various state legislatures debate measures that would alter gun laws for the nation or for the individual states. As a result, there are plenty of opportunities to get involved.

Issues in the debate include child-safety features on guns and the regulation of gun dealers who sell firearms at gun shows. Proponents of gun control seek safety locks and more restrictions on gun purchases. Proponents of firearms claim that possessing firearms is a constitutional right and meets a vital defense need for individuals. They contend that the problem lies not in the sale and ownership of weapons but in their use by criminals.

The Coalition to Stop Gun Violence takes the position that handguns "serve no valid purpose, except to kill people." In contrast, the National Rifle Association (NRA) of America supports the rights of gun owners. The NRA, founded in 1871, is currently one of the most powerful single-issue groups in the United States. The NRA believes that gun laws will not reduce the number of crimes. It is illogical to assume, according to the NRA, that persons who refuse to obey laws prohibiting rape, murder, and other crimes will obey a gun law.

In recent years, gun rights advocates have been strikingly successful in accomplishing their objectives. One sign of this is the affirmation by the United States Supreme Court that individuals have a constitutional right to bear arms. The NRA and other organizations have also been effective in winning state laws that allow citizens to carry concealed weapons in an ever-greater number of environments, including college campuses.

To find out more about the NRA's positions, you can enter "nra" into your favorite Internet search engine. Organizations that advocate gun controls include the Coalition to Stop Gun Violence and the Brady Campaign to Prevent Gun Violence. You can locate the first of these organizations by searching on "csgv" and the second by typing in "brady campaign."

Questions for Discussion and Analysis

1. Review the *Which Side Are You On?* feature on page 226. Given that most of the world's oil is produced and consumed by countries other than the United States, is it reasonable to argue that greater oil production in North America can have a significant effect on gasoline prices? Why or why not?
2. Some interest groups are much more influential than others. Some interest groups famous for their clout are the National Rifle Association, AARP, business groups such as the National Federation of Independent Business, the American Israel Public Affairs Committee, and the American Association for Justice (formerly the Association of Trial Lawyers of America). What factors might make each of these groups powerful?
3. "If guns are outlawed, only outlaws will have guns." This is a key slogan used by opponents of gun control. How much truth do you think there is to this slogan? Explain your reasoning.
4. About half of the paid lobbyists in Washington are former government staff members or former members of Congress. Why would interest groups employ such people? Why might some reformers want to limit the ability of interest groups to employ them? On what basis might an interest group argue that such limits are unconstitutional?

Key Terms

boycott 235
climate control 234
direct technique 230
free rider problem 219
indirect technique 230
interest group 217
labor movement 222
latent interests 218
lobbyist 217
material incentive 219
public interest 226
purposive incentive 220
service sector 222
social movement 218
solidary incentive 219

Chapter Summary

1. An interest group is an organization whose members share common objectives and actively attempt to influence government policy. Interest groups proliferate in the United States because they can influence government at many points in the political structure and because they offer solidary, material, and purposive incentives to their members. Interest groups are often created out of social movements.
2. Major types of interest groups include business, agricultural, labor, public employee, professional, and environmental groups. Other important groups may be considered public-interest, single-interest, ideological, and identity groups. In addition, foreign governments and corporations lobby our government.
3. Interest groups use direct and indirect techniques to influence government. Direct techniques include testifying before committees and rulemaking agencies, providing information to legislators, rating legislators' voting records, building alliances, and aiding political campaigns. Indirect techniques to influence government include campaigns to rally public sentiment, letter-writing campaigns, efforts to influence the climate of opinion, and the use of constituents to lobby for the group's interest. Unconventional methods of applying pressure include demonstrations and boycotts.
4. The 1946 Legislative Reorganization Act was the first attempt to control lobbyists and their activities through registration requirements. The United States Supreme Court narrowly construed the act as applying only to lobbyists who directly seek to influence federal legislation.
5. In 1995, Congress approved new legislation requiring anyone who spends 20 percent of his or her time influencing legislation to register as a lobbyist. Also, any organization spending more than $24,500 semiannually and any individual who is paid more than $6,000 semiannually for his or her work must register. Semiannual reports must include the names of clients, the bills in which they are interested, and the branches of government contacted. The lobbying efforts of grassroots and tax-exempt organizations are exempt from the rules.
6. In 2007, in response to lobbying scandals, Congress tightened rules on giving gifts to legislators and increased reporting requirements for lobbyists to four times a year. Under the 2007 reform legislation, lobbyists now have to report contributions to coalition efforts. Congress has created a searchable online database of lobbying information.

Quiz Multiple Choice

1. When individuals benefit by the actions of an interest group but do not support that group, they are:
   a. **free riders.**
   b. **freeloaders.**
   c. **usually just waiting to join the group.**

2. Farmers receive a disproportionate share of taxpayer subsidies because:
   a. **food is more important than clothes.**
   b. **they have very powerful and well-organized interest groups.**
   c. **they live throughout the United States.**

3. Union membership in the United States has:
   a. **been growing, especially since 2000.**
   b. **stayed about the same since the Great Depression.**
   c. **been declining in recent years, except in the public sector.**

4. Defining the public interest is:
   a. **difficult because most people have no opinions on most issues.**
   b. **difficult because no public policy can benefit everyone.**
   c. **difficult because so few people are interested in politics.**

5. Ideological interest groups include:
   a. **the Democratic and Republican parties.**
   b. **the National Rifle Association.**
   c. **Americans for Democratic Action and the Tea Party movement.**

6. Interest groups today find it easier to communicate with their members because:
   a. **more Americans are interested in politics than ever before.**
   b. **the Internet and especially new social media are pervasive.**
   c. **the cost of mailing letters has fallen.**

7. There are many direct techniques that interest groups can use to affect legislation. They include:
   a. **sending out large numbers of direct-mail advertising pieces.**
   b. **attempts at weakening other interest groups.**
   c. **hiring lobbyists to argue their positions in Congress.**

8. When interest groups try to influence government policy by working through others, they are engaging in:
   a. **direct techniques.**
   b. **indirect techniques.**
   c. **unconventional techniques.**

ANSWERS: 1. a, 2. b, 3. c, 4. b, 5. c, 6. b, 7. c, 8. b.

Quiz Fill-Ins

9. When individuals have definite interests, but choose not to become a member of an interest group that represents these interests, their concerns are called ______________ interests.

10. The U.S. Chamber of Commerce is an example of a ______________ interest group.

11. Elderly Americans, those of particular races, and those of a particular sex, often participate in ______________-based groups.

12. Most lobbying today is undertaken by ______________, who often work in Washington, D.C., law firms.

13. Some interest groups hire public relations firms to improve the public image of an industry or a group. This is called ______________ ______________.

14. Interest groups can attempt to influence government policies by making ______________ ______________ to members of Congress who intend to run for reelection.

15. When a large segment of the population expresses a desire to change the economic, political, or social system, they are creating a ______________ ______________.

16. When an interest group offers its members a sense of belonging, companionship, and the pleasure of associating with others, we call these ______________ ______________ for that group's members.

ANSWERS: 9. latent, 10. business, 11. identity, 12. professionals, 13. climate control, 14. campaign contributions, 15. social movement, 16. solidary incentives.

(© Aleksandar Jovicic/iStockphoto)

Selected Print & Media Resources

SUGGESTED READINGS

Baker, Dean. *The End of Loser Liberalism: Making Markets Progressive.* Washington, D.C.: Center for Economic and Policy Research, 2011. Baker, co-founder of the Center for Economic Policy and Research, argues that under current conditions it is actually possible to promote liberal ends by reducing the scope of government. He calls for repealing tax breaks and special programs that benefit privileged special interests, especially at the state and local levels.

Dubofsky, Melvyn, and Foster Rhea Dulles. *Labor in America: A History.* Wheeling, Ill.: Harlan Davidson, 2010. This work is probably the best general history of American labor. Dubofsky, a history professor at SUNY Binghamton, has given the text a complete update.

Feldman, Richard. *Ricochet: Confessions of a Gun Lobbyist.* Hoboken, N.J.: Wiley, 2007. Feldman, a former NRA lobbyist and an engaging writer, tells the story of the NRA's lobbying efforts and its internal politics. Feldman strongly favors gun owners' rights, but his description of the NRA's internal conflicts is wry and cynical.

Grossman, Matt. *The Not-So-Special Interests: Interest Groups, Public Representation, and American Governance.* Stanford, Calif.: Stanford University Press, 2012. Grossman, a political science professor at Michigan State University, explains why some interest groups succeed and others fail.

MEDIA RESOURCES

Casino Jack and the United States of Money—This 2010 documentary, directed by Alex Gibney, details the life and crimes of super-lobbyist Jack Abramoff. The story involves Indian casinos, Russian spies, Chinese sweatshops, and a mob-style killing in Miami. In the end, Abramoff is headed for prison.

Norma Rae—This 1979 Hollywood movie about an attempt by a northern union organizer to unionize workers in the southern textile industry; stars Sally Field, who won an Academy Award for her performance.

(© PashaIgnatov/iStockphoto)

E-mocracy INTEREST GROUPS AND THE INTERNET

The Internet may have a strong equalizing effect in the world of lobbying and government influence. The first organizations to use electronic means to reach their constituents and drum up support for action were the large economic coalitions, including the U.S. Chamber of Commerce and the National Association of Manufacturers. Groups such as these, as well as groups representing a single product such as tobacco, quickly realized that they could set up Web sites and mailing lists to provide information more rapidly to their members. Members could check the Web every day to see how legislation was developing in Congress or anywhere in the world. National associations could send e-mail to all of their members with one keystroke, mobilizing them to contact their representatives in Congress.

LOGGING ON

Today, almost every interest group or association has its own Web site. To find one, use your favorite search engine (such as Google), and search for the association by name. For a sense of the breadth of the kinds of interest groups that have Web sites, take a look at one or two of those listed here.

1. You can learn more about the labor movement by visiting the AFL-CIO's site. Search on "aflcio."
2. For a business perspective, locate the U.S. Chamber of Commerce site by typing in "uschamber."
3. AARP (formerly the American Association of Retired Persons) can be found by looking for "aarp."
4. It's worth taking a look at the site of the American Israel Public Affairs Committee—enter "aipac."
5. Information on environmental issues is available at a number of sites.
   - The Environmental Defense Fund's site can be found by searching on "edf."
   - You can also go to the Natural Resources Defense Council's site by typing in "nrdc."

8 Political Parties

President Obama greets supporters after a speech at Florida Atlantic University in Boca Raton, Florida. Which major political party would most of these people support?

(Kevin Lamarque/Reuters/Landov)

The seven learning outcomes below are designed to help improve your understanding of this chapter. After reading this chapter, you should be able to:

- Learning Outcome 1: **Define the term *political party*, and cite some of the major activities of the parties.**
- Learning Outcome 2: **Explain how the history of U.S. political parties has resulted in the two major parties that exist today.**
- Learning Outcome 3: **Summarize key economic and cultural positions taken by the two major parties.**
- Learning Outcome 4: **Describe three faces of a party: the party-in-the-electorate, the party organization, and the party-in-government.**
- Learning Outcome 5: **Give some of the reasons why the two-party system has endured in America.**
- Learning Outcome 6: **Evaluate the impact of third parties on U.S. politics.**
- Learning Outcome 7: **Discuss some of the ways in which support for the parties can change, and explain the increasing importance of independents.**

(John G. Mabanglo/EPA/Landov)

UNLIKE MOST CALIFORNIA politicians, Governor Jerry Brown supported the "Top Two Candidates" initiative.

WE CHOSE CANDIDATES THROUGH BIPARTISAN PRIMARY ELECTIONS?

BACKGROUND

In recent years, American politics have been characterized by severe political polarization. Supporters of the two major political parties have often seen the other party as not merely mistaken, but evil. One common result of polarization: competition among candidates to be the most unwavering advocate of their party's philosophy. We see such contests during *primary elections,* in which voters choose the candidates who will represent each party in the November general election. During the 2011–2012 Republican presidential debates and primaries, candidates competed fiercely for the "most conservative" label.

Is there a way to eliminate such "purity" contests? California and Washington recently adopted systems designed to do just that. Under a "Top Two Candidates" primary system, all candidates appear on a single ballot. Candidates can list their party but are not required to do so. More than one candidate from each party can appear on the ballot. The two candidates receiving the most votes—regardless of party—then appear on the general election ballot. In the general election, two Republicans might face each other in a conservative district. In a highly Democratic district, the top two finishers could both be Democrats.

WHAT IF WE CHOSE CANDIDATES THROUGH BIPARTISAN PRIMARY ELECTIONS?

A Top Two Candidates primary could increase voter participation. Parties would no longer have the option of controlling who votes for their candidates in the primary election. Candidates therefore would need to appeal to a broader range of opinion. The assumption is that candidates would take more moderate stands to appeal to independents or members of the other party. For example, in a conservative district, two Republican candidates might be forced to compete on the basis of who could add the most independent and even Democratic voters to their Republican support.

THE MAJOR POLITICAL PARTIES MIGHT SUFFER

A Top Two Candidates election could reduce the influence of the two major parties. According to Ron Nehring, a former chair of the California Republican Party, "It's a misnomer to call this an open primary. It's the abolition of primaries." Indeed, a Top Two election is not really a partisan primary—it is not a way in which parties can decide whom to support. Rather, it can be viewed as the first half of a two-part general election process.

Still, under the Top Two system, political parties would continue to have the right to endorse candidates for the various offices. The parties could publicize these candidates and could spend, within legal limits, as much as they wanted in campaigning for them. The parties could not, however, automatically place their preferred candidates on the November ballot.

WHAT WOULD HAPPEN TO CAMPAIGN SPENDING?

Some predict that if every state used a Top Two system, fewer campaign dollars would be spent. These people believe that partisan politics leads to more campaign spending. Candidates and their supporters spend whatever they can for negative, mudslinging ads on television and the Internet. Others contend that more, rather than less, spending would be necessary, because candidates would have to reach the entire electorate, not just a part of it.

FOR CRITICAL ANALYSIS

1. *If you were a relatively unknown candidate, would you prefer a Top Two Candidates system or an ordinary partisan primary? Why?*
2. *Assume you are a California Republican in a heavily Democratic congressional district. How could you best influence the outcome of your Top Two election?*

The state of the political parties is a matter of constant concern for the media. Even when an election is relatively far off, commentators obsessively assess the relative fortunes of the Republican and Democratic parties. As elections draw closer, polls concentrate on determining which political party individual voters "belong" to or support. Prior to an election, a typical poll usually asks the following question: "Do you consider yourself to be a Republican, a Democrat, or an independent?" For many years, Americans were divided fairly evenly among these three choices. Today, about 40 percent of all voters call themselves **independents.** Of course, independents are not represented as such in Congress, and three-quarters or more of all independents lean toward either the Republicans or the Democrats. Still, the power of independents might be enhanced if changes were made in the way that we choose candidates, as discussed in the chapter-opening *What If . . .* feature.

Independent
A voter or candidate who does not identify with a political party.

Political Party
A group of political activists who organize to win elections, operate the government, and determine public policy.

Faction
A group or bloc in a legislature or political party that is trying to obtain power or benefits.

After the elections are over, the media publish the election results. Among other things, Americans learn which party will control the presidency and how many Democrats and Republicans will be sitting in the House of Representatives and the Senate when the new Congress convenes.

Notice that earlier, when discussing party membership, we put the word *belong* in quotation marks. We did this because hardly anyone actually "belongs" to a political party in the sense of being a card-carrying member. To become a member of a political party, you do not have to pay dues, pass an examination, or swear an oath of allegiance. Therefore, we can ask an obvious question: If it takes almost nothing to be a member of a political party, what, then, is a political party?

■ Learning Outcome 1: **Define the term *political party,* and cite some of the major activities of the parties.**

What Is a Political Party?

A **political party** might be formally defined as a group of political activists who organize to win elections, operate the government, and determine public policy. Political parties are thus quite different from interest groups, which seek to influence, not run, the government.

Political parties also differ from **factions,** which are smaller groups that are trying to obtain power or benefits.[1] Factions preceded the formation of political parties in American history, and the term is still used to refer to groups within parties that follow a particular leader or share a regional identification or an ideological viewpoint. For example, until fairly recently the Democratic Party was seen as containing a southern faction that was much more conservative than the rest of the party. Factions are subgroups within parties that may try to capture a nomination or get a position adopted by the party. A key difference between factions and parties is that factions do not have a permanent organization, whereas political parties do.

Political parties in the United States engage in a wide variety of activities, many of which are discussed in this chapter. Through these

These three individuals are members of the Craven County Republican Party in New Bern, North Carolina.

(AP Photo/*The New Bern Sun Journal*/Chuck Beckley, File)

1. See James Madison's comments on factions in *Federalist Paper* No. 10 in Appendix C at the end of this book.

activities, parties perform a number of functions for the political system. These functions include the following:

1. *Recruiting candidates for public office.* Because it is the goal of parties to gain control of government, they must work to recruit candidates for all elective offices.
2. *Organizing and running elections.* Although elections are a government activity, political parties actually organize voter-registration drives, recruit volunteers to work at the polls, provide much of the campaign activity to stimulate interest in the election, and work to increase voter participation.
3. *Presenting alternative policies to the electorate.*
4. *Accepting responsibility for operating the government.* When a party elects the president or governor—or the majority of the members of a legislative body—it accepts the responsibility for running the government. This includes developing linkages among elected officials in the various branches of government to gain support for policies and their implementation.
5. *Acting as the organized opposition to the party in power.* The "out" party, or the one that does not control the government, is expected to articulate its own policies and oppose the winning party when appropriate.

The major functions of American political parties are carried out by a small, relatively loose-knit nucleus of party activists. This arrangement is quite different from the more highly structured, mass-membership organization typical of many European parties. American parties concentrate on winning elections rather than on signing up large numbers of deeply committed, dues-paying members who believe passionately in the party's program.

■ Learning Outcome 2: **Explain how the history of U.S. political parties has resulted in the two major parties that exist today.**

A History of Political Parties in the United States

Two-Party System
A political system in which only two parties have a reasonable chance of winning.

The United States has a **two-party system,** and that system has been around since before 1800. The function and character of the political parties, as well as the emergence of the two-party system itself, have much to do with the unique historical forces operating from this country's beginning as an independent nation. Indeed, James Madison linked the emergence of political parties to the form of government created by our Constitution.

Generally, we can divide the evolution of our nation's political parties into seven periods:

1. The formation of parties, from 1789 to 1816.
2. The era of one-party rule, from 1816 to 1828.
3. The period from Andrew Jackson's presidency to the eve of the Civil War, from 1828 to 1856.
4. The Civil War and post–Civil War period, from 1856 to 1896.
5. The Republican ascendancy and the progressive period, from 1896 to 1932.
6. The New Deal period, from 1932 to about 1968.
7. The modern period, from approximately 1968 to the present.

Thomas Jefferson was particularly adamant about his dislike of political parties. Nonetheless, he helped create a new party that we call the Jeffersonian Republicans. Why did he find it necessary to engage in party politics?

(AP Photo)

The Formative Years: Federalists and Anti-Federalists

The first partisan political division in the United States occurred before the adoption of the Constitution. As you will recall from Chapter 2, the Federalists were those who pushed for the adoption of the Constitution, whereas the Anti-Federalists were against ratification.

In September 1796, George Washington, who had served as president for two terms, decided not to run again. In his farewell address, he made a somber assessment of the nation's future. Washington felt that the country might be destroyed by the "baneful [harmful] effects of the spirit of party." He viewed parties as a threat to both national unity and the concept of popular government.

Nevertheless, in the years after the ratification of the Constitution, Americans came to realize that something more permanent than a faction would be necessary to identify candidates for office and represent political differences among the people. The result was two political parties.

Federalists and Republicans. One party was the Federalists, which included John Adams, the second president (1797–1801). The Federalists represented commercial interests such as merchants and large planters. They supported a strong national government.

Thomas Jefferson led the other party, which came to be called the Republicans, or Jeffersonian Republicans. (These Republicans should not be confused with the later Republican Party of Abraham Lincoln.[2]) Jefferson's Republicans represented artisans and farmers. They strongly supported states' rights. In 1800, when Jefferson defeated Adams in the presidential contest, one of the world's first peaceful transfers of power from one party to another was achieved.

The One-Party Interlude. From 1800 to 1820, a majority of U.S. voters regularly elected Jeffersonian Republicans to the presidency and to Congress. By 1816, the Federalist Party had nearly collapsed, and two-party competition did not really exist at the national level. Because there was no real political opposition to the Jeffersonian Republicans and thus little political debate, the administration of James Monroe (1817–1825) came to be known as the era of good feelings.

Democrats and Whigs

Organized two-party politics returned after 1824. Following the election of John Quincy Adams as president, the Jeffersonian Republican Party split in two. The supporters of Adams called themselves National Republicans. The supporters of Andrew Jackson, who defeated Adams in 1828, formed the **Democratic Party.** Later, the National Republicans took the name **Whig Party,** which had been a traditional name for British liberals. The Whigs stood for, among other things, federal spending on "internal improvements," such as roads.

The Democrats opposed this policy. The Democrats, who were the stronger of the two parties, favored personal liberty and opportunity for the "common man." It was understood implicitly that the "common man" was a white man—hostility toward African Americans was an important force holding the disparate Democratic groups together.[3]

The Civil War Crisis

In the 1850s, hostility between the North and the South over the issue of slavery divided both parties. The Whigs were the first to split in two. The Whigs had been the party of an active federal government, but southerners had come to believe that "a government strong enough to build roads is a government strong enough to free your slaves." The southern Whigs therefore ceased to exist as an organized party. In 1854, the northern Whigs united with antislavery Democrats and members of the radical antislavery Free Soil Party to found the modern **Republican Party.**

2. To avoid confusion, some scholars refer to Jefferson's party as the Democratic-Republicans, but this name was never used during the time that the party existed.
3. Edward Pessen, *Jacksonian America: Society, Personality, and Politics* (Homewood, Ill.: Dorsey Press, 1969). See especially pages 246–247. The small number of free blacks who could vote were overwhelmingly Whig.

did you know?

The political party with the most seats in the House of Representatives chooses the Speaker of the House, makes any new rules it wants, obtains a majority of the seats on each important committee, chooses committee chairs, and hires most of the congressional staff.

Democratic Party
One of the two major American political parties evolving out of the Republican Party of Thomas Jefferson.

Whig Party
A major party in the United States during the first half of the nineteenth century, formally established in 1836. The Whig Party was anti-Jackson and represented a variety of regional interests.

Republican Party
One of the two major American political parties. It emerged in the 1850s as an antislavery party and consisted of former northern Whigs and antislavery Democrats.

Andrew Jackson earned the name "Old Hickory" for his exploits during the War of 1812. In 1828, Jackson was elected president as the candidate of the new Democratic Party.

(Corbis/Bettmann)

GOP
A nickname for the Republican Party; stands for "grand old party."

Abraham Lincoln ran on the Republican ticket for president in 1860. What political groups banded together to form the modern Republican Party?

(Courtesy of the Ohio Historical Society)

The Post–Civil War Period

After the Civil War, the Democratic Party was able to heal its divisions. Southern resentment of the Republicans' role in defeating the South and fears that the federal government would intervene on behalf of African Americans ensured that the Democrats would dominate the white South for the next century. It was in this period that the Republicans adopted the nickname **GOP,** which stands for "grand old party."

Cultural Politics. Northern Democrats feared a strong government for other reasons. The Republicans thought that the government should promote business and economic growth, but many Republicans also wanted to use the power of government to impose evangelical Protestant moral values on society. Democrats opposed what they saw as culturally coercive measures. Many Republicans wanted to limit or even prohibit the sale of alcohol. They favored the establishment of public schools—with a Protestant curriculum. As a result, Catholics were strongly Democratic.

The Triumph of the Republicans. In this period, the parties were very evenly matched in strength. In the 1890s, however, the Republicans gained a decisive edge. In that decade, the Populist movement emerged in the West and South to champion the interests of small farmers, who were often greatly in debt. Populists supported inflation, which benefited debtors by reducing the real value of outstanding debts. In 1896, when William Jennings Bryan became the Democratic candidate for president, the Democrats embraced populism.

As it turned out, the few western farmers who were drawn to the Democrats by this step were greatly outnumbered by urban working-class voters who believed that inflation would reduce the purchasing power of their paychecks and who therefore became Republicans. William McKinley, the Republican candidate, was elected with a solid majority of the votes. Figure 8–1 below shows the states taken by Bryan and McKinley. Political scientists use the term *realignment* to refer to this kind of large-scale change in support for the two major parties. (Realignment is discussed in more detail later in this chapter.) From 1896 until 1932, the GOP was successful at presenting itself as the party that knew how to manage the economy.

Figure 8–1 ▸ The 1896 Presidential Elections

In 1896, the agrarian, Populist appeal of Democrat William Jennings Bryan (blue states) won western states for the Democrats at the cost of losing more populous eastern states to Republican William McKinley (red states). This pattern held in subsequent presidential elections.

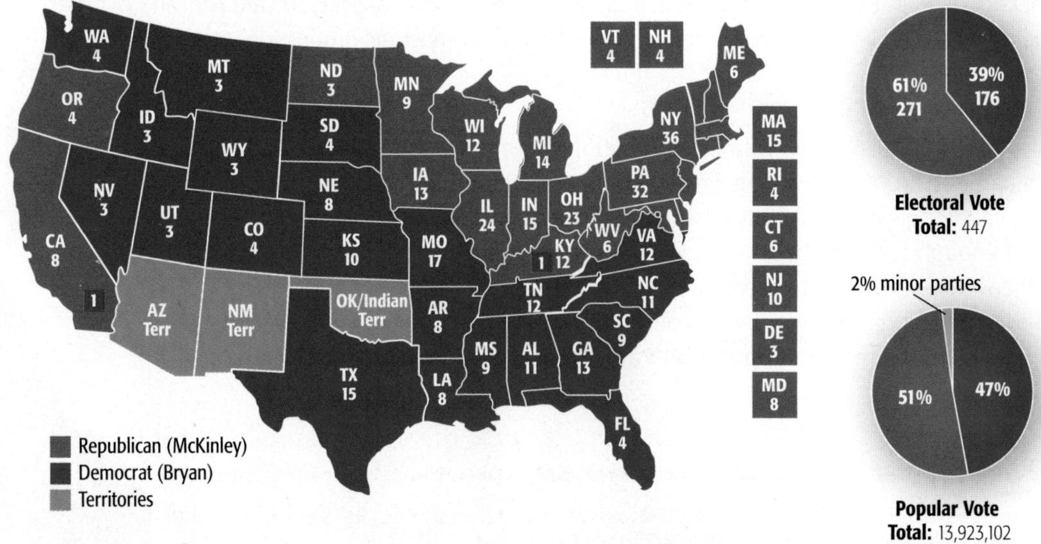

The Progressive Interlude

In the early 1900s, a spirit of political reform arose in both major parties. Called *progressivism,* this spirit was compounded of a fear of the growing power of large corporations and a belief that honest, impartial government could regulate the economy effectively. In 1912, the Republican Party temporarily split as former Republican president Theodore Roosevelt campaigned for the presidency on a third-party Progressive ticket. The Republican split permitted the election of Woodrow Wilson, the Democratic candidate, along with a Democratic Congress.

Like Roosevelt, Wilson considered himself a progressive, although he and Roosevelt did not agree on how progressivism ought to be implemented. Wilson's progressivism marked the beginning of a radical change in Democratic policies. Dating back to its very foundation, the Democratic Party had been the party of limited government. Under Wilson, the Democrats became for the first time at least as receptive as the Republicans to government action in the economy. (Wilson's progressivism did not extend to race relations—for African Americans, the Wilson administration was something of a disaster.)

President Woodrow Wilson (1913–1921) considered himself a progressive. Did he change Democratic policies very much?

The New Deal Era

The Republican ascendancy resumed after Wilson left office. It ended with the election of 1932, in the depths of the Great Depression. Republican Herbert Hoover was president when the Depression began in 1929. Although Hoover took some measures to fight the Depression, they fell far short of what the public demanded. Significantly, Hoover opposed federal relief for the unemployed and the destitute. In 1932, Democrat Franklin D. Roosevelt was elected president by an overwhelming margin. As with the election of 1896, the vote in 1932 constituted a major political realignment.

The Great Depression shattered the working-class belief in Republican economic competence. Under Roosevelt, the Democrats began to make major interventions in the economy in an attempt to combat the Depression and to relieve the suffering of the unemployed. Roosevelt's New Deal relief programs were open to all citizens, both black and white. As a result, African Americans began to support the Democratic Party in large numbers—a development that would have stunned any American politician of the 1800s.

Roosevelt's political coalition was broad enough to establish the Democrats as the new majority party, in place of the GOP. In the 1950s, Republican Dwight D. Eisenhower, the leading U.S. general during World War II, won two terms as president. Otherwise, with minor interruptions, the Democratic ascendancy lasted until about 1968.

did you know?

The Democrats and the Republicans each had exactly one woman delegate at their conventions in 1900.

An Era of Divided Government

The New Deal coalition managed the unlikely feat of including both African Americans and whites who were hostile to African American advancement. This balancing act came to an end in the 1960s, a decade that was marked by the civil rights movement, by several years of "race riots" in major cities, and by increasingly heated protests against the Vietnam War (1965–1975). For many economically moderate, socially conservative voters, especially in the South, social issues had become more important than economic ones, and these individuals left the Democratic Party. These voters outnumbered the new voters who joined the Democrats—newly enfranchised African Americans and former liberal Republicans in New England and the upper Midwest.

The Parties in Balance. The result, after 1968, was a slow-motion realignment that left the nation almost evenly divided in politics. In presidential elections, the Republicans had more success than the Democrats. Until the 1990s, Congress remained Democratic, but official party labels can be misleading. Some of the Democrats were southern

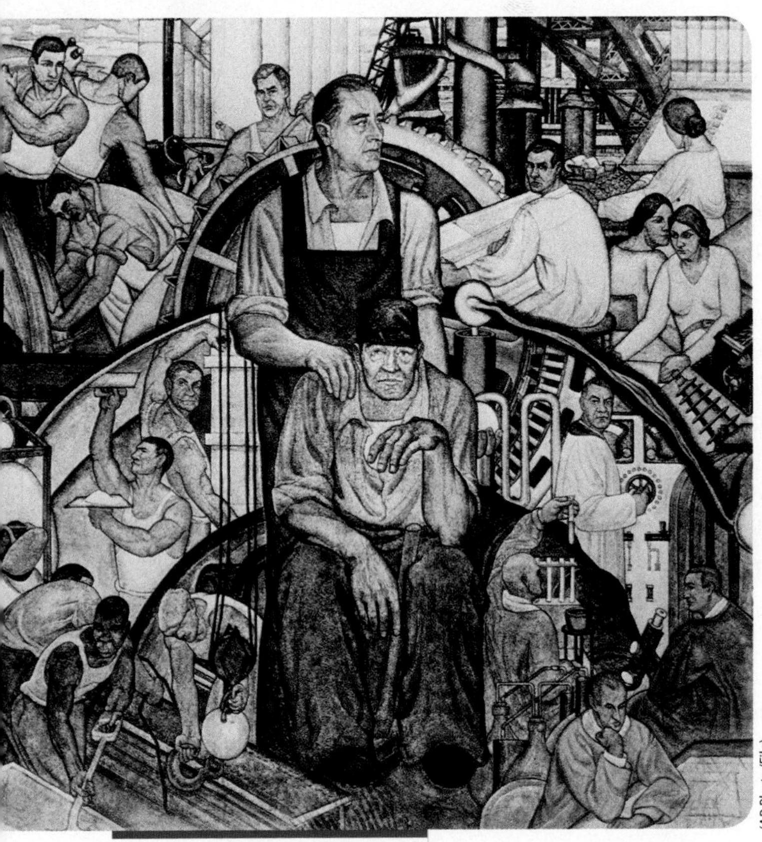
(AP Photo/File)

A mural fresco titled *The New Deal* depicts President Franklin D. Roosevelt, standing at center, and was dedicated to him by the artist, Conrad Albrizio. What aspects of Roosevelt's economic program are depicted here?

conservatives who normally voted with the Republicans on issues. As these conservative Democrats retired, they were largely replaced by Republicans. In 1994, Republicans were able to take control of both the House and the Senate for the first time in many years.

Red State, Blue State. Nothing demonstrated the nation's close political divisions more clearly than the 2000 presidential elections. Democratic presidential candidate Al Gore won the popular vote, but lost the electoral college by a narrow margin to Republican George W. Bush. The closeness of the vote in the electoral college led the press to repeatedly publish the map of the results state by state. Commentators discussed at length the supposed differences between the Republican "red states" and the Democratic "blue states."

An interesting characteristic of the red state–blue state division is that it is an almost exact reversal of the presidential elections of 1896 (see Figure 8–1 on page 250). Except for the state of Washington, every state that supported Democrat William Jennings Bryan in 1896 supported Republican George W. Bush in 2000 and 2004. This reversal parallels the transformation of the Democrats from an anti–civil rights to a pro–civil rights party and from a party that supported limited government to a party that favors expanded positive government action.

A Series of "Wave" Elections

Not only was the presidential election of 2000 very close, but the partisan balance in the U.S. Congress was also very close in the opening years of the twenty-first century. It is true that from 1995 until the elections of 2006, the Republicans had majorities in the House of Representatives and—except for a brief interval—in the Senate. The margin of control in the Senate, however, was frequently no more than a single vote. GOP margins in the House were also very narrow. In those years, both parties had positive images among a majority of poll respondents. Both parties enjoyed approval levels of just over 50 percent.

From time to time, voters demonstrate that they are relatively dissatisfied with the performance of one or another of the major parties. This dissatisfaction can produce a "wave" of support for the other party. Unlike realignments, the effects of wave elections are temporary. The first decade of the twenty-first century was marked by a series of wave elections in which the voters punished first one party and then the other. In the end, the major parties were again closely tied in levels of support, but both had lost a substantial amount of popularity.

Wave Elections Sweep out the Republicans. By 2006, the Republicans were in some difficulty. As the war in Iraq dragged on, ever-larger numbers of voters came to believe that U.S. intervention had been a mistake. In the 2006 midterm elections, the Democrats took control of the U.S. House and Senate in a wave election. President Bush's approval ratings were among the lowest ever recorded for a president.

In December 2007, the nation's economy entered a recession—not a good sign for the party that controls the presidency. In September 2008, a worldwide financial panic turned what had been a modest recession into the greatest economic downturn since the Great Depression of the 1930s. The collapse in economic activity was soon dubbed the "Great Recession." The political consequences of such a development on the eve of a presidential election were inevitable.

Democratic presidential candidate Barack Obama was elected with one of the largest margins in recent years—a 7.3 percentage-point margin over Republican candidate John McCain. The Democrats also picked up eight seats in the U.S. Senate and twenty-one seats in the House, giving them commanding majorities in both chambers. From July 2009 through January 2010, the Democrats controlled sixty Senate seats, enough to pass legislation in the face of united Republican opposition.[4]

Democrats in Trouble. By 2010, the Republicans had regained the support they lost during the previous five years. They did not achieve this feat by improving their popularity among the voters, however. Instead, it was the Democrats who lost popularity. Both parties were now polling in the 40 percent range. In the midterm elections of 2010, the Republicans benefited from one of the strongest wave elections in decades. They added a net total of sixty-three seats in the House, gaining control of that body. The Democrats lost six seats in the Senate, but retained control. The Republicans also scored heavily in state-level elections.

What happened to the Democrats? One explanation is that many independents now blamed the Democrats for persistent unemployment. Not until 2010 did the economy actually begin to create more jobs than had been lost, and the recovery was very weak through 2010, 2011, and 2012.

Many observers, however, argued that independents turned away from the Democrats in the belief that the party was expanding the scope of the federal government to an unacceptable degree. The approximately $800 billion stimulus package of February 2009, while initially popular, was eventually seen by many as evidence of government expansion. The Democratic health-care reform package was also crucial in fostering the perception of the party as being committed to "big government." By passing this legislation, the Democrats attained a goal dating back half a century. In the public mind, however, health care had little or no relation to the economic crisis.

Republican Overreach. The incoming class of Republican House members in 2011 included a large contingent loyal to the Tea Party movement, and many incumbent members aligned themselves with the movement as well. These legislators were pledged to oppose any compromise with the Democrats—even though the Democratic Party still controlled the Senate and the presidency. Republican Speaker John Boehner was hard-pressed to maintain unity in his party on legislative matters.

On issues of principle, however, House Republicans easily united behind an aggressive conservative agenda, expressed in the proposals of Budget Committee chair Paul Ryan of Wisconsin. Ryan's bills passed the House on near-party-line votes in 2011 and 2012 but died in the Senate. Republicans contended that the plans would reduce the federal budget deficit by making enormous cuts to domestic spending. Democrats countered that the cuts would do nothing about the deficit because the bills also contained large tax cuts, and that the plans would do serious damage to valued programs such as Medicare.

The uncompromising spirit of the Republicans received its greatest test in June and July of 2011, when House Republicans refused to lift the nation's debt ceiling unless the Democrats accepted large cuts in spending. President Obama and Speaker Boehner reached a compromise at the end of July, but the threat to the nation's ability to meet its

4. The Senate contest in Minnesota was not decided in favor of the Democrats until July 2009, nine months after the elections. In January 2010, the Republicans won a special Senate election in Massachusetts following the death of Senator Edward Kennedy, a Democrat.

coverage to the Medicare program and increased federal support for public schools through the No Child Left Behind law.

With the arrival of the Obama administration, however, the parties appeared to revert to their traditional positions on the size of government. The question remains as to whether the Republicans will maintain their antigovernment now that they lost the presidency again and do not control the Senate. The rise of the Tea Party movement suggests that they might.

Cultural Politics

In recent years, cultural values have played a significant role in defining the beliefs of the two major parties. For example, in 1987 Democrats were almost as likely to favor stricter abortion laws (40 percent) as Republicans were (48 percent). Today, Republicans are twice as likely to favor stricter abortion laws (50 percent to 25 percent).

did you know?

It took 103 ballots for John W. Davis to be nominated at the Democratic National Convention in 1924.

Cultural Politics and Socioeconomic Status. Some years ago, Thomas Frank reported seeing the following bumper sticker at a gun show in Kansas City: "A working person voting for the Democrats is like a chicken voting for Colonel Sanders." (Colonel Sanders is the iconic founder of KFC, a chain of fried-chicken restaurants.) In light of the economic traditions of the two parties, this seems to be an odd statement. In fact, the sticker is an exact reversal of an earlier one directed against the Republicans.

You can make sense of such a sentiment by remembering what you learned in Chapter 6—although economic conservatism is associated with higher incomes, social conservatism is relatively more common among lower-income groups. The individual who displayed the bumper sticker, therefore, was in effect claiming that cultural concerns—in this example, presumably the right to own handguns—were far more important than economic ones. Frank argues that despite Republican control of both the White House and Congress during much of the George W. Bush administration, cultural conservatives continued to view themselves as embattled "ordinary Americans" under threat from a liberal, cosmopolitan elite.[5] Of course, the election of Barack Obama and a strongly Democratic Congress in 2008 certainly magnified such fears. One result was the Tea Party movement.

This supporter of the health-care reform bill displays his view of corporate lobbying against the legislation in 2010.

(Jewel Samod/AFP/Getty Images)

The Regional Factor in Cultural Politics. Conventionally, some parts of the country are viewed as culturally liberal, and others as culturally conservative. On a regional basis, cultural liberalism (as opposed to economic liberalism) may be associated with economic dynamism. The San Francisco Bay Area can serve as an example. The greater Bay Area contains Silicon Valley, the heart of the high-tech industry. It has the highest per capita personal income of any metropolitan area in America. It also is one of the most liberal regions of the country. San Francisco liberalism is largely cultural—one sign of this liberalism is that the city has been called the "capital" of gay America.

To further illustrate this point, we can compare the political preferences of relatively wealthy states with those of relatively poor ones. Of the fifteen states with the highest per capita personal incomes in 2008, fourteen voted for Democrat Barack Obama in the presidential elections of that year. Of the fifteen with the lowest per capita incomes in 2008, thirteen voted for Republican John McCain.

Given these data, it seems hard to believe that upper-income voters really are more Republican than lower-income ones. Still, within any given state or region, upscale voters are more likely to be Republican regardless of whether the area as a whole leans Democratic or

5. Thomas Frank, *What's the Matter with Kansas? How Conservatives Won the Heart of America* (New York: Holt, 2005).

Republican. States that vote Democratic are often northern states that contain large cities. At least part of this **reverse-income effect** may simply be that urban areas are more prosperous, culturally liberal, and Democratic than the countryside, and that the North is more prosperous, culturally liberal, and Democratic than the South.

Reverse-Income Effect
A tendency for wealthier states or regions to favor the Democrats and for less wealthy states or regions to favor the Republicans. The effect appears paradoxical because it reverses traditional patterns of support.

Cultural Divisions within the Democratic Party. The extremely close and hard-fought Democratic presidential primary contest between Senator Barack Obama and Senator Hillary Clinton in 2008 exposed a series of cultural divisions within the Democratic Party that political scientists have been aware of for some time. Of course, African Americans supported Obama strongly, and women tended to favor Clinton. Beyond these obvious patterns, Clinton appeared to do well among older people, white working-class voters, and Latinos, while Obama received more support from the young and from better-educated, upscale Democrats.

Yet the differences between the two candidates on policy issues were actually very small. Likewise, there was no evidence that Obama fans and Clinton backers held significantly different positions on the issues—the two groups may have been somewhat different kinds of people, but they appeared to have similar politics.

To a degree, Obama's narrow victory reflects changes in the Democrats' core constituencies. Traditionally, the candidate with a stronger working-class appeal could expect to win over the largest number of Democrats. As we have noted, however, in recent years well-educated, professional individuals have shifted to the Democrats, even as voters without college degrees have grown more Republican. By 2008, Obama's educated supporters made up a larger share of the Democratic Party than in years past. Still, Obama could not have won without strong support from African Americans of all classes.

did you know?

In his first inaugural address, Thomas Jefferson proclaimed that "We are all Republicans, we are all Federalists."

Cultural Divisions among the Republicans. One wing of the Republican Party, often called the Religious Right, is energized by conservative religious beliefs. These conservatives are often evangelical Protestants but may also be Catholics, Mormons, or adherents of other faiths. For these voters, moral issues such as abortion and gay marriage are key. The other wing of the GOP is more oriented toward economic issues and business concerns. These voters often are small-business owners or have some other connection to commercial enterprise. Such voters oppose high tax rates and are concerned about government regulations that interfere with the conduct of business.

Of course, many Republicans are pro-business and also support the Religious Right. Some economically oriented Republicans, however, are strongly libertarian and dislike government regulation of social issues as well as economic ones. Likewise, some on the Religious Right are not particularly committed to the free market ethos of the party's business wing and are willing to support a variety of government interventions in the economy.

Successful Republican presidential candidates appeal to both wings of the party. Former Massachusetts governor Mitt Romney, the Republican candidate for president in 2012, initially found it hard to appeal to the Religious Right. Romney's moderate positions on a number of issues in the past had led many to doubt his conservatism (which is actually quite strong). In the end, however, Romney was able to unite his party behind him. Both business-oriented Republicans and the Religious Right were solid in their opposition to the Obama administration.

Moderate and Radical Republicans. During the Obama administration, a new fault line appeared to be opening up in the Republican Party—between moderate conservatives and more radical ones. The more radical wing was often highly critical of the existing Republican Party leadership, accusing it of being little better than the Democrats. The Tea Party movement was strongly identified with this point of view. Together with groups such as the Club for Growth, Tea Party activists sought to purge the Republicans of so-called RINOs (Republicans In Name Only). Between the newly

Tea Party protesters marked "tax day" April 15 with exhortations against "gangster government" and appeals to Republicans seeking their grassroots clout in November elections, a prospect both tempting and troubling to those in the loose movement. Why are Tea Party supporters against higher taxes?

WE WILL
REMEMBER
IN NOVEMBER
NO
VAT
TAX
TAXES
KILL
JOBS

(AP Photo/Steve Bloom/The Olympian)

resurgent political right and the apparent legislative overreach of the Democrats during 2009 and 2010, it may be worth asking whether the two major parties are becoming too radical. We address that issue in this chapter's *Which Side Are You On?* feature on the facing page.

■ Learning Outcome 4: **Describe three faces of a party: the party-in-the-electorate, the party organization, and the party-in-government.**

The Three Faces of a Party

Although American parties are known by a single name and, in the public mind, have a common historical identity, each party really has three major components. The first component is the **party-in-the-electorate.** This phrase refers to all those individuals who claim an attachment to the political party. They need not participate in election campaigns. Rather, the party-in-the-electorate is the large number of Americans who feel some loyalty to the party or who use partisanship as a cue to decide who will earn their vote. Party membership is not really a rational choice. Rather, it is an emotional tie somewhat analogous to identifying with a region or a baseball team. Although individuals may hold a deep loyalty to or identification with a political party, there is no need for members of the party-in-the-electorate to speak out publicly, to contribute to campaigns, or to vote all Republican or all Democratic. Nevertheless, the party leaders pay close attention to their members in the electorate.

Party-in-the-Electorate
Those members of the general public who identify with a political party or who express a preference for one party over another.

Party Organization
The formal structure and leadership of a political party, including election committees; local, state, and national executives; and paid professional staff.

Party-in-Government
All of the elected and appointed officials who identify with a political party.

National Convention
The meeting held every four years by each major party to select presidential and vice-presidential candidates, write a platform, choose a national committee, and conduct party business.

Party Platform
A document drawn up at each national convention, outlining the policies, positions, and principles of the party.

The second component, the **party organization,** provides the structural framework for the political party by recruiting volunteers to become party leaders, identifying potential candidates, and organizing caucuses, conventions, and election campaigns for its candidates, as will be discussed in more detail shortly. It is the party organization and its active workers that keep the party functioning between elections, as well as ensure that the party puts forth electable candidates and clear positions in the elections. If the party-in-the-electorate declines in numbers and loyalty, the party organization must try to find a strategy to rebuild the grassroots following.

The **party-in-government** is the third component of American political parties. The party-in-government consists of those elected and appointed officials who identify with a political party. Generally, elected officials do not also hold official party positions within the formal organization, although they often have the informal power to appoint party executives.

Party Organization

Each of the American political parties is often seen as having a pyramid-shaped organization, with the national chairperson and committee at the top and the local precinct chairperson on the bottom. This structure, however, does not accurately reflect the relative power of the individual components of the party organization. If it did, the national chairperson of the Democratic Party or the Republican Party, along with the national committee, could simply dictate how the organization was to be run, just as if it were ExxonMobil or Apple. In reality, the political parties have a confederal structure, in which each unit has significant autonomy and is linked only loosely to the other units.

Supporters of President Barack Obama hold signs near a campaign stop for Republican presidential candidate Mitt Romney.

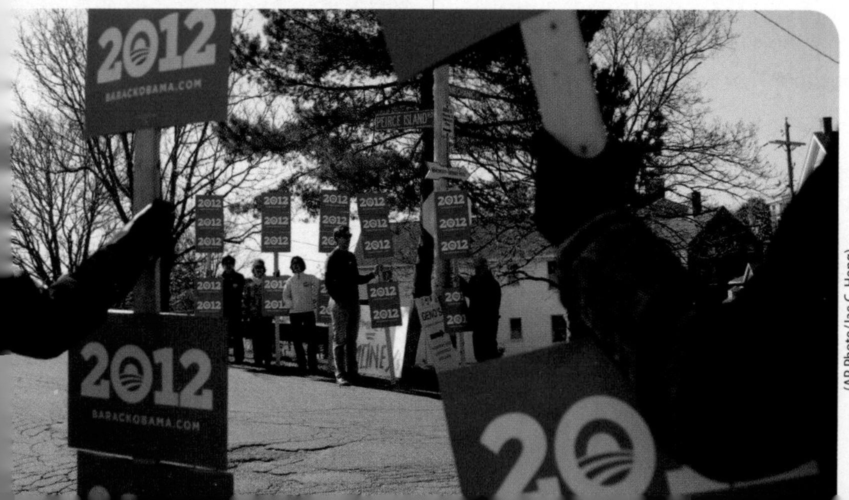

(AP Photo/Jae C. Hong)

The National Party Organization. Each party has a national organization, the most conspicuous part of which is the **national convention,** held every four years. The convention is used to officially nominate the presidential and vice-presidential candidates. In addition, the **party platform** is

Which Side Are You On?

ARE THE PARTIES BECOMING TOO RADICAL?

In recent years, political rhetoric seemed to reach new heights of hysteria. Many Americans on the political right believed that President Obama was foreign-born and ineligible to be president—even though Obama produced his Hawaii birth certificate and the birth was announced in Honolulu newspapers. In one poll, a majority of Republicans affirmed that Obama was a Muslim.

Meanwhile, the Democrats in Congress pushed through their health-care reform program, a massive change in how we fund one-sixth of the nation's economy. No national consensus existed in support of the program, but the Democrats proceeded regardless.

Irresponsible rhetoric, adventurous legislation—were these manifestations of a new radical spirit? Some observers contend that they were.

THE PARTIES HAVE NEVER BEEN SO RADICAL

Those who believe that our politics exhibits unprecedented levels of radicalism point to the extreme language used on the Web, on the airwaves, and in Congress. In addition, both parties seem willing to undertake ideologically motivated steps that can only hurt them. If passing health-care legislation that will damage you politically is not radical, what is?

On their side, Republicans sought to purge their party of candidates showing the least sign of moderation, even when purity meant losing elections. In 2009, for example, national figures such as Sarah Palin intervened to force Republican congressional candidate Dede Scozzafava out of a race in upstate New York on the ground that she was insufficiently conservative. They supported Conservative Party candidate Doug Hoffman instead. Hoffman then lost to Democrat Bill Owens. Parts of the district had not previously voted for a Democrat since the Civil War era.

RADICALISM EXISTS, ALL RIGHT, BUT IT IS NOT NEW

Anyone who thinks that the beliefs of the far right are unprecedentedly "out there" needs to learn more history. In 1958, Robert Welch, leader of the right-wing John Birch Society, claimed in all seriousness that Republican president Dwight D. Eisenhower was a "dedicated, conscious agent of the Communist conspiracy." That beats anything we've heard recently from a prominent figure.

As for the Democrats, passage of health-care legislation doesn't mean that the party has become more radical. It only means that with large majorities in the House and Senate, the party found itself in a position to pass measures it had supported for decades. If the Republicans had the power to win certain long-sought objectives supported by all wings of the party, they would surely do the same.

(© kyoshino / iStockphoto) (© Dean Mitchell / iStockphoto)

developed at the national convention. The platform sets forth the party's position on the issues and makes promises to initiate certain policies if the party wins the presidency.

After the convention, the platform sometimes is neglected or ignored when party candidates disagree with it. Because candidates are trying to win votes from a wide spectrum of voters, it can be counterproductive to emphasize the fairly narrow and sometimes controversial goals set forth in the platform. Still, once elected, the parties do try to carry out platform promises, and many of the promises eventually become law. Of course, some general goals, such as economic prosperity, are included in the platforms of both parties.

Convention Delegates. The party convention provides the most striking illustration of the difference between the ordinary members of a party, or party identifiers, and party activists. As a series of studies by the *New York Times* shows, delegates to the national party conventions are different from ordinary party identifiers. Delegates to the Democratic National

Supporters of Republican presidential candidate and former governor of Massachusetts Mitt Romney hold up campaign signs during his primary night rally in Milwaukee, Wisconsin.

(Darren Hauck/Reuters/Landov)

Convention, as shown in Table 8–1 below, often take stands on issues that are far more liberal than the positions of ordinary Democratic voters. Delegates to the Republican National Convention are often more conservative than ordinary Republicans. Why does this happen? In part, it is because a person, to become a delegate, must be appointed by party leaders or gather votes in a primary election from party members who care enough to vote in a primary.

In addition, the primaries generally pit presidential candidates against one another on intraparty issues. Competition within each party tends to pull candidates away from the center, and delegates even more so. Often, the most important activity for the convention is making peace among the delegates who support different candidates and helping them accept a party platform that will appeal to the general electorate.

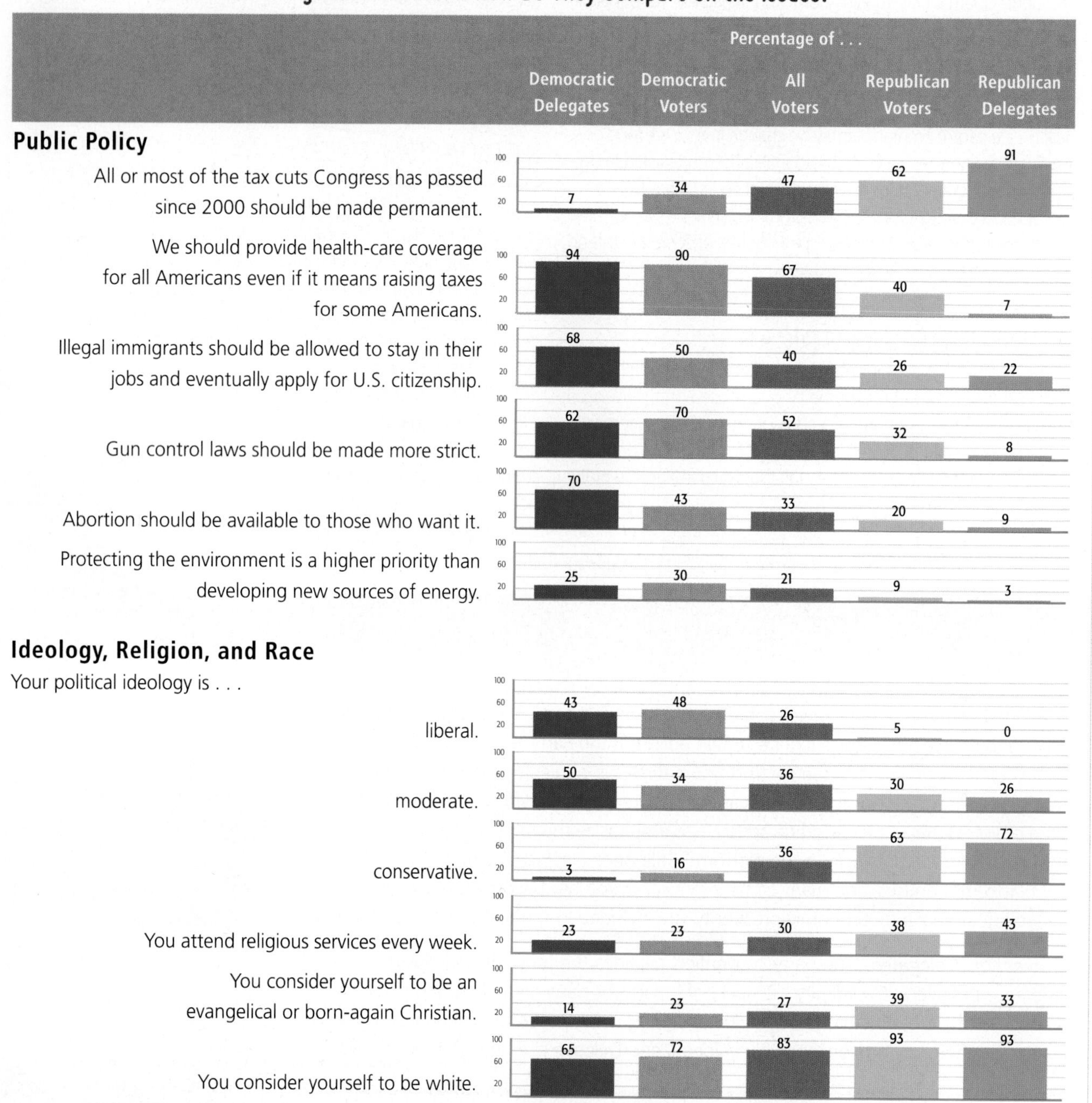

Table 8–1 ▸ Convention Delegates and Voters: How Do They Compare on the Issues?

	Percentage of . . .				
	Democratic Delegates	Democratic Voters	All Voters	Republican Voters	Republican Delegates
Public Policy					
All or most of the tax cuts Congress has passed since 2000 should be made permanent.	7	34	47	62	91
We should provide health-care coverage for all Americans even if it means raising taxes for some Americans.	94	90	67	40	7
Illegal immigrants should be allowed to stay in their jobs and eventually apply for U.S. citizenship.	68	50	40	26	22
Gun control laws should be made more strict.	62	70	52	32	8
Abortion should be available to those who want it.	70	43	33	20	9
Protecting the environment is a higher priority than developing new sources of energy.	25	30	21	9	3
Ideology, Religion, and Race					
Your political ideology is . . .					
liberal.	43	48	26	5	0
moderate.	50	34	36	30	26
conservative.	3	16	36	63	72
You attend religious services every week.	23	23	30	38	43
You consider yourself to be an evangelical or born-again Christian.	14	23	27	39	33
You consider yourself to be white.	65	72	83	93	93

Source: Excerpted and adapted from *The New York Times*/CBS News poll, July 23–August 26, 2008.
Note: These responses are from delegates to the 2008 national conventions. Delegates to the 2012 conventions were not surveyed.

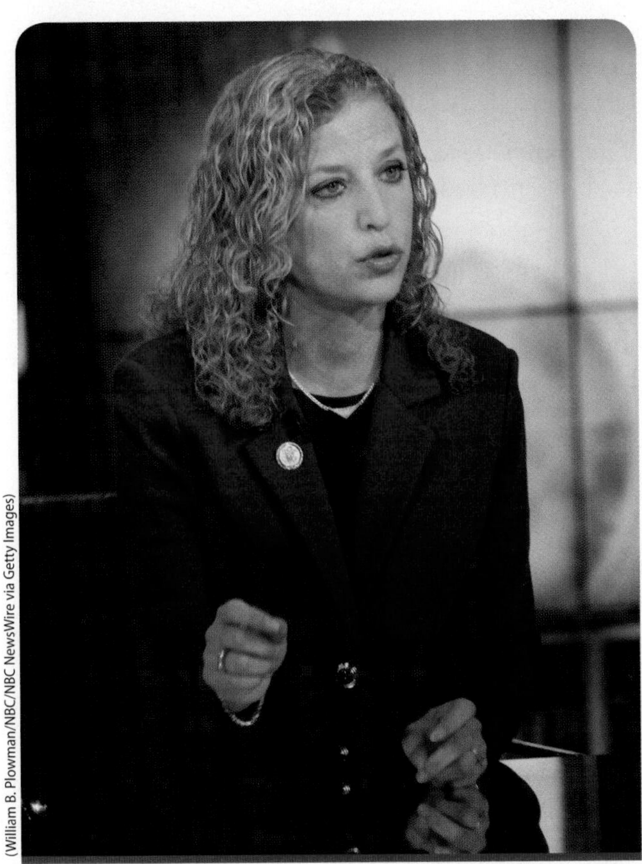

(William B. Plowman/NBC/NBC NewsWire via Getty Images)

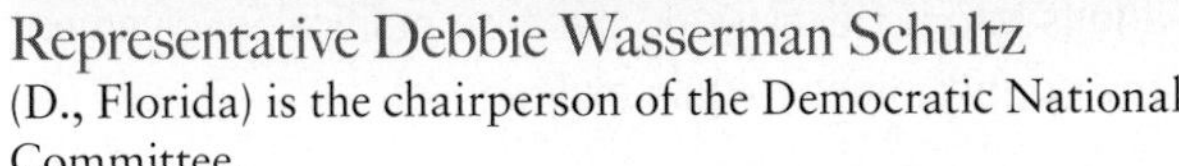

Representative Debbie Wasserman Schultz (D., Florida) is the chairperson of the Democratic National Committee.

(Rod Lamkey, Jr./*The Washington Times*/Landov)

Reince Priebus is the chairperson of the Republican National Committee. Do all registered Republicans vote for this position?

The National Committee. At the national convention, each of the parties formally chooses a national standing committee, elected by the individual state parties. This **national committee** directs and coordinates party activities during the following four years.

National Committee
A standing committee of a national political party established to direct and coordinate party activities between national party conventions.

One of the jobs of the national committee is to ratify the presidential nominee's choice of a national chairperson, who in principle acts as the spokesperson for the party. The national chairperson and the national committee plan the next campaign and the next convention, obtain financial contributions, and publicize the national party.

Picking a National Chairperson. In general, the party's presidential candidate chooses the national chairperson. (If that candidate loses, however, the chairperson is often changed.) The national chairperson performs such jobs as establishing a national party headquarters, raising campaign funds and distributing them to state parties and to candidates, and appearing in the media as a party spokesperson. The national chairperson, along with the national committee, attempts to maintain some sort of communication among the different levels of the party organization. The fact, though, is that the real strength and power of the party are at the state level.

The State Party Organization. Because every state party is unique, it is impossible to describe what an "average" state political party is like. Nonetheless, state parties have several organizational features in common. Each state party has a chairperson, a committee, and a number of local organizations. In theory, the role of the **state central committee**—the principal organized structure of each political party within each state—is similar in the various states. The committee has responsibility for carrying out the policy decisions of the party's state convention.

State Central Committee
The principal organized structure of each political party within each state. This committee is responsible for carrying out policy decisions of the party's state convention.

Also, like the national committee, the state central committee has control over the use of party campaign funds during political campaigns. Usually, the state central committee has little, if any, influence on party candidates once they are elected.

Local Party Machinery: The Grassroots. The lowest layer of party machinery is the local organization, supported by district leaders, precinct or ward captains, and party workers.

Patronage
The rewarding of faithful party workers and followers with government employment or contracts.

Patronage and City Machines. In the 1800s, the institution of **patronage**—the rewarding of the party faithful with government jobs or contracts—held the local organization together. For immigrants and the poor, the political machine often furnished important services and protections. The big-city machine was the archetypal example. The last big-city political machine to exercise substantial power was run by Chicago mayor Richard J. Daley (1955–1978), who was also an important figure in national Democratic politics. City machines are now dead, mostly because their function of providing social services (and reaping the reward of votes) has been taken over by state and national agencies.

did you know?

It takes about seven hundred thousand signatures to qualify to be on the ballot as a presidential candidate in all fifty states.

Local Party Organizations Today. Local political organizations are still able to provide the foot soldiers of politics—individuals who pass out literature and get out the vote on Election Day, which can be crucial in local elections. In many regions, local Democratic and Republican organizations still exercise some patronage, such as awarding courthouse jobs, contracts for street repair, and other lucrative construction contracts. The constitutionality of awarding—or not awarding—contracts on the basis of political affiliation has been subject to challenge, however. The Supreme Court has ruled that firing or failing to hire individuals because of their political affiliation is an infringement of the employees' First Amendment rights to free expression.[6] Local party organizations are also the most important vehicles for recruiting young adults into political work, because political involvement at the local level offers activists many opportunities to gain experience.

The Party-in-Government

After the election is over and the winners are announced, the focus of party activity shifts from getting out the vote to organizing and controlling the government. As you will see in Chapter 10, party membership plays an important role in the day-to-day operations of Congress, with partisanship determining everything from office space to committee assignments and power on Capitol Hill. For the president, the political party furnishes a pool of qualified applicants for political appointments to run the government. (Although it is uncommon to do so, presidents can and occasionally do appoint executive personnel, such as cabinet members, from the opposition party.) As we note in Chapter 11, there are not as many of these appointed positions as presidents might like, and presidential power is limited by the permanent bureaucracy. Judicial appointments also offer a great opportunity to the winning party. For the most part, presidents are likely to appoint federal judges from their own party.

Senator Kirsten Gillibrand of New York is an up-and-coming Democratic politician. She was a candidate for reelection in 2012.

(Flickr/Gillibrand2010)

Divided Government. All of these party appointments suggest that the winning political party, whether at the national, state, or local level, has a great deal of control in the American system. The degree of control that a winning party can actually exercise, however, depends on several factors. At the national level, an important factor is whether the party controls both the executive and the legislative branches of government. If it does, the party leadership in Congress may be reluctant to exercise congressional checks on presidential powers. If Congress cooperates in implementing legislation approved by the president, the president, in turn, will not feel it necessary to exercise the veto power. Certainly, this situation existed

6. *Rutan v. Republican Party of Illinois*, 497 U.S. 62 (1990).

while the Republicans controlled both the legislative and the executive branches of government from January 2003 to January 2007, and when the Democrats controlled the government in the two years following Obama's inauguration in January 2009.

The winning party has less control over the government when the government is divided. A **divided government** is one in which the executive and legislative branches are controlled by different parties. After the 2010 elections, this was the situation facing the nation. Even though the Democrats still controlled the presidency and the U.S. Senate, they could not pass legislation unless it was also supported by the Republicans in the House. Although House Republicans could not pass legislation either, they energetically sought to use what bargaining power they had.

Divided Government
A situation in which one major political party controls the presidency and the other controls one or more chambers of Congress, or in which one party controls a state governorship and the other controls part or all of the state legislature.

The Limits of Party Unity. There are other ways in which the power of the parties is limited. Consider how major laws are passed in Congress. Traditionally, legislation was rarely passed by a vote strictly along party lines. Although most Democrats might oppose a bill, for example, some Democrats would vote for it. Their votes, combined with the votes of Republicans, were often enough to pass the bill. Similarly, support from some Republicans enabled bills sponsored by the Democrats to pass.

One reason that the political parties traditionally found it so hard to rally all of their members in Congress to vote along party lines was that candidates who won most elections largely did so on their own, without significant help from a political party. A candidate generally gained a nomination through her or his own hard work and personal political organization. In many other countries, most candidates are selected by the party organization, not by primary elections. This means, though, that in the United States the parties have very little control over the candidates who run under the party labels. In fact, a candidate could run as a Republican, for example, and advocate beliefs repugnant to the national party, such as racism. No one in the Republican Party organization could stop this person from being nominated or even elected.

Party Polarization. In recent years, it has become increasingly difficult for legislators in either party to obtain support for important legislation from members of the other party. More and more, voting takes place strictly along party lines. Discipline within the party caucuses has never been greater. The Republicans, who took the lead in the development of party unity, presented a united front throughout much of the 1990s. By 2009, the Democrats had largely caught up, although even then the party's congressional delegation contained a number of dissidents, notably the conservative Blue Dog caucus in the U.S. House. One reason for party-line voting is that political overlap between the two parties has essentially vanished. Political scientists calculated that in 2009, the most conservative Blue Dog Democrat in the House was still more liberal than the most liberal Republican—if a term such as *liberal Republican* still makes any sense.

For much of the twentieth century, however, liberal Republicans were a real presence in the nation's politics, and so were extremely conservative Democrats. Millions of Americans formed their party attachments not through ideology, but on the basis of tradition and sentiment. Old-stock New England Yankees were Republicans because New England Yankees had always been Republicans. White southerners were, by and large, Democrats because that party affiliation was part of what it meant to be a southerner. Ideologically, however, most of the southerners were well to the right of the average Yankee. Likewise, Yankee Republicans were, on average, more liberal than most southern Democrats. Today, liberal Yankees are usually Democrats, and conservative southerners are Republicans.

Republicans believe that Senator Susana Martinez of New Mexico has a bright future in their party.

(Mark Holm/The New York Times)

Blocking Tactics. One effect of the new polarization is that interpersonal relationships between members of the parties have deteriorated. True,

(© Danny Shanahan/The New Yorker Collection/www.cartoonbank.com)

"I think it was an election year."

some senators and representatives are able to maintain friendships across party lines, but such friendships have become less common. A second effect is the growing tactic of blocking bills to make the other party appear ineffective, without any attempt to reach a compromise. Republicans pioneered this tactic in the 1990s under House Speaker Newt Gingrich in an attempt to embarrass Democratic president Bill Clinton, and they tried it again in 2010 and 2011, with varying degrees of success.

Democrats contended that the tactic demonstrated Republican irresponsibility. It is also possible to propose—rather than oppose—legislation for political ends, however. For example, in 2010 the Democrats introduced an immigration reform package, in the apparent hopes that it would mobilize their support among Latino voters, even though it had little chance of passing or even coming to a vote.

Why Has the Two-Party System Endured?

There are several reasons why two major parties have dominated the political landscape in the United States for almost two centuries. These reasons have to do with (1) the historical foundations of the system, (2) political socialization and practical considerations, (3) the winner-take-all electoral system, and (4) state and federal laws favoring the two-party system.

■ **Learning Outcome 5:** **Give some of the reasons why the two-party system has endured in America.**

The Historical Foundations of the Two-Party System

As we have seen, at many times in American history one preeminent issue or dispute has divided the nation politically. In the beginning, Americans were at odds over ratifying the Constitution. After the Constitution went into effect, the power of the federal government became the major national issue. Thereafter, the dispute over slavery divided the nation, North versus South. At times—for example, in the North after the Civil War—cultural differences have been important, with advocates of government-sponsored morality (such as banning alcoholic beverages) pitted against advocates of personal liberty.

During much of the twentieth century, economic differences were preeminent. In the New Deal period, the Democrats became known as the party of the working class, while the Republicans became known as the party of the middle and upper classes and commercial interests. In situations like these, when politics is based on an argument between two opposing points of view, advocates of each viewpoint can mobilize most effectively by forming a single, unified party. The result is a two-party system. When such a system has been in existence for almost two centuries, it becomes difficult to imagine an alternative.

Political Socialization and Practical Considerations

Given that the majority of Americans identify with one of the two major political parties, it is not surprising that most children learn at a fairly young age to think of themselves as either Democrats or Republicans. This generates a built-in mechanism to perpetuate a two-party system. Also, most politically oriented people who aspire to work for change consider that the only realistic way to capture political power in this country is to be either a Republican or a Democrat.

The Winner-Take-All Electoral System

Plurality
A number of votes cast for a candidate that is greater than the number of votes for any other candidate but not necessarily a majority.

At almost every level of government in the United States, the outcome of elections is based on the **plurality,** winner-take-all principle. In a plurality system, the winner is the person who obtains the most votes, even if that person does not receive a majority (more than 50 percent) of the votes. Whoever gets the most votes gets everything. Most legislators in the United States are elected from single-member districts in which only one person represents the constituency, and the candidate who finishes second in such an election receives nothing for the effort.

Presidential Voting. The winner-take-all system also operates in the election of the U.S. president. Recall that the voters in each state do not vote for a president directly but vote for **electoral college** delegates who are committed to the various presidential candidates. These delegates are called *electors*.

Electoral College
A group of persons, called electors, who are selected by the voters in each state. This group officially elects the president and the vice president of the United States.

In all but two states (Maine and Nebraska), if a presidential candidate wins a plurality in the state, then *all* of the state's electoral votes go to that candidate. This is known as the *unit rule*. For example, suppose that the electors pledged to a particular presidential candidate receive a plurality of 40 percent of the votes in a state. That presidential candidate will receive all of the state's votes in the electoral college. Minor parties have a difficult time competing under such a system. Because voters know that minor parties cannot win any electoral votes, they often will not vote for minor-party candidates, even if the candidates are in tune with them ideologically.

Popular Election of the Governors and the President. In most of Europe, the chief executive (usually called the prime minister) is elected by the legislature, or parliament. If the parliament contains three or more parties, as is usually the situation, two or more of the parties can join together in a coalition to choose the prime minister and the other leaders of the government. In the United States, however, the people elect the president and the governors of all fifty states. There is no opportunity for two or more parties to negotiate a coalition. Here, too, the winner-take-all principle discriminates powerfully against any third party.

Proportional Representation. Many other nations use a system of proportional representation. If, during the national election, party X obtains 12 percent of the vote, party Y gets 43 percent of the vote, and party Z gets the remaining 45 percent of the vote, then party X gets 12 percent of the seats in the legislature, party Y gets 43 percent of the seats, and party Z gets 45 percent of the seats.

Some nations implement proportional representation by creating districts that elect multiple representatives. Such a system, however, can require the creation of districts that are uncomfortably large. The nation of Israel, for example, is a single, large electoral district. Every party runs nationwide.

An alternate system is to let voters choose both a local representative and a preferred party. Germany uses such a system to elect members of the Bundestag, its parliament. Suppose that the Green Party wins the support of 10 percent of the voters in a particular German state, but only a few Greens win in their local districts. If this happens, enough Greens will be added from the party's statewide list of candidates to boost its Bundestag delegation to 10 percent of the total from that state.

(Bill Clark/Roll Call/Getty Images)

Congressional pages carry the electoral college votes to the House chamber where the election of Barack Obama as the forty-fourth president of the United States was certified on January 8, 2009. What effect does the electoral college have on the political system?

did you know?

The Reform Party, established in 1996, used a vote-by-mail process for the first step of its nominating convention and also accepted votes cast by e-mail.

Regardless of how proportional representation is implemented, the system gives smaller parties a greater incentive to organize than in the United States.

State and Federal Laws Favoring the Two Parties

Many state and federal election laws offer a clear advantage to the two major parties. In some states, the established major parties need to gather fewer signatures to place their candidates on the ballot than minor parties or independent candidates do. The criterion for determining how many signatures will be required is often based on the total party vote in the last general election, thus penalizing a new political party that did not compete in that election.

At the national level, minor parties face different obstacles. All of the rules and procedures of both houses of Congress divide committee seats, staff members, and other privileges on the basis of party membership. A legislator who is elected on a minor-party ticket, such as the Conservative Party of New York, must choose to be counted with one of the major parties to obtain a committee assignment.

The Federal Election Commission (FEC) rules for campaign financing also place restrictions on minor-party candidates. Such candidates are not eligible for federal matching funds in either the primary or the general election. In the 1980 elections, John Anderson, running for president as an independent, sued the FEC for campaign funds. The commission finally agreed to repay part of his campaign costs after the election in proportion to the votes he received. Giving funds to a candidate when the campaign is over is, of course, much less helpful than providing funds while the campaign is still under way.

■ Learning Outcome 6:
Evaluate the impact of third parties on U.S. politics.

The Role of Minor Parties in U.S. Politics

For the reasons just discussed, minor parties have a difficult, if not impossible, time competing within the American two-party political system. Nonetheless, minor parties have played an important role in our political life. Parties other than the Republicans or Democrats are usually called **third parties.** (Technically, of course, there could be fourth, fifth, or sixth parties as well, but we use the term *third party* because it has endured.) Third parties can come into existence in a number of ways. They may be founded from scratch by individuals or groups who are committed to a particular interest, issue, or ideology. They can split off from one of the major parties when a group becomes dissatisfied with the major party's policies. Finally, they can be organized around a particular charismatic leader and serve as that person's vehicle for contesting elections.

Third Party
A political party other than the two major political parties (Republican and Democratic).

Frequently, third parties have acted as barometers of change in the political mood, forcing the major parties to recognize new issues or trends in the thinking of Americans. Political scientists believe that third parties have acted as safety valves for dissident groups, preventing major confrontations and political unrest. In some instances, third parties have functioned as way stations for voters en route from one of the major parties to the other. On the facing page, Table 8–2 lists significant third-party presidential campaigns in American history, and Table 8–3 provides a brief description of third-party beliefs.

Social Media IN POLITICS

Using social media, you can follow the two largest minor parties—the Green Party and the Libertarian Party. You'll find either on Facebook simply by entering a full name, for example "libertarian party" or "green party." On Twitter, it's a bit more complicated: search on "@gpus" for the Greens and "@lpnational" for the Libertarians.

Ideological Third Parties

The longest-lived third parties have been those with strong ideological foundations that are typically at odds with the majority mind-set. The Socialist Party is an example. The party was founded in 1901 and lasted until 1972, when it was finally dissolved. (A smaller party later took up the name.) The Socialists were never very popular in the United States. Indeed, the term *socialist* has recently gained currency as a conservative insult directed at President Obama. In Europe, however, socialist parties became very important, and *socialist* is merely a description. We take a look at the "real" socialists in the *Beyond Our Borders* feature on page 268.

Table 8-2 ▸ The Most Successful Third-Party Presidential Campaigns since 1864

The following list includes all third-party candidates winning more than 5 percent of the popular vote or any electoral votes since 1864. (We ignore isolated "unfaithful electors" in the electoral college who failed to vote for the candidate to which they were pledged.)

Year	Major Third Party	Third-Party Presidential Candidate	Percent of the Popular Vote	Electoral Votes	Winning Presidential Candidate and Party
1892	Populist	James Weaver	8.5	22	Grover Cleveland (D)
1912	Progressive	Theodore Roosevelt	27.4	88	Woodrow Wilson (D)
	Socialist	Eugene Debs	6.0	—	
1924	Progressive	Robert LaFollette	16.6	13	Calvin Coolidge (R)
1948	States' Rights	Strom Thurmond	2.4	39	Harry Truman (D)
1960	Independent Democrat	Harry Byrd	0.4	15*	John F. Kennedy (D)
1968	American Independent	George Wallace	13.5	46	Richard Nixon (R)
1980	National Union	John Anderson	6.6	—	Ronald Reagan (R)
1992	Independent	Ross Perot	18.9	—	Bill Clinton (D)
1996	Reform	Ross Perot	8.4	—	Bill Clinton (D)

*Byrd received fifteen electoral votes from unpledged electors in Alabama and Mississippi.

Source: *Dave Leip's Atlas of U.S. Presidential Elections* at **www.uselectionatlas.org**.

Table 8-3 ▸ Policies of Selected American Third Parties since 1864

Populist: This pro-farmer party of the 1890s advocated progressive reforms. It also advocated replacing gold with silver as the basis of the currency in hopes of creating a mild inflation in prices. (It was believed by many that inflation would help debtors and stimulate the economy.)

Socialist: This party advocated a "cooperative commonwealth" based on government ownership of industry. It was pro-labor, often antiwar, and in later years, anti-Communist. It was dissolved in 1972 and replaced by nonparty advocacy groups (Democratic Socialists of America and Social Democrats USA).

Communist: This left-wing breakaway from the Socialists was the U.S. branch of the worldwide Communist movement. The party was pro-labor and advocated full equality for African Americans. It was also closely aligned with the Communist-led Soviet Union, which provoked great hostility among most Americans.

Progressive: This name was given to several successive splinter parties built around individual political leaders. Theodore Roosevelt, who ran in 1912, advocated federal regulation of industry to protect consumers, workers, and small businesses. Robert LaFollette, who ran in 1924, held similar views.

American Independent: Built around George Wallace, this party opposed any further promotion of civil rights and advocated a militant foreign policy. Wallace's supporters were mostly former Democrats who were soon to be Republicans.

Libertarian: This party opposes most government activity.

Reform: The Reform Party was initially built around businessman H. Ross Perot but later was taken over by others. Under Perot, the party was a middle-of-the-road group opposed to federal budget deficits. Under Patrick Buchanan, it came to represent right-wing nationalism and opposition to free trade.

Green: The Greens are a left-of-center pro-environmental party. They are also generally hostile to globalization.

Beyond Our Borders
THE REAL SOCIALISTS

Not many American politicians accept the socialist label, although Vermont senator Bernie Sanders answers to it. In most Western European nations, however, the main left-of-center party comes out of the socialist tradition. Examples include the British Labour Party, the Socialist Party of France, and the Social Democratic Party of Germany. A hundred years ago, these parties were much more radical than they are today. Most called for the abolition of capitalism. Instead, the state, democratically elected by the people, would own the factories and shops, the banks and railroads. (Some socialists advocated ownership by employee cooperatives instead.) Karl Marx was a patron saint of the movement. Many of these parties—most notably the British Labour Party—were tightly linked to labor unions.

From 1918 to 1920, some of the radical fervor left the socialist parties as revolutionaries withdrew to form the new communist movement. In Russia, the communists actually succeeded in replacing capitalism with government ownership, but their methods were so brutal as to taint everything they did. In time, experiments revealed that government ownership of businesses was not helpful in democratic countries either. In the years following World War II, one by one the socialist parties formally gave up the goal of replacing capitalism. What was left was a commitment to a strong welfare state and to the labor movement.

Despite their growing moderation, substantial differences remain between Western European socialists and American liberals. Socialists continue to champion a much larger and more active government than liberals ever would. European tax burdens prove the point.

FOR CRITICAL ANALYSIS

Socialist parties were far more effective at winning elections after World War II than before the war. What might have been the reason?

Ideology has at least two functions in such parties. First, the members of the party regard themselves as outsiders and look to one another for support—ideology provides great psychological cohesiveness. Second, because the rewards of ideological commitment are partly psychological, these parties do not think in terms of immediate electoral success. A poor showing at the polls therefore does not dissuade either the leadership or the grassroots participants from continuing their quest for change in American government (and, ultimately, American society).

Today's active ideological parties include the Libertarian Party and the Green Party. As you learned in Chapter 1, the Libertarian Party supports a *laissez-faire* ("let it be") capitalist economic program, together with a hands-off policy on regulating matters of moral conduct. The Green Party began as a grassroots environmentalist organization with affiliated political parties across North America and Western Europe. It was established in the United States as a national party in 1996 and nominated Ralph Nader to run for president in 2000. Nader campaigned against what he called "corporate greed," advocated universal health insurance, and promoted environmental concerns. He ran again for president as an independent in 2004 and 2008.

Splinter Parties

Some of the most successful minor parties have been those that split from major parties. The impetus for these **splinter parties,** or factions, has usually been a situation in which a particular personality was at odds with the major party. The most successful of these splinter parties was the "Bull Moose" Progressive Party, formed in 1912 to support Theodore Roosevelt for president. The Republican national convention of that year denied Roosevelt the nomination, despite the fact that he had won most of the primaries. He therefore left the GOP and ran against Republican "regular" William Howard Taft in the

Splinter Party
A new party formed by a dissident faction within a major political party. Often, splinter parties have emerged when a particular personality was at odds with the major party.

general election. Although Roosevelt did not win the election, he did split the Republican vote so that Democrat Woodrow Wilson became president.

Third parties have also been formed to back individual candidates who were not rebelling against a particular party. H. Ross Perot, for example, who challenged Republican George H. W. Bush and Democrat Bill Clinton in 1992, had not previously been active in a major party. Perot's supporters probably would have split their votes between Bush and Clinton had Perot not been in the race. In theory, Perot ran in 1992 as a nonparty independent. In practice, he had to create a campaign organization. By 1996, Perot's organization was formalized as the Reform Party.

(Library of Congress)

Eugene V. Debs, a union leader, became a socialist around 1895. He ran for president of the United States five times as the Socialist Party candidate. Why have socialists had such a hard time gaining public support in this country?

The Impact of Minor Parties

Third parties have rarely been able to affect American politics by actually winning elections. (One exception is that third-party and independent candidates have occasionally won races for state governorships—for example, Jesse Ventura was elected governor of Minnesota on the Reform Party ticket in 1998.) Instead, the impact of third parties has taken two forms. First, third parties can influence one of the major parties to take up one or more issues. Second, third parties can determine the outcome of a particular election by pulling votes from one of the major-party candidates in what is called the "spoiler effect."

Influencing the Major Parties. One of the most clear-cut examples of a major party adopting the issues of a minor party took place in 1896, when the Democratic Party took over the Populist demand for "free silver"—that is, a policy of coining enough new money to create an inflation. As you learned on page 250, however, absorbing the Populists cost the Democrats votes overall.

Affecting the Outcome of an Election. The presidential elections of 2000 were one instance in which a minor party may have altered the outcome. Green Party candidate Ralph Nader received almost 100,000 votes in Florida, a majority of which would probably have gone to Democrat Al Gore if Nader had not been in the race.

The real question, however, is not whether the Nader vote had an effect—clearly, it did—but whether the effect was important. The problem is that in elections as close as the presidential elections of 2000, any factor with an impact on the outcome can be said to have determined the results of the elections.

Mechanisms of Political Change

■ **Learning Outcome 7:** **Discuss some of the ways in which support for the parties can change, and explain the increasing importance of independents.**

In the future, could one of the two parties decisively overtake the other and become the "natural party of government"? The Republicans held this status from 1896 until 1932, and the Democrats enjoyed it for many years after the election of Franklin D. Roosevelt in 1932.

Realignment

One mechanism by which a party might gain dominance is **realignment.** In this process, major constituencies shift their allegiance from one party to another, creating a long-term alteration in the political environment. Realignment has often been associated with particular elections, called *realigning elections.* The election of 1896, which established a Republican ascendancy, was clearly a realigning election. So was the election of 1932, which made the Democrats the leading party.

Realignment
A process in which a substantial group of voters switches party allegiance, producing a long-term change in the political landscape.

Realignments in American Politics. A number of myths exist about the concept of realignment. One is that in realignment a newly dominant party must replace

Why Should You Care about... POLITICAL PARTIES?

Why should you, as an individual, care about political parties? The most exciting political party event, staged every four years, is the national convention. State conventions also take place on a regular basis. These may seem like remote activities. Surprising as it might seem, though, there are opportunities for the individual voter to become involved in nominating delegates to a state or national convention or to become a delegate.

YOU CAN BE A CONVENTION DELEGATE

How would you like to exercise a small amount of real political power yourself—power that goes beyond simply voting in an election? You might be able to become a delegate to a county, district, or even state party convention. Many of these conventions nominate candidates for various offices. For example, in Michigan, the state party conventions nominate the candidates for the Board of Regents of the state's three top public universities. The regents set university policies, so these are nominations in which students have an obvious interest. In Michigan, if you are elected as a party precinct delegate, you can attend your party's state convention.

In much of the country, there are more openings for precinct-level delegates than there are people willing to serve. In such circumstances, almost anyone can become a delegate by collecting a handful of signatures on a nominating petition or by mounting a small-scale write-in campaign. You are then eligible to take part in one of the most educational political experiences available to an ordinary citizen. You will get a firsthand look at how political persuasion takes place, how resolutions are written and passed, and how candidates seek out support among their fellow party members. In some states, party caucuses bring debate even closer to the grassroots level.

HOW YOU CAN MAKE A DIFFERENCE

When the parties choose delegates for the national convention, the process begins at the local level—either the congressional district or the state legislative district. Delegates may be elected in party primary elections or chosen in neighborhood or precinct caucuses. Persons who want to run for delegate positions must first file petitions with the local board of elections. If you are interested in committing yourself to a particular presidential candidate and running for the delegate position, check with the local county committee or with the party's national committee about the rules you must follow.

It is even easier to get involved in the grassroots politics of presidential caucuses. In some states, delegates are first nominated at the local precinct caucus. According to the rules of the Iowa caucuses, anyone can participate in a caucus if he or she is eighteen years old, a precinct resident, and registered as a party member. These caucuses select delegates to the county conventions who are pledged to specific presidential candidates. This is the first step toward the national convention.

At the county caucus and the convention levels, both parties try to find younger members to fill some of the seats. Contact the state or county political party to find out when the caucuses or primaries will be held. Then gather local supporters, and prepare to join in an occasion during which political debate is at its best.

For further information about these opportunities, contact the state party office or your local state legislator. You can also contact the national committee for information on how to become a delegate. Use your favorite Web search engine to locate the Republican National Committee by entering "gop" or the Democratic National Committee by typing in "democrats."

Questions for Discussion and Analysis

1. Review the *Which Side Are You On?* feature on page 259. Suppose that the United States Supreme Court were to reverse itself on *Roe v. Wade,* thus giving the national and state governments the power to outlaw abortions. How might the Republican Party, with its strong right-to-life platform, respond to such a ruling? How might Republicans who support freedom of choice react to their party's actions?

2. In America, party candidates for national office are typically chosen through primary elections. In some other countries, a party's central committee picks the party's candidates. How might primary elections limit the ability of political parties to present a united front on the issues?

3. Do you support (or lean toward) one of the major political parties today? If so, would you have supported the same party in the late 1800s—or would you have supported a different party? Explain your reasoning.

4. During 2011 and 2012, what political developments had an impact on the support that voters gave to the Republican and Democratic parties? What impact did the state of the economy appear to have on the results of the 2012 elections?

Key Terms

dealignment 270
Democratic Party 249
divided government 263
electoral college 265
faction 247
GOP 250
independent 247
national committee 261
national convention 258
party identification 270
party-in-government 258
party-in-the-electorate 258
party organization 258
party platform 258
patronage 262
plurality 264
political party 247
realignment 269
Republican Party 249
reverse-income effect 257
splinter party 268
split-ticket voting 271
state central committee 261
straight-ticket voting 271
swing voters 271
third party 266
tipping 271
two-party system 248
Whig Party 249

Chapter Summary

1. A political party is a group of political activists who organize to win elections, operate the government, and determine public policy. Political parties recruit candidates for public office, organize and run elections, present alternative policies to the voters, assume responsibility for operating the government, and act as the opposition to the party in power.

2. The evolution of our nation's political parties can be divided into seven periods: (a) the formation of political parties from 1789 to 1816; (b) the era of one-party rule from 1816 to 1828; (c) the period from Andrew Jackson's presidency to the eve of the Civil War, from 1828 to 1856; (d) the Civil War and post–Civil War period, from 1856 to 1896; (e) the Republican ascendancy and progressive period, from 1896 to 1932; (f) the New Deal period, from 1932 to about 1968; and (g) the modern period, from approximately 1968 to the present. Throughout most of the modern period, the parties have been closely matched in strength.

3. Many of the differences between the two parties date from the time of Franklin D. Roosevelt's New Deal. The Democrats have advocated government action to help labor and minorities, and the Republicans have championed self-reliance and limited government. Today, cultural differences are at least as important as economic issues in determining party allegiance.

4. A political party consists of three components: the party-in-the-electorate, the party organization, and the party-in-government. Each party component maintains linkages to the others to keep the party strong. Each level of the party—local, state, and national—has considerable autonomy. The national party organization is responsible for holding the national convention in presidential election years, writing the party platform, choosing the national committee, and conducting party business.

5. The party-in-government comprises all of the elected and appointed officeholders of a party. Increased ideological coherence in both major parties has resulted in growing political polarization.

6. Two major parties have dominated the political landscape in the United States for almost two centuries. The reasons for this include (a) the historical foundations of the system, (b) political socialization and practical considerations, (c) the winner-take-all electoral system, and (d) state and

federal laws favoring the two-party system. For these reasons, minor parties have found it extremely difficult to win elections.

7. Minor, or third, parties have emerged from time to time, sometimes as dissatisfied splinter groups from within major parties, and have acted as barometers of change in the political mood. Third parties can affect the political process (even if they do not win) if major parties adopt their issues or if they determine which major party wins an election.

8. One mechanism of political change is realignment, in which major blocs of voters switch allegiance from one party to another. Realignments were manifested in the elections of 1896 and 1932. Some scholars speak of dealignment—that is, the loss of strong party attachments. In fact, the share of the voters who describe themselves as independents has grown, and the share of self-identified Democrats has shrunk. Many independents actually vote as if they were Democrats or Republicans, however. Demographic change can also "tip" a district or state from one party to another.

Quiz Multiple Choice

1. The key difference between an interest group and a political party is that:
   - **a. interest groups want to take over the government.**
   - **b. interest groups seek to influence, not run, the government.**
   - **c. interest groups are much larger in number than political parties.**

2. One of the main activities of political parties is to:
   - **a. organize and run elections.**
   - **b. ensure that the candidates they support are scandal-free.**
   - **c. support the policies of the president, even if he or she is from the opposite party.**

3. The United States has a party system that can be characterized as a:
   - **a. multi-party system.**
   - **b. single-party system.**
   - **c. two-party system.**

4. The New Deal era under Democratic President Franklin D. Roosevelt occurred:
   - **a. at the beginning of the twentieth century.**
   - **b. during the 1960s.**
   - **c. during the Great Depression of the 1930s.**

5. The three faces of a political party include:
   - **a. the party-in-the-electorate, the party organization, and the members of the party.**
   - **b. the party organization, the party-in-government, and the party-in-the-electorate.**
   - **c. the party-in-government, the party-in-the-electorate, and the lobbyists for that party.**

6. At the national party convention:
   - **a. the presidential and vice-presidential candidates will already have been officially nominated.**
   - **b. the party platform is developed.**
   - **c. the head of each major party determines who will run for president and vice president.**

7. At almost every level of government in this country, the outcome of elections is based on the plurality voting system, which means that:
   - **a. the candidate with the largest number of votes wins, even if the winner does not receive 50 percent or more of the votes.**
   - **b. when no one receives 50 percent of the vote, a runoff election is held.**
   - **c. there is no need for everyone to vote in each election.**

8. We typically call parties other than the Democratic or Republican parties:
   - **a. outlier parties.**
   - **b. fringe parties.**
   - **c. third parties.**

ANSWERS: 1. b, 2. a, 3. c, 4. c, 5. b, 6. b, 7. a, 8. c.

Quiz Fill-Ins

9. In an election, when a voter casts ballots for candidates of two or more parties, we call this ______________-______________ voting.

10. Those who vote for all of the candidates of one party are engaging in ______________-______________ voting.

11. Groups within a party that seek to obtain power or benefits are called _______________.

12. The first political division in the United States was between the _______________ and the _______________-_______________.

13. When voters are temporarily dissatisfied with the performance of one or another of the major parties, the result may be a _______________ election.

14. Both political parties have _____________ _____________ that direct and coordinate party activities during the four years after each presidential election.

15. Usually the parties' presidential candidates choose the _______________ _______________.

16. When the executive and legislative branches of the government are controlled by more than one party, we call this _______________ _______________.

ANSWERS: 9. split-ticket, 10. straight-ticket, 11. factions, 12. Federalists; Anti-Federalists, 13. "wave," 14. national committees, 15. national chairpersons, 16. divided government.

(© Aleksandar Jovicic/iStockphoto)

Selected Print & Media Resources

SUGGESTED READINGS

Alterman, Eric, and Kevin Mattson. *The Cause: The Fight for American Liberalism from Franklin Roosevelt to Barack Obama.* New York: Viking Adult, 2012. Alterman, the principal author of this history of American liberalism, is a journalism professor at Brooklyn College and a self-professed ardent liberal. Alterman believes that liberal Democrats can succeed when they emphasize economics.

Dalton, Russell J. *The Apartisan American: Dealignment and Changing Electoral Politics.* Washington, D.C.: CQ Press, 2012. In this study of the independent voter, Dalton, a political science professor at University of California Irvine, reviews decades of polling data.

Dochuk, Darren. *From Bible Belt to Sunbelt: Plain-Folk Religion, Grassroots Politics, and the Rise of Evangelical Conservatism.* New York: W. W. Norton & Co., 2010. Dochuk uses new research to describe the impact of evangelicals on the conservative movement from the Barry Goldwater years to the time of Ronald Reagan. The book won the Allan Nevins prize awarded by the Society of American Historians.

Ellis, Christopher, and James A. Stimson. *Ideology in America.* New York: Cambridge University Press, 2012. In principle, Americans are more likely to advocate conservatism than liberalism. When it comes to what the government actually does, however, liberal policies tend to be more popular. In this work, two professors of political science analyze this paradox.

MEDIA RESOURCES

The American President—This 1995 film stars Michael Douglas as a president who must balance partisanship and friendship (Republicans in Congress promise to approve the president's crime bill only if he modifies an environmental plan sponsored by his liberal girlfriend).

A Third Choice—This award-winning 2011 PBS documentary provides a colorful look at the history of third parties and how they changed America.

(© PashaIgnatov/iStockphoto)

E-mocracy POLITICAL PARTIES AND THE INTERNET

Today's political parties use the Internet to attract voters, organize campaigns, obtain campaign contributions, and the like. Voters, in turn, can go online to learn more about specific parties and their programs. Those who use the Internet for information on the parties, though, need to exercise some caution. Even the official party sites are filled with misinformation or outright lies about the policies and leaders of the other party. Besides the parties' official sites, there are satirical sites mimicking the parties, sites distributing misleading information about the parties, and sites that are raising money for their own causes rather than for political parties.

LOGGING ON

1. The political parties all have Web sites. As we noted earlier, you can use your favorite Web search engine to locate the Republican National Committee by entering "gop" or the Democratic National Committee by typing in "democrats."
2. The two leading third parties are the Libertarian Party and the Green Party. Find their Web sites by searching on "libertarians" and "green party," respectively. Ron Gunzburger's Politics1 site provides a list of more than forty U.S. parties, all of them tiny. Search on "politics1."
3. The Pew Research Center for the People and the Press offers survey data online on how the parties fared during the most recent elections, voter typology, and numerous other issues. Search on "people-press" to access its site.

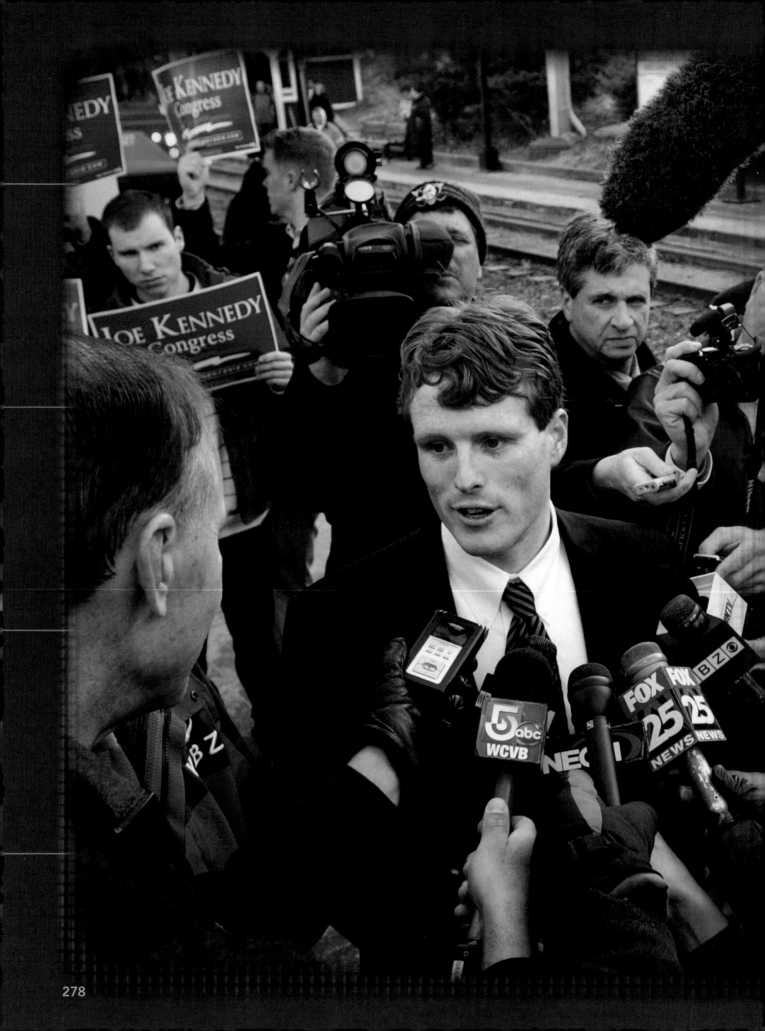

9 Campaigns, Elections, and the Media

The eight learning outcomes below are designed to help improve your understanding of this chapter. After reading this chapter, you should be able to:

- Learning Outcome 1: **Discuss who runs for office and how campaigns are managed.**
- Learning Outcome 2: **Describe the current system of campaign finance.**
- Learning Outcome 3: **Summarize the process of choosing a president of the United States.**
- Learning Outcome 4: **Explain the mechanisms through which voting takes place on Election Day.**
- Learning Outcome 5: **Discuss voter turnout in the United States and the types of people most likely to vote.**
- Learning Outcome 6: **Describe the different types of media and the changing roles that they play in American society.**
- Learning Outcome 7: **Summarize the impact of the media on the political process.**
- Learning Outcome 8: **Consider some of the issues facing today's media, including concentrated ownership, freedom of speech for broadcasters, and political bias.**

Joseph Kennedy III sought media coverage to announce his candidacy for a seat in the U.S. House of Representatives.

(AP Photo/Steven Senne)

(Andrew Cutraro/Redux)

BOB WOODWARD READS the *Washington Post*, for which he is an associate editor. Do many Americans read newspapers?

What if... THERE WERE NO NEWSPAPERS?

BACKGROUND

At the end of the Revolutionary War, Americans could buy any of a total of forty-three newspapers. By 1910, newspapers throughout the country looked much as they do today. Currently, however, many newspapers face extinction. Great newspapers in Chicago, Minneapolis, Philadelphia, and other cities have filed for bankruptcy protection. Some, such as the *Baltimore Examiner* and the *Cincinnati Post,* have folded completely. Some people have speculated that, ultimately, newspapers will disappear altogether. What would such a world look like?

WHAT IF THERE WERE NO NEWSPAPERS?

The trend is already here. Since 1994, the share of Americans saying they read a daily newspaper has dropped from almost 60 percent to around 30 percent. If this trend continues, newspapers could for the most part vanish. Gone, too, would be their reporters and management.

By 2010, for the first time, more people obtained their national and international news from the Internet than from newspapers. Obviously, without newspapers, everyone would obtain their news from the Internet, broadcast and cable television, and to a lesser extent, news magazines. Without newspapers, these other sources of news would increase in size, scope, and availability.

THE DEATH OF THE STANDARD NEWS PACKAGE

When you open a metropolitan newspaper today, it has a "newspaper look." When you visit that newspaper's Web site, it often has the same look, one that dates back a hundred years. You'll find a mixture of local, national, business, sports, and international news, plus weather forecasts. What you see online is not much different from what is in print, although it may be easier to access.

If newspapers disappeared, the conventional news package also would disappear. People would find their news using online portals such as Yahoo and Google News. Their news format consists of headlines, a sentence, and a link. Such operations are cheap to run. Google News has no editors as such—everything is automated. Of course, if newspapers disappeared, Google News would not be able to access newspaper stories. Such stories would have to be found elsewhere online.

NEWS BLOGS AND CABLE NEWS CHANNELS WOULD GAIN VIEWERS

Without newspapers, news blogs would grow. Currently, the Huffington Post (nicknamed HuffPo) has a total staff of two hundred. It has an unpaid army of about three thousand bloggers.

As of 2010, Fox News was the most popular cable news channel, but we also have MSNBC, CNN, and others. Without newspapers, more people would obtain some of their news from these cable sources. New cable news channels might pop up to serve niche audiences.

LOCAL NEWS WITHOUT NEWSPAPERS

Newspaper owners claim that it is not possible to obtain local news without the services of a local newspaper. Yet start-up companies are now creating "hyperlocal" news sites. These sites let people zoom in on what is happening in their neighborhoods. Check out **www.patch.com**, **outside.in**, and **www.everyblock.com**. These sites collect links to articles and blogs and often obtain data from municipal governments and other local sources.

FOR CRITICAL ANALYSIS

1. *Would the quality of news gathering diminish if newspapers no longer existed?*
2. *Many news blogs are definitely biased, and often proud of it. Should this attitude worry us? Why or why not?*

Free elections are the cornerstone of the American political system. Voters choose one candidate over another to hold political office by casting ballots in local, state, and federal elections. In 2012, the voters chose Democrats Barack Obama and Joe Biden to be president and vice president of the United States for the following four years. In 2012, voters also elected all of the members of the House of Representatives and one-third of the members of the Senate. The campaigns were bitter, long, and expensive.

Voters and candidates frequently criticize the American electoral process. It is said to favor wealthier candidates, to further the aims of special interest groups, and to be dominated by older voters and those with better education and higher incomes. Campaign fund-raising has grown by leaps and bounds as the United States Supreme Court has progressively reduced limits on the fund-raising process.

The media play a major role in the political process and in election campaigns. Even though newspapers have become less important, new forms of media have taken their place, as we explained in the opening *What If . . .* feature. The role of the media is discussed in greater depth later in this chapter.

■ **Learning Outcome 1: Discuss who runs for office and how campaigns are managed.**

The Twenty-First-Century Campaign

There are thousands of elective offices in the United States. Although the major political parties strive to provide a slate of candidates for every election, recruiting candidates is easier for some offices than for others. Political parties may have difficulty finding candidates for the board of the local water control district, for example, but they generally find a sufficient number of candidates for county commissioner or sheriff. The "higher" the office and the more prestige attached to it, the more candidates are likely to want to run. In many areas of the country, however, one major party may be considerably stronger than the other is. In those situations, the minority party may have difficulty finding nominees for elections in which victory is unlikely.

Presidential Primary
A statewide primary election of delegates to a political party's national convention, held to determine a party's presidential nominee.

The presidential campaign provides the most colorful and exciting look at candidates and how they prepare to compete for office—in this instance, the highest office in the land. The men and women who wanted to be the Republican candidate in the 2012 presidential campaign faced a long and obstacle-filled path. First, they needed to raise sufficient funds to tour the nation, particularly the states with early **presidential primaries,** to see if they had enough local supporters. They needed funds to create an organization and win primary votes. Finally, when nominated as the party's candidate, the winner required funds to finance a successful campaign for president. Always, at every turn, there was the question of whether there were enough funds to effectively compete against their opponents, and eventually against President Barack Obama.

Former Massachusetts governor Mitt Romney spent almost two years attending campaign events prior to the 2012 elections.

(Benjamin Myers/Reuters/Landov)

Who Is Eligible?

There are few constitutional restrictions on who can be elected to national office in the United States. As detailed in the Constitution, the formal requirements are as follows:

1. *President.* Must be a natural-born citizen, have attained the age of thirty-five years, and be a resident of the country for fourteen years by the time of inauguration.
2. *Vice president.* Must meet the same requirements as the president and also not be a resident of the same state as the president.[1]
3. *Senator.* Must be a citizen for at least nine years, have attained the age of thirty by the time of taking office, and be a resident of the state from which elected.

1. Technically, a presidential and vice-presidential candidate on the same ticket can be from the same state, but if they are, one of the two must forfeit the electoral votes of his or her home state.

(Brian Kersey/UPI/Landov)

During the primary season, why would a sitting president give many news conferences even though he or she is not facing a primary opponent?

4. *Representative*. Must be a citizen for at least seven years, have attained the age of twenty-five by the time of taking office, and be a resident of the state from which elected.

The qualifications for state legislators are set by the state constitutions and likewise include age, place of residence, and citizenship. (Usually, the requirements for the upper chamber of a legislature are somewhat higher than those for the lower chamber.) The legal qualifications for serving as governor or other state office are similar.

Who Runs?

In spite of these minimal legal qualifications for office at both the national and the state levels, a quick look at the slate of candidates in any election—or at the current members of Congress—will reveal that not all segments of the population enjoy these opportunities equally. Holders of political office in the United States are predominantly white and male. Until the twentieth century, presidential candidates were exclusively of northern European origin and of Protestant heritage.[2] Laws that effectively denied voting rights made it impossible to elect African American public officials in many areas in which African Americans constituted a significant portion of the population. As a result of the passage of major civil rights legislation in the 1960s, however, the number of African American public officials has increased throughout the United States, and in a groundbreaking vote, the nation elected an African American president in 2008.

Women as Candidates. Until recently, women generally were considered to be appropriate candidates only for lower-level offices, such as state legislator or school board

2. A number of early presidents were Unitarian. The Unitarian Church is not Protestant, but it is historically rooted in the Protestant tradition.

U.S. Republican presidential candidates (from left to right) Ron Paul, Rick Santorum, Mitt Romney, and Newt Gingrich during one of numerous primary debates in 2011 and the winter of 2012.

(Joshua Lott/Reuters/Landov)

member. The past twenty years have seen a tremendous increase in the number of women who run for office, not only at the state level but for the U.S. Congress as well. Figure 9–1 below shows the increase in female candidates. In 2012, 181 women ran for the House or Senate on major-party tickets, and 88 were elected. Today, a majority of Americans say they would vote for a qualified woman for president of the United States. Indeed, Hillary Clinton came close to winning the Democratic presidential nomination in 2008, a year in which the eventual Democratic nominee was favored to win the general election.

did you know?

Five women received votes for vice president at the Democratic convention in 1924, the first held after women received the right to vote in 1920.

Professional Status. Candidates are likely to be professionals, particularly lawyers. Political campaigning and officeholding are simply easier for some occupational groups than for others, and political involvement can make a valuable contribution to certain careers. Lawyers, for example, have more flexible schedules than do many other professionals, can take time off for campaigning, and can leave their jobs to hold public office full-time. Furthermore, holding political office is good publicity for their professional practice. Perhaps most important, many jobs that lawyers aspire to—federal or state judgeships, state's attorney offices, or work in a federal agency—can be attained by political appointment.

Managing the Campaign

After the candidates have been nominated, typically through a **primary election,** the most exhausting and expensive part of the election process begins—the **general election** campaign, which actually fills the offices at stake. Political campaigns are becoming more complex and more sophisticated with every election. Even with the most appealing of candidates, today's campaigns require a strong organization with (1) expertise in political polling and marketing, (2) professional assistance in fund-raising, accounting, and financial management, and (3) technological capabilities in every aspect of the campaign.

Primary Election
An election in which political parties choose their candidates for the general election.

General Election
An election open to all eligible voters, normally held on the first Tuesday in November, that determines who will fill various elected positions.

The Changing Campaign. The goal is the same for all campaigns—to convince voters to choose a candidate or a slate of candidates for office. Part of the reason for the

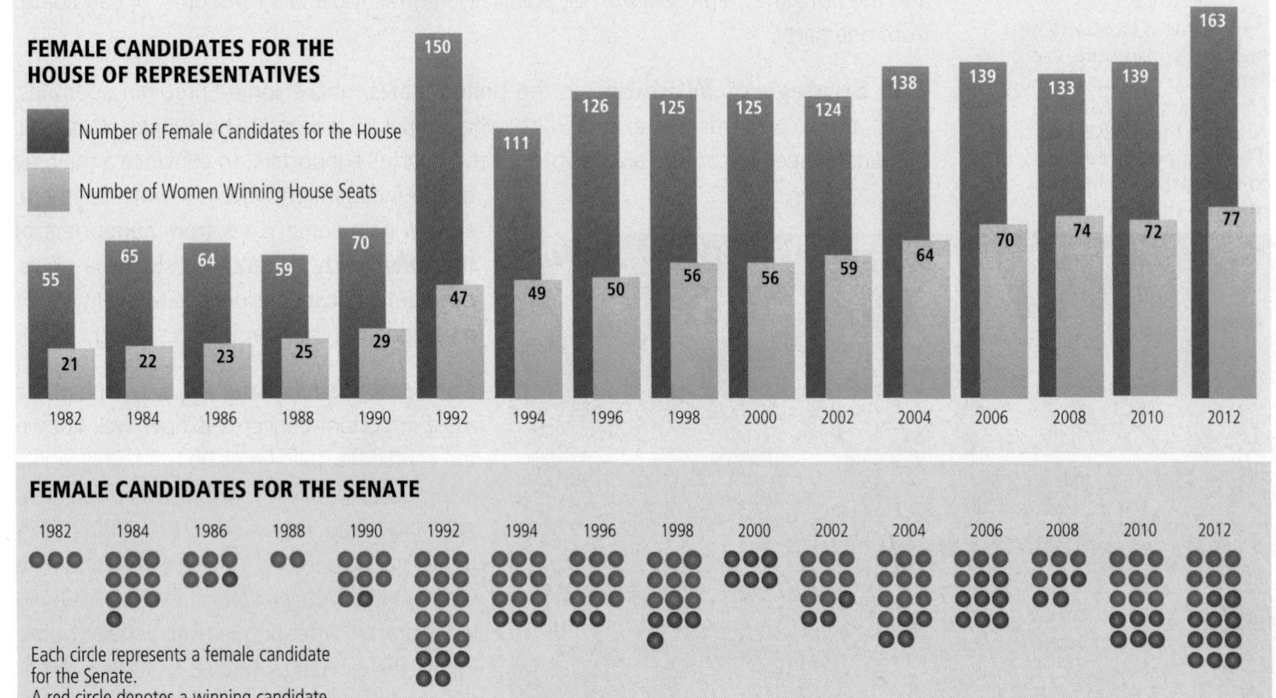

did you know?

Since 1945, the stock market (the Dow Jones Industrial Average) has gone up an average of 6.6 percent in years when a Republican was president—and 9.4 percent when the president was a Democrat.

increased intensity of campaigns in the last decade is that they are now centered on the candidate, not on the party. The candidate-centered campaign emerged in response to changes in the electoral system, the increased importance of television in campaigns, technological innovations such as the Internet, and the increased cost of campaigning.

To run a successful and persuasive campaign, the candidate's organization must be able to raise funds for the effort, obtain coverage from the media, and produce and pay for political commercials and advertising. In addition, the organization needs to schedule the candidate's time effectively, convey the candidate's position on the issues to the voters, and conduct research on the opposing candidate. Finally, the campaign must get the voters to go to the polls.

When party identification was stronger among voters and before the advent of television campaigning, a strong party organization at the local, state, or national level could furnish most of the services and expertise that the candidate needed. Parties used their precinct organizations to distribute literature, register voters, and get out the vote on election day. Less effort was spent on advertising each candidate's positions and character, because the party label presumably communicated that information to many voters.

One of the reasons that campaigns no longer depend on parties is that fewer people identify with them (see Chapter 8), as is evident from the increased number of independent voters. In 1954, fewer than 20 percent of adults identified themselves as independents, whereas today that number is about 40 percent.

The Professional Campaign. Whether the candidate is running for the state legislature, for the governor's office, for the U.S. Congress, or for the presidency, every campaign has some fundamental tasks to accomplish. Today, in national elections most of these tasks are handled by paid professionals rather than volunteers or amateur politicians.

Political Consultant
A paid professional hired to devise a campaign strategy and manage a campaign.

The most sought-after and possibly the most criticized campaign expert is the **political consultant,** who, for a large fee, takes charge of the candidate's campaign. Political consultants began to displace volunteer campaign managers in the 1960s, about the same time that television became a force in campaigns. The paid consultant devises a campaign strategy and theme, oversees advertising, and plans media appearances. The consultants and the firms they represent are not politically neutral. Most will work only for candidates from one party.

The Strategy of Winning. In the United States, unlike some European countries, there are no rewards for a candidate who comes in second. The winner takes all. Candidates seek to capture all the votes of their party's supporters, to convince a majority of the independent voters to vote for them, and to gain some votes from supporters of the other party. To accomplish these goals, candidates must consider their visibility, their message, and their campaign strategy.

Candidate Visibility and Appeal. One of the most important concerns is how well known the candidate is. If she or he is a highly visible incumbent, there may be little need for campaigning except to remind voters of the officeholder's good deeds. If, however, the candidate is an unknown challenger or a largely unfamiliar character attacking a well-known public figure, the campaign requires a strategy to get the candidate before the public.

Two of the best-known political consultants are James Carville for the Democrats and Mary Matalin for the Republicans. They happen to be married to each other. What functions do they perform?

(AP Photo/Odessa American/Albert Cesare)

The Use of Opinion Polls. One of the major sources of information for both the media and the candidates is opinion polls. Poll taking is widespread during the primaries. Presidential hopefuls have private polls taken to make sure that there is at least some chance they could be nominated and, if nominated, elected. During the presidential campaign itself, polling is even more frequent. Polls are taken not only by the regular pollsters—Gallup, Pew Research, and others—but also privately by each candidate's campaign organization. These private polls are for the exclusive and secret use of the candidate and his or her campaign organization. As the election approaches, many candidates use **tracking polls,** which are polls taken almost every day, to find out how well they are competing for votes. Tracking polls enable consultants to fine-tune the advertising and the candidate's speeches in the last days of the campaign.

Tracking Poll
A poll taken on a nearly daily basis as election day approaches.

Focus Group
A small group of individuals who are led in discussion by a professional consultant in order to gather opinions on and responses to candidates and issues.

Focus Groups. Another tactic used by campaign organizations to gain insights into public perceptions of the candidate is a **focus group.** Professional consultants organize a discussion of the candidate or of certain political issues among ten to fifteen ordinary citizens. The citizens are selected from specific target groups in the population—for example, working women, blue-collar men, senior citizens, or young voters.

Recent campaigns have tried to reach groups such as "soccer moms," "Walmart shoppers," or "NASCAR dads."[3] The group discusses personality traits of the candidate, political advertising, and other candidate-related issues. Focus groups can reveal more emotional responses to candidates or the deeper anxieties of voters—feelings that consultants believe often are not tapped by more impersonal telephone surveys. The campaign then can shape its messages to respond to those feelings and perceptions.

did you know?

A candidate can buy lists of all the voters in a precinct, county, or state for a few cents per name.

Financing the Campaign

■ **Learning Outcome 2:** **Describe the current system of campaign finance.**

The connection between money and elections is a sensitive issue in American politics. The belief is widespread that large campaign contributions by special interests corrupt the political system. Indeed, spending reached unprecedented heights during the 2011–2012 election cycle. In 2012, total spending for the presidential races alone reached $2.5 billion. All of these funds had to be provided by the candidates and their families, borrowed, or raised by contributions from individuals, organizations, or **political action committees (PACs).** PACs are committees set up under federal or state law for the express purpose of making political donations.

Political Action Committee (PAC)
A committee set up by and representing a corporation, labor union, or special interest group. PACs raise and give campaign donations.

The way campaigns are financed has changed dramatically in the past several years. For decades, candidates and political parties had to operate within the constraints imposed by complicated laws regulating campaign financing. Many of these constraints still exist, but recent developments have opened up the process to a striking degree. Today, there are no limits on how much any person or institution can invest in the political process, and only modest limits on how this spending can take place.

The Evolution of the Campaign Finance System

Throughout much of early American history, campaign financing was unregulated. No limits existed on contributions, and no data were collected on campaign funding. During the twentieth century, however, a variety of federal corrupt practices acts were adopted to regulate campaign financing. The first, passed in 1925, contained many loopholes and proved to be ineffective. The **Hatch Act** (Political Activities Act) of 1939 is best known for restricting the political activities of civil servants. The act also made it unlawful for a political group to spend more than $3 million in any campaign and limited individual

Hatch Act
An act passed in 1939 that restricted the political activities of government employees. It also prohibited a political group from spending more than $3 million in any campaign and limited individual contributions to a campaign committee to $5,000.

3. NASCAR stands for the National Association for Stock Car Auto Racing.

contributions to a campaign committee to $5,000. Of course, such restrictions were easily circumvented by creating additional political organizations.

did you know?

Abraham Lincoln sold pieces of fence rail that he had split as political souvenirs to finance his campaign.

The Federal Election Campaign Act. The Federal Election Campaign Act (FECA) of 1971, which became effective in 1972, replaced all past laws. The act restricted the amount that could be spent on campaign advertising. It also limited the amount that candidates could contribute to their own campaigns and required disclosure of all contributions and expenditures over $100. In principle, the FECA limited the role of labor unions and corporations in political campaigns.

Federal Election Commission (FEC) The federal regulatory agency with the task of enforcing federal campaign laws. As a practical matter, the FEC's role is largely limited to collecting data on campaign contributions.

Amendments to the FECA passed in 1974 created the **Federal Election Commission (FEC).** This commission consists of six bipartisan administrators whose duty is to enforce compliance with the requirements of the act. The 1974 amendments also placed limits on the sums that individuals and committees could contribute to candidates.

The principal role of the FEC today is to collect data on campaign contributions. Candidate committees must file periodic reports with the FEC listing who contributed, how much was spent, and for what it was spent. As an enforcement body, however, the FEC is conspicuously ineffective and typically does not determine that a campaign has violated the rules until the elections are over, if then.

The original FECA of 1971 limited the amount that each individual could spend on his or her own behalf. The Supreme Court overturned the provision in 1976, in *Buckley v. Valeo,*[4] stating that it was unconstitutional to restrict in any way the amount congressional candidates could spend on their own behalf. The Court later extended this principle to state elections as well.

Issue Advocacy Advertising paid for by interest groups that support or oppose a candidate or a candidate's position on an issue without mentioning voting or elections.

Soft Money Campaign contributions unregulated by federal or state law, usually given to parties and party committees to help fund general party activities.

Political Action Committees. Changes to the FECA in 1974 and 1976 allowed corporations, labor unions, and other interest groups to set up political action committees (PACs) to raise funds for candidates. PACs can contribute up to $5,000 to each candidate in each election. Each corporation or each union is limited to one PAC. The number of PACs grew significantly after 1976, as did the amounts that they spent on elections. Since the 1990s, however, the number of traditional PACs has leveled off because interest groups and activists have found alternative mechanisms for funneling resources into campaigns.

Issue Advocacy Advertising. Business corporations, labor unions, and other interest groups have also developed ways of making independent expenditures that are not coordinated with those of a candidate or political party. A common tactic is **issue advocacy advertising,** which promotes positions on issues rather than candidates. Although promoting issue positions aligns very closely with promoting candidates who support those positions, the courts repeatedly have held that interest groups have a First Amendment right to advocate their positions. Political parties may also make independent expenditures on behalf of candidates.

Comic Stephen Colbert formed his own super PAC and received more than $1 million in contributions.

(AP Photo/Alex Brandon)

Soft Money. Interest groups and PACs hit upon the additional strategy of generating **soft money**—that is, campaign contributions to political parties that escaped the limits of federal or state election law. No limits existed on contributions to political parties for activities such as voter education and

4. 424 U.S. 1 (1976).

voter-registration drives. This loophole enabled the parties to raise millions of dollars from corporations and individuals.

The Rise and Fall of the McCain-Feingold Act. The Bipartisan Campaign Reform Act of 2002, also known as the McCain-Feingold Act after its chief sponsors in the Senate, took effect on the day after the midterm elections of 2002. The law sought to regulate the new campaign finance practices developed since the passage of the FECA. It banned soft money at the federal level, but it did not ban such contributions to state and local parties. It attempted to curb issue advocacy advertising, but also increased the sums that individuals could contribute directly to candidates.

The constitutionality of the 2002 act was immediately challenged. In December 2003, the Supreme Court upheld almost all of the clauses of the act.[5] In 2007, however, the Court eased the act's restrictions on issue advocacy ads when it ruled that only those ads "susceptible of no reasonable interpretation other than as an appeal to vote for or against a specific candidate" could be restricted prior to an election.[6] Finally, in 2010, *Citizens United v. FEC*[7] swept away almost all remaining restrictions on independent expenditures, leading to the system we have today.

(Mort Gerberg/The New Yorker Collection/www.cartoonbank.com)

"Dear J.J.: Thank you so much for your lovely present of fourteen million dollars for my campaign. It was sweet of you to remember. I promise to spend it on something nice."

The Current Campaign Finance Environment

As of 2012, political campaigns are financed in two distinct ways. One of these is spending by the candidate's own committee. Contributions made directly to candidates are subject to limitations: An individual can donate no more than $2,500 to a candidate in a single election, and contributions by committees are limited as well. In exchange for these limits, candidates have almost complete control over how their own campaign money is spent.

Another way in which campaigns are financed is through **independent expenditures.** These funds may be spent on advertising and other political activities, but in theory the expenditures cannot be coordinated with those of a candidate. No limits exist on how much can be spent in this fashion. This two-part system is the direct result of a 2010 ruling by the United States Supreme Court.

Independent Expenditures
Nonregulated contributions from PACs, organizations, and individuals. The funds may be spent on advertising or other campaign activities, so long as those expenditures are not coordinated with those of a candidate.

Citizens United v. FEC. In January 2010, the Supreme Court ruled that corporations, unions, and nonprofits may spend freely to support or oppose candidates, so long as the expenditures are made independently and are not coordinated with candidate campaigns. The ruling overturned campaign-finance laws dating back decades. Democrats, plus many journalists and bloggers, accused the Court of granting corporations rights that ought to be exercised only by flesh-and-blood humans. Republicans and others defended the ruling as protecting freedom of speech.

Super PACs. *Citizens United* led directly to a new type of political organization: the **super PAC.** Traditional PACs, which continue to exist, are set up to represent a corporation, labor union, or special interest group. The super PAC, in contrast, is established to aggregate unlimited contributions by individuals and organizations and then funnel these sums into

Super PAC
A political organization that aggregates unlimited contributions by individuals and organizations to be spent independently of candidate committees.

5. *McConnell v. FEC,* 540 U.S. 93 (2003).
6. *FEC v. Wisconsin Right to Life,* 551 U.S. 449 (2007).
7. 130 S.Ct. 876 (2010).

(AP Photo/Susan Walsh)

Senate majority whip Richard Durbin (D., Ill.) listens to actor Alec Baldwin endorse public funding of elections. Why would any politician want to be associated with an actor or actress?

independent expenditures. By 2011, every major presidential candidate had a super PAC. It soon became clear that the supposed independence of these organizations is a fiction. Presidential super PACs are usually chaired by individuals who are closely associated with the candidate. Frequently, the chair is a former top member of the candidate's campaign.

A variety of other super PACs were established as well. These groups were often oriented toward a party, rather than a candidate. Such super PACs might seek, for example, to support Republican or Democratic candidates for the U.S. Senate, or to intervene within a particular party. The super PAC founded by the Club for Growth, for example, devotes its considerable resources to supporting strong conservatives in Republican primaries and to running negative advertisements against more moderate Republicans.

One interesting development in 2011–2012 was the tendency for super PACs to be supported primarily by very wealthy individuals, rather than by corporations or other organizations. The funding was still provided by business interests but came from individuals who owned corporations, not from the corporations themselves. A striking example of this phenomenon was a $10 million contribution in January 2012 to the super PAC of Republican presidential candidate Newt Gingrich, former Speaker of the U.S. House. The contribution, supplied by casino magnate Sheldon Adelson and his wife, amounted to almost half of all the funds that Gingrich raised throughout the entire primary season. Without this contribution, Gingrich would have been forced to end his campaign much earlier than he actually did. Are super PACs such as these bad for democracy? We address that question in this chapter's *Which Side Are You On?* feature on the facing page.

The 527 Organization. Well before *Citizens United,* interest groups realized that they could set up new organizations outside the parties to encourage voter registration and to run issue ads aimed at energizing supporters. So long as these committees did not endorse candidates, they faced no limits on fund-raising. These tax-exempt groups, called 527 organizations after the section of the tax code that provides for them, first made a major impact during the 2003–2004 election cycle. Since then, they have largely been replaced by super PACs, but a number continue to be active to the present day.

The 501(c)4 Organization. In the 2007–2008 election cycle, campaign-finance lawyers began recommending a new type of independent group—the 501(c)4 organization, which, like the 527 organization, is named after the relevant provision of the tax code. A 501(c)4 is ostensibly a "social welfare" group and, unlike a 527, is not required to disclose the identity of its donors or to report spending to the Federal Election Commission (FEC).

Lawyers then began suggesting that 501(c)4 organizations claim a special exemption that would allow the organization to ask people to vote for or against specific candidates as long as a majority of the group's effort was devoted to issues. Only those funds spent directly to support candidates had to be reported to the FEC, and the 501(c)4 could continue to conceal its donors.

Which Side Are You On?

ARE SUPER PACS BAD FOR DEMOCRACY?

The 2010 Supreme Court decision *Citizens United v. FEC* allowed corporations, unions, and individuals to donate unlimited sums to entities that are "independent" of the candidates. So was born the super PAC. A super PAC can raise sums without limit. Those monies can be spent on both positive and negative campaign ads. Not surprisingly, some very rich people donated millions of dollars to various super PACs during 2011 and 2012. Hollywood mogul Jeffrey Katzenberg gave $2 million to a super PAC supporting President Obama. One of the founders of PayPal, Peter Thiel, donated $2.6 million to a super PAC of Republican presidential candidate Ron Paul. To make fun of these organizations, TV personality Stephen Colbert created his own super PAC, which managed to raise more than $1 million—a very expensive joke. The question is, do super PACs mean the end of democracy as we know it?

JUST ANOTHER WAY FOR BIG MONEY TO RULE AMERICA

Those who oppose super PACs argue that money should not determine the outcome of elections. Super PACs allow America's millionaires and billionaires to donate unlimited funds to influence the outcome of congressional and presidential elections. How can the "little people" keep up? Super PACs are supposed to be independent, but in reality, the majority are run by candidates' former staff members. Obama's super PAC, Priorities USA Action, was organized by two ex–White House staffers, Bill Burton and Sean Sweeney. The pro-Romney super PAC, Restore Our Future, was managed by Romney's former lawyer.

Almost all the advertising purchased by super PACs is negative—the candidates can remain upbeat while their super PACs do the dirty work. These attack ads are themselves a corruption of the political process. Finally, some super PACs manage to hide the identity of many of their donors. A number of public-interest groups have called for a constitutional amendment to overturn *Citizens United*. We need some such step to keep the United States from becoming a republic of the rich, by the rich, and for the rich.

SUPER PACS: GOOD FOR DEMOCRACY AND FREE SPEECH, TOO

Those who support super PACs argue that people should have the right to say whatever they want. Corporations and unions are made up of individuals, and so organizations as well as individuals should be able to express their views by donating to campaign organizations. In 2012, super PACs kept Republican primary candidates viable much longer than would have been possible otherwise. That gave voters more opportunities to support the candidate of their choice. Certainly, Mitt Romney, Newt Gingrich, Rick Santorum, and the other candidates felt the heat from all of those negative ads about their alleged deficiencies. Yet negative ads are one of the richest sources of information for voters.

You do not have to be rich to contribute to a super PAC—consider Stephen Colbert's super PAC. Further, spending lots of campaign dollars does not guarantee election. Past a certain point, the spending is just wasted. In California's 2010 contest for governor, Republican Meg Whitman, a former CEO of eBay and a billionaire, faced Democrat Jerry Brown. She outspent Brown by a huge margin but still lost the election. Brown had just enough in funds to make his point, and he did so effectively. Whitman's endless ads, in contrast, simply annoyed many Californians.

One result was to make it all but impossible to determine exactly how much was spent by independent groups on the 2008 and 2010 elections. Critics claimed that 501(c)4s were being used illegally. The FEC has never ruled on their validity, however. Like the 527 organizations, 501(c)4 groups were eclipsed by super PACs in 2011–2012, but they continue to be a valuable tool for those donors who prefer to conceal their political contributions. For the top independent committees contributing to federal candidates in 2011–2012, see Table 9–1 on the following page.

Presidential Candidate Committees. Despite the limits on contributions to candidate committees, these organizations continued to collect large sums. The committees of

Table 9-1 ▸ The Twenty Top Groups Making Independent Expenditures during the 2011–2012 Cycle

Independent expenditures only. Some groups, such as the party committees, have designated only a small part of their total fundraising as independent expenditures.

Committee	Affiliation	Raised by October 2012	Type	Disclosure of Contributors
American Crossroads & Crossroads GPS	Republican	$129,099,398	Super PAC, 501c	partial
Restore Our Future	Mitt Romney	$117,405,715	Super PAC	full
National Republican Congressional Committee	Republican	$57,052,468	Party committee	full
Priorities USA Action	Barack Obama	$56,816,026	Super PAC	partial
Democratic Congressional Campaign Committee	Democratic	$46,351,273	Party committee	full
Democratic Senatorial Campaign Committee	Democratic	$42,272,748	Party committee	full
Americans for Prosperity	Koch brothers (conservative)	$30,800,720	501c	none
Republican National Committee	Republican	$29,196,231	Party committee	full
US Chamber of Commerce	business	$28,873,817	501c	none
Service Employees International Union	labor	$28,069,574	Super PAC, 527S	full
Majority PAC	Senate Democrats	$27,114,691	Super PAC	full
National Republican Senatorial Committee	Republican	$21,537,108	Party committee	full
House Majority PAC	Democratic	$21,377,797	Super PAC	full
Winning Our Future	Newt Gingrich	$17,002,762	Super PAC	full
Club for Growth	anti-tax	$15,781,250	Super PAC, 501c	partial
American Federation of State, County & Municipal Employees	labor	$12,002,066	501c	full
FreedomWorks	Dick Armey (conservative)	$11,858,959	Super PAC	partial
Americans for Job Security	conservative	$11,387,275	501c	no
Americans for Tax Reform	anti-tax	$11,225,018	501c	no
American Future Fund	conservative	$10,113,905	501c	no

Source: Center for Responsive Politics.

major-party nominees, such as Mitt Romney and Barack Obama, were able to amass hundreds of millions of dollars, often from relatively small contributions.

Candidate committees are much more generously funded than in the past. From 1976 through 2004, most presidential candidates relied on a system of public funding financed by a checkoff on federal income tax forms. This system provided funds to match what a candidate could raise during the primary season. During the general election campaign, the system would pay for a candidate's entire campaign. Publicly funded candidates, however, could not raise funds independently for the general election or exceed the program's overall spending limits.

The system began to break down after 2000, when many candidates rejected public support during the primaries in the belief that they could raise larger sums privately. In 2008, Barack Obama became the first candidate since the program was founded to opt out of federal funding for the general elections as well. By 2012, the public financing system was essentially out of business. None of the major candidates in either party was willing to use it. Public funds continued to be available to support the parties' national conventions, but in 2012 Congress revoked funding for conventions in future election years.

During 2011 and 2012, a division of effort developed between candidate committees and outside organizations such as super PACs. Candidate committees would run positive advertisements that portrayed the candidate to best advantage. Independent organizations would run negative ads aimed at tearing down the candidate's opponents. The belief was that because super PACs and other groups were technically independent, a candidate could deny responsibility for the negative campaign. Over time, however, such denials grew less and less credible.

Running for President: The Longest Campaign

■ Learning Outcome 3: **Summarize the process of choosing a president of the United States.**

The American presidential election is the culmination of two different campaigns: the presidential primary campaign and the general election campaign following the party's national convention. Traditionally, both the primary campaigns and the final campaigns take place during the first ten months of an election year. Increasingly, though, the states are holding their primaries earlier in the year, which has motivated the candidates to begin their campaigns earlier as well. Indeed, candidates in the 2012 presidential races began campaigning in early 2011, thus launching one of the longest presidential campaigns to date in U.S. history.

Primary elections were first mandated in 1904 in Wisconsin for state officials. The purpose of the primary was to open the nomination process to ordinary party members and to weaken the influence of party bosses. Until 1968, however, there were fewer than twenty primary elections for the presidency. They were often *"beauty contests,"* in which the candidates competed for popular votes but the results did not control the selection of delegates to the national convention. National conventions were meetings of the party elite—legislators, mayors, county chairpersons, and loyal party workers—who were mostly appointed to their delegations. The leaders of large blocs of delegates could direct their delegates to support a favorite candidate.

did you know?

In 1910, Oregon established the first presidential primary in which elected delegates were pledged to vote for specific candidates, and although New Hampshire began using primary elections in 1916, it elected only unpledged delegates until 1952.

Reforming the Primaries

In recent decades, the character of the primary process and the makeup of the national convention have changed dramatically. The public, rather than party elites, now generally controls the nomination process. After the disruptive riots outside the doors of the 1968 Democratic convention in Chicago, many party leaders pushed for serious reforms of the convention system.

2012 elections

FINANCING THE PRESIDENTIAL RACES

In 2012, major contributions to the Democratic and Republican presidential campaigns came from very different kinds of people. Mitt Romney did much better than Barack Obama in winning large donations from wealthier individuals. Obama bested Romney in smaller contributions.

An even more interesting distinction appears when we look at the organizations that employ major presidential donors. The five institutions whose employees were most generous to Obama were, in order, the University of California, Microsoft, Google, Harvard, and the federal government itself. The five equivalent Republican groups were Goldman Sachs, Bank of America, Morgan Stanley, JPMorgan Chase, and the Credit Suisse Group—five banks.

Federal employees have an obvious interest in a Democratic administration. The reason that the other four groups gave to Obama probably has more to do with the kinds of people who work at the University of California or Microsoft than any other factor. These institutions attract liberal employees. The bank employees are a more interesting case. In 2008, these people were quite generous to Obama. What changed their minds was the Dodd-Frank financial regulation law, passed in 2010. The financial industry was dead-set against this measure, and Romney promised to get it repealed.

The Democratic National Committee appointed a special commission to study the problems of the primary system. During the next several years, the group—called the McGovern-Fraser Commission—formulated new rules for delegate selection that had to be followed by state Democratic parties beginning in 1972.

The reforms instituted by the Democratic Party, which were mostly imitated by the Republicans, revolutionized the nomination process for the presidency. The most important changes require that a majority of the convention delegates be elected by the voters in primary elections, in caucuses held by local parties, or at state conventions. Delegates are normally pledged to a particular candidate, although the pledge is not always formally binding at the convention. The delegation from each state must also include a proportion of women, younger party members, and representatives of the minority groups within the party. At first, almost no special privileges were given to party leaders and elected party officials, such as senators and governors. In 1984, however, many of these individuals returned to the Democratic convention as **superdelegates.**

Superdelegate
A party leader or elected official who is given the right to vote at the party's national convention. Superdelegates are not selected at the state level.

Primaries and Caucuses

Various types of primaries are used by the states. One notable difference is between proportional and winner-take-all primaries. Another important consideration is whether independent voters can take part in a primary. Some states also use caucuses and conventions to choose candidates for various offices.

Direct Primary
A primary election in which voters decide party nominations by voting directly for candidates.

Indirect Primary
A primary election in which voters choose convention delegates, and the delegates determine the party's candidate in the general election.

Direct and Indirect Primaries. A **direct primary** is one in which voters decide party nominations by voting directly for candidates. In an **indirect primary,** voters instead choose convention delegates, and the delegates determine the party's candidate in the general election. Delegates may be pledged to a particular candidate. Indirect primaries are used almost exclusively in presidential elections. Most candidates in state and local elections are chosen by direct primaries.

Proportional and Winner-Take-All Primaries. Most primaries are *winner-take-all. Proportional* primaries are used mostly to elect delegates to the national conventions of the two major parties—delegates who are pledged to one or another candidate for president. Under the proportional system, if one candidate for president wins 40 percent of the vote in a primary, that candidate receives about 40 percent of the pledged delegates.

In recent years, the Democrats have used the proportional system for all of their presidential primaries and caucuses. For the most part, the Republicans have relied on the winner-take-all principle. In 2012, however, the Republican National Committee ruled that any state choosing national convention delegates before April 1 would be required to use the proportional system. States voting later could adopt whatever method they preferred. A number of early-voting states, such as Arizona and Florida, refused to follow the rules and used winner-take-all systems. Still, a majority of the states now allocate Republican National Convention delegates on a proportional basis.

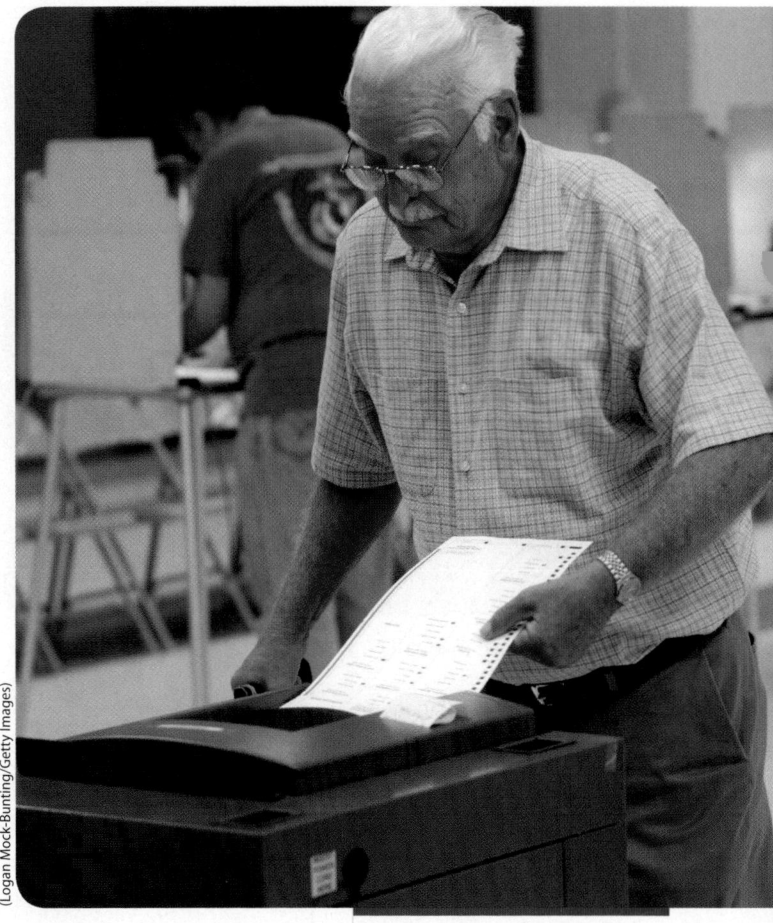

(Logan Mock-Bunting/Getty Images)

This voter submits his primary election ballot at the Codington Elementary School in Wilmington, North Carolina. Do you think fewer people vote in primary elections than in general elections?

Closed Primary. A closed primary is one of several types of primaries distinguished by how independent voters are handled. In a **closed primary,** only declared members of a party can vote in that party's primary. In other words, voters must declare their party affiliation, either when they register to vote or at the primary election. In a closed-primary system, voters cannot cross over into the other party's primary in order to nominate the weakest candidate of the opposing party or to affect the ideological direction of that party.

Open Primary. In an **open primary,** any voter can vote in either party's primary without declaring a party affiliation. Basically, the voter makes the choice in the privacy of the voting booth. The voter must, however, choose one party's list from which to select candidates.

Closed Primary
A type of primary in which the voter is limited to choosing candidates of the party of which he or she is a member.

Open Primary
A primary in which any registered voter can vote (but must vote for candidates of only one party).

Blanket Primary. A *blanket primary* is one in which the voter can vote for candidates of more than one party. Until 2000, a few states, including Alaska, California, and Washington, had blanket primaries. In 2000, however, the United States Supreme Court abolished the system. The Court ruled that the blanket primary violated political parties' First Amendment right of association. Because the nominees represent the party, party members—not the general electorate—should have the right to choose the party's nominee.[8]

Run-Off Primary. Some states have a two-primary system. If no candidate receives a majority of the votes in the first primary, the top two candidates must compete in another primary, called a *run-off primary.*

The "Top-Two" Primary. Louisiana has long used a special type of primary for filling some offices. Under the system, all candidates appear on a single ballot. A party cannot prevent a candidate from appearing on the primary ballot—an insurgent Republican, for

did you know?

When David Leroy Gatchell changed his middle name to None of the Above and ran for the U.S. Senate representing Tennessee, a court ruled that he could not use his middle name on the ballot.

8. *California Democratic Party v. Jones,* 530 U.S. 567 (2000).

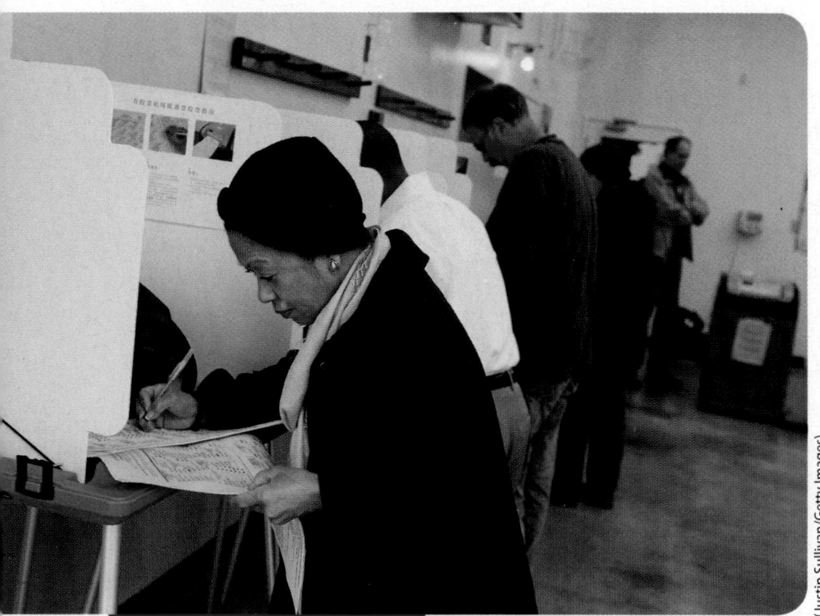
(Justin Sullivan/Getty Images)

These voters are manually filling out their primary election ballots in Oakland, California. What offices are at issue during such elections?

example, could appear on the ballot alongside the party-supported Republican. The two candidates receiving the most votes, regardless of party, then move on to the general election. Following the abolition of the blanket primary, the state of Washington adopted this system. In 2008, the United States Supreme Court upheld the new plan.[9] In 2010, Californians voted to use the type of primary, beginning in 2012. For more detail on this type of primary, see the *What If* . . . feature in Chapter 8 on page 246.

Conventions. While primary elections are the most common way in which a party's candidates are selected, there are other procedures in use. State party conventions may nominate candidates for various offices. Those who attend meetings below the statewide level may participate in nominating candidates as well. The most famous of such meetings are the caucuses that help nominate a party's candidate for president of the United States.

Caucus
A meeting of party members to select candidates and propose policies.

Caucuses. In 2012, sixteen states relied at least in part on **caucuses** for choosing delegates to the Republican and Democratic national conventions. Some of these states used a combined system. Strictly speaking, the caucus system is actually a caucus/convention system. In North Dakota, for example, local citizens, who need not be registered as party members, gather in party meetings, called caucuses, at the precinct level. They choose delegates to district conventions. The district conventions elect delegates to the state convention, and the state convention actually chooses the delegates to the national convention. The national delegates, however, are pledged to reflect the presidential preferences that voters expressed at the caucus level.

Front-Loading the Primaries

When politicians and potential presidential candidates realized that winning as many primary elections as possible guaranteed them the party's nomination for president, their tactics changed dramatically. Candidates began to concentrate on building organizations in states that held early, important primary elections. By the 1970s, candidates recognized that winning early contests, such as the Iowa caucuses and the New Hampshire primary election (both now held in January), meant that the media instantly would label the winner as the **front-runner,** thus increasing the candidate's media exposure and escalating the pace of contributions to his or her campaign.

Front-Runner
The presidential candidate who appears to be ahead at a given time in the primary season.

Front-Loading
The practice of moving presidential primary elections to the early part of the campaign to maximize the impact of these primaries on the nomination.

The Rush to Be First. The state political parties began to see that early primaries had a much greater effect on the outcome of the presidential contest than did later ones. Accordingly, in successive presidential elections, more and more states moved their primaries into the first months of the year, a process known as **front-loading** the primaries. One result was a series of "Super Tuesdays," when multiple states held simultaneous primaries. In 2008, twenty-four states held their primaries or caucuses on February 5, making it the largest Super Tuesday ever. So many states were in play on February 5 that it was impossible for the candidates to campaign strongly in all of them. Rather than winning more attention, many Super Tuesday states found that they were ignored. Because the Democratic race was not decided until the very end of the process in June, the later

9. *Washington State Grange v. Washington State Republican Party,* 552 U.S. 442 (2008).

Democratic primaries, such as those in Indiana, North Carolina, Ohio, Pennsylvania, and Texas, were hotly contested.

Front-loading, in short, had become counterproductive. As a result, in 2012 Super Tuesday was held on March 6, a month later than in 2008. Ten states participated instead of twenty-four.

Social Media IN POLITICS

One of the best people to follow on Twitter for information on elections is *New York Times* blogger Nate Silver. Find him at "fivethirtyeight," the name of his blog.

The National Parties Seek to Regain Control. The process of front-loading the primaries alarmed many observers, who feared that a front-runner might wrap up the nomination before voters were able to make a thorough assessment of the candidates. In the many months between the early primaries and the general election, the voters might come to regret their decision.

In response, the national Democratic and Republican parties took steps to regain control of the primary schedule. Such steps included a ban on primaries or caucuses held before a specified date. States would need special permission to choose delegates before that date. Traditional lead-off states such as Iowa and New Hampshire were allowed to go first, and a limited number of other states also received such permission.

Not all states were willing to follow the official schedule, however. In principle, the national parties had all the power they needed to enforce the rules—they could cut the number of delegates a state was authorized to send to the national convention, or even refuse to seat a state delegation altogether. The two national committees found it politically difficult to impose tough punishments, however. In both 2008 and 2012, several states succeeded in breaking the rules without penalty.

Credentials Committee
A committee used by political parties at their national conventions to determine which delegates may participate. The committee inspects the claim of each prospective delegate to be seated as a legitimate representative of his or her state.

On to the National Convention

Presidential candidates have been nominated by the convention method in every election since 1832. Extra delegates are allowed from states that had voting majorities for the party in the preceding elections. Parties also accept delegates from the District of Columbia, the territories, and U.S. citizens living abroad.

Seating the Delegates. At the convention, each political party uses a **credentials committee** to determine which delegates may participate. Controversy may arise when rival groups claim to be the official party organization. For example, the Mississippi Democratic Party split in 1964 at the height of the civil rights movement, and two sets of delegates were selected. After much debate, the credentials committee seated the mixed-race, pro–civil rights delegation and excluded those who represented the traditional "white" party.

Convention Activities. Most delegates arrive at the convention committed to a presidential candidate. No convention since 1952 has required more than one ballot to choose a nominee. Conventions normally last four days. On each night, featured speakers seek to rally the party faithful and to draw in uncommitted voters who are watching on television. On day three, the vice-presidential nominee is featured. On day four, the presidential candidate gives an acceptance speech. The national networks limit their coverage to the major speeches, but several cable networks and Internet sites provide gavel-to-gavel coverage.

At the 2012 Republican convention, Mitt Romney attempted to present himself as compassionate, in contrast to descriptions offered by Democrats. Judging from the polls, he was not entirely successful. Barack Obama, in contrast, received an unexpected lift from his convention. In a speech, former president Bill Clinton made a better case for Obama than the president was able to make for himself.

(Roger L. Wollenberg/UPI/Landov)

Massachusetts governor Deval Patrick was a keynote speaker at the 2008 Democratic National Convention in Denver, Colorado.

did you know?

The 1976 Republican National Convention, where incumbent president Gerald Ford narrowly defeated former California governor Ronald Reagan, was the last major-party convention at which the party's nominee was not decided before the convention began.

Elector
A member of the electoral college, which selects the president and vice president. Each state's electors are chosen in each presidential election year according to state laws.

The Electoral College

Some people who vote for the president and vice president think that they are voting directly for a candidate. In actuality, they are voting for **electors** who will cast their ballots in the electoral college. Article II, Section 1, of the Constitution outlines in detail the method of choosing electors for president and vice president. The framers of the Constitution did not want the president and vice president to be selected by the "excitable masses." Rather, they wished the choice to be made by a few supposedly dispassionate, reasonable men (but not women).

The Choice of Electors. Electors are selected during each presidential election year. The selection is governed by state laws. After the national party convention, the electors are pledged to the candidates chosen. Each state's number of electors equals that state's number of senators (two) plus its number of representatives. The total number of electors today is 538, equal to 100 senators, 435 members of the House, and 3 electors for the District of Columbia. (The Twenty-third Amendment, ratified in 1961, added electors for the District of Columbia.)

The Electors' Commitment. A plurality of voters in a state chooses a slate of electors (except in Maine and Nebraska, where electoral votes are partly based on congressional districts). Those electors are pledged to cast their ballots on the first Monday after the second Wednesday in December in the state capital for the presidential and vice-presidential candidates of their party. The Constitution does not, however, *require* the electors to cast their ballots for the candidates of their party, and on rare occasions so-called *faithless electors* have voted for a candidate to whom they were not pledged.

The ballots are counted and certified before a joint session of Congress early in January. The candidates who receive a majority (270) of the electoral votes are certified as president-elect and vice president-elect. According to the Constitution, if no candidate receives a majority of the electoral votes, the election of the president is decided in the House from among the candidates with the three highest numbers of votes, with each state having one vote (decided by a plurality of each state delegation). The selection of the vice president is determined by the Senate in a choice between the two candidates with the most votes, each senator having one vote. The House was required to choose the president in 1801 (Thomas Jefferson) and again in 1825 (John Quincy Adams).

South Carolina senator Lindsey Graham speaks at the 2008 Republican National Convention in St. Paul, Minnesota. What types of individuals are normally invited to speak at national party conventions?

(AP Photo/Ron Edmonds)

Problems with the Electoral College System. It is possible for a candidate to become president without obtaining a majority of the popular vote. There have been many presidents in our history who did not win a majority of the popular vote, including Abraham Lincoln, Woodrow Wilson, Harry Truman, John F. Kennedy, Richard Nixon (in 1968), Bill Clinton, and George W. Bush (in 2000). Such an event becomes more likely when there are important third-party candidates.

Perhaps more distressing is the possibility of a candidate's being elected when an opposing candidate receives a plurality of the popular vote. This has occurred on four occasions—in the elections of John Quincy Adams in 1824, Rutherford B. Hayes in 1876, Benjamin Harrison in 1888, and George W. Bush in 2000. All of these candidates won elections in which an opponent received more popular votes than they did. Such results have led to calls for replacing the electoral college with a popular-vote system. We described one such system in the *What If . . .* feature in Chapter 2 on page 32.

How Are Elections Conducted?

■ Learning Outcome 4:
Explain the mechanisms through which voting takes place on Election Day.

The United States uses the **Australian ballot**—a secret ballot that is prepared, distributed, and counted by government officials at public expense. Since 1888, all states have used the Australian ballot. Before that, many states used the alternatives of oral voting or differently colored ballots prepared by the parties. Obviously, knowing which way a person was voting made it easy to apply pressure on the person to change his or her vote, and vote buying was common.

Australian Ballot
A secret ballot prepared, distributed, and tabulated by government officials at public expense. Since 1888, all states have used the Australian ballot rather than an open, public ballot.

Office-Block and Party-Column Ballots

Two types of Australian ballots are used in the United States in general elections. The first, called an **office-block ballot,** or sometimes a **Massachusetts ballot,** groups all the candidates for a particular elective office under the title of that office. Parties dislike the office-block ballot because it places more emphasis on the office than on the party. It discourages straight-ticket voting and encourages split-ticket voting. Most states now use this type of ballot.

A **party-column ballot** is a form of general election ballot in which all of a party's candidates are arranged in one column under the party's label and symbol. It is also called an **Indiana ballot.** In some states, it allows voters to vote for all of a party's candidates for local, state, and national offices by simply marking a single "X" or by pulling a single lever. Because it encourages straight-ticket voting, the two major parties favor this form. When a party has an exceptionally strong presidential or gubernatorial candidate to head the ticket, the use of the party-column ballot increases the **coattail effect** (the influence of a popular candidate on the success of other candidates on the same party ticket).

Office-Block, or Massachusetts, Ballot
A form of general election ballot in which candidates for elective office are grouped together under the title of each office. It emphasizes voting for the office and the individual candidate, rather than for the party.

Party-Column, or Indiana, Ballot
A form of general election ballot in which all of a party's candidates for elective office are arranged in one column under the party's label and symbol. It emphasizes voting for the party, rather than for the office or individual.

Coattail Effect
The influence of a popular candidate on the success of other candidates on the same party ticket.

Voting by Mail

Voting by mail has been accepted for absentee ballots for many decades (for example, for individuals who are doing business away from home or for members of the armed forces). Recently, several states have offered mail ballots to all of their voters. The rationale for using the mail ballot is to make voting easier for the voters and increase turnout. Oregon has gone one step further: since 1998, that state has employed postal ballots exclusively, and there are no polling places. (Voters who do not prepare their ballot in time for the U.S. Postal Service to deliver it can drop off their ballots at drop boxes on Election Day.) In addition, most counties in Washington State now use mail ballots exclusively. By national standards, voter turnout in these two states has been high, but not exceptionally so.

Voting Fraud and Mistakes

Voting fraud is something regularly suspected but seldom proved. Voting in the 1800s, when secret ballots were rare and people had a cavalier attitude toward the open buying of votes, was probably much more conducive to fraud than modern elections are. Still, some observers claim that the potential for voting fraud is high in many states, particularly through the use of phony voter registrations and absentee ballots. Other observers claim, however, that errors due to fraud are trivial in number and that a few mistakes are inevitable in a system involving millions of voters. These people argue that an excessive concern with voting fraud makes it harder for minorities and poor people to vote.

Voter ID Requirements. In recent years, many states have adopted laws requiring enhanced proof of identity before voters can cast their ballots. Indiana imposed the nation's toughest voter identification (ID) law in 2005. Indiana legislators claimed that they were motivated by a desire to prevent voting fraud, but critics argued that they were really trying to suppress voter turnout among minority group members and the poor—the

did you know?

When President Grover Cleveland lost the election of 1888, his wife told the White House staff to change nothing because the couple would be back in four years—and she was right.

(AP Photo/Darron Cummings)

In February 2012, Charlie White, Indiana's secretary of state and chief elections official, was convicted of six felony counts including one for vote fraud.

individuals least likely to possess adequate identification. In 2008, the United States Supreme Court upheld the Indiana voter ID law.[10]

In the wake of the Court's ruling, dozens of states moved to tighten voter ID requirements. By the spring of 2012, thirty-two states had enacted voter ID requirements, and sixteen of these states mandated photo IDs. Not all of these laws were actually in effect, however. In Wisconsin, a state court held that the new law violated the state constitution. Also, most southern states with a history of racial discrimination must obtain pre-clearance from the federal government for any significant change to their voting laws and procedures. The Department of Justice has refused to pre-clear voter ID laws in South Carolina and Texas on the ground that the laws impose a greater burden on minority voters than on whites.

Republicans provided almost all of the support for the new ID laws, which were often based on model legislation from the American Legislative Exchange Council. (We described this group in *Politics and the States* in Chapter 7 on page 232.) More than 239,000 registered voters in South Carolina lacked the identification needed to vote under that state's proposed law. While a state-issued photo ID card is technically free, getting it requires a birth certificate, passport, or other documentation, which can be troublesome to obtain.

Reforming the Voting Process. In Florida in 2000, serious problems with the punch-card voting system may have determined the outcome of the presidential election. In response, Congress enacted the Help America Vote Act (HAVA) of 2002. The act provided funds to the states to help them implement a number of reforms. Among other things, the states were asked to replace outdated voting equipment with newer electronic voting systems. Critics of HAVA pointed out that by urging the adoption of electronic voting equipment, the act may have traded old problems for newer, more complicated ones.

These problems became particularly apparent during the 2006 midterm elections, when more than twenty-five states reported trouble at the polls on Election Day. Many of the problems involved failures in the new voting machines. In one Florida county, it was estimated that nearly eighteen thousand votes may have gone unrecorded by electronic voting machines, thus changing the outcome of a congressional election.

In 2008, therefore, many localities—including almost the entire state of California—retreated to using old-fashioned paper ballots. These ballots slowed the vote count, but they largely eliminated the problems with voting system errors that had plagued recent elections.

In 2010 and 2012, voters reported isolated problems with voting systems, but the issue was not as serious as in earlier years. A growing problem that may require attention was voter intimidation and misinformation. Voters in some minority neighborhoods, for example, purportedly were told by "shadowy" groups that they would face legal trouble if they tried to vote.

Sometimes, ballots are disputed and must be recounted. This occurred after the votes were tallied for the U.S. senatorial candidates in Minnesota in 2008. Is there any way to reform the voting process to avoid such disputes?

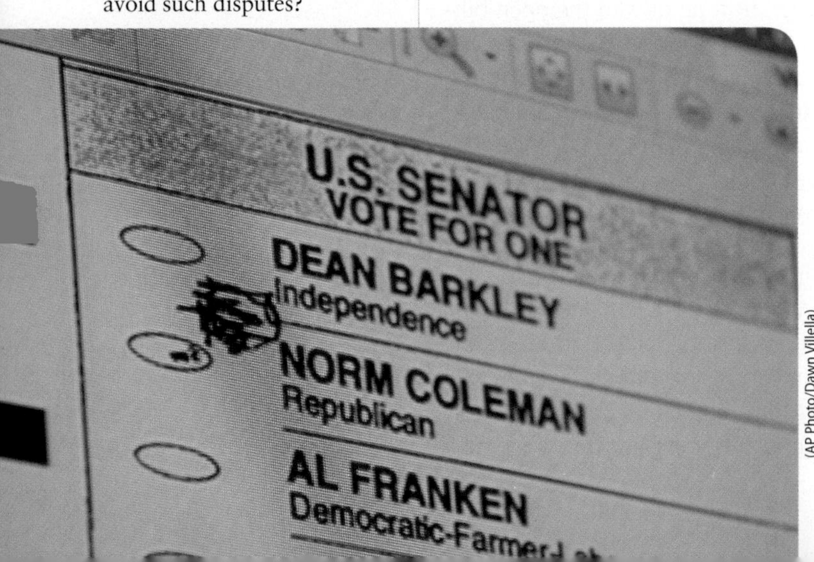

(AP Photo/Dawn Villella)

10. *Crawford v. Marion County Election Board,* 553 U.S. 181 (2008).

Turning Out to Vote

■ Learning Outcome 5: **Discuss voter turnout in the United States and the types of people most likely to vote.**

In 2010, the number of Americans eligible to vote was about 218.05 million people. Of that number, about 90.5 million, or 41.7 percent of the eligible population, actually cast a ballot. When voter turnout is this low, it means, among other things, that the winner of a close election may be voted in by only about one-fifth of those eligible to vote.

Figure 9–2 below shows **voter turnout** for presidential and congressional elections from 1910 to 2012. Each of the peaks in the figure represents voter turnout in a presidential election. Thus, we can also see that turnout for congressional elections is influenced greatly by whether there is a presidential election in the same year. Whereas voter turnout during the presidential elections of 2012 was 60 percent, it was, as noted, only 41.7 percent in the **midterm elections** of 2010.

Voter Turnout
The percentage of citizens taking part in the election process; the number of eligible voters that actually "turn out" on election day to cast their ballots.

Midterm Elections
National elections in which candidates for president are not on the ballot. In midterm elections, voters choose all members of the U.S. House of Representatives and one-third of the members of the U.S. Senate.

The same is true at the state level. When there is a race for governor, more voters participate both in the general election for governor and in the election for state representatives. Voter participation rates in gubernatorial elections are also greater in presidential election years. The average turnout in state elections is about 14 percentage points higher when a presidential election is held.

Now consider local elections. In races for mayor, city council, county auditor, and the like, it is fairly common for only 25 percent or less of the electorate to vote. Is something amiss here? It would seem that people should be more likely to vote in elections that directly affect them. At the local level, each person's vote counts more (because there are fewer voters). Furthermore, the issues—crime control, school bonds, sewer bonds, and the like—touch the immediate interests of the voters. In reality, however, potential voters are most interested in national elections when a presidential choice is involved. Otherwise, voter participation in our representative government is very low (and, as we have seen, it is not overwhelmingly high even in presidential elections).

did you know?
Computer software now exists that can identify likely voters and likely campaign donors by town, neighborhood, and street.

The Effect of Low Voter Turnout

There are two schools of thought concerning low voter turnout. Some view low voter participation as a threat to representative democratic government. Too few individuals are deciding who wields political power in society. In addition, low voter participation

Figure 9–2 ▸ Voter Turnout for Presidential and Midterm Elections, 1910–2012

The peaks represent voter turnout in presidential election years; the troughs represent voter turnout in off-presidential election years.

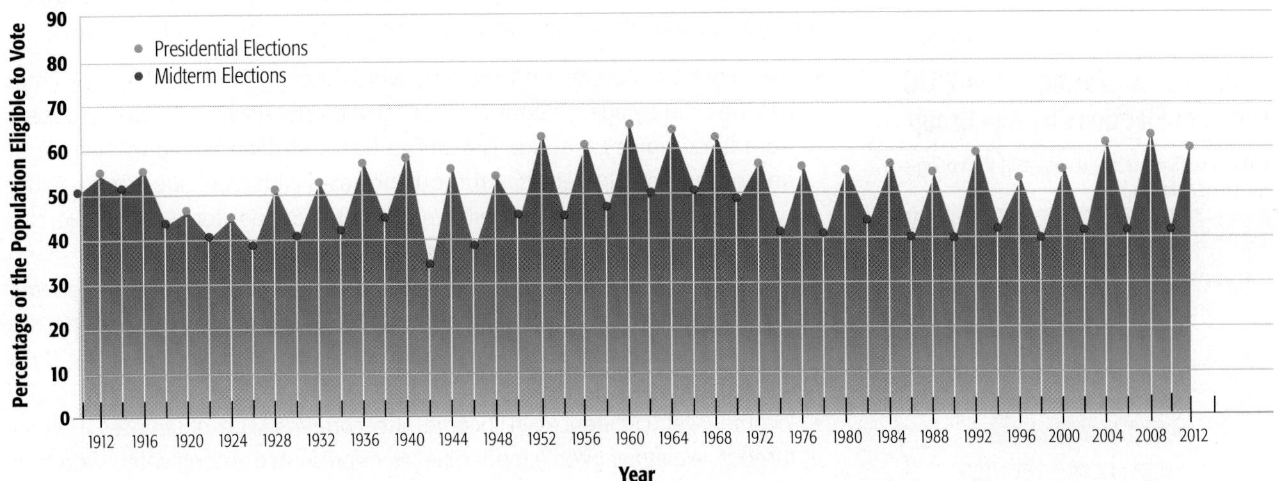

Note: Prior to 1948, the voting-age population is used as a proxy for the population eligible to vote.

Sources: Historical Data Archive, Inter-university Consortium for Political and Social Research; Michael P. McDonald and Samuel L. Popkin, "The Myth of the Vanishing Voter," *American Political Science Review*, Vol. 95, No. 4 (December 2001), p. 966, and the United States Elections Project.

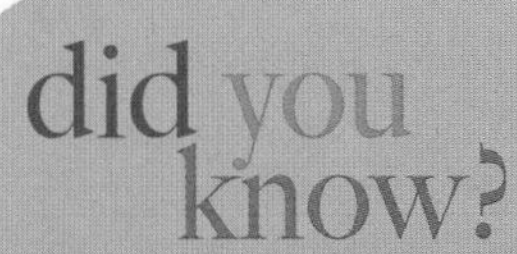

Noncitizens were allowed to vote in some states until the early 1920s.

presumably signals apathy about the political system in general. It also may signal that potential voters simply do not want to take the time to learn about the issues.

Others are less concerned about low voter participation. They contend that low voter participation simply indicates more satisfaction with the status quo. Also, they believe that representative democracy is a reality even if a very small percentage of eligible voters vote. If everyone who does not vote thinks that the outcome of the election will accord with his or her own desires, then representative democracy is working. The nonvoters are obtaining the type of government—with the type of people running it—that they want to have anyway.

Is Voter Turnout Declining?

During the last decades of the twentieth century, the media regularly voiced concern that voter turnout was declining. Indeed, Figure 9–2 on the previous page shows relatively low voter turnout from 1972 through 2002—though turnout has gone back up in the past few elections. Pundits have blamed the low turnout on negative campaigning and broad public cynicism about the political process. But is voter turnout actually as low as it seems?

Voting-Age Population The number of people of voting age living in the country at a given time, regardless of whether they have the right to vote.

One problem with widely used measurements of voter turnout is that they compare the number of people who actually vote with the **voting-age population,** not the population of *eligible voters.* These figures are not the same. The figure for the voting-age population includes felons and former felons who have lost the right to vote. Above all, it includes new immigrants who are not yet citizens. Finally, it does not include Americans living abroad, who can cast absentee ballots.

In 2010, the measured voting-age population included 3.1 million ineligible felons and former felons, and an estimated 19.6 million noncitizens. It did not include 5.0 million Americans living abroad. The voting-age population in 2010 was 235.8 million people. The **vote-eligible population,** however, was only 218.05 million. Using the voting-age population to calculate national turnout would reduce the turnout percentage from 41.7 to 38.2 percent—a substantial error.

Vote-Eligible Population The number of people who, at a given time, enjoy the right to vote in national elections.

As you learned in Chapter 5, the United States has experienced high rates of immigration in recent decades. The very low voter turnout reported in many sources after 1972 may have been a function of the increasing size of the ineligible population, chiefly due to immigration.

Factors Influencing Who Votes

A clear association exists between voter participation and the following characteristics: age, educational attainment, income level, minority status, and ideology.

Table 9–2 ▸ Voting in the 2010 Midterm Elections by Age Group

Turnout is given as a percentage of the voting-age citizen population.

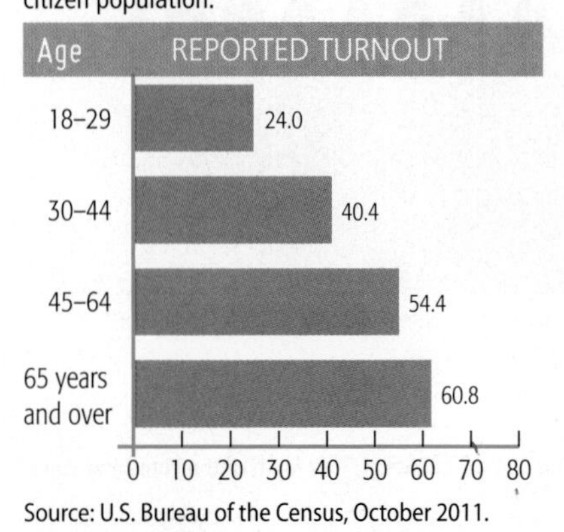

Source: U.S. Bureau of the Census, October 2011.

- *Age.* Look at Table 9–2 on the left, which shows the breakdown of voter participation by age group for the 2010 midterm elections. It would appear from these figures that age is a strong factor in determining voter turnout on Election Day. The reported turnout increases with older age groups. Older voters are more settled in their lives, are already registered, and have had more time to experience voting as an expected activity.
- *Educational attainment.* Education also influences voter turnout. In general, the more education you have, the more likely you are to vote. This pattern is clearly evident in the 2010 election results, as you can see in Table 9–3 on the facing page.
- *Income level.* Differences in income also correlate with differences in voter turnout. Wealthier people tend to be overrepresented among voters who turn out on Election Day. In recent presidential elections, voter turnout for those with the highest annual family incomes has approached three times the turnout of those with the lowest annual family incomes.

- *Minority status.* African Americans and Hispanics traditionally have not turned out to vote at the same rate as non-Hispanic whites. Minority group members, however, tend to have less education and lower incomes than non-Hispanic whites. On average, minority group members are younger. Many Latinos are immigrants who have not yet obtained citizenship. If, however, we correct for such factors as socioeconomic status, age, citizenship, and loss of the right to vote due to a felony conviction, the difference in turnout due to minority status largely disappears.
- *Ideology.* Depending on the issues at stake in a particular election year, political ideology may have a large impact on turnout. Either Republicans or Democrats may be discouraged from voting in a year that looks especially good for the other party. In 2008, for example, turnout among conservatives was relatively low for a presidential election year. In contrast, conservatives voted in very large numbers in 2010, while more liberal voters, especially young people, often stayed home.

Table 9–3 ▸ Voting in the 2010 Midterm Elections by Education Level

Turnout is given as a percentage of the voting-age citizen population.

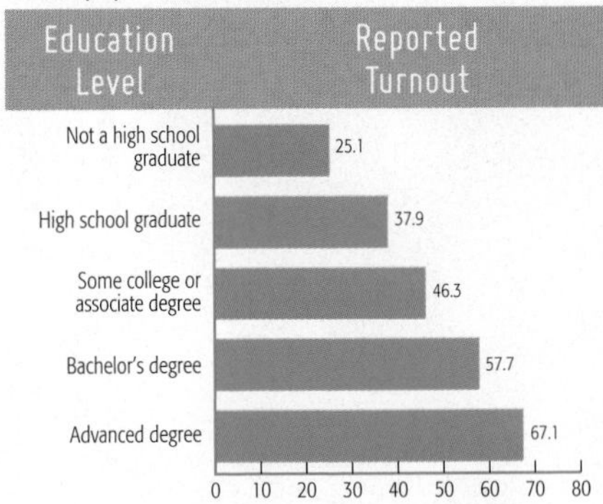

Education Level	Reported Turnout
Not a high school graduate	25.1
High school graduate	37.9
Some college or associate degree	46.3
Bachelor's degree	57.7
Advanced degree	67.1

Source: U.S. Bureau of the Census, October 2011.

Legal Restrictions on Voting

Legal restrictions on voter registration have existed since the founding of our nation. Most groups in the United States have been concerned with the suffrage (the right to vote, also called the franchise) issue at one time or another. In colonial times, only white males who owned property with a certain minimum value were eligible to vote, leaving more Americans ineligible to take part in elections than were eligible.

Property Requirements. Many government functions concern property rights and the distribution of income and wealth, and some of the founders of our nation believed it was appropriate that only people who had an interest in property should vote on these issues. The idea of extending the vote to all citizens was, according to Charles Pinckney, a South Carolina delegate to the Constitutional Convention, merely "theoretical nonsense."

The writers of the Constitution allowed the states to decide who should vote. Thus, women were allowed to vote in Wyoming in 1870 but not in the entire nation until the Nineteenth Amendment was ratified in 1920. By about 1850, most white adult males in nearly all the states could vote without any property qualification. North Carolina was the last state to eliminate its property test for voting—in 1856.

Further Extensions of the Franchise. Extension of the franchise to black males occurred with the passage of the Fifteenth Amendment in 1870. This enfranchisement was short lived, however, as the "redemption" of the South by white racists had rolled back those gains by the end of the century. As discussed in Chapter 5, it was not until the 1960s that African Americans, both male and female, were able to participate in the electoral process in all states. Women received full national voting rights with the Nineteenth Amendment in 1920. The most recent extension of the franchise occurred when the voting age was reduced to eighteen by the Twenty-sixth Amendment in 1971. One result of lowering the voting age was to depress voter turnout beginning in 1972, as you can see in Figure 9–2 on page 299. Young people are less likely to vote than older citizens.

Is the Franchise Still Too Restrictive? There continue to be certain classes of people who do not have the right to vote. These include noncitizens and, in most states, convicted felons who have been released from prison. They also include current prison inmates, election law violators, and people who are mentally incompetent. Also, no one under the age of eighteen can vote. A number of political activists have argued that some of these groups should be allowed to vote. Most other democracies do not prevent

(AP Photo/Wausau Daily Herald/Dan Young)

This would-be voter shows the pieces of identification that were not accepted in Wisconsin to allow her to register. Why weren't they considered sufficient?

convicts from voting after they have completed their sentences. In the 1800s, many states let noncitizen immigrants vote.

One discussion concerns the voting rights of convicted felons who are no longer in prison or on parole. Those who oppose letting these people vote contend that voting should be a privilege, not a right, and we should not want the types of people who commit felonies participating in decision making. Others believe that it is wrong to further penalize those who have paid their debt to society. These people argue that barring felons from the polls injures minority groups, because minorities make up a disproportionately large share of former prison inmates.

Current Eligibility and Registration Requirements. Voting generally requires **registration,** and to register, a person must satisfy the following voter qualifications, or legal requirements: (1) citizenship, (2) age (eighteen or older), and (3) residency—the duration varies widely from state to state and with types of elections. Since 1972, states cannot impose residency requirements of more than thirty days.

Registration
The entry of a person's name onto the list of registered voters for elections. To register, a person must meet certain legal requirements of age, citizenship, and residency.

Each state has different qualifications for voting and registration. In 1993, Congress passed the "motor voter" bill, which requires that states provide voter-registration materials when people receive or renew driver's licenses, that all states allow voters to register by mail, and that voter-registration forms be made available at a wider variety of public places and agencies. In general, a person must register well in advance of an election, although voters in the District of Columbia, Idaho, Iowa, Maine, Minnesota, Montana, New Hampshire, North Carolina, Wisconsin, and Wyoming are allowed to register up to, or even on, Election Day. North Dakota has no voter registration at all.

Some argue that registration requirements are responsible for much of the nonparticipation in our political process. There also is a partisan dimension to the debate over registration and nonvoting. Republicans generally fear that an expanded electorate would help to elect more Democrats—because more Democrats than Republicans are the kinds of persons who have trouble registering.[11]

Voter-Registration Drives. Given the registration system, voter-registration drives are a familiar part of the political landscape. In the year leading up to any presidential or midterm election, public-interest groups and political organizations fan out across the land to register new voters. Registration drives are particularly common on college campuses and in low-income neighborhoods, where large numbers of unregistered voters may be found.

Long seen as noncontroversial, voter-registration drives suddenly became a political issue in 2010, when Acorn, a community-organizing group, was accused of violating election laws in its campaigns. Conservatives claimed that Acorn posed a major threat to the integrity of the voting process. Liberals contended that the controversy was overblown. Still, Acorn was forced to dissolve in 2010. Many former members later organized new groups.

In 2011 and 2012, Republican-controlled legislatures in a number of states tightened the laws governing voter-registration drives. Florida adopted the most stringent of these laws. In that state, organizations conducting registration drives were required to hand in all new registrations within forty-eight hours on penalty of a $50 fine for each late form. No allowance was made for days when state offices are closed—thus effectively banning

11. According to a 2006 study of voting behavior by the Pew Research Center for People & the Press, of the approximately one-fifth of the U.S. voting-age population who are not registered to vote, 20 percent are Democrats and 14 percent are Republicans.

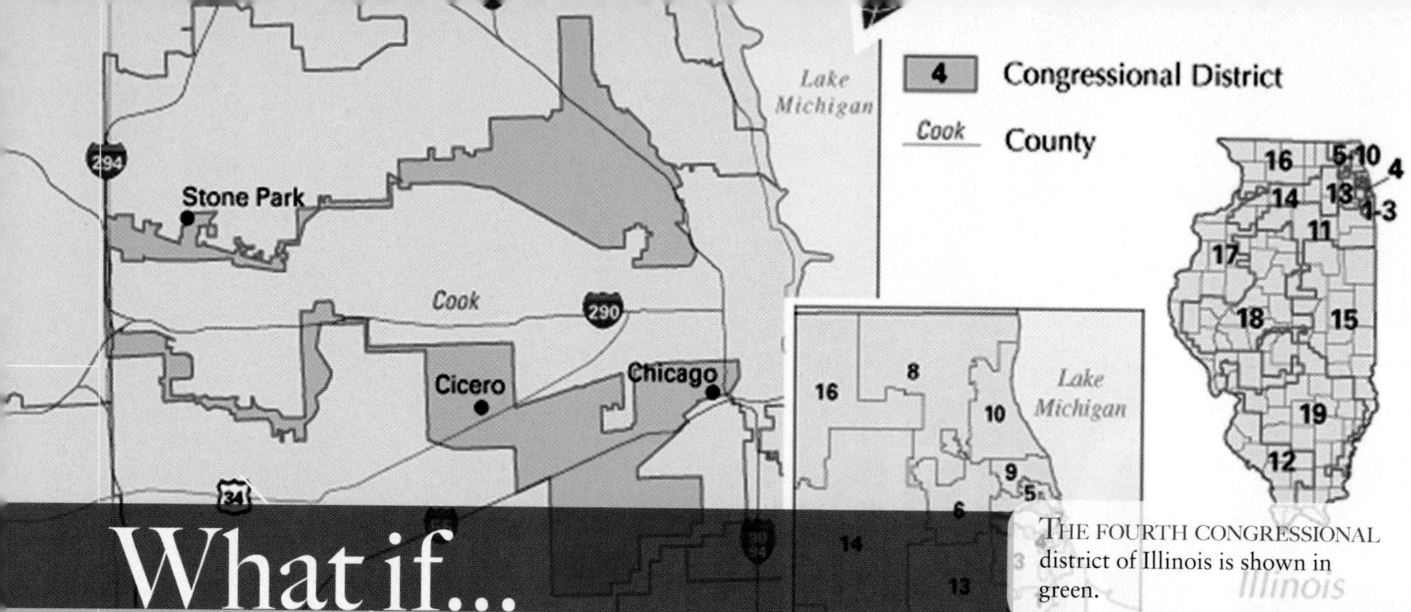

Lake Michigan

4 Congressional District

Cook County

(National Atlas of the United States®/ United States Department of the Interior)

THE FOURTH CONGRESSIONAL district of Illinois is shown in green.

What if... NONPARTISAN PANELS DREW ELECTION DISTRICTS?

BACKGROUND

It used to be that, on Election Day, Americans chose their representatives. Today, the opposite seems to happen—representatives are choosing their voters through political redistricting. Reelection is practically guaranteed in many jurisdictions where congressional districts are designed to be "safe seats" for one or another of the major political parties. This process is called *gerrymandering*.

In most states, district lines are drawn by a small group of party leaders in the state legislature. If one party dominates, it will try to maximize the number of safe seats for its members. Following the 2010 census, Republicans in Texas crafted district boundaries heavily biased in their favor, and Democrats in Illinois did the same. If power is divided between the parties in a particular state, legislators may design districts that benefit incumbents of both parties. In 2002, following such a redistricting in California, not a single state assembly, state senate, or U.S. House seat experienced a change in party control.

Even in the 2010 elections, when Republicans displaced large numbers of Democrats, only a fifth of the 435 U.S. House districts were competitive—that is, decided by 10 percentage points or less. In 160 districts, the winner got more than two-thirds of the vote.

WHAT IF NONPARTISAN PANELS DREW ELECTION DISTRICTS?

If nonpartisan panels or state commissions were used to draw congressional districts every ten years, an immediate question would be: Who should be the members? Some have suggested retired judges. Above all, the members of the panels or commissions would have to be nonpartisan—they could receive no benefit from redistricting.

Some states, such as Arizona, Iowa, and Minnesota, already have nonpartisan redistricting, using panels of retired judges to draw district lines. These states have a larger number of competitive districts than we see in other states. Three of Iowa's five districts are competitive, as are half the districts in Arizona. California instituted nonpartisan redistricting after the 2010 census. Its panel contains equal numbers of Democrats, Republicans, and independents. Panel members are chosen by an elaborate lottery process aimed at reducing the influence of party hierarchies. As a result, California races were more competitive in 2012.

IMPLICATIONS OF NONPARTISAN REDISTRICTING

Some have argued that competitive seats reduce extreme political partisanship because winning candidates cannot appeal only to members of their own party. In fact, this would probably not be an important result. Gerrymandering is impossible in the U.S. Senate, where every member represents an entire state. Yet senators are almost as partisan as members of the House.

More competitive congressional races would surely result, however, from nonpartisan redistricting. One consequence might be increased spending by challengers who have a greater chance of winning. Incumbents facing viable challengers would have to step up their spending, too. We would also expect both candidates to use sophisticated Web campaigns to raise funds and get their messages across. The makeup of Congress could change. There would be fewer "old-timers" holding the reins of power in the House. Newcomers could bring new ideas, but higher turnover could result in the loss of many experienced members.

FOR CRITICAL ANALYSIS

1. *What types of people do you think would be the most unbiased participants in a redistricting panel? Why?*
2. *Some argue that districts with large numbers of supporters of both parties might result in elections that are more divisive. Do you believe this might be a problem? Why or why not?*

voter registration on Fridays and any Saturday falling in a three-day weekend. Early voting days were also drastically curtailed. As a result, the League of Women Voters and Rock the Vote, major sponsors of voter-registration drives, suspended activities in Florida and sued to block the new law. The political parties, however, vowed to press on. In May 2012, a federal district judge suspended most of the voter registration requirements.

The Voting Rights Act. As we discussed in Chapter 5, the Voting Rights Act was enacted in 1965 to ensure that African Americans had equal access to the polls. Any new voting practices or procedures in jurisdictions with a history of discrimination in voting have to be approved by the U.S. Department of Justice or the federal district court in Washington, D.C., before being implemented. As noted earlier in this chapter, the federal government has recently used its powers under the act to reject voter ID laws in several states.

A provision of the Voting Rights Act permits jurisdictions to "bail out" of coverage if they can demonstrate a clean record on discrimination during the previous ten years. By 2009, however, seventeen Virginia counties were the only jurisdictions in the country to successfully bail out. In June 2009, the United States Supreme Court permitted a Texas utility district to file for a bailout and strongly indicated that relief from the requirements of the act should be granted more freely. Indeed, several justices speculated on whether the act was still constitutional under modern circumstances, but the Court drew back from resolving that issue.[12]

■ Learning Outcome 6: **Describe the different types of media and the changing roles that they play in American society.**

The Media and Politics

The study of people and politics must take into account the role played by the media. Historically, the print media played the most important role in informing public debate. The print media developed, for the most part, our understanding of how news is to be reported. Today, however, 69 percent of Americans use television news as their primary source of information. In addition, the Internet has become a major source for news, political communication, and fund-raising. The Internet is now the second most widely used source of information—34 percent of all persons consider it their primary source of news.

Only 22 percent of the public now relies on newspapers as a primary news source. As Internet use grows, the system of gathering and sharing news and information is changing from one in which the media have a primary role to one in which the individual citizen may play a greater part.

Conservative radio talk-show host and Fox TV personality Sean Hannity has increased his audience regularly.

(AP Photo/Dr. Scott M. Lieberman)

The Roles of the Media

The mass media perform a number of different functions in any country. In the United States, we can list at least six media functions. Almost all of them can have political implications, and some are essential to the democratic process. These functions are: (1) entertainment, (2) reporting the news, (3) identifying public problems, (4) socializing new generations, (5) providing a political forum, and (6) making profits.

Entertainment. By far the greatest number of radio and television hours are dedicated to entertaining the public. The battle for prime-time ratings indicates how important successful entertainment is to the survival of networks and individual stations. A number of network shows have a highly political content. Many younger people report that they get much of their

12. *Northwest Austin Municipal Utility District No. One v. Holder,* 557 U.S. 193 (2009).

political information from two programs on the Comedy Central network, hosted by Jon Stewart and Stephen Colbert. Both are liberal, although as part of his routine, Colbert pretends to be a conservative.

For many Americans, especially younger ones, the Internet is replacing television as a source of entertainment. While much time on the Internet may be spent chatting with friends on Skype or even watching television programs online, politics is often a topic. YouTube, in particular, offers a large number of politically oriented videos, many of which are satirical. Talk radio and television shows that feature talk-radio personalities are another form of politically oriented entertainment—one that is dominated by the political right.

did you know?

The first "wire" story transmitted by telegraph was sent in 1846.

Reporting the News. A primary function of the mass media in all their forms is the reporting of news. The media provide words and pictures about events, facts, personalities, and ideas. The protections of the First Amendment are intended to keep the flow of news as free as possible, because it is an essential part of the democratic process. If citizens cannot obtain unbiased information about the state of their communities and their leaders' actions, how can they make voting decisions? One of the most incisive comments about the importance of the media was made by James Madison, who said, "A people who mean to be their own governors must arm themselves with the power knowledge gives. A popular government without popular information or the means of acquiring it, is but a prologue to a farce or a tragedy or perhaps both."[13]

Public Agenda
Issues that are perceived by the political community as meriting public attention and governmental action.

Identifying Public Problems. The power of the media is important not only in revealing what the government is doing but also in determining what the government ought to do—in other words, in setting the **public agenda.** The mass media identify public issues. An example is the release of convicted sex offenders into residential neighborhoods after the end of their prison terms. The media have influenced the passage of legislation, such as "Megan's Law," which requires police to notify neighbors about the release and/or resettlement of certain sex offenders. American journalists also work in a long tradition of uncovering public wrongdoing, corruption, and bribery and of bringing such wrongdoing to the public's attention.

Closely related to this investigative function is that of presenting policy alternatives. Public policy is often complex and difficult to make entertaining, but programs devoted to public policy are often scheduled for prime-time television, especially on cable networks. For its part, the Web offers an enormous collection of political sites, with policy proposals representing every point of view.

Young people (and others) often obtain their political information from political satire shows such as the one hosted by Jon Stewart on Comedy Central. How accurate are the impressions that viewers obtain from watching such shows?

(Ethan Miller/Getty Images for Comedy Central)

Socializing New Generations. As mentioned in Chapter 6, the media strongly influence the beliefs and opinions of Americans. Because of this influence, the media play a significant role in the political socialization of the younger generation and of immigrants to this country. Through the transmission of historical information (sometimes fictionalized), the presentation of American culture, and the portrayal of the diverse regions and groups in the United States, the media teach young people and immigrants about what it means to be an American. Many children's television shows are designed not only to entertain young viewers but also to instruct them in the moral values of American society.

As more young Americans turn to the Internet, they participate in political forums, obtain information for writing assignments, and, in general, obtain much of their socialization from this new medium.

Providing a Political Forum. As part of their news function, the media also provide a political forum for leaders and the public. Candidates for office

13. James Madison, "Letter to W. T. Barry" (August 4, 1822), in Gaillard P. Hunt, ed., *The Writings of James Madison*, Vol. 103 (1910).

use news reporting to sustain interest in their campaigns, while officeholders use the media to gain support for their policies or to present an image of leadership. Presidential trips abroad are one way for the chief executive to get colorful, positive, and exciting news coverage that makes the president look "presidential." The media also offer ways for citizens to participate in public debate, through letters to the editor, blog posts, and other channels.

Making Profits. Most of the news media in the United States are private, for-profit corporate enterprises. In general, profits are made as a result of charging for advertising. Advertising revenues usually are related directly to circulation or to listener/viewer ratings.

Several well-known media outlets, in contrast, are publicly owned—public television stations in many communities and National Public Radio. These operate without extensive commercials, are locally supported, and are often subsidized by the government and corporations.

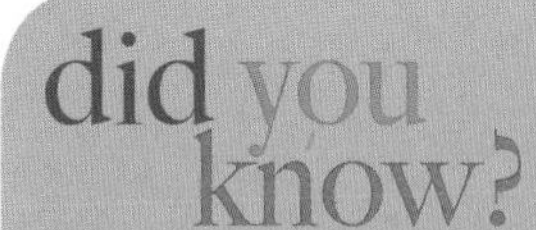

The number of people watching the television networks during prime time has declined by almost 25 percent in the past ten years.

Pressure by Advertisers. For the most part, however, the media depend on advertisers to obtain revenues to make profits. Consequently, reporters may feel pressure from media owners and from advertisers. If an important advertiser does not like the political bent of a particular newspaper, for example, the reporter could be asked to alter his or her "style" of writing. According to the Pew Research Center's Project for Excellence in Journalism, 38 percent of local print and broadcast journalists know of instances in which their newsrooms were encouraged to do a story because it related to an owner, advertiser, or sponsor.[14]

Newspapers in Crisis. Lately, newspapers have found it increasingly difficult to make a profit. Newspaper revenues have fallen because online services such as Craigslist have taken over a greater share of classified advertising. The recent economic crisis, which depressed advertising spending, pushed many large daily newspapers over the edge. Newspapers in Chicago, Denver, and Seattle went out of business. Even some famous papers, such as the *New York Times,* the *Chicago Tribune,* and the *Boston Globe,* were in serious financial trouble.

Although all major newspapers are now online, they have found it difficult to turn a profit on their Web editions. News sites typically cannot sell enough advertising to meet their costs. One problem is that most online advertising revenue is collected by sites that provide search and aggregation services but do not create original content. Google, for example, collects a full 41 percent of all online ad revenue but provides almost no original material. In response to this problem, major newspapers have begun charging for online access, a process dubbed *retreating behind a paywall.* Access charges, however, reduce the number of users who are willing to view a site. We provided additional details on the troubles of the newspaper industry in the *What If . . .* feature that introduced this chapter.

Television versus the New Media

As we explained earlier, new forms of media are displacing older ones as sources of information on politics and society in general. Although it is only recently that newspapers have experienced severe economic difficulties, they were losing ground to television as early as the 1950s. Today, the Internet has begun to displace television.

New Patterns of Media Consumption. Not everyone, however, migrates to new media at the same rate. Among Americans older than sixty-five years of age, only 11 percent obtain information about political campaigns by going online, up from 5 percent in 2000. In

14. Pew Research Center for the People & the Press, *The State of the News Media 2007: An Annual Report on American Journalism.*

this older generation, 31 percent still rely on a daily newspaper, although that is down from 58 percent in 2000.[15]

The media consumption patterns of "early adopters" of new technology are different. Many older high-income persons are among the early adopters, but the new media are most popular among youth. Indeed, many younger people have abandoned e-mail, relying on Facebook, texting, and other systems for messages. Many have moved on from Facebook to newer, more innovative social-networking platforms. Television becomes something to watch only if you cannot find online the program you want to see.

Young early adopters may find much of the older media irrelevant to their lives. It does not matter whether national television news shows are willing to pay personalities such as Diane Sawyer or Matt Lauer millions of dollars if you never watch these shows. Yet television news, cable networks, talk radio, and other older forms of media are not irrelevant to American politics. Older voters outnumber younger ones by a wide margin. As of the 2010 census, about 99 million Americans were age fifty or older. U.S. residents age eighteen through twenty-nine numbered about 52 million. Older voters are more likely to make it to the polls—and many early adopters of new media technology are too young to vote. It follows that television remains essential to American politics.

The Continuing Influence of Television. Television's continuing influence on the political process today is recognized by all who engage in that process. Television news is often criticized for being superficial, particularly compared with the detailed coverage available in newspapers and magazines. In fact, television news is constrained by its technical characteristics, the most important being the limitations of time—stories must be reported in only a few minutes.

did you know?

The average length of a quote, or sound bite, by a candidate decreased from forty-nine seconds in 1968 to less than nine seconds today.

The most interesting aspect of television—and of online videos—is that it relies on pictures rather than words to attract the viewer's attention. Therefore, a video that is chosen for a particular political story has exaggerated importance. Viewers do not know what other photos may have been taken or what other events may have been recorded—they see only those appearing on their screens. Television news can also use well-constructed stories to exploit the potential for drama. Some critics suggest that there is pressure to produce television news that has a story line, like a novel or movie. The story should be short, with exciting pictures and a clear plot. In extreme cases, the news media are satisfied with a **sound bite,** a several-second comment selected or crafted for its immediate impact on the viewer.

Sound Bite
A brief, memorable comment that easily fits into news broadcasts.

It has been suggested that these formatting characteristics of television increase its influence on political events. As you are aware, real life is usually not dramatic, nor do all events have a plot that is neat or easily understood. Political campaigns are continuing events, lasting perhaps as long as two years. The significance of their daily turns and twists is only apparent later. The "drama" of Congress, with its 535 players and dozens of important committees and meetings, is also difficult for the media to present. Television requires, instead, dozens of daily three-minute stories.

The Media and Political Campaigns

■ Learning Outcome 7: **Summarize the impact of the media on the political process.**

All forms of the media—television, newspapers, radio, magazines, online services—have a significant political impact on American society. It is not too much of an exaggeration to say that almost all national political figures, starting with the president, plan every public appearance and statement to attract media coverage.

15. Pew Research Center for the People & the Press, "Cable Leads the Pack as Campaign News Source," February 7, 2012.

Television Coverage

Although younger voters get a relatively small share of their news from television, it remains the primary news source for older voters. Therefore, candidates and their consultants spend much of their time devising strategies that use television to their benefit. Three types of TV coverage are generally employed in campaigns for the presidency and other offices: political advertising (including negative ads), management of news coverage, and campaign debates.

Political Advertising. Political advertising has become increasingly important for the profitability of television station owners. Hearst Television, for example, obtains more than 10 percent of its revenues from political ads during an election year. During 2012, total spending on the media by candidates at all levels totaled close to $7 billion.

Negative Advertising. Perhaps one of the most effective political ads of all time was a thirty-second spot created by President Lyndon Johnson's media adviser in 1964. Johnson's opponent in the campaign was Barry Goldwater, a conservative Republican candidate known for his expansive views on the role of the U.S. military. In this ad, a little girl stood in a field of daisies. As she held a daisy, she pulled the petals off and quietly counted to herself. Suddenly, when she reached number ten, a deep bass voice cut in and began a countdown: "10, 9, 8, 7, 6 . . . ." When the voice intoned "zero," the mushroom cloud of an atomic bomb began to fill the screen. Then President Johnson's voice was heard: "These are the stakes. To make a world in which all of God's children can live, or to go into the dark. We must either love each other or we must die." At the end of the commercial, the message read, "Vote for President Johnson on November 3."

Since the daisy girl advertisement, negative advertising has come into its own. In recent elections, an ever-increasing percentage of political ads have been negative in nature.

The public claims not to like negative advertising, but as one consultant put it, "Negative advertising works."Negative ads can backfire, however, when there are

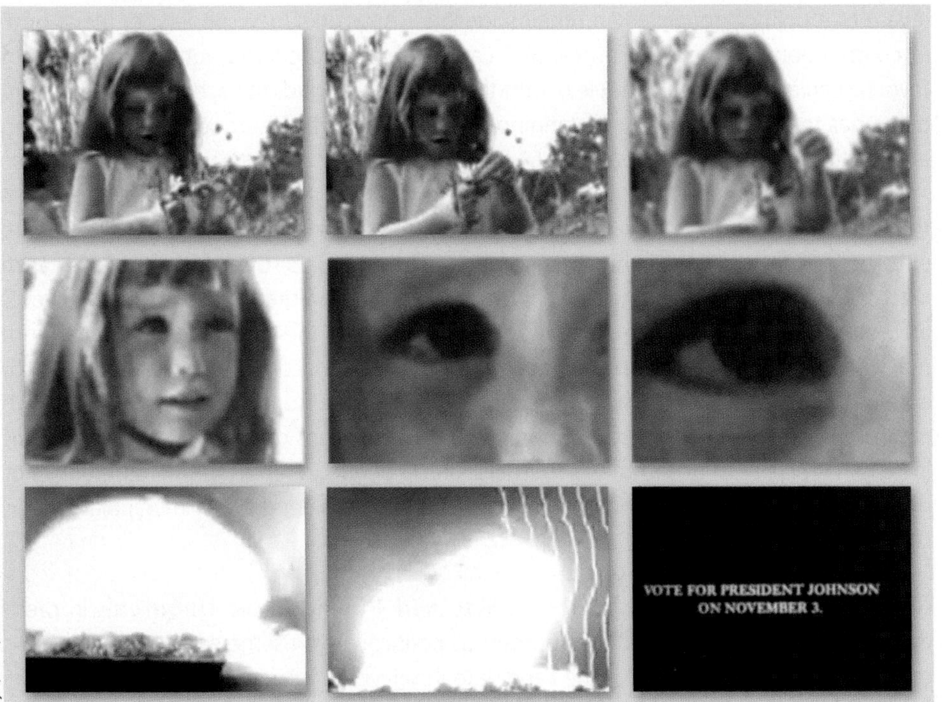

(Doyle, Dane, Bernbach)

These are stills of a short television advertisement used by presidential candidate Lyndon Johnson in 1964. The daisy girl ad contrasted the innocence of childhood with the horror of an atomic bomb. How effective was this negative TV ad?

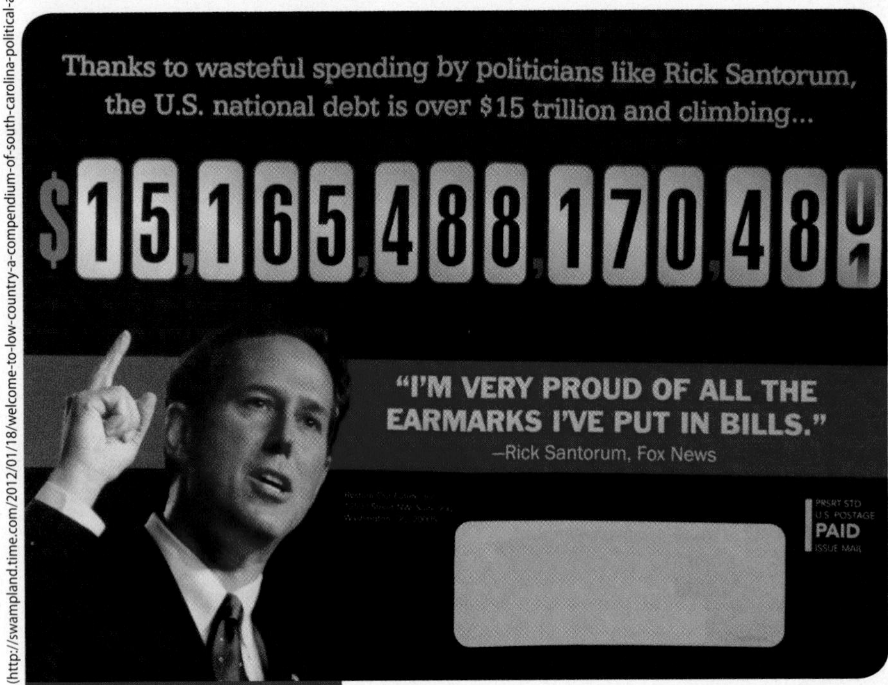

(http://swampland.time.com/2012/01/18/welcome-to-low-country-a-compendium-of-south-carolina-political-ads/)

During the Republican presidential primaries, Rick Santorum's competitors used negative ads to question his conservative credentials.

three or more candidates in the race, a typical state of affairs in the early presidential primaries. If one candidate attacks another, the attacker as well as the candidate who is attacked may come to be viewed negatively by the public. A candidate who "goes negative" may thus unintentionally boost the chances of a third candidate who is not part of the exchange. As an example of this effect, negative advertising by Newt Gingrich in the 2012 Republican presidential primaries may have temporarily injured Mitt Romney, but the eventual leader of the anti-Romney forces turned out to be Rick Santorum, not Gingrich. Santorum ran very few negative ads.

Management of News Coverage. Using political advertising to get a message across to the public is a very expensive tactic. Coverage by the news media, however, is free. The campaign simply needs to ensure that coverage takes place. In recent years, campaign managers have shown increasing sophistication in creating newsworthy events for journalists to cover.

The campaign staff uses several methods to try to influence the quantity and type of coverage the campaign receives. First, the staff understands the technical aspects of media coverage—camera angles, necessary equipment, timing, and deadlines—and plans political events to accommodate the press. Second, the campaign organization is aware that political reporters and their sponsors—networks, newspapers, or blogs—are in competition for the best stories and can be manipulated through the granting of favors, such as a personal interview with the candidate. Third, the scheduler in the campaign has the important task of planning events that will be photogenic and interesting enough for the evening news.

A related goal, although one that is more difficult to attain, is to convince reporters that a particular interpretation of an event is true. Today, the art of putting the appropriate **spin** on a story or event is highly developed. Press advisers, often referred to as **spin doctors,** try to convince journalists that the advisers' interpretations of the political events are correct. For example, the Obama administration and the Republicans engaged in a major spinning duel over the health-care reforms passed by Congress in March 2010. The administration called the legislation essential to provide insurance for everyone and to control the growth in health-care spending. The Republicans described it as a dangerous increase in the size of government. Journalists have begun to report on the different spins placed on events and on how candidates and officeholders try to manipulate news coverage.

Spin
An interpretation of campaign events or election results that is favorable to the candidate's campaign strategy.

Spin Doctor
A political campaign adviser who tries to convince journalists of the truth of a particular interpretation of events.

Going for the Knockout Punch—Televised Presidential Debates. In presidential elections, perhaps just as important as political advertisements and general news coverage is the performance of the candidate in televised presidential debates. After the first such debate in 1960, in which John Kennedy, the young senator from Massachusetts, took on the vice president of the United States, Richard Nixon, candidates became aware of the great potential of television for changing the momentum of a campaign. In general, challengers have much more to gain from debating than do incumbents. Challengers hope that the incumbent will make a mistake in the debate and undermine the "presidential" image. Incumbent presidents are loath to debate their challengers because it puts their opponents on an equal footing with them, but the debates have become so widely anticipated that it is difficult for an incumbent to refuse to participate.

(Library of Congress)

A family watches the 1960 Kennedy-Nixon debates on television. After the debate, TV viewers thought Kennedy had won, whereas radio listeners thought Nixon had the edge. Why have televised presidential debates become major media events?

The 2011–2012 Republican Primary Debates. Presidential candidates have often debated during primary election campaigns, but traditionally such debates have not attracted much interest. The Republican presidential primary race in 2011 and 2012 was a dramatic exception. Between May 2011 and March 2012, the Republicans held twenty-seven debates, shown on such networks as ABC, CNN, Fox News, and NBC. The number of viewers frequently exceeded 5 million, and many more watched the debates in reruns and online.

The debates shaped the course of the Republican campaigns in 2011. The political context was the belief of many strong conservatives that Mitt Romney, the eventual winner, was not really one of them. To be sure, Romney's positions during the primaries were as conservative as anyone might wish, but his earlier record, especially as governor of Massachusetts, was moderate. Romney, therefore, was challenged by a series of anti-Romney candidates.

The first successful anti-Romney contender was Texas governor Rick Perry. His genial style and impressive résumé propelled him into first place in September 2011. Perry, however, was a disastrously poor debater, and by October he was out of the running. He was replaced by Herman Cain, an African American and the former head of Godfather's Pizza, who had almost no experience relevant to the presidency. Still, Cain's brilliant performance in the debates lifted him to first place in October. A series of scandals then destroyed his campaign. Former House Speaker Newt Gingrich's debating skills elevated him to the top of the field twice, in December 2011 and again in January 2012.

By the end of January, however, campaign finance began to reclaim its normal role. In the Florida primary on January 31, Romney buried Gingrich beneath $10 million of negative campaign ads. Former Pennsylvania senator Rick Santorum became the ultimate anti-Romney candidate, but Romney triumphed in the end.

Obama-Romney Debates. The 2012 presidential debates in October turned out to be among the more consequential debates in years. As noted earlier, Obama's team had tried to present Romney as a rich financier who cared only for the interests of other wealthy Americans. Through September, this characterization appeared to be damaging Romney's campaign considerably. In the first of three debates, however, Romney was successful in presenting himself as compassionate, reasonable, and above all, moderate. Obama, meanwhile, gave the appearance of being half asleep. Obama did much better in the next two debates, and polls suggested that he won them on points. The effect of the last two debates, however, was not enough to counteract the impact of the first one. Romney's debate performance tightened up the elections substantially, but not by enough to grant him victory in November.

HOME PAGE | TODAY'S PAPER | VIDEO | MOST POPULAR | Edition: U.S. / Global | Help

The New York Times
Friday, June 8, 2012

Politics

Search All NYTimes.com | Go | ING DIRECT

WORLD | U.S. | N.Y. / REGION | BUSINESS | TECHNOLOGY | SCIENCE | HEALTH | SPORTS | OPINION | ARTS | STYLE | TRAVEL | JOBS | REAL ESTATE | AUTOS

THE CAUCUS | FIVETHIRTY EIGHT | ELECTION 2012 | G.O.P. PRIMARY | INSIDE CONGRESS | POLL WATCH | VIDEO

LATEST FROM POLITICS
4:18 PM ET Senator Raises Questions About Nominee for...
4:23 PM ET Obama Backs Away From 'Fine' Comment
4:19 PM ET Republicans Take Aim at Obama's 'Doing Fine'...

Lobby E-Mails Show Depth of Obama Ties to Drug Industry
By PETER BAKER 2:01 PM ET
A new batch of e-mails between administration officials and drug industry lobbyists underscore the compromises the president made to secure support for his health care overhaul.
· Document: E-Mails Offer Look at Deal-Making Over Health Care Law
Post a Comment | Read (137)

THE CAUCUS
Obama Backs Off Comment That 'Private Sector Is Doing Fine'
By MICHAEL D. SHEAR 8 minutes ago
Republicans had seized on comments President Obama made in which he repeatedly said hiring at private businesses was doing well, while hiring by governments was not.
· The Caucus: Republicans Take Aim at Obama's 'Doing Fine' Comments
· The Caucus: Obama Prods Congress, Citing Euro Crisis

ON POLITICS
2012 May Lack Drama, but Not Significance
By RICHARD W. STEVENSON
Though the current election season is producing very few goose bumps, the 2012 presidential race is shaping up to be more important to the direction of the country than the 2008 campaign was.

Campaigns Blitz 9 Swing States in a Battle of Ads
By JEREMY W. PETERS
The presidential campaigns and their allies have been bombarding a shrinking pool of swing voters with the earliest concentration of advertisements in the modern political era.

POLITICAL MEMO
Demographic Shifts in Key States Could Aid Obama in Fall
By JOHN HARWOOD 12:52 PM ET
Polls show that President Obama holds a thin cushion against economic and political woes in many states: minority voters and the shape-shifting

The Opinion Pages »
TAKING NOTE
The Most Expensive Campaign Ever
If you live in Iowa, Colorado or Nevada, your TV-watching experience must be pretty dreary.
· Krugman: Reagan Was a Keynesian
· Editorial: The Bills to Nowhere
· Campaign Stops: 'You're Likable Enough, Mitt.'
· Room for Debate: Winning Without Wall Street?

FiveThirtyEight Forecast
Nov. 6 Forecast | Now-cast
291.3 Electoral vote 246.7

FIVETHIRTYEIGHT
Election Forecast: Obama Begins With Tenuous Advantage
By NATE SILVER
Introducing the 2012 FiveThirtyEight presidential forecast, which now shows President Obama as a very slight favorite to win re-election.

The Election 2012 App »

The Electoral Map: The Swing States »
217 Solid + Leaning Obama | 115 Tossup | Solid + Leaning Romney 206

Primary Resources
CONGRESS: The Race for the Senate
CAMPAIGN FINANCE: Candidates | Independent Groups

Republican Delegate Tally » UPDATED JUNE 8

Candidate	June 5	Total to date
Romney	264	1480
Santorum	0	267
Gingrich	0	138
Paul	0	137

Source: A.P. 1,144 needed

(http://www.nytimes.com/)

All major papers and magazines have their own Web sites, such as this one for the *New York Times*. How effective are these Web sites at informing the public about political matters?

The Internet, Blogging, and Podcasting

Today, the campaign staff of every candidate running for a significant political office includes an Internet campaign strategist—a professional hired to create and maintain the campaign Web site, social media, blogs, and podcasts (blogs and podcasts will be discussed shortly). The work of this strategist includes designing a user-friendly and attractive Web site for the candidate, managing the candidate's e-mail communications, tracking campaign contributions made through the site, hiring bloggers to push the candidate's agenda on the Web, and monitoring Web sites for favorable or unfavorable comments or video clips about the candidate. Additionally, all major interest groups in the United States now use the Internet to promote their causes. Prior to elections, various groups engage in issue advocacy from their Web sites. At little or no cost, they can promote positions taken by favored candidates and solicit contributions.

Online Fund-raising. Two politicians stand out as pioneers of online fund-raising. The first of these is Ron Paul, a Republican member of Congress from Texas, who has run for president several times on a strongly libertarian platform. Paul's support has been especially strong among heavy Internet users, and these supporters introduced the idea of the *moneybomb.* The San José *Mercury News* described a moneybomb as "a one-day fund-raising frenzy." Two moneybomb events in late 2007 raised more than $10 million for the Paul campaign.

Paul's fund-raising success was overshadowed in 2008, however, by Barack Obama's online fund-raising machine. In that year, Obama obliterated every political fund-raising and spending record in history. In total, his campaign raised more than $650 million, much of it in small donations solicited through the Internet. A key characteristic of successful Internet campaigns has been decentralization. The nature of the Internet has allowed candidates to assemble thousands of individual activists who serve as fund-raisers.

Obama was even more dependent on small Internet donations in 2012 than he had been in 2008, in part because his campaign rhetoric aimed at the wealthy led to a precipitous drop in donations from high-income individuals. One successful tactic was a "dinner with Barack" contest that supporters could enter with a relatively modest donation.

Romney's campaign, in contrast, found it easy to collect large donations but initially had difficulties with smaller donors. The campaign developed a number of innovative techniques to improve its small-donor performance, including iPhone and Android apps to collect donations using a card reader. Romney also encouraged supporters to create individualized "MyMitt" donation pages using a template supplied by the campaign.

Social Media IN POLITICS

For politics, Facebook and Twitter may be two of the most important social media sites, but there are many others of general interest. *Pinterest* is an online pinboard that is wildly popular with women. *Instagram* lets you share smartphone photos. (Facebook bought it out in 2012.) For the truly self-interested, *Klout* measures your influence on your social networks.

Blogging. Within the past few years, politicians have also felt obligated to post regular blogs on their Web sites. The word *blog* comes from *Web log,* a regular updating of one's ideas at a specific Web site. Of course, many people besides politicians are also posting blogs. Not all of the millions of blogs posted daily are political in nature. Many are, though, and they can have a dramatic influence on events, giving rise to the term *blogosphere politics.*

Blogs are clearly threatening the mainstream media. They can be highly specialized, highly political, and highly entertaining. And they are cheap. The *Washington Post* requires thousands of employees, paper, and ink to generate its offline product and incurs delivery costs to get it to readers. A blogging organization such as RealClearPolitics can generate its political commentary with fewer than ten employees.

Podcasting. Once blogs—written words—became well established, it was only a matter of time before they ended up as spoken words. Enter **podcasting,** so called because the first Internet-communicated spoken blogs were downloaded onto Apple's iPods. Podcasts, though, can be heard on a computer or downloaded onto any portable listening device. Podcasting can also include videos. Hundreds of thousands of podcasts are now generated every day. Basically, anyone who has an idea can easily create a podcast and make it available for downloading. Like blogs, podcasting threatens traditional media sources. Publications that sponsor podcasts find it hard to make them profitable.

Podcasting
A method of distributing multimedia files, such as audio or video files, for downloading onto mobile devices or personal computers.

Although politicians have been slower to adopt this form of communication, many now are using podcasts to keep in touch with their constituents, and there are currently thousands, if not tens of thousands, of political podcasts.

Media Problems

■ Learning Outcome 8:
Consider some of the issues facing today's media, including concentrated ownership, freedom of speech for broadcasters, and political bias.

Journalists and other members of the media community are well known for devoting considerable energy to self-analysis. Numerous Web sites, social media, blogs, and other platforms continually review the performance of the various media outlets. Several issues rank high when the media contemplates itself—these include the effects of concentrated ownership, government interference, and bias by reporters.

Concentrated Ownership of the Media

Many media outlets are now owned by corporate conglomerates. A single entity may own a television network; the studios that produce shows, news, and movies; and the means to deliver that content to the home via cable, satellite, or the Internet. The question to be faced in the future is how to ensure competition in the delivery of news so that citizens have access to multiple points of view from the media.

2012 elections
THE MEDIA AND THE ELECTIONS

The 2012 elections generated a number of important media stories. One of these was the surprising ineffectiveness of the vast flow of negative ads bought by super PACs. True, negative ads did score a number of successes. Probably the most important negative ad campaign, however, was not sponsored by an outside committee, but by Barack Obama's own operation. That was the long-running attempt to discredit Romney, which placed Romney in some jeopardy during September. Overall, though, millions of dollars were simply wasted. Observers wondered whether some super PAC organizers hadn't played many of their wealthy contributors for suckers.

A second story was the presidential debates in October. It is hard to overstate how important the first of these debates was for Romney. On the eve of that debate, Romney's campaign was on the ropes. A few days after the first debate, however, Romney had pulled even with Obama in some opinion polls and was leading in others. Romney made a major move to the political center, a move that appears to have caught Obama off guard. During the first debate, Romney appeared relaxed and reasonable. Obama seemed aloof and detached from the entire process. Obama had fallen into a trap that has caught many incumbent presidents. After four years in office, he was not used to the rough-and-tumble debate format. Obama did not make the same mistake twice and was much sharper in the second and third debates. Unfortunately for Romney, much of his "bounce" in the polls from the first debate had worn off by Election Day.

Today, all of the prime-time television networks are owned by major American corporations and are part of corporate conglomerates. The Turner Broadcasting/CNN network was purchased by a major corporation, Time Warner. Fox Broadcasting Company has always been a part of Rupert Murdoch's publishing and media empire. Many of these companies have also formed partnerships with computer software makers, such as Microsoft, for joint electronic-publishing ventures.

The greatest concern advanced by observers of concentrated media ownership is that it could lead to a decline in democratic debate. Also, media owners might use their power to steer the national agenda in a direction that they prefer. Indeed, several news organizations have clear conservative or liberal viewpoints. Among the most famous and successful of these is Fox News, part of Rupert Murdoch's media empire. Murdoch's U.S. newspapers and networks have not been shy about promoting conservative politics. Some observers, however, believe that the emergence of independent news Web sites, blogs, and podcasts provides an ample counterweight to the advocacy of media moguls.

did you know?

A thirty-second television advertisement shown during the Super Bowl costs more than $2.6 million.

Murdoch's dominance has been more of an issue in Britain, where newspapers, radio networks, and television networks owned by his News International enjoy a very large share of the total market. For years, politicians in all major British parties believed that it was potentially fatal to get on the wrong side of the Murdoch empire. In 2011, however, Murdoch's position was seriously undercut by a major scandal. Apparently, staff at Murdoch's *News of the World,* Britain's best-selling Sunday paper, illegally hacked into the cell phones of hundreds of people, including crime victims, celebrities, and members of the royal family. Bribery of police officers was also alleged. The *News of the World* was forced to close as a result of these revelations, and several News International executives faced criminal charges.

Rebekah Brooks was the editor of Britain's *News of the World* newspaper during a phone-hacking scandal. Why would a newspaper want to engage in such hacking?

(AP Photo)

Government Control of Content

The United States has one of the freest presses in the world. Nonetheless, regulation of the media, particularly of the electronic media, does exist. We discussed some aspects of this regulation in Chapter 4, when we examined First Amendment rights and the press.

The First Amendment does not mention electronic media, which did not exist when the Bill of Rights was written. For many reasons, the government has much greater control over electronic media than it does over print media. The Federal Communications Commission (FCC) regulates communications by radio, television, wire, and cable. For many years, the FCC has controlled the number of radio stations, even though technologically we could have many more radio stations than now exist. Also, the FCC created the environment in which for many decades the three major TV networks (NBC, CBS, and ABC) dominated broadcasting.

On the face of it, the First Amendment would seem to apply to all media. In fact, the United States Supreme Court has often been slow to extend free speech and free press guarantees to new media. For example, in 1915 the Court held that "as a matter of common sense," free speech protections did not apply to movies. Only in 1952 did the Court find that motion pictures were covered by the First Amendment.[16] In contrast, the Court extended full protection to the Internet almost immediately by striking down provisions of the 1996 Telecommunications Act.[17] Cable TV also received broad protection in 2000.[18]

While the Court has held that the First Amendment is relevant to radio and television, it has never extended full protection to these

16. *Joseph Burstyn, Inc. v. Wilson*, 343 U.S. 495 (1952).
17. *Reno v. American Civil Liberties Union*, 521 U.S. 844 (1997).
18. *United States v. Playboy Entertainment Group*, 529 U.S. 803 (2000).

media. The Court has used a number of arguments to justify this stand—initially, the scarcity of broadcast frequencies. The Court later held that the government could restrict "indecent" programming based on the "pervasive" presence of broadcasting in the home.[19] On this basis, the FCC has the authority to fine broadcasters for indecency or profanity. In June 2012, the Court ruled that the FCC's ban on momentary nudity and "fleeting expletives"—unscripted expletives uttered in live broadcasts—was unconstitutionally vague. The Court did not, however, address the underlying issue of the FCC's authority in this area.[20]

"Welcome to 'All About the Media,' where members of the media discuss the role of the media in media coverage of the media."

Bias in the Media

For decades, the contention that the mainstream media have a liberal **bias** has been repeated time and again. Bernard Goldberg, formerly a CBS broadcaster and now a commentator for Fox News, is among the most prominent of these critics. Goldberg argues that liberal bias, which "comes naturally to most reporters," has given viewers reason to distrust the big news networks. Some progressives, however, believe that conservatives find liberal bias even in reporting that is scrupulously accurate. In the words of humorist Stephen Colbert: "Reality has a well-known liberal bias."

Bias
An inclination or preference that interferes with impartial judgment.

Other observers claim that, on the whole, the media actually have a conservative bias, especially in their coverage of economic issues. In an analysis of visual images on television news, political scientist Maria Elizabeth Grabe concluded that "image bites" (as opposed to sound bites) more often favor the Republicans.[21] Certainly, the almost complete dominance of talk radio by conservatives has given the political right an outlet that the political left cannot counter. The rise of the blogosphere and other online outlets has complicated the picture of media bias considerably. Neither the left nor the right clearly dominates in this arena.

Other Theories of Media Bias. Some writers have concluded that the mainstream media are really biased toward stories that involve conflict and drama—the better to attract viewers. Still others contend the media are biased against "losers," and when a candidate falls behind in a race, his or her press quickly becomes negative. The Republican primary campaigns in 2011 and 2012 provided many opportunities for candidates to complain about such bias, as one candidate after another shot up in the polls, only to be rejected by respondents a month or two later.

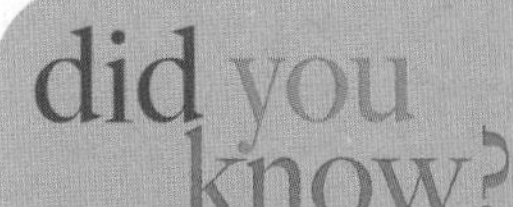

The average age of CNN viewers is forty-four, and most people who watch the evening network news programs are over age fifty.

A Scientific Test for Bias? Communications professor Tim Groeling has devised a test for media bias that may provide accurate results regardless of whether political events favor the Democrats or the Republicans. He has examined how ABC, CBS, NBC, and Fox News reported public opinion polls that assessed the job performances of Democratic president Bill Clinton and Republican president George W. Bush. Confirming what many suspect, Groeling found that ABC, CBS, and NBC gave Clinton more favorable coverage than Bush—and that Fox gave Bush more favorable coverage than Clinton.[22]

19. *FCC v. Pacifica Foundation,* 438 U.S. 726 (1978). In this case, the Court banned seven swear words (famously used by the late comedian George Carlin) during hours when children could hear them.
20. *FCC v. Fox Television Stations,* ___ U.S. ___ (2012).
21. Maria Elizabeth Grabe and Erik Page Bucy, *Image Bite Politics: News and the Visual Framing of Elections* (New York: Oxford University Press, 2009).
22. Tim Groeling, "Who's the Fairest of Them All? An Empirical Test for Partisan Bias on ABC, CBS, NBC, and Fox News," *Presidential Studies Quarterly,* December 2008, p. 631.

Why Should You Care about... THE MEDIA?

Why should you, as an individual, care about the media? Even if you do not plan to engage in political activism, you have a stake in ensuring that your beliefs are truly your own and that they represent your values and interests. To guarantee this result, you need to obtain accurate information from the media and avoid being swayed by subliminal appeals, loaded terms, or outright bias. If you do not take care, you could find yourself voting for a candidate who is opposed to what you believe in or voting against measures that are in your interest.

THE MEDIA AND YOUR LIFE

Television, print media, and the Internet provide a wide range of choices for Americans who want to stay informed. Still, critics of the media argue that a substantial amount of what you read and see is colored either by the subjectivity of editors and bloggers or by the demands of profit making. Even when journalists themselves are relatively successful in an attempt to remain objective, they will of necessity give airtime to politicians and interest group representatives who are far from impartial. The ratio of opinion to fact is even greater on the Web than in the traditional media.

It is worth your while to become a critical consumer of the news. You need the ability to determine what motivates the players in the political game and to what extent they are "shading" the news or even propagating outright lies. You also need to determine which news sources are reliable.

HOW YOU CAN MAKE A DIFFERENCE

To become a critical news consumer, you must develop a critical eye and ear. For example, ask yourself what stories are given prominence at the top of a newspaper Web site. For a contrast to most daily papers, visit the sites of publications with explicit points of view, such as the *National Review* (search on "national review") or the *New Republic* (search on "tnr"). Take note of how they handle stories.

Sources such as blogs often have strong political preferences, and you should try to determine what these are. Does a blog merely give opinions, or does it back up its arguments with data? It is possible to select anecdotes to support almost any argument—does a particular anecdote represent typical circumstances, or is it a rare occurrence highlighted to make a point?

Watching the evening news can be far more rewarding if you look at how much the news depends on video effects. You will note that stories on the evening news tend to be no more than three minutes long, that stories with excellent videos get more attention, and that considerable time is taken up with "happy talk" or human interest stories.

Another way to critically evaluate news coverage is to compare how the news is covered by different outlets. For example, you might compare the coverage of events on Fox News with the presentation on MSNBC, or compare the radio commentary of Rush Limbaugh with that of National Public Radio's *All Things Considered*. When does a show cross the line between news and opinion?

A variety of organizations try to monitor news sources for accuracy and bias. Consider visiting the following Web sites:

1. The American Journalism Review covers a wide variety of journalistic issues, including the migration from print media to online sources. Find its site by entering "ajr."
2. The Committee of Concerned Journalists is a professional organization concerned with journalistic ethics. Search on "concerned journalists."
3. Fairness and Accuracy in Reporting is a media watchdog with a strong liberal viewpoint. Visit it by entering "fair reporting" in a search engine.
4. Accuracy in Media takes a combative conservative position on media issues. Find its site by entering "accuracy in media."

Questions for Discussion and Analysis

1. Review the *Which Side Are You On?* feature on page 289. Some have argued that limits on campaign spending violate First Amendment guarantees of freedom of speech. How strong is this argument? Can such spending be seen as a form of protected expression? Under what circumstances can contributions be seen instead as a method of bribing elected officials?
2. Many observers believe that holding so many presidential primary elections at such an early point in an election year is a serious problem. How might the problem be resolved? Also, is it fair and appropriate that New Hampshire always holds the first presidential primary and Iowa always conducts the first caucuses? Why or why not?
3. Some people are more likely to vote than others. Older persons vote more frequently than younger people. Wealthy voters make it to the polls more often than poor voters. What might cause older and wealthier individuals to exhibit greater turnout?
4. Conservatives have long accused traditional media outlets of having a liberal bias. Are they correct? If so, to what degree? Regardless of whether this particular accusation is correct, what other kinds of bias might affect the reporting of prominent journalists? To the extent that the press exhibits political bias, what factors might cause this bias?

Key Terms

Australian ballot 297
bias 313
caucus 294
closed primary 293
coattail effect 297
credentials committee 295
direct primary 292
elector 296
Federal Election Commission (FEC) 286
focus group 285
front-loading 294
front-runner 294
general election 283
Hatch Act 285
independent expenditures 287
indirect primary 292
issue advocacy 286
midterm elections 299
office-block, or Massachusetts, ballot 297
open primary 293
party-column, or Indiana, ballot 297
podcasting 311
political action committee (PAC) 285
political consultant 284
presidential primary 281
primary election 283
public agenda 304
registration 302
soft money 286
sound bite 306
spin 308
spin doctor 308
superdelegate 292
super PAC 287
tracking poll 285
vote-eligible population 300
voter turnout 299
voting-age population 300

Chapter Summary

1. The legal qualifications for holding political office are minimal at both the state and the local levels, but holders of political office still are predominantly white and male and are likely to be from the professional class.
2. American political campaigns are lengthy and extremely expensive. In the past decade, they have become more candidate centered than party centered in response to technological innovations and decreasing party identification. Candidates have begun to rely on paid professional consultants to perform the various tasks necessary to wage a political campaign. The crucial task of professional political consultants is image building. The campaign organization devises a campaign strategy to maximize the candidate's chances of winning. Candidates use public opinion polls and focus groups to gauge their popularity and to test the mood of the country.
3. Under current conditions, finance for federal campaigns is supplied in two ways: candidate committees and independent expenditures. Candidate committees are under the complete control of the candidate. They have few limits on how they can spend their resources, but individual and organizational contributions to the committees face strict limits. Presidential candidate committees formerly accepted public financing, but candidates no longer participate in that system because they can raise more funds on their own. Independent organizations are not allowed to coordinate their expenditures with candidate campaigns, although this restriction is something of a fiction. These groups, which include super PACs and 501(c)4 organizations, can raise unlimited sums. Modern independent groups are the result of a 2010 Supreme Court ruling, *Citizens United v. FEC.*
4. After the Democratic convention of 1968, the McGovern-Fraser Commission formulated new rules for primaries, which were adopted by Democrats and, in most cases, by Republicans. These reforms opened up the nomination process for the presidency to all voters.
5. A presidential primary is a statewide election to help a political party determine its presidential nominee at the national convention. Some states use the caucus method of choosing convention delegates. The primary campaign recently has been shortened to the first few months of the election year.

6. A voter technically does not vote directly for president but instead chooses between slates of presidential electors. In most states, the slate that wins the most popular votes throughout the state gets to cast all the electoral votes for the state. The candidate receiving a majority (270) of the electoral votes wins. The United States uses the Australian ballot, a secret ballot that is prepared, distributed, and counted by government officials.

7. Voter participation in the United States is often considered to be low, especially in elections that do not feature a presidential contest. Turnout is lower when measured as a percentage of the voting-age population than it is when measured as a percentage of the population actually eligible to vote. There is an association between voter turnout and a person's age, education, and income level.

8. In colonial times, only white males with a certain minimum amount of property were eligible to vote. The suffrage issue has concerned, at one time or another, most groups in the United States. Today, to register to vote, a person must satisfy citizenship, age, and residency requirements. Each state has different qualifications.

9. The media are enormously important in American politics today. They perform a number of functions, including (a) entertainment, (b) news reporting, (c) identifying public problems, (d) socializing new generations, (e) providing a political forum, and (f) making profits.

10. The political influence of the media is most obvious during political campaigns. Today's campaigns use political advertising and expert management of news coverage. For presidential candidates, how they appear in presidential debates is of major importance. Internet blogs, podcasts, and Web sites such as YouTube are transforming today's political campaigns.

11. Frequently, the mainstream media have been accused of liberal bias, although some observers contend that these accusations result from true stories that offend conservatives. Other possible media biases include a bias against political "losers."

Quiz Multiple Choice

1. To be eligible to serve as president of the United States, you must be:
   - **a. a natural-born citizen, a resident of the country for fourteen years, and at least forty-two years old.**
   - **b. a naturalized citizen, at least thirty-five years old, and a resident of the country for fourteen years.**
   - **c. at least thirty-five years old, a resident of the country for fourteen years, and a natural-born citizen.**

2. Organizations set up under federal or state law with the express purpose of making political donations are called:
   - **a. political action committees (PACs).**
   - **b. political activities conventions.**
   - **c. political parties.**

3. The benefit of creating a super PAC is that:
   - **a. it can be used only for negative campaigning.**
   - **b. it can aggregate unlimited contributions by individuals and organizations and funnel these sums into independent expenditures.**
   - **c. it can give unused campaign contributions directly to candidates' families.**

4. Today, presidential candidates do not accept matching public funds because:
   - **a. candidates can raise far more outside of the public system than they would receive if they participated in it.**
   - **b. once candidates accept public funds for the primaries, they must match public funds in the ratio of five to one for the general elections.**
   - **c. public funds are no longer available.**

5. One reason the Federal Election Commission (FEC) has proven to be ineffective is:
   - **a. it has only six members.**
   - **b. it is not allowed to collect data on campaign contributions.**
   - **c. it normally does not rule that a campaign has violated the law until well after the elections are over.**

6. In an indirect primary:
   - **a. voters decide party nominations by voting directly for candidates.**
   - **b. voters make no decisions directly about convention delegates.**
   - **c. voters choose convention delegates, and those delegates determine the party's candidate in the general election.**

7. Today, because the Constitution created the electoral college:
   - **a. individual votes for president and vice president are added up to determine who fills these offices.**
   - **b. voters choose electors who have announced how they will cast their ballots as part of the electoral college.**
   - **c. voters choose members of the electoral college, and those electors decide whom they will support.**

8. In the United States today, all states use secret ballots that are prepared, distributed, and counted by government officials at public expense. This system is called:
   - **a. the Australian ballot.**
   - **b. the Massachusetts ballot.**
   - **c. the office-block ballot.**

ANSWERS: 1. c, 2. a, 3. b, 4. a, 5. c, 6. c, 7. b, 8. a.

Quiz Fill-Ins

9. In statistics on voter participation, the voting-age population is typically larger than the ____________ - ____________ population.

10. The writers of the Constitution allowed the states to decide who should vote. Not until the ratification of the ____________ ____________ in 1920 did all women in the United States have the right to vote.

11. One of the most significant developments in fund-raising over the past few years is the growth in __________ fund-raising.

12. Sometimes, a candidate's supporters launch a/an ____________, which is a one-day fund-raising frenzy.

13. To be eligible to run for senator, an individual must have been a ________ for at least ___ years and be at least ___ years old by the time of taking office.

14. The most sought-after (and most criticized) campaign expert is the __________ __________, who for a large fee takes over the candidate's campaign.

15. The most recent Supreme Court ruling on campaign contributions was ___________ *v. FEC.*

16. In a/an __________ __________, any voter can vote in either party primary without declaring a party affiliation.

17. A/an __________ - __________ ballot groups all the candidates for a particular elective office under the title of that office.

ANSWERS: 9. vote-eligible, 10. Nineteenth Amendment, 11. online, 12. moneybomb, 13. citizen; nine; thirty, 14. political consultant, 15. *Citizens United*, 16. open primary, 17. office-block.

(© Aleksandar Jovicic/iStockphoto)

Selected Print & Media Resources

SUGGESTED READINGS

Cicero, Quintus Tullius, translated by Phillip Freeman. *How to Win an Election: An Ancient Guide for Modern Politicians.* Princeton, N.J.: Princeton University Press, 2012. In 64 B.C.E., when the great Roman orator Marcus Cicero ran for high office, his brother Quintus decided that Marcus needed advice. The resulting recommendations could have been ripped from today's headlines. Freeman, a classics professor, reveals that the more things change, the more they remain the same.

Lehrer, Jim. *Tension City: Inside the Presidential Debates.* New York: Random House Trade Paperbacks, 2012. This volume reveals the background stories of more than forty years of presidential debates. A PBS journalist, Lehrer has presided over eleven presidential and vice-presidential debates.

Martinez, Michael D. *Does Turnout Matter?* Boulder, Colo.: Westview Press, 2009. Scholars have expended much effort in examining why voter turnout is lower in the United States than in many other countries, but the question of whether low turnout actually matters has received less attention. Martinez is a professor of political science at the University of Florida.

McChesney, Robert W., and Victor Pickard, eds. *Will the Last Reporter Please Turn Out the Lights: The Collapse of Journalism and What Can Be Done to Fix It.* New York: The New Press, 2011. In this volume, two communications professors assemble a series of essays that provides a comprehensive introduction to the current crisis in the media.

MEDIA RESOURCES

All the President's Men—A film, produced by Warner Bros. in 1976, starring Dustin Hoffman and Robert Redford as the two *Washington Post* reporters, Carl Bernstein and Bob Woodward, who broke the story on the Watergate scandal. The film is an excellent portrayal of the *Washington Post* newsroom and the decisions that editors make in such situations.

Citizen Kane—A 1941 film, based on the life of William Randolph Hearst and directed by Orson Welles, that has been acclaimed as one of the best movies ever made. Welles himself stars as the newspaper tycoon. The film also stars Joseph Cotten and Alan Ladd.

***Page One: Inside the* New York Times**—This 2011 documentary covers a year in the life of the *New York Times*, a media giant that has been hit hard by the collapse in advertising revenue and the rise of the new media.

The Social Network—In this 2010 Hollywood blockbuster, director David Fincher tells the story of Facebook founder Mark Zuckerberg. The film received eight Academy Award nominations and won three Oscars, including one for best adapted screenplay. It swept the Golden Globe awards, winning for best drama, best director, and best screenplay.

E-mocracy CAMPAIGNS, ELECTIONS, AND THE MEDIA

Today's voters have a significant advantage over those in past decades. It is now possible to obtain extensive information about candidates and issues simply by going online. Some sites present point-counterpoint articles about the candidates or issues in an upcoming election. Other sites support some candidates and positions and oppose others. The candidates themselves all have Web sites that you can visit if you want to learn more about them and their positions. You can also obtain information online about election results by going to sites such as those listed in the *Logging On* section.

The Internet also offers a great opportunity to those who want to access the news. All of the major news organizations, including radio and television stations and newspapers, are online. Most local newspapers include at least some of their news coverage and features on their Web sites, and all national newspapers are online. Even foreign newspapers can now be accessed online within a few seconds.

Also available are purely Web-based news publications, including e-zines (online news magazines) such as *Slate* and *Salon*. Because it is relatively simple for anyone or any organization to put up a home page or Web site, a wide variety of sites have appeared that critique the news media or give alternative interpretations of the news and the way it is presented.

LOGGING ON

For detailed information about current campaign-financing laws and for the latest filings of finance reports, locate the site maintained by the Federal Election Commission by entering "fec" into your favorite search engine.

1. To find excellent reports on where campaign money comes from and how it is spent, be sure to view the site maintained by the Center for Responsive Politics by typing in "opensecrets."
2. Another Web site for investigating voting records and campaign-financing information is that of Project Vote Smart. Find it by searching on its name.
3. To view *Slate*, the e-zine of politics and culture published by Microsoft, enter "slate."
4. To gain an international perspective on the news, you can check foreign news Web sites in English. The following sites all have broad worldwide coverage:
   - The British Broadcasting Corporation: "bbc"
   - China Network Television (surprisingly informative, given that it is owned by a Communist-controlled government): "cntv"
   - The Japan Broadcasting Corporation: "nhk daily"
   - Al Jazeera (the Arab world's number-one television news network): "jazeera"
   - New Delhi Television (India): "ndtv"
   - *Der Spiegel* (Germany): "spiegel international"

10 The Congress

The six learning outcomes below are designed to help improve your understanding of this chapter. After reading this chapter, you should be able to:

■ Learning Outcome 1: **Describe the various roles played by Congress and the constitutional basis of its powers.**

■ Learning Outcome 2: **Explain some of the differences between the House and the Senate and some of the privileges enjoyed by members of Congress.**

■ Learning Outcome 3: **Examine the implications of apportioning House seats.**

■ Learning Outcome 4: **Describe the committee structure of the House and the Senate.**

■ Learning Outcome 5: **Specify the key leadership positions in each chamber.**

■ Learning Outcome 6: **Discuss the process by which a bill becomes law and how the federal government establishes its budget.**

The Capitol building in Washington, D.C., is the home of the United States Congress.

(Gilles Rolla/REA/Redux)

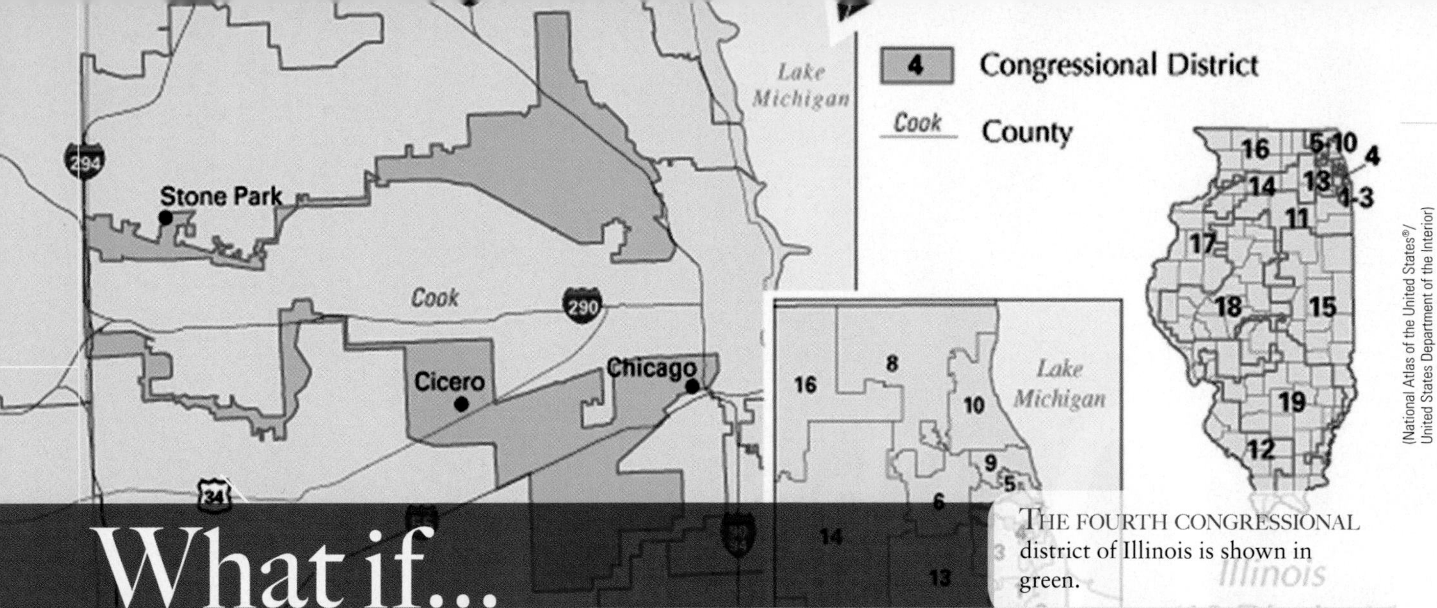

THE FOURTH CONGRESSIONAL district of Illinois is shown in green.

(National Atlas of the United States®/ United States Department of the Interior)

What if...

NONPARTISAN PANELS DREW ELECTION DISTRICTS?

BACKGROUND

It used to be that, on Election Day, Americans chose their representatives. Today, the opposite seems to happen—representatives are choosing their voters through political redistricting. Reelection is practically guaranteed in many jurisdictions where congressional districts are designed to be "safe seats" for one or another of the major political parties. This process is called *gerrymandering*.

In most states, district lines are drawn by a small group of party leaders in the state legislature. If one party dominates, it will try to maximize the number of safe seats for its members. Following the 2010 census, Republicans in Texas crafted district boundaries heavily biased in their favor, and Democrats in Illinois did the same. If power is divided between the parties in a particular state, legislators may design districts that benefit incumbents of both parties. In 2002, following such a redistricting in California, not a single state assembly, state senate, or U.S. House seat experienced a change in party control.

Even in the 2010 elections, when Republicans displaced large numbers of Democrats, only a fifth of the 435 U.S. House districts were competitive—that is, decided by 10 percentage points or less. In 160 districts, the winner got more than two-thirds of the vote.

WHAT IF NONPARTISAN PANELS DREW ELECTION DISTRICTS?

If nonpartisan panels or state commissions were used to draw congressional districts every ten years, an immediate question would be: Who should be the members? Some have suggested retired judges. Above all, the members of the panels or commissions would have to be nonpartisan—they could receive no benefit from redistricting.

Some states, such as Arizona, Iowa, and Minnesota, already have nonpartisan redistricting, using panels of retired judges to draw district lines. These states have a larger number of competitive districts than we see in other states. Three of Iowa's five districts are competitive, as are half the districts in Arizona. California instituted nonpartisan redistricting after the 2010 census. Its panel contains equal numbers of Democrats, Republicans, and independents. Panel members are chosen by an elaborate lottery process aimed at reducing the influence of party hierarchies. As a result, California races were more competitive in 2012.

IMPLICATIONS OF NONPARTISAN REDISTRICTING

Some have argued that competitive seats reduce extreme political partisanship because winning candidates cannot appeal only to members of their own party. In fact, this would probably not be an important result. Gerrymandering is impossible in the U.S. Senate, where every member represents an entire state. Yet senators are almost as partisan as members of the House.

More competitive congressional races would surely result, however, from nonpartisan redistricting. One consequence might be increased spending by challengers who have a greater chance of winning. Incumbents facing viable challengers would have to step up their spending, too. We would also expect both candidates to use sophisticated Web campaigns to raise funds and get their messages across. The makeup of Congress could change. There would be fewer "old-timers" holding the reins of power in the House. Newcomers could bring new ideas, but higher turnover could result in the loss of many experienced members.

FOR CRITICAL ANALYSIS

1. *What types of people do you think would be the most unbiased participants in a redistricting panel? Why?*
2. *Some argue that districts with large numbers of supporters of both parties might result in elections that are more divisive. Do you believe this might be a problem? Why or why not?*

Most Americans view Congress in a less-than-flattering light. In recent years, Congress has appeared to be deeply split, highly partisan in its conduct, and not very responsive to public needs. Polls show that recently, fewer than 20 percent of the public have had a favorable opinion about Congress as a whole. Yet individual members of Congress often receive much higher approval ratings from the voters in their districts. This is one of the paradoxes of the relationship between the people and Congress. Members of the public hold the institution in relatively low regard compared with the satisfaction they express with their individual representatives.

Part of the explanation for these seemingly contradictory appraisals is that members of Congress spend considerable time and effort serving their **constituents.** If the federal bureaucracy makes a mistake, the office of the constituent's senator or representative tries to resolve the issue. On a personal level, what most Americans see, therefore, is the work of these local representatives in their home states.

Constituent
A person represented by a legislator or other elected or appointed official.

Congress, however, was created to work not just for local constituents but also for the nation as a whole. As shown in the chapter-opening *What If . . .* feature, reformers have often proposed changes to the way we elect members of Congress in the hope of encouraging members to consider the national interest. Understanding the nature of the institution and the process of lawmaking is an important part of understanding how the policies that shape our lives are made. In this chapter, we describe the functions of Congress, including constituent service, representation, lawmaking, and oversight of the government. We review how the members of Congress are elected and how Congress organizes itself when it meets. We also examine how bills pass through the legislative process and become laws, and how the federal budget is established.

The Nature and Functions of Congress

■ Learning Outcome 1:
Describe the various roles played by Congress and the constitutional basis of its powers.

The founders of the American republic believed that the bulk of the power that would be exercised by a national government should be in the hands of the legislature. The leading role envisioned for Congress in the new government is apparent from its primacy in the Constitution. Article I deals with the structure, the powers, and the operation of Congress.

Bicameralism

The **bicameralism** of Congress—its division into two legislative houses—was in part the result of the Connecticut Compromise, which tried to balance the large-state population advantage, reflected in the House, and the small-state demand for equality in policymaking, which was satisfied in the Senate. Beyond that, the two chambers of Congress also reflected the social class biases of the founders. They wished to balance the interests and the numerical superiority of the common citizens with the property interests of the less numerous landowners, bankers, and merchants. They achieved this goal by providing that members of the House of Representatives should be elected directly by "the People," whereas members of the Senate were to be chosen by the elected representatives sitting in state legislatures, who were more likely to be members of the elite. (The latter provision was changed in 1913 by the passage of the Seventeenth Amendment, which provides that senators are also to be elected directly by the people.)

Bicameralism
The division of a legislature into two separate assemblies.

The logic of the bicameral Congress was reinforced by differences in length of tenure. Members of the House are required to face the electorate every two years, whereas senators can serve for a much more secure term of six years—even longer than the four-year term provided for the president. Furthermore, the senators' terms are staggered so that only one-third of the senators face the electorate every two years, along with all of the House members.

The bicameral Congress was designed to perform certain functions for the political system. These functions include lawmaking, representation, service to constituents, oversight (regulatory supervision), public education, and conflict resolution. Of these, the two most important and the ones that most often interfere with each other are lawmaking and representation.

The Lawmaking Function

Lawmaking The process of establishing the legal rules that govern society.

Logrolling An arrangement in which two or more members of Congress agree in advance to support each other's bills.

Earmarks Special provisions in legislation to set aside funds for projects that have not passed an impartial evaluation by agencies of the executive branch. Also known as *pork*.

Representation The function of members of Congress as elected officials representing the views of their constituents as well as larger national interests.

Trustee A legislator who acts according to her or his conscience and the broad interests of the entire society.

Instructed Delegate A legislator who is an agent of the voters who elected him or her and who votes according to the views of constituents regardless of personal beliefs.

The principal and most obvious function of any legislature is **lawmaking.** Congress is the highest elected body in the country charged with making binding rules for all Americans. This does not mean, however, that Congress initiates most of the ideas for legislation that it eventually considers. A majority of the bills that Congress acts on originate in the executive branch, and many other bills are traceable to interest groups and political party organizations. Through the processes of compromise and **logrolling** (offering to support a fellow member's bill in exchange for that member's promise to support your bill in the future), as well as debate and discussion, backers of legislation attempt to fashion a winning majority coalition. Traditionally, logrolling often involved agreements to support another member's legislative **earmarks,** also known as *pork*.

Earmarks are special provisions in legislation to set aside funds for projects that have not passed an impartial evaluation by agencies of the executive branch. (Normal spending projects pass through such evaluations.) Recent attempts to ban pork have not succeeded in eliminating the process altogether but have significantly reduced its frequency.

The Representation Function

Representation includes both representing the desires and demands of the constituents in the member's home district or state and representing larger national interests, such as the nation's security or the environment. Because the interests of constituents in a specific district may be at odds with the demands of national policy, the representation function is often a source of conflict for individual lawmakers—and sometimes for Congress as a whole. For example, although it may be in the interest of the nation to reduce defense spending by closing military bases, such closures are not in the interest of the states and districts that will lose jobs and local spending. Every legislator faces votes that set local representational issues against lawmaking realities.

How should the legislators fulfill the representation function? There are several views on how this task should be accomplished.

The Trustee View of Representation. One approach to the question of how representation should be achieved is that legislators should act as **trustees** of the broad interests of the entire society. They should vote against the narrow interests of their constituents if their conscience and their perception of national needs so dictate. For example, in 2011 Congress approved trade agreements with Colombia, Panama, and South Korea, despite the widely held belief that such agreements cost Americans jobs.

Senator Maria Cantwell (D., Wash.) is shown on the right with Senator Mary Landrieu (D., La.). Do senators from the same party but from different states sometimes support opposing legislation? If so, why?

(Kevin Dietsch/UPI/Landov)

The Instructed-Delegate View of Representation. Directly opposed to the trustee view of representation is the notion that members of Congress should behave as **instructed delegates.** That is, they should mirror the views of the majority of the constituents who elected them. On the surface, this approach is plausible and rewarding. For it to work, however, we must assume that constituents actually have well-formed views on the issues that are decided in Congress and, further, that they have clear-cut preferences about these issues. Neither condition is likely to be satisfied very often.

Generally, most legislators hold neither a pure trustee view nor a pure instructed-delegate view. Typically, they combine both perspectives in a pragmatic mix.

did you know?

Fewer than three in ten people can name the House member from their district, and fewer than half can name even one of the two senators from their state.

Service to Constituents

Individual members of Congress are expected by their constituents to act as brokers between private citizens and the imposing, often faceless federal government. This function of providing service to constituents usually takes the form of **casework.** The legislator and her or his staff spend a considerable portion of their time in casework activities, such as tracking down a missing Social Security check, explaining the meaning of particular bills to people who may be affected by them, promoting a local business interest, or interceding with a regulatory agency on behalf of constituents who disagree with proposed agency regulations.

Legislators and many analysts of congressional behavior regard this **ombudsperson** role as an activity that strongly benefits the members of Congress. A government characterized by a large, confusing bureaucracy and complex public programs offers innumerable opportunities for legislators to come to the assistance of (usually) grateful constituents.

Casework
Personal work for constituents by members of Congress.

Ombudsperson
A person who hears and investigates complaints by private individuals against public officials or agencies. (From the Swedish word *ombudsman,* meaning "representative.")

Oversight
The process by which Congress follows up on laws it has enacted to ensure that they are being enforced and administered in the way Congress intended.

The Oversight Function

Oversight of the bureaucracy is essential if the decisions made by Congress are to have any force. **Oversight** is the process by which Congress follows up on the laws it has enacted to ensure that they are being enforced and administered in the way Congress intended. This is done by holding committee hearings and investigations, changing the size of an agency's budget, and cross-examining high-level presidential nominees to head major agencies.

Senators and representatives traditionally have seen their oversight function as a critically important part of their legislative activities. In part, oversight is related to the concept of constituency service, particularly when Congress investigates alleged arbitrariness or wrongdoing by bureaucratic agencies.

A problem with oversight is that it has become entangled in partisan politics. During the past two decades, members of Congress have tended to ease up on oversight whenever the president is of their political party. In contrast, oversight can become intense, and even excessive, when the president faces a chamber of Congress that is controlled by the other party.

Social Media IN POLITICS

Two Facebook pages worth investigating if you are interested in Congress are sponsored by Politico, a political news blog, and *Roll Call,* a newspaper covering Congress. You can also follow these organizations on Twitter.

The Public-Education Function

Educating the public is a function that Congress performs whenever it holds public hearings, exercises oversight over the bureaucracy, or engages in committee and floor debate on such major issues and topics as immigration, global warming, and the concerns of small businesses. In so doing, Congress presents a range of viewpoints on pressing national questions. Congress also decides what issues will come up for discussion and decision. This **agenda setting** is a major facet of its public-education function.

Agenda Setting
Determining which public-policy questions will be debated or considered.

The Conflict-Resolution Function

Congress is commonly seen as an institution for resolving conflicts within American society. Organized interest groups and spokespersons for different racial, religious, economic, and ideological interests look on Congress as an access point for airing their grievances and seeking help. This puts Congress in the position of trying to resolve the differences among competing points of view by passing laws to accommodate as many interested parties as possible. To the extent that Congress meets pluralist expectations in accommodating competing interests, it tends to build support for the entire political process.

The Powers of Congress

The Constitution is both highly specific and extremely vague about the powers that Congress may exercise. The first seventeen clauses of Article I, Section 8, specify most of the **enumerated powers** of Congress—that is, powers expressly given to that body.

Enumerated Power
A power specifically granted to the national government by the Constitution. The first seventeen clauses of Article I, Section 8, specify most of the enumerated powers of Congress.

Enumerated Powers. The enumerated, or expressed, powers of Congress include the right to:

- Impose a variety of taxes, including tariffs on imports.
- Borrow funds.
- Regulate interstate commerce and international trade.
- Establish procedures for naturalizing citizens.
- Make laws regulating bankruptcies.
- Coin (and print) currency, and regulate its value.
- Establish standards of weights and measures.
- Punish counterfeiters.
- Establish post offices and post roads.
- Regulate copyrights and patents.
- Establish the federal court system.
- Punish illegal acts on the high seas.
- Declare war.
- Raise and regulate an army and a navy.
- Call up and regulate the state militias to enforce laws, to suppress insurrections, and to repel invasions.
- Govern the District of Columbia.

The most important of the domestic powers of Congress, listed in Article I, Section 8, are the rights to collect taxes, to spend, and to regulate commerce. The most important foreign policy power is the power to declare war. Other sections of the Constitution allow Congress to establish rules for its own members, to regulate the electoral college, and to override a presidential veto. Congress may also regulate the extent of the Supreme Court's authority to review cases decided by the lower courts, regulate relations among states, and propose amendments to the Constitution.

Powers of the Senate. Some functions are restricted to one chamber. The Senate must advise on, and consent to, the ratification of treaties and must accept or reject presidential nominations of ambassadors, Supreme Court justices, other federal judges, and "all other Officers of the United States." But the Senate may delegate to the president or lesser officials the power to make lower-level appointments.

These specific powers granted to the Senate mean that the Senate is a more powerful chamber than the House. The United States is unique among the world's economically advanced nations in that its "upper house"—the Senate—is more powerful than the "lower house." In every nation with a parliamentary system, the lower house in effect chooses the nation's chief executive officer, the prime minister. We describe a few of the world's upper houses in the *Beyond Our Borders* feature on the facing page.

One of the expressed powers of Congress is the power to impose and collect taxes. Every year on April 15 (if it falls on a weekday), U.S. residents line up in front of post office buildings across America to file their tax returns before the midnight deadline. These New Yorkers have waited until the last minute and are standing in line inside the James A. Farley Post Office building.

(Mario Tama/Getty Images)

Constitutional Amendments. Amendments to the Constitution provide for other congressional powers. Congress must certify the election of a president and a vice president or itself choose those officers if no candidate has a majority of the electoral vote (Twelfth Amendment). It may levy an income tax (Sixteenth Amendment) and determine who will be acting president in case of the death or incapacity of the president or vice president (Twentieth Amendment and Twenty-fifth Amendment).

The Necessary and Proper Clause. Beyond these numerous specific powers, Congress enjoys the right under Clause 18 of Article I, Section 8 (the "elastic," or "necessary and proper," clause), "to make all Laws which shall be necessary and proper for carrying into Execution the foregoing Powers [of Article I], and all other Powers vested by this Constitution in the Government of the United States, or in any Department or Officer thereof." As discussed in Chapter 3, this vague statement of congressional responsibilities has provided, over time, the basis for a greatly expanded national government. It also has constituted, at least in theory, a check on the expansion of presidential powers.

House–Senate Differences and Congressional Perks

■ Learning Outcome 2: **Explain some of the differences between the House and the Senate and some of the privileges enjoyed by members of Congress.**

Congress is composed of two markedly different—but co-equal—chambers. Although the Senate and the House of Representatives exist within the same legislative institution, each has developed certain distinctive features that clearly distinguish one from the other. A summary of these differences is given in Table 10–1 on the next page.

Beyond Our Borders

THE EXCEPTIONAL POWER OF THE U.S. SENATE

Political scientists refer to the U.S. Senate as the "upper house" of Congress. Each senator represents an entire state and is one out of only a hundred, so he or she commands more prestige and press than a representative. The Senate is also more powerful than the "lower house"—the House of Representatives. The Senate must approve treaties. It advises and consents to presidential appointments. The House does not have such powers. In most of the world, however, the "lower house" is far more powerful than the upper one. (Latin America is the one region of the world where the U.S. model dominates.) Consider some examples:

- Canada has a Senate, but it mainly revises legislation passed by the lower house, the House of Commons. Only on rare occasions does it reject such bills altogether. Its seats are entirely filled by appointment—members are often former cabinet members and provincial leaders.
- In Britain, the House of Lords is almost powerless. Until 1958, all seats were inherited, thereby giving that body no democratic legitimacy. Finally, in 1999, all but ninety-two of the hereditary peers were expelled, and today, most members are appointed "life peers." The Conservative-Liberal government in Britain has proposed making the Lords elective. The Lords are limited to making minor improvements to bills passed by the House of Commons.
- The senate in France, which is elected by local government officials, has an excellent wine cellar, but that is about it. When Charles de Gaulle became French president in 1959, he wondered aloud about the senate: "What is that little thing?"

FOR CRITICAL ANALYSIS

Why is the Senate so powerful in the United States?

Table 10–1 ▸ Differences between the House and the Senate

House*	Senate*
Members chosen from local districts	Members chosen from an entire state
Two-year term	Six-year term
Originally elected by voters	Originally (until 1913) elected by state legislatures
May impeach (indict) federal officials	May convict federal officials of impeachable offenses
Larger (435 voting members)	Smaller (100 members)
More formal rules	Fewer rules and restrictions
Debate limited	Debate extended
Less prestige and less individual notice	More prestige and more media attention
Originates bills for raising revenues	Has power to advise the president on, and to consent to, presidential appointments and treaties
Local or narrow leadership	National leadership
More partisan	Somewhat less party loyalty

*Some of these differences, such as the term of office, are provided for in the Constitution. Others, such as debate rules, are not.

Size and Rules

The central difference between the House and the Senate is simply that the House is much larger than the Senate. The House has 435 representatives, plus delegates from the District of Columbia, Puerto Rico, Guam, American Samoa, and the Virgin Islands, compared with just 100 senators. This size difference means that a greater number of formal rules are needed to govern activity in the House, whereas correspondingly looser procedures can be followed in the less-crowded Senate.

This difference is most obvious in the rules governing debate on the floors of the two chambers. The Senate usually permits extended debate on all issues that arise before it. In contrast, the House generally operates with an elaborate system in which its **Rules Committee** proposes time limitations on debate for any bill, and a majority of the entire body accepts or modifies those suggested time limits. As a consequence of its stricter time limits on debate, the House, despite its greater size, often is able to act on legislation more quickly than the Senate.

Rules Committee
A standing committee of the House of Representatives that provides special rules under which specific bills can be debated, amended, and considered by the House.

As a consequence of the greater size of the House, representatives generally cannot achieve as much individual recognition and public prestige as can members of the Senate. Senators are better able to gain media exposure and to establish careers as spokespersons for large national constituencies.

Debate and Filibustering

Filibuster
The use of the Senate's tradition of unlimited debate as a delaying tactic to block a bill.

The Senate tradition of the **filibuster,** or the use of unlimited debate as a blocking tactic, dates back to 1790.[1] In that year, a proposal to move the U.S. capital from New York to Philadelphia was stalled by such time-wasting maneuvers. This unlimited-debate tradition—which also existed in the House until 1811—is not absolute, however.

1. *Filibuster* comes from a Spanish word for pirate, which in turn came from the Dutch term *vrijbuiter,* or freebooter. The word was first used in 1851 to accuse senators of pirating or hijacking debate.

Cloture. Under Senate Rule 22, debate may be ended by invoking *cloture*. Cloture shuts off discussion on a bill. Amended in 1975 and 1979, Rule 22 states that debate may be closed off on a bill if sixteen senators sign a petition requesting it and if, after two days have elapsed, three-fifths of the entire membership (sixty votes, assuming no vacancies) vote for cloture. After cloture is invoked, each senator may speak on a bill for a maximum of one hour before a vote is taken.

Increased Use of the Filibuster. Traditionally, filibusters were rare, and the tactic was employed only on issues of principle. Filibustering senators spoke for many hours, sometimes reading names from a telephone book. By the twenty-first century, however, filibusters could be invoked without such speeches, and senators were threatening to filibuster almost every significant piece of legislation to come before the body. The threats were sufficient to create a new, ad hoc rule that important legislation needed the support of sixty senators, not fifty. As a result of the increased use of the filibuster, some senators have called for its abolition. We discuss that issue in this chapter's *Which Side Are You On?* feature below.

Reconciliation. An additional way of bypassing the filibuster is known as **reconciliation.** Budget bills sent from the House of Representatives to the Senate can be handled under special reconciliation rules that do not permit filibusters. Under the rules,

did you know?

Felons are not barred from serving in Congress, though a chamber can expel a convicted member by a two-thirds vote.

Reconciliation
A special rule that can be applied to budget bills sent from the House of Representatives to the Senate. Reconciliation measures cannot be filibustered.

Which Side Are You On?
IS IT TIME TO GET RID OF THE FILIBUSTER?

It is not in the Constitution, but it is an important institution. It is the filibuster, and it follows from Senate Rule 22, which allows for unlimited debate. Throughout American history, senators could tie up the Senate's business by talking indefinitely. In 1975, Rule 22 was revised. Since that year, a vote by sixty senators is required to stop floor debate instead of the previous sixty-seven. A second significant change in Senate practice developed, however—today, senators don't actually have to *talk* to hold a filibuster. All they have to do to maintain a filibuster is to announce that a filibuster exists. The practical effect has been to create a new rule that all important legislation requires sixty votes in the Senate. Some want the filibuster abolished. Others do not agree.

THE FILIBUSTER IS NOT EVEN CONSTITUTIONAL

Critics of the filibuster argue that it has no constitutional basis and implicitly violates many actual provisions of the Constitution. After all, the Constitution requires a *supermajority*—more than a simple majority—only for special situations such as ratifying treaties, proposing constitutional amendments, overriding presidential vetoes, and convicting impeached officials.

Consider this statement by Alexander Hamilton in *Federalist Paper* No. 75: "All provisions which require more than a majority of any [legislative] body to its resolutions have a direct tendency to embarrass the operations of the government and an indirect one to subject the sense of the majority to that of the minority." Hamilton was writing about a proposal to require that more than half of a chamber's members be present to convene a session, but his argument certainly applies to whether a body should need more than a majority of its members to take a vote.

THE FILIBUSTER AS DAMAGE CONTROL

True, filibusters today are not as colorful as they were before 1975, when senators were forced to read out of a telephone book or even wear diapers to keep a filibuster going. Yet the current filibuster system continues to provide an important protection for minority rights. Why shouldn't Congress be forced to obtain broad support for important legislation? It would be dangerous to allow major taxation and spending measures to be decided by a bare majority vote. Public opinion polling has shown that the filibuster is quite popular among the public at large. Clearly, Americans see the importance of slowing down legislation created by only a single party in Congress. The filibuster still serves a useful purpose, so let's keep it.

(© kyoshino / iStockphoto) (© Dean Mitchell / iStockphoto)

(Philip Scott Andrews/The *New York Times*)

Senator Marco Rubio (R., Fla.) was mentioned as a possible running mate for Mitt Romney in 2012. If he had been picked, he would have been the first Latino on a major party ticket.

reconciliation can be used *only* to handle budgetary matters. Also, in principle, the procedure is to be invoked only for measures that would have the net effect of reducing the federal deficit. This last restriction, however, has frequently been avoided by misleading bookkeeping.

One of the most striking examples of reconciliation took place in March 2010, when the Democrats used the procedure to make a series of amendments to the just-passed Patient Protection and Affordable Care Act, also known as Obamacare. Reconciliation was necessary because at the end of January the Republicans won a special U.S. Senate election, thus reducing the number of Democratic senators to fifty-nine.

Congresspersons and the Citizenry: A Comparison

Members of the Senate and the House of Representatives are not typical American citizens. Members of Congress are older than most Americans, partly because of constitutional age requirements and partly because a good deal of political experience normally is an advantage in running for national office. Members of Congress are also disproportionately white, male, and trained in high-status occupations. Lawyers are by far the largest occupational group among congresspersons, although the proportion of lawyers in the House is lower now than it was in the past. Compared with the average American citizen, members of Congress are well paid. Annual congressional salaries are now $174,000.

Increasingly, members of Congress are also much wealthier than the average citizen. Whereas about 3 percent of Americans have assets exceeding $1 million (not including their homes), almost half of the members of Congress are millionaires. Table 10–2 on the facing page summarizes selected characteristics of the members of Congress.

Perks and Privileges

Legislators have many benefits that are not available to most people. For example, members of Congress are granted generous **franking** privileges that permit them to mail newsletters, surveys, and other correspondence to their constituents for free.[2] The annual cost of congressional mail is now about $10 million to $15 million a year. Typically, the costs for these mailings rise substantially during election years. The use of franking has dropped since 1990 due to the growth of Web home pages, e-mail, blogs, Facebook, and Twitter.

Franking
A policy that enables members of Congress to send material through the mail by substituting their facsimile signature (frank) for postage.

did you know?

Before the Republicans reorganized House services in 1995, all members had buckets of ice delivered to their offices each day, at an annual cost of $500,000.

Permanent Professional Staffs. More than thirty thousand people are employed in the Capitol Hill bureaucracy. About half of them are personal and committee staff members. The personal staff includes office clerks and assistants; professionals who deal with media relations, draft legislation, and satisfy constituency requests for service; and staffers who maintain local offices in the member's home district or state.

The average Senate office on Capitol Hill employs about thirty staff members, and twice that number work on the personal staffs of senators from the most populous states.

2. The word *franking* derives from the Latin *francus,* which means "free."

Table 10-2 ▸ Characteristics of the 113th Congress, 2013–2015

Characteristic	U.S. Population	House	Senate
Age (median)	36.8	56.2	61.5
Percentage minority	34.9	18.2	5
Religion			
Percentage church or synagogue members	66.4	84.8	90
Percentage Roman Catholic	23.9	30.3	28
Percentage Protestant	51.3	50.1	51
Percentage Jewish	1.7	5.1	10
Percentage female	50.7	18.2	17
Percentage with advanced degrees			
Persons age 25 or above only	10.1	64.6	75
Occupation			
Percentage lawyers of those employed	0.8	36.8	56
Percentage blue-collar workers of those employed	23.0	1.1	0
Family income			
Percentage of families earning over $50,000 annually	44.9	100.0	100
Personal wealth*			
Percentage with assets over $1 million	4.7	53.3	80

*112th Congress.
Sources: CIA Factbook, 2010; Census Bureau; Association of Religion Data Archives; and authors' updates.

did you know?

The most recently constructed dormitory for Senate pages cost about $8 million, or $264,200 per bed, compared with the median cost of a university dormitory of $22,600 per bed.

House office staffs typically are about half as large as those of the Senate. The number of staff members has increased dramatically since 1960.

Congress also benefits from the expertise of the professional staffs of agencies that were created to produce information for members of the House and Senate. For example, the Congressional Research Service, the Government Accountability Office, and the Congressional Budget Office all provide reports, audits, and policy recommendations for review by members of Congress.

Congressional Caucuses: Another Source of Support. The typical member of Congress is part of a variety of caucuses. The most important caucuses are those established by the parties in each chamber. These Democratic and Republican meetings provide information to the members and devise legislative strategy for the party. Other caucuses

Michele Bachmann (R., Minn.) is the head of the Tea Party Caucus in the U.S. House of Representatives.

(AP Photo/Cliff Owen)

did you know?

One result of President Obama's 2008 election was that thirty-two African Americans ran for Congress as Republicans in 2010, the largest number to run as Republicans since the years following the Civil War.

have been founded, such as the Democratic Study Group and the Congressional Black Caucus, to support subgroups of members. Many caucuses are established to promote special interests, such as the Potato Caucus and the Sportsmen's Caucus. These caucuses deal with a limited range of legislation. Ideological caucuses, in contrast, may take up any issue. Two of the most important ideological caucuses are the conservative Tea Party Caucus and the liberal Progressive Caucus, both in the House.

Privileges and Immunities under the Law. Members of Congress also benefit from a number of special constitutional protections. Under Article I, Section 6, of the Constitution, for example, "for any Speech or Debate in either House, they shall not be questioned in any other Place." The "speech or debate" clause means that a member may make any allegations or other statements he or she wishes in connection with official duties and normally not be sued for libel or slander or otherwise be subject to legal action.

■ Learning Outcome 3: **Examine the implications of apportioning House seats.**

Congressional Elections and Apportionment

The process of electing members of Congress is decentralized. Congressional elections are conducted by the individual state governments. The states, however, must conform to the rules established by the U.S. Constitution and by national statutes. The Constitution states that representatives are to be elected every second year by popular ballot, and the number of seats awarded to each state is to be determined every ten years by the results of the census. Each state has at least one representative, with most congressional districts having about seven hundred thousand residents. Senators are elected by popular vote (since the passage of the Seventeenth Amendment) every six years; approximately one-third of the seats are chosen every two years. Each state has two senators.

Under Article I, Section 4, of the Constitution, state legislatures are given control over "the Times, Places and Manner of holding Elections for Senators and Representatives"; however, "the Congress may at any time by Law make or alter such Regulations."

Only states can elect members of Congress. Therefore, territories such as Puerto Rico and Guam are limited to electing nonvoting delegates to the House. The District of Columbia is also represented only by a nonvoting delegate.

Candidates for Congressional Elections

Congressional campaigns have changed considerably in the past two decades. Like all other campaigns, they are much more expensive, with the average cost of a winning Senate campaign now $9 million and a winning House campaign averaging more than

Representative Marcy Kaptur is the most senior member of Ohio's congressional delegation as well as the longest-serving woman in the House.

(John Kuntz/The Plain Dealer/Landov)

$1.5 million. In addition, large sums are spent on congressional campaigns by independent committees, as explained in Chapter 9. Once in office, legislators spend time almost every day raising funds for their next campaign.

Most candidates for Congress must win the nomination through a direct primary, in which **party identifiers** vote for the candidate who will be on the party ticket in the general election. To win the primary, candidates may take more liberal or more conservative positions to get the votes of party identifiers. In the general election, they may moderate their views to attract the votes of independents and voters from the other party.

Presidential Effects. Congressional candidates are always hopeful that a strong presidential candidate on their ticket will have "coattails" that will sweep in senators and representatives of the same party. In fact, in some recent presidential elections coattail effects have not materialized at all. One way to measure the coattail effect is to look at the subsequent midterm elections, held in the even-numbered years following the presidential contests. In these years, voter turnout falls sharply. The party controlling the White House frequently loses seats in Congress in the midterm elections, in part because the coattail effect ceases to apply. Table 10–3 on the right shows the pattern for midterm elections since 1946.

The Power of Incumbency. The power of incumbency in the outcome of congressional elections cannot be overemphasized. Table 10–4 on the following page shows that a sizable majority of representatives and a slightly smaller proportion of senators who decide to run for reelection are successful. This conclusion holds for both presidential-year and midterm elections. Even in 2010, when the Republicans made very large gains, most incumbents were safe. A number of scholars contend that the pursuit of reelection is the strongest motivation behind the activities of members of Congress.

Table 10–3 ▸ Midterm Gains and Losses by the Party of the President, 1946–2010

Seats Gained or Lost by the Party of the President in the House of Representatives		
Year	President's Party	Outcome
1946	D.	-55
1950	D.	-29
1954	R.	-18
1958	R.	-47
1962	D.	-4
1966	D.	-47
1970	R.	-12
1974	R.	-48
1978	D.	-15
1982	R.	-26
1986	R.	-5
1990	R.	-8
1994	D.	-52
1998	D.	+5
2002	R.	+5
2006	R.	-30
2010	D.	-64

Apportionment of the House

Two of the most complicated aspects of congressional elections are apportionment issues—**reapportionment** (the allocation of seats in the House to each state after each census) and **redistricting** (the redrawing of the boundaries of the districts within each state). In a landmark six-to-two vote in 1962, the United States Supreme Court made the districting of state legislative districts a **justiciable** (that is, a reviewable) **question.**[3] The Court did so by invoking the Fourteenth Amendment principle that no state can deny to any person "the equal protection of the laws." In 1964, the Court held that *both* chambers of a state legislature must be designed so that all districts are equal in population.[4] Later that year, the Court applied this "one person, one vote" principle to U.S. congressional districts on the basis of Article I, Section 2, of the Constitution, which requires that members of the House be chosen "by the People of the several States."[5]

Severe malapportionment of congressional districts before 1964 resulted in some districts containing two or three times the populations of other districts in the same state, thereby diluting the effect of a vote cast in the more populous districts. This system generally benefited the conservative populations of rural areas and small towns and harmed the interests of the more heavily populated and liberal cities.

Party Identifier
A person who identifies with a political party.

Reapportionment
The allocation of seats in the House of Representatives to each state after each census.

Redistricting
The redrawing of the boundaries of the congressional districts within each state.

Justiciable Question
A question that may be raised and reviewed in court.

3. *Baker v. Carr,* 369 U.S. 186 (1962). The word *justiciable* is pronounced juhs-*tish*-a-buhl.
4. *Reynolds v. Sims,* 377 U.S. 533 (1964).
5. *Wesberry v. Sanders,* 376 U.S. 1 (1964).

Table 10-4 ▸ The Power of Incumbency

	1986	1988	1990	1992	1994	1996	1998	2000	2002	2004	2006	2008	2010	2012
House														
Number of incumbent candidates	394	409	406	368	387	384	402	403	393	404	405	404	397	390
Reelected	385	402	390	325	349	361	395	394	383	397	382	381	338	351
Percentage of total	97.7	98.3	96.0	88.3	90.2	94.0	98.3	97.8	97.5	98.3	94.3	94.3	85.1	80.7
Defeated	9	7	16	43	38	23	7	9	10	7	23	23	59	39
In primary	3	1	1	19	4	2	1	3	3	1	2	5	4	14
In general election	6	6	15	24	34	21	6	6	7	6	21	18	55	25
Senate														
Number of incumbent candidates	28	27	32	28	26	21	29	29	28	26	29	30	24	23
Reelected	21	23	31	23	24	19	26	23	24	25	23	26	20	21
Percentage of total	75.0	85.2	96.9	82.1	92.3	90.5	89,7	79.3	85.7	96.2	79.3	86.7	83.3	91.3
Defeated	7	4	1	5	2	2	3	6	4	1	6	4	4	2
In primary	0	0	0	1	0	1	0	0	1	0	1*	0	3*	1
In general election	7	4	1	4	2	1	3	6	3	1	6	3	2	1

*In 2006, Joe Lieberman of Connecticut lost the Democratic primary but won the general election as an independent. He then caucused with the Democrats. In 2010, Alaska's Lisa Murkowski lost the Republican primary but won the general election as a write-in candidate. She continued to caucus with the Republicans.

Sources: Norman Ornstein, Thomas E. Mann, and Michael J. Malbin, *Vital Statistics on Congress, 2001–2002* (Washington, D.C.: The AEI Press, 2002); and authors' updates.

2012 elections

PARTY CONTROL OF CONGRESS AFTER THE 2012 ELECTIONS

Early in 2012, Senate Democrats seemed to be in trouble. Many of the seats they were defending were in normally Republican states. Political scientists predicted that the Democrats would lose control of the Senate. In the end, the Democrats gained two seats for a total of fifty-five. True, the gains could be chalked up to weak Tea Party Republican candidates. Even with more moderate Republicans, however, the Democrats would have kept their existing margin.

In the House, the Democrats apparently added a net eight seats, for a total of two hundred and one. The Republicans stayed in control with two hundred and thirty-four seats. The outlook for the Republicans was less rosy than these numbers suggest, however. The 2010 elections handed the Republicans many state legislatures right on the eve of the redistricting required by the 2010 census. Republicans took advantage of their opportunities.

Consider Pennsylvania. It went for Obama in 2012, and Democratic senator Bob Casey enjoyed an easy victory. In House contests, with 98 percent of precincts in, Democratic candidates had won 2.72 million votes. Republican candidates received 2.65 million. How many representatives did these votes elect? Five Democrats and thirteen Republicans. That is how effective a good gerrymander can be. There were states with Democratic gerrymanders, such as Illinois. But Florida, Indiana, Michigan, North Carolina, Ohio, and Texas all had Republican gerrymanders. The Republican problem is that gerrymanders do not last forever. In the long run, parties need votes.

Gerrymandering. Although the general issue of apportionment has been dealt with fairly successfully by the one person, one vote principle, the **gerrymandering** issue has not yet been resolved. This term refers to the legislative-boundary-drawing tactics that were used under Elbridge Gerry, the governor of Massachusetts, in the 1812 elections. (See Figure 10–1 alongside.) A district is said to have been gerrymandered when its shape is altered substantially by the dominant party to maximize its electoral strength at the expense of the minority party.

Figure 10–1 ▸ The Original Gerrymander

The practice of "gerrymandering"—the excessive manipulation of the shape of a legislative district to benefit a certain incumbent or party—is probably as old as the republic, but the name originated in 1812. In that year, the Massachusetts legislature carved out of Essex County a district that historian John Fiske said had a "dragonlike contour." When the painter Gilbert Stuart saw the misshapen district, he penciled in a head, wings, and claws and exclaimed, "That will do for a salamander!" Editor Benjamin Russell replied, "Better say a Gerrymander" (after Elbridge Gerry, then governor of Massachusetts).

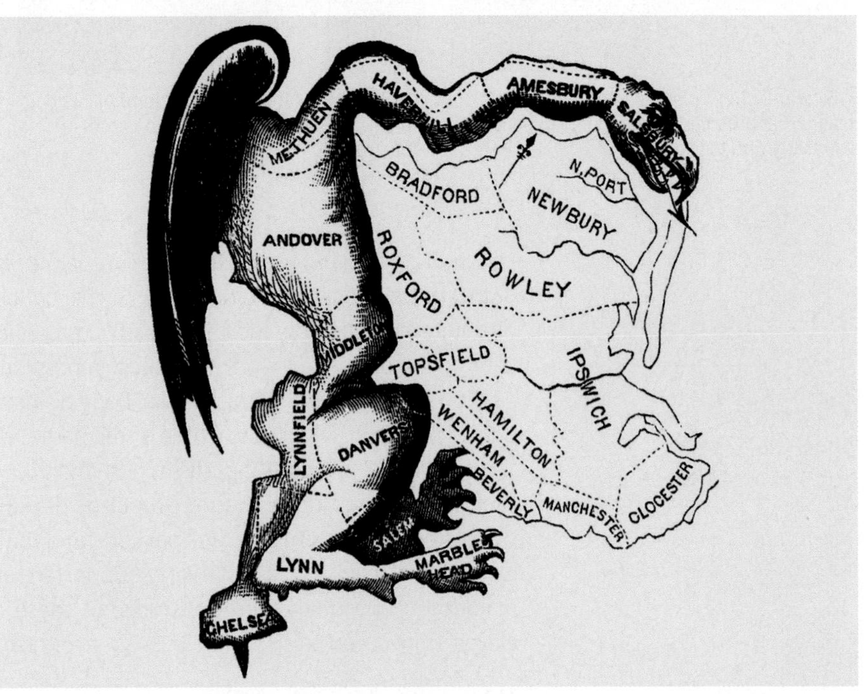

Source: *Congressional Quarterly's Guide to Congress,* 3d ed. (Washington, D.C.: Congressional Quarterly Press, 1982), p. 695.

In 1986, the Supreme Court heard a case that challenged gerrymandered congressional districts in Indiana. The Court ruled for the first time that redistricting for the political benefit of one group could be challenged on constitutional grounds. In this specific case, *Davis v. Bandemer,*[6] however, the Court did not agree that the districts had been drawn unfairly, because it could not be proved that a group of voters would consistently be deprived of influence at the polls as a result of the new districts.

Gerrymandering
The drawing of legislative district boundary lines for the purpose of obtaining partisan or factional advantage. A district is said to be gerrymandered when its shape is manipulated by the dominant party to maximize electoral strength at the expense of the minority party.

In 2004, the United States Supreme Court reviewed an obviously political redistricting scheme in Pennsylvania. The Court concluded, however, that the federal judiciary would not address purely political gerrymandering claims.[7] Two years later, the Supreme Court reached a similar conclusion with respect to most of the new congressional districts created by the Republicans in the Texas legislature in 2003. Again, except for one district in Texas, the Court refused to intervene in what was clearly a political gerrymandering plan.[8] Still, gerrymandering is widely seen as unfair, and for that reason several states have passed laws aimed at outlawing the process. We discussed these reforms in the chapter-opening *What If. . .* feature.

How Gerrymandering Works. Congressional and state legislative redistricting decisions are often made by a small group of political leaders within a state legislature. Typically, their goal is to shape voting districts in such a way as to maximize their party's chances of winning state legislative seats, as well as seats in Congress. Two of the techniques in use are called *packing* and *cracking*. By employing powerful computers and software, voters supporting the opposing party are "packed" into as few districts as possible or the opposing party's supporters are "cracked" into different districts.

Figure 10–2 on the following page illustrates the redistricting process. In these three examples, sixty-four individuals must be distributed among four districts, each of which has a population of sixteen. Two major political parties are involved: the O Party and the X Party.

6. 478 U.S. 109 (1986).
7. *Vieth v. Jubelirer,* 541 U.S. 267 (2004).
8. *League of United Latin American Citizens v. Perry,* 548 U.S. 399 (2006).

Figure 10-2 ▸ Examples of Districting

O	O	O	O	X	X	X	X
O	O	O	O	X	X	X	X
O	O	O	O	X	X	X	X
O	O	O	O	X	X	X	X
X	X	X	X	O	O	O	O
X	X	X	X	O	O	O	O
X	X	X	X	O	O	O	O
X	X	X	X	O	O	O	O

Example 1. A "bipartisan gerrymander" aimed at protecting incumbents in both the O Party and the X Party.

O	O	O	O	X	X	X	X
O	O	O	O	X	X	X	X
O	O	O	O	X	X	X	X
O	O	O	O	X	X	X	X
X	X	X	X	O	O	O	O
X	X	X	X	O	O	O	O
X	X	X	X	O	O	O	O
X	X	X	X	O	O	O	O

Example 2. An unstable system. All districts have the same number of supporters in each party.

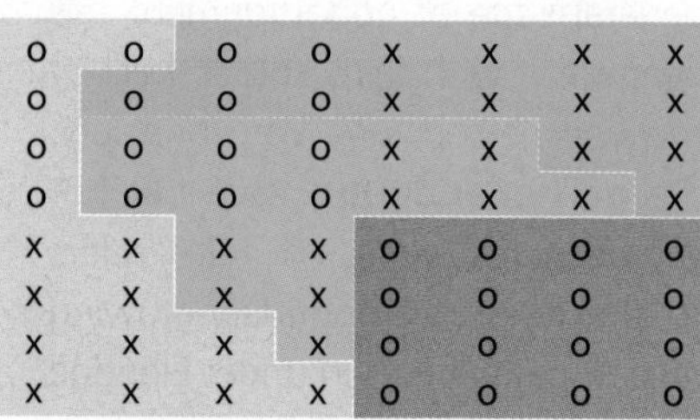

Example 3. A classic partisan gerrymander. The X Party is almost guaranteed to carry three districts.

In Example 1, supporters of the two parties are sorted so that each differently colored district contains only one kind of voter. Such a pattern sometimes appears when the members of a state legislature are most interested in preserving the seats of incumbents, regardless of party. In this example, it would be almost impossible to dislodge a sitting member in a general election. Example 2 is the reverse case. Every district is divided evenly between the parties, and even a very slight swing toward one of the parties could give that party all four seats.

Example 3 is a classic partisan gerrymander benefiting the X Party. The orange district in the lower right is an example of packing—the maximum possible number of supporters of the O Party are packed into that district. The other three districts are examples of cracking. The O Party supporters are cracked so that they do not have a majority in any of the three districts. In these districts, the X Party has majorities of eleven to five, ten to six, and eleven to five, respectively.

"Minority-Majority" Districts. Under the mandate of the Voting Rights Act of 1965, the Justice Department issued directives to states after the 1990 census instructing them to create congressional districts that would maximize the voting power of minority groups—that is, create districts in which minority group voters were the majority. The result was a number of creatively drawn congressional districts.

Many of these "minority–majority" districts were challenged in court by citizens who claimed that creating districts based on race or ethnicity alone violates the equal protection clause of the Constitution. In 2001, for example, the Supreme Court reviewed, for a second time, a case involving North Carolina's Twelfth District.

The district was 165 miles long, following Interstate 85 for the most part. According to a local joke, the district was so narrow that a car traveling down the interstate highway with both doors open would kill most of the voters in the district. In 1996, the Supreme Court had held that the district was unconstitutional because race had been the dominant factor in drawing the district's boundaries. Shortly thereafter, the boundaries were redrawn, but the district was again challenged as a racial gerrymander. In 2001, however, the Supreme Court held that there was insufficient evidence that race had been the dominant factor when the boundaries were redrawn.[9] The Twelfth District's boundaries remained in place.

■ Learning Outcome 4: **Describe the committee structure of the House and the Senate.**

The Committee Structure

Most of the actual work of legislating is performed by the committees and subcommittees within Congress. Thousands of bills are introduced in every session of Congress, and no single member can possibly be adequately informed on all the issues that arise. The

9. *Easley v. Cromartie,* 532 U.S. 234 (2001).

committee system is a way to provide for specialization, or a division of the legislative effort. Members of a committee can concentrate on just one area or topic—such as taxation or energy—and develop sufficient expertise to draft appropriate legislation when needed. The flow of legislation through both the House and the Senate is determined largely by the speed with which the members of these committees act on bills and resolutions.

(Brooks Kraft/Corbis)

Senator Daniel Inouye (D., Hawaii) is the highest-ranking Asian American politician in U.S. history. He is the most senior member of the Senate and holds the honorary post of Senate president pro tem. What are the benefits of seniority?

The Power of Committees

Sometimes called "little legislatures," committees usually have the final say on pieces of legislation.[10] Committee actions may be overturned on the floor by the House or Senate, but this rarely happens. Legislators normally defer to the expertise of the chairperson and other members of the committee who speak on the floor in defense of a committee decision. Chairpersons of committees exercise control over the scheduling of hearings and formal actions on bills. They also decide which subcommittee will act on legislation falling within their committee's jurisdiction. Committees normally have the power to kill proposed legislation by refusing to act on it—by never sending it to the entire chamber for a vote.

Committees only very rarely are deprived of control over bills—although this kind of action is provided for in the rules of each chamber. In the House, if a bill has been considered by a standing committee for thirty days, the signatures of a majority (218) of the House membership on a **discharge petition** can pry a bill out of an uncooperative committee's hands. From 1909 to 2012, however, although over nine hundred such petitions were initiated, only slightly more than two dozen resulted in successful discharge efforts. Of those, twenty resulted in bills that passed the House.[11]

Discharge Petition
A procedure by which a bill in the House of Representatives can be forced (discharged) out of a committee that has refused to report it for consideration by the House. The petition must be signed by an absolute majority (218) of representatives and is used only on rare occasions.

Standing Committee
A permanent committee in the House or Senate that considers bills within a certain subject area.

Types of Congressional Committees

Over the past two centuries, Congress has created several different types of committees, each of which serves particular needs of the institution.

Standing Committees. By far, the most important committees in Congress are the **standing committees**—permanent bodies that are established by the rules of each chamber and that continue from session to session. A list of the standing committees of the 113th Congress is presented in Table 10–5 on the following page. In addition, most of the standing committees have created subcommittees to carry out their work. For example, the 113th Congress has 73 subcommittees in the Senate and 104 in the House. Each standing committee is given a specific area of legislative policy jurisdiction, and almost all legislative measures are considered by the appropriate standing committees.

Because of the importance of their work and the traditional influence of their members in Congress, certain committees are considered to be more prestigious than others. Seats on standing committees that handle spending issues are especially sought after because members can use these positions to benefit their constituents. Committees that control spending include the Appropriations Committee in either chamber and the Ways and Means Committee in the House. Members also normally seek seats on committees that handle matters of special interest to their constituents. A member of the House from

10. The term *little legislatures* is from Woodrow Wilson, *Congressional Government* (Mineola, N.Y.: Dover Books, 2006 [first published in 1885]).
11. Congressional Quarterly, Inc., *Guide to Congress*, 7th ed. (Washington, D.C.: CQ Press, 2012).

Table 10-5 ▸ Standing Committees of the 113th Congress, 2013–2015

House Committees	Senate Committees
Agriculture	Agriculture, Nutrition, and Forestry
Appropriations	Appropriations
Armed Services	Armed Services
Budget	Banking, Housing, and Urban Affairs
Education and the Workforce	Budget
Energy and Commerce	Commerce, Science, and Transportation
Ethics	Energy and Natural Resources
Financial Services	Environment and Public Works
Foreign Affairs	Finance
Homeland Security	Foreign Relations
House Administration	Health, Education, Labor, and Pensions
Judiciary	Homeland Security and Governmental Affairs
Natural Resources	Judiciary
Oversight and Government Reform	Rules and Administration
Rules	Small Business and Entrepreneurship
Science, Space, and Technology	Veterans' Affairs
Small Business	
Transportation and Infrastructure	
Veterans' Affairs	
Ways and Means	

an agricultural district, for example, will have an interest in joining the House Agriculture Committee.

Select Committee
A temporary legislative committee established for a limited time period and for a special purpose.

Select Committees. In principle, a **select committee** is created for a limited time and for a specific legislative purpose. For example, a select committee may be formed to investigate a public problem, such as child nutrition or aging. In practice, a select committee, such as the Select Committee on Intelligence in each chamber, may continue indefinitely. Select committees rarely create original legislation.

Joint Committee
A legislative committee composed of members from both chambers of Congress.

Joint Committees. A **joint committee** is formed by the concurrent action of both chambers of Congress and consists of members from each chamber. Joint committees, which may be permanent or temporary, have dealt with the economy, taxation, and the Library of Congress.

Conference Committee
A special joint committee appointed to reconcile differences when bills pass the two chambers of Congress in different forms.

Conference Committees. Special joint committees—**conference committees**—are formed for the purpose of achieving agreement between the House and the Senate on the exact wording of legislative acts when the two chambers pass legislative proposals in different forms. No bill can be sent to the White House to be signed into law unless it first passes both chambers in identical form. Conference committees are in a position to make significant alterations to legislation and frequently become the focal point of policy debates.

The House Rules Committee. Due to its special "gatekeeping" power over the terms on which legislation will reach the floor of the House of Representatives, the House Rules Committee holds a uniquely powerful position. A special committee rule sets the time limit on debate and determines whether and how a bill may be amended. The Rules Committee has the unusual power to convene while the House is meeting as a whole, to have its resolutions considered immediately on the floor and to initiate legislation on its own.

The Selection of Committee Members

In both chambers, members are appointed to standing committees by the steering committee of their party. The majority-party member with the longest term of continuous service on a standing committee is given preference when the committee selects its chairperson. The most senior member of the minority party is called the *ranking committee member* for that party. This **seniority system** is not required by law but is an informal, traditional process, and it applies to other significant posts in Congress as well. The system, although it deliberately treats members unequally, provides a predictable means of assigning positions of power within Congress.

Seniority System
A custom followed in both chambers of Congress specifying that the member of the majority party with the longest term of continuous service will be given preference when a committee chairperson (or a holder of some other significant post) is selected.

The general pattern until the 1970s was that members of the House or Senate who represented safe seats would be reelected continually and eventually could accumulate enough years of continuous committee service to enable them to become the chairpersons of their committees. In the 1970s, reforms in the chairperson selection process somewhat modified the seniority system in the House. The reforms introduced the use of a secret ballot in electing House committee chairpersons and allowed for the possibility of choosing a chairperson on a basis other than seniority. The Democrats immediately replaced three senior chairpersons who were out of step with the rest of their party. In 1995, under Speaker Newt Gingrich, the Republicans chose relatively junior House members as chairpersons of several key committees, thus ensuring conservative control of the committees. The Republicans also passed a rule limiting the term of a chairperson to six years.

The Formal Leadership

■ Learning Outcome 5:
Specify the key leadership positions in each chamber.

The limited amount of centralized power that exists in Congress is exercised through party-based mechanisms. Congress is organized by party. When the Democratic Party, for example, wins a majority of seats in either the House or the Senate, Democrats control the official positions of power in that chamber, and every important committee has a Democratic chairperson and a majority of Democratic members. The same process holds when Republicans are in the majority.

Leadership in the House

The House leadership is made up of the Speaker, the majority and minority leaders, and the party whips.

The Speaker. The foremost power holder in the House of Representatives is the **Speaker of the House.** The Speaker's position is technically a nonpartisan one, but in fact, for the better part of two centuries, the Speaker has been the official leader of the majority party in the House. When a new Congress convenes in January of odd-numbered years, each party nominates a candidate for Speaker. All Republican members of the

Speaker of the House
The presiding officer in the House of Representatives. The Speaker is always a member of the majority party and is the most powerful and influential member of the House.

(Courtesy of the U.S. Congress)

(AP Photo/Cliff Owen)

(Courtesy of the U.S. Congress)

When the Republicans took control of the House of Representatives following the 2010 midterm elections, they elected John Boehner of Ohio, left, as Speaker of the House, and Eric Cantor of Virginia, center, as House majority leader. Democrat Nancy Pelosi of California, right, formerly the Speaker, became House minority leader. These three leaders are expected to be reelected by their caucuses in the leadership elections that are held in late November 2012.

House are expected to vote for their party's nominee, and all Democrats are expected to support their candidate. The vote to organize the House is the one vote in which representatives must vote with their party. In a sense, this vote defines a member's partisan status.

The major formal powers of the Speaker include the following:

- Presiding over meetings of the House.
- Appointing members of joint committees and conference committees.
- Scheduling legislation for floor action.
- Deciding points of order and interpreting the rules with the advice of the House parliamentarian.
- Referring bills and resolutions to the appropriate standing committees of the House.

A Speaker may take part in floor debate and vote, as can any other member of Congress, but recent Speakers usually have voted only to break a tie.

Majority Leader of the House
The majority leader of the House of Representatives is selected by the majority party in caucus or conference to foster cohesion among party members and to act as spokesperson for the majority party in the House.

The Majority Leader. The **majority leader of the House** is elected by a caucus of the majority party to foster cohesion among party members and to act as a spokesperson for the party. The majority leader influences the scheduling of debate and acts as the chief supporter of the Speaker. The majority leader cooperates with the Speaker and other party leaders, both inside and outside Congress, to formulate the party's legislative program and to guide that program through the legislative process in the House. The parties have often recruited future Speakers from those who hold the position of majority leader.

Minority Leader of the House
The party leader elected by the minority party in the House.

The Minority Leader. The **minority leader of the House** is the candidate nominated for Speaker by a caucus of the minority party. Like the majority leader, the leader of the minority party has as her or his primary responsibility the maintaining of cohesion within the party's ranks. The minority leader works for cooperation among the party's members and speaks on behalf of the president if the minority party controls the White House. In relations with the majority party, the minority leader consults with both the Speaker and the majority leader on recognizing members who wish to speak on the floor, on House rules and procedures, and on the scheduling of legislation. Minority leaders have no actual power in these areas, however.

Whips. The leadership of each party includes assistants to the majority and minority leaders, known as **whips.**[12] The whips are members of Congress who assist the party leaders by passing information down from the leadership to party members and by ensuring that members show up for floor debate and cast their votes on important issues. Whips conduct polls among party members about the members' views on legislation, inform the leaders about whose vote is doubtful and whose is certain, and may exert pressure on members to support the leaders' positions.

Whip
A member of Congress who aids the majority or minority leader of the House or the Senate.

Leadership in the Senate

The Senate is less than one-fourth the size of the House. This fact alone probably explains why a formal, complex, and centralized leadership structure is not as necessary in the Senate as it is in the House.

The two highest-ranking formal leadership positions in the Senate are essentially ceremonial in nature. Under the Constitution, the vice president of the United States is the president (that is, the presiding officer) of the Senate and may vote to break a tie. The vice president, however, is only rarely present for a meeting of the Senate. The Senate elects instead a **president pro tempore** ("pro tem") to preside over the Senate in the vice president's absence. Ordinarily, the president pro tem is the member of the majority party with the longest continuous term of service in the Senate. As mentioned, the president pro tem is mostly a ceremonial position. More junior senators take turns actually presiding over the sessions of the Senate.

President Pro Tempore
The temporary presiding officer of the Senate in the absence of the vice president.

The real leadership power in the Senate rests in the hands of the **Senate majority leader,** the **Senate minority leader,** and their respective whips. The Senate majority and minority leaders have the right to be recognized first in debate on the floor and generally exercise the same powers available to the House majority and minority leaders. They control the scheduling of debate on the floor in conjunction with the majority party's policy committee, influence the allocation of committee assignments for new members or for senators attempting to transfer to a new committee, influence the selection of other party officials, and participate in selecting members of conference committees. The leaders are expected to mobilize support for partisan legislative or presidential initiatives. They act as liaisons with the White House when the president is of their party, try to obtain the

Senate Majority Leader
The chief spokesperson of the majority party in the Senate, who directs the legislative program and party strategy.

Senate Minority Leader
The party officer in the Senate who commands the minority party's opposition to the policies of the majority party and directs the legislative program and strategy of his or her party.

12. *Whip* comes from "whipper-in," a fox-hunting term for someone who keeps the hunting dogs from straying.

(Courtesy of Senator Reid)

(Courtesy of Senator McConnell)

After the Democrats took control of the U.S. Senate in the 2006 elections, Republican senator Mitch McConnell of Kentucky, right, was elected Senate minority leader. Democratic senator Harry Reid of Nevada, left, who had been the Senate minority leader, became the Senate majority leader. Both leaders are expected to be reelected by their caucuses in the leadership elections that are held in late November 2012.

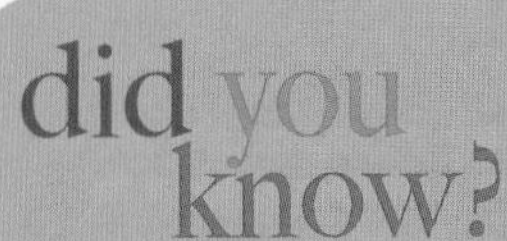

The Constitution does not require that the Speaker of the House of Representatives be an elected member of the House.

cooperation of committee chairpersons, and seek to facilitate the smooth functioning of the Senate through the senators' unanimous consent. The majority and minority leaders are elected by their respective party caucuses. Senate party whips, like their House counterparts, maintain communication within the party on platform positions and try to ensure that party colleagues are present for floor debate and important votes. The Senate whip system is far less elaborate than its counterpart in the House, because there are fewer members to track and senators have a greater tradition of independence. A list of the candidates expected to become the formal party leaders of the 113th Congress is presented in Table 10–6 below.

Lawmaking and Budgeting

■ Learning Outcome 6: **Detail the process by which a bill becomes law and how the federal government establishes its budget.**

Each year, Congress and the president propose and approve many laws. Some are budget and appropriations laws that require extensive bargaining but must be passed for the government to continue to function. Other laws are relatively free of controversy and are passed with little dissension. Still other proposed legislation is extremely controversial and reaches to the roots of differences between Republicans and Democrats.

Figure 10–3, on the facing page, shows that each law begins as a bill, which must be introduced in either the House or the Senate. Often, similar bills are introduced in both chambers. A "money bill," however, must start in the House. In each chamber, the bill follows similar steps. It is referred to a committee and its subcommittees for study, discussion, hearings, and markup (rewriting). When the bill is reported out to the full chamber, it must be scheduled for debate (by the Rules Committee in the House and by the leadership in the Senate). After the bill has been passed in each chamber, if it contains different provisions, a conference committee is formed to write a compromise bill, which must be approved by both chambers before it is sent to the president to sign or veto.

Table 10-6 ▸ Party Leaders in the 113th Congress, 2013–2015

The named individuals were the leading contenders for the various positions in the 2012 leadership elections.

Position	Incumbent	Party/State	Leader Since
House			
Speaker	John Boehner	R., Ohio	Jan. 2011
Majority leader	Eric Cohen	R., Va.	Jan. 2011
Majority whip	Kevin McCarthy	R., Calif.	Jan. 2011
Chair of the Republican Conference	Jeb Hensarling	R., Texas	Jan. 2011
Minority leader	Nancy Pelosi	D., Calif.	Jan. 2011
Minority whip	Steney Hoyer	D., Md.	Jan. 2011
Chair of the Democratic Conference	John Larson	D., Conn.	Jan. 2009
Senate			
President pro tempore	Daniel Inouye	D., Hawaii	June 2010
Majority leader	Harry Reid	D., Nev.	Jan. 2007
Majority whip	Dick Durbin	D., Ill.	Jan. 2007
Chair of the Democratic Conference	Harry Reid	D., Nev.	Jan. 2007
Minority leader	Mitch McConnell	R., Ky.	Jan. 2007
Minority whip	Jon Kyl	R., Ariz.	Dec. 2007
Chair of the Republican Conference	Lamar Alexander	R., Tenn.	Dec. 2007

Figure 10-3 ▸ How a Bill Becomes Law

This illustration shows the most typical way in which proposed legislation is enacted into law. Most legislation begins as similar bills introduced into the House and the Senate. The process is illustrated here with two hypothetical bills, House bill No. 100 (HR 100) and Senate bill No. 200 (S 200). The path of HR 100 is shown on the left, and that of S 200 on the right.

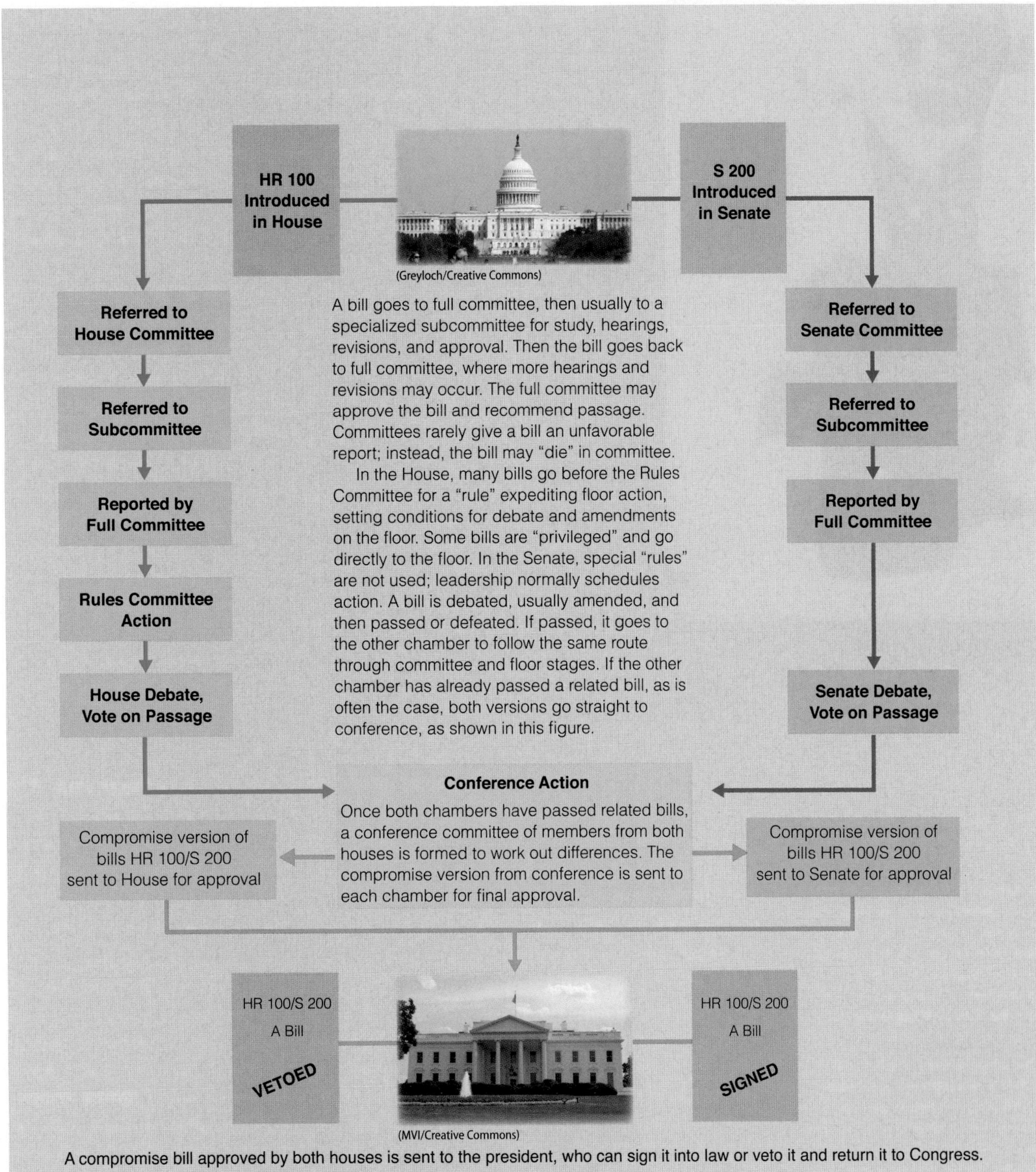
HR 100 Introduced in House
S 200 Introduced in Senate
(Greyloch/Creative Commons)
Referred to House Committee
Referred to Subcommittee
Reported by Full Committee
Rules Committee Action
House Debate, Vote on Passage
Referred to Senate Committee
Referred to Subcommittee
Reported by Full Committee
Senate Debate, Vote on Passage
A bill goes to full committee, then usually to a specialized subcommittee for study, hearings, revisions, and approval. Then the bill goes back to full committee, where more hearings and revisions may occur. The full committee may approve the bill and recommend passage. Committees rarely give a bill an unfavorable report; instead, the bill may "die" in committee.
In the House, many bills go before the Rules Committee for a "rule" expediting floor action, setting conditions for debate and amendments on the floor. Some bills are "privileged" and go directly to the floor. In the Senate, special "rules" are not used; leadership normally schedules action. A bill is debated, usually amended, and then passed or defeated. If passed, it goes to the other chamber to follow the same route through committee and floor stages. If the other chamber has already passed a related bill, as is often the case, both versions go straight to conference, as shown in this figure.
Conference Action
Once both chambers have passed related bills, a conference committee of members from both houses is formed to work out differences. The compromise version from conference is sent to each chamber for final approval.
Compromise version of bills HR 100/S 200 sent to House for approval
Compromise version of bills HR 100/S 200 sent to Senate for approval
HR 100/S 200 A Bill VETOED
HR 100/S 200 A Bill SIGNED
(MVI/Creative Commons)
A compromise bill approved by both houses is sent to the president, who can sign it into law or veto it and return it to Congress. Congress may override a presidential veto by a two-thirds majority in both chambers; the bill then becomes law without the president's signature.

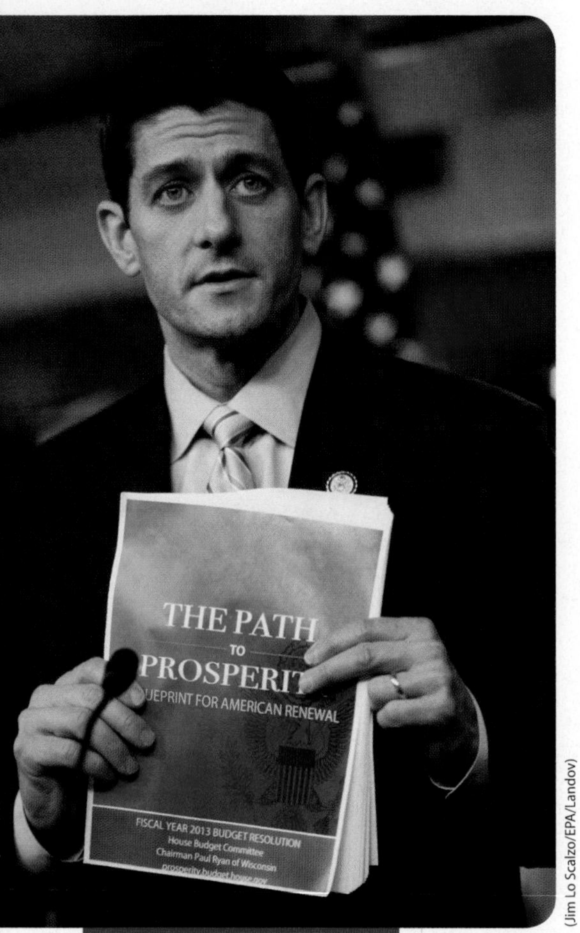

(Jim Lo Scalzo/EPA/Landov)

Congressman Paul Ryan (R., Wisc.) presented a budget plan that was accepted by the House but not the Senate.

How Much Will the Government Spend?

The Constitution is very clear about where the power of the purse lies in the national government: all taxing or spending bills must originate in the House of Representatives. Today, much of the business of Congress is concerned with approving government expenditures through the budget process and with raising the revenues to pay for government programs.

From 1922, when Congress required the president to prepare and present to the legislature an **executive budget,** until 1974, the congressional budget process was so disjointed that it was difficult to visualize the total picture of government finances. The president presented the executive budget to Congress in January. It was broken down into thirteen or more appropriations bills. Some time later, after all of the bills had been debated, amended, and passed, it was more or less possible to estimate total government spending for the next year.

Frustrated by the president's ability to impound, or withhold, funds and dissatisfied with the entire budget process, Congress passed the Budget and Impoundment Control Act of 1974 to regain some control over the nation's spending. The act required the president to spend the funds that Congress had appropriated, ending the president's ability to kill programs by withholding funds. The other major result of the act was to force Congress to examine total national taxing and spending at least twice in each budget cycle.

Even though Congress has a firm grasp on what the federal government's revenues and expenditure will be, it does not follow that the federal budget will be balanced. In the *Politics and Economics* feature on the facing page, we provide background on a crisis in taxing and spending that took place following the elections of 2012.

The budget cycle of the federal government is described in the rest of this section. (See Figure 10–4 on page 346 for a graphic illustration of the budget cycle.)

Executive Budget
The budget prepared and submitted by the president to Congress.

Fiscal Year (FY)
A twelve-month period that is used for bookkeeping, or accounting, purposes. Usually, the fiscal year does not coincide with the calendar year. For example, the federal government's fiscal year runs from October 1 through September 30.

Spring Review
The annual process in which the Office of Management and Budget (OMB) requires federal agencies to review their programs, activities, and goals and submit their requests for funding for the next fiscal year.

Fall Review
The annual process in which the OMB, after receiving formal federal agency requests for funding for the next fiscal year, reviews the requests, makes changes, and submits its recommendations to the president.

Preparing the Budget. The federal government operates on a **fiscal year (FY)** cycle. The fiscal year runs from October through September, so that fiscal year 2014, or FY14, runs from October 1, 2013, through September 30, 2014. Eighteen months before a fiscal year starts, the executive branch begins preparing the budget. The Office of Management and Budget (OMB) receives advice from the Council of Economic Advisers and the Treasury Department. The OMB outlines the budget and then sends it to the various departments and agencies. Bargaining follows, in which—to use only two of many examples—the Department of Health and Human Services argues for more welfare spending, and the armed forces argue for more defense spending.

Even though the OMB has fewer than 550 employees, it is one of the most powerful agencies in Washington. It assembles the budget documents and monitors federal agencies throughout each year. Every year, it begins the budget process with a **spring review**, in which it requires all of the agencies to review their programs, activities, and goals. At the beginning of each summer, the OMB sends out a letter instructing agencies to submit their requests for funding for the next fiscal year. By the end of the summer, each agency must submit a formal request to the OMB.

In actuality, the "budget season" begins with the **fall review.** At this time, the OMB looks at budget requests and, in almost all cases, routinely cuts them back. Although the OMB works within guidelines established by the president, specific decisions often are left to the OMB director and the director's associates. By the beginning of November, the

Politics AND Economics

THE THREAT OF TAXMAGEDDON

Armageddon is the great battle between good and evil predicted to take place during the "end times." Just such a catastrophic scenario—Taxmageddon—was predicted by many if Democrats and Republicans could not reach a compromise over the federal budget after the 2012 elections.

THE FEDERAL BUDGET DEFICIT

For decades, the federal government has spent much more than it has collected through taxes and other revenues. (The years 1998 through 2001 were an exception—revenues exceeded expenditures.) After the onset of the Great Recession in 2007, deficits grew sharply because of falling tax collections, increases in social spending due to high unemployment, and the Obama stimulus measures. In 2010, the deficit peaked at more than 10 percent of the nation's total income—a budget hole of about $1.3 *trillion*. As you might imagine, the size of the deficit was a major political issue during both the 2010 and 2012 election seasons.

TAXMAGEDDON—THE DETAILS

Ironically, Congress had created a situation such that if it did absolutely nothing, the federal budget deficit would drop on December 31, 2012. A vast number of tax breaks were scheduled to expire, all at the same time. Tax cuts passed under President George W. Bush were to end, raising rates on investment income, inheritances, and earnings at all levels. The "marriage penalty" for joint filers would be resurrected, and the value of the child credit was to be cut in half. The Social Security payroll tax would pop back up to 6.2 percent from 4.2 percent, and new Medicare taxes to fund President Obama's health-care initiative would for the first time strike high-income households. Finally, huge cuts in military and domestic spending, part of a 2011 budget deal, were scheduled to take effect. No matter how this crisis was handled, higher taxes seemed inevitable.

THE IMPACT ON THE ECONOMY

Why would Taxmageddon be a disaster? Wouldn't it be a good idea to address the federal budget deficit? Certainly, in the long run, the deficit must be addressed. In the short run, however, enormous tax increases could create equally enormous problems. Economists and political leaders of all stripes agreed on that, although they did not agree on why.

A traditional view was based on the thinking of John Maynard Keynes, a British economist. Keynes believed that when unemployment was high and the economy was operating below its potential, the federal government should run a deficit. The increased demand from government spending would stimulate the economy. Huge tax increases and spending reductions while the economy was still weak would restart the Great Recession. The budget should not be balanced until the economy was in better shape.

Conservatives who rejected Keynesian economics argued that the spending cuts by themselves would be positive—they would enhance confidence. But enormous permanent tax increases would destroy initiative in the private sector and "kill jobs."

Regardless of how Taxmageddon was handled, and no matter which school of economics was right, one point was clear. Spending obligations taken on by the federal government—especially commitments to health care for the elderly—were not compatible with the tax system. Something would have to give. After all, at the height of the recession, the national government was collecting only $3 for every $5 it spent.

FOR CRITICAL ANALYSIS

How might you react to a big increase in the taxes you pay to the federal government?

director's review begins. The director meets with cabinet secretaries and budget officers. Time becomes crucial. The budget must be completed by January so that it can be included in the *Economic Report of the President*.

The Election-Year Budget. The schedule just described cannot apply to a year in which the voters elect a new president or to a year in which a new president is inaugurated. In 2008, George W. Bush did not engage in a fall review of the FY 2010 budget, because he would no longer be in office when the budget went into effect in October 2009. Barack Obama could hardly have undertaken the fall review either, given that he was still campaigning for the presidency.

Figure 10-4 ▶ The Budget Cycle

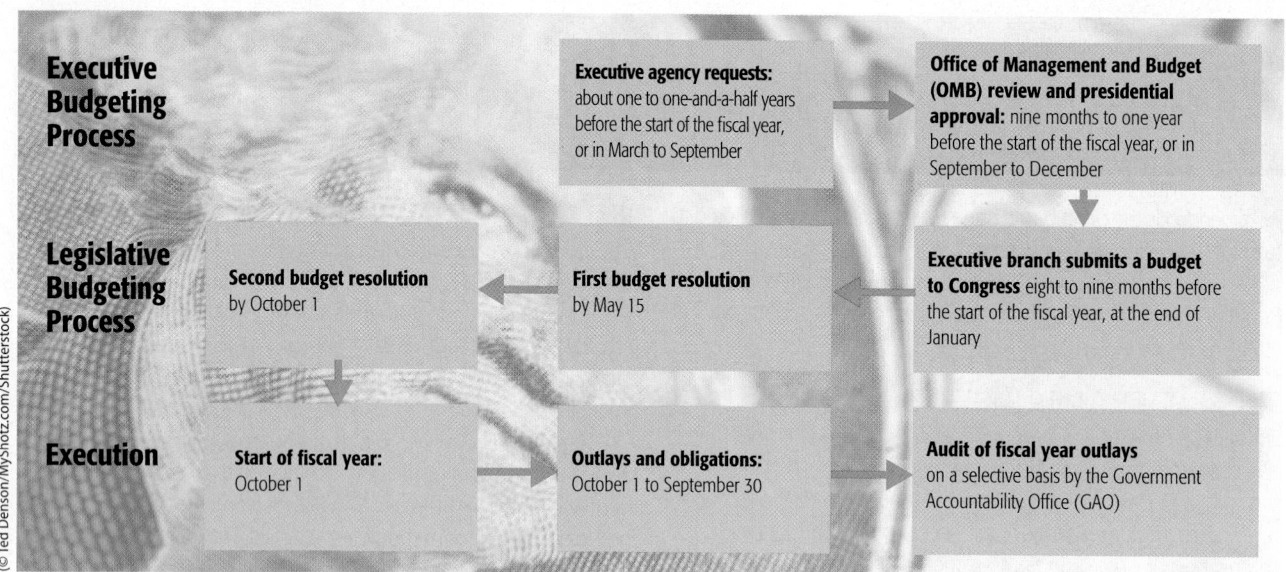
Executive Budgeting Process
Executive agency requests: about one to one-and-a-half years before the start of the fiscal year, or in March to September
Office of Management and Budget (OMB) review and presidential approval: nine months to one year before the start of the fiscal year, or in September to December
Legislative Budgeting Process
Second budget resolution by October 1
First budget resolution by May 15
Executive branch submits a budget to Congress eight to nine months before the start of the fiscal year, at the end of January
Execution
Start of fiscal year: October 1
Outlays and obligations: October 1 to September 30
Audit of fiscal year outlays on a selective basis by the Government Accountability Office (GAO)

Authorization
A formal declaration by a legislative committee that a certain amount of funding may be available to an agency. Some authorizations terminate in a year; others are renewable automatically without further congressional action.

Appropriation
The passage, by Congress, of a spending bill specifying the amount of authorized funds that actually will be allocated for an agency's use.

Following the election of a new president, the budget process is compressed into the first months of the new administration. Indeed, Barack Obama released a budget document for FY 2010 on February 26, 2009, barely a month after he was inaugurated.

Congress Faces the Budget. In January, nine months before the fiscal year starts, the president takes the OMB's proposed budget, approves it, and submits it to Congress. Then the congressional budgeting process takes over. The budgeting process involves two steps. First, Congress must authorize funds to be spent. The **authorization** is a formal declaration by the appropriate congressional committee that a certain amount of funding may be available to an agency. Congressional committees and subcommittees look at the proposals from the executive branch and the Congressional Budget Office in making the decision to authorize funds.

"The only solution I can see is to hold a series of long and costly hearings in order to put off finding a solution."

After the funds have been authorized, they must be appropriated by Congress. The appropriations committees of both the House and the Senate forward spending bills to their respective bodies. The **appropriation** of funds occurs when the final bill is passed. In this process, large sums are in play. Representatives and senators who chair key committees have traditionally found it relatively easy to slip additional spending proposals into a variety of bills. These proposals may have nothing to do with the ostensible purpose of the bill. Such *earmarked* appropriations, known as "pork," have their defenders. Many members of Congress believe that they have a better understanding of the needs of their districts than does any executive branch agency.

In March 2010, the Republican-controlled House implemented rules designed to eliminate earmarks. The new rules have substantially reduced the amount of pork inserted into appropriations bills, but lawmakers have been creative in attempting to circumvent the ban. In some instances, legislators have simply denied that a particular funding request is actually an earmark. More commonly, members have lobbied the various executive agencies to include projects that benefit their districts. According to the OMB definition, spending requested by executive agencies is not pork. Further, the White House itself frequently inserts special requests into the executive budget, thus making the president the biggest "porkmeister" of all.

First Budget Resolution A resolution passed by Congress in May that sets overall revenue and spending goals for the following fiscal year.

Second Budget Resolution A resolution passed by Congress in September that sets "binding" limits on taxes and spending for the following fiscal year.

Continuing Resolution A temporary funding law that Congress passes when an appropriations bill has not been decided by the beginning of the new fiscal year on October 1.

Budget Resolutions. The **first budget resolution** by Congress is due in May. It sets overall revenue goals and spending targets. Spending and tax laws that are drawn up over the summer are supposed to be guided by the first budget resolution. By September, Congress is scheduled to pass its **second budget resolution,** one that will set binding limits on taxes and spending for the fiscal year beginning October 1.

In actuality, Congress has finished the budget on time in only three years since 1977. The budget is usually broken up into a series of appropriations bills. If Congress has not passed one of these bills by October 1, it normally passes a **continuing resolution** that allows the affected agencies to keep on doing whatever they were doing the previous year with the same amount of funding. By the 1980s, continuing resolutions had ballooned into massive measures.

Budget delays reached a climax in 1995 and 1996, when, in a spending dispute with Democratic president Bill Clinton, the Republican Congress refused to pass any continuing resolutions. As a result, some nonessential functions of the federal government were shut down for twenty-seven days. Since 1997, Congress has generally managed to limit continuing resolutions to their original purpose. That does not mean, however, that such resolutions have been easy to pass. The government again came very close to a partial shutdown in April 2011, when the two parties reached a budget deal only hours before the deadline.

These U.S. Senators discuss their response to the latest budget prepared by the administration. Why would senators wish to criticize a presidential proposed budget?

(Jim Lo Scalzo/EPA/Landov)

Why Should You Care about... THE CONGRESS?

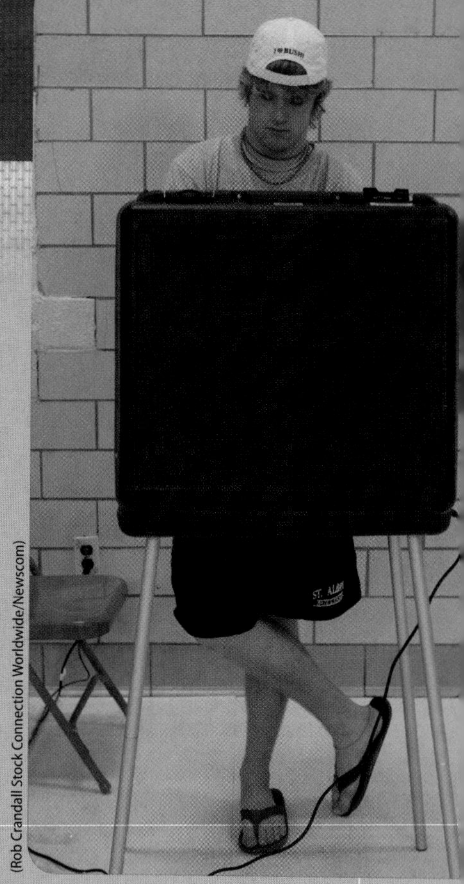
(Rob Crandall Stock Connection Worldwide/Newscom)

Why should you, as an individual, care about Congress? Do you even know the names of your senators and your representative in Congress? A surprising number of Americans do not. Even if you know the names and parties of your elected delegates, there is still much more you could learn about them that would be useful.

CONGRESS AND YOUR LIFE

The legislation that Congress passes can directly affect your life. Consider, for example, the Medicare prescription drug benefit passed in November 2003. Some might think that such a benefit, which helps only persons over the age of sixty-five, would be of no interest to college students. Actually, legislation such as this could affect you long before you reach retirement age. Funding this benefit may mean that you will have to pay higher taxes when you join the workforce. Also, some students may be affected even sooner than that. Most students are part of a family, and family finances are often important in determining whether a family will help pay for the student's tuition. There are families in which the cost of medicine for the oldest members is a substantial burden.

You can make a difference in our democracy simply by going to the polls on Election Day and voting for the candidates you would like to represent you in Congress. It goes without saying, though, that to cast an informed vote, you need to know how your congressional representatives stand on the issues and, if they are incumbents, how they have voted on bills that are important to you.

HOW YOU CAN MAKE A DIFFERENCE

To contact a member of Congress, start by going to the Web sites of the U.S. House of Representatives (search on "us house") and the U.S. Senate ("senate").

Although you can communicate easily with your representatives by e-mail, using e-mail has some drawbacks. Representatives and senators are now receiving large volumes of e-mail from constituents, which they rarely read themselves. They have staff members who read and respond to e-mail instead. Many interest groups argue that U.S. mail, or even express mail or a phone call, is more likely to capture the attention of a representative than e-mail. You can contact your representatives and senators using one of the following addresses or phone numbers:

United States House of Representatives
Washington, DC 20515
202-224-3121

United States Senate
Washington, DC 20510
202-224-3121

Interest groups also track the voting records of members of Congress and rate the members on the issues. Project Vote Smart tracks the performance of more than thirteen thousand political leaders, including their campaign finances, issue positions, and voting records. You can locate the Web site of Project Vote Smart by entering "votesmart" into a search engine.

Finally, if you want to know how your representatives funded their campaigns, contact the Center for Responsive Politics (CRP), a research group that tracks money in politics, campaign fundraising, and similar issues. You can see the CRP site by typing in "opensecrets."

Questions for Discussion and Analysis

1. Review the *Which Side Are You On?* feature on page 329. Is the filibuster a legitimate legislative provision? Why or why not? Even if filibusters are legitimate, are they currently overused? Give your reasons. If filibusters were to be limited in frequency, how might this be done?
2. The District of Columbia is not represented in the Senate and has a single, nonvoting delegate to the House. Should the District of Columbia be represented in Congress by voting legislators? Why or why not? If it should be represented, how? Would it make sense to admit it as a state? To give it back to Maryland? Explain your reasoning.
3. Identify some advantages to the nation that might follow when one party controls the House, the Senate, and the presidency. Identify some of the disadvantages that might follow from such a state of affairs.
4. When the Senate was first created, Americans were often more loyal to their individual states than they are today. Confederate general Robert E. Lee, for example, believed that his native land was Virginia, not the United States. Given the strong sense of national identity that exists in the country today, is it fair that the Senate gives equal representation to all states regardless of how many people live in each? Why or why not? If not, what (if anything) could be done to address the issue?

Key Terms

agenda setting 325
appropriation 346
authorization 346
bicameralism 323
casework 325
conference committee 338
constituent 323
continuing resolution 347
discharge petition 337
earmarks 324
enumerated power 326
executive budget 344
fall review 344
filibuster 328
first budget resolution 347
fiscal year (FY) 344
franking 330
gerrymandering 335
instructed delegate 324
joint committee 338
justiciable question 333
lawmaking 324
logrolling 324
majority leader of the House 340
minority leader of the House 340
ombudsperson 325
oversight 325
party identifier 333
president pro tempore 341
reapportionment 333
reconciliation 329
redistricting 333
representation 324
Rules Committee 328
second budget resolution 347
select committee 338
Senate majority leader 341
Senate minority leader 341
seniority system 339
Speaker of the House 339
spring review 344
standing committee 337
trustee 324
whip 341

Chapter Summary

1. The authors of the Constitution believed that the bulk of national power should be in the legislature. The Connecticut Compromise established a balanced legislature, with the membership in the House of Representatives based on population and the membership in the Senate based on the equality of states.
2. The functions of Congress include (a) lawmaking, (b) representation, (c) service to constituents, (d) oversight, (e) public education, and (f) conflict resolution.
3. The Constitution specifies most of the enumerated, or expressed, powers of Congress, including the right to impose taxes, to borrow funds, to regulate commerce, and to declare war. Congress also enjoys the right to "make all Laws which shall be necessary and proper for carrying into Execution the foregoing Powers, and all other Powers vested by this Constitution in the Government of the United States, or in any Department or Officer thereof." This is called the elastic, or necessary and proper, clause.
4. There are 435 members in the House of Representatives and 100 members in the Senate. Owing to its larger size, the House has a greater number of formal rules. The Senate tradition of unlimited debate dates back to 1790 and has been used over the years to frustrate the passage of bills.
5. Most candidates for Congress win nomination through a direct primary. Most incumbent representatives and senators who run for reelection are successful. Apportionment is the allocation of legislative seats to constituencies. The Supreme Court's "one person, one vote" rule means that the populations of legislative districts must be effectively equal.
6. Members of Congress are not typical American citizens. They are older and wealthier than most Americans, disproportionately white and male, and more likely to be lawyers.
7. Members of Congress are well paid and enjoy benefits such as free postage. Members have personal and committee staff and enjoy a number of legal privileges and immunities.
8. Most of the work of legislating is performed by committees and subcommittees within Congress. Legislation introduced into the House or Senate is assigned to standing committees for review. Joint committees are formed by the action of both chambers and consist of members from

each. Conference committees are joint committees set up to achieve agreement between the House and the Senate on the exact wording of legislative acts that were passed by the chambers in different forms. The seniority rule, which is usually followed, specifies that the longest-serving member of the majority party will be the chairperson of a committee.

9. The foremost power holder in the House of Representatives is the Speaker of the House. Other leaders are the House majority leader, the House minority leader, and the majority and minority whips. Formally, the vice president is the presiding officer of the Senate. Actual leadership in the Senate rests with the majority leader, the minority leader, and their whips.

10. A bill becomes law by progressing through both chambers of Congress and their appropriate standing and joint committees before submission to the president.

11. The budget process for a fiscal year begins with the preparation of an executive budget by the president. This is reviewed by the Office of Management and Budget and then sent to Congress, which is supposed to pass a final budget by the end of September. Since 1978, Congress generally has not followed its own time rules.

Quiz Multiple Choice

1. The bicameralism of Congress means that:
   - **a. every district has two members.**
   - **b. every state has two senators.**
   - **c. congress is divided into two legislative bodies.**

2. In Article 1, Section 8, the Constitution provides most of the enumerated powers of Congress, which include the power to:
   - **a. establish national school standards.**
   - **b. regulate interstate commerce.**
   - **c. create presidential primaries.**

3. The central difference between the House and the Senate is that:
   - **a. the House is much larger than the Senate.**
   - **b. the Senate is much larger than the House.**
   - **c. the Senate meets only occasionally, but the House meets all of the time.**

4. The 435 congressional districts are apportioned every ten years based on:
   - **a. the results of the latest U.S. Census.**
   - **b. the results of a nationwide opinion poll.**
   - **c. nothing—because the districts do not change.**

5. Congressional redistricting often involves gerrymandering, which means that the redistricting:
   - **a. results in an equal number of Democratic and Republican districts.**
   - **b. results in strange-shaped districts designed to favor one party.**
   - **c. results in districts that have almost no representation.**

6. There are several types of committees in Congress. They include:
   - **a. standing committees, sitting committees, and joint committees.**
   - **b. sitting committees, joint committees, and select committees.**
   - **c. standing committees, select committees, and joint committees.**

7. The most powerful leader in the Senate is the:
   - **a. president pro tempore.**
   - **b. vice president, because she or he presides over the Senate.**
   - **c. senate majority leader.**

8. When an appropriations bill has not been passed by the beginning of the new fiscal year, Congress may pass a temporary funding law called:
   - **a. a continuing resolution.**
   - **b. a second budget resolution.**
   - **c. a temporary authorization.**

ANSWERS: 1. c, 2. b, 3. a, 4. a, 5. b, 6. c, 7. c, 8. a.

Quiz Fill-Ins

9. The process of compromise in which members of Congress support each other's bills is called ______________.

10. In contrast to the House, only the Senate has the power to accept or reject presidential nominations of ______________ and ______________ ______________ ______________.

11. A high percentage of senators and representatives are reelected, and we describe this as due to the power of ______________.

12. ______________ committees are permanent bodies that are established by the rules of each chamber of Congress.

13. One of the most important committees in the House is the __________ __________ Committee, because it has the power to decide which legislation will reach the floor of the House.

14. The representative with the most power in the House is the ________ ___ ___ _____ because he or she is the official leader of the majority party.

15. __________ are members of Congress who pass information from the leadership to party members and from members to the leaders.

16. In contrast to the calendar year, which starts January 1 and ends on December 31, the federal government's __________ year runs from October 1 through September 30.

ANSWERS: 9. logrolling, 10. ambassadors, Supreme Court justices, 11. incumbency, 12. Standing, 13. House Rules, 14. Speaker of the House, 15. Whips, 16. fiscal.

(© Aleksandar Jovicic/iStockphoto)

Selected Print & Media Resources

SUGGESTED READINGS

Hacker, Jacob S., and Paul Pierson. *Winner-Take-All Politics: How Washington Made the Rich Richer—and Turned Its Back on the Middle Class.* New York: Simon & Schuster, 2011. In this book, two political scientists seek the cause of current high levels of economic inequality. They conclude that the interests of the very wealthy have come to dominate the congressional consensus of both parties.

Koger, Gregory. *Filibustering: A Political History of Obstruction in the House and Senate.* Chicago: University of Chicago Press, 2010. Many people don't know it, but the rules under which the House and Senate consider legislation have changed considerably over the years. Koger traces the lively history of congressional obstruction.

Schweizer, Peter. *Throw Them All Out.* New York: Houghton Mifflin Harcourt Trade, 2011. Schweizer exposes one of the biggest scandals in American politics: the effective exemption of congressional members and staff from the rules against "insider trading" on Wall Street. This exemption allows the permanent political class to make millions based on information unavailable to the rest of us. In response to this exposé, Congress has recently taken steps to curb the practice.

MEDIA RESOURCES

Charlie Wilson's War—One of the best movies of 2007, starring Tom Hanks and Julia Roberts. This hilarious film is based on the true story of how Wilson, a hard-living, hard-drinking representative from Texas, almost single-handedly wins a billion dollars in funding for the Afghans who are fighting a Russian invasion. When equipped with heat-seeking missiles, the Afghans win. Philip Seymour Hoffman steals the show portraying a rogue CIA operative.

Gerrymandering—This 2010 documentary by director Jeff Reichert manages to uncover a surprising amount of drama in the process of redrawing district lines, in part by focusing on some of the most outrageous recent examples.

Mr. Smith Goes to Washington—A 1939 film in which Jimmy Stewart plays a naïve congressman who is quickly educated in Washington. A true American political classic.

(© PashaIgnatov/iStockphoto)

E-mocracy CONGRESS AND THE WEB

Almost all senators and representatives have Web sites that you can find simply by keying in their names in a search engine. You can learn the names of your congressional representatives by going to the Web site of the House or the Senate (see the following *Logging On* section to find these sites). Once you know the names of your representatives, you can go to their Web sites to learn more about them and their positions on specific issues.

Note that some members of Congress also provide important services to their constituents via their Web sites. Some sites, for example, allow constituents to apply for internships in Washington, D.C.; apply for appointments to military academies; order flags; sign up for tours of the Capitol; and register complaints electronically. Other sites may provide forms from certain government agencies, such as the Social Security Administration, that constituents can use to request assistance from those agencies or to register complaints.

LOGGING ON

To find out about the schedule of activities taking place in Congress, go to the Web sites of the U.S. House and Senate.

1. The Congressional Budget Office is online—search on "cbo."
2. You can locate the U.S. Government Printing Office by entering "gpo."
3. For the real inside facts about what's going on in Washington, D.C., you can look at the following resources:
   - *RollCall,* the newspaper of the Capitol, is available by searching on "rollcall."
   - You can find Politico, a major Web site of political news, by typing its name into a search engine.
   - *The Hill,* a newspaper that investigates various activities of Congress, can be found at "thehill."

SEAL OF THE PRESIDENT OF THE UNITED STATES

11 The President

President Barack Obama presents his campaign themes to the American public at Buckley Air Force Base in Aurora, Colorado, in 2012.

(Gary C. Caskey/UPI/Landov)

The six learning outcomes below are designed to help improve your understanding of this chapter. After reading this chapter, you should be able to:

- Learning Outcome 1: **Identify the types of people who typically undertake serious campaigns for the presidency.**
- Learning Outcome 2: **Distinguish some of the major roles of the president, including head of state, chief executive, commander in chief, chief diplomat, and chief legislator.**
- Learning Outcome 3: **Discuss the president's role as a politician and party chief, as well as the importance of public approval of the president.**
- Learning Outcome 4: **Describe some of the special powers of the president, and tell how a president can be removed from office.**
- Learning Outcome 5: **Explain the organization of the executive branch and, in particular, the executive office of the president.**
- Learning Outcome 6: **Evaluate the role of the vice president, and describe what happens if the presidency becomes vacant.**

(EPA/Rainer Jensen)

GERMAN CHANCELLOR Angela Merkel is part of what type of political system?

What if... CONGRESS CHOSE THE PRESIDENT?

BACKGROUND

The founders intended that the electoral college would keep the voters at large from choosing the president. That scheme failed. A second goal of the electoral college was a success, however—it kept the choice of president out of the hands of Congress. This arrangement was a major part of the Madisonian model—that is, the separation of powers among multiple branches of government. Today, most Americans would consider it a major infringement of their rights if Congress, not the voters, chose the chief executive. In a majority of democratic countries, however, the legislature does exactly that. Such nations have *parliamentary systems.* Almost all European nations and much of Asia and Africa have such systems.

In a parliamentary system, the people in each district elect one or more members of parliament. Typically, voters can choose among candidates from more than two parties. Sometimes dozens of parties are active. Following the election, the largest party or coalition of parties names an executive team—the cabinet—led by a prime minister, premier, or chancellor. The cabinet, also called "the government," takes office when it wins a vote in the lower house of parliament. If at any point the prime minister and cabinet lose the support of the lower house, they are out. If an alternative coalition cannot be formed, the prime minister is reduced to a caretaker role, and an election is called on short notice. Would the American system have looked like this if the founders had let Congress pick the president?

WHAT IF CONGRESS CHOSE THE PRESIDENT?

If the founders had stuck with one of the initial constitutional proposals, such as the Virginia Plan, it is quite possible that the United States might have ended up with a parliamentary system. These initial proposals called for an executive elected by Congress. It is also possible, however, that the U.S. system would have been somewhat different, perhaps unique in the world. It is not clear, under the Virginia Plan, that if Congress elected the president, Congress would also have the power to *remove* the president by any measure short of impeachment and conviction. If the president did not serve at the pleasure of the legislature as a prime minister does, then following a midterm election, the chief executive and the majority in the legislature could be of different parties. That is not possible under a parliamentary system.

EFFECTIVE VERSUS LIMITED GOVERNMENT

Under a parliamentary system, the executive and the majority in the legislature must be of the same party (or coalition of parties). As a result, the executive has little difficulty in passing its preferred programs. A parliamentary majority has few restraints on what it can do—a state of affairs known as *effective government.* The American system, with multiple points at which various powers can block action, is more likely to result in *limited government.*

Any system in which Congress chooses the president would result in more "effective" government. Much of the time, a united Congress and president could exercise power in ways that are currently unusual. In fact, for a time during the first two years of the Obama administration, Congress and the president were united in this fashion. Such circumstances are rare in the United States, however. Even under a semi-parliamentary system in which Congress could not easily remove the president from office, such circumstances would be commonplace.

FOR CRITICAL ANALYSIS

1. ***How might your vote for the U.S. House of Representatives change if you knew that you were simultaneously voting for a national executive leader?***
2. ***If the House always chose the president, what effect would that have on the role of the U.S. Senate?***

The writers of the Constitution had no models to follow when they created the presidency of the United States. Nowhere else in the world was there an elected head of state. What the founders did not want was a king. The two initial plans considered by the founders—the Virginia and New Jersey plans—both called for an executive elected by Congress. As we explain in the chapter-opening *What If* . . . feature, under such plans our political system would be very different from what it is today. As it happened, other delegates, especially those who had witnessed the need for a strong leader in the Revolutionary Army, believed a strong executive would be necessary for the new republic. The delegates, after much debate, created a chief executive who had enough powers granted in the Constitution to balance those of Congress.

In this chapter, after looking at who can become president and at the process involved, we examine closely the nature and extent of the constitutional powers held by the president.

did you know?

President William McKinley's salary of $50,000 in 1900 would be worth $1,320,000 in today's dollars.

Who Can Become President?

The president receives a salary of $400,000, plus $169,000 for expenses and a vast array of free services, beginning with residence in the White House. The requirements for becoming president, as outlined in Article II, Section 1, of the Constitution, are not overwhelmingly stringent:

> *No person except a natural born Citizen, or a Citizen of the United States, at the time of the Adoption of this Constitution, shall be eligible to the Office of President; neither shall any Person be eligible to that Office who shall not have attained to the Age of thirty-five Years, and been fourteen Years a Resident within the United States.*

■ Learning Outcome 1:
Identify the types of people who typically undertake serious campaigns for the presidency.

A "Natural Born Citizen"

The only question that arises about these qualifications relates to the term *natural born Citizen.* Does that mean only citizens born in the United States and its territories? What about a child born to a U.S. citizen visiting or living in another country? Although the question has not been dealt with directly by the Supreme Court, it is reasonable to expect that someone would be eligible if her or his parents were Americans.

These questions were debated when George Romney, who was born in Chihuahua, Mexico, made a serious bid for the Republican presidential nomination in the 1960s.[1] The issue came up again when opponents of President Barack Obama claimed that Obama was not a natural born citizen. In reality, Obama was born in Honolulu, Hawaii, in 1961, two years after Hawaii became a state. Those who disputed Obama's birth claimed that the short-form birth certificate released by the Obama campaign was a forgery—despite the fact that Obama's birth was also recorded by two Honolulu newspapers. Agitation by the "birthers," as they came to be called, subsided in 2011 after the White House released Obama's long-form birth certificate, which was endorsed as valid by every relevant Hawaiian official, Republican and Democrat.

Social Media IN POLITICS

In no field is the president more powerful, relative to the rest of the government, than in foreign policy. If you have an interest in that topic, consider following *Foreign Policy* magazine on Facebook. Simply search on "foreign policy."

Presidential Characteristics

The American dream is symbolized by the statement that "anybody can become president of this country." It is true that in modern times, presidents have included a haberdasher (Harry Truman—for a short period of time), a peanut farmer (Jimmy Carter), and an actor (Ronald Reagan). But if you examine the list of presidents in Appendix F at the end of this book, you will see that the most common previous occupational field of

1. George Romney was governor of Michigan from 1963 to 1969. Romney was not nominated for the presidency, and the issue remains unresolved. George Romney was the father of Mitt Romney, the 2012 Republican presidential candidate.

The youngest president ever elected was John F. Kennedy (1961–1963).

(AP Photo)

The oldest president ever elected was Ronald Reagan (1981–1989).

(AP Photo)

presidents in this country has been the law. Out of forty-four presidents, twenty-seven have been lawyers, and many have been wealthy.

Although the Constitution states that the minimum-age requirement for the presidency is thirty-five years, most presidents have been much older than that when they assumed office. John F. Kennedy, at the age of forty-three, was the youngest elected president, and the oldest was Ronald Reagan, at age sixty-nine. The average age at inauguration has been fifty-four. There has clearly been a demographic bias in the selection of presidents. All have been male, white, and from the Protestant tradition, except for John F. Kennedy, a Roman Catholic, and Barack Obama, an African American. Should voters care about the religion of a presidential candidate? We discuss that question in this chapter's *Which Side Are You On?* feature on the facing page.

The Process of Becoming President

Major and minor political parties nominate candidates for president and vice president at national conventions every four years. As discussed in Chapter 9, the nation's voters do not elect a president and vice president directly but rather cast ballots for presidential electors, who then vote for president and vice president in the electoral college.

did you know?

The only president in U.S. history to be elected with every possible electoral vote was George Washington.

Because victory goes to the candidate with a majority in the electoral college, it is conceivable that someone could be elected to the office of the presidency without having a plurality of the popular vote cast. Indeed, on four occasions, candidates won elections even though their major opponents received more popular votes. One of those elections occurred in 2000, when George W. Bush won the electoral college vote and became president even though his opponent, Al Gore, won the popular vote. In elections in which more than two candidates were running for office, many presidential candidates have won with less than 50 percent of the total popular votes cast for all candidates—including Abraham Lincoln, Woodrow Wilson, Harry Truman, John F. Kennedy, Richard Nixon, and, in 1992, Bill Clinton.

Thus far, on two occasions the electoral college has failed to give any candidate a majority. At this point, the election is thrown into the House of Representatives. The president is then chosen from among the three candidates having the most electoral college votes, as noted in Chapter 9. In 1800, Thomas Jefferson and Aaron Burr tied in

Which Side Are You On?

SHOULD VOTERS CARE ABOUT THE PRESIDENT'S RELIGION?

The U.S. Constitution in Article VI, Section 3, states, "[N]o religious Test shall ever be required as a Qualification to any Office or public Trust under the United States." In other words, our government cannot bar someone from public office because of her or his religious faith (or lack of any religious faith, for that matter). What the Constitution says and how voters pick candidates, though, are two separate matters. Currently, polls report that two-thirds of Americans want their president to be a person of faith. Under such circumstances, an avowed atheist could not become president of the United States. But what about a candidate's specific religious beliefs? Should voters care about these? Opinions differ.

RELIGION SHOULD HAVE NO PART IN CHOOSING CANDIDATES

Today, Americans do not accept that those seeking public office must be of a particular gender or ethnic group. Many people would argue that voters should not consider a candidate's church or faith affiliation either. If the framers of the Constitution wanted to make sure that we do not choose our government officials based on their religion, why should we care more than two centuries later? Men and women of faith can govern just as badly as those who have no faith or the "wrong" faith. A candidate's claim, say, to be a practicing Christian guarantees nothing. The religious convictions of our presidential candidates are not good predictors of how they will face real-world problems. Our votes should be based on character, policies, or party, not on a candidate's religious convictions.

RELIGION DOES, AND SHOULD, MATTER

Others agree that voters should be willing to vote for candidates of any religion, as long as the candidate takes no orders from religious authorities. Even if voters disregard denomination, however, they should care about how a candidate's religious beliefs affect his or her actions. Many Christians believe, for example, that their religion commands that families and individuals be self-reliant, and that government action in the economic sphere undercuts this obligation. Other Christians, observing how Jesus constantly advocated for the poor, believe their religion calls for social services that benefit the needy. Religious beliefs can affect how people view abortion, gay and lesbian rights, the death penalty, and even matters of war and peace. Voters need to understand the impact of a candidate's beliefs on such issues.

(© kyoshino / iStockphoto) (© Dean Mitchell / iStockphoto)

the electoral college. This happened because the Constitution had not been explicit in indicating which of the two electoral votes was for president and which was for vice president. In 1804, the **Twelfth Amendment** clarified the matter by requiring that the president and vice president be chosen separately. In 1824, the House again had to make a choice, this time among William H. Crawford, Andrew Jackson, and John Quincy Adams. It chose Adams, even though Jackson had more electoral and popular votes.

Twelfth Amendment
An amendment to the Constitution, adopted in 1804, that requires the separate election of the president and the vice president by the electoral college.

The Many Roles of the President

■ **Learning Outcome 2:** Distinguish some of the major roles of the president, including head of state, chief executive, commander in chief, chief diplomat, and chief legislator.

The Constitution speaks briefly about the duties and obligations of the president. Based on this brief list of powers and on the precedents of history, the presidency has grown into a very complicated job that requires balancing at least five constitutional roles. These are (1) head of state, (2) chief executive, (3) commander in chief of the armed forces, (4) chief diplomat, and (5) chief legislator of the United States. Here we examine each of these significant presidential functions, or roles. It is worth noting that one person plays all these roles simultaneously and that the needs of the roles may at times come into conflict.

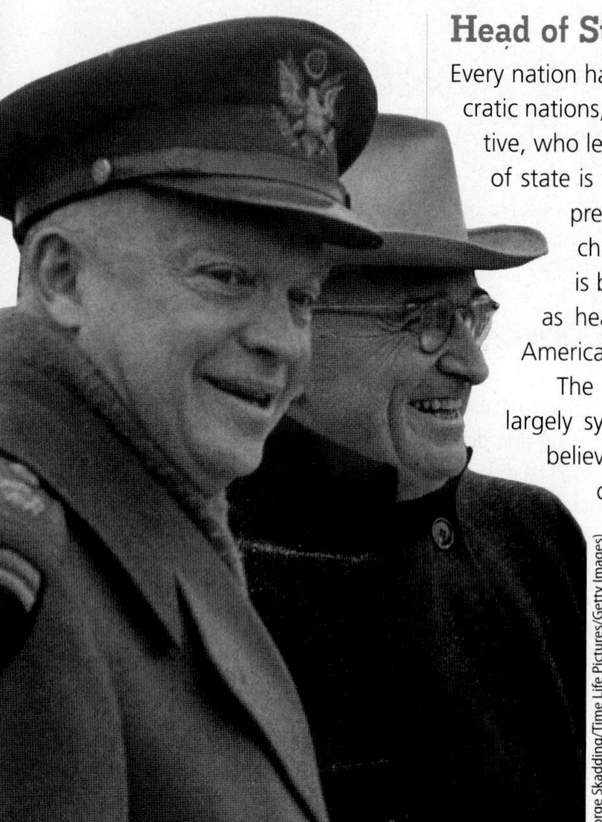
(George Skadding/Time Life Pictures/Getty Images)

American president Harry Truman (1945–1953), stands with General Dwight Eisenhower in 1951. A year later, Eisenhower successfully ran for president. Why might a general make a good president?

Head of State

Every nation has at least one person who is the ceremonial head of state. In most democratic nations, the role of **head of state** is given to someone other than the chief executive, who leads the executive branch of government. In Britain, for example, the head of state is the queen. In much of Europe, the head of state is a relatively powerless president. The prime minister is the chief executive, as we explained in the chapter-opening *What If . . .* feature. But in the United States, the president is both chief executive and head of state. According to William Howard Taft, as head of state the president symbolizes the "dignity and majesty" of the American people.

The president, as head of state, engages in a number of activities that are largely symbolic or ceremonial. Some students of the American political system believe that having the president serve as both the chief executive and the head of state drastically limits the time available to do "real" work. Not all presidents have agreed with this conclusion, however—particularly those presidents who have skillfully blended these two roles with their role as a politician. Being head of state gives the president tremendous public exposure, which can be an important asset in a campaign for reelection. When that exposure is positive, it helps the president deal with Congress over proposed legislation and increases the chances of being reelected—or getting the candidates of the president's party elected.

Chief Executive

According to the Constitution, "The executive Power shall be vested in a President of the United States of America . . . . [H]e may require the Opinion, in writing, of the principal Officer in each of the executive Departments, upon any Subject relating to the Duties of their respective Offices . . . and he shall nominate, and by and with the Advice and Consent of the Senate, shall appoint . . . Officers of the United States. . . . [H]e shall take Care that the Laws be faithfully executed." As **chief executive,** the president is constitutionally bound to enforce the acts of Congress, the judgments of federal courts, and treaties signed by the United States. The duty to "faithfully execute" the laws has been a source of constitutional power for presidents.

Head of State
The role of the president as ceremonial head of the government.

Chief Executive
The role of the president as head of the executive branch of the government.

Civil Service
A collective term for the body of employees working for the government. Generally, "civil service" is understood to apply to all those who gain government employment through a merit system.

Appointment Power
The authority vested in the president to fill a government office or position. Positions filled by presidential appointment include those in the executive branch and the federal judiciary, commissioned officers in the armed forces, and members of the independent regulatory commissions.

The Powers of Appointment and Removal. To assist in the various tasks of the chief executive, the president has a federal bureaucracy (see Chapter 12), which currently consists of 2.2 million federal civilian employees, not counting the U.S. Postal Service (650,000 employees). You might think that the president, as head of the largest bureaucracy in the United States, wields enormous power. The president, however, only nominally runs the executive bureaucracy. Most government positions are filled by **civil service** employees, who generally gain government employment through a merit system rather than presidential appointment.[2] Therefore, even though the president has important **appointment power,** it is limited to cabinet and subcabinet jobs, federal judgeships, agency heads, and several thousand lesser jobs—about eight thousand positions in total.

This means that most of the 2.85 million federal employees owe no political allegiance to the president. They are more likely to owe loyalty to congressional committees or to interest groups representing the sector of the society that they serve. Table 11–1 on the facing page shows what percentage of the total employment in each executive department is available for political appointment by the president.

The president's power to remove from office those officials who are not doing a good job or who do not agree with the president is not explicitly granted by the Constitution

2. See Chapter 12 for a discussion of the Civil Service Reform Act.

Table 11–1 ▶ Total Civilian Positions in Cabinet Departments Available for Political Appointment by the President

Executive Department	Total Number of Employees	Political Appointments Available	Percentage
Agriculture	92,217	372	0.40
Commerce	45,737	336	0.73
Defense	657,347	695	0.11
Education	4,642	293	6.31
Energy	16,140	536	3.32
Health and Human Services	85,257	475	0.56
Homeland Security	198,658	287	0.14
Housing and Urban Development	9,459	146	1.54
Interior	69,866	296	0.42
Justice	115,746	474	0.41
Labor	16,366	226	1.38
State	12,588	555	4.41
Transportation	57,324	268	0.47
Treasury	105,612	202	0.19
Veterans Affairs	317,620	376	0.12

Sources: *Policy and Supporting Positions* (Washington, D.C.: Government Printing Office, 2008). This text, known as "Plum Book" (see Chapter 12), is published after each presidential election. Also, U.S. Office of Personnel Management. Figures are for December 2011.

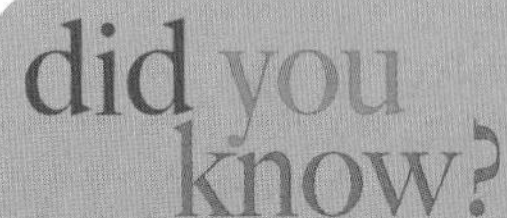

Thomas Jefferson was the first president to be inaugurated in Washington, D.C., where he walked to the Capitol from a boardinghouse, took the oath, made a brief speech in the Senate chamber, and then walked back home.

and has been limited. In 1926, however, a Supreme Court decision prevented Congress from interfering with the president's ability to fire those executive-branch officials whom the president had appointed with Senate approval.[3] There are ten agencies whose directors the president can remove at any time. These agencies include the Commission on Civil Rights, the Environmental Protection Agency, the General Services Administration, and the Small Business Administration. In addition, the president can remove all heads of cabinet departments, all individuals in the Executive Office of the President, and all of the political appointees listed in Table 11–1 above.

Harry Truman spoke candidly of the difficulties a president faces in trying to control the executive bureaucracy. On leaving office, he referred to the problems that Dwight Eisenhower, as a former general of the army, was going to have: "He'll sit here and he'll say do this! do that! and nothing will happen. Poor Ike—it won't be a bit like the Army. He'll find it very frustrating."[4]

Reprieve
A formal postponement of the execution of a sentence imposed by a court of law.

Pardon
A release from the punishment for, or legal consequences of, a crime. A pardon can be granted by the president before or after a conviction.

The Power to Grant Reprieves and Pardons. Section 2 of Article II of the Constitution gives the president the power to grant **reprieves** and **pardons** for offenses

3. *Meyers v. United States*, 272 U.S. 52 (1926).
4. Quoted in Richard E. Neustadt, *Presidential Power: The Politics of Leadership* (New York: Wiley, 1960), p. 9. Note that Truman may not have considered the amount of politics involved in decision making in the upper ranks of the army.

(Pete Souza/Corbis)

The president often meets in the Cabinet Room in the White House with our military leaders and secretary of defense. Shown here from left to right, General Martin Dempsey, Leon Panetta, Admiral James G. Stavridis, and General Douglas M. Fraser.

against the United States except in cases of impeachment. All pardons are administered by the Office of the Pardon Attorney in the Department of Justice.

The Supreme Court upheld the president's power to grant reprieves and pardons in a 1925 case concerning a pardon granted by the president to an individual convicted of contempt of court. A federal circuit court had contended that only judges had the authority to convict individuals for contempt of court when court orders were violated and that the courts should be free from interference by the executive branch. The Supreme Court simply stated that the president could grant reprieves or pardons for all offenses "either before trial, during trial, or after trial, by individuals, or by classes, conditionally or absolutely, and this without modification or regulation by Congress."[5]

President Andrew Johnson set the record for the largest number of persons ever pardoned in 1868 when he issued a blanket amnesty to all former Confederate soldiers. In 1974, in a controversial decision, President Gerald Ford pardoned former president Richard Nixon for his role in the Watergate affair before any charges were brought in court. In 1977, President Jimmy Carter issued a blanket pardon to Vietnam War–era draft resisters, a group that probably included more than 100,000 persons.

Commander in Chief

The president, according to the Constitution, "shall be Commander in Chief of the Army and Navy of the United States, and of the Militia of the several States, when called into the actual Service of the United States." In other words, the armed forces are under civilian, rather than military, control.

Commander in Chief
The role of the president as supreme commander of the military forces of the United States and of the state National Guard units when they are called into federal service.

Wartime Powers. Those who wrote the Constitution had George Washington in mind when they made the president the **commander in chief.** Although we do not expect our president to lead the troops into battle, presidents as commanders in chief have wielded dramatic power. Harry Truman made the awesome decision to drop atomic bombs on Hiroshima and Nagasaki in 1945 to force Japan to surrender and thus bring World War II to an end. Lyndon Johnson ordered bombing missions against North Vietnam

5. *Ex parte Grossman,* 267 U.S. 87 (1925).

in the 1960s, and he personally selected some of the targets. Richard Nixon decided to invade Cambodia in 1970. Ronald Reagan sent troops to Lebanon and Grenada in 1983 and ordered U.S. fighter planes to attack Libya in 1986. George H. W. Bush sent troops to Panama in 1989 and to the Middle East in 1990. Bill Clinton sent troops to Haiti in 1994 and to Bosnia in 1995, ordered missile attacks on alleged terrorist bases in 1998, and sent American planes to bomb Serbia in 1999. George W. Bush ordered the invasion of Afghanistan in 2001 and of Iraq in 2003, and most recently, Barack Obama ordered additional troops into Afghanistan in 2009 and authorized air strikes in Libya in 2011.

The president is the ultimate decision maker in military matters. Everywhere the president goes, so too goes the "football"—a briefcase filled with all of the codes necessary to order a nuclear attack. Only the president has the power to order the use of nuclear force.

As commander in chief, the president probably exercises more authority than in any other role. Constitutionally, Congress has the sole power to declare war, but the president can send the armed forces into situations that are certainly the equivalent of war. Harry Truman dispatched troops to Korea in 1950. Kennedy, Johnson, and Nixon waged an undeclared war in Southeast Asia, where more than 58,000 Americans were killed and 300,000 were wounded. In neither of these situations had Congress declared war.

did you know?

Twenty-one presidents have served only one term in office.

Power over the National Guard. One of the president's powers as commander in chief is the right to assume authority over National Guard units—that is, state militias. Throughout American history, presidents have "nationalized" the Guard to handle domestic problems such as natural disasters or severe social disturbances, including strikes or urban riots. President George W. Bush sent 6,000 members of the National Guard to the Mexican border in 2006–2008 to assist the Border Patrol, and in 2010 President Obama sent 1,200 Guard troops to the border for the same purpose.

The president also has the ability to send National Guard units abroad to supplement the regular armed forces. Both Bush and Obama sent Guard forces abroad on a massive scale. In 2005, National Guard troops comprised a larger percentage of frontline fighting forces than in any war in U.S. history—about 43 percent in Iraq and 55 percent in Afghanistan. Since then, the number of National Guard troops sent abroad has declined.

The War Powers Resolution. In an attempt to gain more control over such military activities, in 1973 Congress passed the **War Powers Resolution**—over President Nixon's veto—requiring that the president consult with Congress when sending American forces into action. Once they are sent, the president must report to Congress within forty-eight hours. Unless Congress approves the use of troops within sixty days or extends the sixty-day time limit, the forces must be withdrawn.

War Powers Resolution
A law passed in 1973 spelling out the conditions under which the president can commit troops without congressional approval.

In spite of the War Powers Resolution, the powers of the president as commander in chief are more extensive today than they were in the past. The so-called war on terrorism, which began after the terrorist attacks of September 11, 2001, led to an especially notable increase in presidential powers. Many people believe that recent administrations have claimed powers that were excessive or even unconstitutional. We discuss this controversy in the *Politics and Terrorism* feature on the following page.

Chief Diplomat

The Constitution gives the president the power to recognize foreign governments, to make treaties with the **advice and consent** of the Senate, and to make special agreements with other heads of state that do not require congressional approval. In addition, the president nominates U.S. ambassadors to other countries. As **chief diplomat,** the president dominates American foreign policy, a role that has been supported many times by the Supreme Court.

Advice and Consent
Terms in the Constitution describing the U.S. Senate's power to review and approve treaties and presidential appointments.

Chief Diplomat
The role of the president in recognizing foreign governments, making treaties, and effecting executive agreements.

Politics AND Terrorism

GEORGE W. OBAMA

During his 2008 presidential campaign, Barack Obama claimed that George W. Bush's antiterrorism policies violated civil liberties and were at odds with American values. One example: holding prisoners indefinitely without charges at the Guantánamo Bay naval base in Cuba. Not long after Obama became president, however, it became clear that his policies were at least as tough as those employed by Bush—hence the gibe "George W. Obama." President Obama did not suffer politically by violating his campaign promises on antiterrorism. By 2012, his antiterrorism policies enjoyed firm support from ordinary voters, regardless of whether they were liberal Democrats or conservative Republicans.

WHEN DID ANTITERRORISM POLICY REALLY CHANGE?

Columnist David Brooks of the *New York Times* has made an interesting observation: the real shift in America's antiterrorism policy took place during the Bush administration. By 2006, dubious interrogation techniques such as waterboarding had been banned. The Bush administration was frantically—and unsuccessfully—seeking ways to close the Guantánamo prison. In short, questionable practices advocated by figures such as Vice President Dick Cheney were no longer operational. Cheney himself was no longer Bush's preeminent adviser and had lost much of his once-formidable power. According to Brooks, the real difference between the two administrations was in the packaging of antiterrorism policy. Whereas the Bush administration was indifferent to process and how policy was presented to the public, the Obama administration was far more concerned about public opinion, at home and abroad.

OBAMA PLAYS HARDBALL

After an initial attempt to close the Guantánamo prison, Obama abandoned the effort and continued the policy of indefinite detention without charges. Earlier, the Supreme Court had ruled that the Constitution grants *habeas corpus* rights even to foreign nationals at Guantánamo, because the Guantánamo base is on American soil. Guantánamo prisoners, in other words, have a right to challenge their detention in court. Bush got around this ruling by shipping detainees to the Bagram Air Base in Afghanistan, and Obama continued that policy. In May 2010, the D.C. Circuit Court of Appeals ruled that the Bush/Obama position was legal—even detainees abducted outside Afghanistan, but shipped there, have no *habeas corpus* rights.

In fact, Obama initiated new antiterrorism policies that went beyond those of the Bush administration. These included a major campaign to assassinate Taliban and al Qaeda leaders in Pakistan, using unmanned drone aircraft. In May 2011, Obama authorized a raid into Pakistan that killed Osama bin Laden, the al Qaeda leader responsible for the 9/11 terror attacks. In September 2011, an American drone killed Anwar al-Awlaki in Yemen. Al-Awlaki was an al Qaeda leader, but he was also a U.S. citizen who had never been indicted or convicted of a crime. Finally, the Obama administration repeatedly pressed felony charges against "whistleblowers" who allegedly shared national secrets with reporters. No such charges were ever filed under President Bush.

FOR CRITICAL ANALYSIS

If Republican presidential candidate Mitt Romney had won, do you think he would have changed any of Obama's antiterrorism policies? Why or why not?

Diplomatic Recognition
The formal acknowledgment of a foreign government as legitimate.

Diplomatic Recognition. An important power of the president as chief diplomat is that of **diplomatic recognition,** or the power to recognize—or to refuse to recognize—foreign governments. In the role of ceremonial head of state, the president has always received foreign diplomats. In modern times, the simple act of receiving a foreign diplomat has been equivalent to accrediting the diplomat and officially recognizing his or her government. Such recognition of the legitimacy of another country's government is a prerequisite to diplomatic relations or treaties between that country and the United States.

Deciding when to recognize a foreign power is not always simple. The United States, for example, did not recognize the Soviet Union until 1933—sixteen years after the Russian Revolution of 1917. It was only after all attempts to reverse the effects of that revolution—including military invasion of Russia and diplomatic isolation—had proved futile that Franklin D. Roosevelt extended recognition to the Soviet government. In December 1978, long after the Communist victory in China in 1949, President Jimmy Carter granted official recognition to the People's Republic of China.[6]

(AP Photo/Barry Thumma)

President George H. W. Bush (1989–1993) is shown here meeting with the foreign minister of Saudi Arabia. Why would a president spend time in such a meeting?

Proposal and Ratification of Treaties. The president has the sole power to negotiate treaties with other nations. These treaties must be presented to the Senate, where they must be approved by a two-thirds vote. After ratification, the president can approve the treaty as adopted by the Senate. Approval poses a problem when the Senate has tacked on substantive amendments or reservations to a treaty, particularly when such changes may require reopening negotiations with the other signatory governments. Sometimes, a president may decide to withdraw a treaty if the senatorial changes are too extensive—as Woodrow Wilson did with the Versailles Treaty in 1919, which concluded World War I. Wilson believed that the senatorial reservations would weaken the treaty so much that it would be ineffective.

President Jimmy Carter (1977–1981) was successful in lobbying for the treaties that provided for the return of the Panama Canal to Panama by the year 2000 and neutralizing the canal. President Bill Clinton won a major political and legislative victory in 1993 by persuading Congress to ratify the North American Free Trade Agreement (NAFTA). In so doing, he had to overcome opposition from Democrats and most of organized labor.

Before September 11, 2001, President George W. Bush indicated his intention to steer the United States in a unilateral direction on foreign policy. After the terrorist attacks of September 11, 2001, however, Bush sought cooperation from U.S. allies in the war on terrorism. Bush's return to multilateralism was exemplified in the signing of a nuclear weapons reduction treaty with Russia in 2002. Nonetheless, his attempts to gain international support for a war against Iraq to overthrow that country's government were not as successful as he had hoped.

In April 2010, President Obama and then–Russian president Dmitry Medvedev signed the New START Treaty, a follow-up to earlier arms control treaties. The ten-year pact will cut the number of nuclear warheads allowed to each party by 30 percent, to 1,550 warheads. The number of permitted missile launchers will be cut in half. The treaty includes a verification process. The U.S. Senate ratified the treaty in December 2010.

Executive Agreements. Presidential power in foreign affairs is enhanced greatly by the use of **executive agreements** made between the president and other heads of state. Such agreements do not require Senate approval, although the House and the Senate may refuse to appropriate the funds necessary to implement them. Whereas treaties are binding on all succeeding administrations, executive agreements require each new president's consent to remain in effect.

Executive Agreement
An international agreement made by the president, without senatorial ratification, with the head of a foreign state.

Among the advantages of executive agreements are speed and secrecy. The former is essential during a crisis. The latter is important when the administration fears that open

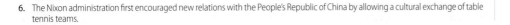

6. The Nixon administration first encouraged new relations with the People's Republic of China by allowing a cultural exchange of table tennis teams.

senatorial debate may be detrimental to the best interests of the United States or to the interests of the president.[7] There have been far more executive agreements (about 9,000) than treaties (about 1,300). Many executive agreements contain secret provisions calling for American military assistance or other support.

Chief Legislator

Chief Legislator
The role of the president in influencing the making of laws.

Constitutionally, presidents must recommend to Congress legislation that they judge necessary and expedient. Not all presidents have wielded their powers as **chief legislator** in the same manner. Some presidents have been almost completely unsuccessful in getting their legislative programs implemented by Congress. Presidents Franklin Roosevelt and Lyndon Johnson, however, saw much of their proposed legislation put into effect.

State of the Union Message
An annual message to Congress in which the president proposes a legislative program. The message is addressed not only to Congress but also to the American people and to the world.

Creating the Congressional Agenda. In modern times, the president has played a dominant role in creating the congressional agenda. In the president's annual **State of the Union message,** which is required by the Constitution (Article II, Section 3) and is usually given in late January shortly after Congress reconvenes, the president presents a legislative program. The message gives a broad, comprehensive view of what the president wishes the legislature to accomplish during its session. It is as much a message to the American people and to the world as it is to Congress. Its impact on public opinion can determine the way in which Congress responds to the president's agenda.

Since 1913, the president has delivered the State of the Union message in a formal address to Congress. Today, this address is one of the great ceremonies of American governance, and many customs have grown up around it. For example, one cabinet member, the "designated survivor," stays away to ensure that the country will always have a president, even if someone manages to blow up the Capitol building. Everyone gives the president an initial standing ovation out of respect for the office, but this applause does not necessarily represent support for the individual who holds the office. During the speech, senators and House members either applaud or remain silent to indicate their opinion of the policies that the president announces.

did you know?

President William Henry Harrison gave the longest inaugural address (8,445 words) of any American president, lasting two hours (the weather was chilly and stormy, and Harrison caught a cold, developed pneumonia and pleurisy, and died a month later).

Getting Legislation Passed. The president can propose legislation, but Congress is not required to pass—or even introduce—any of the administration's bills. How, then, does the president get those proposals made into law? One way is by exercising the power of persuasion. The president writes to, telephones, and meets with various congressional leaders. He or she makes public announcements to influence public opinion. Finally, as head of the party, the president exercises leadership over the party's members in Congress. A president whose party holds a majority in both chambers of Congress usually has an easier time getting legislation passed than does a president who faces a hostile Congress.

Veto Message
The president's formal explanation of a veto when legislation is returned to Congress.

Saying No to Legislation. The president has the power to say no to legislation through use of the veto,[8] by which the White House returns a bill unsigned to Congress with a **veto message** attached. Because the Constitution requires that every bill passed by the House and the Senate be sent to the president before it becomes law, the president must act on each bill:

1. If the bill is signed, it becomes law.
2. If the bill is not sent back to Congress after ten congressional working days, it becomes law without the president's signature.
3. The president can reject the bill and send it back to Congress with a veto message setting forth objections. Congress then can change the bill, hoping to secure

7. The Case Act of 1972 requires that all executive agreements be transmitted to Congress within sixty days after the agreement takes effect. Secret agreements are transmitted to the foreign relations committees as classified information.
8. Veto in Latin means "I forbid."

presidential approval, and repass it. Or Congress can simply reject the president's objections by overriding the veto with a two-thirds roll-call vote of the members present in both the House and the Senate.

4. If the president refuses to sign the bill and Congress adjourns within ten working days after the bill has been submitted to the president, the bill is killed for that session of Congress. This is called a **pocket veto.** If Congress wishes the bill to be reconsidered, the bill must be reintroduced during the following session.

Presidents employed the veto power infrequently until after the Civil War, but it has been used with increasing vigor since then (see Table 11–2 on the following page). The total number of vetoes from George Washington's administration through the end of George W. Bush's second term in office was 2,562, with about two-thirds of those vetoes being exercised by Grover Cleveland, Franklin Roosevelt, Harry Truman, and Dwight Eisenhower.

(AP Photo/Charles Dharapak)

President George W. Bush (2001–2009) gives a State of the Union address while Vice President Dick Cheney and Speaker of the House Nancy Pelosi listen. Where is that address given?

George W. Bush was the first president since Martin Van Buren (1837–1841) to serve a full term in office without exercising the veto power. Bush, who had the benefit of a Republican Congress, did not veto any legislation during his first term. Only in the summer of 2006 did Bush finally issue a veto, saying "no" to stem-cell research legislation passed by Congress. After the Democrats took control of Congress in January 2007, however, the president issued eleven vetoes, four of which were overridden. President Obama, who for two years also enjoyed a Congress dominated by his own party, issued only two vetoes through Election Day 2012.

Pocket Veto
A special veto exercised by the chief executive after a legislative body has adjourned. Bills not signed by the chief executive die after a specified period of time. If Congress wishes to reconsider such a bill, it must be reintroduced in the following session of Congress.

Line-Item Veto
The power of an executive to veto individual lines or items within a piece of legislation without vetoing the entire bill.

The Line-Item Veto. Ronald Reagan lobbied strenuously for Congress to give another tool to the president—the **line-item veto,** which would allow the president to veto *specific* spending provisions of legislation that was passed by Congress. Reagan saw the line-item veto as the only way that he could control overall congressional spending. In 1996, Congress passed the Line Item Veto Act, which provided for the line-item veto. President Clinton used the line-item veto on several occasions, but the act was challenged in court. In 1998, by a six-to-three vote, the United States Supreme Court agreed with the veto's opponents and overturned the act. The Court stated that "there is no provision in the Constitution that authorizes the president to enact, to amend or to repeal statutes."[9]

Congress's Power to Override Presidential Vetoes. A veto is a clear-cut indication of the president's dissatisfaction with congressional legislation. Congress, however, can override a presidential veto, although it rarely exercises this power. Consider that two-thirds of the members of each chamber who are present must vote to override the president's veto in a roll-call vote. This means that if only one-third plus one of the members

9. *Clinton v. City of New York,* 524 U.S. 417 (1998).

Table 11-2 ▸ Presidential Vetoes, 1789 to Present

Years	President	Regular Vetoes	Vetoes Overridden	Pocket Vetoes	Total Vetoes
1789–1797	Washington	2	0	0	2
1797–1801	J. Adams	0	0	0	0
1801–1809	Jefferson	0	0	0	0
1809–1817	Madison	5	0	2	7
1817–1825	Monroe	1	0	0	1
1825–1829	J. Q. Adams	0	0	0	0
1829–1837	Jackson	5	0	7	12
1837–1841	Van Buren	0	0	1	1
1841–1841	Harrison	0	0	0	0
1841–1845	Tyler	6	1	4	10
1845–1849	Polk	2	0	1	3
1849–1850	Taylor	0	0	0	0
1850–1853	Fillmore	0	0	0	0
1853–1857	Pierce	9	5	0	9
1857–1861	Buchanan	4	0	3	7
1861–1865	Lincoln	2	0	5	7
1865–1869	A. Johnson	21	15	8	29
1869–1877	Grant	45	4	48	93
1877–1881	Hayes	12	1	1	13
1881–1881	Garfield	0	0	0	0
1881–1885	Arthur	4	1	8	12
1885–1889	Cleveland	304	2	110	414
1889–1893	Harrison	19	1	25	44
1893–1897	Cleveland	42	5	128	170
1897–1901	McKinley	6	0	36	42
1901–1909	T. Roosevelt	42	1	40	82
1909–1913	Taft	30	1	9	39
1913–1921	Wilson	33	6	11	44
1921–1923	Harding	5	0	1	6
1923–1929	Coolidge	20	4	30	50
1929–1933	Hoover	21	3	16	37
1933–1945	F. Roosevelt	372	9	263	635
1945–1953	Truman	180	12	70	250
1953–1961	Eisenhower	73	2	108	181
1961–1963	Kennedy	12	0	9	21
1963–1969	L. Johnson	16	0	14	30
1969–1974	Nixon	26*	7	17	43
1974–1977	Ford	48	12	18	66
1977–1981	Carter	13	2	18	31
1981–1989	Reagan	39	9	39	78
1989–1993	G. H. W. Bush	29	1	15	44
1993–2001	Clinton	36†	2	1	37
2001–2009	G. W. Bush	11	4	1	12
2009–	Obama	2	0	0	2
TOTAL		1,497	110	1,067	2,564

*Two pocket vetoes by President Nixon, overruled in the courts, are counted here as regular vetoes.
†President Clinton's line-item vetoes are not included.
Sources: Office of the Clerk; plus authors' updates through 2012.

voting in one of the chambers of Congress do not agree to override the veto, the veto holds. In American history, only about 7 percent of all vetoes have been overridden.

The President as Party Chief and Superpolitician

■ Learning Outcome 3: **Discuss the president's role as a politician and party chief, as well as the importance of public approval of the president.**

Presidents are by no means above political partisanship, and one of their many roles is that of chief of party. Although the Constitution says nothing about the function of the president within a political party (the mere concept of political parties was abhorrent to most of the authors of the Constitution), today presidents are the actual leaders of their parties.

The President as Chief of Party

As party leader, the president chooses the national committee chairperson and can try to discipline party members who fail to support presidential policies. One way of exerting political power within the party is through **patronage**—appointing individuals to government or public jobs. This power was more extensive in the past, before the establishment of the civil service in 1883 (see Chapter 12), but the president still retains important patronage power. As we noted earlier, the president can appoint several thousand individuals to jobs in the cabinet, the White House, and the federal regulatory agencies.

Patronage
The practice of rewarding faithful party workers and followers with government employment and contracts.

Perhaps the most important partisan role that the president has played in the 1990s and early 2000s has been that of fund-raiser. The president is able to raise large sums for the party through appearances at dinners, speaking engagements, and other social occasions. President Clinton may have raised more than half a billion dollars for the Democratic Party during his two terms. President George W. Bush was even more successful than Clinton. Barack Obama's spectacular success in raising funds for his presidential campaigns indicates that he has carried on this fund-raising tradition.

Presidents have a number of other ways of exerting influence as party chief. The president may make it known that a particular congressperson's choice for federal judge will not be appointed unless that member of Congress is more supportive of the president's legislative program.[10] The president may agree to campaign for a particular program or for a particular candidate. Presidents also reward loyal members of Congress with support for the funding of local projects, tax breaks for regional industries, and other forms of "pork."

did you know?
With a single exception, a Bush was on the ballot in every presidential election from 1980 through 2004.

Constituencies and Public Approval

All politicians worry about their constituencies, and presidents are no exception. Presidents are also concerned with public approval ratings.

Presidential Constituencies. Presidents have many constituencies. In principle, they are beholden to the entire electorate—the public of the United States—even those who did not vote. Presidents are certainly beholden to their party, because its members helped to put them in office. The president's constituencies also include members of the opposing party whose cooperation the president needs. Finally, the president must take into consideration a constituency that has come to be called the **Washington community** (also known as those "inside the beltway").[11] This community consists of individuals who—whether in or out of political office—are intimately familiar with the workings of government, thrive on gossip, and measure on a daily basis the political power of the president.

Washington Community
Individuals regularly involved with politics in Washington, D.C.

10. "Senatorial courtesy" (see Chapter 13) often puts the judicial appointment in the hands of the Senate, however.
11. The *beltway* refers to Interstate 495, which circles the capital, passing through Maryland and Virginia suburbs.

(Bettmann/Corbis)

President Gerald Ford (1974–1977) addresses a convention of the Veterans of Foreign Wars while in Chicago.

Public Approval. All of these constituencies are impressed by presidents who maintain a high level of public approval, partly because doing so is very difficult to accomplish. Presidential popularity, as measured by national polls, gives the president an extra political resource to use in persuading legislators or bureaucrats to pass legislation.

As you can see from Figure 11–1 below, President George W. Bush enjoyed spectacularly high approval ratings immediately after the terrorist attacks of 9/11. This popularity allowed him to win national security legislation such as the USA Patriot Act. It also allowed him to undertake a robust foreign policy that included the overthrow of the Afghan government and the occupation of Iraq. Bush's popularity declined steadily after 9/11. Obama's initial popularity figures were also very high. Much of his support in early 2009, however, came from Republicans, and it was bound to dissipate. By the beginning of 2010, the public was almost evenly split in their opinions of Obama, and those attitudes remained constant through 2012. True, in some periods—late 2010 and the last half of 2011—his approval rate fell into the low forties, and at other times—the first part of 2011—his popularity rose above 50 percent.

These were variations within relatively narrow margins, however. They suggested that the voters remained split down the middle and that the 2012 elections would be close. Clearly, the state of the economy would have a major effect on the outcome of that election, as we explain in the *Politics and Economics* feature on the facing page.

Figure 11–1 ▸ Public Popularity of Modern Presidents

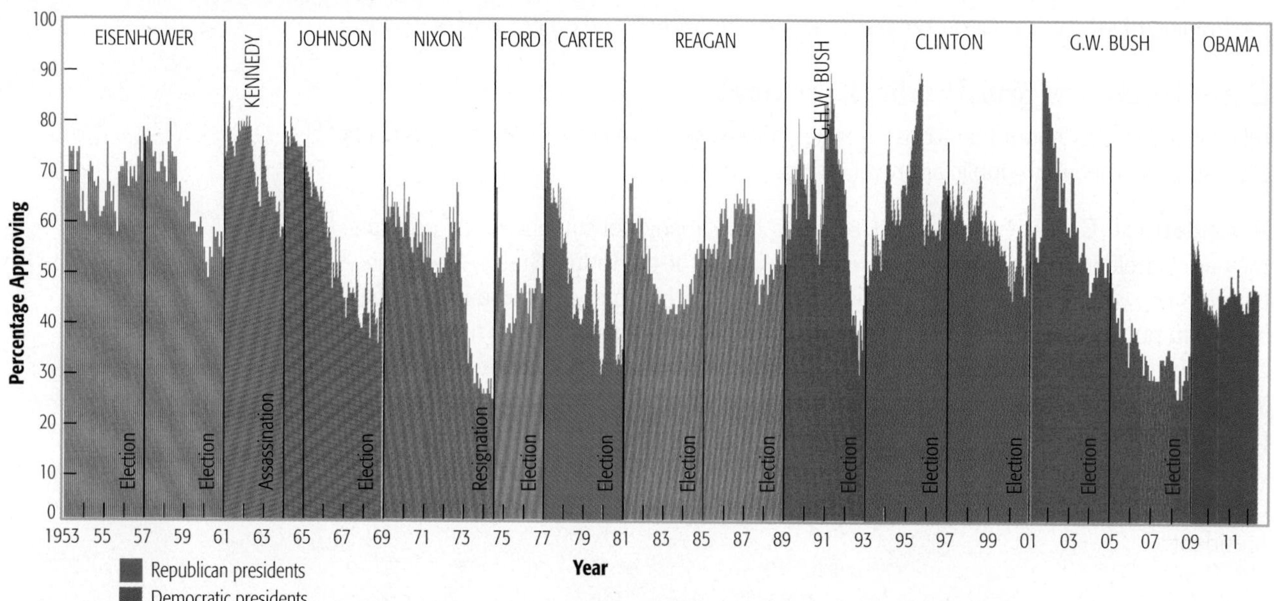

Sources: Adapted from the Roper Center for Public Opinion Research: Gallup and *USA Today*/CNN polls, March 1992 through June 2012 and Real Clear Politics.

Politics AND Economics

THE ECONOMY AND THE RACE FOR PRESIDENT

Some years ago, a presidential campaign adviser coined a memorable saying: "It's the economy, stupid." The adviser meant to say that the state of the economy would determine the outcome of the election. Since then, political scientists have constantly argued over how much of an effect the economy has on presidential elections.

THE REELECTION CHANCES OF INCUMBENTS

One conclusion jumps out of the data: the state of the economy is much more important when an incumbent president is running for reelection than when both major party candidates are new. Voters are not so likely to blame a fresh face for bad economic conditions. In contrast, voters clearly judge incumbent presidents based on the employment situation.

Consider Figure 11–2, which shows the last six presidential reelection bids before 2012. The variables are the incumbent's popular vote margin on the vertical axis and the annualized percentage growth in payrolls during the six months before the election on the horizontal axis. The relationship is strikingly close. Note that we do not use the unemployment rate as a measure. Surprisingly, the unemployment rate has no predictive power at all. What matters is not whether unemployment is high or low, but whether it is getting better or worse.

THE FRAGILITY OF ECONOMIC MODELS

Figure 11–2 would seem to prove that economic variables can tell us almost everything about presidential election outcomes, at least when an incumbent is running. Still, you should take the chart with a grain of salt. We only have six cases here, and the chances are good that the apparently powerful relationship may be in part a coincidence.

Consider an earlier model developed by political scientist Douglas Hibbs using growth in per-person income and the number of military deaths. The model seemed to explain almost 90 percent of the variation in presidential election results from 1952 through 1988. Yet Nate Silver, statistics guru at the *New York Times*, showed that the Hibbs model performed badly in 1996 and 2000. Also, if you look at the years before 1952, the model is almost worthless.

Figure 11–2 ▸ Jobs and Votes

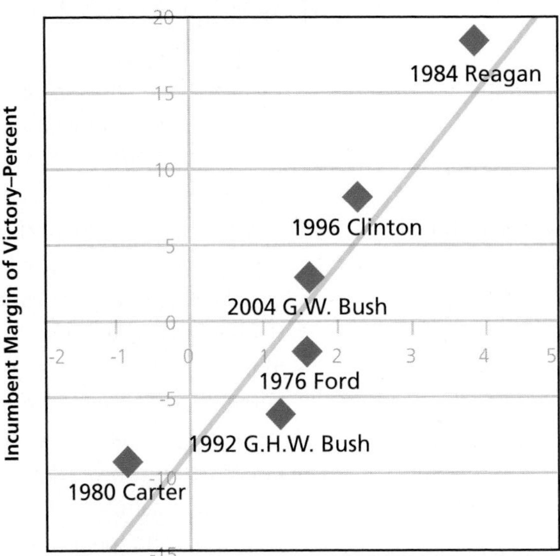

Source: Bureau of Labor Statistics and Dave Leip's *Atlas of U.S. Presidential Elections.*

The payroll-growth model in Figure 11–2 shows some similar flaws. If you plug in Lyndon Johnson's reelection bid in 1964 and Richard Nixon's bid in 1972, both incumbents do much better than the model predicts.

As it happens, Johnson was very successful in portraying his Republican opponent, Barry Goldwater, as politically extreme. Nixon also succeeded in depicting Democrat George McGovern as way too radical. In 2012, Obama tried to damage Romney in this way. Obama had limited success in this attempt, but he did win reelection. His payroll growth figure was 1.24 percent and his provisional popular vote margin was 2.7 percent.

FOR CRITICAL ANALYSIS

Why should the economy be so important in determining how people vote?

"Going Public." Since the early 1900s, presidents have spoken more to the public and less to Congress. In the 1800s, only 7 percent of presidential speeches were addressed to the public. Since 1900, 50 percent have been addressed to the public. Presidents frequently go over the heads of Congress and the political elites, taking their cases directly to the people.

This strategy, dubbed "going public," gives the president additional power through the ability to persuade and manipulate public opinion. By identifying their own positions so clearly, presidents can weaken the legislators' positions. In times when the major political parties are highly polarized, however, the possibility of compromise with the opposition party may actually be reduced if the president openly "nails his colors to the mast."

■ Learning Outcome 4: **Describe some of the special powers of the president, and tell how a president can be removed from office.**

Presidential Powers

Presidents have at their disposal a variety of special powers and privileges not available in the other branches of the U.S. government. The powers of the president discussed earlier in this chapter in the section on the roles of the president are called **constitutional powers,** because their basis lies in the Constitution. In addition, Congress has established by law, or statute, numerous other presidential powers—such as the ability to declare national emergencies. These are called **statutory powers.** Both constitutional and statutory powers have been labeled the **expressed powers** of the president, because they are expressly written into the Constitution or into law.

Constitutional Power
A power vested in the president by Article II of the Constitution.

Statutory Power
A power created for the president through laws enacted by Congress.

Expressed Power
A power of the president that is expressly written into the Constitution or into statutory law.

Inherent Power
A power of the president derived from the statements in the Constitution that "the executive Power shall be vested in a President" and that the president should "take Care that the Laws be faithfully executed"; defined through practice rather than through law.

Presidents also have what have come to be known as **inherent powers.** These depend on the statements in the Constitution that "the executive Power shall be vested in a President" and that the president should "take Care that the Laws be faithfully executed." The most common example of inherent powers is those emergency powers invoked by a president during wartime. Franklin Roosevelt, for example, used his inherent powers to move the Japanese and Japanese Americans living in the United States into internment camps for the duration of World War II. President George W. Bush often justified expanding the powers of his presidency by saying that such powers were necessary to fight the war on terrorism. Additional powers enjoyed by the president include (1) emergency powers, (2) executive orders, (3) executive privilege, and (4) signing statements.

Emergency Powers

If you were to read the Constitution, you would find no mention of the additional powers that the executive office may exercise during national emergencies. Indeed, the Supreme Court has stated that an "emergency does not create power."[12] But it is clear that presidents have made strong use of their inherent powers during times of emergency, particularly in the realm of foreign affairs. The **emergency powers** of the president were first enunciated in the Supreme Court's decision in *United States v. Curtiss-Wright Export Corp.*[13] In that case, President Franklin Roosevelt, without authorization by Congress, ordered an embargo on the shipment of weapons to two warring South American countries. The Court recognized that the president may exercise inherent powers in foreign affairs and that the national government has primacy in these affairs.

Emergency Power
An inherent power exercised by the president during a period of national crisis.

Examples of emergency powers are abundant, coinciding with crises in domestic and foreign affairs. Abraham Lincoln suspended civil liberties at the beginning of the Civil War (1861–1865) and called the state militias into national service. These actions and his subsequent governance of conquered areas—and even of areas of northern states—were justified by claims that they were essential to preserve the Union. Franklin Roosevelt declared an "unlimited national emergency" following the fall of France in World War II (1939–1945) and mobilized the federal budget and the economy for war.

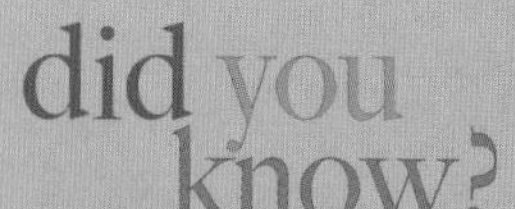

The shortest inaugural address was George Washington's second one, at 135 words.

President Harry Truman authorized the federal seizure of steel plants and their operation by the national government in 1952 during the Korean War. Truman claimed that he was using his inherent emergency power as chief executive and commander in chief to

12. *Home Building and Loan Association v. Blaisdell,* 290 U.S. 398 (1934).
13. 299 U.S. 304 (1936).

safeguard the nation's security, as an ongoing strike by steelworkers threatened the supply of weapons to the armed forces. The Supreme Court did not agree, holding that the president had no authority under the Constitution to seize private property or to legislate such action.[14] According to legal scholars, this was the first time a limit had been placed on the exercise of the president's emergency powers.

Executive Orders

Congress allows the president (as well as administrative agencies) to issue *executive orders* that have the force of law. These executive orders can do the following: (1) enforce legislative statutes, (2) enforce the Constitution or treaties with foreign nations, and (3) establish or modify rules and practices of executive administrative agencies.

An executive order, then, represents the president's legislative power. The only apparent requirement is that under the Administrative Procedure Act of 1946, all executive orders must be published in the ***Federal Register,*** a daily publication of the U.S. government. Executive orders have been used to implement national affirmative action regulations, to restructure the White House bureaucracy, and, under emergency conditions, to ration consumer goods and to administer wage and price controls. They have also been used to classify government information as secret, to regulate the export of restricted items, and to establish military tribunals for suspected terrorists.

Federal Register
A publication of the U.S. government that prints executive orders, rules, and regulations.

Executive Privilege
The right of executive officials to withhold information from or to refuse to appear before a legislative committee.

President George W. Bush made use of such orders in executing the war on terrorism, and more generally in expanding presidential powers. President Obama's executive orders have covered such matters as regulating the pay and practices of members of the executive branch, raising the fuel efficiency standards of cars and trucks, permitting federal grants to international organizations that support abortion, and lifting restrictions on the federal funding of embryonic stem-cell research.

Executive Privilege

Another inherent executive power that has been claimed by presidents concerns the right of the president and the president's executive officials to withhold information from or refuse to appear before Congress or the courts. This is called **executive privilege,** and it relies on the constitutional separation of powers for its basis.

Presidents have frequently invoked executive privilege to avoid having to disclose information to Congress about actions of the executive branch. Executive privilege rests on the assumption that a certain degree of secrecy is essential to national security. Critics of executive privilege believe that it can be used to shield from public scrutiny actions of the executive branch that should be open to Congress and to the American citizenry.

Limits to executive privilege went untested until the Watergate affair in the early 1970s. Five men had broken into the headquarters of the Democratic National Committee and were caught searching for documents that might damage the candidacy of the Democratic nominee, George McGovern. Later investigation showed that the break-in had been planned by members of Richard Nixon's campaign committee and that Nixon and his closest advisers had devised a strategy for impeding the investigation of the crime. After it became known that all of the conversations held in the Oval Office had been recorded on a secret system, Nixon was ordered to turn over the tapes to the special prosecutor in charge of the investigation.

President Richard Nixon (1969–1974) says goodbye outside the White House after his resignation on August 9, 1974, as he prepares to board a helicopter for a flight to nearby Andrews Air Force Base. Was Nixon impeached?

(AP Photo)

14. *Youngstown Sheet and Tube Co. v. Sawyer,* 343 U.S. 579 (1952).

When the President Becomes Incapacitated. According to the Twenty-fifth Amendment, when a president believes that he or she is incapable of performing the duties of office, the president must inform Congress in writing. Then the vice president serves as acting president until the president can resume normal duties. When the president is unable to communicate, a majority of the cabinet, including the vice president, can declare that fact to Congress. Then the vice president serves as acting president until the president resumes normal duties. If a dispute arises over the return of the president's ability, a two-thirds vote of Congress is required to allow the vice president to remain acting president. Otherwise, the president resumes normal duties.

When the Vice Presidency Becomes Vacant. The Twenty-fifth Amendment also addresses the issue of how the president should fill a vacant vice presidency. Section 2 of the amendment simply states, "Whenever there is a vacancy in the office of the Vice President, the President shall nominate a Vice President who shall take office upon confirmation by a majority vote of both Houses of Congress." This is exactly what occurred when Richard Nixon's first vice president, Spiro Agnew, resigned in 1973 because of his alleged receipt of construction contract kickbacks during his tenure as governor of Maryland. Nixon turned to Gerald Ford as his choice for vice president. After extensive hearings, both chambers of Congress confirmed the appointment.

did you know?

President Richard Nixon served 56 days without a vice president, and that President Gerald Ford served 132 days without a vice president.

Then, when Nixon resigned on August 9, 1974, Ford automatically became president and nominated as his vice president Nelson Rockefeller. Congress confirmed Ford's choice. For the first time in the history of the country, neither the president nor the vice president had been elected to their positions.

The Succession Act of 1947. The question of who shall be president if both the president and the vice president die is answered by the Succession Act of 1947. If the president and vice president die, resign, or are disabled, the Speaker of the House will become president, after resigning from Congress. Next in line is the president pro tem of the Senate, followed by the cabinet officers in the order of the creation of their departments (see Table 11–3 below).

Table 11–3 ▸ Line of Succession to the Presidency of the United States

1. Vice President	10. Secretary of Commerce
2. Speaker of the House of Representatives	11. Secretary of Labor
3. Senate President Pro Tempore	12. Secretary of Health and Human Services
4. Secretary of State	13. Secretary of Housing and Urban Development
5. Secretary of the Treasury	14. Secretary of Transportation
6. Secretary of Defense	15. Secretary of Energy
7. Attorney General (head of the Justice Department)	16. Secretary of Education
8. Secretary of the Interior	17. Secretary of Veterans Affairs
9. Secretary of Agriculture	18. Secretary of Homeland Security

Why Should You Care about... THE PRESIDENCY?

(PhotoDisc by Getty Images)

When it comes to caring about the presidency, most people do not need much encouragement. The president is our most important official. The president serves as the public face of the government and, indeed, of the nation as a whole. Many people, however, believe the president is such a remote figure that nothing they can do will affect what he or she does. That is not always true. On many issues, your voice—combined, of course, with the voices of many others—can have an impact. Writing to the president is a traditional way for citizens to express their opinions. Every day, the White House receives several thousand letters and other communications.

THE PRESIDENT AND YOUR LIFE

The president can influence many issues that directly affect your life. For example, in 2010, many voices began to raise the question of whether anything could be done soon about reforming the nation's immigration policies. If any change to immigration policies were to succeed, it would need strong support from the president. Immigration might be a topic on which you have strong opinions. If you have opinions on a subject such as this, you may well want to "cast your vote" by adding your letter to the many others that the president receives on the issue.

Lobbying the president on an issue such as immigration may have an impact, but there may also be issues on which the president refuses to consider popular opinion. President George W. Bush refused to be swayed by the public about the war in Iraq, even after the voters turned Congress over to the Democrats, and President Obama did not consult the opinion polls when pushing through health-care reform. The determination of these presidents should remind you of the importance of learning about presidential candidates and their positions on important issues, and then making sure to vote. Once a candidate is elected, it is possible that neither public opinion nor Congress will be able to alter presidential policies to any significant degree.

HOW YOU CAN MAKE A DIFFERENCE

The most traditional form of communication with the White House is, of course, by letter. Letters to the president should be addressed to

The President of the United States
The White House
1600 Pennsylvania Avenue N.W.
Washington, DC 20500

Letters may be sent to the First Lady at the same address. Will you get an answer? Almost certainly. The White House mail room is staffed by volunteers and paid employees who sort the mail for the president and tally the public's concerns. You may receive a standard response to your comments or a more personal, detailed response.

It is possible to call the White House on the telephone and leave a message for the president or First Lady. To call the switchboard, call 202-456-1414. In most circumstances, a better choice is the round-the-clock comment line, which you can reach at 202-456-1111. When you call that number, an operator will take down your comments and forward them to the president's office.

To find the home page for the White House, type "white house" into any major search engine. The site is designed to be entertaining and to convey information about the president. You can also send your comments and ideas to the White House using e-mail. Send comments to the president at

comments@whitehouse.gov

Address e-mail to the vice president at

vice_president@whitehouse.gov

Questions for Discussion and Analysis

1. Review the *Which Side Are You On?* feature on page 357. Can you think of examples, either in your own life or in the lives of your friends and relatives, where particular religious beliefs have shaped political ideas? If so, describe these influences.
2. What characteristics do you think voters look for when choosing a president? Might these characteristics change as a result of changes in the political environment and the specific problems facing the nation? If you believe voters almost always look for the same characteristics when selecting a president, why is this? If voters seek somewhat different people as president depending on circumstances, which circumstances favor which kinds of leaders?
3. In recent years, many presidents have been lawyers by profession, though George W. Bush was a businessman, Ronald Reagan was an actor, and Jimmy Carter was a naval officer and peanut farmer. What advantages might these three presidents have gained from their career backgrounds? In particular, what benefits might Ronald Reagan have derived from his experience as an actor?
4. Refer to Figure 11–1 on page 368. Note that with a single exception, every eight years since 1961 the presidency has been taken over by the other party. The only exception is Reagan's first term—had Carter been reelected instead, the pattern would have been perfect: eight of Democrats Kennedy and Johnson, eight of Republicans Nixon and Ford, eight of Democrat Carter, eight of Republicans Reagan and G. H. W. Bush, eight of Democrat Clinton, eight of Republican G. W. Bush, and finally a Democrat again, Barack Obama. Why might the voters prefer to pick a president from the other party every few years?

Key Terms

advice and consent 361
appointment power 358
cabinet 373
chief diplomat 361
chief executive 358
chief legislator 364
chief of staff 375
civil service 358
commander in chief 360
constitutional power 370
diplomatic recognition 362
emergency power 370
executive agreement 363
Executive Office of the President (EOP) 374
executive privilege 371
expressed power 370
Federal Register 371
head of state 358
impeachment 372
inherent power 370
kitchen cabinet 373
line-item veto 365
National Security Council (NSC) 376
Office of Management and Budget (OMB) 375
pardon 359
patronage 367
pocket veto 365
reprieve 359
signing statement 372
State of the Union message 364
statutory power 370
Twelfth Amendment 357
Twenty-fifth Amendment 377
veto message 364
War Powers Resolution 361
Washington community 367
White House Office 375

Chapter Summary

1. The office of the presidency in the United States, combining as it does the functions of chief of state and chief executive, was unique at the time of its creation. The framers of the Constitution were divided over whether the president should be a weak or a strong executive.
2. The requirements for the office of the presidency are outlined in Article II, Section 1, of the Constitution. The president's roles include both formal and informal duties. The constitutional roles of the president include head of state, chief executive, commander in chief, chief diplomat, and chief legislator. The president also acts as party chief.
3. As head of state, the president is ceremonial leader of the government. As chief executive, the president is bound to enforce the acts of Congress, the judgments of the federal courts, and treaties. The chief executive has the power of appointment and the power to grant reprieves and pardons.
4. As commander in chief, the president is the ultimate decision maker in military matters. As chief diplomat, the president recognizes foreign governments, negotiates treaties, signs agreements, and nominates and receives ambassadors.
5. The role of chief legislator includes recommending legislation to Congress, lobbying for the legislation, approving laws, and exercising the veto power. Presidents are also leaders of their political parties. Presidents rely on their personal popularity to help them fulfill these functions.
6. In addition to constitutional and inherent powers, the president has statutory powers written into law by Congress.

Presidents also have a variety of special powers not available to the other branches of the government. These include emergency powers and the power to issue executive orders, to invoke executive privilege, and to issue signing statements.

7. Abuses of executive power are dealt with by Articles I and II of the Constitution, which authorize the House and Senate to impeach and remove the president, vice president, or other officers of the federal government for committing "Treason, Bribery, or other high Crimes and Misdemeanors."

8. The president receives assistance from the cabinet and from the Executive Office of the President (including the White House Office).

9. The vice president is the constitutional officer assigned to preside over the Senate and to assume the presidency in the event of the death, resignation, removal, or disability of the president. The Twenty-fifth Amendment, passed in 1967, established procedures to be followed in case of presidential incapacity, death, or resignation and when filling a vacant vice presidency.

Quiz Multiple Choice

1. Anyone can become president of the United States, as long as she or he:
   - **a. is at least 35 years old.**
   - **b. is at least 35 years old and a natural-born citizen.**
   - **c. is at least 40 years old and a natural-born citizen.**
2. Our president is both head of state and chief executive, which means that the president:
   - **a. engages in ceremonial activities both at home and abroad, as well as faithfully ensures that the acts of Congress are enforced.**
   - **b. designates the vice president to represent the United States in public ceremonies abroad.**
   - **c. makes sure that treaties are upheld but delegates other actions to the cabinet.**
3. One of the powers of the president is to appoint certain individuals to federal positions, which include:
   - **a. managers in the U.S. Postal Service, the head of the CIA, and school superintendents.**
   - **b. state governors, the head of the FBI, and the head of the CIA.**
   - **c. federal judges, members of the president's cabinet, and the head of the CIA.**
4. The president is the commander in chief of all U.S. military forces, which allows the president to:
   - **a. assume authority over National Guard units and order a nuclear attack.**
   - **b. order troops to fight abroad for as long as necessary without the approval of Congress.**
   - **c. order troops to fight abroad, but with Congress's approval after one year.**
5. As chief diplomat, the president has the sole power to negotiate treaties with other nations. Therefore, any treaty that the president signs:
   - **a. binds the United States to that treaty.**
   - **b. binds the United States for a period of no less than five years.**
   - **c. only binds the United States if the U.S. Senate approves the treaty by a two-thirds vote.**
6. When the president vetoes legislation passed by Congress, that legislation:
   - **a. can never become law.**
   - **b. can become law if Congress overrides the veto with a two-thirds vote in both chambers.**
   - **c. becomes law if Congress overrides the president's veto by a simple majority vote in both chambers.**
7. When the president issues an executive order, such action represents:
   - **a. the president's legislative power.**
   - **b. the president's power over tax policy.**
   - **c. the president's power over the federal judiciary.**
8. Upon impeachment, the president:
   - **a. must leave office immediately.**
   - **b. cannot run for reelection.**
   - **c. is tried by the Senate.**

ANSWERS: 1. b, 2. a, 3. c, 4. a, 5. c, 6. b, 7. a, 8. c.

Quiz Fill-Ins

9. The White House chief of staff, the ambassador to the United Nations, and the head of the Environmental Protection Agency have at different times been named members of the president's __________.

10. The Council of Economic Advisers, the Office of Management and Budget, and the Office of the U.S. Trade Representative are all part of the __________ __________ of the President.

11. The Office of Chief of Staff, the Office of Scheduling and Advance, and the Office of the Staff Secretary are all part of the __________ __________ __________.

12. The president, vice president, secretaries of State and Defense, and national security adviser are part of the __________ __________ __________.

13. If the president dies, the vice president takes over. If the vice president is also unavailable, then the __________ of the __________ of __________ becomes president.

14. A president who disagrees with a part of legislation that he or she has signed into law can make a written declaration regarding the law's enforcement. This declaration is called a __________ __________.

15. The president has the power to grant __________ and __________ for offenses against the United States.

16. Every January, the president delivers a formal address to Congress. It is called the __________ of the __________ __________.

ANSWERS: 9. cabinet, 10. Executive Office, 11. White House Office, 12. National Security Council, 13. Speaker, House, Representatives, 14. signing statement, 15. reprieves, pardons, 16. State, Union, message.

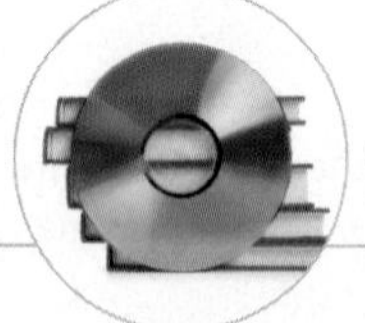

(© Aleksandar Jovicic/iStockphoto)

Selected Print & Media Resources

SUGGESTED READINGS

Gibbs, Nancy, and Michael Duffy. *The Presidents Club: Inside the World's Most Exclusive Fraternity.* New York: Simon & Schuster, 2012. In this book, two journalists examine the often fascinating relationships between former and current presidents.

Kranish, Michael, and Scott Helman. *The Real Romney.* New York: Harper, 2012. Several biographies of Mitt Romney appeared in the run-up to the 2012 presidential elections. This one, by two reporters at the *Boston Globe,* rates high for objectivity and depth.

Scheiber, Noam. *The Escape Artists: How Obama's Team Fumbled the Recovery.* New York: Simon & Schuster, 2012. This nuanced account of economic decision making in the Obama White House is in part a story of failure. Still, Scheiber doubts that it was possible to do much better under the circumstances. Scheiber is senior editor at the *New Republic.*

MEDIA RESOURCES

The American President—A 1995 romantic comedy with plenty of ideas about both romance and government. Michael Douglas is the widower president who falls for a lobbyist, played by Annette Bening. Douglas's comedic performance has been called his best.

My Life—President Bill Clinton's autobiography is essential source material on a fascinating national leader. Many people consider the print version of this work to be excessively padded, so it is best experienced through the Random House audiobook—the CD version of *My Life* is nicely abridged. Clinton's own narration adds considerable flavor to the production.

(© PashaIgnatov/iStockphoto)

E-mocracy THE PRESIDENCY AND THE INTERNET

Today, the Internet has become such a normal part of most Americans' lives that it is almost hard to imagine what life was like without it. Certainly, accessing the latest press releases from the White House was much more difficult twenty years ago than it is today. It was not until the Clinton administration (1993–2001) that access to the White House via the Internet became possible.

Correspondence with the president and the First Lady quickly moved from ordinary handwritten letters to e-mail. Most agencies of the government, as well as congressional offices, also began to provide access and information on the Internet. You can access the White House Web site (see the following *Logging On* section) to find White House press releases, presidential State of the Union messages and other speeches, historical data on the presidency, and much more.

LOGGING ON

1. The White House Web site offers extensive information on the White House and the presidency. You can locate it by entering "white house" into your favorite search engine.
2. You can find inaugural addresses of American presidents from George Washington to Barack Obama by searching on "bartleby 124."
3. You can find an excellent collection of data and maps describing all U.S. presidential elections at Dave Leip's Atlas of U.S. Presidential Elections. Simply type "leip" into your search engine.

12 The Bureaucracy

The six learning outcomes below are designed to help improve your understanding of this chapter. After reading this chapter, you should be able to:

- Learning Outcome 1: **Name the different models that describe the behavior of bureaucracies.**
- Learning Outcome 2: **Identify the largest federal agencies by number of employees and the largest federal spending programs.**
- Learning Outcome 3: **Describe the various types of agencies and organizations that make up the federal executive branch.**
- Learning Outcome 4: **Explain how government employees are hired and how they are administered.**
- Learning Outcome 5: **Evaluate different methods that have been put into place to reform bureaucracies and make them more efficient.**
- Learning Outcome 6: **Discuss how federal agencies make rules and the role of Congress in this process.**

This federal service worker repairs the head of George Washington in Mount Rushmore National Memorial. The worker represents just one small part of our government bureaucracy. (Paul Horsted Stock Connection Worldwide/Newscom)

(NASA/Bill Ingalls/Newscom)

OUR SPACE EXPLORATION program has always been undertaken by the federal government. Could the private sector do the job?

PARTS OF THE FEDERAL GOVERNMENT WERE PRIVATIZED?

BACKGROUND

Many federal government agencies, such as the Central Intelligence Agency, provide services that are highly sensitive. Others, such as the U.S. Postal Service, provide for-fee services that in effect compete with private-sector businesses. Agencies such as the U.S. Weather Service provide their services to the U.S. public at no charge. The Weather Service, nonetheless, is in competition with private weather prediction organizations. The Tennessee Valley Authority (TVA) generates electric power for a seven-state region at relatively low rates. It is in direct competition with private companies that generate electricity.

WHAT IF PARTS OF THE FEDERAL GOVERNMENT WERE PRIVATIZED?

In recent decades, governments throughout the world have sold government-owned agencies and companies to private investors. Certainly, we cannot imagine auctioning off the Central Intelligence Agency to the highest private bidder. Nonetheless, many federal government agencies could be privatized. There are many methods by which privatization could take place. One option would be to issue and sell shares directly to anybody who wants to buy them. Eventually, a group would control a large enough percentage of shares to elect a board of directors so that the group could control the newly privatized agency.

Another option would be to offer to sell government agencies to existing corporations that already might be engaged in similar lines of business. The U.S. Postal Service, for example, could be offered for sale to existing delivery companies such as FedEx and UPS. The TVA could be sold in parts to private electric utility companies. The Federal Aviation Administration could be offered for sale in small chunks. For example, each airport control system could be offered for sale to investors in that particular city.

NOT EVERYONE WOULD BENEFIT FROM PRIVATIZATION

Any federal government agency that became privatized would be subject to the rigors of the marketplace. If the TVA were privatized, it would be forced to take account of the true costs of all of its operations. Ultimately, it might have to raise the price of electricity to its customers.

Consider other examples. The U.S. Postal Service probably would be run more like FedEx and UPS. If it were, U.S. postal workers, who now have a very strong union, would find private postal management much less willing to accept union demands for higher wages. Mail delivery to rural Americans might become more expensive—a private postal service might have to charge the true cost of delivering mail to out-of-the-way residents and businesses. If rural mail delivery service to remote areas became extremely expensive, some people might move closer to town.

If the National Mediation Board were privatized, it would have to bill unions and businesses for the full cost of its mediation services in labor-management disputes. As a result, some labor-management disputes might take longer to resolve because the parties would be reluctant to pay for mediation services.

FOR CRITICAL ANALYSIS

1. ***Which additional agencies and government operations are likely candidates for privatization? Why?***
2. ***Which government agencies and operations clearly are not candidates for privatization? Why?***

Faceless bureaucrats—this image provokes a negative reaction from many, if not most, Americans. Polls consistently report that the majority of Americans support "less government." The same polls, however, report that the majority of Americans support almost every specific program that the government undertakes. The conflict between the desire for small government and the desire for the benefits that only a large government can provide has been a constant feature of American politics. For example, the goal of preserving endangered species has widespread support. At the same time, many people believe that restrictions imposed under the Endangered Species Act violate the rights of landowners. Helping the elderly pay their medical bills is a popular objective, but hardly anyone enjoys paying the Medicare tax that supports this effort.

In this chapter, we describe the size, organization, and staffing of the federal bureaucracy. We review modern attempts at bureaucratic reform and the process by which Congress exerts ultimate control over the bureaucracy. We also discuss the bureaucracy's role in making rules and setting policy.

(Hulton Archive/Getty Images)

German sociologist Max Weber (1864–1920) created the classic model of the modern bureaucracy. Does the power in the classic bureaucracy flow upward, downward, or horizontally?

The Nature of Bureaucracy

Bureaucracy is the name given to an organization that is structured hierarchically to carry out specific functions. Generally, bureaucracies are characterized by an organizational chart. The units of the organization are divided according to the specialization and expertise of the employees.

■ Learning Outcome 1: **Name the different models that describe the behavior of bureaucracies.**

Bureaucracy
An organization that is structured hierarchically to carry out specific functions.

Public and Private Bureaucracies

We should not think of bureaucracy as unique to government. Any large corporation or university can be considered a bureaucratic organization. The fact is that the handling of complex problems requires a division of labor. Individuals must concentrate their skills on specific, well-defined aspects of a problem and depend on others to solve the rest of it.

Public, or government, bureaucracies differ from private organizations in some important ways, however. A private corporation has a single leader—its chief executive officer (CEO). Public bureaucracies do not have a single leader. Although the president is the chief administrator of the federal system, all agencies are subject to the dictates of Congress for their funding, staffing, and, indeed, their continued existence. Public bureaucracies supposedly serve all citizens, while private ones serve private interests.

One other important difference between private corporations and government bureaucracies is that government bureaucracies are not organized to make a profit. Rather, they are supposed to perform their functions as efficiently as possible to conserve taxpayers' dollars. Perhaps it is this ideal that makes citizens hostile toward government bureaucracy when they experience inefficiency and red tape.

Every modern president, at one time or another, has proclaimed that his administration was going to "fix government." All modern presidents also have put forth plans to end government waste and inefficiency. (See Table 12–1 on the following page.) Their success has been, in a word, underwhelming. Presidents generally have been powerless to significantly affect the structure and operation of the federal bureaucracy.

Models of Bureaucracy

Several theories have been offered to help us better understand the ways in which bureaucracies function. Each of these theories focuses on specific features of bureaucracies.

Weberian Model
A model of bureaucracy developed by the German sociologist Max Weber, who viewed bureaucracies as rational, hierarchical organizations in which decisions are based on logical reasoning.

Weberian Model. The classic model, or **Weberian model,** of the modern bureaucracy was proposed by the German sociologist Max Weber.[1] He argued that the

1. Max Weber, *Theory of Social and Economic Organization,* ed. Talcott Parsons (New York: Oxford University Press, 1974).

Table 12-1 ▸ Selected Presidential Plans to End Government Inefficiency

President	Plan
Lyndon Johnson (1963–1969)	Programming, planning, and budgeting systems
Richard Nixon (1969–1974)	Management by Objectives
Jimmy Carter (1977–1981)	Zero-Based Budgeting
Ronald Reagan (1981–1989)	President's Private Sector Survey on Cost Control (the Grace Commission)
George H. W. Bush (1989–1993)	Right-Sizing Government
Bill Clinton (1993–2001)	Reinventing Government
George W. Bush (2001–2009)	Performance-Based Budgeting
Barack Obama (2009–present)	Appointment of a chief performance officer

increasingly complex nature of modern life, coupled with the steadily growing demands placed on governments by their citizens, made the formation of bureaucracies inevitable. According to Weber, most bureaucracies—whether in the public or private sector—are organized hierarchically and governed by formal procedures. The power in a bureaucracy flows from the top downward. Decision-making processes in bureaucracies are shaped by detailed technical rules that promote similar decisions in similar situations.

Bureaucrats are specialists who attempt to resolve problems through logical reasoning and data analysis instead of "gut feelings" and guesswork. Individual advancement in bureaucracies is supposed to be based on merit rather than on political connections. Indeed, the modern bureaucracy, according to Weber, should be an apolitical organization.

Acquisitive Model
A model of bureaucracy that views top-level bureaucrats as seeking to expand the size of their budgets and staffs to gain greater power.

Monopolistic Model
A model of bureaucracy that compares bureaucracies to monopolistic business firms. Lack of competition in either circumstance leads to inefficient and costly operations.

Acquisitive Model. Other theorists do not view bureaucracies in terms as benign as Weber's. Some believe that bureaucracies are acquisitive in nature. Proponents of the **acquisitive model** argue that top-level bureaucrats will always try to expand, or at least to avoid any reductions in, the size of their budgets. Although government bureaucracies are not-for-profit enterprises, bureaucrats want to maximize the size of their budgets and staffs, which are the most visible trappings of power in the public sector. These efforts are also prompted by the desire of bureaucrats to "sell" their products—such as national defense, public housing, or agricultural subsidies—to both Congress and the public.

Monopolistic Model. Because government bureaucracies seldom have competitors, some theorists have suggested that these bureaucratic organizations may be explained best by a **monopolistic model.** The analysis is similar to that used by economists to examine the behavior of monopolistic firms. Monopolistic bureaucracies—like monopolistic firms—essentially have no competitors and act accordingly. Because monopolistic bureaucracies usually are not penalized for chronic inefficiency, they have little reason to adopt cost-saving measures or to make more productive use of their resources. Some economists have argued that such problems can be cured only by privatizing certain bureaucratic functions, as we discussed in this chapter's opening *What If . . .* feature.

Social Media IN POLITICS

Most federal agencies now have a social media presence, and the Centers for Disease Control offers one of the best. For up-to-the-minute health advice, follow CDCgov on Twitter. For hilarious advice on what to do in a natural disaster, search on "cdc zombie apocalypse" on Twitter.

The Size of the Bureaucracy

In 1789, the new government's bureaucracy was tiny. There were three departments—State (with nine employees), War (with two employees), and Treasury (with thirty-nine employees)—and the Office of the Attorney General (which later became the Department of Justice). The bureaucracy was still small in 1798. At that time, the secretary of state had seven clerks and spent a total of $500 (about $9,800 in 2013 dollars) on stationery and printing. In that same year, an appropriations act allocated $1.4 million (or $27.5 million in 2013 dollars) to the War Department.[2]

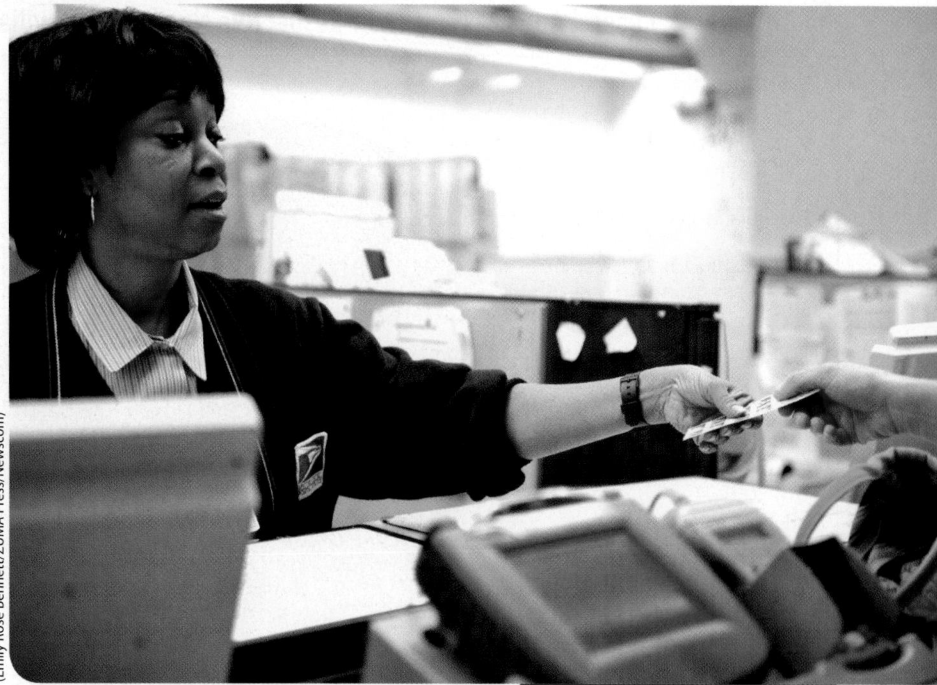

(Emily Rose Bennett/ZUMA Press/Newscom)

The U.S. Postal Service employs more than 550,000 workers.

Government Employment Today

Times have changed, as we can see in Figure 12–1 on the following page, which shows various federal agencies and the number of civilian employees in each. Excluding military service members but including employees of the legislative and judicial branches and the U.S. Postal Service, the federal bureaucracy includes approximately 2.9 million employees. That number has remained relatively stable for the past several decades. It is somewhat deceiving, however, because many other individuals work directly or indirectly for the federal government as subcontractors or consultants.

■ **Learning Outcome 2: Identify the largest federal agencies by number of employees and the largest federal spending programs.**

Conventionally, attempts to measure the size of the federal bureaucracy also leave out the men and women of the Army, Navy, Air Force, and Marines. In 2012, these personnel numbered 1,410,000. Despite their service ethos, it cannot be denied that the armed forces are gigantic bureaucracies with all the characteristics of bureaucracies everywhere. We look at some resulting issues in the *Politics and Bureaucracy* feature on page 391.

The figures for federal government employment are only part of the story. Figure 12–2 on the following page shows the growth in government employment at the federal, state, and local levels. From 1982 to 2008, this growth was mainly at the state and local levels.

If all government employees are included, more than 16 percent of all civilian employment is accounted for by government. Costs are commensurately high. Spending by all levels of government was equivalent to only about 11 percent of the nation's gross domestic product in 1929. For fiscal year 2013, it is approximately 39 percent.

The Great Recession and its aftermath had a major impact on government spending and employment. During 2009, increased social spending due to high rates of unemployment—together with President Barack Obama's stimulus programs—resulted in sharp increases in federal spending. At the same time, the rest of the economy was collapsing. Government spending therefore became a larger part of a smaller economy. Spending peaked at more than 42 percent of the economy in 2009, the largest share since World War II.

In 2009, the number of state and local government workers began to fall, because these governments could not collect enough revenue to fund their previous levels of activity. From August 2008 to the end of 2011, state and local government employment fell by about 660,000.

Federal Spending

While Figure 12–1 provides a good overview of the number of federal employees, it does not accurately depict federal spending. For example, employees of the U.S. Postal Service (USPS) make up about a quarter of the pie chart. Yet for decades the postal service has

2. Leonard D. White, *The Federalists: A Study in Administrative History, 1789–1801* (New York: Free Press, 1948).

Figure 12-1 ▸ Federal Agencies and Their Respective Numbers of Civilian Employees

- Executive Office of the President 1,725
- Legislative Branch 29,930
- Judicial Branch 33,754

Independent Agencies and Corporations 756,973

- U.S. Postal Service 574,000
- All Other Independent Agencies 182,973

Executive Departments 2,100,905

- Defense 657,347
- Veterans Affairs 317,620
- Homeland Security 198,658
- Justice 115,746
- Treasury 105,612
- Agriculture 92,217
- Health and Human Services 85,257
- Interior 69,866
- Transportation 57,324
- Commerce 45,737
- Labor 16,366
- Energy 16,140
- State 12,588
- Housing and Urban Development 9,459
- Education 4,642

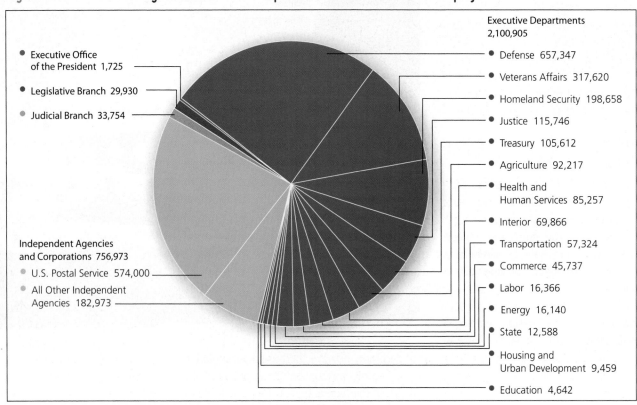

Sources: U.S. Office of Personnel Management, December 2011; and the U.S. Postal Service.

been entirely self-supporting and has drawn no funds from the government at all. (Recent financial troubles have raised the question of whether the USPS can remain self-supporting in the future, however.) In contrast, the employees of the Social Security Administration make up only 3 percent of the federal workforce, but they are responsible for 20 percent of what the federal government spends.

Studies repeatedly show that most Americans have a very inaccurate idea of how the federal budget is spent. Figure 12–3 on page 392 can help. This pie chart demonstrates that about a third of all federal spending goes to two programs that benefit older Americans—Social Security and Medicare. Additional social programs, many aimed at low-income individuals and families, push the total amount of social spending past the 50 percent mark. In short, the federal government spends much more on the poor than many people realize. Medicaid, a joint federal-state program that provides health-care services, is the largest of these programs. (CHIP is the Children's Health Insurance Program, and SNAP is the Supplementary Nutrition Assistance Program, better known as food stamps.) In contrast, traditional cash welfare—Temporary Assistance for Needy Families (TANF)—accounts for only 0.4 percent of the budget ($18 billion) and is buried in the "Miscellaneous low-income and disability support" slice.

Military defense and veterans' benefits are an additional quarter of the whole. Interest payments on the national debt are

Figure 12-2 ▸ Government Employment at the Federal, State, and Local Levels

There are more local government employees than federal and state employees combined.

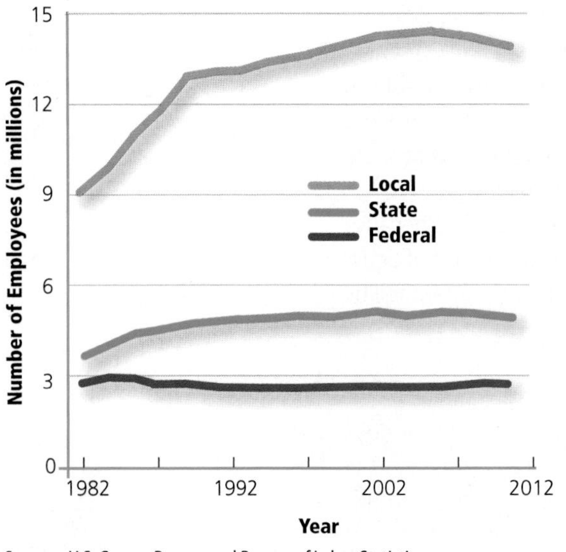

Sources: U.S. Census Bureau and Bureau of Labor Statistics.

Politics AND Bureaucracy

HAVE ARMY RULES CAUSED UNNECESSARY FATALITIES?

During the first years of the Vietnam War (1965–1975), the Army supplied inappropriate ammunition for its new M-16 rifles. As a result, rifles jammed and some of our soldiers died. Eventually, the Army corrected the error. At the beginning of the Iraq War in 2003, the enemy used improvised explosive devices (IEDs) to incapacitate or destroy U.S. Army vehicles. Despite heated requests from the field, years passed before the Army was able to provide adequate supplies of vehicular armor to reduce the danger from IEDs. In the meantime, many American lives were lost.

Apparently, both the M-16 ammo and the vehicular armor problems were the result of rulings at the secretary of defense level. These decisions interfered with the Army's ability to provide its soldiers with necessary equipment in a timely fashion. To this day, rules made at or near the top of the military's immense bureaucracy sometimes create dangerous situations.

THE ARMY MEDEVAC HELICOPTER CONTROVERSY

In 2012, a controversy arose over the Army's medevac helicopters. The triggering incident was the death of Army Specialist Chazray Clark, who was severely wounded by an IED. Clark needed immediate medical attention, but it took the Army more than an hour to get a medevac helicopter to him, even though one was stationed minutes away at Kandahar Air Base. Why the delay? Army rules. Specifically, medevac helicopters must be accompanied by helicopter gunships for protection, and no gunship was immediately available.

SHOULD ARMY MEDEVAC HELICOPTERS BE ARMED?

Army medevac helicopters are unarmed and display large Red Cross emblems to conform to rules of the Geneva Conventions. That means that they could be shot down by an enemy—such as the Taliban—that does not abide by the Geneva Conventions. The medevacs therefore need armed escort for protection. Meanwhile, medevac helicopters used by the Air Force, the Marines, and the Navy—and, for that matter, the British—are unmarked. They are also extremely heavily armed and can fly without escort. A number of soldiers, plus members of Congress, have argued that the Army's medevac helicopters should be armed as well.

THE ARMY'S RESPONSE

The Army's response is that its medevac helicopters are special. They carry much more equipment than Air Force or Navy medevacs and can airlift several injured individuals at once. The added weight of the guns would make it impossible to carry so much equipment. Further, gunships pack more firepower than the door gunners in the medevacs used by the other services.

The Army's critics find these arguments to be unpersuasive. They also note that, in the case of Specialist Clark, an armed Air Force medevac helicopter was immediately available at Kandahar Air Base. Army rules, however, prohibit requests to the Air Force for medevac assistance.

FOR CRITICAL ANALYSIS

Why would it be difficult to create uniform rules for all parts of the U.S. military?

(© kyoshino / iStockphoto) (© Evelyn Peyton / iStockphoto)

5 percent. Education and training, transportation, and "everything else" amount to only 16 percent of the budget. Foreign aid, which is included in the "Everything else" slice, is 1.4 percent, or $56 billion. This is a substantial sum, but it is much smaller than many people imagine. Frequently, politicians will claim that they can balance the federal budget by making large cuts to this 16 percent slice of federal spending. A quick look at Figure 12–3 reveals that such claims are not based on reality.

Figure 12-3 ▸ Federal Government Spending, Fiscal Year 2012

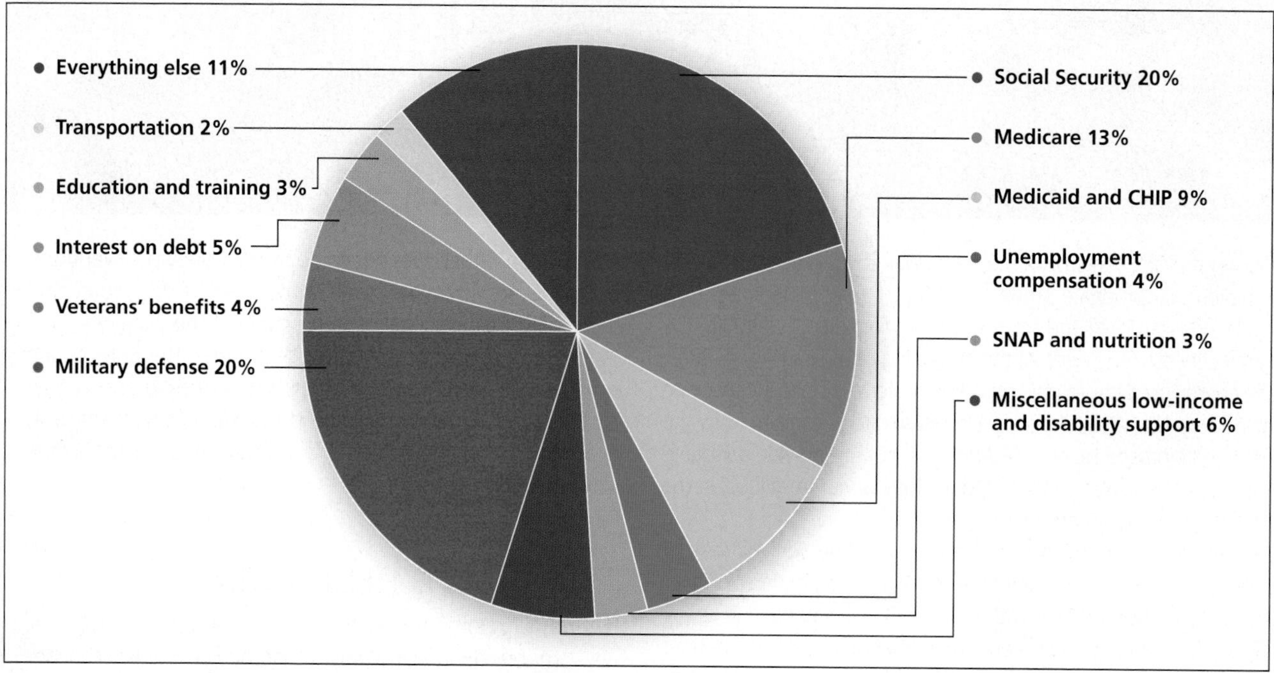

Source: usgovernmentspending.com.

The Organization of the Federal Bureaucracy

■ Learning Outcome 3: **Describe the various types of agencies and organizations that make up the federal executive branch.**

Within the federal bureaucracy are a number of different types of government agencies and organizations. Figure 12–4 on the facing page outlines the several bodies within the executive branch, as well as the separate organizations that provide services to Congress, to the courts, and directly to the president.

The executive branch, which employs most of the government's staff, has four major types of structures. They are (1) cabinet departments, (2) independent executive agencies, (3) independent regulatory agencies, and (4) government corporations. Each has a distinctive relationship to the president, and some have unusual internal structures, overall goals, and grants of power.

Cabinet Departments

Cabinet Department
One of the fifteen major departments of the executive branch.

Line Organization
In the federal government, an administrative unit that is directly accountable to the president.

The fifteen **cabinet departments** are the major service organizations of the federal government. They can also be described in management terms as **line organizations.** This means that they are directly accountable to the president and are responsible for performing government functions, such as printing money and training troops. These departments were created by Congress when the need for each department arose. The first department to be created was State, and the most recent one was Homeland Security, established in 2003. A president might ask that a new department be created or an old one abolished, but the president has no power to do so without legislative approval from Congress.

Each department is headed by a secretary (except for the Justice Department, which is headed by the attorney general). Each department also has several levels of undersecretaries, assistant secretaries, and other personnel.

Figure 12–4 ▶ Organizational Chart of the Federal Government

THE GOVERNMENT OF THE UNITED STATES

THE CONSTITUTION

LEGISLATIVE BRANCH

THE CONGRESS

SENATE **HOUSE**

Architect of the Capitol
United States Botanic Garden
Government Accountability Office
Government Printing Office
Library of Congress
Congressional Budget Office

EXECUTIVE BRANCH

THE PRESIDENT
THE VICE PRESIDENT

Executive Office of the President

White House Office
Office of the Vice President
Council of Economic Advisers
Council on Environmental Quality
National Security Staff
Office of Administration
Office of Management and Budget
Office of National Drug Control Policy
Office of Science and Technology Policy
Office of the U.S. Trade Representative

JUDICIAL BRANCH

THE SUPREME COURT OF THE UNITED STATES

United States Courts of Appeals
United States District Courts
Territorial Courts
United States Court of International Trade
United States Court of Federal Claims
United States Court of Appeals for the Armed Forces
United States Tax Court
United States Court of Appeals for Veterans Claims
Administrative Office of the United States Courts
Federal Judicial Center
United States Sentencing Commission

DEPARTMENT OF AGRICULTURE | **DEPARTMENT OF COMMERCE** | **DEPARTMENT OF DEFENSE** | **DEPARTMENT OF EDUCATION** | **DEPARTMENT OF ENERGY** | **DEPARTMENT OF HEALTH AND HUMAN SERVICES** | **DEPARTMENT OF HOMELAND SECURITY** | **DEPARTMENT OF HOUSING AND URBAN DEVELOPMENT**

DEPARTMENT OF THE INTERIOR | **DEPARTMENT OF JUSTICE** | **DEPARTMENT OF LABOR** | **DEPARTMENT OF STATE** | **DEPARTMENT OF TRANSPORTATION** | **DEPARTMENT OF THE TREASURY** | **DEPARTMENT OF VETERANS AFFAIRS**

INDEPENDENT ESTABLISHMENTS AND GOVERNMENT CORPORATIONS

African Development Foundation
Broadcasting Board of Governors
Central Intelligence Agency
Commodity Futures Trading Commission
Consumer Product Safety Commission
Corporation for National and Community Service
Defense Nuclear Facilities Safety Board
Environmental Protection Agency
Equal Employment Opportunity Commission
Export-Import Bank of the U.S.
Farm Credit Administration
Federal Communications Commission
Federal Deposit Insurance Corporation
Federal Election Commission
Federal Housing Finance Agency
Federal Labor Relations Authority
Federal Maritime Commission
Federal Mediation and Conciliation Service
Federal Mine Safety and Health Review Commission
Federal Reserve System
Federal Retirement Thrift Investment Board
Federal Trade Commission
General Services Administration
Inter-American Foundation
Merit Systems Protection Board
National Aeronautics and Space Administration
National Archives and Records Administration
National Capital Planning Commission
National Credit Union Administration
National Foundation on the Arts and the Humanities
National Labor Relations Board
National Mediation Board
National Railroad Passenger Corporation (AMTRAK)
National Railroad Retirement Board
National Science Foundation
National Transportation Safety Board
Nuclear Regulatory Commission
Occupational Safety and Health Review Commission
Office of the Director of National Intelligence
Office of Government Ethics
Office of Personnel Management
Office of Special Counsel
Overseas Private Investment Corporation
Panama Canal Commission
Peace Corps
Pension Benefit Guaranty Corporation
Postal Regulatory Commission
Securities and Exchange Commission
Selective Service System
Small Business Administration
Social Security Administration
Tennessee Valley Authority
Trade and Development Agency
U.S. Agency for International Development
U.S. Commission on Civil Rights
U.S. International Trade Commission
U.S. Postal Service

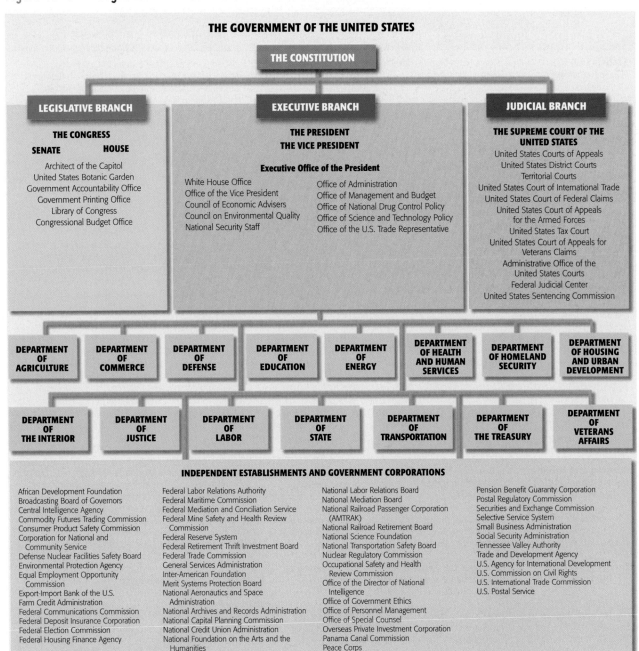

Source: *United States Government Manual*, 2011 (Washington, D.C.: U.S. Government Printing Office, 2011).

Presidents theoretically have considerable control over the cabinet departments, because presidents are able to appoint or fire all of the top officials. Even cabinet departments do not always respond to the president's wishes, though. One reason why presidents are frequently unhappy with their departments is that the entire bureaucratic structure below the top political levels is staffed by permanent employees. Many of these employees are committed to established programs or procedures and resist change. Table 12–2 on the following page shows that each cabinet department employs thousands of individuals, only a handful of whom are under the direct control of the president. The table also describes some of the functions of each of the departments.

Federal, state, and local governments together spend about $1 billion every 78 minutes, every day of the year.

Table 12-2 ▶ Executive Departments

Department and Year Established	Principal Functions	Selected Subagencies
State (1789) (12,588 employees)	Negotiates treaties; develops foreign policy; protects citizens abroad.	Passport Services Office; Bureau of Diplomatic Security; Foreign Service; Bureau of Human Rights and Humanitarian Affairs; Bureau of Consular Affairs.
Treasury (1789) (105,612 employees)	Pays all federal bills; borrows funds; collects federal taxes; mints coins and prints paper currency; supervises national banks.	Internal Revenue Service; U.S. Mint.
Interior (1849) (69,866 employees)	Supervises federally owned lands and parks; supervises Native American affairs.	U.S. Fish and Wildlife Service; National Park Service; Bureau of Indian Affairs; Bureau of Land Management.
Justice (1870)* (115,746 employees)	Furnishes legal advice to the president; enforces federal criminal laws; supervises federal prisons.	Federal Bureau of Investigation; Drug Enforcement Administration; Bureau of Prisons.
Agriculture (1889) (92,217 employees)	Provides assistance to farmers and ranchers; conducts agricultural research; works to protect forests.	Soil Conservation Service; Agricultural Research Service; Food Safety and Inspection Service; Federal Crop Insurance Corporation; Commodity Credit Corporation; Forest Service.
Commerce (1913)[†] (45,737 employees)	Grants patents and trademarks; conducts a national census; monitors the weather; protects the interests of businesses.	Bureau of the Census; Bureau of Economic Analysis; Patent and Trademark Office; National Oceanic and Atmospheric Administration.
Labor (1913)[†] (16,366 employees)	Administers federal labor laws; promotes the interests of workers.	Occupational Safety and Health Administration; Bureau of Labor Statistics; Employment Standards Administration; Employment and Training Administration.
Defense (1947)[‡] (657,347 employees)	Manages the armed forces (army, navy, air force, and marines); operates military bases; is responsible for civil defense.	National Security Agency; Joint Chiefs of Staff; Departments of the Air Force, Navy, Army; Defense Advanced Research Projects Agency; Defense Intelligence Agency; the service academies.
Housing and Urban Development (1965) (9,459 employees)	Deals with the nation's housing needs; develops and rehabilitates urban communities; oversees resale of mortgages.	Government National Mortgage Association; Office of Community Planning and Development; Office of Fair Housing and Equal Opportunity.
Transportation (1967) (57,324 employees)	Finances improvements in mass transit; develops and administers programs for highways, railroads, and aviation.	Federal Aviation Administration; Federal Highway Administration; National Highway Traffic Safety Administration; Federal Transit Administration.
Energy (1977) (16,140 employees)	Promotes the conservation of energy and resources; analyzes energy data; conducts research and development.	Federal Energy Regulatory Commission; National Nuclear Security Administration.
Health and Human Services (1979)[§] (85,257 employees)	Promotes public health; administers Medicare and Medicaid; enforces pure food and drug laws; conducts and sponsors health-related research.	Food and Drug Administration; Public Health Service; Centers for Disease Control and Prevention; National Institutes of Health; Centers for Medicare and Medicaid Services.
Education (1979)[§] (4,642 employees)	Coordinates federal programs and policies for education; administers aid to education; promotes educational research.	Office of Special Education and Rehabilitation Service; Office of Elementary and Secondary Education; Office of Postsecondary Education; Office of Vocational and Adult Education; Office of Federal Student Aid.
Veterans Affairs (1988) (317,620 employees)	Promotes the welfare of veterans of the U.S. armed forces.	Veterans Health Administration; Veterans Benefits Administration; National Cemetery Systems.
Homeland Security (2003) (198,658 employees)	Attempts to prevent terrorist attacks within the United States, control America's borders, and minimize the damage from natural disasters.	U.S. Customs and Border Protection; U.S. Coast Guard; Secret Service; Federal Emergency Management Agency; U.S. Citizenship and Immigration Services; U.S. Immigration Customs Enforcement.

*Formed from the Office of the Attorney General (created in 1789).
[†]Formed from the Department of Commerce and Labor (created in 1903).
[‡]Formed from the Department of War (created in 1789) and the Department of the Navy (created in 1798).
[§]Formed from the Department of Health, Education, and Welfare (created in 1953).

Independent Executive Agencies

Independent executive agencies are bureaucratic organizations that are not located within a department but report directly to the president, who appoints their chief officials. When a new federal agency is created—the Environmental Protection Agency, for example—Congress decides where it will be located in the bureaucracy. In recent decades, presidents often have asked that a new organization be kept separate or independent rather than added to an existing department, particularly if a department may be hostile to the agency's creation. Table 12–3 below describes the functions of selected independent executive agencies.

Independent Executive Agency
A federal agency that is not part of a cabinet department but reports directly to the president.

Independent Regulatory Agencies

Typically, an **independent regulatory agency** is responsible for a specific type of public policy. Its function is to make and implement rules and regulations in a particular sphere of action to protect the public interest. The earliest such agency was the Interstate Commerce Commission (ICC), which was established in 1887 when Americans began to seek some form of government control over the rapidly growing business and industrial sector. This new form of organization, the independent regulatory agency, was supposed to make technical, nonpolitical decisions about rates, profits, and rules that would be for the benefit of all and that did not require congressional legislation. In the years that followed the creation of the ICC, other agencies were formed to regulate such areas as

Independent Regulatory Agency
An agency outside the major executive departments that is charged with making and implementing rules and regulations.

Table 12–3 ▸ Selected Independent Executive Agencies

Name	Date Formed	Principal Functions
The Smithsonian Institution (4,852 employees)	1846	Runs the government's museums and the National Zoo.
Central Intelligence Agency (CIA) (number of employees is classified; estimated to be about 20,000)	1947	Gathers and analyzes political and military information about foreign countries; conducts covert operations outside the United States.
General Services Administration (GSA) (12,729 employees)	1949	Purchases and manages property of the federal government; acts as the business arm of the federal government in overseeing federal government spending projects; discovers overcharges in government programs.
National Science Foundation (NSF) (1,508 employees)	1950	Promotes scientific research; provides grants to all levels of schools for instructional programs in the sciences.
Small Business Administration (SBA) (4,581 employees)	1953	Protects the interests of small businesses; provides low-cost loans and management information to small businesses.
National Aeronautics and Space Administration (NASA) (18,354 employees)	1958	Is responsible for the U.S. space program, including the building, testing, and operating of space vehicles.
Environmental Protection Agency (EPA) (18,662 employees)	1970	Undertakes programs aimed at reducing air and water pollution; works with state and local agencies to help fight environmental hazards.
Social Security Administration (SSA)* (65,911 employees)	1995	Manages the government's Social Security programs, including Retirement and Survivors Insurance, Disability Insurance, Supplemental Security Income, and international programs.

*Separated from the Department of Health and Human Services (created in 1979).

(USA-KT/SIPA/Newscom)

The officers of Freddie Mac and Fannie Mae, government-sponsored enterprises that deal with home financing, face a grilling by members of Congress. They were accused of earning excessively high salaries. Why can Congress question those salaries?

communication (the Federal Communications Commission) and nuclear power (the Nuclear Regulatory Commission). (The ICC was abolished in 1995.)

did you know?

The Commerce Department's U.S. Travel and Tourism Administration once gave $440,000 in disaster relief loans to western ski resort operators because there hadn't been enough snow.

The Purpose and Nature of Regulatory Agencies. In practice, regulatory agencies are administered independently of all three branches of government. They were set up because Congress felt it was unable to handle the complexities and technicalities required to carry out specific laws in the public interest. Regulatory agencies and commissions actually combine some functions of all three branches of government—legislative, executive, and judicial. They are legislative in that they make rules that have the force of law. They are executive in that they provide for the enforcement of those rules. They are judicial in that they decide disputes involving the rules they have made.

Heads of regulatory agencies and members of agency boards or commissions are appointed by the president with the consent of the Senate, although they do not report to the president. When an agency is headed by a board, rather than an individual, the members of the board cannot, by law, all be from the same political party. Presidents can influence regulatory agency behavior by appointing people of their own parties or individuals who share their political views when vacancies occur, in particular when the chair is vacant. Members may be removed by the president only for causes specified in the law creating the agency. Table 12–4 on the facing page describes the functions of selected independent regulatory agencies.

Agency Capture. Over the last several decades, some observers have concluded that regulatory agencies, although nominally independent, may in fact not always be so. They contend that many agencies have been **captured** by the very industries and firms that they were supposed to regulate, and therefore make decisions based on the interests of the industry, not the general public. The results have been less competition rather than more competition, higher prices rather than lower prices, and less choice rather than more choice for consumers.

Capture
The act by which an industry being regulated by a government agency gains direct or indirect control over agency personnel and decision makers.

Deregulation and Reregulation. During the presidency of Jimmy Carter (1977–1981), significant deregulation (the removal of regulatory restraints—the opposite of regulation) was initiated. For example, Carter appointed a chairperson of the Civil Aeronautics Board (CAB) who gradually eliminated regulation of airline fares and routes. Deregulation continued under President Ronald Reagan (1981–1989), who eliminated the CAB in January 1985.

Table 12-4 ▶ Selected Independent Regulatory Agencies

Name	Date Formed	Principal Functions
Federal Reserve System Board of Governors (Fed) (757 federal employees; employment in the entire Fed is 20,310)	1913	Determines policy on interest rates, credit availability, and the money supply.
Federal Trade Commission (FTC) (1,118 employees)	1914	Prevents businesses from engaging in unfair trade practices; stops the formation of monopolies in the business sector; protects consumer rights.
Securities and Exchange Commission (SEC) (3,853 employees)	1934	Regulates the nation's stock exchanges, in which shares of stock are bought and sold; requires full disclosure of the financial profiles of companies that wish to sell stocks and bonds to the public.
Federal Communications Commission (FCC) (1,730 employees)	1934	Regulates communications by radio, television, wire, satellite, and cable.
National Labor Relations Board (NLRB) (1,669 employees)	1935	Protects employees' rights to join unions and bargain collectively with employers; attempts to prevent unfair labor practices by both employers and unions.
Equal Employment Opportunity Commission (EEOC) (2,415 employees)	1964	Works to eliminate discrimination based on religion, gender, race, color, national origin, age, or disability; examines claims of discrimination.
Nuclear Regulatory Commission (NRC) (3,995 employees)	1974	Ensures that electricity-generating nuclear reactors in the United States are built and operated safely; regularly inspects the operations of such reactors.

During the administration of George H. W. Bush (1989–1993), calls for reregulation of many businesses increased. Indeed, during that administration, the Americans with Disabilities Act of 1990, the Civil Rights Act of 1991, and the Clean Air Act Amendments of 1991, all of which increased or changed the regulation of many businesses, were passed. Additionally, the Cable Reregulation Act of 1992 was passed.

Under President Bill Clinton (1993–2001), the Interstate Commerce Commission was eliminated, and the banking and telecommunications industries, along with many other sectors of the economy, were deregulated. At the same time, there was extensive regulation to protect the environment, a trend somewhat attenuated by the George W. Bush administration.

Regulation Today. After the financial crisis of September 2008, many people saw inadequate regulation of the financial industry as a major cause of the nation's economic difficulties. During President Obama's administration, therefore, reregulation of that industry became a major objective. After intense debate, Congress passed a comprehensive financial industry regulation plan in 2010.

Americans have had conflicting views about the amount of regulation that is appropriate for various industries ever since the government began to undertake serious regulatory activities. Many people find regulation to be contrary to the spirit of free enterprise and the American tradition of individualism. Yet in cases such as BP's Deepwater Horizon oil spill disaster in the Gulf of Mexico in April 2010, citizens of all political stripes were

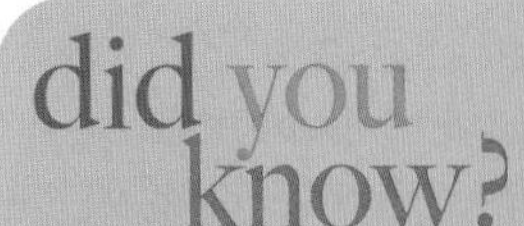

The Pentagon and the Central Intelligence Agency once spent more than $11 million on psychics who were supposed to provide special insights regarding various foreign threats.

outraged to learn that the relevant regulatory agency, the Minerals Management Service, had failed to do its job. Even so, real limits exist as to the ability of the federal government to protect the public, as you will learn in the *Politics and National Security* feature on the facing page.

Government Corporations

Government Corporation An agency of government that administers a quasi-business enterprise. These corporations are used when government activities are primarily commercial.

Another form of bureaucratic organization in the United States is the **government corporation.** Although the concept is borrowed from the world of business, there are important differences between public and private corporations.

A private corporation has shareholders (stockholders) who elect a board of directors, who in turn choose the corporate officers, such as the CEO. When a private corporation makes a profit, it must pay taxes (unless it avoids them through various legal loopholes). It distributes the after-tax profits to shareholders as dividends or plows the profits back into the corporation to make new investments, or both.

A government corporation has a board of directors and managers, but it does not usually have any stockholders. The public cannot buy shares of stock in a typical government corporation, and if the entity makes a profit, it does not distribute the profit as dividends. Nor does it have to pay taxes on profits—the profits remain in the corporation. Table 12–5 below describes the functions of selected government corporations.

Bankruptcy. The federal government can also take effective control of a private corporation in a number of different circumstances. One is bankruptcy. When a company files for bankruptcy, it asks a federal judge for relief from its creditors. The judge, operating under bankruptcy laws established by Congress (as specified in the Constitution), is ultimately responsible for the fate of the enterprise. When a bank fails, the government has a special interest in protecting customers who have deposited funds with the bank. For that reason, the failing institution is taken over by the Federal Deposit Insurance Corporation (FDIC), which ensures continuity of service to bank customers.

Table 12–5 ▸ Selected Government Corporations

Name	Date Formed	Principal Functions
Tennessee Valley Authority (TVA) (12,000 employees)	1933	Operates a Tennessee River control system and generates power for a seven-state region and for the U.S. aeronautics and space programs; promotes the economic development of the Tennessee Valley region; controls floods and promotes the navigability of the Tennessee River.
Federal Deposit Insurance Corporation (FDIC) (8,206 employees)	1933	Insures individuals' bank deposits up to $250,000; oversees the business activities of banks.
Export-Import Bank of the United States (Ex-Im Bank) (402 employees)	1933	Promotes the sale of American-made goods abroad; grants loans to foreign purchasers of American products.
National Railroad Passenger Corporation (AMTRAK) (20,000 employees)	1970	Provides a national and intercity rail passenger service; controls more than 21,000 miles of track and serves 500 communities.
U.S. Postal Service (USPS)* (574,000 employees)	1970	Delivers mail throughout the United States and its territories; is the largest government corporation.

*Formed from the Post Office Department (an executive department).

Politics AND National Security

BUREAUCRATS CAN'T PROTECT US FROM EVERY THREAT

Since the terrorist attacks of September 11, 2001, billions have been spent to create a bureaucracy designed to protect Americans. Thousands of pages of regulations concerning airline travel as well as cargo movement into the United States have been written and applied. We are told by many, including those in government, that terrorism is the greatest threat facing the American people.

TERRORISM IS ONE THREAT AMONG OTHERS

While not downplaying the seriousness of the terrorist threat, we should put it into perspective. Compared to the few thousands who have died during and since 9/11, each year almost forty thousand Americans perish on our highways. Each year, between thirty thousand and fifty thousand of us die from seasonal flu. Each year, thousands die in household accidents. Terrorism is real, but so, too, are the other threats to our lives.

THE BUREAUCRATIC RESPONSE TO TERRORISM

Why must we take off our shoes to fly? Why the three-ounce bottles of shampoo and conditioner? Do such measures really help keep us safe? Possibly not. If once upon a time a terrorist smuggled explosives onto a plane in his shoes, the next terrorist will probably try something else. But for the Transportation Security Agency and its staff members, the worst thing that could possibly happen is a repetition of a successful attack. After such a repetition, no excuses, however reasonable, for having failed to prevent the attack would be accepted. So shoes will be checked forever after. Some people, however, believe that current airport security measures are an overreaction and send the wrong message.

ORDINARY AMERICANS ARE KEY TO OUR SECURITY

The only successful antiterrorist action on September 11, 2001, was undertaken not by the government but by the passengers of United Airlines Flight 93. (The passengers learned that their captors were on a suicide mission through surreptitious cell phone calls.) Since 2001, regular people without training or weapons have been primarily responsible for thwarting attacks aboard commercial airplanes once the attack was under way. On Christmas Day in 2009, passengers and flight attendants subdued the "underwear bomber" on board a plane flying into Detroit. The "thanks" that the passengers and crew received in Detroit was to be held in the baggage area for more than five hours without food—or the right to use their cell phones.

Realistically, it is ordinary people who are best positioned to see and respond to terrorist activities, according to Stephen Flynn, president of the Center for National Policy. Flynn does believe that better technology helps, but it is not enough. Flynn's solution? The government should "support regular people in being able to withstand, rapidly recover, and adapt to foreseeable risk."

FOR CRITICAL ANALYSIS

Our presidents have repeatedly assured us that the federal government is doing everything in its power to keep us safe. What limits the government's ability to do this?

(© kyoshino / iStockphoto) (© Evelyn Peyton / iStockphoto)

Government Ownership of Private Enterprises. The federal government can also obtain partial or complete ownership of a private corporation by purchasing its stock. Before 2008, such takeovers were rare, although they occasionally happened. When Continental Illinois, then the nation's seventh-largest bank, failed in 1984, the FDIC wound up in control of the institution for ten years before it could find a buyer. Significantly, the FDIC took over Continental Illinois by purchasing *preferred stock* newly issued by the bank. **Preferred stock** is a special type of investment that typically pays interest but does not let the holders vote for the corporation's board of directors. By purchasing the stock, the FDIC pumped $4.5 billion of new capital—provided by the taxpayers—into the bank, ensuring its solvency.

Preferred Stock A special share of ownership in a corporation that typically confers no right to vote for the company's board of directors, but does pay interest.

The Bank Bailout. The Continental Illinois rescue provided a blueprint for the massive bank bailout initiated by Henry Paulson, President George W. Bush's Treasury secretary, in

October 2008. The Troubled Asset Relief Program (TARP) gave the Treasury the authority to spend up to $700 billion. Of this sum, about $400 billion was actually disbursed by Paulson and by Timothy Geithner, Obama's Treasury secretary. The government bought preferred stock and similar investment devices from more than eight hundred businesses, including banks, automobile companies, and the giant insurance company AIG.

The bailout program was tremendously unpopular, but by 2011 most banks had paid back the government's investments. The auto companies and AIG had announced plans to do likewise. In 2012, the Congressional Budget Office estimated that TARP's final cost to the taxpayers would be about $32 billion.

Government-Sponsored Enterprises. An additional type of corporation is the government-sponsored enterprise, a business created by the federal government itself, which then sells part or all of the corporation's stock to private investors. Until 2008, the leading examples of this kind of company were the Federal Home Loan Mortgage Corporation, known as Freddie Mac, and the Federal National Mortgage Association, commonly known as Fannie Mae. Both of these firms buy mortgages from banks and bundle them into securities that can be sold to investors. When the housing market collapsed during the Great Recession, so—eventually—did Freddie Mac and Fannie Mae.

Investors had always assumed that the federal government backed up the obligations of the two enterprises, even though the government had never issued an explicit guarantee. In September 2008, the implicit guarantee became real when Treasury secretary Paulson placed the two mortgage giants under a federal "conservatorship" and pumped billions in fresh capital—also provided by the taxpayers—into them through purchases of preferred and common stock. In contrast to the TARP investments, the sums invested in Freddie Mac and Fannie Mae appear to be lost forever. In 2011, the Federal Housing Finance Agency estimated that the bailouts of the two companies would ultimately cost taxpayers $124 billion.

Staffing the Bureaucracy

There are two categories of bureaucrats: political appointees and civil servants. As noted earlier, the president can make political appointments to most of the top jobs in the federal bureaucracy. The president also can appoint ambassadors to foreign posts. All of the

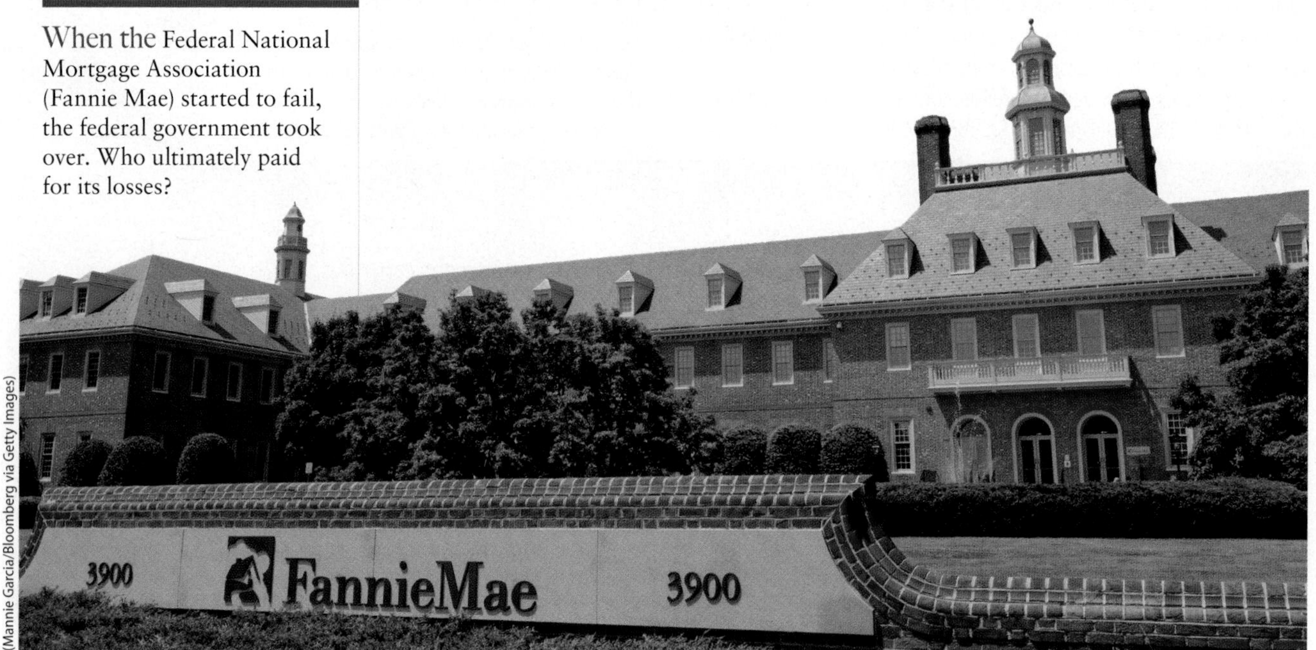

When the Federal National Mortgage Association (Fannie Mae) started to fail, the federal government took over. Who ultimately paid for its losses?

(Mannie Garcia/Bloomberg via Getty Images)

jobs that are considered "political plums" and that usually go to the politically well connected are listed in *Policy and Supporting Positions,* a book published by the Government Printing Office after each presidential election. Informally (and appropriately), this has been called the "Plum Book." The rest of the national government's employees belong to the civil service and obtain their jobs through a much more formal process.

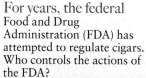

■ Learning Outcome 4:
Explain how government employees are hired and how they are administered.

Political Appointees

To fill the positions listed in the "Plum Book,"[3] the president and the president's advisers solicit suggestions from politicians, businesspersons, and other prominent individuals. Appointments to these positions offer the president a way to pay off outstanding political debts. Presidents often use ambassadorships to reward individuals for their campaign contributions. But the president must also take into consideration such things as the candidate's work experience, intelligence, political affiliations, and personal characteristics. Presidents have differed in the importance they attach to appointing women and minorities to plum positions.

The Aristocracy of the Federal Government. Political appointees are in some sense the aristocracy of the federal government. But their powers, although they appear formidable on paper, are often exaggerated. Like the president, a political appointee will occupy her or his position for a comparatively brief time. Political appointees often leave office before the president's term actually ends. In fact, the average term of service for political appointees is less than two years. As a result, most appointees have little background for their positions and may be mere figureheads. Often, they only respond to the paperwork that flows up from below. Additionally, the professional civil servants who make up the permanent civil service may not feel compelled to carry out their current chief's directives quickly, because they know that he or she will not be around for very long.

The Difficulty in Firing Civil Servants. This inertia is compounded by the fact that it is very difficult to discharge civil servants. In recent years, fewer than 0.1 percent of federal employees have been fired for incompetence. Because discharged employees may appeal their dismissals, many months or even years can pass before the issue is resolved conclusively. This occupational rigidity helps to ensure that most political appointees, no matter how competent or driven, will not be able to exert much meaningful influence over their subordinates, let alone implement dramatic changes in the bureaucracy itself.

History of the Federal Civil Service

When the federal government was formed in 1789, it had no career public servants but rather consisted of amateurs who were almost all Federalists. When Thomas Jefferson took over as president, few federal administrative jobs were held by members of his party, so he fired more than one hundred officials and replaced them with his own supporters. Then, for the next twenty-five years, a growing body of federal administrators gained experience and expertise, becoming in the process professional public servants. These administrators stayed in office regardless of who was elected

For years, the federal Food and Drug Administration (FDA) has attempted to regulate cigars. Who controls the actions of the FDA?

(AP Photo/Steve Helber)

3. See Table 11–1 on page 359 for a list of the number of positions available for presidential appointments in the most recent edition of the "Plum Book."

(Library of Congress)

President James A. Garfield was assassinated in 1881 by a disappointed office seeker, Charles J. Guiteau. The long-term effect of this event was to replace the spoils system with a permanent career civil service. This process began with the passage of the Pendleton Act in 1883, which established the Civil Service Commission.

president. The bureaucracy had become a self-maintaining, long-term element within government.

To the Victor Belong the Spoils. When Andrew Jackson took over the White House in 1828, he could not believe how many appointed officials (appointed before he became president, that is) were overtly hostile toward him and his Democratic Party. Because the bureaucracy was reluctant to carry out his programs, Jackson did the obvious: he fired federal officials—more than had been fired by all his predecessors combined. The **spoils system**—an application of the principle that to the victor belong the spoils—became the standard method of filling federal positions. Whenever a new president was elected from a party different from the party of the previous president, there would be an almost complete turnover in the staffing of the federal government.

Spoils System
The awarding of government jobs to political supporters and friends.

Merit System
The selection, retention, and promotion of government employees on the basis of competitive examinations.

Pendleton Act (Civil Service Reform Act)
An act that established the principle of employment on the basis of merit and created the Civil Service Commission to administer the personnel service.

Civil Service Commission
The initial central personnel agency of the national government; created in 1883.

The Civil Service Reform Act of 1883. Jackson's spoils system survived for a number of years, but it became increasingly corrupt. In addition, the size of the bureaucracy increased by 300 percent between 1851 and 1881. As the bureaucracy grew larger, the cry for civil service reform became louder. Reformers began to look to the example of several European countries—in particular, Germany. That country had established a professional civil service that operated under a **merit system** in which job appointments were based on competitive examinations.

In 1883, the **Pendleton Act**—or **Civil Service Reform Act**—was passed, placing the first limits on the spoils system. The act established the principle of employment on the basis of open, competitive examinations and created the **Civil Service Commission** to administer the personnel service. Only 10 percent of federal employees were covered by the merit system initially. Later laws, amendments, and executive orders, however, increased the coverage to more than 90 percent of federal employees. The effects of these reforms were felt at all levels of government.

The Supreme Court strengthened the civil service system in *Elrod v. Burns*[4] in 1976 and *Branti v. Finkel*[5] in 1980. In those two cases, the Court used the First Amendment to forbid government officials from discharging or threatening to discharge public employees solely for not being supporters of the political party in power unless party affiliation is an appropriate requirement for the position. Additional enhancements to the civil service system were added in *Rutan v. Republican Party of Illinois*[6] in 1990. The Court's ruling effectively prevented the use of partisan political considerations as the basis for hiring, promoting, or transferring most public employees. An exception was permitted, however, for senior policymaking positions, which usually go to officials who will support the programs of the elected leaders.

The Civil Service Reform Act of 1978. In 1978, the Civil Service Reform Act abolished the Civil Service Commission and created two new federal agencies to perform its duties. To administer the civil service laws, rules, and regulations, the act created the Office of Personnel Management (OPM). The OPM is empowered to recruit, interview, and test potential government workers and determine who should be hired. The OPM makes recommendations to the individual agencies as to which persons meet the standards

4. 427 U.S. 347 (1976).
5. 445 U.S. 507 (1980).
6. 497 U.S. 62 (1990).

(typically, the top three applicants for a position), and the agencies then decide whom to hire. To oversee promotions, employees' rights, and other employment matters, the act created the Merit Systems Protection Board (MSPB). The MSPB evaluates charges of wrongdoing, hears employee appeals of agency decisions, and can order corrective action against agencies and employees.

Federal Employees and Political Campaigns. In 1933, when President Franklin D. Roosevelt set up his New Deal, an army of civil servants was hired to staff the many new agencies that were created. Because the individuals who worked in these agencies owed their jobs to the Democratic Party, it seemed natural for them to campaign for Democratic candidates. The Democrats who controlled Congress in the mid-1930s did not object. But in 1938, a coalition of conservative Democrats and Republicans took control of Congress and forced through the Hatch Act—or Political Activities Act—of 1939. The act prohibited federal employees from actively participating in the political management of campaigns. It also forbade the use of federal authority to influence nominations and elections, and it outlawed the use of bureaucratic rank to pressure federal employees to make political contributions.

The Hatch Act created a controversy that lasted for decades. Many contended that the act deprived federal employees of their First Amendment freedoms of speech and association. In 1972, a federal district court declared the act unconstitutional. The United States Supreme Court, however, reaffirmed the challenged portion of the act in 1973, stating that the government's interest in preserving a nonpartisan civil service was so great that the prohibitions should remain.[7] Twenty years later, Congress addressed the criticisms of the Hatch Act by passing the Federal Employees Political Activities Act of 1993. This act, which amended the Hatch Act, lessened the harshness of the 1939 act in several ways. Among other things, the 1993 act allowed federal employees to run for office in nonpartisan elections, participate in voter-registration drives, make campaign contributions to political organizations, and campaign for candidates in partisan elections.

did you know?

According to a recent report, federal employees earn an average of $108,476 in total compensation (including benefits) for jobs equivalent to those in the private sector, while the comparable private-sector employees average $69,928.

Modern Attempts at Bureaucratic Reform

■ Learning Outcome 5: **Evaluate different methods that have been put into place to reform bureaucracies and make them more efficient.**

As long as the federal bureaucracy exists, attempts to make it more open, efficient, and responsive to the needs of U.S. citizens will continue. The most important actual and proposed reforms in the last several decades include sunshine and sunset laws, privatization, incentives for efficiency and productivity, and more protection for so-called whistleblowers.

Sunshine Laws before and after 9/11

In 1976, Congress enacted the **Government in the Sunshine Act.** It required for the first time that all multiheaded federal agencies—agencies headed by a committee instead of an individual—hold their meetings regularly in public session. The bill defined meetings as almost any gathering, formal or informal, of agency members, including a conference telephone call. The only exceptions to this rule of openness are discussions of matters such as court proceedings or personnel problems, and these exceptions are specifically listed in the bill. Sunshine laws now exist at all levels of government.

Government in the Sunshine Act
A law that requires all committee-directed federal agencies to conduct their business regularly in public session.

Information Disclosure. In 1966, the federal government passed the Freedom of Information Act (FOIA), which required federal government agencies, with certain exceptions, to disclose to individuals information contained in government files. (You will learn more about this act in the *Why Should You Care about . . .* feature at the end of this chapter.)

7. *United States Civil Service Commission v. National Association of Letter Carriers,* 413 U.S. 548 (1973).

"Who do I see to get big government off my back?"

FOIA requests are helpful not just to individuals. Indeed, the major beneficiaries of the act have been news organizations, which have used it to uncover government waste, scandals, and incompetence. For example, reporters learned that much of the $5 billion allocated to help small businesses recover from the effects of the 9/11 terrorist attacks went to companies that did not need such relief, including a South Dakota country radio station, a dog boutique in Utah, an Oregon winery, and a variety of Dunkin' Donuts and Subway franchises.

Curbs on Information Disclosure. Since the terrorist attacks of September 11, 2001, the trend toward open government has been reversed at both the federal and the state levels. Within weeks after September 11, 2001, federal agencies removed hundreds, if not thousands, of documents from Internet sites, public libraries, and the reading rooms found in various federal government departments. Information contained in some of the documents included diagrams of power plants and pipelines, structural details on dams, and safety plans for chemical plants. The military also immediately began restricting information about its current and planned activities, as did the Federal Bureau of Investigation. These agencies were concerned that terrorists could make use of this information to plan attacks.

It is possible, however, that whenever the public starts to believe that the threat has lessened, some groups will take state and local governments to court in an effort to increase public access to state and local records by reimposing the sunshine laws that were in effect before 9/11.

Sunset Legislation
Laws requiring that existing programs be reviewed regularly for their effectiveness and be terminated unless specifically extended as a result of these reviews.

Sunset Laws

The size and scope of the federal bureaucracy can potentially be controlled through **sunset legislation,** which places government programs on a definite schedule for congressional consideration. Unless Congress specifically reauthorizes a particular federally operated program at the end of a designated period, the program will be terminated automatically—that is, its sun will set.

The idea of sunset legislation was initially suggested by Franklin Roosevelt when he created the host of New Deal agencies in the 1930s. His adviser (and later Supreme Court justice), William O. Douglas, recommended that each agency's charter should include a provision allowing for its termination in ten years. Only an act of Congress could revitalize it. The proposal was never adopted. It was not until 1976 that a state legislature—Colorado's—adopted sunset legislation for state regulatory

A Federal Emergency Management Agency (FEMA) official inspects tornado damage in Moscow, Ohio.

(AP Photo/Al Behrman)

commissions, giving them a life of six years before their "suns set." Today, most states have some type of sunset law.

Privatization

Another approach to bureaucratic reform is **privatization,** which occurs when government services are replaced by services from the private sector. For example, the government has contracted with private firms to operate prisons. Supporters of privatization argue that some services can be provided more efficiently by the private sector. A similar scheme involves furnishing vouchers to government "clients" in lieu of services. For example, instead of supplying housing, the government could offer vouchers that recipients could use to "pay" for housing in privately owned buildings. (We discussed privatization in the chapter-opening *What If . . .* feature.)

Privatization
The replacement of government services with services provided by private firms.

The privatization, or contracting-out, strategy has been most successful on the local level. Some municipalities have contracted with private companies for such services as trash collection. This approach is not a cure-all, however, because many functions, particularly on the national level, cannot be contracted out in any meaningful way. For example, the federal government could not contract out many of the Defense Department's functions to private firms.

The increase in the amount of government work being contracted out to the private sector has led to significant controversy in recent years. Some have criticized the lack of competitive bidding for many contracts that the government has awarded. Another concern is the perceived lack of government oversight of the work done by private contractors.

did you know?

Federal officials spent $333,000 building a deluxe, earthquake-proof outhouse for hikers in Pennsylvania's remote Delaware Water Gap recreation area.

Incentives for Efficiency and Productivity

An increasing number of state governments are beginning to experiment with schemes to run their operations more efficiently and capably. These plans focus on maximizing the efficiency and productivity of government workers by providing incentives for improved performance. Some of the most promising measures have included such tactics as permitting agencies that do not spend their entire budgets to keep some of the difference and rewarding employees with performance-based bonuses.

Government Performance and Results Act. At the federal level, the Government Performance and Results Act of 1997 was designed to improve efficiency in the federal workforce. The act requires all government agencies (except the Central Intelligence Agency) to describe their goals and establish methods for determining whether those goals are being met. Goals may be broadly crafted (for example, reducing the time it takes to test a new drug before allowing it to be marketed) or narrowly crafted (for example, reducing the number of times a telephone rings before it is answered).

(Robert Weber/The New Yorker Collection/www.cartoonbank.com)

"These projected figures are a figment of our imagination. We hope you like them."

Saving Costs through E-Government. Many contend that the communications revolution brought about by the Internet has not only improved the efficiency with which government agencies deliver services to the public but also helped to reduce the cost of government. Agencies can

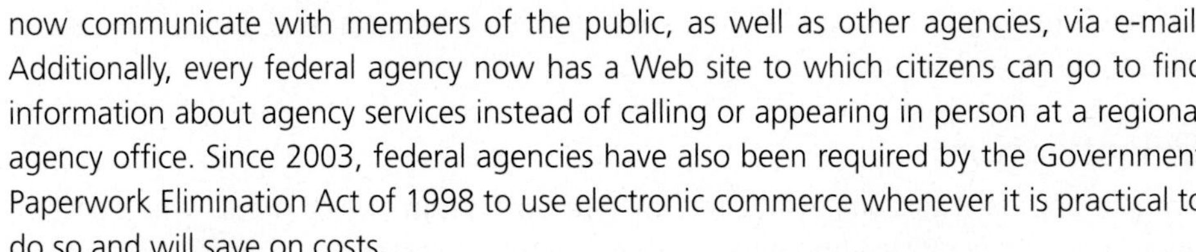

now communicate with members of the public, as well as other agencies, via e-mail. Additionally, every federal agency now has a Web site to which citizens can go to find information about agency services instead of calling or appearing in person at a regional agency office. Since 2003, federal agencies have also been required by the Government Paperwork Elimination Act of 1998 to use electronic commerce whenever it is practical to do so and will save on costs.

Although data-rich high-tech systems have provided new, efficient ways of accomplishing the government's work, privacy concerns have become an issue when the government collects data on individuals. As one example, the American public has never accepted the concept of a national ID card, even though many other nations require their citizens to obtain such ID. Even in the United States, it is difficult to live a normal life without a Social Security number and a state-issued ID such as a driver's license. Lack of adequate ID can also be a tremendous burden to the world's poorest people, as we explain in the *Beyond Our Borders* feature on the facing page.

did you know?

A report by the Government Accountability Office (GAO) revealed that the Department of Agriculture sent $1.1 billion in farm payments to more than 170,000 dead people over a seven-year period.

Helping Out the Whistleblowers

A **whistleblower** is someone who blows the whistle on (brings to public attention) a gross governmental inefficiency or an illegal action. Whistleblowers may be clerical workers, managers, or even specialists, such as scientists.

Whistleblower
Someone who brings to public attention gross governmental inefficiency or an illegal action.

Laws Protecting Whistleblowers. The 1978 Civil Service Reform Act prohibits reprisals against whistleblowers by their superiors, and it set up the Merit Systems Protection Board as part of this protection. Many federal agencies also have toll-free hotlines that employees can use anonymously to report bureaucratic waste and inappropriate behavior. About 35 percent of all calls result in agency action or follow-up. Further protection for whistleblowers was provided in 1989, when Congress passed the Whistleblower Protection Act. That act established an independent agency, the Office of Special Counsel (OSC), to investigate complaints brought by government employees who have been demoted, fired, or otherwise sanctioned for reporting government fraud or waste.

Some state and federal laws encourage employees to blow the whistle on their employers' wrongful actions by providing monetary incentives to the whistleblowers. At the federal level, the False Claims Act of 1986 allows a whistleblower who has disclosed information about a fraud against the U.S. government to receive a monetary award. If the government chooses to prosecute the case and wins, the whistleblower receives between 15 and 25 percent of the proceeds. If the government declines to intervene, the whistleblower can bring a suit on behalf of the government and, if the suit is successful, will receive between 25 and 30 percent of the proceeds.

Two FBI whistleblowers testify on Capitol Hill in Washington before the House Crime, Terrorism, and Homeland Security subcommittee hearing.

(AP Photo/J. Scott Applewhite)

The Problem Continues. Despite these efforts to help whistleblowers, there is little evidence that they truly receive much protection. More than 41 percent of the employees who turned to the OSC for assistance in a recent three-year period stated that they were no longer employees of the government agencies on which they had blown the whistle.

Additionally, in 2006 the United States Supreme Court placed restrictions on lawsuits brought by public workers. The case, *Garcetti v. Ceballos,*[8] involved an assistant district attorney, Richard Ceballos, who wrote a memo asking if a county sheriff's deputy had lied in a search warrant affidavit. Ceballos claimed that he was subsequently demoted and denied a promotion. The outcome of the case turned on whether an employee has

8. 547 U.S. 410 (2006).

Beyond Our Borders

BIOMETRIC IDS FOR MORE THAN ONE BILLION CITIZENS OF INDIA

(© kyoshino / iStockphoto) (© mattjeacock / iStockphoto)

India has a population of 1.2 billion people. By mid-century, it will have 1.5 billion citizens and surpass China as the world's most populous nation. India's economy is growing, but hundreds of millions of its citizens remain desperately poor. Not surprisingly, the nation is badly governed and famous for corruption and a sluggish bureaucracy. India is also a country with booming high-tech industries, however. Beginning in 2010, the Indian government rolled out a high-tech plan to provide biometric IDs for every one of its citizens. Identifications are based on fingerprints and iris scans, and they are entered into the world's largest online ID database. Why is India undertaking this massive project?

THE ANONYMOUS POOR

The primary beneficiaries of the project are expected to be India's poorest citizens. Until now, few poor Indians have had good ways of proving who they are. They had no passport, no driver's license, and no birth certificate. Often, they live in villages where dozens of people share the same name. As a result, they could not open bank accounts or undertake dozens of other activities. The Indian government provides a variety of welfare programs for its poorest citizens, including subsidized grain allotments and make-work schemes. Without proper identification, however, poor Indians have struggled to obtain the services they have been promised. Much of the make-work funding has been stolen by officials who collect the wages of fictitious "ghost workers."

ENTERING THE MODERN WORLD

A secure online identity changes a poor person's relationship with the modern world. Banks are more willing to lend to people they can trace. Mobile phone companies can more easily extend credit. It becomes possible to shop online. India's poor are visibly enthusiastic about the project. People continue to line up day after day to obtain their twelve-digit ID numbers. By the beginning of 2013, a third of all Indians were enrolled.

PRIVACY CONCERNS

The program has its critics. Naturally, these include the corrupt officials who have benefited from the previous situation. More principled critics have raised concerns about India's lack of privacy and data-protection laws. Some claim the scheme could be used to expel illegal immigrants back to Bangladesh, a nation even more impoverished than India. Others point out, however, that people who are destitute have few expectations of privacy.

FOR CRITICAL ANALYSIS

In what ways could India's biometric ID program be abused?

a First Amendment right to criticize an employment-related action. The Court deemed that when he wrote his memo, Ceballos was speaking as an employee, not a citizen, and was thus subject to his employer's disciplinary actions. The ruling will affect millions of governmental employees.

Protecting whistleblowers was an Obama campaign promise. Many observers believe, however, that in practice the Obama administration's record on whistleblowers is one of the worst ever. We discuss that question in this chapter's *Which Side Are You On?* feature on the following page.

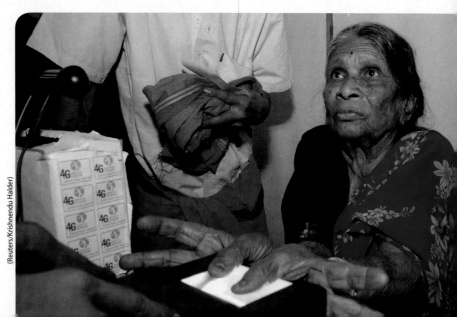

(Reuters/Krishnendu Halder)

An Indian woman gets her fingerprint scanned for identification purposes.

Which Side Are You On?

NATIONAL SECURITY WHISTLEBLOWERS—HEROES OR CRIMINALS?

(© kyoshino / iStockphoto) (© Dean Mitchell / iStockphoto)

Espionage has always been a crime. In 1917, shortly after the United States entered World War I, Congress passed the Espionage Act to punish citizens who gave aid to our enemies. Since that time, it has been used very rarely. In 2010, however, the government brought charges under the act against Private First Class Bradley Manning, an Army intelligence analyst who stole thousands of secret documents and passed them to Wikileaks, a Web site. Wikileaks then posted much of this material on the Web, causing considerable embarrassment to the United States. From 2010 through 2012, the government brought charges against five other people under the act. Are these prosecutions a crackdown on espionage—or an attempt to target legitimate whistleblowers?

THE FEDERAL GOVERNMENT HAS BECOME PARANOID

Some argue that most of these Espionage Act cases involve whistleblowing, not espionage. Consider Thomas A. Drake, formerly of the National Security Agency (NSA). He was prosecuted under the Espionage Act and faced thirty-five years in prison. His "crime" was suggesting to a reporter that the NSA should not spend hundreds of millions of dollars on a private-sector digital-data-monitoring program. He thought that an internally developed project would cost less and be more effective. In the end, the government's case against him collapsed, and he pled guilty to one misdemeanor count that carried no jail time.

"The Obama administration has been quite hypocritical about its promises about openness, transparency, and accountability," said Jesselyn Radack, director for national security and human rights at the Government Accountability Project. "Pursuing whistleblowers as spies is heavy-handed and beyond the scope of the law." The Obama administration has charged more people with leaking government secrets than all previous presidencies combined.

CRIMINALS, NOT HEROES

Others believe that it is right to use the Espionage Act to prosecute those who leak critical secrets. There is a difference between a "leaker" and a whistleblower. A leak of classified information may endanger American soldiers and intelligence officers. It can let our enemies know the methods we use to gather information. Consider the case of former CIA officer Jeffrey Sterling. He was charged with giving classified information to a *New York Times* reporter about U.S. attempts to sabotage the Iranian nuclear program. The reporter later published this information in a book. We can assume that the government of Iran was very interested in reading that work. It appears that Sterling sought revenge for the CIA's refusal to let him publish his memoirs or to settle his racial discrimination suit against the agency. Some call former CIA officer John Kiriakou a hero for exposing the agency's use of the waterboarding interrogation technique, widely considered to be a form of torture. Kiriakou also revealed the name of at least one other CIA agent, however. Such leaks can endanger lives, and thus the leakers deserve prosecution.

Bureaucrats as Politicians and Policymakers

Enabling Legislation
A statute enacted by Congress that authorizes the creation of an administrative agency and specifies the name, purpose, composition, functions, and powers of the agency being created.

Because Congress is unable to oversee the day-to-day administration of its programs, it must delegate certain powers to administrative agencies. Congress delegates power to agencies through **enabling legislation.** For example, the Federal Trade Commission was created by the Federal Trade Commission Act of 1914, the Equal Employment Opportunity Commission was created by the Civil Rights Act of 1964, and the Occupational Safety and Health Administration was created by the Occupational Safety and Health Act of 1970. The enabling legislation generally specifies the name, purpose, composition, functions, and powers of the agency.

In theory, the agencies should put into effect laws passed by Congress. Laws are often drafted in such vague and general terms, however, that they provide limited guidance to agency administrators as to how they should be implemented. This means that the agencies themselves must decide how best to carry out the wishes of Congress.

The discretion given to administrative agencies is not accidental. Congress has long realized that it lacks the technical expertise and the resources to monitor the implementation of its laws. Hence, administrative agencies are created to fill the gaps. This gap-filling role requires an agency to formulate administrative rules (regulations) to put flesh on the bones of the law. But it also forces the agency itself to become an unelected policymaker.

The Rulemaking Environment

Rulemaking does not occur in a vacuum. Suppose that Congress passes a new air-pollution law. The Environmental Protection Agency (EPA) might decide to implement the new law through a technical regulation on factory emissions. This proposed regulation would be published in the *Federal Register,* a daily government publication, so that interested parties would have an opportunity to comment on it. Individuals and companies that opposed parts or all of the rule might then try to convince the EPA to revise or redraft the regulation. Some parties might try to persuade the agency to withdraw the proposed regulation altogether. In any event, the EPA would consider these comments in drafting the final version of the regulation.

■ Learning Outcome 6: **Discuss how federal agencies make rules and the role of Congress in this process.**

Waiting Periods and Court Challenges. Once the final regulation has been published in the *Federal Register,* there is a sixty-day waiting period before the rule can be enforced. During that period, businesses, individuals, and state and local governments can ask Congress to overturn the regulation. After the sixty-day period has lapsed, the regulation can still be challenged in court by a party having a direct interest in the rule, such as a company that expects to incur significant costs in complying with it. The company could argue that the rule misinterprets the applicable law or goes beyond the agency's statutory purview. An allegation by the company that the EPA made a mistake in judgment probably would not be enough to convince the court to throw out the rule. The company instead would have to demonstrate that the rule itself was "arbitrary and capricious."

Controversies. How agencies implement, administer, and enforce legislation has resulted in controversy. For example, decisions made by agencies charged with administering the Endangered Species Act have led to protests from farmers, ranchers, and others whose economic interests have been harmed.

At times, a controversy may arise when an agency *refuses* to issue regulations to implement a particular law. When the EPA refused to issue regulations designed to curb the emission of carbon dioxide and other greenhouse gases, state and local governments, as well as a number of environmental groups, sued the agency. Those bringing the suit claimed that the EPA was not fulfilling its obligation to implement the provisions of the Clean Air Act. Ultimately, the Supreme Court held that the EPA had the authority to—and should—regulate such gases.[9]

All vehicles that use internal combustion engines discharge carbon dioxide, which many researchers believe contributes to the threat of global warming. Who should regulate carbon dioxide emissions?

(Daniel Acker/Bloomberg via Getty Images)

Negotiated Rulemaking

Since the end of World War II in 1945, companies, environmentalists, and other special interest groups have challenged government regulations in court. In the 1980s, however, the sheer wastefulness of attempting to regulate through litigation became increasingly apparent. Today, a growing number of federal

9. *Massachusetts v. EPA,* 549 U.S. 497 (2007).

did you know?

Each year, federal administrative agencies produce rules that fill an average of 7,500 pages in the *Code of Federal Regulations.* The regulations now contained in this code cover 144,000 pages.

agencies encourage businesses and public-interest groups to become directly involved in drafting regulations. Agencies hope that such participation may help to prevent later courtroom battles over the regulations.

Congress formally approved such a process, which is called *negotiated rulemaking,* in the Negotiated Rulemaking Act of 1990. The act authorizes agencies to allow those who will be affected by a new rule to participate in the rule-drafting process. If an agency chooses to engage in negotiated rulemaking, it must publish in the *Federal Register* the subject and scope of the rule to be developed, the names of parties that will be affected significantly by the rule, and other information. Representatives of the affected groups and other interested parties then may apply to be members of the negotiating committee. The agency is represented on the committee, but a neutral third party (not the agency) presides over the proceedings. Once the committee members have reached agreement on the terms of the proposed rule, a notice is published in the *Federal Register,* followed by a period for comments by any person or organization interested in the proposed rule. Negotiated rulemaking often is conducted under the condition that the participants promise not to challenge in court the outcome of any agreement to which they were a party.

Bureaucrats as Policymakers

Theories of public administration once assumed that bureaucrats do not make policy decisions but only implement the laws and policies promulgated by the president and legislative bodies. A more realistic view is that the agencies and departments of government play important roles in policymaking. As we have seen, many government rules, regulations, and programs are in fact initiated by the bureaucracy, based on its expertise and scientific studies. How a law passed by Congress eventually is translated into action—from the forms to be filled out to decisions about who gets the benefits—usually is determined within each agency or department. Even the evaluation of whether a policy has achieved its purpose usually is based on studies that are commissioned and interpreted by the agency administering the program.

Iron Triangle
The three-way alliance among legislators, bureaucrats, and interest groups to make or preserve policies that benefit their respective interests.

The bureaucracy's policymaking role has often been depicted as an *iron triangle.* Recently, many political scientists have come to see the concept of an *issue network* as a more accurate description of the policymaking process.

Iron Triangles. In the past, scholars often described the bureaucracy's role in the policymaking process by using the concept of an **iron triangle**—a three-way alliance among legislators in Congress, bureaucrats, and interest groups. Consider as an example the development of agricultural policy. Congress, as one component of the triangle, includes two major committees concerned with agricultural policy, the House Committee on Agriculture and the Senate Committee on Agriculture, Nutrition, and Forestry. The Department of Agriculture, the second component of the triangle, has almost 100,000 employees, plus thousands of contractors and consultants. Agricultural interest groups, the third component of the triangle, include many large and powerful associations, such as the American Farm Bureau Federation, the National Cattlemen's Beef Association, and the Corn Growers Association. These three components of the iron triangle work together, formally or informally, to create policy.

These farmers raise beef cattle on an Iowa farm. To which part of the iron triangle in agriculture do they belong?

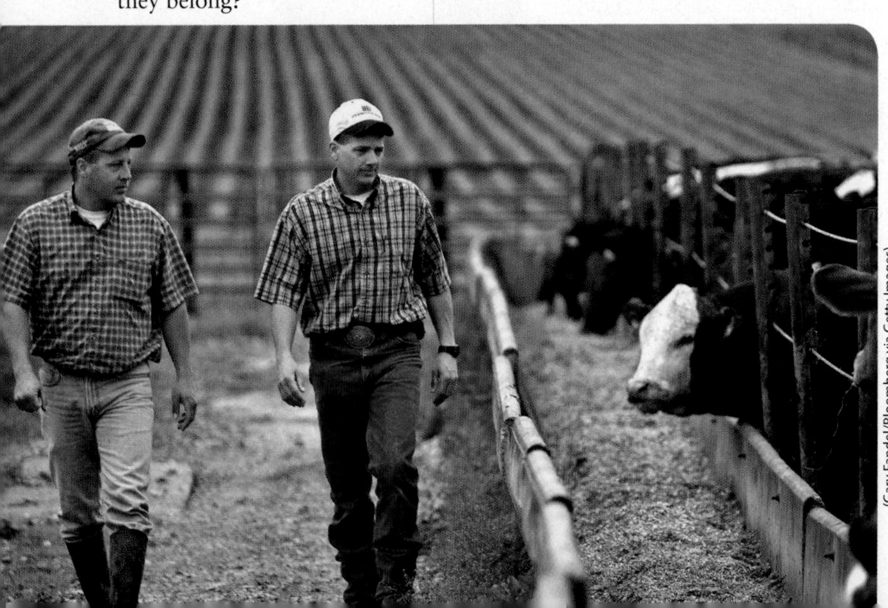

(Gary Fandel/Bloomberg via Getty Images)

For example, the various agricultural interest groups lobby Congress to develop policies that benefit their groups' economic welfare. Members of Congress cannot afford to ignore the wishes of interest groups because those groups are potential sources of voter support and campaign contributions. The legislators in Congress also work closely with the Department of Agriculture, which, in implementing a policy, can develop rules that benefit—or at least do not hurt—certain industries or groups. The Department of Agriculture, in turn, supports policies that enhance the department's budget and powers. In this way, according to theory, agricultural policy is created that benefits all three components of the iron triangle.

Issue Networks. With the growth in the complexity of government, policymaking also has become more complicated. The bureaucracy is larger, Congress has more committees and subcommittees, and interest groups are more powerful than ever. Although iron triangles still exist, often they are inadequate as descriptions of how policy is made today. Frequently, different interest groups concerned about a certain area of policy have conflicting demands, making agency decisions difficult. Additionally, during periods of divided government, departments are pressured by the president to take one approach and by Congress to take another.

Many scholars now use the term *issue network* to describe the policymaking process. An **issue network** consists of individuals or organizations that support a particular policy position on the environment, taxation, consumer safety, or some other issue. Typically, an issue network includes legislators and/or their staff members, interest group leaders, bureaucrats, scholars and other experts, and representatives from the media. Members of a particular issue network work together to influence the president, members of Congress, administrative agencies, and the courts to affect public policy on a specific issue. Each policy issue may involve conflicting positions taken by two or more issue networks.

Issue Network
A group of individuals or organizations—which may consist of legislators and legislative staff members, interest group leaders, bureaucrats, scholars and other experts, and media representatives—that supports a particular policy position on a given issue.

Congressional Control of the Bureaucracy

Many political pundits doubt whether Congress can meaningfully control the federal bureaucracy. These commentators forget that Congress specifies in an agency's "enabling legislation" the powers of the agency and the parameters within which it can operate. Additionally, Congress has the power of the purse and theoretically could refuse to authorize or appropriate funds for a particular agency (see the discussion of the budgeting process in Chapter 10). Whether Congress would actually take such a drastic measure would depend on the circumstances. It is clear, however, that Congress does have the legal authority to decide whether or not to fund administrative agencies.

Congress can also exercise oversight over agencies. Congressional committees conduct investigations and hold hearings to oversee an agency's actions, reviewing them to ensure compliance with congressional intentions. The agency's officers and employees can be ordered to testify before a committee about the details of various actions. Through the questions and comments of members of the House or the Senate during the hearings, Congress indicates its positions on specific programs and issues.

Congress can ask the Government Accountability Office (GAO) to investigate particular agency actions as well. The Congressional Budget Office (CBO) also conducts oversight studies. The results of a GAO or CBO study may encourage Congress to hold further hearings or make changes in a law. Even if the law is not changed explicitly by Congress, however, the views expressed in any investigations and hearings are taken seriously by agency officials, who often act on those views.

Why Should You Care about... THE BUREAUCRACY?

Why should you, as an individual, care about the bureaucracy? You might consider that the federal government collects billions of pieces of information on tens of millions of Americans each year. These data are stored in files and sometimes are exchanged among agencies. You are probably the subject of several federal records (for example, in the Social Security Administration, the Internal Revenue Service, and, if you are a male, the Selective Service).

(AP Photo/L.G. Patterson)

These students are accessing their personal records to see if they are accurate.

THE BUREAUCRACY AND YOUR LIFE

Verifying the information that the government has on you can be important. On several occasions, the records of two people with similar names have become confused. Sometimes innocent persons have had the criminal records of other persons erroneously inserted in their files. Such disasters are not always caused by bureaucratic error. One of the most common crimes in today's world is "identity theft," in which one person makes use of another person's personal identifiers (such as a Social Security number) to commit fraud. In some instances, identity thieves have been arrested and even jailed under someone else's name.

HOW YOU CAN MAKE A DIFFERENCE

The 1966 Freedom of Information Act (FOIA) requires that the federal government release, at your request, any identifiable information it has about you or about any other subject. Ten categories of material are exempted, however (classified material, confidential material on trade secrets, internal personnel rules, personal medical files, and the like). To request material, write directly to the Freedom of Information Act officer at the agency in question (say, the Department of Education). You must have a relatively specific idea about the document or information you want to obtain.

A second law, the Privacy Act of 1974, gives you access specifically to information the government may have collected about you. This law allows you to review records on file with federal agencies and to check those records for possible inaccuracies.

If you want to look at any records or find out if an agency has a record on you, write to the agency head or Privacy Act officer, and address your letter to the specific agency. State that "under the provisions of the Privacy Act of 1974, 5 U.S.C. 522a, I hereby request a copy of (or access to) ______." Then describe the record that you wish to investigate.

The General Services Administration (GSA) has published a citizen's guide, *Your Right to Federal Records,* that explains both the FOIA and the Privacy Act, and how to go about using them. You can locate this manual by entering its name into your favorite search engine.

Questions for Discussion and Analysis

1. Review the *Which Side Are You On?* feature on page 408. Under what circumstances is it inappropriate for whistle-blowers to take their concerns to the press, even when they believe the government is doing something wrong?
2. Consider the paradox described at the beginning of this chapter: the public believes strongly in "small government" but endorses almost all the activities that government actually performs. Why do you think Americans hold such contradictory beliefs?
3. If Congress tried to make civil servants easier to fire, what political forces might stand in the way?
4. The U.S. attorney general, head of the Justice Department, is appointed by the president and is frequently the president's close political ally. Should the attorney general and other U.S. attorneys be appointed on a partisan basis? Why or why not?

Key Terms

acquisitive model 388
bureaucracy 387
cabinet department 392
capture 396
Civil Service Commission 402
enabling legislation 408
government corporation 398
Government in the Sunshine Act 403
independent executive agency 395
independent regulatory agency 395
iron triangle 410
issue network 411
line organization 392
merit system 402
monopolistic model 388
Pendleton Act (Civil Service Reform Act) 402
preferred stock 399
privatization 405
spoils system 402
sunset legislation 404
Weberian model 387
whistleblower 406

Chapter Summary

1. Bureaucracies are hierarchical organizations characterized by a division of labor and extensive procedural rules. In addition to governments, major corporations and universities have bureaucratic organizations.
2. Several theories have been offered to describe bureaucracies. The Weberian model posits that bureaucracies are rational, hierarchical organizations in which decisions are based on logical reasoning. The acquisitive model views top-level bureaucrats as pressing for ever-larger budgets and staffs to augment their power. The monopolistic model focuses on the environment in which most government bureaucracies operate, stating that bureaucracies are inefficient and excessively costly to operate because they have no competitors.
3. Since the founding of the United States, the federal bureaucracy has grown from 50 to about 2.9 million employees (including the U.S. Postal Service, but excluding the military). Federal, state, and local employees together make up more than 16 percent of the nation's civilian labor force. The federal bureaucracy consists of fifteen cabinet departments, as well as a large number of independent executive agencies, independent regulatory agencies, and government corporations. These entities enjoy varying degrees of autonomy, visibility, and political support.
4. A federal bureaucracy of career civil servants was formed during Thomas Jefferson's presidency. Andrew Jackson implemented a spoils system through which he appointed his own political supporters. A civil service based on professionalism and merit was the goal of the Civil Service Reform Act of 1883. Concerns that the civil service be freed from the pressures of politics prompted the passage of the Hatch Act in 1939. Significant changes in the administration of the civil service were made by the Civil Service Reform Act of 1978.
5. There have been many attempts to make the federal bureaucracy more open, efficient, and responsive to the needs of U.S. citizens. The most important reforms have included sunshine and sunset laws, privatization, strategies to provide incentives for increased efficiency and productivity, and protection for whistleblowers.
6. Congress delegates much of its authority to federal agencies when it creates new laws. The bureaucrats who run these agencies may become important policymakers because Congress has neither the time nor the technical expertise to oversee the administration of its laws. In the agency rulemaking process, a proposed regulation is published. A comment period follows, during which interested parties may offer suggestions for changes. Because companies and other organizations have challenged many regulations in

court, federal agencies now are authorized to allow parties that will be affected by new regulations to participate in the rule-drafting process.

7. Congress exerts ultimate control over all federal agencies because it controls the federal government's purse strings. It also establishes the general guidelines by which regulatory agencies must abide. The appropriations process provides a way to send messages of approval or disapproval to particular agencies, as do congressional hearings and investigations of agency actions.

Quiz Multiple Choice

1. Bureaucracies exist in the private and in the public sectors. The main difference is that:
   a. **Public bureaucracies are organized to make a profit.**
   b. **Public bureaucracies do not have a single leader.**
   c. **Public bureaucracies determine their own spending limits.**
2. Local, state, and federal government employment averages about:
   a. **35 percent of total employment.**
   b. **5 percent of total employment.**
   c. **16 percent of total employment.**
3. The executive branch of our federal government has four major types of structures. One of the following is not included:
   a. **Cabinet departments.**
   b. **Independent regulatory agencies.**
   c. **Government employees' unions.**
4. In terms of federal dollars spent, the most important programs are:
   a. **Social programs including Social Security and Medicare.**
   b. **The military and subsidies for corporations.**
   c. **Foreign aid.**
5. The heads of independent executive agencies report to:
   a. **Congress.**
   b. **The president.**
   c. **The judiciary.**
6. Federal regulatory agencies are administered independently of all three branches of government. Nonetheless, the heads of regulatory agencies and members of agency boards and commissions are appointed by:
   a. **The Speaker of the House.**
   b. **The president with the consent of the Senate.**
   c. **The Supreme Court.**
7. The first significant legislation aimed at making the federal civil service nonpartisan and independent was:
   a. **The Civil Service Act of 1978.**
   b. **The Hatch Act.**
   c. **The Pendleton Act of 1883.**
8. An issue network consists of individuals or organizations that support a particular policy position. A typical issue network includes:
   a. **Congress, the president's cabinet, and the Supreme Court.**
   b. **Federal judges, congressional staff, and the heads of certain private corporations.**
   c. **Legislators (or their staff), interest group leaders, bureaucrats, scholars, and the media.**

ANSWERS: 1. b, 2. c, 3. c, 4. a, 5. b, 6. b, 7. c, 8. c.

Quiz Fill-Ins

9. Congress can attempt to control the bureaucracy by holding congressional committee ____________. Also, Congress can ask the ____________ ____________ ____________ to investigate particular agency actions.
10. There are many models of bureaucratic behavior. One argues that top-level bureaucrats always want to expand their bureaucracies. This is called the ____________ model.
11. When a federal agency's function is to make and implement rules and regulations to protect the public interest, it is called an ____________ ____________ ____________.
12. Government corporations have boards of directors and managers, but typically they do not have ____________.
13. The listing of politically appointed federal government positions is found in the *Policy and Supporting Positions* book. This book is usually called the ____________ ____________.

14. In the early days of this country, when one party won the presidency, government employees were often fired and replaced with those who supported the incoming president's party. This was called the ____________ ____________.

15. Because Congress cannot oversee the daily administration of its many programs, it delegates power to agencies through ____________ ____________.

16. All proposed federal regulation can be found in a daily government publication called the ____________ ____________.

ANSWERS: 9. hearings, Government Accountability Office, 10. acquisitive, 11. independent regulatory agency, 12. shareholders, 13. *Plum Book*, 14. spoils system, 15. enabling legislation, 16. *Federal Register*.

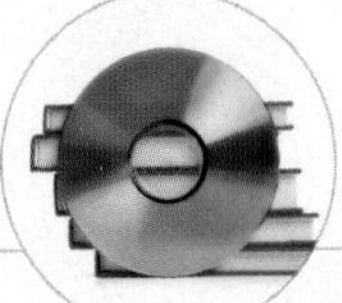
(© Aleksandar Jovicic/iStockphoto)

Selected Print & Media Resources

SUGGESTED READINGS

Aab, Stacy Parker. *Government Girl: Young and Female in the White House.* New York: Ecco, 2010. In this delightfully written coming-of-age tale, Aab begins as an intern and graduates to becoming a staffer in the Clinton White House. The reader learns what it is like to work in a pressure-cooker environment populated by type A personalities.

Conn, Steven. *To Promote the General Welfare: The Case for Big Government.* New York: Oxford University Press, 2012. This collection of essays shows the many ways in which government programs have improved the quality of life in America. Conn is a history professor at Ohio State.

Simmons, Randy T. *Beyond Politics: The Roots of Government Failure.* Oakland, Calif.: Independent Institute, 2011. Simmons believes that citizens often ask their government to do too much, with negative results. An economics professor at Utah State, he is an advocate of the public choice theory of politics. This edition is a completely revised and up-to-date version of a classic.

Yglesias, Matthew. *The Rent Is Too Damn High: What to Do about It and Why It Matters More Than You Think.* New York: Simon & Schuster Digital Sales, 2012. This e-book contends that some of the most damaging examples of bureaucratic over-regulation take place at the local level, where zoning restrictions drive up the cost of housing. Yglesias is a blogger currently writing on the Slate Web site.

MEDIA RESOURCES

When the Levees Broke: A Requiem in Four Acts—A strong treatment of Hurricane Katrina's impact on New Orleans by renowned African American director Spike Lee. We learn about the appalling performance of authorities at every level and the suffering that could have been avoided. Lee's anger at what he sees adds spice to this 2006 production.

Yes, Minister—A new member of the British cabinet bumps up against the machinations of a top civil servant in a comedy of manners. This popular 1980 BBC comedy is available on DVD.

(© PashaIgnatov/iStockphoto)

E-mocracy THE BUREAUCRACY AND THE INTERNET

All federal government agencies (and nearly all state agencies) have Web pages. Citizens can access these Web sites to find information and forms that, in the past, could normally be obtained only by going to a regional or local branch of the agency. For example, if you or a member of your family wants to learn about Social Security benefits available on retirement, you can simply access the Social Security Administration's Web site to find that information. A number of federal government agencies have also been active in discovering and prosecuting fraud perpetrated on citizens through the Internet.

LOGGING ON

1. Numerous links to federal agencies and information on the federal government can be found at the U.S. government's official Web site. Locate it by entering "usagov" into a search engine.
2. You may want to examine two publications available from the federal government to learn more about the federal bureaucracy. The first is the *Federal Register,* which is the official publication for executive-branch documents. You can find it by searching on its name. The second is the *United States Government Manual,* which describes the origins, purposes, and administrators of every federal department and agency. Type "gov manual" into a search engine.
3. The "Plum Book," which lists the bureaucratic positions that can be filled by presidential appointment, is online. Search on "plumbook."
4. To find telephone numbers for government agencies and personnel, enter "govt agencies."

APPELLANTS

13 The Courts

The six learning outcomes below are designed to help improve your understanding of this chapter. After reading this chapter, you should be able to:

- Learning Outcome 1: **Explain the main sources of American law, including constitutions, statutes and regulations, and the common law tradition.**
- Learning Outcome 2: **Describe the structure of the federal court system and such basic judicial requirements as jurisdiction and standing to sue.**
- Learning Outcome 3: **Discuss the procedures used by the United States Supreme Court and the various types of opinions it hands down.**
- Learning Outcome 4: **Evaluate the manner in which federal judges are selected.**
- Learning Outcome 5: **Consider the ways in which the Supreme Court makes policy, giving examples from the Rehnquist and Roberts courts.**
- Learning Outcome 6: **Explain the forces that limit the activism of the courts in making policy.**

These New York judges are listening to oral arguments. The attorney in front of them represents a client who is appealing a trial court's decision. (AP Photo/Hans Pennink)

(AP Photo/Dana Verkouteren)

BECAUSE THE UNITED STATES Supreme Court does not allow television cameras, no one can watch the nine justices depicted in this drawing. Should we be able to see "the real thing"?

What if...

ARGUMENTS BEFORE THE SUPREME COURT WERE TELEVISED?

BACKGROUND

Since 1955, the United States Supreme Court has allowed audio recordings of oral arguments before the Court. Also, during every session of the Supreme Court, a court reporter transcribes every word that is spoken, even with indications when there is laughter. You can find written transcripts and audio recordings of each oral argument by entering "supreme oral argue" into an online search engine. On the page "Oral Arguments—Supreme Court of the United States," scroll down until you see "Argument Transcripts" and "Argument Audio." Today, many states have gone one step further—they allow appellate court sessions to be televised. The federal appellate courts and the Supreme Court have resisted televising their proceedings, however.

WHAT IF ARGUMENTS BEFORE THE SUPREME COURT WERE TELEVISED?

Presumably, coverage of Supreme Court proceedings would be undertaken in the same way that sessions in the Senate and the House of Representatives are televised by C-SPAN. The C-SPAN coverage includes no commentaries about the proceedings in the chambers of Congress. The television coverage is straightforward, word for word, and often quite boring.

In the Supreme Court, similar television coverage would consist of one or two cameras and their operators discreetly positioned in the courtroom where the nine justices hear oral arguments and question the attorneys. Another third C-SPAN channel might have to be created to televise Supreme Court proceedings. A low-cost alternative would be Internet video streaming. Available anywhere in the world, Internet video streaming would thereby allow the rest of the world to better understand the American judicial system.

The Supreme Court could follow the states, which have already developed a wide variety of rules governing television coverage of court proceedings.[a] Most states' rules allow the presiding judge to limit or prohibit coverage. Most states also allow the parties to object to television coverage, and some require the parties' consent.

If Supreme Court proceedings were televised, we could expect a media "mini-industry" to follow, particularly on the Internet. There might be new Web sites with portions of Supreme Court proceedings shown in video along with commentary by legal and political experts.

GRANDSTANDING—A POSSIBILITY?

Certain sitting judges and others have argued against televising Supreme Court sessions because of the possibility of "grandstanding." In other words, they are worried that justices might ask questions and make comments during the proceedings in the hopes that such comments would become sound bites on the evening news. Justice Anthony M. Kennedy has said that televising proceedings would "change our collegial dynamic." Grandstanding by lawyers presenting oral arguments is also a possible danger.

In contrast, Judge Diarmuid O'Scannlain of the U.S. Court of Appeals for the Ninth Circuit believes that the concerns about grandstanding and politicking in the courtroom are "overstated." He argues that televising appellate court proceedings depoliticizes them and improves the public's perception of the legal process.

FOR CRITICAL ANALYSIS

1. *How wide an audience do you believe the television proceedings of the Supreme Court would have?*
2. *Do you think that televised proceedings of the Supreme Court would significantly increase public awareness of Supreme Court decisions? Why or why not?*

a. See the information provided by the Radio Television Digital News Association by searching on "state court camera."

As Alexis de Tocqueville, a French commentator on American society in the 1800s, noted, "scarcely any political question arises in the United States that is not resolved, sooner or later, into a judicial question."[1] Our judiciary forms part of our political process. The instant that judges interpret the law, they become actors in the political arena—policymakers working within a political institution.

The most important political force within our judiciary is the United States Supreme Court. The justices of the Supreme Court are not elected but rather are appointed by the president and confirmed by the Senate. The same is true for all other federal court judges. Because Supreme Court justices are so important in our governmental system, it has been suggested that arguments before the Court should be televised, as this chapter's opening *What If . . .* feature discussed.

How do courts make policy? Why do the federal courts play such an important role in American government? The answers to these questions lie, in part, in our colonial heritage. Most of American law is based on the English system, particularly the English *common law tradition.* In that tradition, the decisions made by judges constitute an important source of law. We open this chapter with an examination of this tradition and of the various other sources of American law. We then look at the federal court system—how it is organized, how its judges are selected, how these judges affect policy, and how they are restrained by our system of checks and balances.

Social Media IN POLITICS

Unlike the other branches of government, the courts tend to view social media as a serious annoyance. Judges do not want jurors to discuss or research their cases, but Twitter, Facebook, and the Internet in general make it hard to enforce these rules. In San Francisco, a jury pool of six hundred people was dismissed because *all* of them had researched a high-profile case.

Sources of American Law

The body of American law includes the federal and state constitutions, statutes passed by legislative bodies, administrative law, and case law—the legal principles expressed in court decisions. Case law is based in part on the common law tradition, which dates to the earliest English settlements in North America.

■ Learning Outcome 1: **Explain the main sources of American law, including constitutions, statutes and regulations, and the common law tradition.**

The Common Law Tradition

In 1066, the Normans conquered England, and William the Conqueror and his successors began the process of unifying the country under their rule. One of the ways in which they did this was to establish king's courts. Before the conquest, disputes had been settled according to local custom. The king's courts sought to establish a common, or uniform, set of rules for the whole country. As the number of courts and cases increased, portions of the most important decisions of each year were gathered together and recorded in *Year Books.* Judges who were settling disputes similar to ones that had been decided before used the *Year Books* as the basis for their decisions. If a case was unique, judges had to create new rules, but they based their decisions on the general principles suggested by earlier cases. The body of judge-made law that developed under this system is still used today and is known as the **common law.**

The practice of deciding new cases with reference to former decisions—that is, according to **precedent**—became a cornerstone of the English and American judicial systems and is embodied in the doctrine of ***stare decisis*** (pronounced *ster*-ay dih-*si*-ses), a Latin phrase that means "to stand on decided cases." The doctrine of *stare decisis* obligates judges to follow the precedents set previously by their own courts or by higher courts that have authority over them.

For example, a lower state court in California would be obligated to follow a precedent set by the California Supreme Court. That lower court, however, would not be obligated to follow a precedent set by the supreme court of another state, because each state court system is independent. Of course, when the United States Supreme Court decides

Common Law
Judge-made law that originated in England from decisions shaped according to prevailing custom. Decisions were applied to similar situations and gradually became common to the nation.

Precedent
A court rule bearing on subsequent legal decisions in similar cases. Judges rely on precedents in deciding cases.

Stare Decisis
To stand on decided cases; the judicial policy of following precedents established by past decisions.

1. Alexis de Tocqueville, *Democracy in America* (New York: Harper & Row, 1966), p. 248.

an issue, all of the nation's other courts are obligated to abide by the Court's decision—because the Supreme Court is the highest court in the land.

Constitutions

The constitutions of the federal government and the states set forth the general organization, powers, and limits of government. The U.S. Constitution is the supreme law of the land. A law in violation of the Constitution, no matter what its source, may be declared unconstitutional and thereafter cannot be enforced. Similarly, the state constitutions are supreme within their respective borders (unless they conflict with the U.S. Constitution or federal laws and treaties made in accordance with it). The Constitution thus defines the political playing field on which state and federal powers are reconciled.

Statutes and Administrative Regulations

Although the English common law provides the basis for both our civil and our criminal legal systems, statutes (laws enacted by legislatures) have become increasingly important in defining the rights and obligations of individuals. Federal statutes may relate to any subject that is a concern of the federal government and may apply to areas ranging from hazardous waste to federal taxation. State statutes include criminal codes, commercial laws, and laws covering a variety of other matters. Cities, counties, and other local political bodies also pass statutes, which are called *ordinances*. These ordinances may deal with such issues as real estate zoning proposals and public safety.

Rules and regulations issued by administrative agencies are another source of law. Today, much of the work of the courts consists of interpreting these laws and regulations and applying them to the specific circumstances of the cases that come before the courts.

Case Law
Judicial interpretations of common law principles and doctrines, as well as interpretations of constitutional law, statutory law, and administrative law.

Case Law

Because we have a common law tradition, in which the doctrine of *stare decisis* plays an important role, the decisions rendered by the courts also form an important body of law, collectively referred to as **case law.** Case law includes judicial interpretations of common law principles and doctrines, as well as interpretations of constitutional provisions, statutes, and administrative agency regulations. As you learned in previous chapters, it is up to the courts—and ultimately, if necessary, the Supreme Court—to decide what a constitutional provision or a statutory phrase means. In doing so, the courts, in effect, establish law.

Courts in many of the nations formerly governed or settled by Britain—Australia, Canada, Ireland, the United States, and others—exhibit some broad similarities. All make use of the common law, as well as statutes and administrative regulations. All share the basic judicial requirements that you will learn about shortly. In some lands formerly ruled by Britain, such as India, Nigeria, and Pakistan, the common law is supplemented by local traditional law.

Nations that do not share the common law tradition typically rely on a statutory code alone, in what is called the civil law system. Judges under the civil law system are not bound by precedent in the way that judges are under the common law system. Should American judges be banned from considering "foreign" laws? We discuss one such controversy in the *Beyond Our Borders* feature on the facing page.

The plaintiffs standing on the steps of the Supreme Court represented a large class of female employees who alleged that Walmart had discriminated against them. What might motivate them to pursue their legal claim?

(Reuters/Larry Downing)

Beyond Our Borders
AMERICAN COURTS AND FOREIGN LAW

Nations are sovereign entities. As such, they determine their own national laws and how to interpret and to enforce them. The United States does so as well. Indeed, many Americans argue that foreign or international laws should have no applicability in the United States. One manifestation of this belief is the movement to prohibit the use of *sharia*, the moral code of Islam, in American courts. Sharia is a guide to Muslims in their personal and professional dealings. Many Americans have heard of sharia only in the context of limiting women's rights or handing down harsh corporal punishments in Saudi Arabia and in other Muslim nations.

(© kyoshino / iStockphoto) (© mattjeacock / iStockphoto)

SOME STATES ATTEMPT TO BAN THE USE OF FOREIGN LAWS

In recent years, a number of conservatives have denounced sharia. For example, Newt Gingrich, former Speaker of the House and a Republican presidential candidate, declared, "We should have a federal law that says sharia law cannot be recognized by any court in the United States." Several states have responded with legislation.

Louisiana's legislation states that foreign law may not be applied if it violates a state or national constitutional protection. Sharia is not mentioned, although discussion in the state legislature and in the press dealt with little else. The Louisiana measure has no practical effect because it restates a long-standing principle of American law. In contrast, an Oklahoma ballot measure, passed in 2010, forbids courts from considering or using either international law or sharia law under any circumstances whatsoever. In 2012, a federal appeals court blocked the Oklahoma measure on First Amendment grounds.

MEDIATION IS REALLY THE ISSUE

In reality, sharia law has been used in the United States only in mediation and arbitration procedures within the Muslim community. One example is the use of sharia principles when dividing property in a divorce settlement. American courts have long encouraged the use of mediation and arbitration services, and many contracts specify that disputes under the contract will be settled by arbitration, rather than a state or federal court. Most such services are secular, but some are based on Orthodox Jewish or evangelical Christian principles.

Decisions by an arbitrator or mediator can be enforced by a court of law, but two conditions apply. First, both parties must have agreed to the arbitration in advance. Second, the courts will review the decision to ensure that arbitrators were neutral, and that the decision is not grossly unfair and does not undermine public policy. Whether provided by a secular service, a Jewish rabbi, or a sharia expert, all mediation and arbitration must conform to American law.

FOR CRITICAL ANALYSIS

The U.S. Constitution does not privilege any religion over another. Given that, is sharia really "foreign" if two Muslims who are American citizens use it to settle a dispute? Why or why not?

The Federal Court System

■ Learning Outcome 2: **Describe the structure of the federal court system and such basic judicial requirements as jurisdiction and standing to sue.**

The United States has a dual court system, with state courts and federal courts. Each of the fifty states, as well as the District of Columbia, has its own independent system of courts. This means that there are fifty-two court systems in total. Here we focus on the federal courts.

Basic Judicial Requirements

Certain requirements must be met before a case can be brought before a court in any court system, state or federal. Two important requirements are *jurisdiction* and *standing to sue*.

Jurisdiction. A state court can exercise **jurisdiction** (the authority of the court to hear and decide a case) over the residents of a particular geographic area, such as a county or district. A state's highest court, or supreme court, has jurisdictional authority over all residents within the state.

Jurisdiction
The authority of a court to decide certain cases. Not all courts have the authority to decide all cases. Where a case arises and what its subject matter is are two jurisdictional issues.

Because the Constitution established a federal government with limited powers, federal jurisdiction is also limited. Article III, Section 1, of the U.S. Constitution limits the jurisdiction of the federal courts to cases that involve either a federal question or diversity of citizenship. A **federal question** arises when a case is based, at least in part, on the U.S. Constitution, a treaty, or a federal law. A person who claims that her or his rights under the Constitution, such as the right to free speech, have been violated could bring a case in a federal court. **Diversity of citizenship** exists when the parties to a lawsuit are from different states or (more rarely) when the suit involves a U.S. citizen and a government or citizen of a foreign country. The amount in controversy must be at least $75,000 before a federal court can take jurisdiction in a diversity case, however.

Federal Question
A question that has to do with the U.S. Constitution, acts of Congress, or treaties. A federal question provides a basis for federal jurisdiction.

Diversity of Citizenship
The condition that exists when the parties to a lawsuit are citizens of different states or when the parties are citizens of a U.S. state and citizens or the government of a foreign country. Diversity of citizenship can provide a basis for federal jurisdiction.

Given the significant limits on federal jurisdiction, most lawsuits and criminal cases are heard in state, rather than federal, courts. A defendant or a party to a dispute handled by a state court may file an appeal with a state appeals court, or even the state's supreme court. Appeals cannot be taken to a federal court, however, unless there is a federal question at stake. A case could be brought in a federal court on the ground that a state court violated a person's constitutional rights. It is not possible to appeal to a federal court if an individual believes, for example, that the trial court has improperly applied state law to the case in question.

Standing to Sue. Another basic judicial requirement is standing to sue, or a sufficient "stake" in a matter to justify bringing suit. The party bringing a lawsuit must have suffered a harm, or have been threatened by a harm, as a result of the action that led to the dispute in question. Standing to sue also requires that the controversy at issue be a justiciable controversy. A **justiciable controversy** is a controversy that is real and substantial, as opposed to hypothetical or academic. In other words, a court will not give advisory opinions on hypothetical questions.

Justiciable Controversy
A controversy that is real and substantial, as opposed to hypothetical or academic.

Parties to Lawsuits

In most lawsuits, the parties are the plaintiff (the person or organization that initiates the lawsuit) and the defendant (the person or organization against whom the lawsuit is brought). There may be a number of plaintiffs and defendants in a single lawsuit. In the past several decades, many lawsuits have been brought by interest groups (see Chapter 7). Interest groups play an important role in our judicial system, because they **litigate**—bring to trial—or assist in litigating most cases of racial or gender-based discrimination, almost all civil liberties cases, and more than one-third of the cases involving business matters. Interest groups also file ***amicus curiae*** (pronounced ah-*mee*-kous *kur*-ee-eye) **briefs,** or "friend of the court" briefs, in more than 50 percent of these kinds of cases.

Sometimes, interest groups or other plaintiffs will bring a **class-action suit,** in which whatever the court decides will affect all members of a class similarly situated (such as users of a particular product manufactured by the defendant in the lawsuit). The strategy of class-action lawsuits was pioneered by such groups as the National Association for the Advancement of Colored People (NAACP), the Legal Defense Fund, and the Sierra Club, whose leaders believed that the courts would offer a more sympathetic forum for their views than would Congress.

Litigate
To engage in a legal proceeding or seek relief in a court of law; to carry on a lawsuit.

***Amicus Curiae* Brief**
A brief (a document containing a legal argument supporting a desired outcome in a particular case) filed by a third party, or *amicus curiae* (Latin for "friend of the court"), who is not directly involved in the litigation but who has an interest in the outcome of the case.

Class-Action Suit
A lawsuit filed by an individual seeking damages for "all persons similarly situated."

Procedural Rules

Both the federal and the state courts have established procedural rules that shape the litigation process. These rules are designed to protect the rights and interests of the parties and to ensure that the litigation proceeds in a fair and orderly manner. The rules also serve to identify the issues that must be decided by the court—thus saving court time and costs. Court decisions may also apply to trial procedures. For example, the Supreme Court has held that the parties' attorneys cannot discriminate against prospective jurors on the basis of race or gender. Some lower courts have also held that people cannot be excluded from juries because of their sexual orientation or religion.

The parties must comply with procedural rules and with any orders given by the judge during the course of the litigation. When a party does not follow a court's order, the court can cite him or her for contempt. A party who commits *civil* contempt (failing to comply with a court's order for the benefit of another party to the proceeding) can be taken into custody, fined, or both, until that party complies with the court's order. A party who commits *criminal* contempt (obstructing the administration of justice or disrespecting the rules of the court) also can be taken into custody and fined but cannot avoid punishment by complying with a previous order.

Throughout this text, you have read about how technology is affecting all areas of government. The judiciary is no exception. Today's courts post opinions and other information online. Increasingly, lawyers are expected to file court documents electronically. There is little doubt that in the future we will see more court business conducted online.

Types of Federal Courts

As you can see in Figure 13–1 below, the federal court system is basically a three-tiered model consisting of (1) U.S. district courts and various specialized courts of limited jurisdiction (not all of the latter are shown in the figure), (2) intermediate U.S. courts of appeals, and (3) the United States Supreme Court.

U.S. District Courts. The U.S. district courts are trial courts. A **trial court** is what the name implies—a court in which trials are held and testimony is taken. The U.S. district courts are courts of **general jurisdiction,** meaning that they can hear cases involving a broad array of issues. Federal cases involving most matters typically are heard in district courts. The other courts on the lower tier of the model shown in Figure 13–1 are courts of **limited jurisdiction,** meaning that they can try cases involving only certain types of claims, such as tax claims or bankruptcy petitions.

There is at least one federal district court in every state. The number of judicial districts can vary over time owing to population changes and corresponding caseloads. Today,

Trial Court
The court in which most cases begin.

General Jurisdiction
A court's authority to hear cases without significant restriction. A court of general jurisdiction normally can hear a broad range of cases.

Limited Jurisdiction
A court's authority to hear cases with restriction to certain types of claims, such as tax claims or bankruptcy petitions.

Figure 13–1 ▸ The Federal Court System

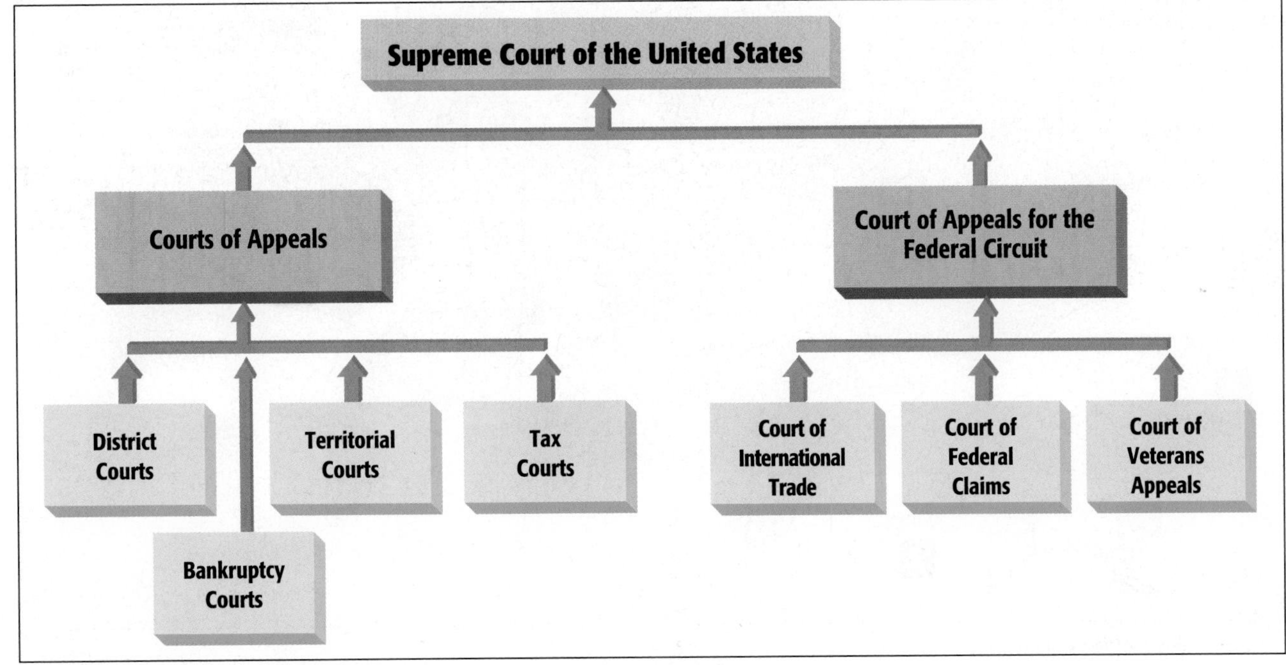

there are ninety-four federal judicial districts. A party who is dissatisfied with the decision of a district court can appeal the case to the appropriate U.S. court of appeals, or federal **appellate court.** Figure 13–2 below shows the jurisdictional boundaries of the district courts (which are state boundaries, unless otherwise indicated by dotted lines within a state) and of the U.S. courts of appeals.

Appellate Court
A court having jurisdiction to review cases and issues that were originally tried in lower courts.

Many federal administrative agencies and most executive departments also employ administrative law judges who resolve disputes arising under the rules governing their agencies. For example, the Social Security Administration might hold a hearing to determine whether a specific class of individuals is entitled to collect a particular benefit. If all internal Social Security appeals processes have been exhausted, a party may have a right to file an appeal in a federal district court. Appeals from the decisions of other agencies may be heard by the district courts, the U.S. courts of appeals, or even a specialized federal court, depending on the agency.

U.S. Courts of Appeals. There are thirteen U.S. courts of appeals—also referred to as U.S. circuit courts of appeals. Twelve of these courts, including the U.S. Court of Appeals for the District of Columbia, hear appeals from the federal district courts located within their respective judicial circuits (geographic areas over which they exercise jurisdiction). The Court of Appeals for the Thirteenth Circuit, called the Federal Circuit, has national appellate jurisdiction over certain types of cases, such as cases involving patent law and those in which the U.S. government is a defendant.

Note that when an appellate court reviews a case decided in a district court, the appellate court does not conduct another trial. Rather, a panel of three or more judges reviews the record of the case on appeal, which includes a transcript of the trial proceedings, and determines whether the trial court committed an error. Usually, appellate courts

Figure 13–2 ▶ Geographic Boundaries of Federal District Courts and U.S. Courts of Appeals

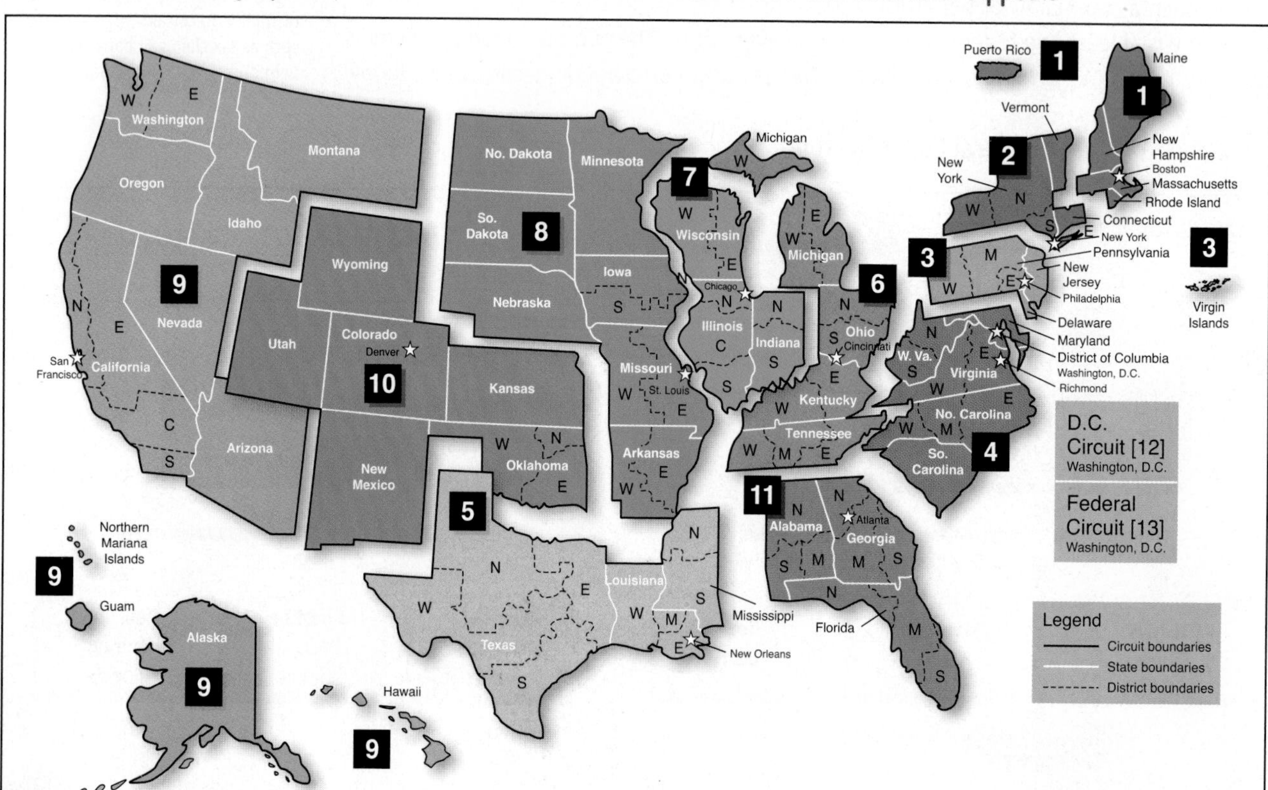

Source: Administrative Office of the United States Courts.

do not look at questions of *fact* (such as whether a party did, in fact, commit a certain action, such as burning a flag) but at questions of *law* (such as whether the act of burning a flag is a form of speech protected by the First Amendment to the Constitution). An appellate court will challenge a trial court's finding of fact only when the finding is clearly contrary to the evidence presented at trial or when there is no evidence to support the finding.

A party can petition the United States Supreme Court to review an appellate court's decision. The likelihood that the Supreme Court will grant the petition is slim, however, because the Court reviews only a small percentage of the cases decided by the appellate courts. This means that decisions made by appellate courts usually are final.

The United States Supreme Court. The highest level of the three-tiered model of the federal court system is the United States Supreme Court. When the Supreme Court came into existence in 1789, it had six justices. In the following years, more justices were added. Since 1869, there have been nine justices on the Court.

According to the language of Article III of the U.S. Constitution, there is only one national Supreme Court. All other courts in the federal system are considered "inferior." Congress is empowered to create other inferior courts as it deems necessary. The inferior courts that Congress has created include the district courts, the federal courts of appeals, and the federal courts of limited jurisdiction.

Although the Supreme Court can exercise original jurisdiction (that is, act as a trial court) in certain cases, such as those affecting foreign diplomats and those in which a state is a party, most of its work is as an appellate court. The Court hears appeals not only from the federal appellate courts but also from the highest state courts. Note, though, that the United States Supreme Court can review a state supreme court decision only if a federal question is involved. Because of its importance in the federal court system, we look more closely at the Supreme Court later in this chapter.

did you know?

The Supreme Court was not provided with a building of its own until 1935, in the 146th year of its existence.

Federal Courts and the War on Terrorism

As noted, the federal court system includes a variety of trial courts of limited jurisdiction, dealing with matters such as tax claims or international trade. The government's attempts to combat terrorism have drawn attention to certain specialized courts that meet in secret. We look next at these courts, as well as at the role of the federal courts with respect to the detainees accused of terrorism.

The FISA Court. The federal government created the first secret court in 1978. In that year, Congress passed the Foreign Intelligence Surveillance Act (FISA), which established a court to hear requests for warrants for the surveillance of suspected spies. Officials can request a warrant without having to reveal to the suspect or to the public the information used to justify the warrant. The FISA court has approved almost all of the thousands of requests for warrants that officials have submitted. There is no public access to the court's proceedings or records. Hence, when the court authorizes surveillance, suspects normally do not even know that they are under scrutiny.

In the aftermath of the terrorist attacks on September 11, 2001, the George W. Bush administration expanded the powers of the FISA court. Previously, FISA had allowed secret domestic surveillance only if the "purpose" was to combat intelligence gathering by foreign powers. Amendments to FISA enacted after 9/11

(AP Photo/Todd Goodrich)

Chief Justice John Roberts, Jr., speaks at the University of Montana in Missoula. Do you think there are some subjects that he would avoid in any of his public speeches?

changed this wording to "a significant purpose"—meaning that warrants may now be requested to obtain evidence that can be used in criminal trials.

Alien "Removal Courts." In 1996, Congress passed the Anti-Terrorism and Effective Death Penalty Act. The new law was a response to the bombing of a federal building in 1995 in Oklahoma City, which killed 168 people. Even though the perpetrators of this crime were white U.S. citizens whose motives were entirely domestic, the new law focused on noncitizens. For example, the act created an alien "removal court" to hear evidence against suspected "alien terrorists." The judges in this court rule on whether there is probable cause for deportation. If so, a public deportation proceeding is held in a U.S. district court. The prosecution does not need to follow procedures that normally apply in criminal cases. In addition, the defendant cannot see the evidence that the prosecution used to secure the hearing.

The Federal Courts and Enemy Combatants. After the 9/11 attacks, the U.S. military took custody of hundreds of suspected terrorists seized in Afghanistan and elsewhere and held them at Guantánamo Bay, Cuba. The detainees were classified as *enemy combatants,* and, according to the Bush administration, they could be held indefinitely. The administration also claimed that because the detainees were not prisoners of war, they were not protected under international laws governing the treatment of prisoners of war. The handling of the prisoners at Guantánamo has been a source of ongoing controversy. The United States Supreme Court held, first in 2004 and then in 2006, that the Bush administration's treatment of these detainees violated the U.S. Constitution.[2]

In response to the Court's 2006 decision, Congress passed the Military Commissions Act of 2006. The act eliminated federal court jurisdiction over challenges by noncitizens held as enemy combatants based on *habeas corpus,* the right of a detained person to challenge the legality of his or her detention before a judge. In June 2008, the Court ruled that the provisions restricting the federal courts' jurisdictional authority over detainees' *habeas corpus* challenges were illegal.[3] The decision gave Guantánamo detainees the right to challenge their detention in federal civil courts.

In 2009, the Obama administration abolished the category of *enemy combatant* and promised to close the Guantánamo prison. (As of January 2013, though, the prison remains open.) President Obama did not, however, move to try all of the detainees in U.S. civil courts. Under the Military Commissions Act of 2009, some of the prisoners were to be tried in a revised system of military commissions. Further, in May 2009, Obama claimed the right to detain certain accused terrorists indefinitely without trial. In May 2010, a federal appeals court ruled that the administration had the right to detain prisoners indefinitely at Bagram Air Base in Afghanistan because the prison is located on foreign soil and within a war zone.[4]

(Al Ross/The New Yorker Collection/www.cartoonbank.com)

"And don't go whining to some higher court."

2. *Hamdi v. Rumsfeld,* 542 U.S. 507 (2004); *Hamdan v. Rumsfeld,* 548 U.S. 557 (2006).
3. *Boumediene v. Bush,* 553 U.S. 723 (2008).
4. *Maqaleh v. Gates,* 605 F.3d 84 (D.C.Cir. 2010).

The Supreme Court at Work

■ Learning Outcome 3: **Discuss the procedures used by the United States Supreme Court and the various types of opinions it hands down.**

The Supreme Court begins its regular annual term on the first Monday in October and usually adjourns in late June or early July of the next year. Special sessions may be held after the regular term ends, but only a few cases are decided in this way. More commonly, cases are carried over until the next regular session.

Of the total number of cases that are decided each year in U.S. courts, those reviewed by the Supreme Court represent less than one in four thousand. Included in these, however, are decisions that profoundly affect our lives. In recent years, the United States Supreme Court has decided issues involving freedom of speech, the right to bear arms, health-care reform, campaign finance, capital punishment, the rights of criminal suspects, affirmative action programs, religious freedom, abortion, sexual harassment, pornography, states' rights, and many other matters with significant consequences for the nation.

Because the Supreme Court exercises a great deal of discretion over the types of cases it hears, it can influence the nation's policies by issuing decisions in some types of cases and refusing to hear appeals in others, thereby allowing lower court decisions to stand. Indeed, the fact that George W. Bush assumed the presidency in 2001 instead of Al Gore, his Democratic opponent, was largely due to a Supreme Court decision to review a Florida court's ruling. The Supreme Court reversed the Florida court's order to recount manually the votes in selected Florida counties—a decision that effectively handed the presidency to Bush.[5]

(David Hume Kennerly/Getty Images)

United States Supreme Court justice Clarence Thomas stands in his chambers with three of his clerks. What type of work do clerks do when they assist a Supreme Court justice?

Which Cases Reach the Supreme Court?

Many people are surprised to learn that in a typical case, there is no absolute right of appeal to the United States Supreme Court. The Court's appellate jurisdiction is almost entirely discretionary—the Court chooses which cases it will decide. The justices never explain their reasons for hearing certain cases and not others, so it is difficult to predict which case or type of case the Court might select.

Factors That Bear on the Decision. A number of factors bear on the decision to accept a case. If a legal question has been decided differently by various lower courts, it may need resolution by the highest court. A ruling may be necessary if a lower court's decision conflicts with an existing Supreme Court ruling. In general, the Court considers whether the issue could have significance beyond the parties to the dispute.

Another factor is whether the solicitor general is asking the Court to take a case. The solicitor general, a high-ranking presidential appointee within the Justice Department, represents the national government before the Supreme Court and promotes presidential policies in the federal courts. He or she decides what cases the government should ask the

5. *Bush v. Gore,* 531 U.S. 98 (2000).

Supreme Court to review and what position the government should take in cases before the Court.

Writ of *Certiorari*
An order issued by a higher court to a lower court to send up the record of a case for review.

Rule of Four
A United States Supreme Court procedure by which four justices must vote to grant a petition for review if a case is to come before the full court.

Oral Arguments
The arguments presented in person by attorneys to an appellate court. Each attorney presents to the court reasons why the court should rule in her or his client's favor.

Granting Petitions for Review. If the Court decides to grant a petition for review, it will issue a **writ of *certiorari*** (pronounced sur-shee-uh-*rah*-ree). The writ orders a lower court to send the Supreme Court a record of the case for review. The vast majority of the petitions for review are denied. A denial is not a decision on the merits of a case, nor does it indicate agreement with the lower court's opinion. (The judgment of the lower court remains in force, however.) Therefore, denial of the writ has no value as a precedent. The Court will not issue a writ unless at least four justices approve of it. This is called the **rule of four.**[6]

Court Procedures

Once the Supreme Court grants *certiorari* in a particular case, the justices do extensive research on the legal issues and facts involved in the case. (Of course, some preliminary research is necessary before deciding to grant the petition for review.) Each justice is entitled to four law clerks, who undertake much of the research and preliminary drafting necessary for the justice to form an opinion.

The Court normally does not hear any evidence, as is true with all appeals courts. The Court's consideration of a case is based on the abstracts, the record, and the briefs. The attorneys are permitted to present **oral arguments.** Unlike the practice in most courts, lawyers addressing the Supreme Court can be (and often are) questioned by the justices at any time during oral arguments. All statements and the justices' questions during oral arguments are recorded.

The justices meet to discuss and vote on cases in conferences held throughout the term. In these conferences, in addition to deciding cases already before the Court, the justices determine which new petitions for *certiorari* to grant. These conferences take place in the oak-paneled chamber and are strictly private—no stenographers, audio recorders, or video cameras are allowed.

did you know?

Before they take their seats on the bench, each justice shakes hands with the others. This practice began with Chief Justice Melville W. Fuller in the late 1800s as a way to remind justices that, although they may have differences of opinion, they share a common purpose.

Opinion
A statement by a judge or a court of the decision reached in a case. An opinion sets forth the applicable law and details the reasoning on which the ruling was based.

Affirm
To declare that a court ruling is valid and must stand.

Reverse
To annul, or make void, a court ruling on account of some error or irregularity.

Remand
To send a case back to the court that originally heard it.

Unanimous Opinion
A Court opinion or determination on which all judges agree.

Decisions and Opinions

When the Court has reached a decision, its opinion is written. The **opinion** contains the Court's ruling on the issue or issues presented, the reasons for its decision, the rules of law that apply, and other information. In many cases, the decision of the lower court is **affirmed,** resulting in the enforcement of that court's judgment or decree. If the Supreme Court believes that the lower court made the wrong decision, however, the decision will be **reversed.** Sometimes the case will be **remanded** (sent back to the court that originally heard the case) for a new trial or other proceeding. For example, a lower court might have held that a party was not entitled to bring a lawsuit under a particular law. If the Supreme Court holds to the contrary, it will remand (send back) the case to the trial court with instructions that the trial go forward.

The Court's written opinion sometimes is unsigned; this is called an opinion *per curiam* ("by the court"). Typically, the Court's opinion is signed by all the justices who agree with it. When in the majority, the chief justice decides who writes the opinion and may choose to write it personally. When the chief justice is in the minority, the senior justice on the majority side assigns the opinion.

Types of Opinions. When all justices unanimously agree on an opinion, the opinion is written for the entire Court (all the justices) and can be deemed a **unanimous opinion.**

6. The "rule of four" is modified when seven or fewer justices participate, which occurs from time to time. When that happens, as few as three justices can grant *certiorari*.

When there is not a unanimous opinion, a **majority opinion** is written, outlining the views of the majority of the justices involved in the case. Often, one or more justices who feel strongly about making or emphasizing a particular point that is not made or emphasized in the majority written opinion will write a **concurring opinion.** That means the justice writing the concurring opinion agrees (concurs) with the conclusion given in the majority written opinion but wants to make or clarify a particular point or to voice disapproval of the grounds on which the decision was made.

Finally, in other than unanimous opinions, one or more **dissenting opinions** are usually written by those justices who do not agree with the majority. The dissenting opinion is important because it often forms the basis of the arguments used years later if the Court reverses the previous decision and establishes a new precedent.

Majority Opinion
A court opinion reflecting the views of the majority of the judges.

Concurring Opinion
A separate opinion prepared by a judge who supports the decision of the majority of the court but who wants to make or clarify a particular point or to voice disapproval of the grounds on which the decision was made.

Dissenting Opinion
A separate opinion in which a judge dissents from (disagrees with) the conclusion reached by the majority of the court and expounds his or her own views about the case.

Publishing Opinions. Shortly after the opinion is written, the Supreme Court announces its decision from the bench. The clerk of the Court also releases the opinion for online publication. Ultimately, the opinion is published in the *United States Reports,* which is the official printed record of the Court's decisions.

The Court's Dwindling Caseload. Some have complained that the Court reviews too few cases each term, thus giving the lower courts insufficient guidance on important issues. Indeed, the number of signed opinions issued by the Court has dwindled notably since the 1980s. For example, in its 1982–1983 term, the Court issued signed opinions in 151 cases. By the early 2000s, this number had dropped to between 70 and 80 per term. In the term ending in June 2012, the number was 77.

■ Learning Outcome 4: **Evaluate the manner in which federal judges are selected.**

The Selection of Federal Judges

All federal judges are appointed. The Constitution, in Article II, Section 2, states that the president is to appoint the justices of the Supreme Court with the advice and consent of the Senate. Congress has established the same procedure for staffing other federal courts. This means that the Senate and the president jointly decide who shall fill every vacant judicial position, no matter what the level.

There are currently 874 federal judicial posts at all levels, although at any given time many of these positions are vacant. Once appointed to a federal judgeship, a person holds that job for life. Judges serve until they resign, retire voluntarily, or die. Federal judges who engage in blatantly illegal conduct may be removed through impeachment, although such action is rare.

In contrast to federal judges, many state judges—including the judges who sit on state supreme courts—are chosen by the voters in elections. Inevitably, judicial candidates must raise campaign funds. What arguments favor the election of judges? What problems can such a system create? We examine such questions in this chapter's *Which Side Are You On?* feature on the following page.

Judicial Appointments

Candidates for federal judgeships are suggested to the president by the Department of Justice, senators, other judges, the candidates themselves, and lawyers' associations and other interest groups. In selecting a candidate to nominate for a judgeship, the president considers not only the person's competence but also other factors, including the person's political philosophy (as will be discussed shortly), ethnicity, and gender.

The nomination process—no matter how the nominees are obtained—always works the same way. The president makes the actual nomination,

Sonia Sotomayor is the first Latina justice on the United States Supreme Court.

(Steve Petteway/Collection of the Supreme Court of the United States)

Which Side Are You On?

SHOULD STATE JUDGES BE ELECTED?

The nation's founders sought to insulate the courts from popular passions, and as a result, all of the judges and justices in the federal court system are appointed by the president and confirmed by the Senate. Federal judges and justices are appointed for life. In thirty-nine states, in contrast, some or all state judges must face election and reelection.

The question of whether state judges should be elected or whether they should be appointed has proved to be very divisive. Many in the legal community agreed with a former Oregon Supreme Court justice, Hans A. Linde, when he pointed out that "to the rest of the world, American adherence to judicial elections is as incomprehensible as our rejection of the metric system." Public opinion polls, however, regularly show strong public support for electing judges.

THE PEOPLE'S WILL SHOULD PREVAIL

Those who advocate the election of state judges see the issue as a simple matter of democracy. Judges cannot be insulated from politics. Governors who appoint judges are highly political creatures and are likely to appoint members of their own party. If politics is going to play a role, the people ought to have their say directly. In addition, researchers at the University of Chicago School of Law found that elected judges wrote more opinions than appointed judges.

We let ordinary people participate in the legal process through the jury system, and they ought to be able to choose judges as well. That way, the people can be confident that judges will respond to popular concerns, such as the fear of crime. Without elections, judges living in safe, upscale neighborhoods may fail to appreciate what it is like to fear for your safety on an everyday basis.

ELECTING JUDGES LEADS TO CORRUPTION

Former United States Supreme Court justice Sandra Day O'Connor condemned the practice of electing judges: "No other nation in the world does that because they realize you are not going to get fair and impartial judges that way." Opponents of judicial elections observe that most voters do not have enough information to make sensible choices when they vote for judicial candidates. Therefore, campaign contributions wind up deciding judicial races.

Judicial candidates raise considerable funds from the lawyers who will appear before them if they win. Additional campaign funds are raised by special interest groups that want "their" candidate elected or reelected to the state court in question. People who want to elect judges think that the candidates they vote for will, for example, be "tough on crime." Often, they are. But those who oppose judicial elections contend that elected judges will also tilt toward the wealthy groups that put them in office, and away from the interests of ordinary people.

(© kyoshino / iStockphoto) (© Dean Mitchell / iStockphoto)

submitting the name to the Senate. To reach a conclusion, the Senate Judiciary Committee (operating through subcommittees) invites testimony, both written and oral, at its various hearings. The Senate then either confirms or rejects the nomination.

Federal District Court Judgeship Nominations. Although the president officially nominates federal judges, in the past the nomination of federal district court judges actually originated with a senator or senators of the president's party from the state in which there was a vacancy (if such a senator existed). In effect, judicial appointments were a form of political patronage. President Jimmy Carter (1977–1981) ended this tradition by establishing independent commissions to oversee the initial nomination process. President Ronald Reagan (1981–1989) abolished Carter's nominating commissions and established complete presidential control of nominations.

Senatorial Courtesy
In federal district court judgeship nominations, a tradition allowing a senator to veto a judicial appointment in his or her state.

A practice used in the Senate, called **senatorial courtesy,** is a constraint on the president's freedom to appoint federal district judges. Senatorial courtesy allows a senator of the president's political party to veto a judicial appointment in her or his state. During much of American history, senators from the "opposition" party (the party to which the president does not belong) have also enjoyed the right of senatorial courtesy, although their veto power has varied over time.

In 2000, Orrin Hatch, Republican chair of the Senate Judiciary Committee, announced that the opposition party (at that point, the Democrats) would no longer be allowed to invoke senatorial courtesy. When the Democrats took over the Senate following the elections of 2006, Senator Patrick J. Leahy (D., Vt.), chair of the Judiciary Committee, let it be known that the old bipartisan system of senatorial courtesy would return. Of course, the Republicans, who were now in the minority, were unlikely to object to a nomination submitted by Republican president George W. Bush, and the old practices did not become truly effective until Democratic president Barack Obama took office.

(AP Photo/ Jennifer Pitts /The Journal Record)

In many states, judges are elected by the voters. What might be some of the problems with this system compared to one in which judges are appointed?

Federal Courts of Appeals Appointments. There are many fewer appointments to the federal courts of appeals than federal district court appointments, but they are more important. Federal appellate judges handle more important matters, and therefore presidents take a keener interest in the nomination process for such judgeships. Also, the U.S. courts of appeals have become "stepping-stones" to the Supreme Court.

Supreme Court Appointments. As we have described, the president nominates Supreme Court justices. Table 13–1 on the following page summarizes the background of all Supreme Court justices to 2013. As you can see, the most common occupational background of the justices at the time of their appointment has been private legal practice or state or federal judgeship. Those nine justices who were in federal executive posts at the time of their appointment held the high offices of secretary of State, comptroller of the Treasury, secretary of the Navy, postmaster general, secretary of the Interior, chairman of the Securities and Exchange Commission, and secretary of Labor. In the "Other" category under "Occupational Position before Appointment" in Table 13–1 are two justices who were professors of law (including William H. Taft, a former president) and one justice who was a North Carolina state employee with responsibility for organizing and revising the state's statutes.

The Special Role of the Chief Justice. The chief justice is not only the head of a group of nine justices who interpret the law. In essence, he or she is also the chief executive officer of a large bureaucracy that includes more than one thousand judges with lifetime tenure, hundreds of magistrates and bankruptcy judges with limited tenure, and a staff of about thirty thousand.

The chief justice is the chair of the Judicial Conference of the United States, a policymaking body that sets priorities for the federal judiciary. This position means that the chief justice indirectly oversees that group's $6 billion budget.

Finally, the chief justice appoints the director of the Administrative Office of the United States Courts. The chief justice and the director select judges who sit on judicial committees that examine international judicial relations, technology, and a variety of other topics.

did you know?

Jimmy Carter is the only president to serve a full term without nominating a Supreme Court justice.

Partisanship and Judicial Appointments. In most circumstances, the president appoints judges or justices who belong to the president's own political party. Presidents see their federal judiciary appointments as the one sure way to institutionalize their political views long after they have left office. By 1993, for example, Presidents Ronald Reagan and George H. W. Bush together had appointed nearly three-quarters of all federal court judges. This preponderance of Republican-appointed federal judges strengthened the

Politics AND the Federal System

PARTISANSHIP AND JUDICIAL CONFIRMATIONS

The Constitution requires that federal judges and justices be chosen with "the advice and consent" of the Senate. Nowhere does the Constitution require that the Senate cross-examine federal judicial nominees, but that is certainly what happens today. Indeed, Senate judicial hearings can sometimes seem like soap operas, particularly when a Supreme Court seat is at stake. Not surprisingly, the three-ring-circus atmosphere of these hearings began with the advent of twenty-four-hour cable television coverage via CNN and other networks.

AREN'T JUDGES SUPPOSED TO BE IMPARTIAL?

In principle, the federal judiciary should act as a counterweight to the other two branches of government, both of which are highly political. Naturally, presidents will try to nominate candidates who share the president's perspectives. Yet we expect all judges to make unbiased decisions based on neutral legal principles. If they did so, then judicial nominees could be confirmed on their qualifications, regardless of whether they were Republicans or Democrats.

The record shows, however, that Democratic presidents hardly ever nominate avowed Republicans and, likewise, Republican presidents do not nominate Democrats. Further, during nomination hearings, Republican senators have made it difficult for Democratic presidents to move their nominees through the process. Democrats have done the same with a Republican as president.

THE RESULT OF PARTISANSHIP IN JUDICIAL NOMINATIONS

When federal judicial nominees are not confirmed in a timely manner, the result is unfilled seats in the federal court system. This weakens the effectiveness of the federal judiciary. By the summer of 2012, nearly 10 percent of all judicial positions were vacant. Delays in confirming judges mean that the business of justice slows down. An old saying comes to mind: "Justice delayed is justice denied." Under President Obama, the number of "judicial emergencies" created by empty seats has risen by 70 percent. While many have blamed Senate Republicans for this state of affairs, it is also a fact that Obama has been slower to make judicial nominations than any president in recent memory.

One legal blogger, Howard Fineman, has made a radical suggestion: stop holding public Supreme Court confirmation hearings. "They make everyone involved look bad. They are worse than a waste of time, because they confuse the public about what the Supreme Court does and undermine respect for law and judges."

FOR CRITICAL ANALYSIS

Why do senators like lengthy televised nomination hearings?

(© kyoshino / iStockphoto) (© Evelyn Peyton / iStockphoto)

that case, in which the Court declared that a law passed by Congress violated the Constitution, the Court claimed such a power for the judiciary:

> *It is emphatically the province and duty of the Judicial Department to say what the law is. Those who apply the rule to a particular case must of necessity expound and interpret that rule. If two laws conflict with each other, the courts must decide on the operation of each.*

If a federal court declares that a federal or state law or policy is unconstitutional, the court's decision affects the application of the law or policy only within that court's jurisdiction. For this reason, the higher the level of the court, the greater the impact of the decision on society. Because of the Supreme Court's national jurisdiction, its decisions have the greatest impact. For example, when the Supreme Court held that an Arkansas state constitutional amendment limiting the terms of congresspersons was unconstitutional, laws establishing term limits in twenty-three other states were also invalidated.[8]

8. *U.S. Term Limits v. Thornton*, 514 U.S. 779 (1995).

Judicial Activism and Judicial Restraint

Judicial scholars like to characterize different judges and justices as being either "activist" or "restraintist."

Judicial Activism. The doctrine of **judicial activism** rests on the conviction that the federal judiciary should take an active role by using its powers to check the activities of Congress, state legislatures, and administrative agencies when those governmental bodies exceed their authority. One of the Supreme Court's most activist eras was the period from 1953 to 1969, when the Court was headed by Chief Justice Earl Warren. The Warren Court propelled the civil rights movement forward by holding, among other things, that laws permitting racial segregation violated the equal protection clause.

Judicial Restraint. In contrast, the doctrine of **judicial restraint** rests on the assumption that the courts should defer to the decisions made by the legislative and executive branches, because members of Congress and the president are elected by the people, whereas members of the federal judiciary are not. Because administrative agency personnel normally have more expertise than the courts do in the areas regulated by the agencies, the courts likewise should defer to agency rules and decisions. In other words, under the doctrine of judicial restraint, the courts should not thwart the implementation of legislative acts and agency rules unless they are clearly unconstitutional.

(AP Photo)

Earl Warren served as chief justice of the United States Supreme Court for thirteen years starting in 1953. Was he known for judicial activism or for judicial restraint?

Political Implications. In the past, judicial activism was often linked with liberalism, and judicial restraint with conservatism. In fact, though, a conservative judge can be activist, just as a liberal judge can be restraintist. In the 1950s and 1960s, the Supreme Court was activist and liberal. Some observers believe that the Rehnquist Court, with its conservative majority, became increasingly activist over time.

After the initial election of Democrat Barack Obama as president, some suggested that the Court's conservative wing became still more activist in its approach to judicial interpretation. The *Citizens United v. Federal Election Commission* decision, in which the Court struck down long-standing campaign finance laws, lends credence to this view. (You learned about this ruling on page 287 in Chapter 9.) Some observers believed that the Court was stepping back from conservative judicial activism when it upheld most of Obama's health-care reform legislation in June 2012. Others, however, note that the Court also blocked the attempt by Congress to force states to expand the Medicaid program. This step was an innovation in limiting the power of Congress.

Judicial Activism
A doctrine holding that the federal judiciary should take an active role by using its powers to check the activities of governmental bodies when those bodies exceed their authority.

Judicial Restraint
A doctrine holding that the courts should defer to the decisions made by the elected representatives of the people in the legislative and executive branches.

Strict Construction
A judicial philosophy that looks to the "letter of the law" when interpreting the Constitution or a particular statute.

Broad Construction
A judicial philosophy that looks to the context and purpose of a law when making an interpretation.

Strict versus Broad Construction

Other terms that are often used to describe a justice's philosophy are *strict construction* and *broad construction.* Justices who believe in **strict construction** look to the "letter of the law" when they attempt to interpret the Constitution or a particular statute. Those who favor **broad construction** try to determine the context and purpose of the law.

As with the doctrines of judicial restraint and judicial activism, strict construction is often associated with conservative political views, whereas broad construction is often linked with liberalism. These traditional political associations sometimes appear to be reversed, however. Consider the Eleventh Amendment to the Constitution, which rules out lawsuits in federal courts "against one of the United States by Citizens of another State, or by Citizens or Subjects of any Foreign State." Nothing is said about citizens suing

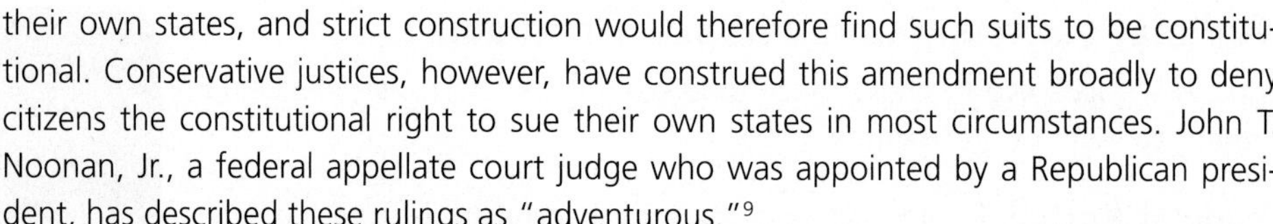

their own states, and strict construction would therefore find such suits to be constitutional. Conservative justices, however, have construed this amendment broadly to deny citizens the constitutional right to sue their own states in most circumstances. John T. Noonan, Jr., a federal appellate court judge who was appointed by a Republican president, has described these rulings as "adventurous."[9]

Broad construction is often associated with the concept of a "living constitution." Supreme Court justice Antonin Scalia, in contrast, has said that "the Constitution is not a living organism, it is a legal document. It says something and doesn't say other things." Scalia believes that jurists should stick to the plain text of the Constitution "as it was originally written and intended."

The Rehnquist Court

William H. Rehnquist, who died in 2005, became the sixteenth chief justice of the Supreme Court in 1986. He was known as a strong anchor of the Court's conservative wing. The rightward movement, which began shortly after Rehnquist became chief justice, continued as other conservative appointments to the bench were made during the Reagan and George H. W. Bush administrations.

did you know?

A proclamation by President George Washington and a congressional resolution established the first national Thanksgiving Day on November 26, 1789. The reason for the holiday was to give thanks for the new Constitution.

Interestingly, some previously conservative justices showed a tendency to "migrate" to a more liberal view of the law. Sandra Day O'Connor, the first female justice, gradually shifted to the left on a number of issues, including abortion. Generally, O'Connor and Justice Anthony Kennedy provided the "swing votes" on the Rehnquist Court.

Although the Court moved to the right during the Rehnquist era, it was closely divided in many cases. Consider the Court's rulings on states' rights. In 1995, the Court held, for the first time in sixty years, that Congress had overreached its powers under the commerce clause when it attempted to regulate the possession of guns in school zones. According to the Court, the possession of guns in school zones had nothing to do with the commerce clause.[10] Yet in a 2005 case, the Court ruled that Congress's power to regulate commerce allowed it to ban marijuana use even when a state's law permitted such use and the growing and use of the drug were strictly local in nature.[11] What these two rulings had in common was that they supported policies generally considered to be conservative—the right to possess firearms on the one hand, and a strong line against marijuana on the other.

The Roberts Court

John Roberts became chief justice in 2005, following the death of Chief Justice Rehnquist. Replacing one conservative chief justice with another did not immediately change the Court's ideological balance. The real change came in January 2006, when Samuel Alito replaced Sandra Day O'Connor. Unlike O'Connor, Alito was firmly in the conservative camp. This fact had consequences. In a 2007 case, for example, the Court upheld a 2003 federal law banning partial birth abortion, by a close (five-to-four) vote.[12] The Supreme Court's conservative drift continued in the following years. In 2008, for example, the Court established the right of individuals to own guns for private use,[13] and it upheld lethal injection as an execution method.[14]

In 2010, the Court issued two major opinions, both of which were major victories for the political right. In *Citizens United v. Federal Election Commission,*

When Elena Kagan was confirmed as a justice of the United States Supreme Court, she became only the fourth woman to hold this position. Why has it taken so long for women to win appointment as Supreme Court justices?

(AP Photo/Alex Brandon)

9. John T. Noonan, Jr., *Narrowing the Nation's Power: The Supreme Court Sides with the States* (Berkeley: University of California Press, 2002).
10. *United States v. Lopez,* 514 U.S. 549 (1995).
11. *Gonzales v. Raich,* 545 U.S. 1 (2005).
12. *Gonzales v. Carhart,* 550 U.S. 124 (2007).
13. *District of Columbia v. Heller,* 554 U.S. 570 (2008).
14. *Baze v. Rees,* 553 U.S. 35 (2008).

Figure 13-3 ▸ The Roberts Court

The members of the United States Supreme Court as of 2013.

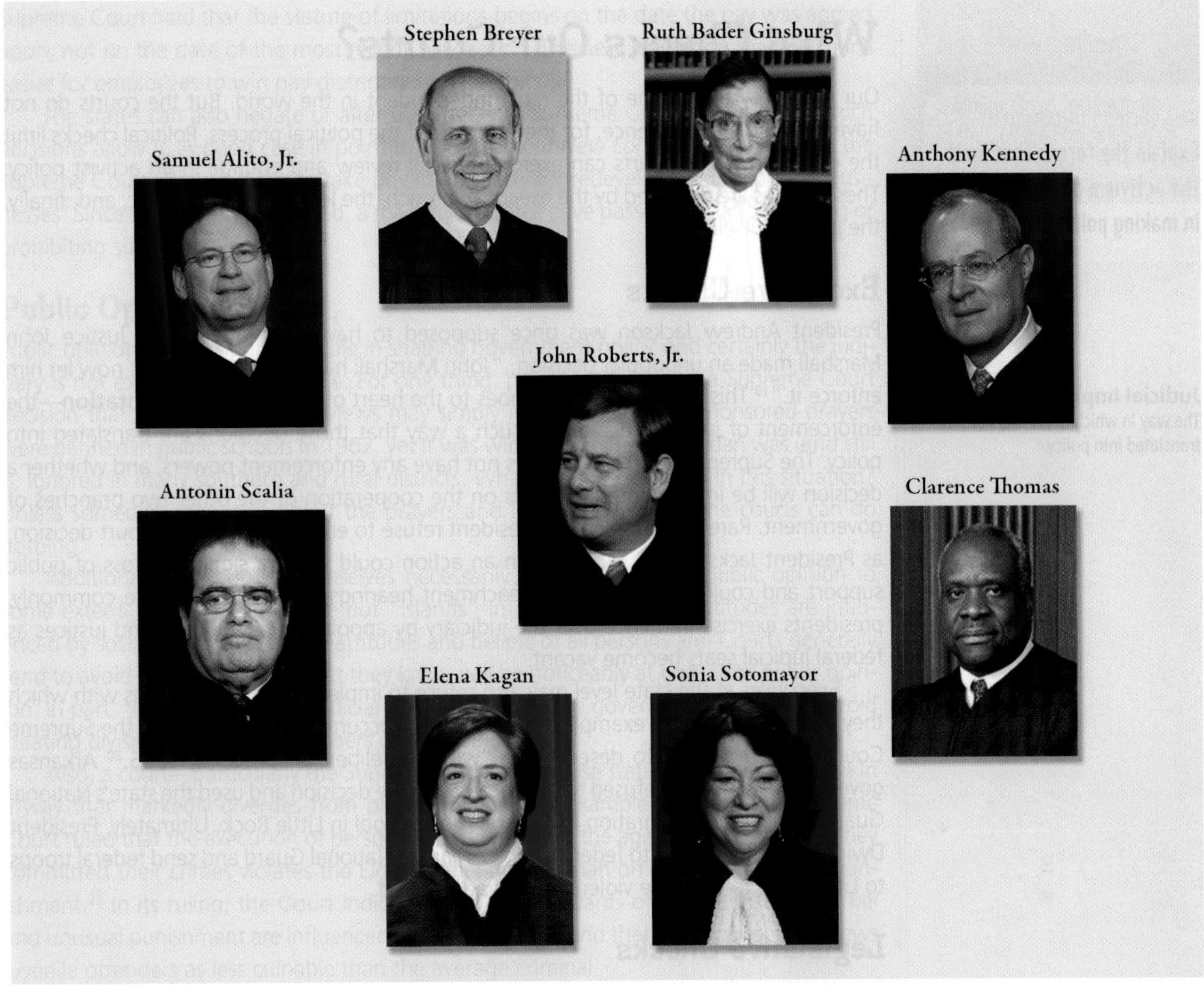

(Kagan—AP Photo/Pablo Martinez Monsivais, File; Sotomayor—AP/Charles Dharapak; remaining photos—The U.S. Supreme Court)

the Court struck down long-standing campaign finance laws.[15] (We discussed *Citizens United* on page 289 in Chapter 9.) A second major ruling was *McDonald v. Chicago,* in which the Court held that all state and local governments are bound to recognize the right to bear arms as an individual right.[16] In these and other key cases, Justice Kennedy continued to cast the deciding vote.

Although the Roberts Court is widely characterized as conservative, its philosophy is not identical with the conservatism of the Republicans in Congress or the broader conservative movement. True, justices such as Scalia and Thomas can rightly be characterized as movement conservatives. Justice Kennedy and even Chief Justice Roberts, however, clearly "march to their own drummer." As one example, the Court has shown a degree of sympathy for the rights of gay men and lesbians that cannot be found in the Republican Party platform. It was Justice Kennedy, after all, who in 2003 wrote the opinion in *Lawrence v. Texas* striking down laws that ban gay sex nationwide.[17] Chief Justice Roberts demonstrated

15. 558 U.S. 50 (2010).
16. 561 U.S. 3025 (2010).
17. 539 U.S. 558 (2003).

Hypothetical and Political Questions. Other judicial doctrines and practices also act as restraints. As already mentioned, the courts will hear only what are called justiciable disputes—disputes that arise out of actual cases. In other words, a court will not hear a case that involves a merely hypothetical issue.

Political Question An issue that a court believes should be decided by the executive or legislative branch—or these two branches acting together.

Additionally, if a political question is involved, the Supreme Court often will exercise judicial restraint and refuse to rule on the matter. A **political question** is one that the Supreme Court declares should be decided by the elected branches of government—the executive branch, the legislative branch, or those two branches acting together. For example, the Supreme Court has refused to rule on whether women in the military should be allowed to serve in combat units, preferring instead to defer to the executive branch's decisions on the matter. Generally, though, fewer questions are deemed political questions by the Supreme Court today than in the past.

The Impact of the Lower Courts. Higher courts can reverse the decisions of lower courts. Lower courts can act as a check on higher courts, too. Lower courts can ignore—and have ignored—Supreme Court decisions. Usually, they do so indirectly. A lower court might conclude, for example, that the precedent set by the Supreme Court does not apply to the exact circumstances in the case before the court. Alternatively, the lower court may decide that the Supreme Court's decision was ambiguous with respect to the issue before the lower court. The fact that the Supreme Court rarely makes broad and clear-cut statements on any issue makes it easier for lower courts to interpret the Supreme Court's decisions in different ways.

(Kevin Dietsch/UPI/Landov)

When opinions are deeply divided about an issue, demonstrations often occur in front of the Supreme Court building in Washington, D.C. Here, protesters show their opposition to a tough new Arizona law targeting illegal immigrants.

Why Should You Care about... THE COURTS?

(AP Photo/Bob Brown/Richmond Times-Dispatch)

This young woman was among the first allowed to attend the Virginia Military Institute. A Supreme Court ruling opened the school to women beginning in August 1997.

Why should you, as an individual, care about the courts? The U.S. legal system may seem too complex to be influenced by one individual, but its power nonetheless depends on the support of individuals. The public has many ways of resisting, modifying, or overturning statutes and rulings of the courts.

THE COURTS AND YOUR LIFE

You may find it worthwhile to attend one or more court sessions to see how the law works in practice. Legislative bodies may make laws and ordinances, but legislation is given its practical form by court rulings. Therefore, if you care about the effects of a particular law, pay attention to how the courts are interpreting it. For example, do you believe that sentences handed down for certain crimes are too lenient—or too strict? Legislative bodies can attempt to establish sentences for various offenses, but the courts inevitably retain considerable flexibility in determining what happens in any particular case.

HOW YOU CAN MAKE A DIFFERENCE

Public opinion can have an effect on judicial policies. Whichever cause may interest you, there is probably an organization that pursues lawsuits to benefit that cause and could use your support. A prime example is the modern women's movement, which undertook a long series of lawsuits to change the way women are treated in American life. The courts only rule on cases that are brought before them, and the women's movement changed American law by filing—and winning—case after case.

- In 1965, a federal circuit court opened a wide range of jobs for women by overturning laws that kept women out of work that was "too hard" for them.
- In 1971, the United States Supreme Court ruled that states could not prefer men when assigning the administrators of estates. (This case was brought by Ruth Bader Ginsburg, who was later to sit on the Court herself.)
- In 1974, the Court ruled that employers could not use the "going market rate" to justify lower wages for women.
- In 1975, it ruled that women could not be excluded from juries.
- In 1978, an Oregon court became the first of many to find that a man could be prosecuted for raping his wife.
- In 1996, the Virginia Military Institute was forced to admit women as cadets.

Today, groups such as the National Organization for Women continue to support lawsuits to advance women's rights.

If you want information about the Supreme Court, contact the following by telephone or letter:

Clerk of the Court
The Supreme Court of the United States
1 First St. N.E.
Washington, DC 20543
(202) 479-3011

You can access an online site for information about the Supreme Court by entering "oyez" into your favorite search engine.

Questions for Discussion and Analysis

1. Review the *Which Side Are You On?* feature on page 430. Why do you think that attorneys, as a group, contribute more to judicial campaigns than do members of other professions?
2. What are the benefits of having lifetime appointments to the United States Supreme Court? What problems might such appointments cause? What would be the likely result if Supreme Court justices faced term limits?
3. On page 436, we described how the Rehnquist Court ruled in favor of states' rights in a gun-control case and against states' rights on a matter concerning marijuana. Why do you think the justices might have come to different conclusions in these two cases?
4. Should Congress ever limit the jurisdiction of the federal courts for political reasons? Should Congress block the Court's ability to rule on cases raised by the prisoners at Guantánamo Bay? Why or why not?

Key Terms

affirm 428
***amicus curiae* brief** 422
appellate court 424
broad construction 435
case law 420
class-action suit 422
common law 419
concurring opinion 429
dissenting opinion 429
diversity of citizenship 422
federal question 422
general jurisdiction 423
judicial activism 435
judicial implementation 438
judicial restraint 435
jurisdiction 421
justiciable controversy 422
limited jurisdiction 423
litigate 422
majority opinion 429
opinion 428
oral arguments 428
political question 440
precedent 419
remand 428
reverse 428
rule of four 428
senatorial courtesy 430
stare decisis 419
strict construction 435
trial court 423
unanimous opinion 428
writ of *certiorari* 428

Chapter Summary

1. American law is rooted in the common law tradition, which is part of our heritage from England. The common law doctrine of *stare decisis* (which means "to stand on decided cases") obligates judges to follow precedents established previously by their own courts or by higher courts that have authority over them. Precedents established by the United States Supreme Court, the highest court in the land, are binding on all lower courts. Fundamental sources of American law include the U.S. Constitution and state constitutions, statutes enacted by legislative bodies, regulations issued by administrative agencies, and case law.
2. Article III, Section 1, of the U.S. Constitution limits the jurisdiction of the federal courts to cases involving (a) a federal question, which is a question based, at least in part, on the U.S. Constitution, a treaty, or a federal law, or (b) diversity of citizenship—which arises when parties to a lawsuit are from different states or when the lawsuit involves a foreign citizen or foreign government. The federal court system is a three-tiered model consisting of (a) U.S. district (trial) courts and various lower courts of limited jurisdiction, (b) intermediate U.S. courts of appeals, and (c) the United States Supreme Court. Cases may be appealed from the district courts to the appellate courts. In most cases, the decisions of the federal appellate courts are final because the Supreme Court hears relatively few cases.
3. The Supreme Court's decision to review a case is influenced by many factors, including the significance of the issues involved and whether the solicitor general is asking the Court to take the case. After a case is accepted, the justices (with the help of their law clerks) undertake research on the issues involved in the case, hear oral arguments from the parties, meet in conference to discuss and vote on the issues, and announce the opinion, which is then released for publication.
4. Federal judges are nominated by the president and confirmed by the Senate. Once appointed, they hold office for life, barring gross misconduct. The nomination and confirmation process, particularly for Supreme Court justices, is often extremely politicized. Democrats and Republicans alike realize that justices may occupy seats on the Court for decades and naturally want to have persons appointed who share their basic views. Nearly 20 percent of all Supreme Court appointments have been either rejected or not acted on by the Senate.
5. In interpreting and applying the law, judges inevitably become policymakers. The most important policymaking

tool of the federal courts is the power of judicial review. This power was not mentioned specifically in the Constitution, but the Supreme Court claimed the power for the federal courts in its 1803 decision in *Marbury v. Madison.*

6. Judges who take an active role in checking the activities of the other branches of government sometimes are characterized as "activist" judges, and judges who defer to the other branches' decisions sometimes are regarded as "restraintist" judges. The Warren Court of the 1950s and 1960s was activist in a liberal direction, whereas the Rehnquist and Roberts Courts became increasingly activist in a conservative direction.

7. When William Rehnquist was appointed chief justice in 1986, the Supreme Court began a rightward shift and over time issued a number of conservative opinions. To date, the Roberts Court appears to be continuing the rightward movement of the Court. The Court, however, is fairly evenly divided between strongly conservative justices and liberal-to-moderate justices, with Justice Kennedy often providing swing votes in key cases before the Court.

8. Checks on the powers of the federal courts include executive checks, legislative checks, public opinion, and judicial traditions and doctrines.

Quiz Multiple Choice

1. One important source of American law is:
   a. **the rights and duties of workers as expressed in employment agreements.**
   b. **case law based in part on the common law tradition.**
   c. **case law based in part on the federal tradition.**

2. When a court feels obligated to base its decisions on precedents—decisions handed down in previous cases—it is adhering to the:
   a. **doctrine of *stare decisis.***
   b. **doctrine of *habeas corpus.***
   c. **concept of federalism.**

3. The supreme law of the land in the United States is:
   a. **state constitutions for actions within each state.**
   b. **state constitutions plus the U.S. Constitution.**
   c. **the U.S. Constitution.**

4. "I'll take it all the way to the Supreme Court." A lawyer cannot truthfully promise this because:
   a. **the Supreme Court may be too far away from the state in which the controversy occurred.**
   b. **the Supreme Court only hears a limited number of cases in which a federal question is involved.**
   c. **the Supreme Court is not in session for a full twelve months each year.**

5. The distinction between federal district courts and federal appellate courts can be summarized by the following statement:
   a. **federal district courts are trial courts that hear evidence, but federal appellate courts do not hear evidence.**
   b. **federal district courts only hear appeals from federal appellate courts.**
   c. **federal appellate courts only accept cases involving state constitutions.**

6. The U.S. Supreme Court chooses which cases it will hear. It decides:
   a. **approximately 200 cases a year.**
   b. **approximately 300 cases a year.**
   c. **fewer than 100 cases a year.**

7. When the U.S. Supreme Court issues an opinion that has the support of the entire Court, it is called a unanimous opinion. Otherwise, the Court issues a majority opinion. Those justices in the minority who do not agree with the majority opinion often write:
   a. **a concurring opinion.**
   b. **a dissenting opinion.**
   c. **a request to retry the case.**

8. When a federal court declares that a federal or state law or policy is unconstitutional, that court is engaging in:
   a. **judicial review.**
   b. **congressional condemnation.**
   c. **administrative oversight.**

ANSWERS: 1. b, 2. a, 3. c, 4. b, 5. a, 6. c, 7. b, 8. a.

Quiz Fill-Ins

9. The doctrine of __________ __________ rests on the conviction that the federal judiciary should actively use its powers to check the laws passed by Congress and state legislatures.

10. When a Supreme Court justice believes in __________ __________, she or he will look to the "letter of the law" when attempting to interpret the Constitution or a particular statute.

11. Whenever a case involves a __________ __________, the Supreme Court normally declares that it should be decided by the elected branches of government—the executive branch, the legislative branch, or both.

12. Sometimes, even when only state laws are at issue, a federal court will hear a case if __________ of __________ exists, meaning that the parties to the lawsuit are from different states. The amount in controversy must be at least __________, though.

13. To bring a lawsuit, a party must show that he or she suffered an actual harm or is threatened by an actual harm as a result of the action that led to the dispute. If so, then that party has __________ to __________.

14. When the federal government wants to engage in surveillance of suspected spies, it can avail itself of the __________ __________ __________ Act passed in 1978.

15. When the United States Supreme Court decides that it wishes to review a case, it will issue a __________ of __________, ordering a lower court to send a record of the case for review.

16. The most important checks on our judicial system are __________ checks, __________ checks, and __________ __________.

ANSWERS: 9. judicial activism, 10. strict construction, 11. political question, 12. diversity; citizenship; $75,000, 13. standing; sue, 14. Foreign Intelligence Surveillance, 15. writ; *certiorari,* 16. executive; legislative; public opinion.

(© Aleksandar Jovicic/iStockphoto)

Selected Print & Media Resources

SUGGESTED READINGS

Bach, Amy. *Ordinary Injustice: How America Holds Court.* New York: Holt Paperbacks, 2010. In an investigation that moves from small-town Georgia to upstate New York and from Chicago to Mississippi, lawyer Amy Bach uncovers the chronic injustice meted out daily to ordinary Americans by a legal system so underfunded and understaffed that it is a menace to the people it is designed to serve.

Friedman, Barry. *The Will of the People: How Public Opinion Has Influenced the Supreme Court and Shaped the Meaning of the Constitution.* New York: Farrar, Straus and Giroux, 2010. It has long been said that the Supreme Court follows the election returns. This history of the Court, by a New York University law professor, seeks to demonstrate that proposition in detail.

Greenhouse, Linda. *The U.S. Supreme Court: A Very Short Introduction.* New York: Oxford University Press, 2012. The Very Short Introduction series has been exceptionally successful in commissioning well-written works by top experts. Greenhouse, the author of this incisive introduction, was the *New York Times* Supreme Court correspondent for thirty years.

Posner, Richard A. *How Judges Think.* Cambridge, Mass.: Harvard University Press (paperback), 2010. Posner, a U.S. appeals court judge, is an astonishingly prolific writer on political, economic, and legal issues. In this volume, he returns to what he knows best, judicial philosophy. Posner contends that judges inevitably rely on their own experiences and prejudices, and that regardless of what Supreme Court justices may say, their rulings are highly political. Posner believes that the best guarantee of impartial justice is to fully understand the true consequences of each decision.

MEDIA RESOURCES

Gideon's Trumpet—A 1980 film, starring Henry Fonda as the small-time criminal James Earl Gideon, which makes clear the path a case takes to the Supreme Court and the importance of cases decided there.

The Supreme Court—A four-part PBS series that won a 2008 Parents' Choice Gold Award. The series follows the history of the Supreme Court from the first chief justice, John Marshall, to the earliest days of the Roberts Court. Some of the many topics discussed are the Court's dismal performance in the Civil War era, its conflicts with President Franklin D. Roosevelt, its role in banning the segregation of African Americans, and its role in the abortion controversy.

E-mocracy COURTS ON THE WEB

Most courts in the United States have sites on the Web. These sites vary in what they include. Some courts simply display contact information for court personnel. Others include recent judicial decisions along with court rules and forms. Many federal courts permit attorneys to file documents electronically. The information available on these sites continues to grow as courts try to avoid being left behind in the Information Age. One day, courts may decide to implement *virtual courtrooms,* in which judicial proceedings take place totally via the Internet. The Internet may ultimately provide at least a partial solution to the twin problems of overloaded dockets and the high time and financial costs of litigation.

LOGGING ON

The home page of the federal courts is a good starting point for learning about the federal court system in general. At this site, you can even follow the path of a case as it moves through the federal court system. You can locate this page by typing "us courts" into an online search engine.

To access the Supreme Court's official Web site, on which Supreme Court decisions are made available within hours of their release, search on "supreme court."

Several Web sites offer searchable databases of Supreme Court decisions. You can access Supreme Court cases since 1970 by searching on "findlaw supreme court."

Cornell University also offers an easily searchable index to Supreme Court opinions, including some important historic decisions. Find it by typing "cornell supct" into your search engine.

You can find information on the justices of the Supreme Court, as well as their decisions, by entering "oyez" into your search engine.

TODAY WE MARCH... TOMORROW WE VOTE!
New American Opportuni
www.cirnow.or
e Are
merica
New American Opportunity Campaign

14 Domestic and Economic Policy

The six learning outcomes below are designed to help improve your understanding of this chapter. After reading this chapter, you should be able to:

- Learning Outcome 1: **Describe the five steps of the policymaking process, using the health-care reform legislation as an example.**
- Learning Outcome 2: **Explain why illegal immigration is seen as a problem, and cite some of the steps that have been taken in response to it.**
- Learning Outcome 3: **Discuss recent developments in crime rates and incarceration.**
- Learning Outcome 4: **Evaluate the federal government's responses to high oil prices and the controversy over global warming.**
- Learning Outcome 5: **Define *unemployment, inflation, fiscal policy, net public debt,* and *monetary policy.***
- Learning Outcome 6: **Describe the various taxes that Americans pay, and discuss some of the controversies surrounding taxation.**

These activists support immigration rights. They want Congress and the president to enact comprehensive reform, a key domestic policy issue.

(EPA/Matthew Cavanaugh)

(mathieukor/iStockphoto)

What if...

So-called hard money—silver and gold—has always had an appeal as currency. Why don't we have a gold standard?

WE RETURNED TO THE GOLD STANDARD?

BACKGROUND

If you look at a dollar bill, you won't find much information about what is "backing" the bill. In fact, the only thing that backs the dollar is your certainty that everyone will accept it in payment for goods, services, and debts. Until 1964, however, the U.S. government issued dollar bills with the statement: "This certifies that there is on deposit in the treasury of the United States of America one dollar in silver payable to the bearer on demand." Apparently, the dollar was backed by silver.

In reality, it was backed by a law that set the value of the currency in terms of a specified quantity of gold. This was the gold standard. Until the 1930s, much of the world was on a gold standard. Nations agreed to redeem their currencies for a fixed amount of gold at the request of any holder of that currency. The heyday of the gold standard was from 1870 to 1914, although Britain had been on a gold standard since the 1820s.

For decades, most economists have assumed that the gold standard was history. In the 2012 Republican presidential primaries, however, some candidates argued for a return to the gold standard. In a public opinion poll taken in late 2011, 44 percent of those questioned favored the idea of a return to gold.

WHAT IF WE RETURNED TO THE GOLD STANDARD?

The first thing that the federal government would have to do is decide on the free convertibility of dollars for gold. If it used current gold prices, you would be able to exchange, say, $1,600 for an ounce of gold. Obviously, if the government declared an exchange rate that was equal to the world price of gold, you would have little incentive to ask a bank to give you gold for your dollars. If you really wanted gold, you would simply buy it on the open market.

INFLATION AND DEFLATION

Those in favor of a gold standard often argue that only "hard money" can prevent inflation, or a sustained rise in average prices and a loss in value of the currency. Indeed, from 1971, when President Richard Nixon eliminated the last vestiges of the gold standard, to 2013, average prices rose by about 5.8 times. In 1971, gold was worth $35 per ounce. If the price of gold had gone up at the same rate as everything else, it would now cost about $200 per ounce. In fact, the price of an ounce today is, as noted, close to $1,600.

If we had remained on the gold standard after 1971, therefore, the dollar might have eight times its 1971 value. That means average prices would have fallen to one-eighth of their previous levels. Instead of inflation, there would have been a massive *deflation,* in which the value of the dollar would have increased hugely while the prices of everything else collapsed.

A gold standard, therefore, does not guarantee price stability. Consider also what would happen if we were suddenly able to mine vast quantities of new gold. This has happened. In the years after 1900, when new South African gold flooded the market, inflation reached 10 percent.

More typically, however, a gold standard threatens to cause deflation, and most economists consider deflation a much more dangerous condition than inflation. Deflation has been associated with severe depressions. In the Great Depression, for example, average prices fell by about 25 percent from 1929 to 1933. It's a good bet, therefore, that if we ever did return to the gold standard, we would probably leave it again soon.

FOR CRITICAL ANALYSIS

1. *If the government creates "fiat money" (money not backed by any commodity), as it now does, how can it avoid inflation or deflation?*
2. *Why does gold hold more fascination as the basis of a monetary system than, say, copper, steel, wheat, corn, or other commodities?*

Part of the public-policy debate in our nation involves domestic problems. **Domestic policy** can be defined as all laws, government planning, and government actions that concern internal issues of national importance. Consequently, the span of such policies is enormous. Domestic policies range from relatively simple issues, such as what the speed limit should be on interstate highways, to more complex ones, such as how best to protect our environment or how we should manage the nation's money supply, as discussed in this chapter's opening *What If . . .* feature. Many of our domestic policies are formulated and implemented by the federal government, but a number of others are the result of the combined efforts of federal, state, and local governments.

Domestic Policy
All laws, government planning, and government actions that concern internal issues of national importance, such as poverty, crime, and the environment.

We can define several types of domestic policy. *Regulatory policy* seeks to define what is and is not legal. Setting speed limits is obviously regulatory policy. *Redistributive policy* transfers income from certain individuals or groups to others, often based on the belief that these transfers enhance fairness. Social Security is an example. *Promotional policy* seeks to foster or discourage various economic or social activities, typically through subsidies and tax breaks. A tax credit for buying a fuel-efficient car would qualify as promotional. Typically, whenever a policy decision is made, some groups will be better off and some groups will be hurt. All policymaking generally involves such a dilemma.

In this chapter, we look at domestic policy issues involving health care, immigration, crime, and energy and the environment. We also examine national economic policies undertaken by the federal government.

The Policymaking Process: Health Care as an Example

■ **Learning Outcome 1:**
Describe the five steps of the policymaking process, using the health-care reform legislation as an example.

How does any issue get resolved? First, of course, the issue must be identified as a problem. Often, policymakers have only to open their local newspapers or letters from their constituents to discover that a problem is brewing. On rare occasions, a crisis—such as that brought about by the terrorist attacks of September 11, 2001—creates the need to formulate policy. Like most Americans, however, policymakers receive much of their information from the national media. Finally, various lobbying groups provide information to members of Congress.

No matter how simple or how complex the problem, those who make policy follow a number of steps. We can divide the process of policymaking into five steps: (1) agenda building, (2) policy formulation, (3) policy adoption, (4) policy implementation, and (5) policy evaluation.

The health-care legislation passed in 2010 can be used to illustrate this process. Regardless of the ultimate fate of the reforms, they are still the most recent large-scale attempt to craft new public policy.

In March 2010, President Barack Obama signed into law the **Patient Protection and Affordable Care Act,** a massive overhaul of the nation's health-care funding system. A few days later, Obama signed the Health Care and Education Reconciliation Act, a series of adjustments to the main legislative package. These two measures constituted the most important political development in the United States between the 2008 and 2010 elections, and the largest expansion in the welfare state since the presidency of Lyndon B. Johnson (1963–1969). The signing of these bills marked the climax of an approximately nine-month debate in the nation and in Congress over the future of our health-care system.

Patient Protection and Affordable Care Act
A law passed in 2010 that seeks, among other things, to ensure health-care insurance for American citizens. The act is supplemented by the Health Care and Education Reconciliation Act and nicknamed "Obamacare" by opponents and journalists.

Health Care: Agenda Building

First of all, an issue must get on the agenda. In other words, Congress must become aware that a problem requires congressional action. Agenda building may occur as the result of a crisis, technological change, or mass media campaign, as well as through the efforts of strong political personalities and effective lobbying groups. To understand how health care came to be an important issue, and how health-care reform became part of the national agenda, we need to examine the background of the issue.

Health Care's Role in the American Economy. As of 2011, health care was estimated to account for 18.2 percent of the total U.S. economy. In 1965, about 6 percent of our national income was spent on health care, but that percentage has been increasing ever since, as you can see in Figure 14–1 below. Per capita spending on health care is greater in the United States than almost anywhere else in the world. Measured by the percentage of the **gross domestic product (GDP)** devoted to health care, America spends almost twice as much as Britain or Japan. (See Figure 14–2 on the facing page.)

Gross Domestic Product (GDP)
The dollar value of all *final* goods and services produced in a one-year period.

As of 2010, when none of the health-care reforms had yet been implemented, government spending on health care constituted about 50 percent of total health-care spending. Private insurance accounted for more than 30 percent of payments for health care. The remainder—less than 20 percent—was paid directly by individuals or by charities. The government programs **Medicare** and **Medicaid** have been the main sources of hospital and other medical benefits for about 100 million Americans—one-third of the nation's population. Many of these people are elderly.

Medicare
A federal health-insurance program that covers U.S. residents over the age of sixty-five. The costs are met by a tax on wages and salaries.

Medicaid
A joint state-federal program that provides medical care to the poor (including indigent elderly persons in nursing homes). The program is funded out of general government revenues.

Medicare. The Medicare program, which was created in 1965 under President Lyndon Johnson, pays hospital and physician bills for U.S. residents over the age of sixty-five. Since 2006, Medicare has also paid for at least part of the prescription drug expenses of the elderly. In return for paying a tax on their earnings (currently set at 2.9 percent of wages and salaries) while in the workforce, retirees are assured that the majority of their hospital and physician bills will be paid for with public funds.

Medicare is now the second-largest domestic spending program, after Social Security. Government expenditures on Medicare have routinely exceeded forecasts. The government has responded in part by imposing arbitrary reimbursement caps on specific medical procedures. The government has also cut rates of reimbursement to individual physicians and physician groups, such as health maintenance organizations (HMOs). As a result, some physicians and HMOs have become reluctant to accept Medicare patients.

Figure 14–1 ▸ Percentage of Total National Income Spent on Health Care in the United States

The portion of total national income spent on health care has risen steadily since 1965.

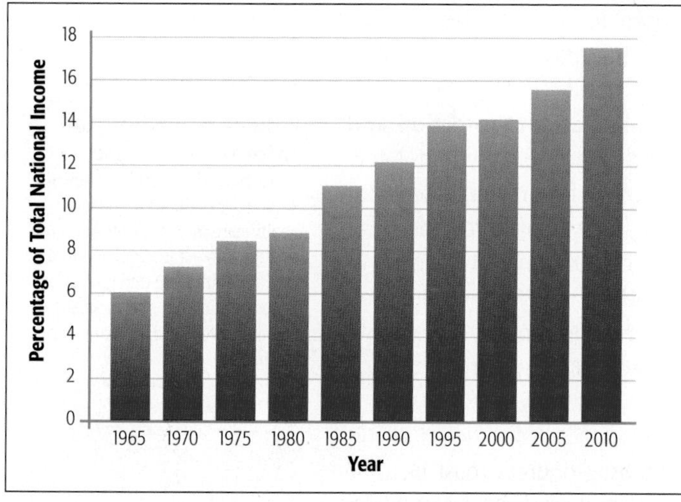

Sources: U.S. Department of Commerce; U.S. Department of Health and Human Services; Deloitte and Touche LLP; VHA, Inc.; and Centers for Medicare and Medicaid Services.

Medicaid. Within a few short years, the joint federal-state taxpayer-funded Medicaid program for the "working poor" has generated one of the biggest expansions of government entitlements ever. In 1990, total Medicaid spending was around $50 billion. By fiscal year 2013, the total cost of Medicaid and the Children's Health Insurance Program (CHIP) was about $325 billion. At the end of the twentieth century, 34 million people were enrolled in the programs. Today, in the wake of the Great Recession, there are more than 60 million.

In recent years, the federal government has paid about 55 percent of Medicaid's total cost. The states pay the rest. Wealthy states must pick up a greater share of the tab than poor ones. Medicaid costs have imposed major strains on the budgets of many states. As you will learn later in this section, the new health-care reform legislation adopted in 2010 will expand considerably the share of the population that is eligible for Medicaid. Much of the extra expense due to the new enrollees will be picked up by federal taxpayers.

The Problem of the Uninsured. In 2010, about 49 million Americans—more than 16 percent of the population—did not have health insurance. The uninsured population has been relatively young, in part due to Medicare, which covers almost everyone over the age of sixty-five. Also, younger workers are more likely to be employed in entry-level jobs without health-insurance benefits.

The traditional system of health care in the United States was based on the assumption that employers would provide health insurance to working-age persons. Many small businesses, however, simply have not been able to afford to offer their workers health insurance. In 2011, employer-provided health insurance cost an average of $5,429 for single coverage and $15,073 for family coverage, according to the Kaiser Family Foundation.

Figure 14-2 ▸ **Cost of Health Care in Economically Advanced Nations**

Cost is given as a percentage of total gross domestic product (GDP). Figures are for 2009 and 2010.

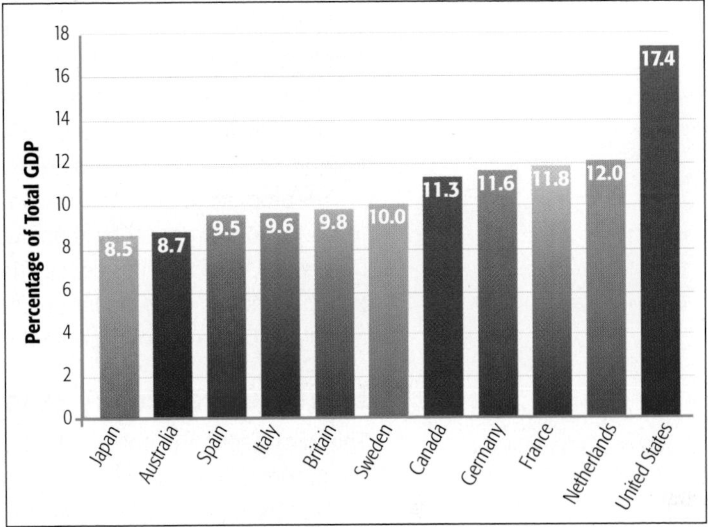

Source: Excerpted and adapted from the Organization for Economic Cooperation and Development, *OECD Health Data*, 2011.

The Problem of High Costs. High medical costs are a problem not only for individuals with inadequate or nonexistent insurance coverage. They are also a problem for the system as a whole. Over the past four decades, per capita spending on health care in the United States grew at an average rate of 4.9 percent per year, even when corrected for inflation. A main driver of the growth in health-care spending was new medical technologies and services. The increased number of elderly persons imposed additional costs.

People over the age of sixty-five run up health-care bills that are far larger than those incurred by the rest of the population. As a federal problem, therefore, health-care spending growth has been and will remain chiefly a Medicare issue, even after the passage of the new health-care measures. In 2011, the government's Medicare trustees reported that by 2024 the Medicare trust fund was projected to run out of funds necessary to pay for all of its obligations. Such prospects explain why the issue of health-care cost containment was almost as important as the issue of universal coverage during the 2009 debates.

The International Experience. The Patient Protection and Affordable Care Act of 2010 attempts to provide **universal health insurance** for American citizens. The concept of universal health insurance is not new. Throughout the twentieth century, most economically advanced nations adopted such systems. By the twenty-first century, the United States was the only advanced industrial country with a large pool of citizens who lacked health insurance. American progressives considered it unacceptable that the United States could not do what these other nations had done—another argument for placing reform on the agenda.

Universal Health Insurance Any of several possible programs to provide health insurance to everyone in a country. The central government does not necessarily provide the insurance itself but may subsidize the purchase of insurance from private insurance companies.

Health Care: Policy Formulation

During the next step in the policymaking process, various policy proposals are discussed among government officials and the public. Such discussions may take place in the printed media, on television, and in the halls of Congress. Congress holds hearings, the president voices the administration's views, and the topic may even become a campaign issue.

Since the time of President Harry Truman (1945–1953), some liberals have sought to establish a national health-insurance system in this country. During his first two years in office, President Bill Clinton (1993–2001) attempted to steer such a proposal through Congress, but his plan failed. In the first decade of the twenty-first century, however, universal health insurance began to reappear as a political issue.

Unlike previous proposals, the new universal health-insurance plans did not provide for a federal monopoly on basic health insurance. Instead, universal coverage would result from a mandate that all citizens must obtain health insurance from some source—an employer, Medicare or Medicaid, or a plan from a private-sector insurance company through a market sponsored by the federal government or a state government. Low-income families would receive a subsidy to help them pay their insurance premiums. Insurers could not reject applicants.

A program of this nature was adopted by the state of Massachusetts in 2006 in response to a proposal by then–Republican governor Mitt Romney. When, in 2008, the Democrats won the presidency and large majorities in both chambers of Congress, such policy proposals were again on the table nationally. Yet several major issues had to be addressed before a policy could be adopted.

Health Care: Policy Adoption

The third step in the policymaking process involves choosing a specific policy from among the proposals that have been discussed.

As president, Barack Obama largely delegated the drafting of a health-care plan to Congress. Obama's willingness to let Congress take the lead was a notable change. Recent presidents, such as George W. Bush and Bill Clinton, had sought to push presidential proposals through the legislative process without significant alteration. Obama's tactics eliminated much of the tug-of-war between Congress and the president that had been commonplace in past decades, but the political cost of letting Congress take the lead was high. Congress took a very long time to pass the necessary legislation, and much of the political maneuvering required for passage was highly unpopular with the public.

Individual Mandate
In health-care reform, the requirement that all citizens obtain health-care insurance coverage from some source, public or private.

The Issue of Mandated Coverage. One issue that needed to be resolved became known as the *individual mandate*. During the 2008 Democratic presidential primary campaigns, Obama's health-care plan did not require adults to obtain coverage, although coverage was required for children. Obama's plan, in other words, had no mandated coverage. Congressional Democrats, however, quickly adopted the **individual mandate** in all of their draft proposals. Without the mandate, there was no way that the numbers would add up: universal coverage was impossible unless everyone—healthy and sick alike—chipped in. Unfortunately for the Democrats, the individual mandate allowed the Republicans to accuse the Democrats of "forcing" people to do something, never a popular position in America.

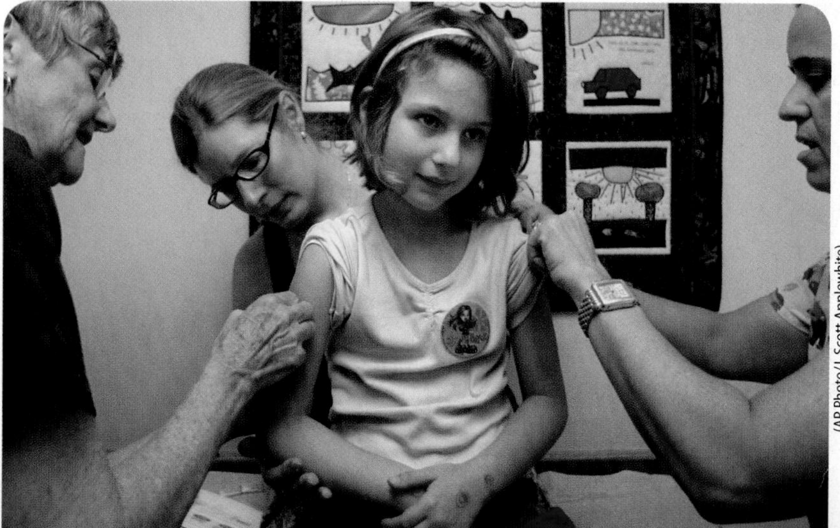

This child is receiving several inoculations at the same time. Are there situations in which her parents won't have to pay for such medical services? If so, what are they?

(AP Photo/J. Scott Applewhite)

New Taxes. Funding the legislation required additional taxes. Democrats in the House called for heavier taxes on the rich, while the Senate proposed taxes on drug and insurance companies. In the end, the two chambers compromised on smaller tax increases on the rich than the House had planned, plus a number of taxes on the health-care corporations.

Public Reaction. Initially, popular support for health-care reform, as reported by opinion polls, was relatively high. Support eroded quickly, however, as Congress took up the actual legislation. Demonstrations against the Democratic proposals began in the late summer of 2009—many were organized by the new Tea Party movement. The process of moving the reform through congressional channels gave the public a close look at how legislatures operate, and many citizens clearly were not happy with what they saw.

did you know?

From 2007 through 2009, the U.S. government mailed out $180 million in benefit checks to twenty thousand Americans—who were dead.

Passage. The House passed its bill in November 2009, and the Senate passed its version in December. Passing the reform legislation became more complicated in January 2010, after Republican Scott Brown won a Massachusetts special election to fill a vacant U.S. Senate seat. The election meant that the Senate Democrats lost their sixtieth vote, which was necessary to end filibusters. If the House and Senate versions of the bill were reconciled in a conference committee—the normal procedure—Senate Democrats would not be able to pass the resulting compromise, and the entire reform effort would collapse.

President Obama and then–House Speaker Nancy Pelosi, however, patiently assembled enough Democratic support in the House to pass the Senate bill unaltered, thus eliminating the need for a conference committee. The House then immediately passed a reconciliation act, which was not subject to Senate filibuster. The Senate accepted it three days later. "Obamacare," as it was nicknamed, was the law of the land. Outraged Republicans accused the Democrats of "ramming" the legislation through Congress. Neither the Senate's bill nor the House's reconciliation measure received the vote of even a single Republican.

Details of the Legislation. Most of the major provisions of the new legislation were not to go into effect until 2014. The long delay was established in part to allow systems such as state insurance pools to be set up more effectively, but the Democrats also wanted to keep costs down during the initial ten-year period. The lengthy implementation, however, presented political problems for the Democrats, who faced two national elections before most of the programs would be in effect. Voters in those elections would receive few of the promised benefits of the programs.

Some provisions took effect quickly, however. Young adults were allowed to stay on their parents' health plans until they turned twenty-six, and insurance companies could not drop people when they became sick.

In 2014, most of the program kicks in, including the following:

- A ban on excluding people with preexisting conditions from insurance plans.
- A requirement that most people obtain insurance or pay an income tax penalty.
- State health-insurance exchanges where individuals and small businesses can buy policies from commercial insurance companies.
- Subsidies to help persons with incomes up to four times the federal poverty level purchase coverage on the exchanges.
- Medicaid coverage for individuals with incomes up to 133 percent of the poverty level.

Significant taxes to pay for the new benefits were to be phased in from 2011 to 2018.

Health Care: Policy Implementation

The fourth step in the policymaking process involves the implementation of the policy alternative chosen by Congress. Government action must be implemented by bureaucrats, the courts, police, and individual citizens.

In the example of health-care reform, implementation was complicated by conservative resistance to the legislation. As you learned in earlier chapters, a large number of state officials challenged the constitutionality of Obamacare. The Supreme Court in 2012

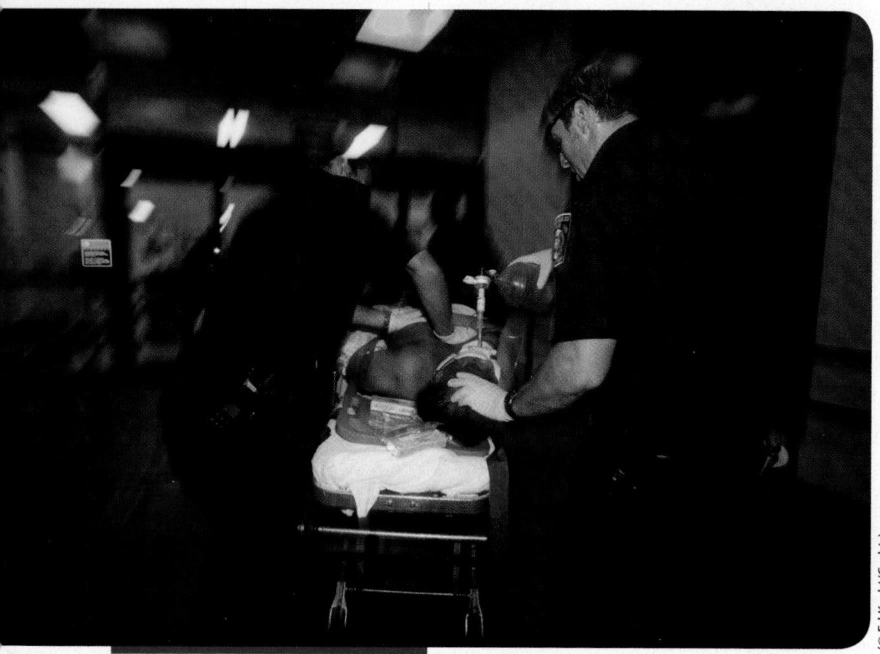
(© Ed Kashi/Corbis)

When uninsured individuals use the hospital emergency services, some of these costs are paid by others, including governments—i.e., taxpayers. Why is that so?

upheld the individual mandate, but made the expansion of the Medicaid program optional for the states. Many Republican governors announced that they would not expand Medicaid or cooperate with other implementation efforts. In Congress, Republicans called for repeal of the legislation. If that should fail, they threatened to block funding necessary to implement various parts of the program.

Complete repeal of the legislation would require the support of not only the Republican-controlled House but also the Senate. The repeal would also have to survive a presidential veto. Repeal, in other words, is almost impossible before 2013, and unlikely even then. Finally, much of the reform package takes the form of an entitlement program, such as Medicare or Social Security. Funding for entitlement programs continues on a year-to-year basis unless it is explicitly altered or abolished. In other words, entitlements do not depend on annual budget votes in Congress for their continued survival. Therefore, even if Republicans in Congress were able to "defund" certain aspects of the reforms, most of the new policies would survive.

Health Care: Policy Evaluation

After a policy has been implemented, it is evaluated. When a policy has been in place for a given period of time, groups inside and outside the government conduct studies to determine how the program has actually worked. Based on this feedback and the perceived success or failure of the policy, a new round of policymaking initiatives may be undertaken to improve on the effort.

As of 2013, the health-care reforms had received very little evaluation. In part, this was because so many of the reforms were yet to be implemented. Also, opponents were more interested in repealing the legislation than improving it. Republicans and Democrats did agree on at least one small fix in 2011, however: they abolished a provision that imposed heavy paperwork requirements on small businesses.

Immigration

■ Learning Outcome 2: **Explain why illegal immigration is seen as a problem, and cite some of the steps that have been taken in response to it.**

In recent years, immigration rates in the United States have been among the highest since their peak in the early twentieth century. Every year, more than 1 million people immigrate to this country legally, a figure that does not include the large number of unauthorized immigrants. Those born on foreign soil now constitute about 13 percent of the U.S. population—more than twice the percentage of thirty years ago.

Since 1977, four out of five immigrants have come from Latin America or Asia. Hispanics have overtaken African Americans as the nation's largest minority. As you learned in Chapter 5, if current immigration rates continue, by 2050 minority groups collectively will constitute the "majority" of Americans. If such groups were to form coalitions, they could increase their political power dramatically. The "old guard" white majority would no longer dominate American politics.

Some regard the high rate of immigration as a plus for America because it offsets the low birthrate and aging population, which we also discussed in Chapter 5. Immigrants expand the workforce and help to support, through their taxes, government programs that benefit older Americans, such as Medicare and Social Security. In contrast, nations that do not have high immigration rates, such as Japan, are experiencing serious challenges due to their aging populations.

A significant number of U.S. citizens, however, believe that immigration—both legal and illegal—negatively affects America. They argue, among other things, that the large number of immigrants seeking work results in lower wages for Americans, especially those with few skills. They also worry about the cost of providing immigrants with services such as education and medical care.

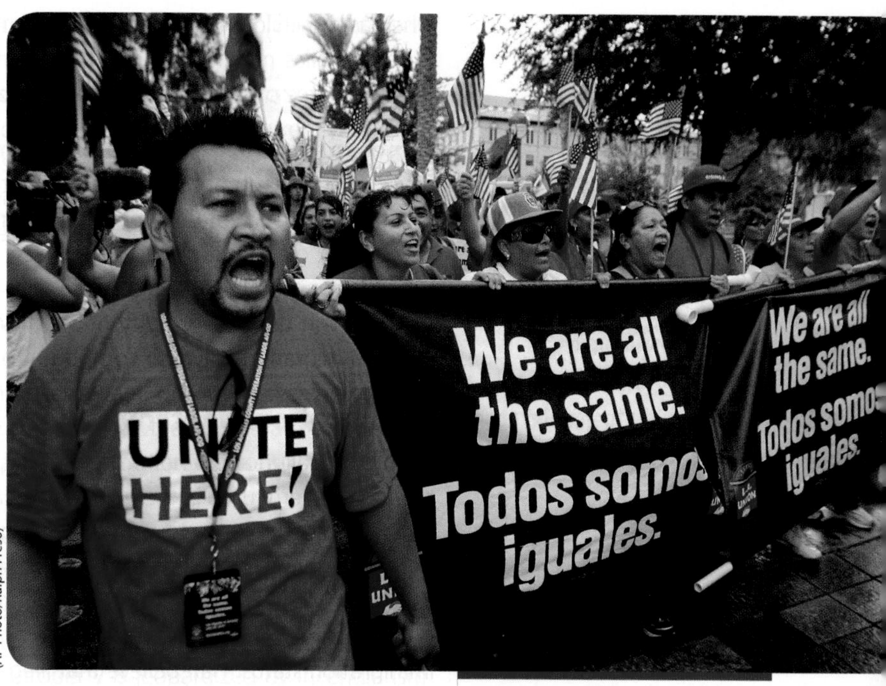

(AP Photo/Ralph Freso)

Immigration remains a "hot button" issue. Why do so many foreigners wish to live in the United States, even if it means entering illegally?

The Issue of Unauthorized Immigration

Illegal immigration—or unauthorized immigration, to use the terminology of the Department of Homeland Security—has been a major national issue for many years. Latin Americans, especially those migrating from Mexico, constitute the majority of individuals entering the United States without permission. In addition, many unauthorized immigrants enter the country legally, often as tourists or students, and then fail to return home when their visa status expires. Naturally, the unauthorized population is hard to count, but the total number clearly has increased each year for several decades. The number of illegal immigrants appears to have peaked in 2007, however, on the eve of the Great Recession, when the number reached 11.8 million. By 2011, the total was down to 11.5 million, according to the Department of Homeland Security, and may have fallen since.

Unauthorized immigrants typically come to the United States to work, and until recently their labor has been in high demand. The housing boom, which came to an abrupt end in the fall of 2007, was partially fueled by the steady stream of unauthorized immigrants seeking jobs. Until the Immigration Reform and Control Act of 1986, there was no law against hiring foreign citizens who lacked proper papers.

Until recently, laws penalizing employers were infrequently enforced. The Obama administration, however, has stepped up enforcement of these laws significantly. In addition, several states, notably Alabama and Arizona, have adopted laws that impose severe sanctions on businesses that employ unauthorized workers. As a result, many agricultural businesses in these states have begun to report labor shortages.

Characteristics of the Undocumented Population. Studies of unauthorized immigrants have revealed that a large share of them eventually return to their home countries, where they frequently set up small businesses or retire. Many send remittances back to relatives in their homeland. In 2011, Mexico received $23 billion in such remittances. In these ways, unauthorized immigrants are acting as immigrants to the United States always have. Throughout American history, immigrants frequently returned home or sent funds to relatives in the "old country."

Unauthorized immigrants very often live in mixed households, in which one or more members of a family have lawful resident status, but others do not. A woman from Guatemala with permanent resident status, for example, might be married to a Guatemalan man who is in the country illegally. Often, the parents in a family are unauthorized,

Figure 14–3 ▸ Homicide Rates

Homicide rates recently declined to levels last seen in the 1960s. (The 2001 rate does *not* include deaths attributed to the 9/11 terrorist attacks.)

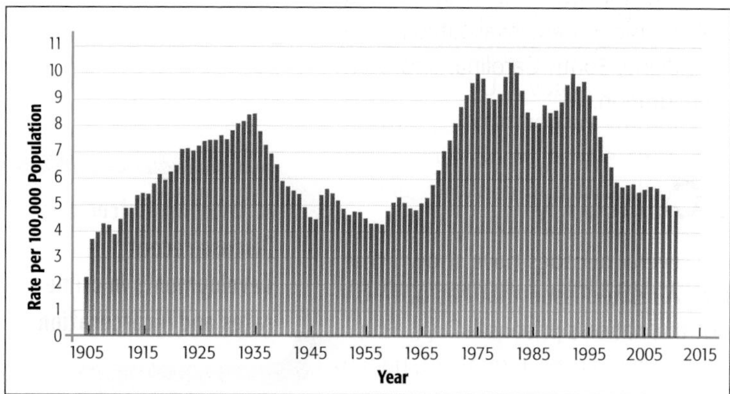

Sources: U.S. Department of Justice; and National Center for Health Statistics, *Vital Statistics.*

Figure 14–4 ▸ Violent Crime Rates

Violent crime rates began a steep decline in 1995. The crimes included in this chart are rape, robbery, aggravated and simple assault, and homicide.

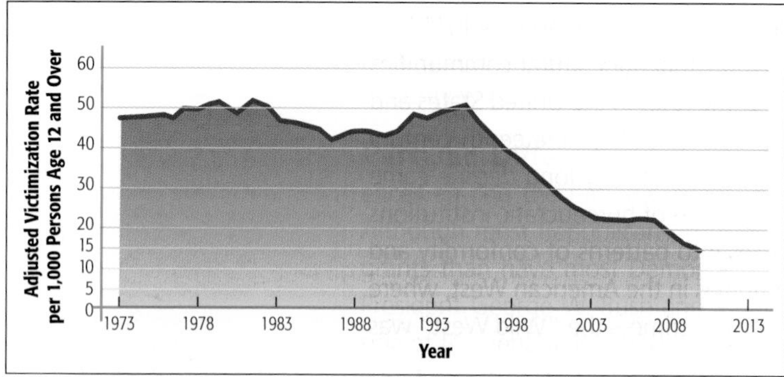

Sources: U.S. Department of Justice; rape, robbery, and assault data are from the *National Crime Victimization Survey;* the homicide data are from the Federal Bureau of Investigation's *Uniform Crime Reports.*

Figure 14–5 ▸ Theft Rates

Theft rates have declined significantly since the 1970s. *Theft* is defined as completed or attempted theft of property or cash without personal contact.

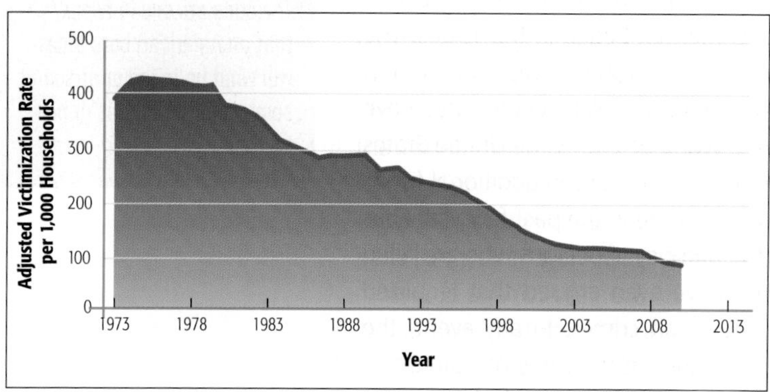

Source: U.S. Department of Justice, *National Crime Victimization Survey.*

The Prison Population Bomb

Many Americans believe that the best solution to the nation's crime problem is to impose stiff prison sentences on offenders. Such sentences, in fact, have become national policy. By 2013, U.S. prisons and jails held 2.4 million people. About two-thirds of the incarcerated population were in state or federal prisons, with the remainder held in local jails. About 60 percent of the persons held in local jails were awaiting court action. The other 40 percent were serving sentences.

The number of incarcerated persons has grown rapidly in recent years. In 1990, for example, the total number of persons held in U.S. jails or prisons was still only 1.1 million. From 1995 to 2002, the incarcerated population grew at an average of 3.8 percent annually. The rate of growth has slowed since 2002, however, and appears to have stabilized in 2011 and 2012.

The Incarceration Rate. Some groups of people are much more likely to find themselves behind bars than others. Men are more than ten times more likely to be incarcerated than women. Prisoners are also disproportionately African American. To measure how frequently members of particular groups are imprisoned, the standard statistic is the **incarceration rate.** This rate is the number of people incarcerated for every 100,000 persons in a particular population group. To put it another way, an incarceration rate of 1,000 means that 1 percent of a particular group is in custody. Using this statistic, we can say that U.S. men have an incarceration rate of 1,398, compared with a rate of 131 for U.S. women.

These figures, close to an all-time high, mean that more than 1 male out of every 100 is in jail or prison in this country. Figure 14–6 on the facing page shows selected incarceration rates by gender, race, and age. Note the very high incarceration rate for African Americans between the ages of thirty and thirty-four—at any given time, almost 11 percent of this group is in jail or prison. How do American incarceration rates compare with those of other countries? We answer that question in this chapter's *Beyond Our Borders* feature on the facing page.

Incarceration Rate
The number of persons held in jail or prison for every 100,000 persons in a particular population group.

Prison Construction and Conditions. To house a growing number of inmates, prison construction and management have become sizable industries in the United States. Ten years ago, prison overcrowding was a major issue. In 1994, for example, state prisons had a rated capacity of about 500,000 inmates but actually held 900,000 people. The prisons were therefore operating at 80 percent above capacity. Today, after a major prison construction program, many state prisons are operating within their capacity, but some state systems are still at 20 percent above capacity or more. The federal prison system is still 37 percent above capacity. Since 1980, Texas has built 120 new prisons, Florida has built 84, and California has built 83. In 1923, there were only 61 prisons in the entire United States.

Figure 14–6 ▸ Incarceration Rates per 100,000 Persons for Selected U.S. Population Groups

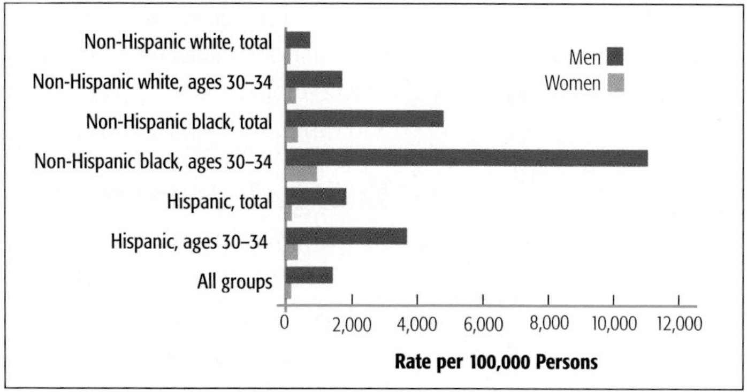

Source: "Prison Inmates at Midyear 2009," *Bureau of Justice Statistics Bulletin,* U.S. Department of Justice (2010).

Effects of Incarceration. When imprisonment keeps truly violent felons behind bars longer, it prevents them from committing additional crimes. The average predatory street criminal commits fifteen or more crimes each year when not behind bars. But most prisoners are in for a relatively short time and are released on parole early, often because of prison overcrowding. Many then find themselves back in prison because they have violated parole, typically by using illegal drugs. Indeed, of the 1.5 million people who are arrested each year, the majority are arrested for drug offenses. Given that from 20 million to 40 million Americans violate one or more drug laws each year, the potential "supply" of prisoners seems almost limitless.

Beyond Our Borders

HOW MANY PEOPLE DO OTHER COUNTRIES SEND TO PRISON?

The United States has more people in jail or prison than any other country in the world. That fact is not necessarily surprising, because the United States also has one of the world's largest total populations. More to the point, the United States has the highest reported incarceration *rate* of any country on earth. North Korea almost certainly has a higher incarceration rate than the United States, but that nation does not report its incarceration statistics. (One human rights organization estimates the North Korean rate as 825 prisoners for every 100,000 inhabitants.) Figure 14–7 on the left compares U.S. incarceration rates, measured by the number of prisoners per 100,000 residents, with incarceration rates in other major countries. The figure for China is not the official figure but an estimate by a human rights group.

Figure 14–7 ▸ Incarceration Rates around the World

Incarceration rates of major nations, measured by the number of prisoners per 100,000 residents.

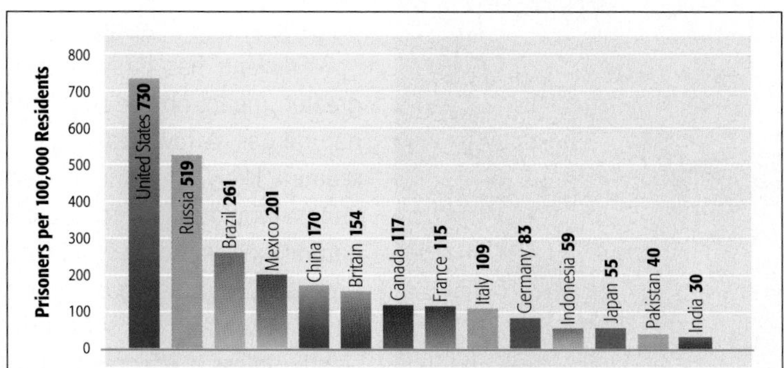

Source: International Centre for Prison Studies, King's College London.

(© kyoshino / iStockphoto) (© mattjeacock / iStockphoto)

■ Learning Outcome 4: **Evaluate the federal government's responses to high oil prices and the controversy over global warming.**

Energy and the Environment

A major part of President Obama's legislative agenda from 2009 to 2012 was directed at energy and environmental issues. Energy policy addresses two major problems: (1) America's reliance on foreign oil, much of which is produced by unfriendly regimes, and (2) global warming purportedly caused by increased emissions of carbon dioxide (CO_2) and other greenhouse gases.

Energy Independence—A Strategic Issue

As of mid-2012, the United States imports about 43 percent of the petroleum it consumes. More than one-third of U.S. imports come from two friendly neighbors, Canada and Mexico, and about one-quarter from Middle Eastern countries, primarily Saudi Arabia. The world's largest oil exporters include a number of nations that are not friends of the United States. Russia is the world's second-largest oil exporter, after Saudi Arabia. Other major exporters include Venezuela and Iran. Both are openly hostile to American interests, and Venezuela is a major source of U.S. oil imports.

While the United States is far from attaining the goal of energy independence, the nation has taken significant steps in that direction. American reliance on foreign oil is down dramatically from what it was only a few years ago. In 2006, almost 60 percent of our oil came from abroad, compared to the current 43 percent. What changes were responsible for this turnaround?

Social Media IN POLITICS

If you check out "fracking" on Twitter, you'll find a large range of tweets for and against the new gas and oil production process.

High Prices and New Production. If the price of a commodity goes up, producers of that commodity have an incentive to produce more of it. The price of gasoline has certainly risen in recent years. In the summer of 2008, before the full impact of the Great Recession, the price of gasoline exceeded $4 for the first time. The price fell during the recession. By the spring of 2011, despite the slow pace of economic recovery, gasoline once again cost more than $4 in many parts of the country. The price has fluctuated since but remains high. Clearly, petroleum producers had an incentive to extract more crude oil, if possible. The question was, could they?

By 2008, some experts doubted that enough new oil could be extracted to keep prices from rising indefinitely. They underestimated the impact of a new technology—*fracking,* short for hydraulic fracturing. Fracking involves injecting a high-pressure solution of water and chemicals into hydrocarbon-bearing rocks, releasing oil or natural gas. The high price of oil made fracking profitable, and it made production from oil sands in Alberta, Canada, affordable as well. (For more on the oil sands, see the *Which Side Are You On?* feature on page 226 in Chapter 7.)

Fracking has had an even greater impact on the supply of natural gas. A few years ago, it seemed likely that the United States would need to import natural gas. Imports would be expensive, because gas cannot be transported by ship efficiently unless it is converted to liquefied natural gas (LNG). By 2012, however, so much natural

(EPA/Jim Lo Scalzo/Landov)

Hydraulic fracturing, or fracking, has transformed many parts of the United States in the last few years. How has this technology changed our energy situation and what are the criticisms of it?

gas was available domestically that the nation had run out of storage space. Plans were under way to export LNG from terminals built to import it. Low natural gas prices plus new air-pollution regulations made coal uncompetitive as a source of electricity. As a result, plans for 168 new coal-based power plants were abandoned, and about 100 existing plants were scheduled for retirement. Despite concerns that fracking might harm drinking-water supplies or otherwise damage the environment, use of the process continues to grow rapidly.

The Politics of Expensive Oil. The high price of gasoline is a political issue, and several presidential candidates claimed that, if elected, they would bring it down. Crude oil prices are set worldwide, however, and the ability of the federal government to affect these prices is very limited. (As noted, natural gas is expensive to transport overseas, so its price has fallen in North America.) Still, the government has taken some steps to encourage increased supplies of gasoline.

President Obama issued higher fuel-efficiency standards for vehicles in 2009 and 2012. By 2016, new cars should average 39 miles per gallon and light trucks should average 30. By 2025, the nation's combined fleet of new cars and light trucks must have an average fuel efficiency of 54.5 miles per gallon.

The federal government also subsidizes the development of alternative fuels. Subsidies to encourage the production of ethanol from corn are controversial. Critics charge that ethanol production is an inefficient method of producing energy. Ethanol also makes food more expensive by driving up the cost of corn. Subsidies for renewable energy sources, such as windmills and solar power panels, have attracted criticisms, too. A problem with wind and especially solar power has been high costs. Prices have fallen rapidly, however, and use of these technologies has risen quickly. Still, they are a small fraction of the nation's power supply.

Disasters in the Energy Industry. For some years, opening new areas for oil and gas drilling has been a major plank in the Republican Party platform. Democrats have been more reluctant, but in March 2010, President Obama announced that major new offshore tracts in the Atlantic would be open to deep-sea drilling. Less than one month later, the BP *Deepwater Horizon* oil spill disaster in the Gulf of Mexico began. The spill, the largest in American history, resulted in a temporary moratorium on new offshore drilling.

Unlike many Democrats, Obama also favored building new energy plants that would use nuclear power. Electric utilities planned several new nuclear plants, but these plans were shelved almost immediately. The major problem was that nuclear power could not compete on cost with natural gas. A second problem was safety. In March 2011, a giant tsunami struck northeast Japan and severely damaged four nuclear reactors located on the coast. The resulting radiation leaks convinced many people that new nuclear power plants would be dangerous. By 2012, every one of Japan's fifty-four reactors had been shut down at least temporarily.

Global Warming

In the 1990s, many scientists working on climate change began to conclude that average world temperatures would rise significantly during the twenty-first century. Gases released by human activity, principally carbon dioxide (CO_2), may be producing a "greenhouse effect," trapping the sun's heat and slowing its release into outer space.

The Global Warming Debate. Most scientists who perform research on the world's climate believe that global warming will be significant, but there is considerable disagreement as to how much warming will actually occur. It is generally accepted that world temperatures have already increased by about 0.74 degrees Celsius over the past century.

The United Nations' Intergovernmental Panel on Climate Change predicts increases ranging from 1.1 to 6.4 degrees Celsius by 2100. This range of estimates is rather wide and reflects the uncertainties involved in predicting the world's climate.

Global warming has become a major political football to be kicked back and forth by conservatives and liberals. Former vice president Al Gore's Oscar-winning and widely viewed documentary on global warming, released in 2006, further fueled the debate. (Gore received the Nobel Peace Prize in 2007 for his work.) Titled *An Inconvenient Truth,* the film stressed that actions to mitigate global warming must be taken now if we are to avert a planet-threatening crisis. Environmental groups and others have been pressing the federal government to do just that.

Their efforts are complicated by the fact that a major share of the American electorate does not believe that global warming is happening or, if it is happening, that it is caused by human activities. Disbelief in global warming is a partisan phenomenon. According to one poll, skepticism about global warming among Republicans rose by 11 percentage points from 2008 to 2009, and a majority of Republicans now believe that global warming does not exist. The opinions of Democrats have not changed—about four-fifths of them accept that global warming is a problem. If there is no global warming, of course, there would be no reason to limit emissions of CO_2 and other greenhouse gases.

Legislative Stalemate. The centerpiece of the Obama administration's legislative program on energy and the environment was a bill designed to limit greenhouse gas emissions. In June 2009, the House passed a 932-page bill replete with concessions to major energy consumers, including utility companies, heavy manufacturers, petroleum refiners, and others. In the Senate, this bill sank without a trace, to the considerable annoyance of House Democratic leaders. Senate attempts to agree on a different bill in 2010 were unsuccessful, and the Republican takeover of the House in the 2010 elections meant that no action on greenhouse gas emissions was likely in the near future.

Despite the lack of government action, CO_2 emissions in 2011 in the United States were actually down from 2008. The most important cause was new power plants using natural gas instead of coal. (Gas does release some CO_2, but less than half as much as coal.) More fuel-efficient cars also contributed to the reduction.

The Politics of Economic Decision Making

■ Learning Outcome 5: **Define *unemployment, inflation, fiscal policy, net public debt,* and *monetary policy.***

Nowhere are the principles of public policymaking more obvious than in the economic decisions made by the federal government. The president and Congress (and to a growing extent, the judiciary) are constantly faced with questions of economic policy. Such issues become especially important when the nation enters a recession.

Good Times, Bad Times

Like any economy that is fundamentally capitalist, the U.S. economy experiences ups and downs. Good times—booms—are followed by lean years. If a slowdown is severe enough, it is called a **recession.** Recessions are characterized by increased **unemployment,** the inability of those who are in the labor force to find a job. The government tries to moderate the effects of such downturns. In contrast, booms are historically associated with another economic problem that the government must address—rising prices, or **inflation.**

Recession
Two or more successive quarters in which the economy shrinks instead of grows.

Unemployment
The inability of those who are in the labor force to find a job; also the number of those in the labor force actively looking for a job, but unable to find one.

Inflation
A sustained rise in the general price level of goods and services.

Measuring Unemployment. Estimates of the number of unemployed are prepared by the U.S. Department of Labor. The Bureau of the Census also generates estimates using survey research data. Critics of the published unemployment rate calculated by the federal government believe that it fails to reflect the true numbers of discouraged workers and "hidden unemployed." There is no exact way to measure discouraged workers, however. The Department of Labor defines them as people who have dropped out of the labor force and are no longer looking for a job because they believe that the job market has little to offer them. To see an alternative depiction of job loss as it occurred in the most recent recession, see Figure 14–8 below. Note that the number of job losses peaked in January 2009, at the very start of the Obama administration. Thereafter, the trend line was up, but that was cold comfort for job seekers. Throughout 2009, the employment picture merely got worse ever more slowly.

Not until 2010 did the economy actually begin creating jobs again, and even then progress was slow and subject to reversals. We discuss the problem of long-term unemployment in the *Politics and Economics* feature on the following page.

Social Media IN POLITICS

If you follow "calculatedrisk" on Twitter, you'll receive a wide range of current data that helps you make sense of the economy.

Inflation. Rising prices, or inflation, can also be a serious economic and political problem. Inflation is a sustained upward movement in the average level of prices. Another way of defining inflation is as a decline in the purchasing power of money over time. The government measures inflation using the *consumer price index,* or CPI. The Bureau of Labor Statistics identifies a market basket of goods and services purchased by the typical consumer, and regularly checks the price of that basket. Over a period of many years, inflation can add up. For example, today's dollar is worth (very roughly) about a twentieth of what it was worth a century ago. In effect, today's dollar is a 1913 nickel.

The Business Cycle. Economists refer to the regular succession of economic expansions and contractions as the *business cycle.* An extremely severe recession is called a *depression,* as in the example of the Great Depression. By 1933, actual output was 35 percent below the nation's productive capacity. Unemployment reached 25 percent. Compared with this catastrophe, recessions since 1945 have usually been mild. Nevertheless, the United States has experienced recessions with some regularity. Recession years since 1960 have included 1970, 1974, 1980, 1982, 1990, 2001, and 2008.

To try to control the ups and downs of the national economy, the government has several policy options. One is to change the level of taxes or government spending. Another possibility involves influencing interest rates and the money side of the economy. We will examine taxing and spending, or **fiscal policy,** first.

Fiscal Policy
The federal government's use of taxation and spending policies to affect overall business activity.

Figure 14–8 ▸ Net Change in U.S. Jobs since 2008

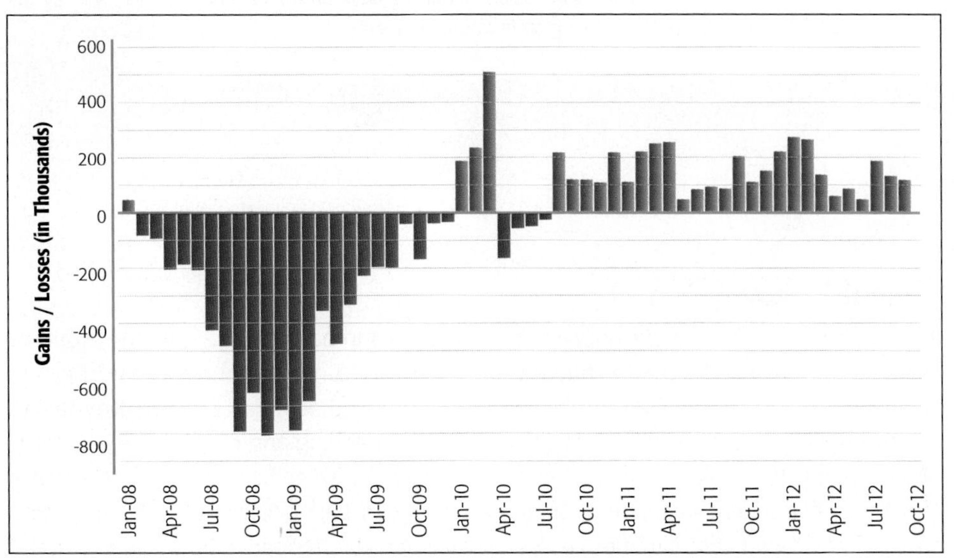

Source: Bureau of Labor Statistics.

Politics AND Economics

THE PROBLEM OF LONG-TERM UNEMPLOYMENT

Although the Great Recession officially ended in 2009, the rate of unemployment remained historically high. Millions of Americans have dropped out of the labor force altogether. Millions of other Americans have been unemployed for longer than six months. They face particular difficulties when trying to find a job.

DISCRIMINATION AGAINST THE LONG-TERM UNEMPLOYED

Many of those who have been unemployed for a long time have experienced discrimination when they attempt to schedule a job interview. Some employers have stated in private that they will not consider applicants who have been unemployed for more than six months. (In some cases, however, these employers may still consider such a job candidate if that person has kept active, for example in volunteer activities.)

At least thirteen states are considering legislation to prohibit employers from discriminating against the long-term unemployed in help-wanted ads. The New York–based National Employment Law Project wants stronger action—it favors an explicit ban on employers and employment agencies that refuse to consider long-term unemployed applicants.

INCREASED GOVERNMENT SPENDING FOR INCOME SECURITY

Although the burden of unemployment falls most heavily on the unemployed themselves, taxpayers also stand to lose. Government expenditures have increased because of the large number of long-term unemployed. At the federal level, income security expenditures rose from about $200 billion in 2007 to almost $440 billion in 2010. The largest share of these income security payments goes to unemployment compensation, Supplemental Security Income, and food stamps (now called the Supplemental Nutrition Assistance Program, or SNAP).

Most of these social programs have been in effect for a long time. To be sure, from 2008 through late 2012, Congress extended the maximum period under which individuals could receive unemployment benefits from twenty-six weeks to thirty-nine weeks and finally to ninety-nine weeks. But Congress issued similar extensions during previous recessions.

Eligibility requirements for one program, however—food stamps—have been reduced significantly in recent years. Until 2002, the food stamp program (SNAP) imposed an *assets test* on potential recipients. If an individual or family had assets such as a savings account, a car, or a house, they could not participate in the program. Many recently unemployed persons simply had assets that were too large to allow them to collect food stamps.

These requirements were relaxed under the Bush administration in 2002 and again in 2008. By 2008, the assets test was effectively repealed. In 2002, only about 20 percent of the households of unemployed persons were participating in SNAP. Today, the figure exceeds 50 percent. SNAP has in effect become a part of the nation's unemployment assistance system.

FOR CRITICAL ANALYSIS

As noted, Congress typically extends the time period for unemployment benefits when unemployment is unusually high. What effect might such payments have on the rate of long-term unemployment?

Fiscal Policy

Keynesian Economics
A school of economic thought that tends to favor active federal government policymaking to stabilize economy-wide fluctuations, usually by implementing discretionary fiscal policy.

Fiscal policy is the domain of Congress. A fiscal policy approach to stabilizing the economy is often associated with the twentieth-century British economist John Maynard Keynes. Keynes (1883–1946) originated the school of thought that today is called **Keynesian economics,** which supports the use of government spending and taxing to help stabilize the economy. (*Keynesian* is pronounced *kayn*-zee-un.) Keynes believed that there was a need for government intervention in the economy, in part because after falling into a recession or depression, a modern economy may become trapped in an ongoing state of less than full employment.

Government Spending and Borrowing. Keynes developed his fiscal policy theories during the Great Depression of the 1930s. He believed that the forces of supply and demand operated too slowly on their own in such a serious recession. Unemployment meant people had less to spend, and because they could not buy things, more businesses failed, creating additional unemployment. It was a vicious cycle. Keynes's idea was simple: in such circumstances, the *government* should step in and engineer the spending that is needed to return the economy to a more normal state.[3]

The spending promoted by the government could take either of two forms. The government could increase its own spending, or it could cut taxes, allowing the taxpayer to undertake the spending instead. To have the effect Keynes wanted, however, it was essential that the spending be financed by borrowing. In other words, the government should run a **budget deficit**—it should spend more than it receives.

Budget Deficit
Government expenditures that exceed receipts.

Discretionary Fiscal Policy. Keynes originally developed his fiscal theories as a way of lifting an economy out of a major disaster such as the Great Depression. Beginning with the presidency of John F. Kennedy (1961–1963), however, policymakers have attempted to use Keynesian methods to "fine-tune" the economy. This is discretionary fiscal policy—*discretionary* meaning left to the judgment or discretion of a policymaker.

Attempts to fine-tune the economy face a timing problem. It takes a while to collect and assimilate economic data. Therefore, time may go by before an economic problem can be identified. After an economic problem is recognized, a solution must be formulated. There will be an action time lag between the recognition of a problem and the implementation of policy to solve it. Getting Congress to act can easily take a year or two. Finally, after fiscal policy is enacted, it takes time for the policy to act on the economy. Because fiscal policy time lags are long and variable, a policy designed to combat a recession may not produce results until the economy is already out of the recession.

Because of the timing problem, attempts by the government to employ fiscal policy in the past fifty years have typically taken the form of tax cuts or increases. Tax changes can take effect more quickly than government spending. In 2009, therefore, the Obama administration was employing an exceptional approach with its economic stimulus spending.

Criticisms of Keynes. There have always been economic schools of thought that consider Keynesian economics to be fatally flawed. These schools argue that either fiscal policy has no effect or it has negative side effects that outweigh any benefits. Some opponents of fiscal policy believe that the federal government should limit itself to monetary policy, which we will discuss shortly. Others believe that it is best for the government to do nothing at all.

It is worth noting that most voters have neither understood nor accepted Keynesian economics. Despite popular attitudes, politicians of both parties accepted Keynesian ideas for many years. Republican president Richard Nixon (1969–1974) is alleged to have said, "We are all Keynesians now." George W. Bush justified many of his policies using Keynesian language. During the first years of Obama's presidency, however, such thinking among Republicans in Congress vanished almost completely. Instead, Republicans rejected countercyclical policies, reflecting the popular belief that during a recession the government should "tighten its belt."

It did not help the Keynesian cause that Obama's economic stimulus package failed to end high rates of unemployment—Keynesian economists argued that the stimulus was less than half of what was needed to accomplish such a goal. When Obama, in his 2010 State of the Union address, employed the belt-tightening metaphor, Keynesians realized that they had lost control of the political discourse.

English economist John Maynard Keynes (1883–1946).

(Walter Stoneman/Samuel Bourne/Getty Images)

3. Robert Skidelsky, *Keynes: The Return of the Master* (New York: Public Affairs, 2010).

During 2011, Obama and the Republicans in the House issued competing federal budget plans that included long-term spending cuts. Republicans also called for immediate cuts in federal and state spending. Yet the unemployment rate remained close to 9 percent, a figure that traditionally would have ruled out short-term efforts to reduce the deficit. As the 2012 elections approached, however, Obama moved away from the theme of deficit reduction and toward a campaign based on opposing economic inequality.

Deficit Spending and the Public Debt

Treasuries
U.S. Treasury securities—bills, notes, and bonds; debt issued by the federal government.

Public Debt, or National Debt
The total amount of debt carried by the federal government.

The federal government typically borrows by selling U.S. Treasury bills, notes, and bonds, known collectively as *Treasury securities* and informally as **treasuries.** The sale of these federal obligations to corporations, private individuals, pension plans, foreign governments, foreign businesses, and foreign individuals adds to this nation's **public debt, or national debt.** In the past few years, foreign governments, especially those of China and Japan, have come to own about 50 percent of the net U.S. public debt. Thirty years ago, the share of the U.S. public debt held by foreigners was only 15 percent.

Deficit Spending. As noted, when the federal government spends more than it receives in revenues, it typically borrows by selling U.S. Treasury securities. Individuals, businesses, and foreigners buy these treasuries. Every time the federal government engages in deficit spending, it increases the size of its total debt.

Can deficit spending go on forever? Certainly, it can go on for quite a long time for the U.S. government. After all, as long as individuals, businesses, and foreigners (especially foreign governments) are willing to purchase Treasury securities, the government can continue to engage in deficit spending. If deficit spending goes on long enough, however, the rest of the world—which owns about 50 percent of all Treasury securities—may lose faith in our government. Consequently, U.S. government borrowing might become more expensive. We, as taxpayers, are responsible for the interest that the federal government pays when it issues treasuries. A vicious cycle might occur—more deficit spending could lead to higher interest rate costs on the U.S. debt, leading in turn to even larger deficits.

So far, however, there has been little sign that such a problem is imminent. On the contrary, following the financial crisis that struck on September 15, 2008, panicked investors piled into treasuries in the belief that these were the safest instruments in existence. The interest that the U.S. government must pay on its borrowing is also very low. In June 2012, the average interest rate on four-week Treasury bills—the shortest-term Treasury obligations—was 0.06 percent—for all practical purposes, an interest rate of zero. Correcting for inflation, anyone buying short-term treasuries was paying the U.S. government for the privilege of making loans to it. After a crisis in which it seemed possible that the government of Greece might default on its debts, investors again began to demand treasuries.

Social Media IN POLITICS

A number of bloggers address economic issues through social media. For a liberal view, see the Facebook page of Matthew Yglesias. For a conservative take, follow Harvard professor Greg Mankiw on Twitter by entering "gregmankiwblog." The politics of both bloggers are moderated by their commitment to economics.

The Public Debt in Perspective. Did you know that the federal government has accumulated trillions of dollars in debt? Does that scare you? It certainly would if you thought that we had to pay it back tomorrow. But we do not.

Gross Public Debt
The net public debt plus interagency borrowings without the government.

Net Public Debt
The accumulation of all past federal government deficits; the total amount owed by the federal government to individuals, businesses, and foreigners.

There are two types of public debt—gross and net. The **gross public debt** includes all federal government interagency borrowings, which really do not matter. This is similar to your taking an IOU ("I owe you") out of your left pocket and putting it into your right pocket. Today, federal interagency borrowings account for about $4.8 trillion of the gross public debt. What is important is the **net public debt**—the public debt that does not include interagency borrowing. Table 14–1 on the facing page shows the net public debt of the federal government since 1950. This table does not take into account two very important variables: inflation and increases in population. A better way to examine the relative importance of the public debt is to compare it with the *gross domestic product (GDP),* as is done in Figure 14–9 on page 468. (Remember from earlier in this chapter that the gross domestic product is the dollar value of all final goods and services produced in a one-year period.) In the figure, you see that the public debt reached its peak during World War II and fell until 1975. From about 1960 to 2008, the net public debt as a percentage of GDP ranged between 30 and 62 percent.

Are We Always in Debt? From 1960 until the last few years of the twentieth century, the federal government spent more than it received in all but two years. Some observers considered those ongoing budget deficits to be the negative result of Keynesian policies. Others argued that the deficits actually resulted from the abuse of Keynesianism. Politicians have been more than happy to run budget deficits in recessions, but they have often refused to implement the other side of Keynes's recommendations—to run a *budget surplus* during boom times.

In 1993, however, President Bill Clinton (1993–2001) obtained a tax increase as the nation emerged from a mild recession. Between the tax increase and the "dot-com boom," the United States had a budget surplus each year from 1998 to 2002. Some commentators predicted that we would be running federal government surpluses for years to come.

Back to Deficit Spending. All of those projections went by the wayside because of several events. One event was the "dot-com bust" followed by the 2001–2002 recession, which lowered the rate of growth of not only the economy but also the federal government's tax receipts. In every recession that we have lived through, tax receipts have always fallen. The "bust" in 2008–2011 was no exception.

A major event took place on September 11, 2001. As a result of the terrorist attacks, the federal government spent much more than it had planned to spend on security against terrorism. Also, the government had to pay for the war in Iraq in 2003 and the occupation of that country thereafter. Finally, Congress authorized major increases in spending on discretionary programs.

The Great Recession dramatically increased the budget deficit and the level of public debt. Tax revenues collapsed, and spending on such items as unemployment compensation rose automatically. In addition, immediately upon taking office, President Obama obtained legislation from Congress that helped push the public debt to levels not seen since World War II. Such high levels of debt became a major political issue.

Table 14-1 ▸ Net Public Debt of the Federal Government

Year	Total (Billions of Current Dollars)
1950	219.0
1960	236.8
1970	283.2
1980	811.9
1990	2,411.6
1995	3,604.4
1996	3,734.1
1997	3,772.3
1998	3,721.1
1999	3,632.4
2000	3,405.3
2001	3,339.3
2002	3,553.2
2003	3,924.1
2004	4,307.3
2005	4,601.2
2006	4,843.1
2007	5,049.3
2008	5,808.7
2009	7,551.9
2010	9,022.8
2011	10,127.0
2012	11,578.1*
2013	12,636.7*

*Estimate.
Sources: 1945–1995, U.S. Office of Management and Budget; 2000–2013, U.S. Treasury.

Monetary Policy

Controlling the rate of growth of the money supply is called **monetary policy.** This policy is the domain of the **Federal Reserve System,** also known simply as the **Fed.** The Fed is the most important regulatory agency in the U.S. monetary system.

The Fed performs a number of important functions. Perhaps the Fed's most important task is regulating the amount of money in circulation, which can be defined loosely as checking account balances and currency. The Fed also provides a system for transferring checks from one bank to another. In addition, it holds reserves deposited by most of the nation's banks, savings and loan associations, savings banks, and credit unions. Finally, it plays a role in supervising the banking industry.

Monetary Policy
The use of changes in the amount of money in circulation to alter credit markets, employment, and the rate of inflation.

Federal Reserve System (the Fed)
The agency created by Congress in 1913 to serve as the nation's central banking organization.

Federal Open Market Committee
The most important body within the Federal Reserve System. The Federal Open Market Committee decides how monetary policy should be carried out.

Organization of the Federal Reserve System. A board of governors manages the Fed. This board consists of seven full-time members appointed by the president with the approval of the Senate. There are twelve Federal Reserve district banks. The most important unit within the Fed is the **Federal Open Market Committee.** This is the body that actually determines the future growth of the money supply and other important economy-wide financial variables. This committee is composed of the members of the Board of Governors, the president of the New York Federal Reserve Bank, and presidents of four other Federal Reserve banks, rotated periodically.

Figure 14-9 ▶ Net Public Debt as a Percentage of Gross Domestic Product

During World War II, the net public debt as a percentage of GDP grew dramatically. It fell thereafter but rose again from 1980 to 1992, under Republicans Reagan and G. H. W. Bush. The percentage fell under Democrat Clinton.

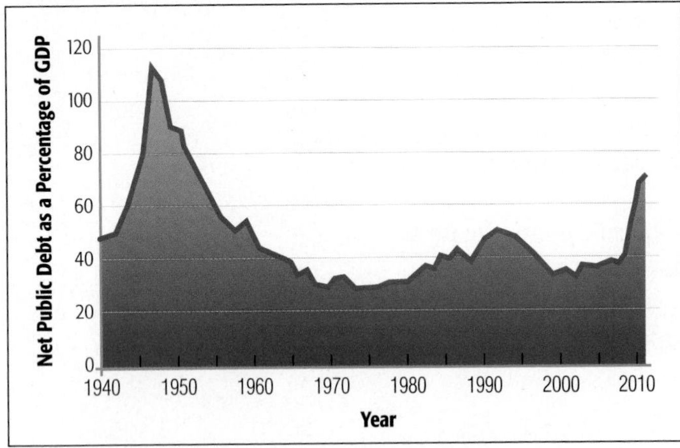

Sources: U.S. Department of the Treasury and Office of Management and Budget.

The Board of Governors of the Federal Reserve System is independent. The president can attempt to influence the board, and Congress can threaten to merge the Fed into the Treasury Department, but as long as the Fed retains its independence, its chairperson and governors can do what they please. Hence, any talk about "the president's monetary policy" or "Congress's monetary policy" is inaccurate. The Fed remains one of the truly independent sources of economic power in the government.

Loose and Tight Monetary Policies. The Federal Reserve System seeks to stabilize nationwide economic activity by controlling the amount of money in circulation. Changing the amount of money in circulation is a major aspect of monetary policy. You may have read a news report in which a business executive complained that money is "too tight" or run across a story about an economist who warned that money is "too loose." In these instances, the terms *tight* and *loose* refer to the monetary policy of the Fed.

Credit, like any good or service, has a cost. The cost of borrowing—the interest rate—is similar to the cost of any other aspect of doing business. When the cost of borrowing falls, businesspersons undertake more investment projects. When it rises, businesspersons undertake fewer projects. Consumers also react to interest rates when deciding whether to borrow funds to buy houses, cars, or other "big-ticket" items.

Loose Monetary Policy Monetary policy that makes credit inexpensive and abundant, possibly leading to inflation.

Tight Monetary Policy Monetary policy that makes credit expensive in an effort to slow inflation.

If the Fed implements a **loose monetary policy** (often called an "expansionary" policy), the supply of credit increases and its cost falls. If the Fed implements a **tight monetary policy** (often called a "contractionary" policy), the supply of credit falls (or fails to grow) and its cost increases. A loose money policy is often implemented to encourage economic growth. You may be wondering why any nation would want a tight money policy. The answer is to control inflation. If money becomes too plentiful too quickly, prices on average increase, and the purchasing power of the dollar decreases.

Time Lags for Monetary Policy. You learned earlier that policymakers who implement fiscal policy—the manipulation of budget deficits and the tax system—experience problems with time lags. The Fed faces similar problems when it implements monetary policy.

Economist Ben Bernanke heads the Federal Reserve. Why is he frequently called to testify before members of Congress?

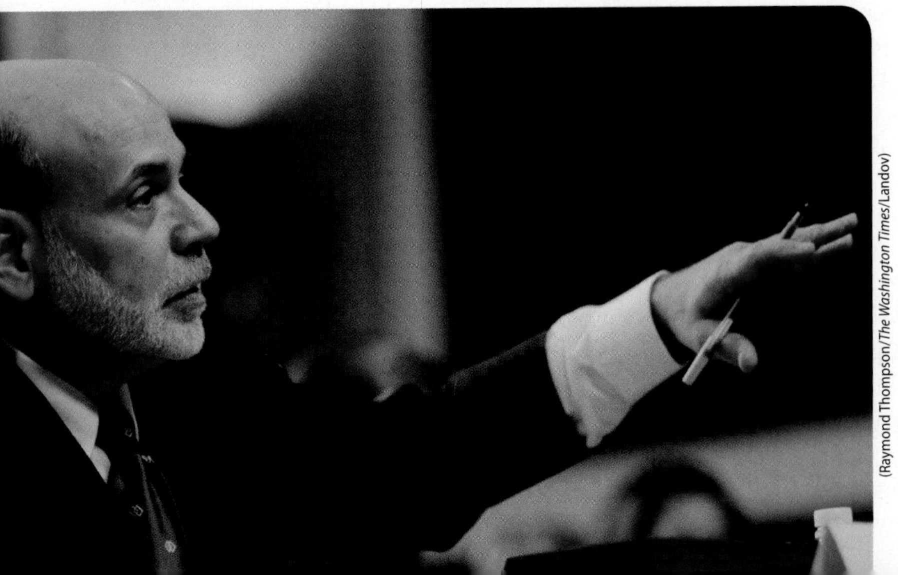

(Raymond Thompson/*The Washington Times*/Landov)

Sometimes, accurate information about the economy is not available for months. Once the state of the economy is known, time may elapse before any policy can be put into effect. Still, the time lag in implementing monetary policy is usually much shorter than the lag in implementing fiscal policy. The Federal Open Market Committee meets eight times a year and can put a policy into effect relatively quickly. A change in the money supply may not have an effect for several months, however.

Monetary Policy during Recessions. A tight monetary policy is effective as a way of taming inflation. (Some would argue that it is the *only* way that inflation can be stopped.) If interest rates go high enough, people *will* stop borrowing. How effective, though, is a loose monetary policy at ending a recession? Under normal conditions, it is very effective. A loose monetary policy will spur an expansion in economic activity.

To combat the Great Recession, however, the Fed reduced its interest rate effectively to zero. It could not go any lower. Yet when consumers had credit, they were still reluctant to make major purchases. Many businesses found that they had little need to borrow to invest in new activities—and no need to hire new staff. Overall demand for goods and services was so low that companies could produce all they needed with their existing capacity and workforce. Monetary policy had run out of steam—using it was like "pushing on a string." The government has little power to force banks to lend, and it certainly has no power to make people borrow and spend. As a result, the Obama administration placed its bets on fiscal policy.

During 2008 and 2009, the Fed developed a new way to respond to the failure of banks to lend. Relying on its ability to create money, it began to make loans itself, without turning to Congress for appropriations. The Fed bought debt issued by corporations. It bought securities that were based on student loans and credit-card debt. By 2009, the Fed had loaned out close to $2 trillion in fresh credit. In 2010 and 2011, the Fed implemented yet another new policy, called *quantitative easing,* in an attempt to make monetary policy more effective. Quantitative easing essentially means buying quantities of long-term treasuries.

Regulating Banks. In addition to managing the money supply, the Federal Reserve has a variety of responsibilities in the area of bank regulation. The Fed ensures that banks have a large enough quantity of reserve capital to back up the loans they are making. It also administers various regulations that protect consumers. In the past, not all banks fell under the regulatory oversight of the Fed. For example, the Fed did not supervise investment banks that do not take deposits from customers. This exemption came to an end in 2008 when the collapse of Bear Stearns, an investment bank, threatened to bring down large numbers of other institutions that had financial ties to the ailing firm. The Fed stepped in to extend Bear Stearns an emergency loan and to force it to sell out to JPMorgan Chase, a much stronger institution, for a nominal price. Subsequently, the president and Congress took action to provide $700 billion to "rescue" other financial firms facing collapse.

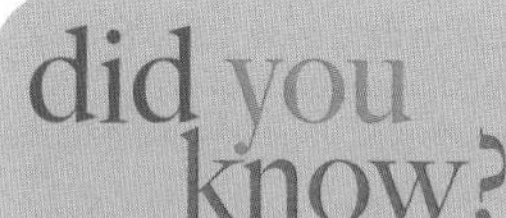

It costs the U.S. Mint 2.41 cents to make a penny and 11.18 cents to make a nickel.

The Politics of Taxes

Federal taxes are enacted by members of Congress. Today, the Internal Revenue Code, which is the federal tax code, encompasses thousands of pages, thousands of sections, and thousands of subsections—our tax system is not very simple.

■ Learning Outcome 6: **Describe the various taxes that Americans pay, and discuss some of the controversies surrounding taxation.**

Americans pay a variety of taxes. At the federal level, the income tax is levied on most sources of income. Social Security and Medicare taxes are assessed on wages and salaries. There is an income tax for corporations, which has an indirect effect on many individuals. The estate tax is collected from property left behind by those who have died. State and local governments also assess taxes on income, sales, and land. Altogether, the value of all taxes collected by the federal government and by state and local governments is about 25 percent of GDP. This is a substantial sum, but it is less than what many other countries collect, as you can see in Figure 14–10 on the following page.

Federal Income Tax Rates

Individuals and businesses pay income taxes based on tax rates. Not all of your income is taxed at the same rate. The first few dollars of income that you earn are not taxed at all. The highest rate is imposed on the "last" dollar you make. This highest rate is the *marginal*

Figure 14–10 ▸ Total Amount of Taxes Collected as a Percentage of Gross Domestic Product (GDP) in Major Industrialized Nations

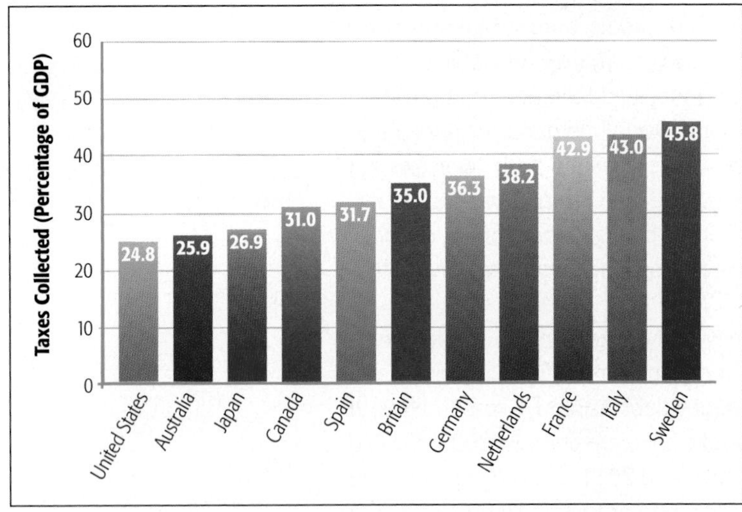

Source: Excerpted and adapted from the Organization for Economic Cooperation and Development.

tax rate. Table 14–2 below shows the 2012 marginal tax rates for individuals and married couples (based on tax forms filed in 2013). The higher the tax rate—the action on the part of the government—the greater the public's reaction to that tax rate. If the highest tax rate you pay on the income you make is 15 percent, then any method you can use to reduce your taxable income by one dollar saves you fifteen cents in tax liabilities that you owe to the federal government.

Individuals paying a 15 percent rate have a relatively small incentive to avoid paying taxes, but consider the individuals who faced a marginal tax rate of 94 percent in the 1940s, during and after World War II. They had a tremendous incentive to find legal ways to reduce their taxable incomes. For every dollar of income that was somehow deemed nontaxable, these taxpayers would reduce tax liabilities by ninety-four cents.

Loopholes and Lowered Taxes

Loophole
A legal method by which individuals and businesses are allowed to reduce the tax liabilities owed to the government.

Individuals and corporations facing high tax rates will adjust their earning and spending behavior to reduce their taxes. They will also make concerted attempts to get Congress to add **loopholes** to the tax law that allow them to reduce their taxable incomes. When Congress imposed very high tax rates on high incomes, it also provided for more loopholes than it does today. For example, special provisions enabled investors in oil and gas wells to reduce their taxable incomes.

Progressive Tax
A tax that rises in percentage terms as incomes rise.

Progressive and Regressive Taxation. As Table 14–2 shows, the greater your taxable income, the higher the marginal tax rate. Persons with large incomes pay a larger share of their income in income tax. A tax system in which rates go up with income is called a **progressive tax** system. The federal income tax is clearly progressive.

Table 14–2 ▸ Marginal Tax Rates for Single Persons and Married Couples (2012)

Single Persons		Married Filing Jointly	
Marginal Tax Bracket	Marginal Tax Rate	Marginal Tax Bracket	Marginal Tax Rate
$ 0–$ 8,700	10%	$ 0–$ 17,400	10%
$ 8,701–$ 35,350	15%	$ 17,401–$ 70,700	15%
$ 35,351–$ 85,650	25%	$ 70,701–$142,700	25%
$ 85,651–$178,650	28%	$142,701–$217,450	28%
$178,651–$388,350	33%	$217,451–$388,350	33%
$388,351 and higher	35%	$388,351 and higher	35%

The income tax is not the only tax you must pay. For example, the federal Social Security tax is levied on all wage and salary income at a flat rate of 6.2 percent. (Employers pay another 6.2 percent, making the total effective rate 12.4 percent.) In 2012, however, there was no Social Security tax on wages and salaries in excess of $110,100. (This "cap" changes from year to year.) Persons with very high salaries, therefore, pay no Social Security tax on much of their wages. In addition, the tax is not levied on investment income (including capital gains, rents, royalties, interest, dividends, and profits from a business). The wealthy receive a much greater share of their income from these sources than others do. As a result, the wealthy pay a much smaller portion of their income in Social Security taxes than do the working poor. The Social Security tax is therefore a **regressive tax.** Note that three-quarters of all taxpayers owe more in payroll taxes, such as Social Security and Medicare taxes, than they do in income taxes.

Regressive Tax
A tax that falls in percentage terms as incomes rise.

The Temporary Payroll Tax Cut. In 2011 and 2012, the portion of the Social Security payroll tax paid by employees was temporarily reduced from 6.2 percent to 4.2 percent. This rate cut was an economic stimulus measure agreed to by President Obama and the Republicans in Congress. While the cut was in line with Keynesian economics, it also appealed to Republican antitax philosophy. The reduction was scheduled to end on the last day of 2012, and its repeal was part of the "taxmageddon" crisis that Congress was forced to address in December 2012. For more details on this crisis, see the *Politics and Economics* feature on page 345 in Chapter 10.

Health-Care Taxes. One aspect of the Patient Protection and Affordable Care Act (Obamacare) is that it raises taxes on upper income persons to offset the act's cost. Beginning in 2013, single taxpayers with more than $200,000 in earned income pay an additional 0.9 percent Medicare tax on all of their income above $200,000. For married taxpayers filing jointly, the tax starts at income above $250,000. Also, single taxpayers with an *adjusted gross income* of more than $200,000 will pay a new 3.8 percent Medicare tax on "unearned" income. Such income includes interest, dividends, rents, royalties, and a variety of other payments. Again, for married taxpayers filing jointly, the tax starts at income above $250,000. Of course, if the Republicans were to succeed in repealing the legislation, these taxes would not go into effect.

Who Pays? The question of whether the tax system should be progressive—and if so, to what degree—is subject to vigorous political debate. Democrats in general and liberals in particular favor a tax system that is significantly progressive. Republicans and conservatives are more likely to prefer a tax system that is proportional or even regressive.

Overall, what kind of tax system do we have? The various taxes Americans pay pull in different directions. The federal estate tax is extremely progressive, because it is not imposed at all on smaller estates. Sales taxes are regressive because the wealthy spend a relatively smaller portion of their income on items subject to the sales tax. Before 2013, the 1.45 percent Medicare payroll tax was entirely flat—that is, neither progressive nor regressive. Because it was not levied on investment income, however, it was regressive overall. The Affordable Care Act, however, turned the tax into a progressive one beginning in 2013, as explained in the previous section. Table 14–3 at right lists the characteristics of major taxes. Add everything up, and the tax system as a whole is slightly progressive. Given all this, should the rich pay even more in taxes? We look at that question in the *Which Side Are You On?* feature on the following page.

Table 14-3 ▸ Progressive versus Regressive Taxes

Progressive Taxes
Federal income tax
State income taxes
Federal corporate income tax
Estate tax
Medicare tax
Regressive Taxes
Social Security tax
State sales taxes
Local real estate taxes

Which Side Are You On?

SHOULD THE RICH PAY EVEN MORE IN TAXES?

The rich have gotten richer during the past few decades—of that we are certain. Go back to 1980. In that year, the top 1 percent of income earners made 9.3 percent of the nation's total income. Thirty years later, the top 1 percent of income earners made more than 20 percent of the nation's income.

WHY SHOULDN'T THE RICH PAY MORE TAXES?

Not only have the rich increased their share of the nation's income, they also have become wealthier. We are increasingly becoming a society divided by class. In the past ten years, the hourly pay of average workers, corrected for inflation, has not risen at all. During the same decade, the number of millionaires and billionaires skyrocketed.

In this context, it seems appropriate to raise taxes on the rich. After all, they are now paying much lower marginal tax rates than during much of the postwar history of the United States. There have been periods when marginal federal income tax rates on the very rich exceeded 90 percent. Today, the rate is 35 percent. In addition, the tax on capital gains, which make up a much larger share of the income of the rich than of other people, is only 15 percent today. Finally, state and local taxes favor the top 1 percent. They pay 8.4 percent of their income to state and local governments, as opposed to 12.4 percent of income paid by those in the bottom 20 percent.

Those who have benefited the most from America's economic system should pay more, particularly when the federal budget deficit is a major concern. Certainly, President Obama has contended that the rich ought to do more to pay down the deficit. The rich argue that they are the "engines of economic growth" and should be encouraged to continue their hard work. Higher taxes, however, are not going to keep the wealthy from striving.

DON'T KILL THE GEESE THAT LAY THE GOLDEN EGGS

It is true that the top 1 percent of income earners now receive more of the national income than they did thirty years ago. Yet in those thirty years, the share of total income taxes paid by the top 1 percent of income earners increased from 18.3 percent to 38 percent. The top 1 percent of income-earning U.S. residents pay more than one-third of all federal income taxes in the United States.

The top-earning 5 percent of taxpayers pay more than the bottom 95 percent—58.7 percent of federal income taxes. The top 50 percent of earners account for 97.3 percent of all income tax paid. The number of those who pay nothing to support the federal government through the income tax continues to rise (although this lower-income group does pay Social Security and Medicare taxes).

An increasingly large number of Americans actually receive more through the federal income tax than they pay. As part of the Earned Income Tax Program, 25 million families and individuals with incomes of up to $48,000 receive payments that substantially reduce their Social Security and Medicare taxes.

If we use taxes to "soak the rich," we will tax the most productive individuals in the country. High marginal tax rates discourage effort. The higher the rate, the greater the discouragement, and this will reduce the rate of economic growth. More income will be redistributed, but is that the ultimate goal of our society? Indeed, Republicans in Congress believe that tax rates on top earners should go down, not up.

(© kyoshino / iStockphoto) (© Dean Mitchell / iStockphoto)

Why Should You Care about... DOMESTIC POLICY?

(Will Seberger/ZUMA Press/Newscom)

This candidate for Congress in Arizona has made the defense of Social Security and Medicaid one of his major campaign planks. Why might this be an effective strategy?

Collectively, programs such as Medicare, Medicaid, Social Security, unemployment compensation, and several others are known as *entitlement programs.* They are called entitlements because if you meet certain qualifications—of age or income, for example—you are entitled to specified benefits. The federal government can estimate how much it will have to pay out in entitlements but cannot set an exact figure in advance. In this way, entitlement spending differs from other government spending. When Congress decides what it will give to the national park system, for example, it allocates an exact sum, and the park system cannot exceed that budget. Along with national defense, entitlements make up by far the greatest share of the federal budget. This fact led a Bush administration staff member to joke: "It helps to think of the government as an insurance company with an army."

ENTITLEMENT REFORM AND YOUR LIFE

What happens to entitlements will affect your life in two major ways. Entitlement spending will largely determine how much you pay in taxes throughout your working lifetime. Entitlement policy will also determine how much support you receive from the federal government when you grow old. Because entitlements make up such a large share of the federal budget, it is not possible to address the issue of budget deficits without considering entitlement spending. Further, as you learned in this chapter, under current policies, spending on Medicare will rise in future years, placing ever-greater pressure on the federal budget. Sooner or later, entitlement reform will be impossible to avoid. However these programs are changed, you will feel the effects in your wallet throughout your life.

HOW YOU CAN MAKE A DIFFERENCE

Should Medicare and Social Security benefits be high, with the understanding that taxes must therefore go up? Should these programs be cut back in the hope of avoiding deficits and tax increases? Do entitlements mean that the old are fleecing the young—or is that argument irrelevant because we will all grow old someday? Progressives and conservatives disagree strongly about these questions. You can develop your own opinions by learning more about entitlement reform. The following organizations take a conservative position on entitlements:

- National Center for Policy Analysis. Find its Web page on entitlement reform by entering "ncpa retirement" into your favorite Internet search engine.
- The Heritage Foundation. See what it has to say by searching on "heritage entitlements."

The following organizations take a liberal stand on entitlements:

- National Committee to Preserve Social Security and Medicare. You can locate the home page of this organization by typing in "ncpssm."
- AARP (formerly the American Association of Retired Persons). To learn this group's position on entitlements, enter "aarp work social."

Questions for Discussion and Analysis

1. Until recently, Congress always opposed the establishment of a universal health-insurance system for the United States. What could the reasons for this stance have been? Are the reasons compelling? What political interests might oppose a universal system, and why?
2. Just how serious an offense should illegal immigration be? Construct arguments in favor of considering it a felony and arguments for viewing it as a mere civil infraction.
3. Should the problem of illegal immigration be addressed by making legal immigration easier? Why or why not?
4. Review the *Which Side Are You On?* feature on page 472. Are the higher income tax rates for wealthy people fair? Why or why not? Is the method of calculating the Social Security tax fair? Why or why not?

Key Terms

budget deficit 465
domestic policy 449
Federal Open Market Committee 467
Federal Reserve System (the Fed) 467
fiscal policy 463
gross domestic product (GDP) 450
gross public debt 466
incarceration rate 458
individual mandate 452
inflation 462
Keynesian economics 464
loophole 470
loose monetary policy 468
Medicaid 450
Medicare 450
monetary policy 467
net public debt 466
Patient Protection and Affordable Care Act 449
progressive tax 470
public debt, or national debt 466
recession 462
regressive tax 471
tight monetary policy 468
treasuries 466
unemployment 462
universal health insurance 451

Chapter Summary

1. Domestic policy consists of all laws, government planning, and government actions that concern internal issues of national importance. Policies are created in response to public problems or public demand for government action. The policymaking process is initiated when policymakers become aware—through the media or from their constituents—of a problem that needs to be addressed by the legislature and the president. The process of policymaking includes five steps: agenda building, policy formulation, policy adoption, policy implementation, and policy evaluation. Policy actions typically result in both costs and benefits for society.
2. Health-care spending accounts for more than 18 percent of the U.S. economy and is growing. Reasons for this growth include the increasing number of elderly persons and advancing technology. A major source of funding is Medicare, the federal program that pays health-care expenses of U.S. residents over the age of sixty-five. The federal government has tried to restrain the growth in Medicare spending.
3. More than 16 percent of the population does not have health insurance—a major political issue. Individual health-insurance policies (not obtained through an employer) are expensive and may be unobtainable at any price. In most wealthy countries, this problem is addressed by a universal health-insurance system under which the government provides basic coverage to all citizens. In 2010, Congress passed a health-care reform package that in time will provide near-universal coverage in the United States. It will require residents not already covered to purchase coverage, which will be subsidized for low-income persons.
4. Today, more than 1 million immigrants enter the United States each year, and about 13 percent of the U.S. population consists of foreign-born persons. Illegal immigrants may number about 11 million. The status of these unauthorized immigrants (the Department of Homeland Security term) is a major political issue. Some people wish to give such persons a legally recognized status and allow them to become citizens someday. Others call for tougher laws against illegal immigration and against hiring illegal entrants.
5. There is widespread concern in this country about violent crime. The overall rate of violent crime has declined since 1995, however. In response to crime concerns, the United States has incarcerated an unusually large number of persons, compared to other countries.

6. Issues concerning energy and the environment are on the nation's agenda today. One problem is our reliance on petroleum imports, given that many petroleum exporters are hostile to American interests. In recent years, however, new production techniques such as fracking have increased the domestic supply of crude oil and especially of natural gas. Global warming, caused by the emission of CO_2 and other greenhouse gases, is a second major problem, although some dispute how serious it actually is.

7. Fiscal policy is the use of taxes and spending to affect the overall economy. Time lags in implementing fiscal policy can create serious difficulties. The federal government has run a deficit in most years since 1960. The deficit is met by U.S. Treasury borrowing. This adds to the public debt of the U.S. government. Although the budget was temporarily in surplus from 1998 to 2002, large deficits now seem likely for many years to come.

8. Monetary policy is controlled by the Federal Reserve System, or the Fed. Monetary policy consists of changing the rate of growth of the money supply in an attempt to either stimulate or cool the economy. A loose monetary policy, in which more money is created, encourages economic growth. A tight monetary policy, in which less money is created, may be the only effective way of ending an inflationary spiral.

9. U.S. taxes are about 25 percent of the gross domestic product. Individuals and corporations that pay taxes at the highest rates will try to pressure Congress into creating exemptions and tax loopholes. Loopholes allow high-income earners to reduce their taxable incomes. The federal income tax is progressive—tax rates increase as income increases. Some other taxes, such as the Social Security tax and state sales taxes, are regressive—they take a larger share of the income of poorer people.

Quiz Multiple Choice

1. The policymaking process includes, but is not limited to:
   - **a. agenda building, policy formulation, and judicial approval.**
   - **b. agenda building, policy formulation, and policy adoption.**
   - **c. agenda building, policy formulation, and state referendums.**

2. Within U.S. borders, there are many illegal immigrants, numbering as high as:
   - **a. 3 million.**
   - **b. 23 million.**
   - **c. 11 million.**

3. The incarceration rate is defined as:
   - **a. the number of people in prison or jail for every 100,000 persons.**
   - **b. the number of people in prison or jail for every 1,000 persons.**
   - **c. the number of people in prison or jail for every 1,000,000 persons.**

4. A major new source of increased energy supplies within the United States comes from:
   - **a. running existing wells at a faster pace.**
   - **b. fracking (hydraulic fracturing).**
   - **c. the new oil boom in Illinois.**

5. Fiscal policy involves:
   - **a. government spending and changes in the money supply in circulation.**
   - **b. government taxation and the changes in the money supply in circulation.**
   - **c. government taxing and spending policies.**

6. Federal government deficit spending leads to:
   - **a. increased taxes and a lower public debt.**
   - **b. increases in the public debt.**
   - **c. increases in government regulation.**

7. Monetary policy in the United States is implemented by:
   - **a. Congress and the president.**
   - **b. Congress and the United States Supreme Court.**
   - **c. the Board of Governors of the Federal Reserve System acting through the Federal Open Market Committee.**

8. The federal personal income tax system can be called:
   - **a. a regressive tax.**
   - **b. a progressive tax.**
   - **c. a degressive tax.**

ANSWERS: 1. b, 2. c, 3. a, 4. b, 5. c, 6. b, 7. c, 8. b.

Quiz Fill-Ins

9. The last two phases of the policymaking process involve policy ____________ and policy ____________.

10. When an economic slowdown is severe enough, it is officially called a ____________, which is characterized by increased ____________.

11. There is a tight relationship between federal government ____________ and the ____________ debt. An increase in the former automatically leads to an increase in the latter.

12. When the Federal Reserve wants to counter a recession, it sometimes engages in ____________ ____________ policy.

13. Fiscal policy and, to a lesser extent, monetary policy do not have their desired effects immediately. Rather, these two policies both suffer from the problem of ____________ ____________.

14. Americans who work for a salary typically pay federal income taxes, as well as ____________ taxes and ____________ taxes.

15. Emissions of carbon dioxide (CO_2) have fallen since 2008 because of the increased use of ____________ ____________ and increased automobile ____________ ____________.

16. Discretionary fiscal policy is often associated with the economic theories of ____________ ____________ ____________.

ANSWERS: 9. implementation; evaluation, 10. recession; unemployment, 11. deficits; public, 12. Loose monetary, 13. time lags, 14. Social Security; Medicare, 15. natural gas; fuel efficiency, 16. John Maynard Keynes.

(© Aleksandar Jovicic/iStockphoto)

Selected Print & Media Resources

SUGGESTED READINGS

Johnson, Simon, and James Kwak. *White House Burning: The Founding Fathers, Our National Debt, and Why It Matters to You.* New York: Pantheon, 2012. The authors provide the history of the national debt, explain why it is a grave problem today, and offer solutions that preserve key social programs. Johnson is an MIT business professor, and Kwak is a law professor at the University of Connecticut.

Krugman, Paul. *End This Depression Now!* New York: W. W. Norton & Company, 2012. Krugman, a Nobel Prize winner and an economics professor at Princeton, is widely considered to be the dean of modern Keynesianism. He argues that the government's failure to adopt sufficiently expansionary fiscal and monetary policies has created a disaster.

Lomborg, Bjørn. *Cool It: The Skeptical Environmentalist's Guide to Global Warming.* New York: Knopf, 2008. Lomborg, a critic of the environmental movement, believes that it would be more practical to take action against global warming later in the century, when the world is (presumably) richer and when renewable energy sources have become more competitive in price.

Miller, Roger LeRoy, *et al.* *The Economics of Public Issues,* 17th ed. Upper Saddle River, N.J.: Prentice Hall, 2011. The authors use short essays of three to seven pages to explain the purely economic aspects of numerous social problems, including health care, the environment, and poverty.

Taylor, John B. *First Principles: Five Keys to Restoring America's Prosperity.* New York: W. W. Norton & Company, 2012. An economics professor at Stanford, Taylor is a leading opponent of expansionary fiscal and monetary policies. Taylor contends that we must return to America's founding principles of economic freedom to place the nation on a sound footing.

MEDIA RESOURCES

An Inconvenient Truth—A 2006 Paramount Classics production of former vice president Al Gore's Oscar-winning documentary on global warming and actions that can be taken in response to this challenge.

De Nadie (Border Crossing)—An award-winning and heartbreaking documentary, this 2007 film follows a group of Central Americans as they attempt to pass through Mexico and enter the United States. Tin Dirdamal is the director.

Sicko—Michael Moore's 2007 effort to take on the U.S. health-care industry. Rather than focusing on the plight of the uninsured, Moore addresses the troubles of those who have been denied coverage by their insurance companies. In his most outrageous stunt ever, Moore assembles a group of 9/11 rescue workers who have been denied proper care and takes them to Cuba, where the government, perfectly aware of the propaganda implications, is more than happy to arrange for their treatment.

(© PashaIgnatov/iStockphoto)

E-mocracy PUBLIC POLICY

Today, the Internet offers opportunities for you to easily access information about any domestic policy issue. The *Logging On* section that follows lists a variety of Web sites where you can learn more about domestic policy issues and how they affect you. Many other sites are available as well. For example, would you like to learn more about prisons and incarceration rates in different countries? The Web site of the International Centre for Prison Studies (ICPS) can help. Find it by entering "prison studies" into a search engine. Would you like to take a turn at proposing a federal budget and allocating spending among different programs, domestic or otherwise? You can find a budget simulation game by searching on "kowal budget." Of course, most news media outlets have their own Web sites, which are useful for keeping up to date on the latest domestic policy developments.

LOGGING ON

1. The National Governors Association offers information on the current status of Medicaid and other topics. For its home page, type in "governors assn."
2. The Federal Bureau of Investigation offers information about crime rates. You can find it by entering "fbi ucr."
3. For information on energy topics, see the Department of Energy Web site by searching on "energy gov."
4. You can keep up with actions taken by the Federal Reserve. Check the home page of the Federal Reserve Bank of San Francisco by typing in "frbsf."
5. For further information on Social Security, access the Social Security Administration's home page by entering "ssa."
6. For information on the 2012 budget of the U.S. government, see the site of the Office of Management and Budget by searching on "omb."

S. ARMY

15 Foreign Policy

Sometimes our foreign and defense policies require that National Guard troops must leave the United States to fight in foreign lands, such as Afghanistan. The troops often have families that they must leave behind. (Jim Weber/ZUMA Press/Corbis)

The five learning outcomes below are designed to help improve your understanding of this chapter. After reading this chapter, you should be able to:

- Learning Outcome 1: **Define *foreign policy,* and discuss moral idealism versus political realism in foreign policy.**
- Learning Outcome 2: **Describe recent foreign policy challenges that involve the use of force, including terrorism and the wars in Afghanistan and Iraq.**
- Learning Outcome 3: **Discuss the use of diplomacy in addressing such issues as nuclear proliferation, the rise of China, the economic crisis in Europe, and the confrontation between Israel and the Palestinians.**
- Learning Outcome 4: **Explain the role of the president, executive agencies, and Congress in making U.S. foreign policy.**
- Learning Outcome 5: **Cite the main themes in the history of U.S. foreign policy.**

(Reuters/Shannon Stapleton)

THESE ARE U.S. ARMY recruits being sworn in. Are they forced to join?

What if... WE BROUGHT BACK THE DRAFT?

BACKGROUND

Young people today have no direct memory of the draft—forced military conscription—because military service became voluntary in 1973. From 1948 to 1973, however, all American males were subject to the draft. Required military service provided large forces to confront the Soviet Union during the Cold War (a period you will read about in this chapter). The draft was used during the war in Vietnam (1965–1975), when it became a heated issue. The idea of bringing back the draft has recently reappeared in public debate. In 2006 and 2007, members of Congress and of George W. Bush's administration suggested that the draft be reinstated. In recent years, however, because of high unemployment and the drawdown of forces in Iraq and Afghanistan, the military has had no difficulty in filling its enlistment quotas. As a result, there has been less talk of a draft.

WHAT IF WE BROUGHT BACK THE DRAFT?

If the draft was reinstated, the U.S. Selective Service would once again be a powerful bureaucratic organization. At the height of the Vietnam War, many young men over the age of eighteen focused much of their attention on avoiding the draft. The same might be true if we brought the draft back today.

Today, the pool of draft-eligible men (and women, if they are included) is much larger than required by the U.S. military. Even though the military has recently been stretched thin, "boots on the ground" are becoming less important as the military continues to evolve toward technological warfare. At the peak of the Vietnam War, there were more than 500,000 U.S. troops in Southeast Asia. As of mid-2012, there were about 90,000 U.S. troops in Afghanistan and 19,000 in the Middle East. Consequently, the Selective Service might have to create more deferments than were available during the Vietnam War.

Another idea is to create a civilian service as an alternative to military service. Persons who opted for such a program might provide care for the elderly or assist with government services in the inner cities.

BENEFITS OF A DRAFT

At various times during the Iraq and Afghanistan wars, the Department of Defense was forced to extend tours of duty for units that were about to be brought home. A draft would prevent these kinds of troop shortages. In particular, a draft would eliminate the unfairness involved in stationing National Guard troops abroad for long periods of time.

If we brought back the draft, the U.S. military would include children of wealthy families, unlike the situation today. In principle, therefore, service to one's country would become more evenly distributed across social and economic classes, promoting fairness. Some argue that a draft would cause Congress and the president to think differently about military operations. If the children of senators and representatives were drafted and sent to dangerous regions, those leaders might be more cautious about going to war.

THE DRAFT AS A TAX ON THE YOUNG

Typically, draftees are paid nominal amounts—less than they could earn in the civilian sector. It is not necessary to pay draftees the relatively high salaries and benefits required to induce young Americans to volunteer for military service. As a result, with a draft, federal expenditures for military pay would decline. The financial burden of staging military actions abroad would fall in part on the draftees themselves. They would effectively be paying a tax consisting of the difference between what they could earn outside the U.S. military and what they were paid by the military.

FOR CRITICAL ANALYSIS

1. *Some argue that the volunteer nature of our U.S. military is responsible for the relatively small antiwar movement in this country today. Why might that be so?*
2. *What alternatives to military service might be possible?*

On September 11, 2001, Americans were forced to change their view of national security and of their relations with the rest of the world—literally overnight. No longer could citizens of the United States believe that national security issues involved only threats overseas or that the American homeland could not be attacked. No longer could Americans believe that regional conflicts in other parts of the world had no direct impact on the United States.

Within a few days, it became known that the 9/11 attacks on the World Trade Center and on the Pentagon had been planned and carried out by a terrorist network named al Qaeda that was directed by the radical Islamist leader Osama bin Laden. The network was closely linked to the Taliban government of Afghanistan, which had ruled that nation since 1996.

Americans were shocked by the success of the attacks. They wondered how our airport security systems could have failed so drastically. Shouldn't our intelligence community have known about and defended against this terrorist network? How could our foreign policy have been so blind to the anger of Islamist groups throughout the world?

In this chapter, we examine the tools of foreign policy and national security policy in light of the many challenges facing the United States today. One such challenge for U.S. foreign policymakers is how best to respond to the threat of terrorism. A question raised by the resulting U.S. military commitments is whether we need to bring back the draft, as we discussed in the chapter-opening *What If . . .* feature. We also review the history of American foreign policy.

■ Learning Outcome 1:
Define *foreign policy,* and discuss moral idealism versus political realism in foreign policy.

Facing the World: Foreign and Defense Policies

The United States is only one nation in a world with almost two hundred independent countries, many located in regions where armed conflict is ongoing. What tools does our nation have to deal with the many challenges to its peace and prosperity? One tool is **foreign policy.** By this term, we mean both the goals the government wants to achieve in the world and the techniques and strategies used to achieve them. These techniques and strategies include **diplomacy, economic aid, technical assistance,** and military intervention. Sometimes foreign policies are restricted to statements of goals or ideas, such as the goal of helping to end world poverty, whereas at other times foreign policies involve comprehensive efforts to achieve particular objectives, such as preventing Iran from obtaining nuclear weapons.

As you will read later in this chapter, in the United States the **foreign policy process** usually originates with the president and those agencies that provide advice on foreign policy matters. Congressional action and national public debate often affect foreign policy formulation as well.

Foreign Policy
A nation's external goals and the techniques and strategies used to achieve them.

Diplomacy
The process by which nations carry on political relations with one another and resolve conflicts by peaceful means.

Economic Aid
Assistance to other nations in the form of grants, loans, or credits to buy the assisting nation's products.

Technical Assistance
The practice of sending experts in such areas as agriculture, engineering, or business to aid other nations.

Foreign Policy Process
The steps by which foreign policy goals are decided and acted on.

National Security Policy
Foreign and domestic policy designed to protect the nation's independence and political integrity; policy that is concerned with the safety and defense of the nation.

Defense Policy
A subset of national security policy having to do with the U.S. armed forces.

National Security and Defense Policies

As one aspect of overall foreign policy, **national security policy** is designed primarily to protect the independence and the political integrity of the United States. It concerns itself with the defense of the United States against actual or potential future enemies.

U.S. national security policy is based on determinations made by the Department of Defense, the Department of State, and a number of other federal agencies, including the National Security Council (NSC). The NSC acts as an advisory body to the president, but it had increasingly become a rival to the State Department in influencing the foreign policy process until the Obama presidency, when Hillary Rodham Clinton became secretary of state.

Defense policy is a subset of national security policy. Generally, defense policy refers to the set of policies that direct the nature and activities of the U.S. armed forces. Defense policy also considers the types of armed forces units we need to have, such as rapid response forces or Marine expeditionary forces, and the types of weaponry that should be developed and maintained for the nation's security. Defense policies are proposed by the leaders of the nation's military forces and the secretary of defense, and these policies are greatly influenced by congressional decision makers.

Diplomacy

Diplomacy is another aspect of foreign policy. Diplomacy includes all of a nation's external relationships, from routine diplomatic communications to summit meetings among heads of state. More specifically, diplomacy refers to the settling of disputes and conflicts among nations by peaceful methods. Diplomacy is also the set of negotiating techniques by which a nation attempts to carry out its foreign policy. Of course, diplomacy can be successful only if the parties are willing to negotiate.

Morality versus Reality in Foreign Policy

Since the earliest years of the republic, Americans have felt that their nation has a special destiny. The American experiment in political and economic liberty, it was thought, would provide the best possible life for its citizens and be a model for other nations. As the United States assumed greater status as a power in world politics, Americans came to believe that the nation's actions on the world stage should be guided by American political and moral principles.

Moral Idealism
A philosophy that sees nations as normally willing to cooperate and agree on moral standards for conduct.

Moral Idealism. This view of America's mission has led to the adoption of many foreign policy initiatives that are rooted in **moral idealism.** This philosophy views the world as fundamentally benign and assumes that most nations can be persuaded to take moral considerations into account when setting their policies.[1] In this perspective, nations should come together and agree to keep the peace, as President Woodrow Wilson (1913–1921) proposed for the League of Nations. Many foreign policy initiatives taken by the United States have been based on this idealistic view of the world. The Peace Corps, which was created by President John F. Kennedy in 1961, is one example of an effort to spread American goodwill and technology.

Political Realism
A philosophy that sees each nation acting principally in its own interests.

Political Realism. In opposition to the moral perspective is **political realism.** Realists see the world as a dangerous place in which each nation strives for its own survival and interests, regardless of moral considerations. The United States must therefore base its foreign policy decisions on cold calculations without regard to morality. Realists believe that the United States must be prepared to defend itself militarily, because other nations are, by definition, dangerous. A strong defense will show the world that the United States is willing to protect its interests.

The practice of political realism in foreign policy allows the United States to sell weapons to military dictators who will support its policies, to support American business around the globe, and to repel terrorism through the use of force.

American Foreign Policy—A Mixture of Both. It is important to note that the United States has never been guided by only one of these principles. Instead, both moral idealism and political realism affect foreign policymaking. At times, idealism and realism can pull in different directions, making it difficult to establish a coherent policy. The so-called Arab Spring of 2011 serves as an example of such crosscurrents in American foreign policy.

1. Eugene R. Wittkopf, Charles W. Kegley, and James M. Scott, *American Foreign Policy*, 7th ed. (Belmont, Calif.: Wadsworth Publishing, 2007).

The Arab Spring: Egypt and Tunisia. Acting on the basis of political realism, the United States had built long-standing relationships with various dictators in the Arab world, including Hosni Mubarak of Egypt. Close relations with Mubarak helped guarantee the peace between Egypt and Israel. Given such alliances, the United States had to determine whether to support existing governments when they came under attack by popular rebellions. The king of Saudi Arabia, for one, demanded that America support its old allies.

President Barack Obama and Secretary of State Hillary Clinton, however, did not believe that realism and idealism were necessarily in conflict. The United States could support democratic movements and remain true to its values. Such a course of action was realistic as well as idealistic because in Egypt and Tunisia, at least, the rebels were winning. Championing popular movements increased the likelihood that America would be on good terms with the new governments in those countries.

(Jamal Nasrallah/EPA/Landov)

Many Syrians fled to Jordan to escape the bloodshed in their own country. Why might the U.S. be concerned about the fighting in Syria?

The Arab Spring: Libya and Syria. Libya proved to be a special challenge, however. In that country, the rebels were immediately successful in taking power only in the eastern region. The United States and its European allies eventually intervened with air power to assist the rebels. By doing so, these nations were able to demonstrate that their support for Arab popular movements was serious and not just rhetorical. Intervention, however, was possible only because the Libyan rebels had liberated at least part of their country.

The rebellion in Syria turned out quite differently. The dictator of that country, Bashar al Assad, was able to retake rebellious cities and neighborhoods by inflicting horrendous casualties on civilians. Short of all-out war against the Syrian regime, foreign governments had little opportunity to affect developments in that country. Western powers did impose sanctions on the Syrian government, but they had little immediate effect. Nevertheless, the rebellion continued into 2012, as previously peaceful rebels began to arm themselves and launch counterattacks. Foreign powers seemed powerless to prevent Syria from descending into a bloody civil war.

Terrorism and Warfare

■ **Learning Outcome 2:** **Describe recent foreign policy challenges that involve the use of force, including terrorism and the wars in Afghanistan and Iraq.**

The foreign policy of the United States—whether idealist, realist, or both—must be formulated to deal with world conditions. Early in its history, the United States was a weak, new nation facing older nations well equipped for war. In the twenty-first century, the United States faces different challenges. Now it must devise foreign and defense policies that will enhance its security in a world in which it is the global superpower. In some instances, these policies have involved the use of force.

The Emergence of Terrorism

Terrorism is a systematic attempt to inspire fear to gain political ends. Typically, terrorism involves the indiscriminate use of violence against noncombatants. We often think of terrorists as nongovernmental agents. The term was first coined, however, to refer to the

Terrorism
A systematic attempt to inspire fear to gain political ends, typically involving the indiscriminate use of violence against noncombatants.

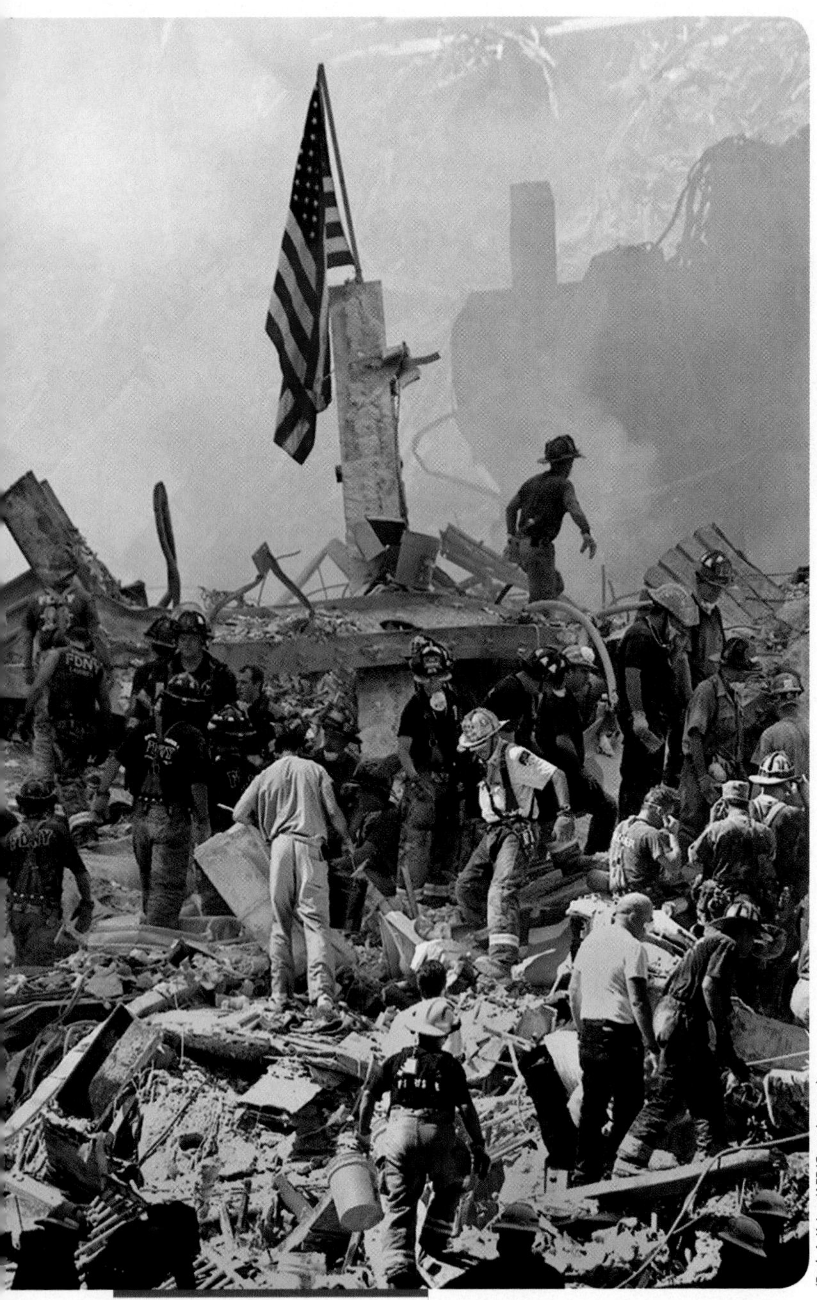

(Beth A. Keiser/AFP/Getty Images)

An American flag stands in the rubble of the World Trade Center towers two days after the September 11, 2001, terrorist attacks. In what ways did the events of 9/11 change U.S. foreign policy?

actions of the radicals who were in control of the government at the height of the French Revolution (1789–1799).

In years past, terrorism was a strategy generally employed by radicals who wanted to change the status of a particular nation or province. For example, over many years the Irish Republican Army undertook terrorist attacks in the British province of Northern Ireland with the aim of driving out the British and uniting the province with the Republic of Ireland. In Spain, the ETA organization has employed terrorism with the goal of creating an independent Basque state in Spain's Basque region. In the twenty-first century, however, the United States has confronted a new form of terrorism that is not associated with such clear-cut aims.

September 11. In 2001, terrorism came home to the United States in ways that few Americans could have imagined. In a well-coordinated attack, nineteen terrorists hijacked four airplanes and crashed three of them into buildings—two into the World Trade Center towers in New York City and one into the Pentagon in Washington, D.C. The fourth airplane crashed in a field in Pennsylvania, after the passengers fought the hijackers.

Why did the al Qaeda network plan and launch attacks on the United States? One reason was that the leaders of the network, including Osama bin Laden, were angered by the presence of U.S. troops on the soil of Saudi Arabia, which they regard as sacred. They also saw the United States as the primary defender of Israel against the Palestinians. The attacks were intended to frighten and demoralize America so that it would withdraw troops from the Middle East.

Al Qaeda's ultimate goals, however, were not limited to forcing the United States to withdraw from the Middle East. Al Qaeda envisioned worldwide revolutionary change, with all nations brought under the theocratic rule of an Islamicist empire. Governments have successfully negotiated with terrorists who profess limited aims—today, radicals associated with the Irish Republican Army are part of a coalition government in Northern Ireland. In contrast, there is no way to negotiate with an organization such as al Qaeda.

Later Islamicist Bombings. Since September 11, 2001, al Qaeda has not succeeded in committing another act of terrorism on American soil. Terrorists influenced by al Qaeda have committed serious crimes in other countries, however. In March 2004, an attack by Islamicist extremists killed 191 people in a railroad bombing in Madrid, Spain. In July 2005, suicide bombers attacked the rapid transit and bus systems in London, with a death toll of 56. Al Qaeda affiliates are responsible for hundreds, perhaps thousands, of deaths in Iraq, Yemen, and other Islamic nations. Almost all of the victims in these countries were Muslims.

The War on Terrorism

After 9/11, President George W. Bush implemented stronger security measures to help ensure homeland security and protect U.S. facilities and personnel abroad. The president sought and received congressional support for heightened airport security, new laws allowing greater domestic surveillance of potential terrorists, and increased funding for the military.

A New Kind of War. In September 2002, President Bush enunciated what became known as the "Bush Doctrine," or the doctrine of preemption. The concept of "preemptive war" as a defense strategy was a new element in U.S. foreign policy. The concept is based on the assumption that in the war on terrorism, self-defense must be *anticipatory*. President Bush stated in March 2003, just before launching the invasion of Iraq, "Responding to such enemies only after they have struck first is not self-defense, it is suicide."

Opposition to the Bush Doctrine. The Bush Doctrine had many critics. Some pointed out that preemptive wars against other nations have traditionally been waged by dictators and rogue states, not democratic nations. By employing such a strategy, the United States would seem to be contradicting its basic values. Others claimed that launching preemptive wars would make it difficult for the United States to pursue world peace in the future. By endorsing such a policy itself, the United States could hardly argue against the decisions of other nations to do likewise when they felt potentially threatened.

Wars in Iraq

In 1990, the Persian Gulf became the setting for a major challenge to the international system set up after World War II (1939–1945). President Saddam Hussein of Iraq sent troops into the neighboring oil sheikdom of Kuwait, occupying that country. This was the most clear-cut case of aggression against an independent nation in half a century.

The First Gulf War. At the request of Saudi Arabia, American troops were dispatched to set up a defensive line at the Kuwaiti border. In January 1991, U.S.-led coalition forces launched a massive air attack on Iraq. After several weeks, the ground offensive began. Iraqi troops retreated from Kuwait a few days later, and the First Gulf War ended.

As part of the cease-fire that ended the First Gulf War, Iraq agreed to allow United Nations (UN) weapons inspectors to oversee the destruction of its missiles and any chemical and nuclear weapons. Economic sanctions would be imposed on Iraq until the weapons inspectors finished their work. In 1999, however, Iraq placed so many obstacles in the path of the UN inspectors that they withdrew from the country.

The Second Gulf War—The Iraq War. In 2002 and early 2003, President Bush called for a "regime change" in Iraq and began assembling an international coalition that might support further military action in Iraq. Bush was unable to convince the UN Security Council that military force was necessary in Iraq, so the United States took the initiative. In March 2003, U.S. and British forces invaded Iraq and within a month had toppled Hussein's decades-old dictatorship. The process of establishing order and creating a new government in Iraq turned out to be extraordinarily difficult, however.

Occupied Iraq. The people of Iraq are divided into three principal ethnic groups. The Kurdish-speaking people of the north were overjoyed by the invasion. The Arabs adhering to the Shiite branch of Islam live principally in the south

In parts of Afghanistan, former Taliban rebels turned in their weapons at the local police stations. U.S. combat involvement in that country was scheduled to end in 2014.

(AP Photo/Hoshang Hashimi, File)

and constitute a majority of the population. The Shiites were glad that Saddam Hussein, who had murdered many thousands of Shiites, was gone. They were deeply skeptical of U.S. intentions, however. The Arabs belonging to the Sunni branch of Islam live mainly to the west of Baghdad. Although the Sunnis constitute only a minority of the population, they had controlled the government under Hussein. Many of them considered the occupation to be a disaster.

Social Media IN POLITICS

The armed forces all have their own Facebook pages. For example, search on "US army." Although official, the page contains a vast array of posts and information.

The Insurgency. In short order, a Sunni guerrilla insurgency arose and launched attacks against the coalition forces. Occupation forces also came under attack by Shiite forces loyal to Muqtada al Sadr, a radical cleric. Coalition forces were soon suffering monthly casualties comparable to those experienced during the initial invasion. Iraq had begun to be a serious political problem for President Bush. By May 2004, a majority of Americans no longer believed that going to war had been the right thing to do.

The Threat of Civil War. At the time of the invasion, al Qaeda did not exist in Iraq. Ironically, the occupation of Iraq soon led to the establishment of an al Qaeda operation in that country, which sponsored suicide bombings and other attacks against coalition troops and the forces of the newly established Iraqi government. Al Qaeda did not limit its hostility to the Americans but issued vitriolic denunciations of the Iraqi Shiites. Rhetoric was followed by violence. While Sunni and Shiite insurgents continued to launch attacks on coalition forces, the major bloodletting in the country now took place between Sunnis and Shiites. By late 2006, polls indicated that about two-thirds of Americans wanted to see an end to the Iraq War—a sentiment expressed in the 2006 elections.

Iraqi Endgame. In January 2007, President Bush announced a major increase, or "surge," in U.S. troop strength. He placed General David Petraeus, the U.S. Army's leading counterinsurgency expert, in charge of all forces in Iraq. Skeptics doubted that either Petraeus or the new troop levels would have much effect on the outcome.

In April 2007, however, Sunni tribal leaders rose up against al Qaeda and called in U.S. troops to help them. The new movement, called the Awakening, spread rapidly. Al Qaeda, it seems, had badly overplayed its hand by terrorizing the Sunni population. Also, in March 2008 the Iraqi government launched an operation to drive Muqtada al Sadr's Shiite militia out of the southern city of Basra. The government forces ultimately prevailed.

During subsequent months, the Iraqi government gained substantial control over its own territory. Still, American attitudes toward the war remained negative. Democratic candidate Barack Obama had opposed the Iraq War from the start, and he called for setting a deadline for the withdrawal of U.S. forces. In 2008, President Bush and Iraqi prime minister Nouri al Maliki negotiated such a deadline. The difference between Obama's position and that of Bush was now merely a matter of months. In February 2009, President Obama announced that U.S. combat forces would leave Iraq by August 2010, and the rest of the American troops would be out by the end of 2011.

General David Petraeus presents his assessment of the situation in Iraq to a congressional committee in 2009. In 2010, Petraeus was named head of our forces in Afghanistan. Who ultimately decides the leadership of our military missions?

(Alex Wong/Getty Images)

War in Afghanistan

The Iraq War was not the only military effort launched by the Bush administration as part of the war on terrorism. The first military effort was directed against al Qaeda camps in Afghanistan and the Taliban regime, which had ruled most of Afghanistan since 1996. In late 2001, after building a coalition of international allies and anti-Taliban rebels within Afghanistan, the United States began an air campaign against the Taliban regime. The anti-Taliban rebels, known as the Northern Alliance, were able to take Kabul, the capital, and oust the Taliban from power. The United States and other members of the international community then fostered the creation of an elected Afghan government.

The Return of the Taliban. The Taliban were defeated, but not destroyed. U.S. forces were unable to locate Osama bin Laden and other top al Qaeda leaders. The Taliban and al Qaeda both retreated to the rugged mountains between Afghanistan and Pakistan, where they were able to establish bases on the Pakistani side of the border. In 2003, the Taliban began to launch attacks against Afghan soldiers, foreign aid workers, and even American troops. Despite increases in coalition forces, the Taliban continued to gain strength. Through 2008 and 2009, the Taliban were able to take over a number of Pakistani districts, even as the United States began attacking suspected Taliban and al Qaeda targets in Pakistan using small unmanned aircraft called drones. In 2009, the government of Pakistan initiated military action in an attempt to retake Taliban-controlled districts.

Obama and Afghanistan. In his presidential campaign, Barack Obama called for increased American troop levels to deal with the emergency, and as president, in February 2009 he dispatched seventeen thousand additional soldiers to Afghanistan. During that year, the administration conducted a policy review of the war. In December 2009, Obama announced that he would send an additional thirty thousand troops to Afghanistan but would begin troop withdrawals in July 2011.

(Reuters/Pentagon)

Osama bin Laden was public enemy number one during Bush's presidency and part of Obama's. He was assassinated in May 2011.

The Death of bin Laden. The CIA and other U.S. intelligence forces were unable to develop information on Osama bin Laden's whereabouts until 2010. In that year and in 2011, the intelligence agencies obtained evidence that bin Laden might be living in a highly secure residential compound in Abbottabad, Pakistan. Pakistan's military academy is located in Abbottabad, which led many observers to surmise that bin Laden was living under the protection of members of Pakistan's military.

On May 1, 2011, U.S. Navy SEALs launched a helicopter raid on the compound from bases in Afghanistan. In a brief firefight, the SEALs killed bin Laden and four others. The SEALs also collected much intelligence material. The only hitch in the operation was that one of the helicopters crashed on landing. No one was seriously injured, but the commandos had to destroy the damaged helicopter because it was an advanced model that employed classified technology.

Americans responded to President Obama's announcement of the operation with relief and satisfaction. Reactions in Pakistan itself were mostly negative—the raid was generally seen as a violation of Pakistan's sovereignty.

■ Learning Outcome 3: **Discuss the use of diplomacy in addressing such issues as nuclear proliferation, the rise of China, the economic crisis in Europe, and the confrontation between Israel and the Palestinians.**

U.S. Diplomatic Efforts

The United States has dealt with many international problems through diplomacy, rather than the use of armed force. Some of these issues include the proliferation of nuclear weapons, the growing power of China, and the confrontation between Israel and the

did you know?

Including the Civil War, more than 1 million American soldiers have been killed in the nation's wars.

Cold War
The ideological, political, and economic confrontation between the United States and the Soviet Union following World War II.

Palestinians. Economic and humanitarian concerns can also be addressed through diplomacy.

Nuclear Weapons

In 1945, the United States was the only nation to possess nuclear weapons. Several nations quickly joined the "nuclear club," however, including the Soviet Union in 1949, Britain in 1952, France in 1960, and China in 1964. Few nations have made public their nuclear weapons programs since China's successful test of nuclear weapons in 1964. India and Pakistan, however, detonated nuclear devices within a few weeks of each other in 1998, and North Korea conducted an underground nuclear explosive test in October 2006. Several other nations are suspected of possessing nuclear weapons or the capability to produce them in a short time. Israel is known to possess more than one hundred nuclear warheads.

With nuclear weapons, materials, and technology available worldwide, it is conceivable that terrorists could obtain a nuclear device and use it in a terrorist act. In fact, a U.S. federal indictment filed in 1998, after the attack on the American embassies in Kenya and Tanzania, charged Osama bin Laden and his associates with trying to buy components for making a nuclear bomb "at various times" since 1992.

Nuclear Stockpiles. More than twenty-two thousand nuclear warheads are known to be stockpiled worldwide, although the exact number is uncertain because some countries do not reveal the extent of their holdings. Although the United States and Russia have dismantled many of their nuclear weapons systems since the end of the **Cold War** and the dissolution of the Soviet Union in 1991 (discussed later in this chapter), both still retain sizable nuclear arsenals. More alarming is the fact that, since the dissolution of the Soviet Union, the security of its nuclear arsenal has declined. There have been reported thefts, smugglings, and illicit sales of nuclear material from the former Soviet Union in the past two decades.

North Korean leader Kim Jong-un and his wife Ri Sol-ju attend the opening ceremony of the Rungna People's Pleasure Ground in Pyongyang.

(KCNA KCNA/Reuters)

Nuclear Proliferation: Iran. For years, the United States, the European Union, and the UN have tried to prevent Iran from becoming a nuclear power. In spite of these efforts, many observers believe that Iran is now in the process of developing nuclear weapons—although Iran maintains that it is interested in developing nuclear power only for peaceful purposes. Continued diplomatic attempts to at least slow down Iran's quest for a nuclear bomb have so far proved ineffectual. The group of nations attempting to talk with Iran includes Britain, China, France, Germany, Russia, and the United States. By 2009, the UN Security Council had already voted three rounds of sanctions against Iran in reaction to its nuclear program.

One problem with the attempt to develop meaningful international sanctions was resistance from Russia and China. By 2010, Russia appeared to have lost patience with Iran, but China was able to limit the impact of the new UN sanctions imposed in that year. China is often reluctant to impose sanctions, and Iran is one of China's major trading partners.

By 2012, it was clear that sanctions against Iran were beginning to damage that country's economy. Of special importance was the U.S. campaign to persuade other nations to stop importing Iranian oil, which enjoyed increasing success. Threats that Israel or even the United States might bomb Iran's nuclear sites added to the pressure. In Washington, D.C., and in Israel, a debate was under way: Should diplomacy be allowed to take its course—or would the use of armed force be necessary to stop Iran from developing nuclear weapons? We discuss that issue in the *Which Side Are You On?* feature on the facing page.

Which Side Are You On?

SHOULD AMERICA—OR ISRAEL—ATTACK IRAN'S NUCLEAR SITES?

(© kyoshino / iStockphoto) (© Dean Mitchell / iStockphoto)

Since at least 2002, Western intelligence services contend that Iran is attempting to develop nuclear weapons. Iran denies this claim, of course. Iran's supreme leader, Ayatollah Ali Khamenei, has even issued a *fatwa* (an Islamic legal ruling) stating that the production and use of nuclear weapons are forbidden under Islam. The Iranian government claims that its uranium enrichment program is aimed only at developing nuclear power. Yet Iran appears to be enriching uranium well past the level needed to fuel a nuclear reactor—its enrichment program is close to producing weapons-grade material.

For several years, Israel has stated that it is prepared to bomb Iranian nuclear sites rather than let that nation obtain nuclear weapons. These threats of action became especially pointed beginning in 2011. Some politicians in the United States have argued that we should support Israel in launching a preemptive strike at Iran's uranium enrichment facilities. Bear in mind that, more than any other nation, Israel may be at risk from a nuclear-equipped Iran. In 2005, Iranian president Mahmoud Ahmadinejad made a statement that was widely translated as "Israel should be wiped off the map." A more accurate translation was "The government of Israel should vanish from the pages of time," a sentiment only marginally less alarming.

THE TIME IS NOW—DESTROY IRAN'S ENRICHMENT SITES

The position of the hawks on this issue is clear: The longer we wait, the harder it will be to destroy Iran's numerous, well-protected, and widely dispersed uranium enrichment facilities. Israel is clearly ready to take the lead but needs U.S. support, not to mention U.S.-supplied "bunker buster" bombs. The hawks do not believe that Iran can retaliate by launching a Middle Eastern war. They point out that the United States has at least two aircraft carriers in the region that would go into action immediately if Iranian aircraft threatened Israel. The fact is, the world cannot allow a nuclear-armed Iran because that country's leaders will attempt to annihilate Israel. Those leaders will also be willing to sell their technology to terrorists.

IRAN IS NOT FOOLISH ENOUGH TO USE A NUCLEAR BOMB

The doves on this issue contend that air strikes could only slow down Iran's nuclear development, not stop it altogether. Doves also do not believe that Iranian leaders would commit national suicide by using nuclear bombs against Israel. Historically, nations have become more risk averse once they acquired nuclear weapons. If Israel, with the support of the United States, were to engage in air strikes against Iran, that nation would respond furiously. Oil shipping in the region would come to a halt. Extremists in many Middle Eastern countries would use the Israeli bombing as an excuse to set the region ablaze. The people of Iran would rally around their leaders—and Iran would now have an even greater motivation to develop nuclear weapons. The majority of Israelis do not want their government to bomb Iran. Why should we?

Nuclear Proliferation: North Korea. North Korea tested a nuclear device in 2006. An agreement reached in February 2007 provided that North Korea would start disabling its nuclear facilities and allow UN inspectors into the country. In return, China, Japan, Russia, South Korea, and the United States—the other members of the six-party negotiations—would provide aid to North Korea. North Korea, however, was allowed to keep its nuclear arsenal, which American intelligence officials believe may include as many as six nuclear bombs or the fuel to make them. In July 2007, North Korea dismantled one of its nuclear reactors and admitted UN inspectors into the country. In October 2008, the United States removed North Korea from its list of states that sponsor terrorism.

By 2009, however, North Korea was pulling back from its treaty obligations. In April, the country tested a long-range missile capable of delivering a nuclear warhead, in violation of a UN Security Council demand that it halt such tests. After the Security Council

Social Media IN POLITICS

If you search on "foreign policy" on Facebook, you'll go to the Facebook page of *Foreign Policy* magazine. It has information on a wide variety of foreign policy topics.

rapidly gained ascendancy over William Rogers, the secretary of state. More recently, Condoleezza Rice played an important role as national security adviser during George W. Bush's first term. Like Kissinger, Rice eventually became secretary of state.

Intelligence Community The government agencies that gather information about the capabilities and intentions of foreign governments or that engage in covert actions.

The Intelligence Community. No discussion of foreign policy would be complete without some mention of the **intelligence community.** This consists of the forty or more government agencies and bureaus that are involved in intelligence activities. The CIA, created as part of the National Security Act of 1947, is the key official member of the intelligence community.

did you know?

In the name of national security, the United States spends at least $11.4 billion annually to keep information classified.

Covert Actions. Intelligence activities consist mostly of overt information gathering, but covert actions also are undertaken. Covert actions, as the name implies, are carried out in secret, and the American public rarely finds out about them. The CIA covertly aided in the overthrow of the Mossadegh regime in Iran in 1953 and was instrumental in destabilizing the Allende government in Chile from 1970 to 1973.

During the mid-1970s, the "dark side" of the CIA was partly uncovered when the Senate undertook an investigation of its activities. One of the major findings of the Senate Select Committee on Intelligence was that the CIA had routinely spied on American citizens domestically, supposedly a prohibited activity. Consequently, the CIA came under the scrutiny of oversight committees within Congress.

By 2001, the agency had come under fire again. Problems included the discovery that one of its agents had been spying on behalf of a foreign power, the inability of the agency to detect the nuclear arsenals of India and Pakistan, and, above all, its failure to obtain advance knowledge about the 9/11 terrorist attacks.

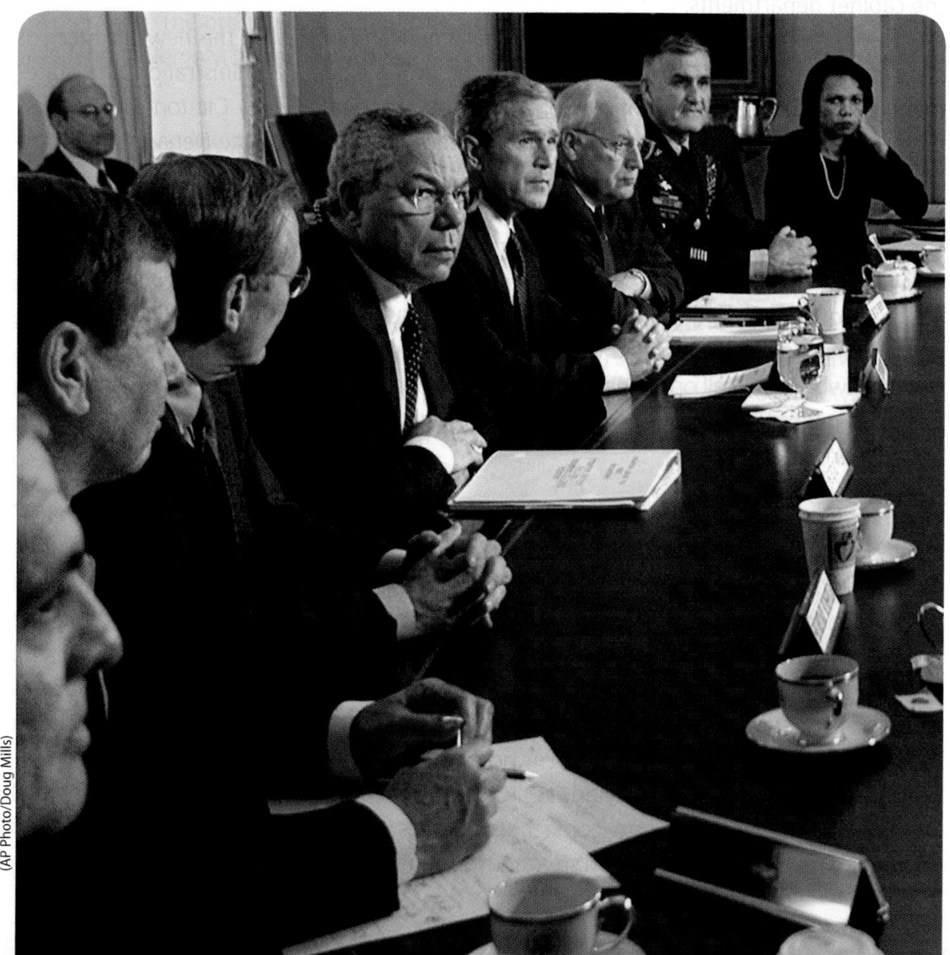

President Bush is shown with his National Security Council (NSC) the day after the terrorist attacks on September 11, 2001. At that time, the NSC consisted of the director of the Central Intelligence Agency, the secretary of defense, the secretary of state, the vice president, the chairman of the joint chiefs of staff, and, of course, the national security adviser. How important is the NSC's role in determining U.S. foreign policy?

(AP Photo/Doug Mills)

The Intelligence Community and the War on Terrorism. With the rise of terrorism as a threat, the intelligence agencies have received more funding and enhanced surveillance powers, but these moves have also provoked fears of civil liberties violations. Legislation enacted in 2004 established the Office of the Director of National Intelligence to oversee the intelligence community.

A simmering controversy that came to a head in 2009 concerned the CIA's use of a technique called *waterboarding* while interrogating several prisoners in the years immediately following 9/11. Before 9/11, the government had defined waterboarding as a form of torture, but former vice president Dick Cheney, a public advocate of the practice, denied that it was. One concern was whether Bush administration officials would face legal action as a result of the practice. In May 2009, President Obama, even as he denounced waterboarding, assured CIA employees that no member of the agency would be penalized for following Justice Department rulings that had legitimized harsh interrogation methods. The Obama administration also declined to pursue cases against the Justice Department officials who made those rulings.

The Department of Defense. The Department of Defense (DOD) was created in 1947 to bring all of the various activities of the American military establishment under the jurisdiction of a single department headed by a civilian secretary of defense. At the same time, the joint chiefs of staff, consisting of the commanders of the various military branches and a chairperson, was created to formulate a unified military strategy.

Although the Department of Defense is larger than any other federal department, it declined in size after the fall of the Soviet Union in 1991. In the subsequent ten years, the total number of civilian employees was reduced by about 400,000, to approximately 665,000. After 9/11, the war on terrorism and combat in Afghanistan and Iraq drove the defense budget up again. The budget leveled off in 2012, however, and as a result of attempts to reduce the federal budget deficit, it may actually decline in 2014.

(AP Photo)

This aerial view of the five-sided Pentagon building shows where many of the defense personnel work in Arlington, Virginia. The Pentagon covers an area of twenty-nine acres. When was the Department of Defense created?

Congress Balances the Presidency

A new interest in the balance of power between Congress and the president on foreign policy questions developed during the Vietnam War. Sensitive to public frustration over the long and costly war and angry at Richard Nixon for some of his other actions as president, Congress attempted to establish limits on the power of the president in setting foreign and defense policy.

The War Powers Resolution of 1973. In 1973, Congress passed the War Powers Resolution over President Nixon's veto. The act limited the president's use of troops in military action without congressional approval (see Chapter 11). Most presidents, however, have not interpreted the "consultation" provisions of the act as meaning that Congress should be consulted before military action is taken. Instead, Presidents Ford, Carter, Reagan, George H. W. Bush, and Clinton ordered troop movements and then informed congressional leaders.

The War Powers Resolution was in the news again in May 2011, sixty days after the United States and several European nations began providing air support to the rebels in

Libya. Sixty days was the deadline for President Obama to seek congressional support for military action. Obama, however, claimed that no authorization was needed because U.S. activities did not amount to "hostilities." In June, the House passed a resolution rebuking the president, but the Senate refused to consider it.

Monroe Doctrine
A policy statement by President James Monroe in 1823, which set out three principles: (1) European nations should not establish new colonies in the Western Hemisphere, (2) European nations should not intervene in the affairs of independent nations of the Western Hemisphere, and (3) the United States would not interfere in the affairs of European nations.

Isolationist Foreign Policy
A policy of abstaining from an active role in international affairs or alliances, which characterized U.S. foreign policy toward Europe during most of the 1800s.

The Power of the Purse. One of Congress's most significant constitutional powers is the so-called power of the purse. The president may order that a certain action be taken, but that order cannot be executed unless Congress funds it. When the Democrats took control of Congress in January 2007, many asked whether the new Congress would use its power of the purse to bring an end to the Iraq War, in view of strong public opposition to the war. Congress's decision was to add conditions to a war-funding request submitted by the president. The conditions required the president to establish timelines for the re-deployment of American troops in Iraq. Bush immediately threatened to veto any bill that imposed conditions on the funding. His threat carried the day.

In this circumstance, the power of Congress was limited by political considerations. Congress did not even consider the option of refusing to fund the war altogether. For one thing, there was not enough support in Congress for such an approach. For another, the Democrats did not want to be accused of placing the troops in Iraq in danger. Additionally, the threat of a presidential veto significantly limited Congress's power. The Democrats simply did not have a large enough majority to override a veto.

■ Learning Outcome 5:
Cite the main themes in the history of U.S. foreign policy.

The Major Foreign Policy Themes

Although some observers might suggest that U.S. foreign policy is inconsistent and changes with the current occupant of the White House, the long view of American diplomatic ventures reveals some major themes underlying foreign policy. In the early years of the nation, presidents and the people generally agreed that the United States should avoid foreign entanglements and concentrate instead on its own development. From the beginning of the twentieth century until the present, however, a major theme has been increasing global involvement. The theme of the post–World War II years was the containment of communism. The theme for at least the first part of the twenty-first century is countering terrorism, as we discussed earlier in this chapter.

James Monroe, the fifth president, is associated most commonly with what foreign policy doctrine?

(AP Photo)

The Formative Years: Avoiding Entanglements

The founders of the United States had a basic mistrust of European governments. This was a logical position at a time when the United States was so weak militarily that it could not influence European developments directly. Moreover, being protected by oceans that took weeks to cross certainly allowed the nation to avoid entangling alliances. During the 1800s, therefore, the United States generally stayed out of European conflicts and politics. In the Western Hemisphere, however, the United States pursued an active expansionist policy. The nation purchased Louisiana in 1803, annexed Texas in 1845, gained substantial territory from Mexico in 1848, purchased Alaska in 1867, and annexed Hawaii in 1898.

The Monroe Doctrine. President James Monroe, in his message to Congress on December 2, 1823, stated that the United States would not accept any new European intervention in the Western Hemisphere. In return, the United States would not meddle in European affairs. The **Monroe Doctrine** was the underpinning of the U.S. **isolationist foreign policy** toward Europe, which continued throughout the 1800s.

The Spanish-American War and World War I. The end of the isolationist policy started with the Spanish-American War in 1898. Winning the war gave the United States possession of Guam, Puerto Rico, and the Philippines (which gained independence in 1946). On the heels of that war came World War I (1914–1918). The United States declared war on Germany in April 1917, because that country refused to give up its campaign of sinking all ships headed for Britain, including passenger ships from America. (Large passenger ships of that time commonly held over a thousand people, so the sinking of such a ship was a disaster comparable to the attack on the World Trade Center.)

In the 1920s, the United States went "back to normalcy," as President Warren G. Harding urged it to do. U.S. military forces were largely disbanded, defense spending dropped to about 1 percent of the total annual national income, and the nation returned to a period of isolationism.

The Era of Internationalism

Isolationism was permanently shattered by the bombing of the U.S. naval base at Pearl Harbor, Hawaii, on December 7, 1941. The surprise attack by the Japanese caused the deaths of 2,403 American servicemen and wounded 1,143 others. Eighteen warships were sunk or seriously damaged, and 188 planes were destroyed at the airfields. President Franklin Roosevelt asked Congress to declare war on Japan immediately, and the United States entered World War II.

At the conclusion of the war, the United States was the only major participating country to emerge with its economy intact, and even strengthened. The United States was also the only country to have control over operational nuclear weapons. President Harry Truman had made the decision to use two atomic bombs in August 1945 to end the war with Japan. (Historians still argue over the necessity of this action, which ultimately killed more than 100,000 Japanese and left an equal number permanently injured.) The United States truly had become the world's superpower.

The Cold War. The United States had become an uncomfortable ally of the Soviet Union after Adolf Hitler's invasion of that country. Soon after World War II ended, relations between the Soviet Union and the West deteriorated. The Soviet Union wanted a weakened Germany, and to achieve this, it insisted that Germany be divided in two, with East Germany becoming a buffer against the West. Little by little, the Soviet Union helped to install Communist governments in Eastern European countries, which began to be referred to collectively as the **Soviet bloc.** In response, the United States encouraged the rearming of Western Europe. The Cold War had begun.[2]

Soviet Bloc
The Soviet Union and the Eastern European countries that installed Communist regimes after World War II and were dominated by the Soviet Union.

Containment Policy. In 1947, a remarkable article was published in *Foreign Affairs* magazine, signed by "X." The actual author was George F. Kennan, chief of the policy-planning staff for the State Department. The doctrine of **containment** set forth in the article became—according to many—the bible of Western foreign policy. "X" argued that whenever and wherever the Soviet Union could successfully challenge the West, it would do so. He recommended that our policy toward the Soviet Union be "firm and vigilant containment of Russian expansive tendencies."[3]

Containment
A U.S. diplomatic policy adopted by the Truman administration to contain Communist power within its existing boundaries.

The containment theory was expressed clearly in the **Truman Doctrine,** which was enunciated by President Harry Truman in 1947. Truman held that the United States must help countries in which a Communist takeover seemed likely. Later that year, he backed the Marshall Plan, an economic assistance plan for Europe that was intended to prevent the expansion of Communist influence there. In 1949, the United States entered into a military alliance with a number of European nations called the North Atlantic Treaty Organization, or

Truman Doctrine
The policy adopted by President Harry Truman in 1947 to halt Communist expansion in southeastern Europe.

2. See John Lewis Gaddis, *The United Nations and the Origins of the Cold War* (New York: Columbia University Press, 1972).
3. X, "The Sources of Soviet Conduct," *Foreign Affairs*, July 1947, p. 575.

Strategic Arms Limitation Treaty (SALT I) A treaty between the United States and the Soviet Union to stabilize the nuclear arms competition between the two countries. SALT I talks began in 1969, and the treaty was signed on May 26, 1972.

As the result of lengthy negotiations under Secretary of State Henry Kissinger and President Nixon, the United States and the Soviet Union signed the **Strategic Arms Limitation Treaty (SALT I)** in May 1972. That treaty limited the number of offensive missiles each country could deploy.

The policy of détente was not limited to the U.S. relationship with the Soviet Union. Seeing an opportunity to capitalize on increasing friction between the Soviet Union and the People's Republic of China, Kissinger secretly began negotiations to establish a new relationship with China. President Nixon eventually visited that nation in 1972. The visit set the stage for the formal diplomatic recognition of that country, which occurred during the Carter administration (1977–1981).

(Reuters/Gary Hershorn/Files GMHSV)

Soviet leader Mikhail Gorbachev (left) stands with U.S. president Ronald Reagan (right) in 1987, shortly after the two men finished negotiations on a major arms-control treaty.

Nuclear Arms Agreements with the Soviet Union. President Ronald Reagan (1981–1989) initially took a hard line against the Soviet Union. In 1987, however, after several years of negotiations, the United States and the Soviet Union signed the Intermediate-Range Nuclear Forces Treaty. The result was the dismantling of four thousand intermediate-range missiles.

In 1991, President George H. W. Bush and the Soviet Union signed the Strategic Arms Reduction Treaty (START). Implementation was complicated by the collapse of the Soviet Union in December 1991. In 1992, however, the treaty was re-signed by Russia and other former Soviet republics.

The Dissolution of the Soviet Union. After the fall of the Berlin Wall in 1989, it was clear that the Soviet Union had relinquished much of its political and military control over the states of Eastern Europe that formerly had been part of the Soviet bloc. No one expected the Soviet Union to dissolve into separate states as quickly as it did, however. Although Soviet leader Mikhail Gorbachev tried to adjust the Soviet constitution and political system to allow greater autonomy for the republics within the union, demands for political, ethnic, and religious autonomy grew. On the day after Christmas in 1991, the Soviet Union was officially dissolved. Figure 15–2 on the facing page shows the situation in Europe today.

Russia after the Soviet Union. In 1991, Boris Yeltsin won the first free presidential election in Russian history. Under Yeltsin, Russia undertook wide-ranging economic reforms aimed at introducing capitalism into what had been a communist country. State-owned enterprises were sold off, frequently at low prices to persons with inside connections. Radical changes resulted in a major economic crisis—Russian GDP declined by 50 percent between 1990 and 1995. Thereafter, oil exports led the way to economic stabilization.

In 2000, Yeltsin resigned because of poor health. He named Vladimir Putin, architect of the Russian military effort against an independence movement in the province of Chechnya, as acting president. A few months later, Putin won the presidency in a national election. Putin chipped away at Russia's democratic institutions, slowly turning the country into what was, in essence, an elected autocracy. When Putin's second term as president came to an end in 2008, he could not immediately run for reelection. He therefore engineered the election of one of his supporters, Dmitry Medvedev, as president. Medvedev

Figure 15-2 ▸ Europe after the Fall of the Soviet Union

This map shows the growth in European unity as marked by participation in transnational organizations. The United States continues to lead NATO (and would be orange if it were on the map). Note the reunification of Germany and the creation of new states from the former Yugoslavia and the former Soviet Union.

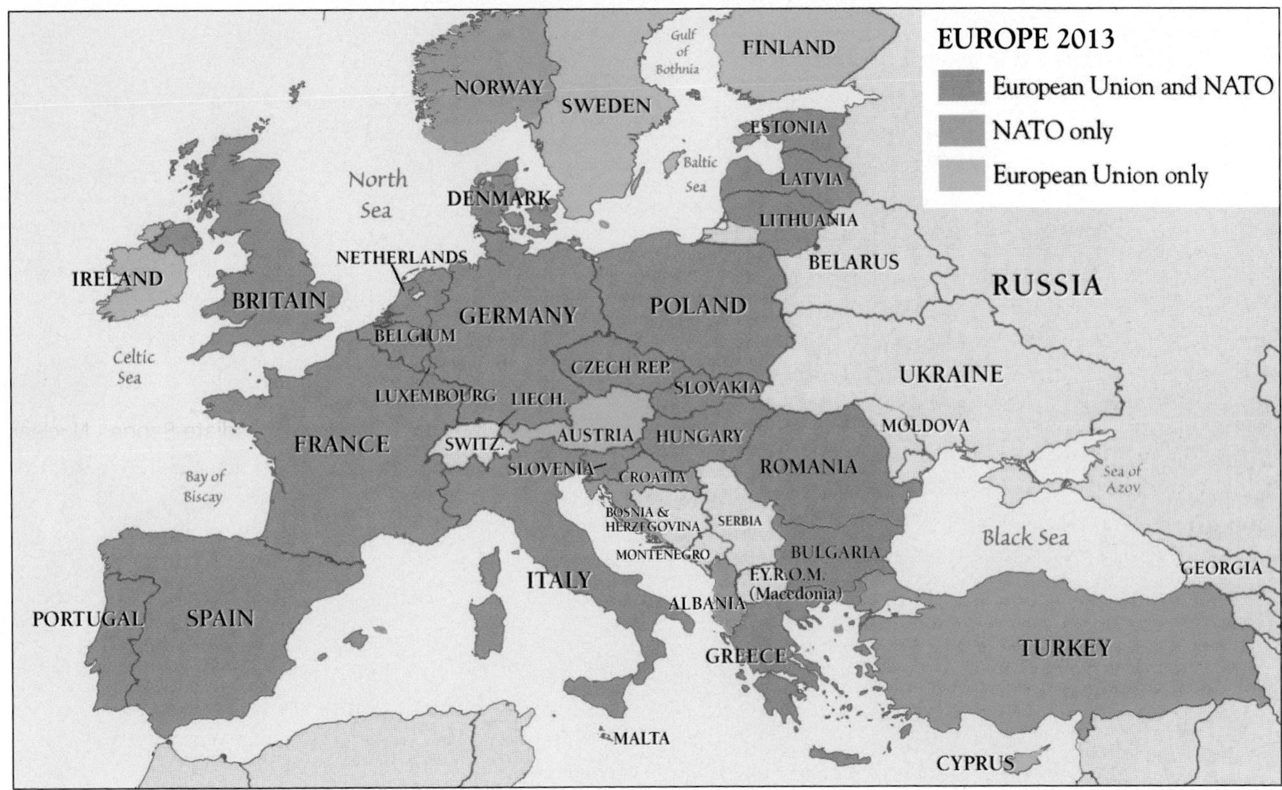

promptly appointed Putin as prime minister. It was clear that Putin retained real power in Russia, and in 2012 Putin again took the presidency.

In recent years, the United States has become concerned over Russia's aggressive attitude toward its neighbors. In 2008, Russian troops entered Georgia to prevent that nation from retaking an autonomous region that was under Russian protection. On several occasions since 2005, Russia has cut off the transmission of natural gas to Europe as a result of disputes. Russia also reacted angrily to U.S. plans for antimissile defenses in Eastern Europe, aimed at protecting Europe from a possible future Iranian attack. Russia appeared to believe that the defenses were directed against it. Still, the United States needed Russian assistance in matters such as curbing Iran's nuclear program.

The 1992 START agreement expired in December 2009, and in April 2010 President Obama and Russian president Medvedev signed New START, a follow-on treaty. New START reduced the number of permitted warheads to 1,550 for each side, a drop of about 30 percent from previous agreements. After some delays, the Senate ratified the treaty in December 2010.

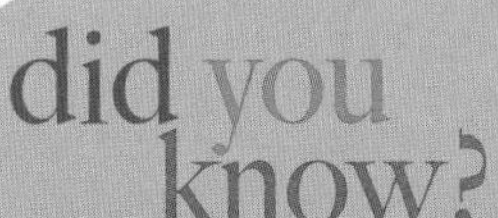

Russia has suffered more battle deaths in putting down the rebellion in Chechnya than the Soviet Union experienced in its decades-long attempt to subdue Afghanistan.

Why Should You Care about... FOREIGN POLICY?

(Karen Bleier/AFP/Getty Images/Newscom)

How do Amnesty International protesters hope to change our country's foreign policy?

One foreign policy issue worth caring about is human rights. In many countries throughout the world, human rights are not protected. In some nations, people are imprisoned, tortured, or killed because they oppose the current regime. In other nations, certain ethnic or racial groups are oppressed by the majority population.

FOREIGN POLICY AND YOUR LIFE

The strongest reason for involving yourself with human rights issues in other countries is simple moral altruism—unselfish regard for the welfare of others. The defense of human rights is unlikely to put a single dollar in your pocket.

A broader consideration, however, is that human rights abuses are often associated with the kind of dictatorial regimes that are likely to provoke wars. To the extent that the people of the world can create a climate in which human rights abuses are unacceptable, they may also create an atmosphere in which national leaders believe that they must display peaceful conduct generally. This, in turn, might reduce the frequency of wars, some of which could involve the United States. Fewer wars would mean preserving peace and human life, not to mention reducing the financial burden imposed by the military.

HOW YOU CAN MAKE A DIFFERENCE

What can you do to work for the improvement of human rights in other nations? One way is to join an organization that attempts to keep watch over human rights violations. (Two such organizations are listed at the end of this feature.) By publicizing human rights violations, such organizations try to pressure nations into changing their practices. Sometimes, these organizations are able to apply enough pressure and cause enough embarrassment that victims may be freed from prison or allowed to emigrate.

Another way to work for human rights is to keep informed about the state of affairs in other nations and to write personally to governments that violate human rights or to their embassies, asking them to cease these violations.

If you want to receive general information about the position of the United States on human rights violations, you can contact the State Department:

U.S. Department of State
Bureau of Democracy, Human Rights, and Labor
2201 C St. N.W.
Washington, DC 20520
202-647-4000
To find the bureau's page online, enter "state human rights" into a search engine.

The following organizations are well known for their watchdog efforts in countries that violate human rights for political reasons:

Amnesty International U.S.A.
5 Penn Plaza
New York, NY 10001
212-807-8400
You can also search on "amnestyusa."

American Friends Service Committee
1501 Cherry St.
Philadelphia, PA 19102
215-241-7000
Type "afsc" into a search engine.

Questions for Discussion and Analysis

1. Review the *Which Side Are You On?* feature on page 489. Under what conditions would it be appropriate to launch an air strike against Iran's nuclear facilities? What results might follow from such a strike?
2. Why do you think that North Korea and Iran might want to possess nuclear weapons, even though they can never hope to match the nuclear arsenals of the original nuclear powers?
3. Some people believe that if no U.S. military personnel were stationed abroad, terrorists would have less desire to harm Americans or the United States. Do you agree? Why or why not?
4. As of late 2012, no terrorist act remotely comparable to the attacks of 9/11 had taken place on U.S. soil. Why do you think that is so? How much credit can the government take? To what extent might terrorists experience practical difficulties in accomplishing anything like the damage inflicted on 9/11?

Key Terms

Cold War 488
containment 501
defense policy 481
détente 503
diplomacy 481
economic aid 481
foreign policy 481
foreign policy process 481
intelligence community 498
isolationist foreign policy 500
Monroe Doctrine 500
moral idealism 482
national security policy 481
negative constituents 497
normal trade relations (NTR) status 490
political realism 482
Soviet bloc 501
Strategic Arms Limitation Treaty (SALT I) 504
technical assistance 481
terrorism 483
Truman Doctrine 501

Chapter Summary

1. Foreign policy includes the nation's external goals and the techniques and strategies used to achieve them. National security policy, which is one aspect of foreign policy, is designed to protect the independence and the political and economic integrity of the United States. Diplomacy involves the nation's external relationships and is an attempt to resolve conflict without resort to arms. U.S. foreign policy is based on both moral idealism and political realism.
2. Terrorism is the attempt to create fear to gain political ends, usually by violence against noncombatants. It has become a major challenge facing the United States and other nations. The United States waged war on terrorism after the attacks of September 11, 2001.
3. In 1991 and again in 2003, the United States sent combat troops to Iraq. The second war in Iraq, begun in 2003, succeeded in toppling that nation's decades-long dictatorship but led to a long, grinding conflict with insurgent forces. The current campaign in Afghanistan, which grew out of the war on terrorism, may prove to be equally difficult.
4. Recent diplomatic efforts by the United States include containing the nuclear ambitions of Iran and North Korea. The rise of China as a world power and eventually a superpower introduces a series of issues the United States must address. American efforts to promote the peace process between Israel and the Palestinians have had limited success.
5. World economic issues, such as trade with China and the European debt crisis, demand U.S. attention. Humanitarian assistance has been a component of American foreign policy, as exemplified by relief efforts following natural disasters.
6. The formal power of the president to make foreign policy derives from the U.S. Constitution, which designates the president as commander in chief of the army and navy. Presidents have interpreted this authority broadly. They also have the power to make treaties and executive agreements. In principle, the State Department is the executive agency with primary authority over foreign affairs. The National Security Council also plays a major role. The

intelligence community consists of government agencies engaged in activities varying from information gathering to covert operations. In response to presidential actions in the Vietnam War, Congress attempted to establish some limits on the power of the president to intervene abroad by passing the War Powers Resolution in 1973.

7. Three major themes have guided U.S. foreign policy. In the early years of the nation, isolationism was the primary strategy. With the start of the twentieth century, isolationism gave way to global involvement. From the end of World War II through the 1980s, the major goal was to contain communism and the influence of the Soviet Union.

8. During the 1800s, the United States stayed out of European conflicts and politics, so these years have been called the period of isolationism. The end of the policy of isolationism toward Europe started with the Spanish-American War of 1898. U.S. involvement in European politics became more extensive when the United States entered World War I in 1917. World War II marked a lasting change in American foreign policy. The United States was the only major country to emerge from the war with its economy intact and the only country with operating nuclear weapons.

9. Soon after World War II, the Cold War began. A policy of containment, which assumed an expansionist Soviet Union, was enunciated in the Truman Doctrine. Following the apparent arms equality of the United States and the Soviet Union, the United States adopted a policy of détente, or loosening of tensions.

10. The United States signed arms control agreements with the Soviet Union under Presidents Nixon, Reagan, and George H. W. Bush. After the fall of the Soviet Union, Russia emerged as a less threatening state. Under President Vladimir Putin, however, Russia has moved away from democracy and in part returned to its old autocratic traditions.

Quiz Multiple Choice

1. As part of foreign policy, national security policy is designed to:
   - **a. ensure that the fifty states respect each others' borders.**
   - **b. ensure that all other countries respect each others' borders.**
   - **c. protect the independence and political integrity of the United States.**

2. Acts of terrorism are:
   - **a. the result of small-country governments' attempts to gain new territory.**
   - **b. systematic attempts to inspire fear to gain political ends.**
   - **c. due to large-country governments that failed in diplomacy.**

3. Since the beginning of this nation, various presidents have involved the United States in numerous undeclared wars, numbering at least:
   - **a. 10.**
   - **b. 500.**
   - **c. 125.**

4. In addition to the president, other sources of foreign policymaking include:
   - **a. the Department of State, the National Security Council, and the Department of Defense.**
   - **b. the Department of State, the Justice Department, and the Department of Defense.**
   - **c. the National Security Council, the Justice Department, and the editors of *Foreign Policy* magazine.**

5. The Cold War refers to a period during which:
   - **a. the Soviet Union and the United States faced off throughout the world.**
   - **b. the United States reverted back to isolationist policies.**
   - **c. the United States engaged in an economic war with many Asian countries.**

6. The concept of "preemptive war" as a defense strategy was a new element in U.S. foreign policy in the 2000s. It has been called:
   - **a. the Obama Doctrine.**
   - **b. the Clinton Doctrine.**
   - **c. the Bush Doctrine.**

7. The intelligence community is involved in foreign policy and consists of:
   - **a. the CIA and the Department of Defense.**
   - **b. over forty government agencies and bureaus involved in intelligence activities.**
   - **c. the CIA and the National Security Council (NSC).**

8. Congress may thwart a president's war-making powers by:
   - **a. censoring the president.**
   - **b. cutting off funding for military actions abroad.**
   - **c. threatening to adjourn.**

ANSWERS: 1. c, 2. b, 3. c, 4. a, 5. a, 6. c, 7. b, 8. b.

Quiz Fill-Ins

9. In 1823, President James Monroe stated that the United States would not accept any new European colonies or intervention in the Western Hemisphere and the United States would not meddle in European affairs. This became known as the __________ __________.

10. Just after World War II, President Harry Truman vowed that the United States must help countries in which a Communist takeover seemed likely. This became known as the __________ __________.

11. During the Cold War, two major adversaries were the __________ __________ and the __________ __________.

12. Two often conflicting principles of foreign policy are __________ __________ and __________ __________.

13. The two countries that today represent the most serious problems with nuclear proliferation are __________ and __________ __________.

14. As part of foreign policy, the Constitution gives the president the power to make __________ provided that the __________ concurs.

15. Much of the foreign policy of U.S. presidents has been carried out through both public and secret __________ __________.

16. In 1947, Congress created an organization to advise the president on the integration of "domestic, foreign, and military policies relating to the national security." It was named the __________ __________ __________.

ANSWERS: 9. Monroe Doctrine, 10. Truman Doctrine, 11. Soviet Union; United States, 12. moral idealism; political realism, 13. Iran; North Korea, 14. treaties; Senate 15. executive agreements, 16. National Security Council.

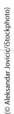

(© Aleksandar Jovicic/iStockphoto)

Selected Print & Media Resources

SUGGESTED READINGS

Acemoglu, Daron, and James Robinson. *Why Nations Fail: The Origins of Power, Prosperity, and Poverty.* New York: Crown Business, 2012. The authors collect fascinating examples to make a simple point: Nations fail when their institutions let rulers extract the nations' wealth in ways that choke off growth. Acemoglu and Robinson are economists at MIT and Harvard, respectively.

Gelvin, James L. *The Arab Uprisings: What Everyone Needs to Know.* New York: Oxford University Press, 2012. This slim volume in a question-and-answer format explores all aspects of the revolutions that have swept the Middle East. Gelvin is a history professor at UCLA.

Myers, B. R. *The Cleanest Race: How North Koreans See Themselves—and Why It Matters.* Brooklyn, N.Y.: Melville House, 2010. Myers argues that North Korean beliefs are not really based on Marxism. The nation's true ideology—shared by both leaders and citizens—is extreme nationalism. Myers, an American, is a professor at a South Korean university.

Rashid, Ahmed. *Pakistan on the Brink: The Future of America, Pakistan, and Afghanistan.* New York: Viking Adult, 2012. A leading journalist of Pakistan, Rashid succinctly describes the dilemmas faced by the United States and by the various political forces in Pakistan and Afghanistan.

Walter, Carl, and Fraser Howie. *Red Capitalism: The Fragile Financial Foundation of China's Extraordinary Rise.* Hoboken, N.J.: Wiley, 2012 (revised). Walter and Howie explain how China has financed the growth of its state-owned enterprises by exploiting the savings of the population. They question whether this model can succeed in the long run.

MEDIA RESOURCES

Black Hawk Down—A 2002 film that recounts the events in Mogadishu, Somalia, in October 1993, during which two U.S. Black Hawk helicopters were shot down. The film, which is based on reporter Mark Bowden's best-selling book by the same name, contains graphic scenes of terrifying urban warfare.

The Ugly American—One of the most intelligent political films of the 1960s, starring Marlon Brando as the U.S. ambassador to a Southeast Asian nation that is bursting with nationalism and beset by a Communist insurgency.

United 93—A 2006 documentary about the fourth airplane hijacked on 9/11. When they learned the fate of the other three planes via their cell phones, the passengers decided to fight back, with the result that the plane crashed in a Pennsylvania field, far from its intended target. *United 93* takes place in real time and is almost unbearably moving. Several critics named it the best film of the year.

(© PashaIgnatov/iStockphoto)

E-mocracy INTERNATIONAL ORGANIZATIONS

For years, international organizations have played a key role in world affairs, and these organizations are likely to become even more important in years to come. In the United States, the Obama administration promised to place greater reliance on multilateral approaches when addressing problems abroad—in contrast to the Bush administration's "go it alone" approach.

International organizations do not only dispense aid, loans, and advice. Several of them also field troops supplied by member nations. The "blue helmets" of the United Nations (UN) take part in seventeen missions, many in the Middle East or Africa. American forces in Afghanistan cooperate with those of other nations through the North Atlantic Treaty Organization (NATO). The UN, NATO, and other multinational organizations all have Web sites where you can learn about the history and status of current international conflicts.

LOGGING ON

- In addition to materials on international crises, the United Nations Web site contains a treasure trove of international statistics. To access this site, enter "un en" into an Internet search engine.
- For news about NATO, search on "nato."
- The European Union, a confederation of twenty-seven nations, is one of the most important international bodies in existence. You can learn more about it by entering "eu" into a search engine.
- The Organisation for Economic Co-operation and Development (OECD) provides another major source of international statistics and economic analysis. You can access the OECD's Web site by searching on "oecd."

APPENDIX A

THE DECLARATION OF INDEPENDENCE

In Congress, July 4, 1776

A Declaration by the Representatives of the United States of America, in General Congress assembled. When in the Course of human Events, it becomes necessary for one People to dissolve the Political Bands which have connected them with another, and to assume among the Powers of the Earth, the separate and equal Station to which the Laws of Nature and of Nature's God entitle them, a decent Respect to the Opinions of Mankind requires that they should declare the causes which impel them to the Separation.

We hold these Truths to be self-evident, that all Men are created equal, that they are endowed by their Creator with certain unalienable Rights, that among these are Life, Liberty, and the Pursuit of Happiness—That to secure these Rights, Governments are instituted among Men, deriving their just Powers from the Consent of the Governed, that whenever any Form of Government becomes destructive of these Ends, it is the Right of the People to alter or to abolish it, and to institute new Government, laying its Foundation on such Principles, and organizing its Powers in such Forms, as to them shall seem most likely to effect their Safety and Happiness. Prudence, indeed, will dictate that Governments long established should not be changed for light and transient Causes; and accordingly all Experience hath shewn, that Mankind are more disposed to suffer, while Evils are sufferable, than to right themselves by abolishing the Forms to which they are accustomed. But when a long Train of Abuses and Usurpations, pursuing invariably the same Object, evinces a Design to reduce them under absolute Despotism, it is their Right, it is their Duty, to throw off such Government, and to provide new Guards for their future Security. Such has been the patient Sufferance of these Colonies; and such is now the Necessity which constrains them to alter their former Systems of Government. The History of the present King of Great-Britain is a History of repeated Injuries and Usurpations, all having in direct Object the Establishment of an absolute Tyranny over these States. To prove this, let Facts be submitted to a candid World.

He has refused his Assent to Laws, the most wholesome and necessary for the public Good.

He has forbidden his Governors to pass Laws of immediate and pressing Importance, unless suspended in their Operation till his Assent should be obtained; and when so suspended, he has utterly neglected to attend to them.

He has refused to pass other Laws for the Accommodation of large Districts of People, unless those People would relinquish the Right of Representation in the Legislature, a Right inestimable to them, and formidable to Tyrants only.

He has called together Legislative Bodies at Places unusual, uncomfortable, and distant from the Depository of their Public Records, for the sole Purpose of fatiguing them into Compliance with his Measures.

He has dissolved Representative Houses repeatedly, for opposing with manly Firmness his Invasions on the Rights of the People.

He has refused for a long Time, after such Dissolutions, to cause others to be elected; whereby the Legislative Powers, incapable of Annihilation, have returned to the People at large for their exercise; the State remaining in the mean time exposed to all the Dangers of Invasion from without, and Convulsions within.

He has endeavoured to prevent the Population of these States; for that Purpose obstructing the Laws for Naturalization of Foreigners; refusing to pass others to encourage their Migrations hither, and raising the Conditions of new Appropriations of Lands.

He has obstructed the Administration of Justice, by refusing his Assent to Laws for establishing Judiciary Powers.

He has made Judges dependent on his Will alone, for the Tenure of their offices, and the Amount and payment of their Salaries.

He has erected a Multitude of new Offices, and sent hither Swarms of Officers to harass our People, and eat out their Substance.

He has kept among us, in Times of Peace, Standing Armies, without the consent of our Legislatures.

He has affected to render the Military independent of, and superior to the Civil Power.

He has combined with others to subject us to a Jurisdiction foreign to our Constitution, and unacknowledged by our Laws; giving his Assent to their Acts of pretended Legislation:

For quartering large Bodies of Armed Troops among us:

For protecting them, by a mock Trial, from Punishment for any Murders which they should commit on the Inhabitants of these States:

For cutting off our Trade with all Parts of the World:

For imposing Taxes on us without our Consent:

For depriving us, in many cases, of the Benefits of Trial by Jury:

For transporting us beyond Seas to be tried for pretended Offences:

For abolishing the free System of English Laws in a neighbouring Province, establishing therein an arbitrary Government, and enlarging its Boundaries, so as to render it at once an Example and fit Instrument for introducing the same absolute Rule into these Colonies:

For taking away our Charters, abolishing our most valuable Laws, and altering fundamentally the Forms of our Governments:

For suspending our own Legislatures, and declaring themselves invested with Power to legislate for us in all Cases whatsoever.

He has abdicated Government here, by declaring us out of his Protection and waging War against us.

He has plundered our Seas, ravaged our Coasts, burnt our towns, and destroyed the Lives of our People.

He is, at this Time, transporting large Armies of foreign Mercenaries to compleat the works of Death, Desolation, and Tyranny, already begun with circumstances of Cruelty and Perfidy, scarcely paralleled in the most barbarous Ages, and totally unworthy the Head of a civilized Nation.

He has constrained our fellow Citizens taken Captive on the high Seas to bear Arms against their Country, to become the Executioners of their Friends and Brethren, or to fall themselves by their Hands.

He has excited domestic Insurrections amongst us, and has endeavoured to bring on the Inhabitants of our Frontiers, the merciless Indian Savages, whose known Rule of Warfare, is an undistinguished Destruction, of all Ages, Sexes and Conditions.

In every state of these Oppressions we have Petitioned for Redress in the most humble Terms: Our repeated Petitions have been answered only by repeated Injury. A Prince, whose Character is thus marked by every act which may define a Tyrant, is unfit to be the Ruler of a free People.

Nor have we been wanting in Attentions to our British Brethren. We have warned them from Time to Time of Attempts by their Legislature to extend an unwarrantable Jurisdiction over us. We have reminded them of the Circumstances of our Emigration and Settlement here. We have appealed to their native Justice and Magnanimity, and we have conjured them by the Ties of our common Kindred to disavow these Usurpations, which, would inevitably interrupt our Connections and Correspondence. They too have been deaf to the Voice of Justice and of Consanguinity. We must, therefore, acquiesce in the Necessity, which denounces our Separation, and hold them, as we hold the rest of Mankind, Enemies in War, in Peace, Friends.

We, therefore, the Representatives of the UNITED STATES OF AMERICA, in General Congress Assembled, appealing to the Supreme Judge of the World for the Rectitude of our Intentions, do, in the Name, and by the Authority of the good People of these Colonies, solemnly Publish and Declare, That these United Colonies are, and of Right ought to be, Free and Independent States; that they are absolved from all Allegiance to the British Crown, and that all political Connection between them and the State of Great-Britain, is and ought to be totally dissolved; and that as Free and Independent States, they have full Power to levy War, conclude Peace, contract Alliances, establish Commerce, and to do all other Acts and Things which Independent States may of right do. And for the support of this declaration, with a firm Reliance on the Protection of divine Providence, we mutually pledge to each other our lives, our Fortunes, and our sacred Honor.

APPENDIX B

HOW TO READ CASE CITATIONS AND FIND COURT DECISIONS

Many important court cases are discussed in references in footnotes throughout this book. Court decisions are recorded and published. When a court case is mentioned, the notation that is used to refer to, or to cite, the case denotes where the published decision can be found.

State courts of appeals decisions are usually published in two places, the state reports of that particular state and the more widely used *National Reporter System* published by West Publishing Company. Some states no longer publish their own reports. The National Reporter System divides the states into the following geographic areas: Atlantic (A. or A.2d, where *2d* refers to *Second Series*), South Eastern (S.E. or S.E.2d), South Western (S.W., S.W.2d, or S.W.3d), North Western (N.W. or N.W.2d), North Eastern (N.E. or N.E.2d), Southern (So. or So.2d), and Pacific (P., P.2d, or P.3d).

Federal trial court decisions are published unofficially in West's *Federal Supplement* (F.Supp. or F.Supp.2d), and opinions from the circuit courts of appeals are reported unofficially in West's *Federal Reporter* (F., F.2d, or F.3d). Opinions from the United States Supreme Court are reported in the *United States Reports* (U.S.), the *Lawyers' Edition of the Supreme Court Reports* (L.Ed. or L.Ed.2d), West's *Supreme Court Reporter* (S.Ct.), and other publications. The *United States Reports* is the official publication of United States Supreme Court decisions. It is published by the federal government. Many early decisions are missing from these volumes. The citations of the early volumes of the *United States Reports* include the names of the actual reporters, such as Dallas, Cranch, or Wheaton. *McCulloch v. Maryland,* for example, is cited as 17 U.S. (4 Wheat.) 316. Only after 1874 did the present citation system, in which cases are cited based solely on their volume and page numbers in the *United States Reports,* come into being. The *Lawyers' Edition of the Supreme Court Reports* is an unofficial and more complete edition of Supreme Court decisions. West's *Supreme Court Reporter* is an unofficial edition of decisions dating from October 1882. These volumes contain headnotes and numerous brief editorial statements of the law involved in each case.

State courts of appeals decisions are cited by giving the name of the case; the volume, name, and page number of the state's official report (if the state publishes its own reports); the volume, unit, and page number of the *National Reporter;* and the volume, name, and page number of any other selected reporter. Federal court citations are also listed by giving the name of the case and the volume, name, and page number of the reports.

In addition to the citation, this textbook lists the year of the decision in parentheses. Consider, for example, the case *National Federation of Independent Business v. Sebelius,* 132 S.Ct. 2566 (2012). The Supreme Court's decision of this case may be found in volume 132 of the *Supreme Court Reporter* on page 2566. The case was decided in 2012.

Today, many courts, including the United States Supreme Court, publish their opinions online. This makes it much easier for students to find and read cases, or summaries of cases, that have significant consequences for American government and politics. To access cases via the Internet, use the URLs given in the *Logging On* section at the end of Chapter 13.

FEDERALIST PAPERS NOS. 10, 51, AND 78

In 1787, after the newly drafted U.S. Constitution was submitted to the thirteen states for ratification, a major political debate ensued between the Federalists (who favored ratification) and the Anti-Federalists (who opposed ratification). Anti-Federalists in New York were particularly critical of the Constitution, and in response to their objections, Federalists Alexander Hamilton, James Madison, and John Jay wrote a series of eighty-five essays in defense of the Constitution. The essays were published in New York newspapers and reprinted in other newspapers throughout the country.

For students of American government, the essays, collectively known as the Federalist Papers, *are particularly important because they provide a glimpse of the founders' political philosophy and intentions in designing the Constitution—and, consequently, in shaping the American philosophy of government.*

We have included in this appendix three of these essays: Federalist Papers *Nos. 10, 51, and 78. Each essay has been annotated by the authors to indicate its importance in American political thought and to clarify the meaning of particular passages.*

Federalist Paper No. 10

Federalist Paper *No. 10, penned by James Madison, has often been singled out as a key document in American political thought. In this essay, Madison attacks the Anti-Federalists' fear that a republican form of government will inevitably give rise to "factions"—small political parties or groups united by a common interest—that will control the government. Factions will be harmful to the country because they will implement policies beneficial to their own interests but adverse to other people's rights and to the public good. In this essay, Madison attempts to lay to rest this fear by explaining how, in a large republic such as the United States, there will be so many different factions, held together by regional or local interests, that no single one of them will dominate national politics.*

Madison opens his essay with a paragraph discussing how important it is to devise a plan of government that can control the "instability, injustice, and confusion" brought about by factions.

Among the numerous advantages promised by a well-constructed Union, none deserves to be more accurately developed than its tendency to break and control the violence of faction. The friend of popular governments never finds himself so much alarmed for their character and fate as when he contemplates their propensity to this dangerous vice. He will not fail, therefore, to set a due value on any plan which, without violating the principles to which he is attached, provides a proper cure for it. The instability, injustice, and confusion introduced into the public councils have, in truth, been the mortal diseases under which popular governments have everywhere perished, as they continue to be the favorite and fruitful topics from which the adversaries to liberty derive their most specious declamations. The valuable improvements made by the American constitutions on the popular models, both ancient and modern, cannot certainly be too much admired; but it would be an unwarrantable partiality to contend that they have as effectually obviated the danger on this side, as was wished and expected. Complaints are everywhere heard from our most considerate and virtuous citizens, equally the friends of public and private faith and of public and personal liberty, that our governments are too unstable, that the public good is disregarded in the conflicts of rival parties, and that measures are too often decided, not according to the rules of justice and the rights of the minor party, but by the superior force of an interested and overbearing majority. However anxiously we may wish that these complaints had no foundation, the evidence of known facts will not permit us to deny that they are in some degree true. It will be found, indeed, on a candid review of our situation, that some of the distresses under which we labor have been erroneously charged on the operation of our governments; but it will be found, at the same time, that other causes will not alone account for many of our heaviest misfortunes; and, particularly, for that prevailing and increasing distrust of public engagements and alarm for private rights which are echoed from one end of the continent to the other. These must be chiefly, if not wholly, effects of the unsteadiness and injustice with which a factious spirit has tainted our public administration.

Madison now defines what he means by the term faction.

By a faction I understand a number of citizens, whether amounting to a majority or minority of the whole, who are united and actuated by some common impulse of passion, or of interest, adverse to the rights of other citizens, or the permanent and aggregate interests of the community.

Madison next contends that there are two methods by which the "mischiefs of faction" can be cured: by removing the causes of faction or by controlling their effects. In the following paragraphs, Madison explains how liberty itself nourishes factions. Therefore, to abolish factions would involve abolishing liberty—a cure "worse than the disease."

There are two methods of curing the mischiefs of faction: the one, by removing its causes; the other, by controlling its effects.

There are again two methods of removing the causes of faction: the one, by destroying the liberty which is essential to its existence; the other, by giving to every citizen the same opinions, the same passions, and the same interests.

It could never be more truly said than of the first remedy that it was worse than the disease. Liberty is to faction what air is to fire, an aliment without which it instantly expires. But it could not be a less folly to abolish liberty, which is essential to political life, because it nourishes faction than it would be to wish the annihilation of air, which is essential to animal life, because it imparts to fire its destructive agency.

The second expedient is as impracticable as the first would be unwise. As long as the reason of man continues fallible, and he is at liberty to exercise it, different opinions will be formed. As long as the connection subsists between his reason and his self-love, his opinions and his passions will have a reciprocal influence on each other; and the former will be objects to which the latter will attach themselves. The diversity in the faculties of men, from which the rights of property originate, is not less an insuperable obstacle to a uniformity of interests. The protection of these faculties is the first object of government. From the protection of different and unequal faculties of acquiring property, the possession of different degrees and kinds of property immediately results; and from the influence of these on the sentiments and views of the respective proprietors ensues a division of the society into different interests and parties.

The latent causes of faction are thus sown in the nature of man; and we see them everywhere brought into different degrees of activity, according to the different circumstances of civil society. A zeal for different opinions concerning religion, concerning government, and many other points, as well of speculation as of practice; an attachment to different leaders ambitiously contending for pre-eminence and power; or to persons of other descriptions whose fortunes have been interesting to the human passions, have, in turn, divided mankind into parties, inflamed them with mutual animosity, and rendered them much more disposed to vex and oppress each other than to co-operate for their common good. So strong is this propensity of mankind to fall into mutual animosities that where no substantial occasion presents itself the most frivolous and fanciful distinctions have been sufficient to kindle their unfriendly passions and excite their most violent conflicts. But the most common and durable source of factions has been the various and unequal distribution of property. Those who hold and those who are without property have ever formed distinct interests in society. Those who are creditors, and those who are debtors, fall under a like discrimination. A landed interest, a manufacturing interest, a mercantile interest, a moneyed interest, with many lesser interests, grow up of necessity in civilized nations, and divide them into different classes, actuated by different sentiments and views. The regulation of these various and interfering interests forms the principal task of modern legislation and involves the spirit of party and faction in the necessary and ordinary operations of government.

No man is allowed to be a judge in his own cause, because his interest would certainly bias his judgment, and, not improbably, corrupt his integrity. With equal, nay with greater reason, a body of men are unfit to be both judges and parties at the same time; yet what are many of the most important acts of legislation but so many judicial determinations, not indeed concerning the rights of single persons, but concerning the rights of large bodies of citizens? And what are the different classes of legislators but advocates and parties to the causes which they determine? Is a law proposed concerning private debts? It is a question to which the creditors are parties on one side and the debtors on the other. Justice ought to hold the balance between them. Yet the parties are, and must be, themselves the judges; and the most numerous party, or in other words, the most powerful faction must be expected to prevail. Shall domestic manufacturers be encouraged, and in what degree, by restrictions on foreign manufacturers? [These] are questions which would be differently decided by the landed and the manufacturing classes, and probably by neither with a sole regard to justice and the public good. The apportionment of taxes on the various descriptions of property is an act which seems to require the most exact impartiality; yet there is, perhaps, no legislative act in which greater opportunity and temptation are given to a predominant party to trample on the rules of justice. Every shilling with which they overburden the inferior number is a shilling saved to their own pockets.

It is in vain to say that enlightened statesmen will be able to adjust these clashing interests and render them all subservient to the public good. Enlightened statesmen will not always be at the helm. Nor, in many cases, can such an adjustment be made at all without taking into view indirect and remote considerations, which will rarely prevail over the immediate interest which one party may find in disregarding the rights of another or the good of the whole.

The inference to which we are brought is that the causes of faction cannot be removed and that relief is only to be sought in the means of controlling its effects.

Having concluded that "the causes of faction cannot be removed," Madison now looks in some detail at the other method by which factions can be cured—by controlling their effects. This is the heart of his essay. He begins by positing a significant question: How can you have self-government without risking the possibility that a ruling faction, particularly a majority faction, might tyrannize over the rights of others?

If a faction consists of less than a majority, relief is supplied by the republican principle, which enables the majority to defeat its sinister views by regular vote. It may clog the administration, it may convulse the society; but it will be unable to execute and mask its violence under the forms of the Constitution. When a majority is included in a faction, the form of popular government, on the other hand, enables it to sacrifice to its ruling passion or interest both the public good and the rights of other citizens. To secure the public good and private rights against the danger of such a faction, and at the same time to preserve the spirit and the form of popular government, is then the great object to which our inquiries are directed. Let me add that it is the great desideratum by which alone this form of government can be rescued from the opprobrium under which it has so long labored and be recommended to the esteem and adoption of mankind.

Madison now sets forth the idea that one way to control the effects of factions is to ensure that the majority is rendered incapable of acting in concert in order to "carry into effect schemes of oppression." He goes on to state that in a democracy, in which all citizens participate personally in government decision making, there is no way to prevent the majority from communicating with each other and, as a result, acting in concert.

By what means is this object attainable? Evidently by one of two only. Either the existence of the same passion or interest in a majority at the same time must be prevented, or the majority, having such coexistent passion or interest, must be rendered, by their number and local situation, unable to concert and carry into effect schemes of oppression. If the impulse and the opportunity be suffered to coincide, we well know that neither moral nor religious motives can be relied on as an adequate control. They are not found to be such on the injustice and violence of individuals, and lose their efficacy in proportion to the number combined together, that is, in proportion as their efficacy becomes needful.

From this view of the subject it may be concluded that a pure democracy, by which I mean a society consisting of a small number of citizens, who assemble and administer the government in person, can admit of no cure for the mischiefs of faction. A common passion or interest will, in almost every case, be felt by a majority of the whole; a communication and concert results from the form of government itself; and there is nothing to check the inducements to sacrifice the weaker party or an obnoxious individual. Hence it is that such democracies have ever been spectacles of turbulence and contention; have ever been found incompatible with personal security or the rights of property; and have in general been as short in their lives as they have been violent in their deaths. Theoretic politicians, who have patronized this species of government, have erroneously supposed that by reducing mankind to a perfect equality in their political rights, they would at the same time be perfectly equalized and assimilated in their possessions, their opinions, and their passions.

Madison now moves on to discuss the benefits of a republic with respect to controlling the effects of factions. He begins by defining a republic and then pointing out the "two great points of difference" between a republic and a democracy: a republic is governed by a small body of elected representatives, not by the people directly; and a republic can extend over a much larger territory and embrace more citizens than a democracy can.

A republic, by which I mean a government in which the scheme of representation takes place, opens a different prospect and promises the cure for which we are seeking. Let us examine the points in which it varies from pure democracy, and we shall comprehend both the nature of the cure and the efficacy which it must derive from the Union.

The two great points of difference between a democracy and a republic are: first, the delegation of the government, in the latter, to a small number of citizens elected by the rest; secondly, the greater number of citizens and greater sphere of country over which the latter may be extended.

In the following four paragraphs, Madison explains how in a republic, particularly a large republic, the delegation of authority to elected representatives will increase the likelihood that those who govern will be "fit" for their positions and that a proper balance will be achieved between local (factional) interests and national interests. Note how he stresses that the new federal Constitution, by dividing powers between state governments and the national government, provides a "happy combination in this respect."

The effect of the first difference is, on the one hand, to refine and enlarge the public views by passing them through the medium of a chosen body of citizens, whose wisdom may best discern the true interest of their country and whose patriotism and love of justice will be least likely to sacrifice it to temporary or partial considerations. Under such a regulation it may well happen that the public voice, pronounced by the representatives of the people, will be more consonant to the public good than if pronounced by the people themselves, convened for the purpose. On the other hand, the effect may be inverted. Men of factious tempers, of local prejudices, or of sinister designs, may, by intrigue, by corruption, or by other means, first obtain the suffrages, and then betray the interests of the people. The question resulting is, whether small or extensive republics are most favorable to the election of proper guardians of the public weal; and it is clearly decided in favor of the latter by two obvious considerations.

In the first place, it is to be remarked that however small the republic may be the representatives must be raised to a certain number in order to guard against the cabals of a few; and that however large it may be, they must be limited to a certain number in order to guard against the confusion of a multitude. Hence, the number of representatives in the two cases not being in proportion to that of the constituents, and being proportionally greater in the small republic, it follows that if the proportion of fit characters be not less in the large than in the small republic, the former will present a greater option, and consequently a greater probability of a fit choice.

In the next place, as each representative will be chosen by a greater number of citizens in the large than in the small republic, it will be more difficult for unworthy candidates to practice with success the vicious arts by which elections are too often carried; and the suffrages of the people being more free, will be more likely to center on men who possess the most attractive merit and the most diffusive and established characters.

It must be confessed that in this, as in most other cases, there is a mean, on both sides of which inconveniencies will be found to lie. By enlarging too much the number of electors, you render the representative too little acquainted with all their local circumstances and lesser interests; as by reducing it too much, you render him unduly attached to these, and too little fit to comprehend and pursue great and national objects. The federal Constitution forms a happy combination in this respect; the great and aggregate interests being referred to the national, the local and particular to the State legislatures.

Madison now looks more closely at the other difference between a republic and a democracy—namely, that a republic can encompass a larger territory and more citizens than a democracy can. In the remaining paragraphs of his essay, Madison concludes that in a large republic, it will be difficult for factions to act in concert. Although a factious group—religious, political, economic, or otherwise—may control a local or regional government, it will have little chance of gathering a national following. This is because in a large republic, there will be numerous factions whose work will offset the work of any one particular faction ("sect"). As Madison phrases it, these numerous factions will "secure the national councils against any danger from that source."

The other point of difference is the greater number of citizens and extent of territory which may be brought within the compass of republican than of democratic government; and it is this circumstance principally which renders factious combinations less to be dreaded in the former than in the latter. The smaller the society, the fewer probably will be the distinct parties and interests composing it; the fewer the distinct parties and interests, the more frequently will a majority be found of the same party; and the smaller the number of individuals composing a majority, and the smaller the compass within which they are placed, the more easily will they concert and execute their plans of oppression. Extend the sphere and you take in a greater variety of parties and interests; you make it less probable that a majority of the whole will have a common motive to invade the rights of other citizens; or if such a common motive exists, it will be more difficult for all who feel it to discover their own strength and to act in unison with each other. Besides other impediments, it may be remarked that, where there is a consciousness of unjust or dishonorable purposes, communication is always checked by distrust in proportion to the number whose concurrence is necessary.

Hence, it clearly appears that the same advantage which a republic has over a democracy in controlling the effects of faction is enjoyed by a large over a small republic—is enjoyed by the Union over the States composing it. Does this advantage consist in the substitution of representatives whose enlightened views and virtuous sentiments render them superior to local prejudices and to schemes of injustice? It will not be denied that the representation of the Union will be most likely to possess these requisite endowments. Does it consist in the greater security afforded by a greater variety of parties, against the event of any one party being able to outnumber and oppress the rest? In an equal degree does the increased variety of parties comprised within the Union increase this security. Does it, in fine, consist in the greater obstacles opposed to the concert and accomplishment of the secret wishes of an unjust and interested majority? Here again the extent of the Union gives it the most palpable advantage.

The influence of factious leaders may kindle a flame within their particular States but will be unable to spread a general conflagration through the other States. A religious sect may degenerate into a political faction in a part of the Confederacy; but the variety of sects dispersed over the entire face of it must secure the national councils against any danger from that source. A rage for paper money, for an abolition of debts, for an equal division of property, or for any other improper or wicked project, will be less apt to pervade the whole body of the Union than a particular member of it, in the same proportion as such a malady is more likely to taint a particular county or district than an entire State.

In the extent and proper structure of the Union, therefore, we behold a republican remedy for the diseases most incident to republican government. And according to the degree of pleasure and pride we feel in being republicans ought to be our zeal in cherishing the spirit and supporting the character of federalists.

Publius
(James Madison)

Federalist Paper No. 51

Federalist Paper No. 51, also authored by James Madison, is another classic in American political theory. Although the Federalists wanted a strong national government, they had not abandoned the traditional American view, particularly notable during the revolutionary era, that those holding powerful government positions could not be trusted to put national interests and the common good above their own personal interests. In this essay, Madison explains why the separation of the national government's powers into three branches—executive, legislative, and judicial—and a federal structure of government offer the best protection against tyranny.

To what expedient, then, shall we finally resort, for maintaining in practice the necessary partition of power among the several departments as laid down in the Constitution? The only answer that can be given is that as all these exterior provisions are found to be inadequate the defect must be supplied, by so contriving the interior structure of the government as that its several constituent parts may, by their mutual relations, be the means of keeping each other in their proper places. Without presuming to undertake a full development of this important idea I will hazard a few general observations which may perhaps place it in a clearer light, and enable us to form a more correct judgment of the principles and structure of the government planned by the convention.

In the next two paragraphs, Madison stresses that for the powers of the different branches (departments) of government to be truly separated, the personnel in one branch should not be dependent on another branch for their appointment or for the "emoluments" (compensation) attached to their offices.

In order to lay a due foundation for that separate and distinct exercise of the different powers of government, which to a certain extent is admitted on all hands to be essential to the preservation of liberty, it is evident that each department should have a will of its own; and consequently should be so constituted that the members of each should have as little agency as possible in the appointment of the members of the others. Were this principle rigorously adhered to, it would require that all the appointments for the supreme executive, legislative, and judiciary magistracies should be drawn from the same fountain of authority, the people, through channels having no communication whatever with one another. Perhaps such a plan of constructing the several departments would be less difficult in practice than it may in contemplation appear. Some difficulties, however, and some additional expense would attend the execution of it. Some deviations, therefore, from the principle must be admitted. In the constitution of the judiciary department in particular, it might be inexpedient to insist rigorously on the principle: first, because peculiar qualifications being essential in the members, the primary consideration ought to be to select that mode of choice which best secures these qualifications; second, because the permanent tenure by which the appointments are held in that department must soon destroy all sense of dependence on the authority conferring them.

It is equally evident that the members of each department should be as little dependent as possible on those of the others for the emoluments annexed to their offices. Were the executive magistrate, or the judges, not independent of the legislature in this particular, their independence in every other would be merely nominal.

In the following passages, which are among the most widely quoted of Madison's writings, he explains how the separation of the powers of government into three branches helps to counter the effects of personal ambition on government. The separation of powers allows personal motives to be linked to the constitutional rights of a branch of government. In effect, competing personal interests in each branch will help to keep the powers of the three government branches separate and, in so doing, will help to guard the public interest.

But the great security against a gradual concentration of the several powers in the same department consists in giving to those who administer each department the necessary constitutional means and personal motives to resist encroachments of the others. The provision for defense must in this, as in all other cases, be made commensurate to the danger of attack. Ambition must be made to counteract ambition. The interest of the man must be connected with the constitutional rights of the place. It may be a reflection on human nature that such devices should be necessary to control the abuses of government. But what is government itself but the greatest of all reflections on human nature? If men were angels, no government would be necessary. If angels were to govern men, neither external nor internal controls on government would be necessary. In framing a government which is to be administered by men over men, the great difficulty lies in this: you must first enable the government to control the governed; and in the next place oblige it to control itself. A dependence on the people is, no doubt, the primary control on the government; but experience has taught mankind the necessity of auxiliary precautions.

This policy of supplying, by opposite and rival interests, the defect of better motives, might be traced through the whole system of human affairs, private as well as public. We see it particularly displayed in all the subordinate distributions of power, where the constant aim is to divide and arrange the several offices in such a manner as that each may be a check on the other—that the private interest of every individual may be a sentinel over the public rights. These inventions of prudence cannot be less requisite in the distribution of the supreme powers of the State.

Madison now addresses the issue of equality between the branches of government. The legislature will necessarily predominate, but if the executive is given an "absolute negative" (absolute veto power) over legislative actions, this also could lead to an abuse of power. Madison concludes that the division of the legislature into two "branches" (parts, or chambers) will act as a check on the legislature's powers.

But it is not possible to give to each department an equal power of self-defense. In republican government, the legislative authority necessarily predominates. The remedy for this inconveniency is to divide the legislature into different branches; and to render them, by different modes of election and different principles of action, as little connected with each other as the nature of their common functions and their common dependence on the society will admit. It may even be necessary to guard against dangerous encroachments by still further precautions. As the weight of the legislative authority requires that it should be thus divided, the weakness of the executive may require, on the other hand, that it should be fortified. An absolute negative on the legislature appears, at first view, to be the natural defense with which the executive magistrate should be armed. But perhaps it would be neither altogether safe nor alone sufficient. On ordinary occasions it might not be exerted with the requisite firmness, and on extraordinary occasions it might be perfidiously abused. May not this defect of an absolute negative be supplied by some qualified connection between this weaker department and the weaker branch of the stronger department, by which the latter may be led to support the constitutional rights of the former, without being too much detached from the rights of its own department?

If the principles on which these observations are founded be just, as I persuade myself they are, and they be applied as a criterion to the several State constitutions, and to the federal Constitution, it will be found that if the latter does not perfectly correspond with them, the former are infinitely less able to bear such a test.

In the remainder of the essay, Madison discusses how a federal system of government, in which powers are divided between the states and the national government, offers "double security" against tyranny.

There are, moreover, two considerations particularly applicable to the federal system of America, which place that system in a very interesting point of view.

First. In a single republic, all the power surrendered by the people is submitted to the administration of a single government; and the usurpations are guarded against by a division of the government into distinct and separate departments. In the compound republic of America, the power surrendered by the people is first divided between two distinct governments, and then the portion allotted to each subdivided among distinct and separate departments. Hence a double security arises to the rights of the people. The different governments will control each other, at the same time that each will be controlled by itself.

Second. It is of great importance in a republic not only to guard the society against the oppression of its rulers, but to guard one part of the society against the injustice of the other part. Different interests necessarily exist in different classes of citizens. If a majority be united by a common interest, the rights of the minority will be insecure. There are but two methods of providing against this evil: the one by creating a will in the community independent of the majority—that is, of the society itself; the other, by comprehending in the society so many separate descriptions of citizens as will render an unjust combination of a majority of the whole very improbable, if not impracticable. The first method prevails in all governments possessing an hereditary or self-appointed authority. This, at best, is but a precarious security; because a power independent of the society may as well espouse the unjust views of the major as the rightful interests of the minor party, and may possibly be turned against both parties. The second method will be exemplified in the federal republic of the United States. Whilst all authority in it will be derived from and dependent on the society, the society itself will be broken into so many parts, interests and classes of citizens, that the rights of individuals, or of the minority, will be in little danger from interested combinations of the majority.

In a free government the security for civil rights must be the same as that for religious rights. It consists in the one case in the multiplicity of interests, and in the other in the multiplicity of sects. The degree of security in both cases will depend on the number of interests and sects; and this may be presumed to depend on the extent of country and number of people comprehended under the same government. This view of the subject must particularly recommend a proper federal system to all the sincere and considerate friends of republican government, since it shows that in exact proportion as the territory of the Union may be formed into more circumscribed Confederacies, or States, oppressive combinations of a majority will be facilitated; the best security, under the republican forms, for the rights of every class of citizen, will be diminished; and consequently the stability and independence of some member of the government, the only other security, must be proportionally increased. Justice is the end of government. It is the end of civil society. It ever has been and ever will be pursued until it be obtained, or until liberty be lost in the pursuit. In a society under the forms of which the stronger faction can readily unite and oppress the weaker, anarchy may as truly be said to reign as in a state of nature, where the weaker individual is not secured against the violence of the stronger; and as, in the latter state, even the stronger individuals are prompted, by the uncertainty of their condition, to submit to a government which may protect the weak as well as themselves; so, in the former state, will the more powerful factions or parties be gradually induced, by a like motive, to wish for a government which will protect all parties, the weaker as well as the more powerful.

It can be little doubted that if the State of Rhode Island was separated from the Confederacy and left to itself, the insecurity of rights under the popular form of government within such narrow limits would be displayed by such reiterated oppressions of factious majorities that some power altogether independent of the people would soon be called for by the voice of the very factions whose misrule had proved the necessity of it. In the extended republic of the United States, and among the great variety of interests, parties, and sects which it embraces, a coalition of a majority of the whole society could seldom take place on any other principles than those of justice and the general good; whilst there being thus less danger to a minor from the will of a major party, there must be less pretext, also, to provide for the security of the former, by introducing into the government a will not dependent on the latter, or, in other words, a will independent of the society itself. It is no less certain than it is important, notwithstanding the contrary opinions which have been entertained, that the larger the society, provided it lie within a practicable sphere, the more duly capable it will be of self-government. And happily for the republican cause, the practicable sphere may be carried to a very great extent by a judicious modification and mixture of the *federal principle.*

Publius
(James Madison)

Federalist Paper No. 78

In this essay, Alexander Hamilton looks at the role of the judicial branch (the courts) in the new government fashioned by the Constitution's framers. The essay is historically significant because, among other things, it provides a basis for the courts' power of judicial review, which was not explicitly set forth in the Constitution (see Chapters 2 and 13).

After some brief introductory remarks, Hamilton explains why the founders decided that federal judges should be appointed and given lifetime tenure. Note how he describes the judiciary as the "weakest" and "least dangerous" branch of government. Because of this, claims Hamilton, "all possible care" is required to enable the judiciary to defend itself against attacks by the other two branches of government. Above all, the independence of the judicial branch should be secured, because if judicial powers were combined with legislative or executive powers, there would be no liberty.

We proceed now to an examination of the judiciary department of the proposed government.

In unfolding the defects of the existing Confederation, the utility and necessity of a federal judicature have been clearly pointed out. It is the less necessary to recapitulate the considerations there urged, as the propriety of the institution in the abstract is not disputed; the only questions which have been raised being relative to the manner of constituting it, and to its extent. To these points, therefore, our observations shall be confined.

The manner of constituting it seems to embrace these several objects: 1st. The mode of appointing the judges. 2d. The tenure by which they are to hold their places. 3d. The partition of the judiciary authority between different courts, and their relations to each other.

First. As to the mode of appointing the judges; this is the same with that of appointing the officers of the Union in general, and has been so fully discussed in the last two numbers, that nothing can be said here which would not be useless repetition.

Second. As to the tenure by which the judges are to hold their places; this chiefly concerns their duration in office; the provisions for their support; the precautions for their responsibility.

According to the plan of the convention, all judges who may be appointed by the United States are to hold their offices during good behavior; which is conformable to the most approved of the State constitutions and among the rest, to that of this State. Its propriety having been drawn into question by the adversaries of that plan, is no light symptom of the rage for objection, which disorders their imaginations and judgments. The standard of good behavior for the continuance in office of the judicial magistracy, is certainly one of the most valuable of the modern improvements in the practice of government. In a monarchy it is an excellent barrier to the despotism of the prince; in a republic it is a no less excellent barrier to the encroachments and oppressions of the representative body. And it is the best expedient which can be devised in any government, to secure a steady, upright, and impartial administration of the laws.

Whoever attentively considers the different departments of power must perceive, that, in a government in which they are separated from each other, the judiciary, from the nature of its functions, will always be the least dangerous to the political rights of the Constitution; because it will be least in a capacity to annoy or injure them. The Executive not only dispenses the honors, but holds the sword of the community. The legislature not only commands the purse, but prescribes the rules by which the duties and rights of every citizen are to be regulated. The judiciary, on the contrary, has no influence over either the sword or the purse; no direction either of the strength or of the wealth of the society; and can take no active resolution whatever. It may truly be said to have neither force nor will, but merely judgment; and must ultimately depend upon the aid of the executive arm even for the efficacy of its judgments.

This simple view of the matter suggests several important consequences. It proves incontestably, that the judiciary is beyond comparison the weakest of the three departments of power; that it can never attack with success either of the other two; and that all possible care is requisite to enable it to defend itself against their attacks. It equally proves, that though individual oppression may now and then proceed from the courts of justice, the general liberty of the people can never be endangered from that quarter; I mean so long as the judiciary remains truly distinct from both the legislature and the Executive. For I agree, that "there is no liberty, if the power of judging is not separated from the legislative and executive powers." And it proves, in the last place, that as liberty can have nothing to fear from the judiciary alone, but would have everything to fear from its union with either of the other departments; that as all the effects of such a union must ensue from a dependence of the former on the latter, notwithstanding a nominal and apparent separation; that as, from the natural feebleness of the judiciary, it is in continual jeopardy of being overpowered, awed, or influenced by its co-ordinate branches; and that as nothing can contribute so much to its firmness and independence as permanency in office, this quality may therefore be justly regarded as an indispensable ingredient in its constitution, and, in a great measure, as the citadel of the public justice and the public security.

Hamilton now stresses that the "complete independence of the courts" is essential in a limited government, because it is up to the courts to interpret the laws. Just as a federal court can decide which of two conflicting statutes should take priority, so can that court decide whether a statute conflicts with the Constitution. Essentially, Hamilton sets forth here the theory of judicial review—the power of the courts to decide whether actions of the other branches of government are (or are not) consistent with the Constitution. Hamilton points out that this "exercise of judicial discretion, in determining between two contradictory laws," does not mean that the judicial branch is superior to the legislative branch. Rather, it "supposes" that the power of the people (as declared in the Constitution) is superior to both the judiciary and the legislature.

The complete independence of the courts of justice is peculiarly essential in a limited Constitution. By a limited Constitution, I understand one which contains certain specified exceptions to the legislative authority; such, for instance, as that it shall pass no bills of attainder, no ex-post-facto laws, and the like. Limitations of this kind can be preserved in practice no other way than through the medium of courts of justice, whose duty it must be to declare all acts contrary to the manifest tenor of the Constitution void. Without this, all the reservations of particular rights or privileges would amount to nothing. Some perplexity respecting the rights of the courts to pronounce legislative acts void, because contrary to the Constitution, has arisen from an imagination that the doctrine would imply a superiority of the judiciary to the legislative power. It is urged that the authority which can declare the acts of another void, must necessarily be superior to the one whose acts may be declared void. As this doctrine is of great importance in all the American constitutions, a brief discussion of the ground on which it rests cannot be unacceptable.

There is no position which depends on clearer principles, than that every act of a delegated authority, contrary to the tenor of the commission under which it is exercised, is void. No legislative act, therefore, contrary to the Constitution, can be valid. To deny this, would be to affirm, that the deputy is greater than his principal; that the servant is above his master; that the representatives of the people are superior to the people themselves; that men acting by virtue of powers, may do not only what their powers do not authorize, but what they forbid.

If it be said that the legislative body are themselves the constitutional judges of their own powers, and that the construction they put upon them is conclusive upon the other departments, it may be answered, that this cannot be the natural presumption, where it is not to be collected from any particular provisions in the Constitution. It is not otherwise to be supposed, that the Constitution could intend to enable the representatives of the people to substitute their will to that of their constituents. It is far more rational to suppose, that the courts were designed to be an intermediate body between the people and the legislature, in order, among other things, to keep the latter within the limits assigned to their authority. The interpretation of the laws is the proper and peculiar province of the courts. A constitution is, in fact, and must be regarded by the judges, as a fundamental law. It therefore belongs to them to ascertain its meaning, as well as the meaning of any particular act proceeding from the legislative body. If there should happen to be an irreconcilable variance between the two, that which has the superior obligation and validity ought, of course, to be preferred; or, in other words, the Constitution ought to be preferred to the statute, the intention of the people to the intention of their agents.

Nor does this conclusion by any means suppose a superiority of the judicial to the legislative power. It only supposes that the power of the people is superior to both; and that where the will of the legislature, declared in its statutes, stands in opposition to that of the people, declared in the Constitution, the judges ought to be governed by the latter rather than the former. They ought to regulate their decisions by the fundamental laws, rather than by those which are not fundamental.

This exercise of judicial discretion, in determining between two contradictory laws, is exemplified in a familiar instance. It not uncommonly happens, that there are two statutes existing at one time, clashing in whole or in part with each other, and neither of them containing any repealing clause or expression. In such a case, it is the province of the courts to liquidate and fix their meaning and operation. So far as they can, by any fair construction, be reconciled to each other, reason and law conspire to dictate that this should be done; where this is impracticable, it becomes a matter of necessity to give effect to one, in exclusion of the other. The rule which has obtained in the courts for determining their relative validity is, that the last in order of time shall be preferred to the first. But this is a mere rule of construction, not derived from any positive law, but from the nature and reason of the thing. It is a rule not enjoined upon the courts by legislative provision, but adopted by themselves, as consonant to truth the propriety, for the direction of their conduct as interpreters of the law. They thought it reasonable, that between the interfering acts of an equal authority, that which was the last indication of its will should have the preference.

But in regard to the interfering acts of a superior and subordinate authority, of an original and derivative power, the nature and reason of the thing indicate the converse of that rule as proper to be followed. They teach us that the prior act of a superior ought to be preferred to the subsequent act of an inferior and subordinate authority; and that accordingly, whenever a particular statute contravenes the Constitution, it will be the duty of the judicial tribunals to adhere to the latter and disregard the former.

It can be of no weight to say that the courts, on the pretense of a repugnancy, may substitute their own pleasure to the constitutional intentions of the legislature. This might as well happen in the case of two contradictory statutes; or it might as well happen in every adjudication upon any single statute. The courts must declare the sense of the law; and if they should be disposed to exercise will instead of judgment, the consequence would equally be the substitution of their pleasure to that of the legislative body. The observation, if it prove anything, would prove that there ought to be no judges distinct from that body.

If, then, the courts of justice are to be considered as the bulwarks of a limited Constitution against legislative encroachments, this consideration will afford a strong argument for the permanent tenure of judicial offices, since nothing will contribute so much as this to that independent spirit in the judges which must be essential to the faithful performance of so arduous a duty.

The independence of the judges is equally requisite to guard the Constitution and the rights of individuals from the effects of those ill humors, which the arts of designing men, or the influence of particular conjunctures, sometimes disseminate among the people themselves, and which, though they speedily give place to better information, and more deliberate reflection, have a tendency, in the meantime, to occasion dangerous innovations in the government, and serious oppressions of the minor party in the community. Though I trust the friends of the proposed Constitution will never concur with its enemies, in questioning that fundamental principle of republican government, which admits the right of the people to alter or abolish the established Constitution, whenever they find it inconsistent with their happiness, yet it is not to be inferred from this principle, that the representatives of the people, whenever a momentary inclination happens to lay hold of a majority of their constituents, incompatible with the provisions of the existing Constitution, would, on that account, be justifiable in a violation of those provisions; or that the courts would be under a greater obligation to connive at infractions in this shape, than when they had proceeded wholly from the cabals of the representative body. Until the people have, by some solemn and authoritative act, annulled or changed the established form, it is binding upon themselves collectively, as well as individually; and no presumption, or even knowledge, of their sentiments, can warrant their representatives in a departure from it, prior to such an act. But it is easy to see, that it would require an uncommon portion of fortitude in the judges to do their duty as faithful guardians of the Constitution, where legislative invasions of it had been instigated by the major voice of the community.

But it is not with a view to infractions of the Constitution only, that the independence of the judges may be an essential safeguard against the effects of occasional ill humors in the society. These sometimes extend no farther than to the injury of the private rights of particular classes of citizens, by unjust and partial laws. Here also the firmness of the judicial magistracy is of vast importance in mitigating the severity and confining the operation of such laws. It not only serves to moderate the immediate mischiefs of those which may have been passed, but it operates as a check upon the legislative body in passing them; who, perceiving that obstacles to the success of iniquitous intention are to be expected from the scruples of the courts, are in a manner compelled, by the very motives of the injustice they meditate, to qualify their attempts. This is a circumstance calculated to have more influence upon the character of our governments, than but few may be aware of. The benefits of the integrity and moderation of the judiciary have already been felt in more States than one; and though they may have displeased those whose sinister expectations they may have disappointed, they must have commanded the esteem and applause of all the virtuous and disinterested. Considerate men, of every description, ought to prize whatever will tend to beget or fortify that temper in the courts; as no man can be sure that he may not be tomorrow the victim of a spirit of injustice, by which he may be a gainer today. And every man must now feel, that the inevitable tendency of such a spirit is to sap the foundations of public and private confidence, and to introduce in its stead universal distrust and distress.

That inflexible and uniform adherence to the rights of the Constitution, and of individuals, which we perceive to be indispensable in the courts of justice, can certainly not be expected from judges who hold their offices by a temporary commission. Periodical appointments, however regulated, or by whomsoever made, would, in some way or other, be fatal to their necessary independence. If the power of making them was committed either to the Executive or legislature, there would be danger of an improper complaisance to the branch which possessed it; if to both, there would be an unwillingness to hazard the displeasure of either; if to the people, or to persons chosen by them for the special purpose, there would be too great a disposition to consult popularity, to justify a reliance that nothing would be consulted but the Constitution and the laws.

Hamilton points to yet another reason why lifetime tenure for federal judges will benefit the public: effective judgments rest on a knowledge of judicial precedents and the law, and such knowledge can only be obtained through experience on the bench. A "temporary duration of office," according to Hamilton, would "discourage individuals [of 'fit character'] from quitting a lucrative practice to serve on the bench" and ultimately would "throw the administration of justice into the hands of the less able, and less well qualified."

There is yet a further and a weightier reason for the permanency of the judicial offices, which is deducible from the nature of the qualifications they require. It has been frequently remarked, with great propriety, that a voluminous code of laws is one of the inconveniences necessarily connected with the advantages of a free government. To avoid an arbitrary discretion in the courts, it is indispensable that they should be bound down by strict rules and precedents, which serve to define and point out their duty in every particular case that comes before them; and it will readily be conceived from the variety of controversies which grow out of the folly and wickedness of mankind, that the records of those precedents must unavoidably swell to a very considerable bulk, and must demand long and laborious study to acquire a competent knowledge of them. Hence it is, that there can be but few men in the society who will have sufficient skill in the laws to qualify them for the stations of judges. And making the proper deductions for the ordinary depravity of human nature, the number must be still smaller of those who unite the requisite integrity with the requisite knowledge. These considerations apprise us, that the government can have no great option between fit character; and that a temporary duration in office, which would naturally discourage such characters from quitting a lucrative line of practice to accept a seat on the bench, would have a tendency to throw the administration of justice into hands less able, and less well qualified, to conduct it with utility and dignity. In the present circumstances of this country, and in those in which it is likely to be for a long time to come, the disadvantages on this score would be greater than they may at first sight appear; but it must be confessed, that they are far inferior to those which present themselves under other aspects of the subject.

Upon the whole, there can be no room to doubt that the convention acted wisely in copying from the models of those constitutions which have established good behavior as the tenure of their judicial offices, in point of duration; and that so far from being blamable on this account, their plan would have been inexcusably defective, if it had wanted this important feature of good government. The experience of Great Britain affords an illustrious comment on the excellence of the institution.

Publius
(Alexander Hamilton)

APPENDIX D

JUSTICES OF THE UNITED STATES SUPREME COURT SINCE 1900

Chief Justices

Name	Years of Service	State App't from	Appointing President	Age at App't	Political Affiliation	Educational Background*
Fuller, Melville Weston	1888–1910	Illinois	Cleveland	55	Democrat	Bowdoin College; studied at Harvard Law School
White, Edward Douglass	1910–1921	Louisiana	Taft	65	Democrat	Mount St. Mary's College; Georgetown College (now University)
Taft, William Howard	1921–1930	Connecticut	Harding	64	Republican	Yale; Cincinnati Law School
Hughes, Charles Evans	1930–1941	New York	Hoover	68	Republican	Colgate University; Brown; Columbia Law School
Stone, Harlan Fiske	1941–1946	New York	Roosevelt, F.	69	Republican	Amherst College; Columbia
Vinson, Frederick Moore	1946–1953	Kentucky	Truman	56	Democrat	Centre College
Warren, Earl	1953–1969	California	Eisenhower	62	Republican	University of California, Berkeley
Burger, Warren Earl	1969–1986	Virginia	Nixon	62	Republican	University of Minnesota; St. Paul College of Law (Mitchell College)
Rehnquist, William Hubbs	1986–2005	Virginia	Reagan	62	Republican	Stanford; Harvard; Stanford University Law School
Roberts, John G., Jr.	2005–present	District of Columbia	G. W. Bush	50	Republican	Harvard; Harvard Law School

Associate Justices

Name	Years of Service	State App't from	Appointing President	Age at App't	Political Affiliation	Educational Background*
Harlan, John Marshall	1877–1911	Kentucky	Hayes	61	Republican	Centre College; studied law at Transylvania University
Gray, Horace	1882–1902	Massachusetts	Arthur	54	Republican	Harvard College; Harvard Law School
Brewer, David Josiah	1890–1910	Kansas	Harrison	53	Republican	Wesleyan University; Yale; Albany Law School
Brown, Henry Billings	1891–1906	Michigan	Harrison	55	Republican	Yale; studied at Yale Law School and Harvard Law School
Shiras, George, Jr.	1892–1903	Pennsylvania	Harrison	61	Republican	Ohio University; Yale; studied law at Yale and privately
White, Edward Douglass	1894–1910	Louisiana	Cleveland	49	Democrat	Mount St. Mary's College; Georgetown College (now University)
Peckham, Rufus Wheeler	1896–1909	New York	Cleveland	58	Democrat	Read law in father's firm
McKenna, Joseph	1898–1925	California	McKinley	55	Republican	Benica Collegiate Institute, Law Department
Holmes, Oliver Wendell, Jr.	1902–1932	Massachusetts	Roosevelt, T.	61	Republican	Harvard College; studied law at Harvard Law School

*Sources: Educational background information derived from Elder Witt, *Guide to the U.S. Supreme Court*, 2d ed. (Washington, D.C.: Congressional Quarterly Press, Inc., 1990). Reprinted with the permission of the publisher. Plus authors' update.

(Continued)

Associate Justices (Continued)

Name	Years of Service	State App't from	Appointing President	Age at App't	Political Affiliation	Educational Background
Day, William Rufus	1903–1922	Ohio	Roosevelt, T.	54	Republican	University of Michigan; University of Michigan Law School
Moody, William Henry	1906–1910	Massachusetts	Roosevelt, T.	53	Republican	Harvard; Harvard Law School
Lurton, Horace Harmon	1910–1914	Tennessee	Taft	66	Democrat	University of Chicago; Cumberland Law School
Hughes, Charles Evans	1910–1916	New York	Taft	48	Republican	Colgate University; Brown University; Columbia Law School
Van Devanter, Willis	1911–1937	Wyoming	Taft	52	Republican	Indiana Asbury University; University of Cincinnati Law School
Lamar, Joseph Rucker	1911–1916	Georgia	Taft	54	Democrat	University of Georgia; Bethany College; Washington and Lee University
Pitney, Mahlon	1912–1922	New Jersey	Taft	54	Republican	College of New Jersey (Princeton); read law under father
McReynolds, James Clark	1914–1941	Tennessee	Wilson	52	Democrat	Vanderbilt University; University of Virginia
Brandeis, Louis Dembitz	1916–1939	Massachusetts	Wilson	60	Democrat	Harvard Law School
Clarke, John Hessin	1916–1922	Ohio	Wilson	59	Democrat	Western Reserve University; read law under father
Sutherland, George	1922–1938	Utah	Harding	60	Republican	Brigham Young Academy; one year at University of Michigan Law School
Butler, Pierce	1923–1939	Minnesota	Harding	57	Democrat	Carleton College
Sanford, Edward Terry	1923–1930	Tennessee	Harding	58	Republican	University of Tennessee; Harvard; Harvard Law School
Stone, Harlan Fiske	1925–1941	New York	Coolidge	53	Republican	Amherst College; Columbia University Law School
Roberts, Owen Josephus	1930–1945	Pennsylvania	Hoover	55	Republican	University of Pennsylvania; University of Pennsylvania Law School
Cardozo, Benjamin Nathan	1932–1938	New York	Hoover	62	Democrat	Columbia University; two years at Columbia Law School
Black, Hugo Lafayette	1937–1971	Alabama	Roosevelt, F.	51	Democrat	Birmingham Medical College; University of Alabama Law School
Reed, Stanley Forman	1938–1957	Kentucky	Roosevelt, F.	54	Democrat	Kentucky Wesleyan University; Foreman Yale; studied law at University of Virginia and Columbia University; University of Paris
Frankfurter, Felix	1939–1962	Massachusetts	Roosevelt, F.	57	Independent	College of the City of New York; Harvard Law School
Douglas, William Orville	1939–1975	Connecticut	Roosevelt, F.	41	Democrat	Whitman College; Columbia University Law School
Murphy, Frank	1940–1949	Michigan	Roosevelt, F.	50	Democrat	University of Michigan; Lincoln's Inn, London; Trinity College
Byrnes, James Francis	1941–1942	South Carolina	Roosevelt, F.	62	Democrat	Read law privately
Jackson, Robert Houghwout	1941–1954	New York	Roosevelt, F.	49	Democrat	Albany Law School
Rutledge, Wiley Blount	1943–1949	Iowa	Roosevelt, F.	49	Democrat	University of Wisconsin; University of Colorado

Associate Justices (Continued)

Name	Years of Service	State App't from	Appointing President	Age at App't	Political Affiliation	Educational Background
Burton, Harold Hitz	1945–1958	Ohio	Truman	57	Republican	Bowdoin College; Harvard Law School
Clark, Thomas Campbell	1949–1967	Texas	Truman	50	Democrat	University of Texas
Minton, Sherman	1949–1956	Indiana	Truman	59	Democrat	Indiana University College of Law; Yale Law School
Harlan, John Marshall	1955–1971	New York	Eisenhower	56	Republican	Princeton; Oxford University; New York Law School
Brennan, William J., Jr.	1956–1990	New Jersey	Eisenhower	50	Democrat	University of Pennsylvania; Harvard Law School
Whittaker, Charles Evans	1957–1962	Missouri	Eisenhower	56	Republican	University of Kansas City Law School
Stewart, Potter	1958–1981	Ohio	Eisenhower	43	Republican	Yale; Yale Law School
White, Byron Raymond	1962–1993	Colorado	Kennedy	45	Democrat	University of Colorado; Oxford University; Yale Law School
Goldberg, Arthur Joseph	1962–1965	Illinois	Kennedy	54	Democrat	Northwestern University
Fortas, Abe	1965–1969	Tennessee	Johnson, L.	55	Democrat	Southwestern College; Yale Law School
Marshall, Thurgood	1967–1991	New York	Johnson, L.	59	Democrat	Lincoln University; Howard University Law School
Blackmun, Harry A.	1970–1994	Minnesota	Nixon	62	Republican	Harvard; Harvard Law School
Powell, Lewis F., Jr.	1972–1987	Virginia	Nixon	65	Democrat	Washington and Lee University; Washington and Lee University Law School; Harvard Law School
Rehnquist, William H.	1972–1986	Arizona	Nixon	48	Republican	Stanford; Harvard; Stanford University Law School
Stevens, John Paul	1975–present	Illinois	Ford	55	Republican	University of Colorado; Northwestern University Law School
O'Connor, Sandra Day	1981–2006	Arizona	Reagan	51	Republican	Stanford; Stanford University Law School
Scalia, Antonin	1986–present	Virginia	Reagan	50	Republican	Georgetown University; Harvard Law School
Kennedy, Anthony M.	1988–present	California	Reagan	52	Republican	Stanford; London School of Economics; Harvard Law School
Souter, David Hackett	1990–present	New Hampshire	G. H. W. Bush	51	Republican	Harvard; Oxford University
Thomas, Clarence	1991–present	District of Columbia	G. H. W. Bush	43	Republican	Holy Cross College; Yale Law School
Ginsburg, Ruth Bader	1993–present	District of Columbia	Clinton	60	Democrat	Cornell University; Columbia Law School
Breyer, Stephen G.	1994–present	Massachusetts	Clinton	55	Democrat	Stanford University; Oxford University; Harvard Law School
Alito, Samuel Anthony, Jr.	2006–present	New Jersey	G. W. Bush	55	Republican	Princeton University; Yale Law School
Sotomayor, Sonia Marie	2009–present	New York	Obama	55	Democrat	Princeton University; Yale Law School
Kagan, Elena	2010–present	District of Columbia	Obama	50	Democrat	Princeton and Oxford Universities; Harvard Law School

APPENDIX E

PARTY CONTROL OF CONGRESS SINCE 1900

Congress	Years	President	Majority Party in House	Majority Party in Senate
57th	1901–1903	McKinley/T. Roosevelt	Republican	Republican
58th	1903–1905	T. Roosevelt	Republican	Republican
59th	1905–1907	T. Roosevelt	Republican	Republican
60th	1907–1909	T. Roosevelt	Republican	Republican
61st	1909–1911	Taft	Republican	Republican
62d	1911–1913	Taft	Democratic	Republican
63d	1913–1915	Wilson	Democratic	Democratic
64th	1915–1917	Wilson	Democratic	Democratic
65th	1917–1919	Wilson	Democratic	Democratic
66th	1919–1921	Wilson	Republican	Republican
67th	1921–1923	Harding	Republican	Republican
68th	1923–1925	Harding/Coolidge	Republican	Republican
69th	1925–1927	Coolidge	Republican	Republican
70th	1927–1929	Coolidge	Republican	Republican
71st	1929–1931	Hoover	Republican	Republican
72d	1931–1933	Hoover	Democratic	Republican
73d	1933–1935	F. Roosevelt	Democratic	Democratic
74th	1935–1937	F. Roosevelt	Democratic	Democratic
75th	1937–1939	F. Roosevelt	Democratic	Democratic
76th	1939–1941	F. Roosevelt	Democratic	Democratic
77th	1941–1943	F. Roosevelt	Democratic	Democratic
78th	1943–1945	F. Roosevelt	Democratic	Democratic
79th	1945–1947	F. Roosevelt/Truman	Democratic	Democratic
80th	1947–1949	Truman	Republican	Democratic
81st	1949–1951	Truman	Democratic	Democratic
82d	1951–1953	Truman	Democratic	Democratic
83d	1953–1955	Eisenhower	Republican	Republican
84th	1955–1957	Eisenhower	Democratic	Democratic
85th	1957–1959	Eisenhower	Democratic	Democratic
86th	1959–1961	Eisenhower	Democratic	Democratic
87th	1961–1963	Kennedy	Democratic	Democratic
88th	1963–1965	Kennedy/Johnson	Democratic	Democratic
89th	1965–1967	Johnson	Democratic	Democratic
90th	1967–1969	Johnson	Democratic	Democratic
91st	1969–1971	Nixon	Democratic	Democratic
92d	1971–1973	Nixon	Democratic	Democratic
93d	1973–1975	Nixon/Ford	Democratic	Democratic
94th	1975–1977	Ford	Democratic	Democratic
95th	1977–1979	Carter	Democratic	Democratic
96th	1979–1981	Carter	Democratic	Democratic
97th	1981–1983	Reagan	Democratic	Republican
98th	1983–1985	Reagan	Democratic	Republican
99th	1985–1987	Reagan	Democratic	Republican
100th	1987–1989	Reagan	Democratic	Democratic
101st	1989–1991	G. H. W. Bush	Democratic	Democratic
102d	1991–1993	G. H. W. Bush	Democratic	Democratic
103d	1993–1995	Clinton	Democratic	Democratic
104th	1995–1997	Clinton	Republican	Republican
105th	1997–1999	Clinton	Republican	Republican
106th	1999–2001	Clinton	Republican	Republican
107th	2001–2003	G. W. Bush	Republican	Democratic
108th	2003–2005	G. W. Bush	Republican	Republican
109th	2005–2007	G. W. Bush	Republican	Republican
110th	2007–2009	G. W. Bush	Democratic	Democratic
111th	2009–2011	Obama	Democratic	Democratic
112th	2011–2013	Obama	Republican	Democratic
113th	2013–2015	Obama	Republican	Democratic

APPENDIX F

PRESIDENTS OF THE UNITED STATES

	Term of Service	Age at Inauguration	Political Party	College or University	Occupation or Profession
1. George Washington	1789–1797	57	None		Planter
2. John Adams	1797–1801	61	Federalist	Harvard	Lawyer
3. Thomas Jefferson	1801–1809	57	Jeffersonian Republican	William and Mary	Planter, Lawyer
4. James Madison	1809–1817	57	Jeffersonian Republican	Princeton	Lawyer
5. James Monroe	1817–1825	58	Jeffersonian Republican	William and Mary	Lawyer
6. John Quincy Adams	1825–1829	57	Jeffersonian Republican	Harvard	Lawyer
7. Andrew Jackson	1829–1837	61	Democrat		Lawyer
8. Martin Van Buren	1837–1841	54	Democrat		Lawyer
9. William H. Harrison	1841	68	Whig	Hampden-Sydney	Soldier
10. John Tyler	1841–1845	51	Whig	William and Mary	Lawyer
11. James K. Polk	1845–1849	49	Democrat	U. of N. Carolina	Lawyer
12. Zachary Taylor	1849–1850	64	Whig		Soldier
13. Millard Fillmore	1850–1853	50	Whig		Lawyer
14. Franklin Pierce	1853–1857	48	Democrat	Bowdoin	Lawyer
15. James Buchanan	1857–1861	65	Democrat	Dickinson	Lawyer
16. Abraham Lincoln	1861–1865	52	Republican		Lawyer
17. Andrew Johnson	1865–1869	56	National Union†		Tailor
18. Ulysses S. Grant	1869–1877	46	Republican	U.S. Mil. Academy	Soldier
19. Rutherford B. Hayes	1877–1881	54	Republican	Kenyon	Lawyer
20. James A. Garfield	1881	49	Republican	Williams	Lawyer
21. Chester A. Arthur	1881–1885	51	Republican	Union	Lawyer
22. Grover Cleveland	1885–1889	47	Democrat		Lawyer
23. Benjamin Harrison	1889–1893	55	Republican	Miami	Lawyer
24. Grover Cleveland	1893–1897	55	Democrat		Lawyer
25. William McKinley	1897–1901	54	Republican	Allegheny College	Lawyer
26. Theodore Roosevelt	1901–1909	42	Republican	Harvard	Author
27. William H. Taft	1909–1913	51	Republican	Yale	Lawyer
28. Woodrow Wilson	1913–1921	56	Democrat	Princeton	Educator
29. Warren G. Harding	1921–1923	55	Republican		Editor
30. Calvin Coolidge	1923–1929	51	Republican	Amherst	Lawyer
31. Herbert C. Hoover	1929–1933	54	Republican	Stanford	Engineer
32. Franklin D. Roosevelt	1933–1945	51	Democrat	Harvard	Lawyer
33. Harry S. Truman	1945–1953	60	Democrat		Businessman
34. Dwight D. Eisenhower	1953–1961	62	Republican	U.S. Mil. Academy	Soldier
35. John F. Kennedy	1961–1963	43	Democrat	Harvard	Author
36. Lyndon B. Johnson	1963–1969	55	Democrat	Southwest Texas State	Teacher
37. Richard M. Nixon	1969–1974	56	Republican	Whittier	Lawyer
38. Gerald R. Ford‡	1974–1977	61	Republican	Michigan	Lawyer
39. James E. Carter, Jr.	1977–1981	52	Democrat	U.S. Naval Academy	Businessman
40. Ronald W. Reagan	1981–1989	69	Republican	Eureka College	Actor
41. George H. W. Bush	1989–1993	64	Republican	Yale	Businessman
42. Bill Clinton	1993–2001	46	Democrat	Georgetown	Lawyer
43. George W. Bush	2001–2009	54	Republican	Yale	Businessman
44. Barack Obama	2009–	47	Democrat	Columbia	Lawyer

*Church preference; never joined any church.

†The National Union Party consisted of Republicans and War Democrats. Johnson was a Democrat.

**Inaugurated Dec. 6, 1973, to replace Agnew, who resigned Oct. 10, 1973.

Religion	Born	Died	Age at Death	Vice President	
1. Episcopalian	Feb. 22, 1732	Dec. 14, 1799	67	John Adams	(1789–1797)
2. Unitarian	Oct. 30, 1735	July 4, 1826	90	Thomas Jefferson	(1797–1801)
3. Unitarian*	Apr. 13, 1743	July 4, 1826	83	Aaron Burr George Clinton	(1801–1805) (1805–1809)
4. Episcopalian	Mar. 16, 1751	June 28, 1836	85	George Clinton Elbridge Gerry	(1809–1812) (1813–1814)
5. Episcopalian	Apr. 28, 1758	July 4, 1831	73	Daniel D. Tompkins	(1817–1825)
6. Unitarian	July 11, 1767	Feb. 23, 1848	80	John C. Calhoun	(1825–1829)
7. Presbyterian	Mar. 15, 1767	June 8, 1845	78	John C. Calhoun Martin Van Buren	(1829–1832) (1833–1837)
8. Dutch Reformed	Dec. 5, 1782	July 24, 1862	79	Richard M. Johnson	(1837–1841)
9. Episcopalian	Feb. 9, 1773	Apr. 4, 1841	68	John Tyler	(1841)
10. Episcopalian	Mar. 29, 1790	Jan. 18, 1862	71		
11. Methodist	Nov. 2, 1795	June 15, 1849	53	George M. Dallas	(1845–1849)
12. Episcopalian	Nov. 24, 1784	July 9, 1850	65	Millard Fillmore	(1849–1850)
13. Unitarian	Jan. 7, 1800	Mar. 8, 1874	74		
14. Episcopalian	Nov. 23, 1804	Oct. 8, 1869	64	William R. King	(1853)
15. Presbyterian	Apr. 23, 1791	June 1, 1868	77	John C. Breckinridge	(1857–1861)
16. Presbyterian*	Feb. 12, 1809	Apr. 15, 1865	56	Hannibal Hamlin Andrew Johnson	(1861–1865) (1865)
17. Methodist*	Dec. 29, 1808	July 31, 1875	66		
18. Methodist	Apr. 27, 1822	July 23, 1885	63	Schuyler Colfax Henry Wilson	(1869–1873) (1873–1875)
19. Methodist*	Oct. 4, 1822	Jan. 17, 1893	70	William A. Wheeler	(1877–1881)
20. Disciples of Christ	Nov. 19, 1831	Sept. 19, 1881	49	Chester A. Arthur	(1881)
21. Episcopalian	Oct. 5, 1829	Nov. 18, 1886	57		
22. Presbyterian	Mar. 18, 1837	June 24, 1908	71	Thomas A. Hendricks	(1885)
23. Presbyterian	Aug. 20, 1833	Mar. 13, 1901	67	Levi P. Morton	(1889–1893)
24. Presbyterian	Mar. 18, 1837	June 24, 1908	71	Adlai E. Stevenson	(1893–1897)
25. Methodist	Jan. 29, 1843	Sept. 14, 1901	58	Garret A. Hobart Theodore Roosevelt	(1897–1899) (1901)
26. Dutch Reformed	Oct. 27, 1858	Jan. 6, 1919	60	Charles W. Fairbanks	(1905–1909)
27. Unitarian	Sept. 15, 1857	Mar. 8, 1930	72	James S. Sherman	(1909–1912)
28. Presbyterian	Dec. 29, 1856	Feb. 3, 1924	67	Thomas R. Marshall	(1913–1921)
29. Baptist	Nov. 2, 1865	Aug. 2, 1923	57	Calvin Coolidge	(1921–1923)
30. Congregationalist	July 4, 1872	Jan. 5, 1933	60	Charles G. Dawes	(1925–1929)
31. Friend (Quaker)	Aug. 10, 1874	Oct. 20, 1964	90	Charles Curtis	(1929–1933)
32. Episcopalian	Jan. 30, 1882	Apr. 12, 1945	63	John N. Garner Henry A. Wallace Harry S. Truman	(1933–1941) (1941–1945) (1945)
33. Baptist	May 8, 1884	Dec. 26, 1972	88	Alben W. Barkley	(1949–1953)
34. Presbyterian	Oct. 14, 1890	Mar. 28, 1969	78	Richard M. Nixon	(1953–1961)
35. Roman Catholic	May 29, 1917	Nov. 22, 1963	46	Lyndon B. Johnson	(1961–1963)
36. Disciples of Christ	Aug. 27, 1908	Jan. 22, 1973	64	Hubert H. Humphrey	(1965–1969)
37. Friend (Quaker)	Jan. 9, 1913	Apr. 22, 1994	81	Spiro T. Agnew Gerald R. Ford**	(1969–1973) (1973–1974)
38. Episcopalian	July 14, 1913	Dec. 26, 2006	93	Nelson A. Rockefeller§	(1974–1977)
39. Baptist	Oct. 1, 1924			Walter F. Mondale	(1977–1981)
40. Disciples of Christ	Feb. 6, 1911	June 5, 2004	93	George H. W. Bush	(1981–1989)
41. Episcopalian	June 12, 1924			J. Danforth Quayle	(1989–1993)
42. Baptist	Aug. 19, 1946			Albert A. Gore	(1993–2001)
43. Methodist	July 6, 1946			Dick Cheney	(2001–2009)
44. United Church of Christ	Aug. 4, 1961			Joe Biden	(2009–)

‡Inaugurated Aug. 9, 1974, to replace Nixon, who resigned that same day.
§Inaugurated Dec. 19, 1974, to replace Ford, who became president Aug. 9, 1974.

GLOSSARY

A

Acquisitive Model A model of bureaucracy that views top-level bureaucrats as seeking to expand the size of their budgets and staffs to gain greater power.

Actual Malice Either knowledge of a defamatory statement's falsity or a reckless disregard for the truth.

Administrative Agency A federal, state, or local government unit established to perform a specific function. Administrative agencies are created and authorized by legislative bodies to administer and enforce specific laws.

Advice and Consent Terms in the Constitution describing the U.S. Senate's power to review and approve treaties and presidential appointments.

Affirm To declare that a court ruling is valid and must stand.

Affirmative Action A policy in educational admissions or job hiring that gives special attention or compensatory treatment to traditionally disadvantaged groups in an effort to overcome present effects of past discrimination.

Agenda Setting Determining which public-policy questions will be debated or considered.

***Amicus Curiae* Brief** A brief (a document containing a legal argument supporting a desired outcome in a particular case) filed by a third party, or *amicus curiae* (Latin for "friend of the court"), who is not directly involved in the litigation but who has an interest in the outcome of the case.

Anarchy The condition of no government.

Anti-Federalist An individual who opposed the ratification of the new Constitution in 1787. The Anti-Federalists were opposed to a strong central government.

Appellate Court A court having jurisdiction to review cases and issues that were originally tried in lower courts.

Appointment Power The authority vested in the president to fill a government office or position. Positions filled by presidential appointment include those in the executive branch and the federal judiciary, commissioned officers in the armed forces, and members of the independent regulatory commissions.

Appropriation The passage, by Congress, of a spending bill specifying the amount of authorized funds that actually will be allocated for an agency's use.

Aristocracy "Rule by the best"; in reality, rule by members of the upper class.

Arraignment The first act in a criminal proceeding, in which the defendant is brought before a court to hear the charges against him or her and enter a plea of guilty or not guilty.

Australian Ballot A secret ballot prepared, distributed, and tabulated by government officials at public expense. Since 1888, all states have used the Australian ballot rather than an open, public ballot.

Authoritarianism A type of regime in which only the government itself is fully controlled by the ruler. Social and economic institutions exist that are not under the government's control.

Authority The right and power of a government or other entity to enforce its decisions.

Authorization A formal declaration by a legislative committee that a certain amount of funding may be available to an agency. Some authorizations terminate in a year; others are renewable automatically without further congressional action.

B

Bias An inclination or preference that interferes with impartial judgment.

Bicameral Legislature A legislature made up of two parts, called chambers. The U.S. Congress, composed of the House of Representatives and the Senate, is a bicameral legislature.

Bicameralism The division of a legislature into two separate assemblies.

Bill of Rights The first ten amendments to the U.S. Constitution.

Block Grants A federal grant that provides funds to a state or local government for a general functional area, such as criminal justice or mental-health programs.

Boycott A form of pressure or protest—an organized refusal to purchase a particular product or deal with a particular business.

Broad Construction A judicial philosophy that looks to the context and purpose of a law when making an interpretation.

Budget Deficit Government expenditures that exceed receipts.

Bureaucracy An organization that is structured hierarchically to carry out specific functions.

C

Cabinet An advisory group selected by the president to aid in making decisions. The cabinet includes the heads of fifteen executive departments and others named by the president.

Cabinet Department One of the fifteen major departments of the executive branch.

Capitalism An economic system characterized by the private ownership of wealth-creating assets, free markets, and freedom of contract.

Capture The act by which an industry being regulated by a government agency gains direct or indirect control over agency personnel and decision makers.

Case Law Judicial interpretations of common law principles and doctrines, as well as interpretations of constitutional law, statutory law, and administrative law.

Casework Personal work for constituents by members of Congress.

Categorical Grants A Federal grants to a states or local government for a specific programs or projects.

Caucus A meeting of party members to select candidates and propose policies.

Checks and Balances A major principle of the American system of government whereby each branch of the government can check the actions of the others.

Chief Diplomat The role of the president in recognizing foreign governments, making treaties, and effecting executive agreements.

Chief Executive The role of the president as head of the executive branch of the government.

Chief Legislator The role of the president in influencing the making of laws.

Chief of Staff The person who is named to direct the White House Office and advise the president.

Civil Disobedience A nonviolent, public refusal to obey allegedly unjust laws.

Civil Law The law regulating conduct between private persons over noncriminal matters, including contracts, domestic relations, and business interactions.

Civil Liberties Those personal freedoms, including freedom of religion and freedom of speech, that are protected for all individuals. The civil liberties set forth in the U.S. Constitution, as amended, restrain the government from taking certain actions against individuals.

Civil Rights Generally, all rights rooted in the Fourteenth Amendment's guarantee of equal protection under the law.

Civil Service A collective term for the body of employees working for the government. Generally, "civil service" is understood to apply to all those who gain government employment through a merit system.

Civil Service Commission The initial central personnel agency of the national government; created in 1883.

Class-Action Suit A lawsuit filed by an individual seeking damages for "all persons similarly situated."

Clear and Present Danger Test The test proposed by Justice Oliver Wendell Holmes for determining when government may restrict free speech. Restrictions are permissible, he argued, only when speech creates a *clear and present danger* to the public order.

Climate Control The use of public relations techniques to create favorable public opinion toward an interest group, industry, or corporation.

Closed Primary A type of primary in which the voter is limited to choosing candidates of the party of which he or she is a member.

Coattail Effect The influence of a popular candidate on the success of other candidates on the same party ticket.

Cold War The ideological, political, and economic confrontation between the United States and the Soviet Union following World War II.

Commander in Chief The role of the president as supreme commander of the military forces of the United States and of the state National Guard units when they are called into federal service.

Commerce Clause The section of the Constitution in which Congress is given the power to regulate trade among the states and with foreign countries.

Commercial Speech Advertising statements, which increasingly have been given First Amendment protection.

Common Law Judge-made law that originated in England from decisions shaped according to prevailing customs. Decisions were applied to similar situations and thus gradually became common to the nation.

Concurrent Powers Powers held jointly by the national and state governments.

Concurring Opinion A separate opinion prepared by a judge who supports the decision of the majority of the court but who wants to make or clarify a particular point or to voice disapproval of the grounds on which the decision was made.

Confederal System A system consisting of a league of independent states, in which the central government created by the league has only limited powers over the states.

Confederation A political system in which states or regional governments retain ultimate authority except for those powers they expressly delegate to a central government; a voluntary association of independent states, in which the member states agree to limited restraints on their freedom of action.

Conference Committee A special joint committee appointed to reconcile differences when bills pass the two chambers of Congress in different forms.

Consensus General agreement among the citizenry on an issue.

Consent of the People The idea that governments and laws derive their legitimacy from the consent of the governed.

Conservatism A set of beliefs that includes a limited role for the national government in helping individuals, support for traditional ideals and life choices, and a cautious response to change.

Conservative Movement An American movement in the 1950s that provided a comprehensive ideological framework for conservative politics.

Constituent A person represented by a legislator or other elected or appointed official.

Constitutional Power A power vested in the president by Article II of the Constitution.

Containment A U.S. diplomatic policy adopted by the Truman administration to contain Communist power within its existing boundaries.

Continuing Resolution A temporary funding law that Congress passes when an appropriations bill has not been decided by the beginning of the new fiscal year on October 1.

Cooperative Federalism A model of federalism in which the states and the national government cooperate in solving problems.

Credentials Committee A committee used by political parties at their national conventions to determine which delegates may participate. The committee inspects the claim of each prospective delegate to be seated as a legitimate representative of his or her state.

Criminal Law The law that defines crimes and provides punishment for violations. In criminal cases, the government is the prosecutor.

D

***De Facto* Segregation** Racial segregation that occurs because of past social and economic conditions and residential racial patterns.

***De Jure* Segregation** Racial segregation that occurs because of laws or administrative decisions by public agencies.

Dealignment A decline in party loyalties that reduces long-term party commitment.

Defamation of Character Wrongfully hurting a person's good reputation. The law imposes a general duty on all persons to refrain from making false, defamatory statements about others.

Defense Policy A subset of national security policy having to do with the U.S. armed forces.

Democracy A system of government in which political authority is vested in the people. The term is derived from the Greek words demos ("the people") and kratos ("authority").

Democratic Party One of the two major American political parties evolving out of the Republican Party of Thomas Jefferson.

Democratic Republic A republic in which representatives elected by the people make and enforce laws and policies.

Détente A French word meaning a relaxation of tensions. The term characterized U.S.-Soviet relations as they developed under President Richard Nixon and Secretary of State Henry Kissinger.

Devolution The transfer of powers from a national or central government to a state or local government.

Diplomacy The process by which nations carry on political relations with one another and resolve conflicts by peaceful means.

Diplomatic Recognition The formal acknowledgment of a foreign government as legitimate.

Direct Democracy A system of government in which political decisions are made by the people directly, rather than by their elected representatives; probably attained most easily in small political communities.

Direct Primary A primary election in which voters decide party nominations by voting directly for candidates.

Direct Technique An interest group activity that involves personal interaction with government officials to further the group's goals.

Discharge Petition A procedure by which a bill in the House of Representatives can be forced (discharged) out of a committee that has refused to report it for consideration by the House. The petition must be signed by an absolute majority (218) of representatives and is used only on rare occasions.

Dissenting Opinion A separate opinion in which a judge dissents from (disagrees with) the conclusion reached by the majority on the court and expounds his or her own views about the case.

Diversity of Citizenship The condition that exists when the parties to a lawsuit are citizens of different states or when the parties are citizens of a U.S. state and citizens or the government of a foreign country. Diversity of citizenship can provide a basis for federal jurisdiction.

Divided Government A situation in which one major political party controls the presidency and the other controls one or more chambers of Congress, or in which one party controls a state governorship and the other controls part or all of the state legislature.

Divided Opinion Public opinion that is polarized between two quite different positions.

Domestic Policy All of the laws, government planning, and government actions that concern internal issues of national importance, such as poverty, crime, and the environment.

Dual Federalism A model of federalism in which the states and the national government each remain supreme within their own spheres. The doctrine looks on nation and state as co-equal sovereign powers. Neither the state government nor the national government should interfere in the other's sphere.

E

Earmarks Special provisions in legislation to set aside funds for projects that have not passed an impartial evaluation by agencies of the executive branch. Also known as pork.

Economic Aid Assistance to other nations in the form of grants, loans, or credits to buy the assisting nation's products.

Elastic Clause, or Necessary and Proper Clause The clause in Article I, Section 8, that grants Congress the power to do whatever is necessary to execute its specifically delegated powers.

Elector A member of the electoral college, which selects the president and vice president. Each state's electors are chosen in each presidential election year according to state laws.

Electoral College A group of persons, called electors, who are selected by the voters in each state. This group officially elects the president and the vice president of the United States.

Elite Theory A perspective holding that society is ruled by a small number of people who exercise power to further their self-interests.

Emergency Power An inherent power exercised by the president during a period of national crisis.

Enabling Legislation A statute enacted by Congress that authorizes the creation of an administrative agency and specifies the name, purpose, composition, functions, and powers of the agency being created.

Enumerated Power Powers specifically granted to the national government by the Constitution. The first seventeen clauses of Article I, Section 8, specify most of the enumerated powers of the national government.

Equality As a political value, the idea that all people are of equal worth.

Establishment Clause The part of the First Amendment prohibiting the establishment of a church officially supported by the national government. It determines the legality of giving state and local government aid to religious organizations and schools, allowing or requiring school prayers, and teaching evolution versus creationism.

Exclusionary Rule A judicial policy prohibiting the admission at trial of illegally obtained evidence.

Executive Agreement An international agreement between chiefs of state that does not require legislative approval.

Executive Budget The budget prepared and submitted by the president to Congress.

Executive Office of the President (EOP) An organization established by President Franklin Roosevelt to assist the president in carrying out major duties.

Executive Order A rule or regulation issued by the president that has the effect of law. Executive orders can implement and give administrative effect to provisions in the U.S. Constitution, treaties, or statutes.

Executive Privilege The right of executive officials to withhold information from or to refuse to appear before a legislative committee.

Expressed Power A power of the president that is expressly written into the Constitution or into statutory law.

F

Faction A group or bloc in a legislature or political party that is trying to obtain power or benefits.

Fairness Doctrine A Federal Communications Commission rule enforced between 1949 and 1987 that required radio and television to present controversial issues and discuss them in a manner that was (in the commission's view) honest, equitable, and balanced.

Fall Review The annual process in which the OMB, after receiving formal federal agency requests for funding for the next fiscal year, reviews the requests, makes changes, and submits its recommendations to the president.

Federal Election Commission (FEC) The federal regulatory agency with the task of enforcing federal campaign laws. As a practical matter, the FEC's role is largely limited to collecting data on campaign contributions.

Federal Mandate A requirement in federal legislation that forces states and municipalities to comply with certain rules.

Federal Open Market Committee The most important body within the Federal Reserve System. The Federal Open Market Committee decides how monetary policy should be carried out.

Federal Question A question that has to do with the U.S. Constitution, acts of Congress, or treaties. A federal question provides a basis for federal jurisdiction.

Federal Register A publication of the U.S. government that prints executive orders, rules, and regulations.

Federal Reserve System (the Fed) The agency created by Congress in 1913 to serve as the nation's central banking organization.

Federal System A system of government in which power is divided between a central government and regional, or subdivisional, governments. Each level must have some domain in which its policies are dominant and some genuine political or constitutional guarantee of its authority.

Federalist The name given to one who was in favor of the adoption of the U.S. Constitution and the creation of a federal union with a strong central government.

Feminism The movement that supports political, economic, and social equality for women.

Fertility Rate A statistic that measures the average number of children that women in a given group are expected to have over the course of a lifetime.

Filibuster The use of the Senate's tradition of unlimited debate as a delaying tactic to block a bill.

First Budget Resolution A resolution passed by Congress in May that sets overall revenue and spending goals for the following fiscal year.

Fiscal Having to do with government revenues and expenditures.

Fiscal Federalism A process by which funds raised through taxation or borrowing by one level of government (usually the national government) are spent by another level (typically state or local governments).

Fiscal Policy The federal government's use of taxation and spending policies to affect overall business activity.

Fiscal Year (FY) A twelve-month period that is used for bookkeeping, or accounting, purposes. Usually, the fiscal year does not coincide with the calendar year. For example, the federal government's fiscal year runs from October 1 through September 30.

Focus Group A small group of individuals who are led in discussion by a professional consultant in order to gather opinions on and responses to candidates and issues.

Foreign Policy A nation's external goals and the techniques and strategies used to achieve them.

Foreign Policy Process The steps by which foreign policy goals are decided and acted on.

Framing Establishing the context of a polling question or a media report. Framing can mean fitting events into a familiar story or activating preconceived beliefs.

Franking A policy that enables members of Congress to send material through the mail by substituting their facsimile signature (frank) for postage.

Free Exercise Clause The provision of the First Amendment guaranteeing the free exercise of religion. The provision constrains the national government from prohibiting individuals from practicing the religion of their choice.

Free Rider Problem The difficulty interest groups face in recruiting members when the benefits they achieve can be gained without joining the group.

Front-Loading The practice of moving presidential primary elections to the early part of the campaign to maximize the impact of these primaries on the nomination.

Front-Runner The presidential candidate who appears to be ahead at a given time in the primary season.

G

Gag Order An order issued by a judge restricting the publication of news about a trial or a pretrial hearing to protect the accused's right to a fair trial.

Gender Discrimination Any practice, policy, or procedure that denies equality of treatment to an individual or to a group because of gender.

Gender Gap The difference between the percentage of women who vote for a particular candidate and the percentage of men who vote for the candidate.

General Election An election open to all eligible voters, normally held on the first Tuesday in November, that determines who will fill various elected positions.

General Jurisdiction A court's authority to hear cases without significant restriction. A court of general jurisdiction normally can hear a broad range of cases.

Generational Effect A long-lasting effect of the events of a particular time on the political opinions of those who came of political age at that time.

Gerrymandering The drawing of legislative district boundary lines for the purpose of obtaining partisan or factional advantage. A district is said to be gerrymandered when its shape is manipulated by the dominant party to maximize electoral strength at the expense of the minority party.

GOP A nickname for the Republican Party that stands for "grand old party."

Government The preeminent institution within society in which decisions are made that resolve conflicts and allocate benefits and privileges. It is unique because it has the ultimate authority for making these decisions.

Government Corporation An agency of government that administers a quasi-business enterprise. These corporations are used when government activities are primarily commercial.

Government in the Sunshine Act A law that requires all committee-directed federal agencies to conduct their business regularly in public session.

Grandfather Clause A device used by southern states to disenfranchise African Americans. It restricted voting to those whose grandfathers had voted before 1867.

Great Compromise The compromise between the New Jersey and Virginia Plans that created one chamber of the Congress based on population and one chamber representing each state equally; also called the Connecticut Compromise.

Gross Domestic Product (GDP) The dollar value of all *final* goods and services produced in a one-year period.

Gross Public Debt The net public debt plus interagency borrowings without the government.

H

Hatch Act An act passed in 1939 that restricted the political activities of government employees. It also prohibited a political group from spending more than $3 million in any campaign and limited individual contributions to a campaign committee to $5,000.

Head of State The role of the president as ceremonial head of the government.

Hispanic Someone who can claim a heritage from a Spanish-speaking country. The term is used only in the United States or other countries that receive immigrants—Spanish-speaking persons living in Spanish-speaking countries do not normally apply the term to themselves.

House Effect In public opinion polling, an effect in which one polling organization's results consistently differ from those reported by other poll takers.

I

Ideology A comprehensive set of beliefs about the nature of people and about the role of an institution or government.

Imminent Lawless Action Test The current standard established by the Supreme Court for evaluating the legality of advocacy speech. Such speech can be forbidden only when it is "directed to inciting . . . imminent lawless action."

Impeachment An action by the House of Representatives to accuse the president, vice president, or other civil officers of the United States of committing "Treason, Bribery, or other high Crimes and Misdemeanors."

Incarceration Rate The number of persons held in jail or prison for every 100,000 persons in a particular population group.

Incorporation Theory The view that most of the protections of the Bill of Rights apply to state governments through the Fourteenth Amendment's due process clause.

Independent A voter or candidate who does not identify with a political party.

Independent Executive Agency A federal agency that is not part of a cabinet department but reports directly to the president.

Independent Expenditures Nonregulated contributions from PACs, organizations, and individuals. The funds may be spent on advertising or other campaign activities, so long as those expenditures are not coordinated with those of a candidate.

Independent Regulatory Agency An agency outside the major executive departments that is charged with making and implementing rules and regulations.

Indirect Primary A primary election in which voters choose convention delegates, and the delegates determine the party's candidate in the general election.

Indirect Technique A strategy employed by interest groups that uses third parties to influence government officials.

Individual Mandate In health-care reform, the requirement that all citizens obtain health-care insurance coverage from some source, public or private.

Inflation A sustained rise in the general price level of goods and services.

Inherent Power A power of the president derived from the statements in the Constitution that "the executive Power shall be vested in a President" and that the president should "take Care that the Laws be faithfully executed"; defined through practice rather than through law.

Initiative A procedure by which voters can propose a law or a constitutional amendment.

Institution An ongoing organization that performs certain functions for society.

Instructed Delegate A legislator who is an agent of the voters who elected him or her and who votes according to the views of constituents regardless of personal beliefs.

Intelligence Community The government agencies that gather information about the capabilities and intentions of foreign governments or that engage in covert actions.

Interest Group An organized group of individuals sharing common objectives who actively attempt to influence policymakers.

Intermediate Scrutiny The standard used by the courts to determine whether a law or government action improperly discriminates against women. Also known as exacting scrutiny.

Interstate Compact An agreement between two or more states. Agreements on minor matters are made without congressional consent, but any compact that tends to increase the power of the contracting states relative to other states or relative to the national government generally requires the consent of Congress.

Iron Triangle The three-way alliance among legislators, bureaucrats, and interest groups to make or preserve policies that benefit their respective interests.

Isolationist Foreign Policy A policy of abstaining from an active role in international affairs or alliances, which characterized U.S. foreign policy toward Europe during most of the 1800s.

Issue Advocacy Advertising paid for by interest groups that support or oppose a candidate or a candidate's position on an issue without mentioning voting or elections.

Issue Network A group of individuals or organizations—which may consist of legislators and legislative staff members, interest group leaders, bureaucrats, scholars and other experts, and media representatives—that supports a particular policy position on a given issue.

J

Joint Committee A legislative committee composed of members from both chambers of Congress.

Judicial Activism A doctrine holding that the federal judiciary should take an active role by using its powers to check the activities of governmental bodies when those bodies exceed their authority.

Judicial Implementation The way in which court decisions are translated into action.

Judicial Restraint A doctrine holding that the courts should defer to the decisions made by the elected representatives of the people in the legislative and executive branches.

Judicial Review The power of the Supreme Court and other courts to declare unconstitutional federal or state laws and other acts of government.

Jurisdiction The authority of a court to decide certain cases. Not all courts have the authority to decide all cases. Where a case arises and what its subject matter is are two jurisdictional issues.

Justiciable Controversy A controversy that is real and substantial, as opposed to hypothetical or academic.

Justiciable Question A question that may be raised and reviewed in court.

K

Keynesian Economics A school of economic thought that tends to favor active federal government policymaking to stabilize economy-wide fluctuations, usually by implementing discretionary fiscal policy.

Kitchen Cabinet The informal advisers to the president.

L

Labor Movement The economic and political expression of working-class interests.

Latent Interests Public-policy interests that are not recognized or addressed by a group at a particular time.

Latino An alternative to the term Hispanic that is preferred by many. Latina is the feminine.

Lawmaking The process of establishing the legal rules that govern society.

Legislature A governmental body primarily responsible for the making of laws.

Legitimacy Popular acceptance of the right and power of a government or other entity to exercise authority.

Libel A written defamation of a person's character, reputation, business, or property rights.

Liberalism A set of beliefs that includes the advocacy of positive government action to improve the welfare of individuals, support for civil rights, and tolerance for political and social change.

Libertarianism A political ideology based on skepticism or opposition toward most government activities.

Liberty The greatest freedom of the individual that is consistent with the freedom of other individuals in the society.

Limited Government A government with powers that are limited either through a written document or through widely shared beliefs.

Limited Jurisdiction A court's authority to hear cases with restriction to certain types of claims, such as tax claims or bankruptcy petitions.

Line Organization In the federal government, an administrative unit that is directly accountable to the president.

Line-Item Veto The power of an executive to veto individual lines or items within a piece of legislation without vetoing the entire bill.

Literacy Test A test administered as a precondition for voting, often used to prevent African Americans from exercising their right to vote.

Litigate To engage in a legal proceeding or seek relief in a court of law; to carry on a lawsuit.

Lobbyist An organization or individual who attempts to influence legislation and the administrative decisions of government.

Logrolling An arrangement in which two or more members of Congress agree in advance to support each other's bills.

Loophole A legal method by which individuals and businesses are allowed to reduce the tax liabilities owed to the government.

Loose Monetary Policy Monetary policy that makes credit inexpensive and abundant, possibly leading to inflation.

M

Madisonian Model A structure of government proposed by James Madison in which the powers of the government are separated into three branches: executive, legislative, and judicial.

Majoritarianism A political theory holding that, in a democracy, the government ought to do what the majority of the people want.

Majority More than 50 percent. Or, the age at which a person is entitled by law to the right to manage her or his own affairs.

Majority Leader of the House The majority leader of the House of Representatives is selected by the majority party in caucus or conference to foster cohesion among party members and to act as spokesperson for the majority party in the House.

Majority Opinion A court opinion reflecting the views of the majority of the judges.

Majority Rule A basic principle of democracy asserting that the greatest number of citizens in any political unit should select officials and determine policies.

Material Incentive A reason or motive based on the desire to enjoy certain economic benefits or opportunities.

Media The channels of mass communication.

Medicaid A joint state-federal program that provides medical care to the poor (including indigent elderly persons in nursing homes). The program is funded out of general government revenues.

Medicare A federal health-insurance program that covers U.S. residents over the age of sixty-five. The costs are met by a tax on wages and salaries.

Merit System The selection, retention, and promotion of government employees on the basis of competitive examinations.

Midterm Elections National elections in which candidates for president are not on the ballot. In midterm elections, voters choose all members of the U.S. House of Representatives and one-third of the members of the U.S. Senate.

Minority Leader of the House The party leader elected by the minority party in the House.

Monetary Policy The use of changes in the amount of money in circulation to alter credit markets, employment, and the rate of inflation.

Monopolistic Model A model of bureaucracy that compares bureaucracies to monopolistic business firms. Lack of competition in either circumstance leads to inefficient and costly operations.

Monroe Doctrine A policy statement made by President James Monroe in 1823, which set out three principles: (1) European nations should not establish new colonies in the Western Hemisphere, (2) European nations should not intervene in the affairs of independent nations of the Western Hemisphere, and (3) the United States would not interfere in the affairs of European nations.

Moral Idealism A philosophy that sees nations as normally willing to cooperate and agree on moral standards for conduct.

N

National Committee A standing committee of a national political party established to direct and coordinate party activities between national party conventions.

National Convention The meeting held every four years by each major party to select presidential and vice-presidential candidates, write a platform, choose a national committee, and conduct party business.

National Security Council (NSC) An agency in the Executive Office of the President that advises the president on national security.

National Security Policy Foreign and domestic policy designed to protect the nation's independence and political integrity; policy that is concerned with the safety and defense of the nation.

Natural Rights Rights held to be inherent in natural law, not dependent on governments. John Locke stated that natural law, being superior to human law, specifies certain rights of "life, liberty, and property." These rights, altered to become "life, liberty, and the pursuit of happiness," are asserted in the Declaration of Independence.

Negative Constituents Citizens who openly oppose the government's policies.

Net Public Debt The accumulation of all past federal government deficits; the total amount owed by the federal government to individuals, businesses, and foreigners.

Normal Trade Relations (NTR) Status A status granted through an international treaty by which each member nation must treat other members as well as it treats the country that receives its most favorable treatment. This status was formerly known as most-favorednation status.

O

Obscenity Sexually offensive material. Obscenity can be illegal if it is found to violate a four-part test established by the United States Supreme Court.

Office of Management and Budget (OMB) A division of the Executive Office of the President. The OMB assists the president in preparing the annual budget, clearing and coordinating departmental agency budgets, and supervising the administration of the federal budget.

Office-Block, or Massachusetts, Ballot A form of general election ballot in which candidates for elective office are grouped together under the title of each office. It emphasizes voting for the office and the individual candidate, rather than for the party.

Oligarchy "Rule by a few."

Ombudsperson A person who hears and investigates complaints by private individuals against public officials or agencies. (From the Swedish word *ombudsman,* meaning "representative.")

Open Primary A primary in which any registered voter can vote (but must vote for candidates of only one party).

Opinion A statement by a judge or a court of the decision reached in a case. An opinion sets forth the applicable law and details the reasoning on which the ruling was based.

Opinion Leader One who is able to influence the opinions of others because of position, expertise, or personality.

Opinion Poll A method of systematically questioning a small, selected sample of respondents who are deemed representative of the total population.

Oral Arguments The arguments presented in person by attorneys to an appellate court. Each attorney presents to the court reasons why the court should rule in her of his client's favor.

Order A state of peace and security. Maintaining order by protecting members of society from violence and criminal activity is the oldest purposes of government.

Oversight The process by which Congress follows up on laws it has enacted to ensure that they are being enforced and administered in the way Congress intended.

P

Pardon A release from the punishment for, or legal consequences of, a crime. A pardon can be granted by the president before or after a conviction.

Party Identification Linking oneself to a particular political party.

Party Identifier A person who identifies with a political party.

Party Organization The formal structure and leadership of a political party, including election committees; local, state, and national executives; and paid professional staff.

Party Platform A document drawn up at each national convention, outlining the policies, positions, and principles of the party.

Party-Column, or Indiana, Ballot A form of general-election ballot in which all of a party's candidates for elective office are arranged in one column under the party's label and symbol. It emphasizes voting for the party, rather than for the office or individual.

Party-in-Government All of the elected and appointed officials who identify with a political party.

Party-in-the-Electorate Those members of the general public who identify with a political party or who express a preference for one party over another.

Patronage The rewarding of faithful party workers and followers with government employment and contracts.

Peer Group A group whose members share common social characteristics. These groups play an important part in the socialization process, helping to shape attitudes and beliefs.

Pendleton Act (Civil Service Reform Act) An act that established the principle of employment on the basis of merit and created the Civil Service Commission to administer the personnel service.

Pluralism A theory that views politics as a conflict among interest groups. Political decision making is characterized by compromise and accommodation.

Plurality A number of votes cast for a candidate that is greater than the number of votes for any other candidate but not necessarily a majority.

Pocket Veto A special veto exercised by the chief executive after a legislative body has adjourned. Bills not signed by the chief executive die after a specified period of time. If Congress wishes to reconsider such a bill, it must be reintroduced in the following session of Congress.

Podcasting A method of distributing multimedia files, such as audio or video files, for downloading onto mobile devices or personal computers.

Police Power The authority to legislate for the protection of the health, morals, safety, and welfare of the people. In the United States, most police power is reserved to the states.

Political Action Committee (PAC) A committee set up by and representing a corporation, labor union, or special interest group. PACs raise and give campaign donations.

Political Consultant A paid professional hired to devise a campaign strategy and manage a campaign.

Political Culture A patterned set of ideas, values, and ways of thinking about government and politics that characterize a people.

Political Party A group of political activists who organize to win elections, operate the government, and determine public policy.

Political Question An issue that a court believes should be decided by the executive or legislative branch—or these two branches acting together.

Political Realism A philosophy that sees each nation acting principally in its own interest.

Political Socialization The process by which political beliefs and values are transmitted to new immigrants and to our children. The family and the educational system are two of the most important sources of the political socialization process.

Political Trust The degree to which individuals express trust in the government and political institutions, usually measured through a specific series of survey questions.

Politics The process of resolving conflicts and deciding "who gets what, when, and how." More specifically, politics is the struggle over power or influence within organizations or informal groups that can grant or withhold benefits or privileges.

Poll Tax A special tax that had to be paid as a qualification for voting. In 1964, the Twenty-fourth Amendment to the Constitution outlawed the poll tax in national elections, and in 1966 the Supreme Court declared it unconstitutional in state elections as well.

Popular Sovereignty The concept that ultimate political authority is based on the will of the people.

Precedent A court rule bearing on subsequent legal decisions in similar cases. Judges rely on precedents in deciding cases.

Preferred Stock A special share of ownership in a corporation that typically confers no right to vote for the company's board of directors, but does pay interest.

President Pro Tempore The temporary presiding officer of the Senate in the absence of the vice president.

Presidential Primary A statewide primary election of delegates to a political party's national convention, held to determine a party's presidential nominee.

Primary Election An election in which political parties choose their candidates for the general election.

Prior Restraint Restraining an activity before it has actually occurred. When expression is involved, this means censorship.

Privatization The replacement of government services with services provided by private firms.

Progressive A popular alternative to the term liberal.

Progressive Tax A tax that rises in percentage terms as incomes rise.

Property Anything that is or may be subject to ownership. As conceived by the political philosopher John Locke, the right to property is a natural right superior to human law (laws made by government).

Public Agenda Issues that are perceived by the political community as meriting public attention and governmental action.

Public Debt, or National Debt The total amount of debt carried by the federal government.

Public Figure A public official or any other person, such as a movie star, known to the public because of his or her position or activities.

Public Interest The best interests of the overall community; the national good, rather than the narrow interests of a particular group.

Public Opinion The aggregate of individual attitudes or beliefs shared by some portion of the adult population.

Purposive Incentive A reason for supporting or participating in the activities of a group that is based on agreement with the goals of the group. For example, someone with a strong interest in human rights might have a purposive incentive to join Amnesty International.

R

Ratification Formal approval.

Rational Basis Review The standard used by the courts to determine the constitutionality of a law or government action if neither strict scrutiny nor intermediate scrutiny applies.

Realignment A process in which a substantial group of voters switches party allegiance, producing a long-term change in the political landscape.

Reapportionment The allocation of seats in the House of Representatives to each state after each census.

Recall A procedure allowing the people to vote to dismiss an elected official from state office before his or her term has expired.

Recession Two or more successive quarters in which the economy shrinks instead of grows.

Reconciliation A special rule that can be applied to budget bills sent from the House of Representatives to the Senate. Reconciliation measures cannot be filibustered.

Redistricting The redrawing of the boundaries of the congressional districts within each state.

Referendum An electoral device whereby legislative or constitutional measures are referred by the legislature to the voters for approval or disapproval.

Registration The entry of a person's name onto the list of registered voters for elections. To register, a person must meet certain legal requirements of age, citizenship, and residency.

Regressive Tax A tax that falls in percentage terms as incomes rise.

Remand To send a case back to the court that originally heard it.

Representation The function of members of Congress as elected officials representing the views of their constituents as well as larger national interests.

Representative Assembly A legislature composed of individuals who represent the population.

Representative Democracy A form of government in which representatives elected by the people make and enforce laws and policies; may retain the monarchy in a ceremonial role.

Reprieve A formal postponement of the execution of a sentence imposed by a court of law.

Republic A form of government in which sovereign power rests with the people, rather than with a king or a monarch.

Republican Party One of the two major American political parties. It emerged in the 1850s as an antislavery party and consisted of former northern Whigs and antislavery Democrats.

Reverse To annul, or make void, a court ruling on account of some error or irregularity.

Reverse Discrimination The situation in which an affirmative action program discriminates against those who do not have minority status.

Reverse-Income Effect A tendency for wealthier states or regions to favor the Democrats and for less wealthy states or regions to favor the Republicans. The effect appears paradoxical because it reverses traditional patterns of support.

Rule of Four A United States Supreme Court procedure by which four justices must vote to grant a petition for review if a case is to come before the full court.

Rules Committee A standing committee of the House of Representatives that provides special rules under which specific bills can be debated, amended, and considered by the House.

S

Sampling Error The difference between a sample's results and the true result if the entire population had been interviewed.

Second Budget Resolution A resolution passed by Congress in September that sets "binding" limits on taxes and spending for the following fiscal year.

Select Committee A temporary legislative committee established for a limited time period and for a special purpose.

Senate Majority Leader The chief spokesperson of the majority party in the Senate, who directs the legislative program and party strategy.

Senate Minority Leader The party officer in the Senate who commands the minority party's opposition to the policies of the majority party and directs the legislative program and strategy of his or her party.

Senatorial Courtesy In federal district court judgeship nominations, a tradition allowing a senator to veto a judicial appointment in his or her state.

Seniority System A custom followed in both chambers of Congress specifying that the member of the majority party with the longest term of continuous service will be given preference when a committee chairperson (or a holder of some other significant post) is selected.

Separate-but-Equal Doctrine The doctrine holding that separate-but-equal facilities do not violate the equal protection clause of the Fourteenth Amendment to the U.S. Constitution.

Separation of Powers The principle of dividing governmental powers among different branches of government.

Service Sector The sector of the economy that provides services— such as health care, banking, and education—in contrast to the sector that produces goods.

Sexual Harassment Unwanted physical or verbal conduct or abuse of a sexual nature that interferes with a recipient's job performance, creates a hostile work environment, or carries with it an implicit or explicit threat of adverse employment consequences.

Signing Statement A written declaration that a president may make when signing a bill into law. Such statements may point out sections of the law that the president deems unconstitutional.

Slander The public uttering of a false statement that harms the good reputation of another. The statement must be made to, or within the hearing of, persons other than the defamed party.

Social Contract A voluntary agreement among individuals to secure their rights and welfare by creating a government and abiding by its rules.

Social Movement A movement that represents the demands of a large segment of the public for political, economic, or social change.

Socialism A political ideology based on strong support for economic and social equality. Socialists traditionally envisioned a society in which major businesses were taken over by the government or by employee cooperatives.

Socioeconomic Status The value assigned to a person due to occupation or income. An upper-class person, for example, has high socioeconomic status.

Soft Money Campaign contributions unregulated by federal or state law, usually given to parties and party committees to help fund general party activities.

Solidary Incentive A reason or motive that follows from the desire to associate with others and to share with others a particular interest or hobby.

Sound Bite A brief, memorable comment that can easily be fit into news broadcasts.

Soviet Bloc The Soviet Union and the Eastern European countries that installed Communist regimes after World War II and were dominated by the Soviet Union.

Speaker of the House The presiding officer in the House of Representatives. The Speaker is always a member of the majority party and is the most powerful and influential member of the House.

Spin An interpretation of campaign events or election results that is favorable to the candidate's campaign strategy.

Spin Doctor A political campaign adviser who tries to convince journalists of the truth of a particular interpretation of events.

Splinter Party A new party formed by a dissident faction within a major political party. Often, splinter parties have emerged when a particular personality was at odds with the major party.

Split-Ticket Voting Voting for candidates of two or more parties for different offices, such as voting for a Republican presidential candidate and a Democratic congressional candidate.

Spoils System The awarding of government jobs to political supporters and friends.

Spring Review The annual process in which the Office of Management and Budget (OMB) requires federal agencies to review their programs, activities, and goals and submit their requests for funding for the next fiscal year.

Standing Committee A permanent committee in the House or Senate that considers bills within a certain subject area.

Stare Decisis To stand on decided cases; the judicial policy of following precedents established by past decisions.

State A group of people occupying a specific area and organized under one government. It may be either a nation or a subunit of a nation.

State Central Committee The principal organized structure of each political party within each state. This committee is responsible for carrying out policy decisions of the party's state convention.

State of the Union Message An annual message to Congress in which the president proposes a legislative program. The message is addressed not only to Congress but also to the American people and to the world.

Statutory Power A power created for the president through laws enacted by Congress.

Straight-Ticket Voting Voting exclusively for the candidates of one party.

Strategic Arms Limitation Treaty (SALT I) A treaty between the United States and the Soviet Union to stabilize the nuclear arms competition between the two countries. SALT I talks began in 1969, and agreements were signed on May 26, 1972.

Strict Construction A judicial philosophy that looks to the "letter of the law" when interpreting the Constitution or a particular statute.

Strict Scrutiny A judicial standard for assessing the constitutionality of a law or government action when the law or action threatens to interfere with a fundamental right or potentially discriminates against members of a suspect classification.

Suffrage The right to vote; the franchise.

Sunset Legislation Laws requiring that existing programs be reviewed regularly for their effectiveness and be terminated unless specifically extended as a result of these reviews.

Super PAC A political organization that aggregates unlimited contributions by individuals and organizations to be spent independently of candidate committees.

Superdelegate A party leader or elected official who is given the right to vote at the party's national convention. Superdelegates are not elected at the state level.

Supremacy Clause The constitutional provision that makes the Constitution and federal laws superior to all conflicting state and local laws.

Supremacy Doctrine A doctrine that asserts the priority of national law over state laws. This principle is stated in Article VI of the Constitution, which provides that the Constitution, the laws passed by the national government under its constitutional powers, and all treaties constitute the supreme law of the land.

Suspect Classification A classification, such as race, religion, or national origin, that triggers strict scrutiny by the courts when a law or government action potentially discriminates against members of the class.

Swing Voters Voters who frequently swing their support from one party to another.

Symbolic Speech Expression made through articles of clothing, gestures, movements, and other forms of nonverbal conduct. Symbolic speech is given substantial protection by the courts.

T

Technical Assistance The practice of sending experts in such areas as agriculture, engineering, or business to aid other nations.

Terrorism A systematic attempt to inspire fear to gain political ends, typically involving the indiscriminate use of violence against noncombatants.

Theocracy "Rule by God," or the gods; in practice, rule by religious leaders, typically self-appointed.

Third Party A political party other than the two major political parties (Republican and Democratic).

Tight Monetary Policy Monetary policy that makes credit expensive in an effort to slow inflation.

Tipping A phenomenon that occurs when a group that is becoming more numerous over time grows large enough to change the political balance in a district, state, or country.

Totalitarian Regime A form of government that controls all aspects of the political, social, and economic life of a nation.

Tracking Poll A poll taken on a nearly daily basis as election day approaches.

Treasuries U.S. Treasury securities—bills, notes, and bonds; debt issued by the federal government.

Trial Court The court in which most cases begin.

Truman Doctrine The policy adopted by President Harry Truman in 1947 to halt Communist expansion in southeastern Europe.

Trustee A legislator who acts according to her or his conscience and the broad interests of the entire society.

Twelfth Amendment An amendment to the Constitution, adopted in 1804, that requires the separate election of the president and vice president by the electoral college.

Twenty-fifth Amendment A 1967 amendment to the Constitution that establishes procedures for filling presidential and vice-presidential vacancies and makes provisions for presidential incapacity.

Two-Party System A political system in which only two parties have a reasonable chance of winning.

U

Unanimous Opinion A Court opinion or determination on which all judges agree.

Unemployment The inability of those who are in the labor force to find a job; also the number of those in the labor force actively looking for a job, but unable to find one.

Unicameral Legislature A legislature with only one legislative chamber, as opposed to a bicameral (two-chamber) legislature, such as the U.S. Congress. Today, Nebraska is the only state in the Union with a unicameral legislature.

Unitary System A centralized governmental system in which ultimate governmental authority rests in the hands of the national, or central, government.

Universal Health Insurance Any of several possible programs to provide health insurance to everyone in the country. The central government does not necessarily provide the insurance itself but may subsidize the purchase of insurance from private insurance companies.

Universal Suffrage The right of all adults to vote for their government representatives.

V

Veto Message The president's formal explanation of a veto when legislation is returned to Congress.

Vote-Eligible Population The number of people who, at a given time, enjoy the right to vote in national elections.

Voter Turnout The percentage of citizens taking part in the election process; the number of eligible voters that actually "turn out" on election day to cast their ballots.

Voting-Age Population The number of people of voting age living in the country at a given time, regardless of whether they have the right to vote.

W

War Powers Resolution A law passed in 1973 spelling out the conditions under which the president can commit troops without congressional approval.

Washington Community Individuals regularly involved with politics in Washington, D.C.

Watergate Break-In The 1972 illegal entry into the Democratic National Committee offices by participants in President Richard Nixon's reelection campaign.

Weberian Model A model of bureaucracy developed by the German sociologist Max Weber, who viewed bureaucracies as rational, hierarchical organizations in which decisions are based on logical reasoning.

Whig Party A major party in the United States during the first half of the nineteenth century, formally established in 1836. The Whig Party was anti-Jackson and represented a variety of regional interests.

Whip A member of Congress who aids the majority or minority leader of the House or the Senate.

Whistleblower Someone who brings to public attention gross governmental inefficiency or an illegal action.

White House Office The personal office of the president, which tends to presidential political needs and manages the media.

White Primary A state primary election that restricts voting to whites only; outlawed by the Supreme Court in 1944.

Writ of *Certiorari* An order issued by a higher court to a lower court to send up the record of a case for review.

Writ of *Habeas Corpus* *Habeas corpus* means, literally, "you have the body." A writ of habeas corpus is an order that requires jailers to bring a prisoner before a court or a judge and explain why the person is being held.

INDEX

D

F

G

H

I

O

Q

R

S

T

U

Y

Z